MW01251170

FIELDING'S
PEOPLE'S
REPUBLIC OF
CHINA
1990

FIELDING'S BERMUDA AND THE BAHAMAS 1990
FIELDING'S BUDGET EUROPE 1990
FIELDING'S CARIBBEAN 1990
FIELDING'S EUROPE 1990
FIELDING'S MEXICO 1990
FIELDING'S PEOPLE'S REPUBLIC OF CHINA 1990
FIELDING'S SELECTIVE SHOPPING GUIDE TO EUROPE 1990

FIELDING'S AFRICAN SAFARIS
FIELDING'S ALASKA AND THE YUKON
FIELDING'S CALIFORNIA
FIELDING'S EUROPE WITH CHILDREN
FIELDING'S FAMILY VACATIONS USA
FIELDING'S FAR EAST 2nd revised edition
FIELDING'S HAVENS AND HIDEAWAYS USA
FIELDING'S LEWIS AND CLARK TRAIL
FIELDING'S LITERARY AFRICA
FIELDING'S MOTORING AND CAMPING EUROPE
FIELDING'S SPANISH TRAILS IN THE SOUTHWEST
FIELDING'S WORLDWIDE CRUISES 4th revised edition

FIELDING'S
PEOPLE'S REPUBLIC OF CHINA
1990

BY
RUTH LOR MALLOY

FIELDING TRAVEL BOOKS
℅ WILLIAM MORROW & COMPANY, INC.
105 Madison Avenue, New York, N.Y. 10016

ISBN: 0-688-08449-4
ISBN: 0-340-51048-X (Hodder & Stoughton)
Printed in the United States of America

Fourth Revised Fielding Edition

1 2 3 4 5 6 7 8 9 10

Text design by Marsha Cohen/Parallelogram

ACKNOWLEDGMENTS

Many people are responsible for this book: travelers who took the time to share their experiences and impressions with us: hotel officials who talked not just of their businesses but of the problems and joys of living and working in China; business travelers on airplanes; and tourists in hotel coffee shops or trains.

I am also particularly grateful to travelers, friends, and travel professionals who gave a great deal of time in sending information or relating their experiences for the *Travel China Newsletter,* its hotel evaluation book, and this book: among the many are Joan Annis, Patricia Appel, Ragni Askevold, B. Atkinson, Lucille Barale, Steve Beaver, Barbara Brechin, Sherm Bullis, Dorothea Coryell, Louise deYoung, Francisca de Zwager, Maurice F. Dubras, Victoria Goettler, Janet H. Halstead, Ying Hope, Lois G. Jackson, Moira Mudie, John Radford, Grace Raube, Adele Rickett, Harriet Sharkey, John T. Shelton, Lisa Sheung, Gloria Spoden, Mary Terchek, Willy Thorogood, Ernestine Van Houten, Franklin L. Wills, and Jane Wright.

What could we do without the input of seasoned travel agents and airlines like Air China, Canadian Airlines International Limited, China Eastern Airlines, China Educational Tours (Boston), Bestway (Vancouver), Tin Bo (Toronto and Ottawa), and US China Travel Service.

I also wish to thank the Chinese consulate in Toronto and the Chinese tourism officials who shared their time and knowledge, and the foreign embassy officials and foreign residents in China who spoke frankly and anonymously. Then there were the many guides who translated and argued my case with dense hotel officials.

Who financed the research? Basically, the buyers of *Fielding's People's Republic of China* and the subscribers to *Travel China Newsletter.* A great deal of help came from the China National Tourist Office in New York and from Mr. Shen Shoujun of the National Tourism Administration of China.

In some cities, I was hosted or assisted by China Travel Service, China International Travel Service, municipal foreign affairs departments, or the tourism administration: Anshan, Beijing, Changchun, Dalian, Fushun, Guangzhou, Harbin, Jilin, Nanjing, Quanzhou, Shanghai, Shantou, Shaoguan, Shenyang, Shenzhen, Suzhou, Xiamen, Yangzhou. I am especially indebted to the tourism administrations of Beijing, Guangdong, Heilongjiang, Liaoning, Jiangsu, Shanghai, Mai Ya Miao, and Michael Sun (Guangzhou), and Lin Feng of C.I.T.S. Fuzhou.

Especially helpful hotels have been the Garden (Guangzhou), Holiday Inn Asia Pacific, Hua Ting Sheraton (Shanghai), Huadu (Beijing), Beijing International (Beijing), Jinling (Nanjing), Jinsha (Shanghai), Longhu (Shantou), Mandarin (Xiamen), Movenpick (Beijing), Nikko (Shanghai), Novotel (Guangzhou), Shangri-la (Beijing), Tian Ma (Shanghai), and Xiqiao (Shanghai).

Information flowed regularly from hotels, travel agencies, and from Kim Chui and Wendy Hughes of Hong Kong.

Though she was unable to work on this edition, my appreciation goes to Priscilla Liang Hsu, who co-authored the 1987 edition and whose touch is still evident in this one. My gratitude also goes to Bob Orchard, publisher of the *Travel China Newsletter* and the *Guide to China's Hotels,* for his optimism and support.

Most of all, this book would not have been possible without the cooperation of my family, especially my husband Michael Malloy (who has no interest in China travel).

To all go my thanks, and the thanks of our readers.

Ruth Lor Malloy

UP-TO-DATE INFORMATION

The logistics of tourism everywhere are constantly changing, especially in China, where new hotels are opening at a furious pace. Yet information about these hotels and the new regulations is difficult to obtain, frequently discovered only upon asking.

Because travelers need information on China as current as possible, we offer the benefit of our resources at a discount to owners of *Fielding's People's Republic of China* for one time only.

For a six-month introductory subscription to the *Travel China Newsletter* with the latest information and changes that have come to our attention, *please send the following coupon and US$20 (or equivalent)*. Yearly subscriptions are regularly available for US$87.

This newsletter has been published monthly since September 1987. You might want to request copies of the six editions prior to your China trip.

AUTHOR'S NOTE

The Beijing Massacre of early June 1989 and subsequent history-making events happened after this book had gone to press. We do believe, however, that by the time you read this China should again be completely safe for tourists. If in doubt, we urge you follow the advice on up-to-date information on page 46.

GOOD FOR A SIX-MONTH TRIAL SUBSCRIPTION

of Ruth Lor Malloy's newsletter
on China's tourism and hotels,
to be used with the 1990 edition of
Fielding's People's Republic of China.

Coupon valid to December 31, 1990

Date of your trip:_____

( ) When do you want your monthly subscription to end?

Please check information needed.

( ) Information **not already** in this book on hotels in China, including telephone numbers, addresses, descriptions, evaluations, and current price of at least a standard double in F.E.C.s—where these are available. Noted will be the hotels that have informed us in writing that they will reconfirm reservations by telex.

( ) Latest information **not already** in this book on visas, customs, credit cards, and currency; new flights, travel from Hong Kong, cities open to foreign visitors, important new tourist attractions with evaluations (if possible). Also travel tips, important address changes, etc.

( ) Latest prices: A sampling of prices for food, film, hotel laundry, taxis, souvenirs, C.I.T.S. service charges, etc.

( ) Travel brochures

Photocopies or facsimiles of this coupon will be ignored.

Please send US$20 to Blendon Information Services, Suite 1, 126 Willowdale Ave., Willowdale, Ont., M2N 4Y2, Canada.

Name: (please type or print)_____

Address:_____

_____

CONTENTS

INTRODUCTION · · · **1**
Why Go to China? / **1**
Background / **1**
Tourism / **6**
Note / **14**

THE BASICS · · · **17**
Where in China? / **17**
When to Go? / **22**
How to Go / **23**
Should You Take Your Children? / **33**
Should You Go If Your Health Is Fragile / **34**
Choosing a Travel Agent / **34**

BEFORE YOU GO · · · **39**
Booking into China / **39**
Booking Domestic Travel / **41**
Formalities / **42**

WHAT TO TAKE · · · **54**

GETTING THERE (AND BACK) · · · **65**

HOTELS · · · **75**
History / **75**
Today / **75**

FOOD · · · **84**
Background / **84**
Some Regional and Special Dishes / **94**

GETTING AROUND · · · **99**
Transportation / **105**
Local Transportation / **113**
Communications / **116**

LOCAL CUSTOMS · · · 119
Does "Yes" Mean "Yes"? / 119
Does "No" Mean "No"? / 119
Ask Questions / 120
Applause / 120
Criticisms and Suggestions / 120
Tipping / 121
Good Manners / 121
Joking about Politics and Sex / 121
Beggars / 122
Flirting / 122
Will You Be Followed? / 122
Photography / 122
If You Get Into Trouble / 123
Smoking / 127
Spitting / 127
Looking Up Specific Chinese Citizens / 127
Chinese Hospitality / 129
If You're Invited to a Wedding / 129
Gift Giving / 129
Religion / 130
People's Feelings / 132
Forms of Address / 133
Politics / 133
Government / 134
Guanxi / 134
Democracy Walls / 134
Triple Standards / 135
If a Chinese Asks for Help / 135
Firecrackers / 135
Endangered Species / 136

SHOPPING · · · 138
Friendship Stores / 139
Arts, Crafts, and Antique Stores / 139
Factories / 139
Department Stores / 139
Free Markets / 139
Overseas Chinese Stores / 140
Specialty Stores / 140
Secondhand Stores / 140
What to Buy / 140

WHAT IS THERE TO SEE AND DO? · · · **148**

DESTINATIONS · · · **182**
Anqing, Anhui, see "Hefei"
Anshan, Liaoning / **185**
Anshun, Guizhou, see "Guiyang"
Antu (Nature Reserve, Changbai Mountains), Jilin, see "Changchun"
Anyang, Henan / **186**
Badaling, see "Great Wall"
Baoji, see "Xi'an"
Baotou, Inner Mongolia / **188**
Beidaihe, Hebei / **190**
Beihai, Guangxi, see "Nanning"
Beijing / **192**
Bengbu, Anhui, see "Hefei"
Benxi, Liaoning, see "Shenyang"
Binxian, Shaanxi, see "Xi'an"
Changchun, Jilin / **226**
Changsha, Hunan / **230**
Changzhou, Jiangsu / **234**
Chaoshan, Guangdong, see "Shantou"
Chaozhou, Guangdong, see "Shantou"
Chengde, Hebei / **235**
Chengdu, Sichuan / **240**
Chongqing, Sichuan / **246**
Ciping, Jiangxi, see "Jinggang Mountain"
Conghua, Guangdong / **251**
Dadiwan, Gansu, see "Lanzhou"
Dali, Yunnan, see "Xiguan"
Dalian, Liaoning / **251**
Dandong, see "Shenyang"
Daqing, Heilongjiang, see "Harbin"
Datong, Shanxi / **255**
Dazhai, Shanxi / **258**
Dazu County, Sichuan / **259**
Dongting Lake, see "Yueyang"
Dunhuang, Gansu / **261**
Ejinhoroq, Inner Mongolia, see "Baotou"
Emei Shan, Sichuan / **263**
Fengdu, Sichuan, see "Chongqing"
Fengjie County, Sichuan, see "Yangtze Gorges"
Fengyang County, Anhui, see "Hefei"

Foshan, Guangdong / **264**
Fushun, Liaoning / **266**
Fuzhou, Fujian / **268**
   Gaochang, Xinjiang, see "Turpan"
Gezhouba, Hubei / **271**
   Golmud, Qinghai, see "Xining"
   Gongxian, Henan, see "Zhengzhou"
Grand Canal / **271**
Great Wall / **272**
Guangzhou, Guangdong / **275**
   Guanxian County, Sichuan, see "Chengdu"
Guilin, Guangxi / **290**
Guiping, Guangxi / **297**
Guiyang, Guizhou / **298**
   Haikou, Guangdong, see "Hainan Island"
Hainan Island, Guangdong / **300**
Handan, Hebei / **302**
Hangzhou, Zhejiang / **303**
   Hankou, Hubei, see "Wuhan"
   Hanyang, Hubei, see "Wuhan"
   Hanzhong, see "Xi'an"
Harbin, Heilongjiang / **312**
Hefei, Anhui / **315**
Hengshan Mountain, Hunan and Shanxi / **319**
Hohhot, Inner Mongolia / **320**
   Huai'an, see "Nanjing"
   Huairou County, see "Great Wall"
   Huangguoshu Waterfall, Guizhou, see "Guiyang"
   Huangling, Shaanxi, see "Yan'an"
Huangshan Mountain, Anhui / **323**
   Huashan, Shanxi, see "Xi'an"
Jiangmen, Guangdong / **325**
   Jiaohe, Xinjiang, see "Turpan"
   Jiayuguan, Gansu, see "Jiuquan"
Jilin, Jilin / **327**
Jinan, Shandong / **328**
Jingdezhen, Jiangxi / **333**
Jinggang Shan, Jiangxi / **334**
   Jinghong, Yunnan, see "Kunming"
   Jingshan Ling, see "Great Wall" and "Chengde"
   Jingzhou, see "Shashi," "Wuhan," and "Yangtze Gorges"
   Jintian, Guangxi, see "Nanning"
   Jinzhou, Liaoning, see "Shenyang"
   Jiuhua Mountain Tourist Resort, Anhui, see "Hefei"
Jiujiang, Jiangxi / **335**

Jiuquan, Gansu / **336**
  Jiuzhaigou, Sichuan, see "Chengdu"
  Jixian, Tianjin see "Tianjin" and "Great Wall"
  Juyongguan, see "Great Wall"
Kaifeng, Henan / **337**
  Kaili, Guizhou, see "Guiyang"
Kashi, Xinjiang / **339**
  Kashgar, see "Kashi"
Kunming, Yunnan / **341**
Lanzhou, Gansu / **346**
Leshan, Sichuan / **349**
Lhasa, Tibet / **351**
  Lianyungang, Jiangsu, see "Nanjing"
  Lijiang, Yunnan, see "Kunming"
  Linfen, Shanxi, see "Taiyuan"
  Lintong, Shaanxi, see "Xi'an"
  Linxi, Gansu, see "Lanzhou"
  Linzi, Shandong, see "Jinan" and "Zibo"
  Liubu, Shandong, see "Jinan"
Liuzhou, Guangxi / **361**
  Luda, Liaoning, see "Dalian"
  Lunan (Stone Forest), Yunnan, see "Kunming"
Luoyang, Henan / **362**
Lushan Mountain, Jiangxi / **367**
  Ma'anshan Mountain, Anhui, see "Hefei"
  Mangshan Mountain, Henan, see "Zhengzhou"
  Meishan County, Sichuan, see "Chengdu"
  Mixian County, Henan, see "Zhengzhou"
  Miyun County, see "Great Wall"
  Mogan Mountain, Zhejiang, see "Hangzhou"
  Mudanjiang, Heilongjiang, see "Harbin"
Nanchang, Jiangxi / **370**
Nanjing, Jiangsu / **372**
Nanning, Guangxi / **383**
  Nanniwan, Shaanxi, see "Yan'an"
  Nantong, see "Nanjing"
Ningbo, Zhejiang / **386**
  Putuo Shan, Zhejiang, see "Ningbo"
Qingdao, Shandong / **390**
Qinhuangdao, Hebei / **395**
  Qiqihar, Heilongjiang, see "Harbin"
  Qonggyai, Tibet, see "Lhasa"
Quanzhou, Fujian / **396**
Qufu, Shandong / **399**
  Sanya, Guangdong, see "Hainan Island"

Ruicheng County, Shanxi, see "Taiyuan"
Shanghai / **404**
Shanhaiguan, Hebei / **424**
  Shannon, Tibet, see "Lhasa"
Shantou, Guangdong / **425**
Shaoguan, Guangdong / **427**
Shaoshan, Hunan / **429**
Shaoxing, Zhejiang / **430**
Shashi, Hubei / **432**
Shekou, Guangdong / **433**
  Shentong, Shandong, see "Jinan"
Shenyang, Liaoning / **434**
Shenzhen, Guangdong / **437**
  Shibaozhai, Sichuan, see "Yangtze Gorges"
Shihezi, Xinjiang / **439**
Shijiazhuang, Hebei / **440**
  Shiqi, Guangdong, see "Zhongshan"
Silk Road / **442**
  Simao, Yunnan, see "Kunming"
  Songshan Mountain, Henan, see "Zhengzhou"
Suzhou, Jiangsu / **444**
Tai'an, Shandong / **451**
Taishan, Guangdong / **453**
  Taishan Mountain, Shandong, see "Tai'an"
Taiyuan, Shanxi / **456**
Tangshan, Hebei / **459**
Tianjin / **459**
  Tianshan Mountain, Xinjiang, see "Urumqi"
  Tianshui, Gansu, see "Lanzhou"
  Tiantai, Zhejiang, see "Hangzhou"
  Tongchuan, see "Xi'an"
  Tonglushan, Hubei, see "Wuhan"
  Tunxi, Anhui, see "Hefei"
Turpan, Xinjiang / **467**
Urumqi, Xinjiang / **470**
  Wanxian, Sichuan, see "Yangtze Gorges"
Weifang, Shandong / **473**
Weihai, Shandong / **474**
  Wolong Nature Preserve, Sichuan, see "Chengdu"
  Wuchang, Hubei, see "Wuhan"
  Wudang Mountains, see "Wuhan"
Wuhan, Hubei / **475**
  Wuhu, Anhui, see "Hefei"
  Wuming, Guangxi, see "Nanning"
  Wutai Mountain, Shanxi, see "Datong"

Wuxi, Jiangsu / **480**
  Wuyi Mountain, Fujian, see "Fuzhou"
Xiaguan, Yunnan / **483**
Xiamen, Fujian / **486**
Xi'an, Shaanxi / **491**
  Xigaze, Tibet, see "Lhasa"
  Xindu, Sichuan, see "Chengdu"
  Xing'an County, Guangxi, see "Guilin"
  Xinglong, Guangdong, see "Hainan Island"
Xinhui, Guangdong / **506**
Xining, Qinghai / **507**
Xiqiao Mountain, Guangdong / **509**
  Xizhou, Yunnan, see "Xiaguan"
  Xumi Mt., Ningxia, see "Yinchuan"
Xuzhou, Jiangsu / **511**
Yan'an, Shaanxi / **512**
  Yangshuo, Guangxi, see "Guilin"
Yangtze Gorges / **515**
Yangzhou, Jiangsu / **519**
Yantai, Shandong / **522**
  Yaxian, Guangdong, see "Hainan"
  Yichang, Hubei, see "Yangtze"
  Yidu, Shandong, see "Jinan"
Yinchuan, Ningxia / **527**
  Yingxian County, see "Datong"
  Yixian, Hebei, see "Zunhua"
Yixing, Jiangsu / **530**
Yueyang, Hunan / **532**
  Yuncheng, Shanxi, see "Taiyuan"
Zhangzhou, Fujian / **533**
  Zhang Jiajie, Hunan, see "Changsha"
  Zhangmu, Tibet, see "Lhasa"
Zhanjiang, Guangdong / **535**
Zhaoqing, Guangdong / **537**
Zhengzhou, Henan / **539**
Zhenjiang, Jiangsu / **543**
  Zhenning, Guizhou, see "Guiyang"
Zhongshan City, Guangdong / **547**
  Zhoukoudian, see "Beijing"
Zhuhai, Guangdong / **549**
Zibo, Shandong / **551**
  Zigong, see "Chengdu"
Zunhua, Hubei / **551**
  Zunyi, Guizhou, see "Guiyang"

SPECIAL FOR OVERSEAS CHINESE · · · 553

SPECIAL FOR BUSINESS PEOPLE · · · 556

USEFUL PHRASES · · · 560

MILESTONES IN CHINESE HISTORY · · · 651

IMPORTANT ADDRESSES AND INFORMATION · · · 664
Some Chinese Missions Abroad / 664
Tour Organizers and Travel Agents / 666
China Friendship Associations / 669
For Scholars, Students and Foreign Experts / 669
Other Important Addresses / 670
Customs Regulations / 674

BIBLIOGRAPHY · · · 676

QUICK REFERENCE · · · 679

BUDGET AND HOTEL QUICK REFERENCE · · · 692
How Much Money Should You Take to China? / 692
Recent Prices / 696
Hotels—Prices and Telephone Numbers / 702
Finances / 714
Salaries / 716
Currency / 716

MAPS · · · 719

INDEX · · · 750

INTRODUCTION

WHY GO TO CHINA?

—Because it is historically and culturally one of the richest countries in the world, and many of its ancient buildings have been restored for all to enjoy.

—Because China has some of the world's most spectacular natural scenery.

—Because what is happening now to the Chinese people is vital and exciting—a recent openness to the outside world in which you, the foreign visitor, can play a part. Here is a drama of immense importance to human history—will China, with its tremendous population of more than one fifth of mankind, achieve its goals of modernization by the year 2000? Can she do this with a minimum of social damage before any adverse reaction to current policies takes place?

—Because the banquet food is rarely duplicated anywhere. Where else can you get dishes shaped like phoenixes or swans or rabbits? And today the art of the great master chefs is being passed on.

—Because you can see for yourself its time-honored handicrafts being made; for example, 45 balls within balls, each intricatcly carved and free-moving.

—Because you can experience a culture very different from your own, and yet in many ways similar.

—Because foreigners have influenced the development of China and traces of that history can still be found and studied.

—Because if you are of Chinese ancestry (in this life or previous lives), you can look for your roots and especially help in the development of your ancestral land.

—Because China is available for the first time in recent history to tourists, and who knows when it may be closed to tourists again?

BACKGROUND

China is a country that has infuriated yet tantalized the rest of the world for centuries. Its arrogant indifference, the wealth and divine right of its emperors have intrigued generations of curious people everywhere.

1

In more recent years, its fanatical adherence to an alien ideology has continued to mystify. Even today, people around the world are asking, "Is it or isn't it?"

China started out as a nation over 2200 years ago. The thousands of years of relative isolation since then allowed the Chinese to indulge in and develop their unique Confucian-based culture until the 19th century. At that time, more advanced technology and greed encouraged many European countries and Japan to grab power and territory in China. The Chinese reacted to foreign victories with bewilderment, various anti-foreigner rebellions, and then, in 1911, with a republican revolution. After a period of embarrassing national disintegration, first under the war lords and then during civil war and Japanese invasion, the country was finally reunited in 1949 under the Communists.

In spite of several drastic setbacks, China has moved ahead since that point to a period of relative prosperity and freedom.

The Chinese people, up until very recently, have been 80% agricultural. Attachment to land has colored their thinking and behavior. Their religion, their loyalties, and their efforts have always been based on pragmatism.

Before 1950, China's economy stemmed primarily from a feudal system, land rented to peasants in return for a percentage of the crops. Landlords ideally had responsibility for the welfare of their serfs, on whom they were largely dependent for their wealth. Although the system was abused frequently, owning land was the goal of millions.

China became a Communist country in 1949. Heady with victory, the Communist leaders embarked on a series of programs religiously following the theories of Mao Zedong, the man who had led them to power. But the Chinese leaders were pragmatists first. When something didn't work, they tried something else.

The Communists started out with a land-to-the-peasants program, and then to collectivization, to communes, and to communes with private plots. During the Cultural Revolution, private plots were abolished, to be reinstated and encouraged later. In the 1970s, it was apparent that even that system was not meeting the needs of the people.

In the early 1980s, an economy largely based on the family replaced that of the communes. Most counties adopted the Responsibility System, whereby rural inhabitants rent land or machines. The government receives an agreed share in the produce while villagers can keep or sell the surplus. Anybody can also work on projects such as handicrafts, livestock, and vegetables, which they can sell for their own gain. These you will see on sale in "free markets." Families and collectives have opened up hotels, restaurants, and factories. It would seem that China has almost come around full circle, with the government replacing the feudal landlords. But has it?

Under the new economic system, the government no longer determines all that is grown or produced and how much; the market now affects most production directly. Many peasants have been working furiously and are making more money than they ever have before. Many villagers now have higher incomes than most salaried city dwellers.

At present, China is thus undergoing another revolution. For the first time, many villages are earning less than 50% of income from agriculture. Over the next few decades even more mechanization of agriculture and urban growth should develop, especially as new airfields, resort complexes with golf courses, new factories and schools eat into existing agricultural land.

The revolutionary slogans of nationalistic self-sufficiency and personal sacrifice of the fifties and sixties have now given way to international cooperation and modernization and some people getting richer faster than others.

The new economic policies also include the opening up of many cities to foreign investment. A concerted effort to attract foreign money has been made in the coastal areas, with a series of regional development zones extending from Dalian in the north to Beihai city in the south, and especially in Shenzhen, Guangzhou, Shanghai, Dalian, and Tianjin. Here foreign investment particularly is being encouraged, and harbors, roads, and telecommunications added to or improved. Factories, office blocks, hotels, and workers' quarters are shooting up everywhere. Many of these and other areas have or will soon have International Direct-Dial (IDD) telephones and international airports. Many cities now have domestic direct-dial facilities, considerably cutting down the time it used to take to make operator-assisted long distance calls.

The effects of the new economic policies are apparent everywhere, as you can see by the many construction cranes wherever you go. A battalion of private souvenir merchants greet you at almost every tourist attraction. Relatively expensive Hong Kong–made clothes hang for sale in front of stores and in the free markets. Groups of former peasants are building hotels, paving roads, and constructing bridges, playgrounds, libraries, and schools. In some areas, you can see a great deal of new peasant housing, some of luxury size.

The one-child birth control program is trying to keep the population from overwhelming the economy. The population of China (including Taiwan, Hong Kong, and Macao) is 1.08 billion, and the leadership hopes it will stay below 1.2 billion.

Problems to be studied include the psychological effect of a child with no siblings but masses of doting aunts, uncles, and grandparents; and the financial support of the growing proportion of elderly people. Recently signs have indicated that birth control regulations may loosen up a bit, especially in the countryside and among minorities, where controls have been less strict, anyway, than in the cities. With the economy based on family enterprises, more children are needed to help out.

You can see the relaxing of the puritanical Maoist ethic in the new freedom to enjoy life. Without the hours spent in political meetings studying the works of Chairman Mao, people now have more leisure. Instead of saving their money for the development of the country, they are eating out in restaurants, and couples are ordering bigger and more elaborate wedding feasts. People are buying videos, color televisions, washing machines, refrigerators, and mopeds. A few private citizens have even bought cars and trucks! But are they so concerned about acquisitions that they are forgetting about sensitivity to others?

Life is less serious now. Lively dance parties are held in every city. Many men and women wear high-heeled shoes and sunglasses, and the women are adding some glamour to their lives with permanent waves, lipsticks, and colorful dresses. Billiard halls, discos, and state lotteries seem to be popular everywhere. And Chinese tourists flock everywhere in China, a few even traveling outside the country.

Whereas anything foreign was considered counterrevolutionary before, today musicians like Wham! and John Denver, innumerable foreign symphony orchestras and dance groups, and artists like Robert Rauschenberg have helped to stimulate an interest in foreign culture. New also is the more mature approach to history, some credit being given to the help of the Nationalists in fighting the Japanese invaders, for example. While before only revolutionary themes could be expressed in the arts, today Marx is treated as a human on stage, and nude models have been used in art classes. References to human sexuality are gingerly appearing for the first time in recent literature and stage plays—but nothing like elsewhere in the world. In the late 1970s, none of this could have been predicted.

After decades of drabness, China is beginning to look more cheerful. It is a nice change.

The current revolution has also affected education. Previously, the government decided solely through examinations who would be paid to go to university and what jobs those graduates would take later. Today, some colleges have been built where students pay fees, choose their own subjects, and find their own jobs after graduation. At least one U.S.-style private university is operating in China (Huanghe University in Zhengzhou) with English as the medium of instruction. Some universities with U.S. ties are granting MBAs. Thousands of Chinese students also have been encouraged to study abroad, not all with government funding. The country's leadership is aware that the former system cannot supply the expertise to modernize the country before its goal, the year 2000.

With any new system come abuses and changes: a great number of such students do not want to come home after finishing their studies abroad.

Recently, an overheated economy produced inflation and many

people panicked. In 1988, those who could went on buying sprees: electronics, gas stoves, etc.—money was going out of style. People in positions to buy foreign motorcycles and videos made a lot of money reselling them.

New classes of wealthy farmers and merchants, and oppressed laborers have developed. Intellectuals are suffering. Many salaried government officials and professionals have been forced to take part-time work to supplement their inflation-eroded wages and higher standards of living. Young people.have become attendants in joint-venture hotels or merchants rather than teachers and doctors. When you compare salaries, it's easy to see why. There is already a shortage of teachers and probably doctors.

Look at the people selling black-market currency outside hotels and clothes in night markets. Look at the people grabbing your bags in the railway stations. Some of them look like intellectuals, trying to make ends meet. A new what's-in-it-for-me generation is developing (out of greed or necessity).

During the late 1980s, controlling inflation was the key to much of government policy. The Communists won support in the 1940s because they promised control of inflation. Now inflation has threatened again. The government has responded with anti-inflationary measures: cutting back on imports and non-capital construction, no more new hotels, and you may notice price quotations in U.S. dollars, a hedge against inflation and possible devaluation of Chinese currency.

China is opening up more and more to Taiwan and the Soviets. By the time you read this, there may have been a Sino-Soviet summit, the first in decades, with trade and cultural exchanges. You may be rubbing shoulders with Soviet tourists.

Now that Taiwan visitors are allowed by their government to visit China, relations with ''little brother'' will probably improve there too. Trading has started and should expand.

In 1987, university students around the country demonstrated for more freedom. The Communist Party general secretary, liberal university officials, and journalists, all of whom encouraged the students, were subsequently forced to resign. China is not a democratic country. The current leaders are pragmatic. They are concerned about economic stability and reaching their goals. When things look like they're getting out of control they do not hesitate to put on the brakes.

On the surface, the Chinese may appear to be moving quickly toward capitalism. This confusion makes a visit to China now particularly intriguing. Have they or haven't they abandoned Communism, or Marxism, or Marxist-Leninism, or whatever they've been following? Some theoreticians argue that it is only Mao Zedong's own brand of Marxist-Leninism that they have abandoned. Among other heresies, Mao based his revolution on the peasants rather than industrial workers. And does the government still control the means of production? Will prosperous Guandong rebel against economic domination by Beijing? Are State Council regulations being ignored? What will happen after the passing of Deng Xiaoping? What has happened to slower workers? Have any gone on strike? Quit? Been fired? Starved? Why don't you check that one out for yourself?

These are just a few of the changes. When you go to China as the decade changes, you will see many others. It is an exciting time to go, and you will experience history being made. But you have to be alert to what is going on.

See also "Milestones in Chinese History."

TOURISM

China has charmed or infuriated its tourists. Some have stomped away vowing never to return again. But a few have stomped away and come back.

Those who hated it obviously weren't prepared. They complain about the difficulty in getting around, smelly toilets, substandard hotels, the crowds, and the lack of service.

Those who liked it saw beyond the problems. Attitude makes a difference.

The successful visitor is one who likes challenges, who approaches every new situation with humor and flexibility. Being stranded with heavy luggage and no porters in a train station is an opportunity to make friends! It might take a while, but eventually someone will come along to help, especially if you look approachable or ask.

China has a lot to offer visitors, and this makes up for the obstacles.

China wants tourists. She needs friends and the foreign exchange they bring.

In 1988, China hosted over 4.3 million overseas tourists in tours (of whom 1.84 million were of non-Chinese origin). In addition to these are millions of Chinese tourists also wanting to climb the Great Wall and peek into the pavilions of the Forbidden City.

In the last few years China has been working hard to develop tourism. Restaurants and hotels of all grades have been opened. She is also building highways, superhighways, airports, and ship quays. She is trying to raise standards of service by having airlines and travel agencies compete with each other for business. She is upgrading more tourist attractions. Over 500 destinations are open to foreigners. This covers all of the important tourist attractions in the country.

The development of tourism is not progressing as quickly as China's leaders or foreign visitors want. While tourism is bringing in more money than expected, the numbers of tourists have not reached expectations;

1989 should be a better year. Many of the new joint-venture hotels have now opened, and many Chinese-managed hotels have reached good Western standards. In a few cases they have better than Western standards with smoke alarms in each guest room, easily monitored by an attendant on each floor. Great restaurants are now available. Communications have improved tremendously. But in some cases tourism is still held back by people in the industry who do not yet fully understand just what foreign visitors need. The biggest problem has been the domestic airlines, which need to learn a lot about public relations and computers. (It is still not easy to get a CAAC schedule in China.) But CAAC is claiming a 91% on-time record. Another major problem is the lack of porters or luggage-carrying facilities for individual travelers at 99% of China's train stations. English-language capability has improved but still leaves much to be desired. And while public toilets have improved considerably in airports and at many tourist attractions, stinking, clogged, dirty toilets still can ruin a good meal.

And someone could make a killing leasing out carpet-cleaning equipment, if he or she could convince Chinese managers of the need.

Prepaid group tourism is still the easiest way to go but individual travel is becoming a lot easier, and can be cheaper than a group tour. An abundance of hotels are now open for individuals willing to pay in the D/B US$85 to US$130 a night range (except in peak periods) in Beijing, Xi'an, and Shanghai. Tianjin, Guilin, and Guangzhou are cheaper. You can still get clean, comfortable, though less luxurious accommodations for US$40 and less. The further down you go, though, the fewer services you get.

Telexes and travel agencies make reservations easy, and hotel drivers can pick up checked luggage at airports. Individual tourists can also get reasonably priced city tours in a few cities. China prefers groups. Government travel agencies charge outrageous prices for packages for individuals because groups are more efficient.

But China is not ignoring the persistent numbers of those individual travelers either, and many on-their-own adventurers have been happy about their experiences in China. These people still cheerfully network among themselves about the best of the cheaper hotels and how to get a cheaper boat trip in Guilin, and avoid C.I.T.S.'s unsatisfactory tours in Tibet. A frontier atmosphere of pioneering and sharing exists among individual travelers—even among jaded business people who have been traveling in China for years.

It is now a little easier and a bit more difficult to get an individual tourist visa. Visas can be obtained in five working days, by applying at a Chinese consulate abroad, with a full, mini, or a custom-designed package (like a hotel reservation). During the high season—May, August, September, and October—it is also necessary to have a telex or letter from C.I.T.S. before a visa will be issued, but some consulates abroad have been satisfied simply with confirmed paid hotel reservations.

If you want to travel more cheaply you can get a visa in Hong Kong for HK$50 or through a travel agent in three hours or so. They are happy even if they only book you a train or into inexpensive hotels.

Group travel has become even easier. Groups of 9 to 30 persons planning to travel together may apply for a group visa and must enter and exit China together. The group organizer collects copies of the main pages of each passport but no individual application forms or photos are needed.

Flights and passenger ship routes have increased over the last year. Airlines flying into China now include Air China, Air Italia, All Nippon Airways, Cathay Pacific Airways, Canadian Airlines International, Dragon Airlines, Finnair, Japan Air Lines, Lufthansa, Northwest Airlines, Pakistan International Airlines, Philippine Airlines, Qantas Airways, Singapore Airlines, Swissair, Thai International and United. Land routes are open from North Korea, the Soviet Union, Nepal, and Pakistan.

More deluxe hotels have been built, usually as joint ventures between foreign companies and Chinese partners. The competition has forced wholly Chinese-managed hotels to modernize and improve services. Even in many medium-priced hotels, one now finds free toothbrush sets, 110/220 volt outlets for shavers, and room smoke alarms. Many hotels have clean public as well as guest toilets. American Standard must be making a killing! Many have bedside television and light controls, a second telephone in the bathroom, and computers that keep track of guests. The lobbies of the older hotels have been completely transformed. Few hotels are without discos!

Some of the new or newly renovated hotels have imported bathroom fixtures: Italian, Spanish, American, or Japanese. Luxury suites might have Jacuzzis. The lovely Nanhai in Shenzhen has even imported a toilet that washes the user with a strategically placed water spray and dries with hot air.

Many of the big new hotels tend to look alike, with a revolving restaurant on top, an architectural style that will characterize the decade. The luxury hotels, at first glance, are equal to or better than those in New York or Toronto. Some lobbies are huge and elegant, rivaling the best of Manila and Bangkok. Many staff members are smartly dressed in beautifully Hong Kong–tailored uniforms or silk *cheong sams/chipaos*. Beijing's Great Wall Hotel is not the only one that served "jet-fresh prime U.S. beef."

You can make reservations for the top hotels by telex, and should get an answer even if they have no rooms available. You can also book rooms through hotel chains in North America, your travel agent, or your airline. See "Important Addresses."

A shortage of staff with international experience means that service is not up to Bangkok or Hong Kong standards—though it can come close. Hotels are furiously training staff, and attempting to fire the hopeless. They are fining workers or giving bonuses, depending on performance and volume of business. Some hotels are allowing attendants to keep tips (though tips cannot be asked or waited for). The resulting polite and eager service is impressive, and should improve even more.

By the end of 1989, many hotels should be officially graded with one to five stars for maintenance, service, facilities, food, etc. Tourism administrations in each city should have a list of hotels, restaurants, and shops approved for foreign visitors. These can be removed from the list if there are complaints of dishonesty, poor service, and poor facilities.

Many hotels now have public relations departments, and you should call on them for help if you have problems. In a move unheard of for any Chinese-managed hotel, the Kunlun (Beijing) recently refunded the trans-Pacific airfare of a Canadian guest. The tourist had broken her ankle in its then inadequately lit partking lot on her second night in the country. The hotel accepted responsibility. But many tours still cannot guarantee their hotels.

The furious pace of hotel construction will probably continue into the early 1990s, although a halt has been called on many proposed projects. The range spans from huge palaces fit for visiting heads of state to tiny temple hostels for pilgrims. One hears now of a glut of luxury-class hotels in Guangzhou, Xi'an, Guilin, Shanghai, and Beijing, all the better for travelers. Hotel prices should come down in the 1990s.

Keep in mind that while new hotels might be very beautiful, they can deteriorate quickly. We have tried to grade hotels, but six months later the quality might be completely different. A renovation then brings the facilities back up to higher standards. (The *Travel China* newsletter publishes evaluations sent in by recent hotel guests regarding the state of hotels used.)

In the Chinese-managed hotels, total renovations are made every two to four years, but in the meantime, soft drinks and spit get hopelessly ground into beautiful wool carpets. On the other hand, the foreign-managed hotels try to practice perpetual maintenance.

The top joint-venture hotels have raised the level of expectations for all hotels. Where before tourists were happy to get a tacky room with a private bath, and then, later, an air-conditioner and television set, today's visitors expect a refrigerator and spotless rugs too.

One must keep reminding oneself that the standards of China's hotels have risen considerably since the days of no shower curtains and no coffee shops, less than a decade ago.

The new economic policies and competition have also given birth to some excellent new restaurants. Many hotels in Guilin, for example, have imported chefs from Hong Kong. Many hotels use imported ingredients and the big favorite in Guangdong is corn soup, made with canned American corn!

Hopefully these are only temporary measures until China can train enough cooks of its own, and grow its own sweet corn. Even a wholly Chinese-managed hotel might house one or two joint-venture restaurants, with higher prices and food closer to Western or Hong Kong tastes. Not having tried them all, we can only say that these new restaurants at least look 100% better than the dumpy old ones. Many look like ancient palaces with attendants in flowing silk robes.

Another recent development is the proliferation in the number of travel agencies. China International Travel Service is no longer the only one serving foreign visitors. New agencies, many of them travel arms of other government departments, have gotten into the act. China Travel Service, long specializing in travel for Overseas Chinese and Compatriots, is now wooing the foreign traveler as well. Where C.I.T.S. won't book train tickets, these others will, and some give lower-priced tours and services as well.

But some agencies charge higher prices too. *Travelers should now shop around.* In early 1989, the price of a trip to the Great Wall and Ming Tombs ranged from ¥12 to ¥150! Some agencies charge about ¥12 to ¥80 to book plane tickets and hotels, yet some hotels will book tickets for free.

In Beijing 47 travel agencies now compete, 17 of these licensed for foreign travelers. Elsewhere, C.I.T.S. branches vie with C.I.T.S. headquarters for customers. It is too early to judge how this situation is working out, or to recommend a good travel agent, but some travel agencies are offering two free tickets instead of one for each 15 people on a tour.

Foreign travel organizations have also become more deeply committed. American Express and Thomas Cook have signed contracts with Chinese agencies, and American Express and MasterCard are issuing credit cards in China.

China's airlines have shown improvement, but are still not up to international standards, especially in their domestic operations. Payment in China can only be made in cash, not by credit card. They are adding many new planes, opening convenient booking offices, and building or expanding airports. But some planes are small and uncomfortable (especially for big foreigners). Some planes have broken seat belts and luggage bins that fall open. Cabin crews are not always careful about safety checks (but service is improving). If you have a choice of planes, study a flight schedule and pick the newer, faster planes.

In 1988, individual travelers could no longer book multiple-destination domestic tickets from abroad. Some North American travel agents have been promising this for late 1989, but it remains to be seen. (In the meantime, if individuals with tight schedules need the assurance of confirmed reservations, we suggest they try flying from Hong Kong directly to the city they want, as flights from Hong Kong can be confirmed. You can also try booking through host units, travel agents, or each of your hotels in China, sending payment and passport numbers. Failing these, you can try flying stand-by after you arrive in China, pleading emergency. The success rate of stand-bys is very high unless you happen to hit a busy travel period.) Group tours can get confirmed flights.

1988 was a bad year for aviation in China. With three plane crashes, (two involving old Russian-built Ilyushins, one due to weather), many planes were pulled out of service for repairs. 200,000 Taiwan visitors and an increasing number of domestic travelers competed for space. Travelers experienced delays, especially out of Chengdu, Chongqing, Guilin, Guangzhou, and Xi'an. Some foreigners spent three days in airports. Some groups had to break up. We suggest you carry snacks, reading material, and playing cards whenever you fly. (Few airports have restaurants.)

Those waiting for delayed flights are rarely given progress reports unless they ask, and nothing more than tea unless they insist.

We also suggest that tours spend more time in fewer cities to minimize time in airports. Beijing, for example, has very interesting side trips—like Chengde within four hours' train ride.

To solve the problem, cheaper airfare for Chinese and compatriot travelers were cancelled on the most popular flights during high season, because reservation clerks were ordered to give preference to foreigners. Direct flights from Hong Kong consequently became harder to get.

Stewardesses smile more frequently now, and give the impression of wanting to help. (You should have seen them before.) They are dressing more smartly these days; they used to wear baggy khaki uniforms. Food on flights seems better but it still isn't very good. CAAC gives away goodies like fans, vases, and business card holders. Safety spiels are mandatory. Attendants ask passengers to fasten seat belts at appropriate times, but they don't check belts very carefully.

The development of new domestic airlines has been slow. The two most prominent have been Shanghai Airlines and China United Airlines, the latter a joint venture with the airforce. CUA uses military planes, pilots, and airports. Compared to CAAC subsidiaries, both have very few flights but seem to offer better services. All domestic airlines charge the same prices and have the same general regulations as CAAC (such as baggage allowances and refunds).

CAAC is still in the process of phasing out its planes and becoming only a regulatory body. Air China (Beijing), China Eastern (Shanghai), and Xiamen Airline have come into being. Other independent airlines should break operational ties with CAAC in 1989 and 1990.

While it is too early to determine which airlines are best, we urge you to send us a copy of your boarding pass with a note regarding date, punctuality, cleanliness, comfort, service, food, safety, and pilots. We will announce results in future editions.

China is also buying more and better passenger trains, and improvements should have started to show by now, but with more people traveling, trains in the late 1980s were even harder to book than planes. Some tour groups expecting soft class found themselves in hard class. Officials have tried to limit demand by canceling group tickets (for all but foreigners). New train cars are still being promised for foreign tourists, including air-conditioned cars (from East Germany) with English-speaking attendants.

· Like some other services, China is trying to keep prices down for domestic travelers. Since railways are subsidized, the more travelers there are, the less money there is available for improvements. China has also had some bad train accidents lately.

Taxi service has improved, but prices have gone up. Shanghai taxis now have meters marked with telephone numbers if you have complaints. Shanghai is one of the cities talking about a much-needed subway. Public mini-buses traveling regular routes are starting to appear. These are more expensive than regular buses but cheaper than taxis.

The improved economy has also meant new problems like traffic jams and shortage of parking spaces. Many cities have now built elevated highways, and superhighways. But be prepared for delays.

The variety of goods on sale for tourists has also improved, both in quantity and quality. Clothing styles are better than before but stores were full of outdated, heavily sequinned party dresses when the style in North America was big sweaters with appliques. (China comes nowhere near surpassing Hong Kong as the place to shop for international fashions.) Jewelry has also proliferated, previously banned by the Cultural Revolution. Upmarket goods are frequently found in the deluxe hotels. China Travel Service has opened "Duty-free stores," selling imported motorcycles, microwave ovens, and computers to those with foreign currency and passports.

But problems have arisen here too. While thefts in hotels are rare, people now have to watch their purses and wallets in crowded areas.

At least one hawker on a boat on Guilin's Li River has tried to pass fake pearls off as real. And some private merchants have become so aggressive, they've scared foreign customers away. One of the worst places is at the Terracotta Army in Xi'an, where little children have been exploited to charm tourists out of their money. And women hard sell their "beautiful" jackets with tears in their eyes.

In Xi'an, too, I bargained one merchant down to "ten" and then he insisted it was "ten U.S. dollars"!

One can now rely more on credit cards, but plastic money is still not as common as in other countries and should not be relied on completely. Take traveler's checks and cash.

A recent trend in several cities has been the development of theme parks with reproductions of ancient buildings. The classic novel *Dream of the Red Chamber (Mansions)* seems to be a favorite. Resort complexes with golf courses are being built, and have even opened in that most hallowed of spots, the Ming Tombs north of Beijing. Whole streets are being renovated in Song, Ming, or Qing architecture.

Tourist attractions are being developed and improved.

There seems to be more awareness of the hazards of cigarette smoking. It is now forbidden on domestic flights, and in some train coaches. A handful of joint-venture hotels have no smoking areas in restaurants and some rooms. But smoking is still very common.

Tourism information is becoming easier to obtain: Information desks have opened at some airports, the government has finally started a twice-a-month tourism newspaper, the National Tourism Administration has published a good booklet on Festivals and C.I.T.S. has one on hotels, and some C.I.T.S. branches have sent representatives to North America who should be able to answer questions about their provinces.

Going on a group tour doesn't eliminate all the problems. But it does mean someone else has to deal with them, and that "someone else" should also be able to find you a clean toilet.

Shortages of trained, experienced staff with a good command of the English language plague all sectors of the industry because it has expanded too quickly. Experienced tour guides have moved on to other positions, and recent group tourists have complained of inexperienced guides, although some are excellent. It is very important to take a list of what you want to do and see. Otherwise, some guides will take you shopping (to stores where they get commissions). Make a list as you read through this book. Some national tours have even had to manage without a national guide. Deciding whether or not to tip, and how much to tip, is still a problem for travelers.

Training still has very high priority. Many new tourism institutes and courses have been started, but it takes time to produce competent graduates. Students have also been sent to the U.S., Australia, and Europe for tourism training.

At the top hotels individuals can also make sure of reservations by giving their credit card numbers, especially during high season. Chinese travel agencies make block hotel bookings to assure sufficient rooms for their clients.

But most hotels honor their reservations!

The horror stories persist—but so do the success stories.

Market forces rather than the state now set most prices. The Chinese also tend to charge what they can get, and if the number of tourists falls, prices should go down.

NOTE

Fielding's People's Republic of China was written for all tourists in China: those on their own and those on escorted tours. It is for business people, foreigners living there, Overseas Chinese and Hong Kong, Macao, and Taiwan Compatriots—anyone wanting to make the most of opportunities in this fascinating country. This guide has been designed to help visitors plan their trips, and to give them an idea of what to expect. It should help you orient yourself, travel around China independently, and make decisions about where to stay, how to get there, and what to do and see. For those on escorted tours, it should give a broader picture of the places you are visiting and the options you have. You should not allow yourself to be at the mercy of tour guides.

Here also are as many Chinese characters as we could get for the names of hotels, restaurants, stores, and tourist attractions. You can communicate by pointing to them so non-English speakers will know where you want to go.

Over 500 cities, counties, towns, and villages are now available to foreign tourists. We have presented what we feel are the most important. Many of the minor destinations are listed as side trips from the larger cities, especially provincial capitals.

Since we couldn't put over 500 names on one map, we have put the names of many of the cities mentioned in this book on maps of the six tourist regions. After each city name in "Destinations" is the region. If you want to find out what other places of interest are in the area, consult that particular map as well as the text on the provincial capital.

China is now producing a great deal of travel literature of its own. We encourage you to supplement the information here with what is available in China, especially the Cartographic Department maps and the China City Guides series.

Please do not consider any guidebook as the only source of information about a country. A guidebook should stimulate your interest as well as give you a lot of essential facts. So please ask many questions in China about what you are experiencing. Only then will you learn, and in learning, enjoy.

Fielding's People's Republic of China is one in a series of eight China guides written by Ruth Lor Malloy since 1973 under a variety of titles. Each one has been updated, expanded, and improved over its predecessor. The 1987 edition was the only one written in collaboration with Priscilla Liang Hsu.

Pinyin spellings: In 1979, China adopted the pinyin system of romanizing its language based on the Beijing pronunciation. This was no easy decision since the language is monosyllabic and the word *ma,* for example, can have at least four totally different meanings depending on the tone. China's recent published literature in English has been using this system. However, many older history books were written in the old Wade-Giles romanization, and in China itself, many historical names like Chiang Kai-shek and Dr. Sun Yat-sen can be found in either form of romanization. We have used the spelling most commonly found now in China.

We have also tried to include the English terminology and new spelling for place names because you will hear both. This might look cumbersome, especially with the Chinese characters; however, we hope all this effort will be helpful to you. The names of dynasties are in the new spelling. A glossary and charts are in the "Quick Reference" section to help straighten things out.

In cases where both the old and new spellings are used, the operative one is the new spelling.

Important to know is that pinyin is phonetic and that "X" is like *sh* as in *she,* "Q" is like *ch* as in *cheek,* "Zh" is like *j* as in *jump,* and "Z" like *z* as in *zero.* See also *How to Pronounce Chinese Letters* in "Quick Reference."

Another confusing area has been whether words like Hong Qiao should be together as one or separated into two words. The tendency now is to combine place names into one word even though they can be very long. Shijiazhuang, for example, would be easier to pronounce if separated into Shi Jia Zhuang, but is found written both ways.

Avoid confusing the provinces Hunan and Henan, Jiangxi and Jiangsu, Shaanxi and Shanxi, Hubei and Hebei, and the cities Jilin and Jinan, the many Hengshan Mountains, and Taishan (in Guangdong) and Taishan (in Shandong). And there is still no standard translation for important place names; for example, Lingyan Si in Jinan has been translated Magic Cliff or Intelligent Rock Temple in different pieces of Jinan tourist literature. It could be difficult to figure out just what is being described.

The imperial dating system has always been used in China: "in the fifth year of the Emperor Hongwu." We have compromised here by giving specific dates and/or the dynasty name or the number of "years ago." Dynastic identification is important because it puts events into context. Some dynasties are more important than others and we hope you will gradually learn them and not have to turn to the "Quick Reference" every time they come up.

From the second Sunday in April to about the second Sunday in September, China is on daylight savings time. Be sure to clarify exact departure and arrival times of trains, ships, and planes.

Note also that the information in this book is as accurate as could be compiled at press time. The situation in China is so fluid that changes will have taken place by the time you visit. When in doubt, ask. And should you find things different, please let us know so we can make changes for future editions. A handy form is in the back of the book.

The travel agencies, hotels, restaurants, and other enterprises listed here free of charge *should* be able to help you. As far as we can see they are reliable, but a mention in this book is not necessarily a recommendation. They are listed to show your options.

Finally, to avoid having to carry a book as heavy as this, cut out the pages you think you'll need in China, and staple each section. Carrying ''Beijing'' and ''Useful Phrases'' is a lot easier than carrying the whole book in Beijing.

Have a great trip!

THE BASICS

WHERE IN CHINA?

First of all, you must decide where in China you want to go. China is full of choices. It is a big country, the third largest in area in the world. It has huge mountains and small mountains, deserts and tropical rain forests, and the second lowest saltwater lake in the world. It has 5000-year-old neolithic sites and pandas in the wild. Among its many ethnic minorities are the Tibetans, who live on the roof of the world and have fascinated people for centuries with their unique customs and religion.

No other country has such variety and vitality, and such a long, continuous history. No other country has such a wealth of temples, pagodas, ancient palaces, gardens, mountains, and elaborate tombs. China has so many valuable cultural relics that one can actually get indigestion from seeing a fraction of what it has to offer.

Careful choices are important if you want to be continually thrilled and surprised. The third set of 500 unique *arhats* can get very boring unless you know what to look for.

The ideal is to take several two-week trips rather than one trip a month long. This gives you a chance to do some digesting and reading in between. Many visitors, unfortunately, have to take longer trips, their perceptions dulled by fatigue toward the end.

Keep in mind your physical capabilities. The most strenuous places to visit are the Silk Road, Inner Mongolia, and, especially, Tibet.

To help you plan your itinerary, make a list of your priorities. If you want to join an existing group tour, see if you can find one that fits. Here are some suggestions. Take one city from any of the following groupings in which you are interested. Take two cities if you want to see more of any particular item. Yes, the hard part is choosing; China has over 500 places open to visit! You have to study a long menu.

If time and money are short, try to confine yourself to one tourist region, such as North China or West China. Staying in one area is cheaper and less time-consuming than hopping all around the country. Currently, you could lose one day (or more) every time you fly.

General interest

For details, see "Destinations." If you can only visit one city, it must be Beijing. Then, in order of priority, Xi'an, and Suzhou, Hangzhou, or Kunming.

Ancient capitals: Best to visit are Xi'an and Beijing; then Luoyang, Chengde, Chengdu, Nanjing, and Shenyang; and finally Anyang, Hangzhou, Kaifeng, Datong, and Suzhou. Well-preserved imperial palaces still only in Beijing, Chengde, and Shenyang.

The Great Wall: See "Great Wall."

Impressive city walls: Nanjing, Kaifeng, and Xi'an.

Imposing imperial tombs: Ming dynasty—better near Beijing, but also the first one in Nanjing and a minor one in Guilin. Qing dynasty—most impressive in Zunhua, but also in Shenyang and Yixian (see "Zunhua"). Qin, Han, and Tang dynasties in Xi'an. The famous Qin Army Vault Museum is visited from Xi'an. Song dynasty near Zhengzhou, but not worth making a special trip.

Important Buddhist sites: Xi'an (including Famen Temple, where they found a finger bone believed to be that of Prince Gautama, the founder of Buddhism), Luoyang, and Beijing. Impressive temples with 500 arhats are in Beijing, Suzhou, Chengdu, and Kunming. The most important Lama temples are, of course, in Tibet, but there are also some exciting ones in Chengde and Beijing. The *Four Sacred Buddhist Mountains are Putuo Shan (Ningbo), Jiuhua Shan (Hefei), Wutai Shan (Datong), and Emei Shan, with many old temples. For **martial arts fans,** Shaolin Temple is reached from Zhengzhou.

Cave temples: The best are in Luoyang, Datong, and Dunhuang. Also impressive: Dazu, Lanzhou, and Leshan.

The *Four Important Taoist Temples: Baiyun Monastery in Beijing, Qingyang Monastery in Chengdu, Taiqing Monastery in Shenyang, and Shangzhen Monastery in Suzhou. For the mythology, there's Yantai, Lushan, and Yueyang.

Important Confucian sites: Best is Qufu, hometown of the sage. Beijing has the second largest temple, now the city museum.

Most important cities with Jewish history: Kaifeng and Shanghai.

---

*Traditional Chinese evaluation.

Important mosques: Guangzhou, Quanzhou, Beijing, Hangzhou, Yangzhou, and Xi'an.

Neolithic site museums: Xi'an, Lanzhou, and Zhengzhou. Many being opened elsewhere too.

Primitive man: Peking Man (Zhoukoudian—see Beijing); Maba Man (see Shaoguan).

Shang dynasty sites: Zhengzhou and Anyang.

Foreign imperialist history: Very little in museums, but much European architecture in Tianjin, Shanghai, Wuhan, Beijing, Harbin, and Qingdao. Some in Xiamen and Guangzhou (Canton). Among the 46 treaty ports were also Zhenjiang, Ningbo, Fuzhou, Xiamen (Amoy), Nanjing, Jiujiang, Shashi, and Chongqing.

Best ancient history museums: Beijing, Shenyang, Xi'an, Zhengzhou, and Wuhan.

24 cities of historical or revolutionary importance protected by the State Council: Beijing, Chengde, Datong, Nanjing, Suzhou, Yangzhou, Hangzhou, Shaoxing, Quanzhou, Jingdezhen, Qufu, Luoyang, Kaifeng, Jiangling, Changsha, Guangzhou, Guilin, Chengdu, Zunyi, Kunming, Dali, Lhasa, Xi'an, and Yan'an. In some cases, whole streets of ancient buildings are being preserved or reconstructed.

Most important revolutionary sites: With good museums—Beijing, Yan'an, Shaoshan, Nanchang, and Jinggang Shan.

Other unusual structures worth seeing: Hengshan for the Temple in Mid-air; Lhasa for the Potala.

Memorable boat rides: The Yangtze Gorges, the Li River from Guilin, and the Grand Canal.

Limestone formations: Very impressive caves in Guilin, but also good at Yixing, Nanning, and Zhaoqing. The Stone Forest at Kunming is celebrated.

Seaside resorts: Beidaihe, Qingdao, Sanya (Hainan Island), Zhuhai, and Shenzhen.

Well-preserved ancient cadavers and their belongings: In museums. The best is in Changsha of a 2100-year-old noblewoman. Also

Zhenjiang and Jingzhou. Large mummy collection in Urumqi. A few
mummies near Turpan.

Best classical Chinese gardens: Summer Palace and Beihai Park
in Beijing, the Yu Garden in Shanghai, and many gardens in Suzhou,
Wuxi, and Hangzhou.

Gorgeous mountain scenery: Guilin—tame; Lushan Mountain,
Chengde, and Jinggang Shan—a little rough, but you can drive around
there; Taishan Mountain (a 4-hour climb, but cable cars available); Huang
Shan (cable car), Emei Shan (cable car), and Hua Shan—very rugged.
Then there are the Himalayas in Tibet and Xinjiang!

Last Emperor: Puyi lived in Beijing, Changchun, Fushun, and Tianjin. Manchu dynasty palace and tombs in Shenyang.

Satellite launch site: Tours now to Xichaing (see Chengdu).

Camel and pony rides, and yurts: Hohhot, and Silk Road.

***Three Most Eminent Halls:**   Tian Kuang Hall in Tai'an; Taihe Hall
in the Imperial Palace, Beijing; and the Dacheng Hall in Qufu's Confucius Temple.

***Five Great Mountains:**   Taishan, Hengshan (Hunan), Hengshan
(Shanxi), Huashan, and Songshan.

Theme Parks: Dream of the Red Chamber in Shanghai and Beijing;
Han City in Guangzhou.

For Those with Special Interests

Musicians   should be interested in the bronze chime bells in Wuhan
and the Chinese musical instruments factory in Suzhou.

Plant lovers   can visit botanical gardens: Lushan, Guangzhou, Nanjing, Hangzhou, etc.

Hot-air ballooning and gliding: Anyang has both. Xi'an says ballooning is permitted there, but bring your own.

Sports: **Mountaineering**—Several peaks, including Qomolangma
(Everest) are open. **Skiing**—Not well developed yet, but lifts near Har-
bin and Jilin. **Scuba diving**—In Zhanjiang and Hainan Island. **Golf**—
In Zhongshan, Zhuhai, Tianjin, Beijing, and soon in Shanghai.

Visits to ancestral villages and relatives: See "Special for Overseas Chinese."

Steam locomotives: No more factory in Datong. Museums in Datong and Shenyang. Real working steam engines in Anshan, Jilin, Shenyang, Changchun and Harbin, best photographed in winter.

Dogs: See Datong.

Performing Pandas: Shanghai Acrobats and Circus. Wuhan Acrobats.

Pandas in a wildlife preserve: Wolong, near Chengdu; Baishuijiang Nature Reserve in Gansu province; Shennonjia in Hubei.

Sister Cities: Many foreign cities have "friendship links" with specific Chinese cities, and you may want to include yours in your itinerary. For example, Melbourne and Tianjin, Edinburgh and Xi'an, Toronto and Chongqing, Chattanooga and Wuxi. Ask your city hall.

Wheel-chair-confined travelers: Hotel rooms with lower sinks, etc., for wheelchair-confined travelers: Hilton (Shanghai), Shangri-la and China World (Beijing), Lakeside (Fuzhou), Holiday Inns Dalian, Xi'an, and City Center (Guangzhou). Ask about these when you book.

As a rule of thumb:

—The cradle of Chinese civilization was along the Yellow River (Zhengzhou, Anyang).

—The Silk Road went west from Xi'an. See *Silk Road*.

—The western imperialists controlled areas along the Yangtze River, and also Changsha. They were active on the east coast between Liaoning province and Hainan Island. The Japanese controlled Northeast China, then known as Manchuria, and, later, most of urban China.

—Most national minorities live mainly in the west, north, and southwest parts of China, especially Guangxi, Yunnan, Guizhou, Sichuan, Xinjiang, Tibet, and Inner Mongolia. Turkish-related Moslem minorities live primarily in Xinjiang, Qinghai, and Gansu.

—The earlier migrations of Chinese to America and Australia in the 19th and early 20th centuries originated from Guangdong province; the migrations to Southeast Asia originated largely from Fujian, but also from Guangdong.

—**The 14 Coastal Cities** earmarked in 1984 for accelerated development are Beihai, Dalian, Fuzhou, Guangzhou, Lianyungang, Nantong, Ningbo, Qingdao, Qinhuangdao, Shanghai, Tianjin, Wenzhou, Yantai, and Zhanjiang. **Special Economic Zones:** Shenzhen, Xiamen,

Shantou, and Zhuhai. The Yangtze and Pearl river deltas including Guangzhou—part of southern Fujian province—including Xiamen, Zhangzhou, and Quanzhou—and the Liaodong and Shandong peninsulas are also S.E.Z.s. Direct international flights to some of these cities have now started.

If you want to avoid crowds, head for cities away from the tourist track, like Changsha, Guiyang, Jingdezhen, Nanning, Quanzhou, Shaoxing, Taishan, Yangzhou, Yantai, Xiamen, Xuzhou, Zhaoqing, Zhengzhou, Zhongshan, and Zibo. These have enough for at least one day's sightseeing, but you could spend a week just exploring by bicycle if you're interested in lifestyles, looking for glimpses of old architecture, and getting chatty with the natives. Taishan (Guangdong) still has most of its old buildings, but come quickly, before it's all replaced by highrises, and take advantages of the classes it offers in Chinese painting, language, *qigong* (Chinese yoga), etc.

—**The Ten Most Popular Tourist Attractions in China,** the result of a poll in the mid-1980s by Chongguo Luyou Bao, China's tourism magazine: Great Wall, Guilin, West Lake (Hangzhou), Imperial Palace (Beijing), Suzhou Gardens, Huangshan, Yangtze Gorges, Sun-Moon Lake (Taiwan), Imperial Summer Resort (Chengde), and the Qin Army Vault Museum (Xi'an). Runners-up were: Lake Taihu (Wuxi), Summer Palace (Beijing), Taishan Mountain (Tai'an), Emei Mountain, Lushan, Huangguoshou Falls (Guiyang), Mogao Grottoes (Dunhuang), Lake Tianchi (Urumqi), Potala Palace (Lhasa), Seven Star Rock (Zhaoqing), and Huashan Mountain.

WHEN TO GO?

If you care about the weather, the best time to visit is May–June or September–October, but these, of course, are the times when most people like to travel. If you go then, you could run into crowds and delays, even if all reservations are confirmed. You could also try April or November and hope for good weather. Do consult each city listed under "Destinations." South China is chilly but fine in January. Kunming has spring temperatures most of the year.

It is important to remember that the Chinese do not heat their buildings as warmly as foreigners do in winter. South of the Yangtze there is no heat at all, except in tourist hotels, even though it can be very chilly. Some low-priced hotels do not have any heat at all. If the cold bothers you, avoid Northeast China, Inner Mongolia, Northwest China, Tibet, Qinghai, and any mountains in winter, especially around the lunar new year (around late January or early February). Even in Guangzhou at that time you need a top coat and a sweater. Avoid the lunar new year especially in Guangzhou and Fujian, as hotels and trains are full of Overseas Chinese visitors and prices are at their highest. Industrial pollution is particularly bad in winter too. But most tour agencies and hotels give discounts in such low seasons! Avoid Guangzhou during its trade fairs.

The hottest time of the year is usually July and early August. Traditionally, the "three furnaces" of China are Nanjing, Wuhan, and Chongqing. There's also Nanchang. Almost all hotels, but few other buildings, are now air-conditioned. Most tourist buses and many taxis are air-conditioned. This is the time to put mountain or seaside resorts at the end of a hot tour.

In late spring, April–May through the summer, rain and high humidity make south China (including Guangzhou and Guilin) quite oppressive, but the greenery is lush and beautiful. Inner Mongolia and the Silk Road have a problem with sandstorms in spring and autumn.

As a rough gauge, China extends from the same latitude as James Bay in Canada to south of Cuba. Beijing is at almost the same latitude as Philadelphia, and Guangzhou as Havana. Take altitude into account: the higher, the colder. Winter begins in mid-November.

Wise tourists who are healthy and not afraid of the cold could plan trips in the winter even in the north. New-fallen snow transforms any city into a wonderland and makes red pavilions and curved gold roofs intensely beautiful. (It also makes roads slippery, and traffic slow-moving.)

Winters in Beijing are about the same as in Philadelphia and Toronto, only the air is drier. Precautions like long underwear should be taken because of the lack of heat in many buildings (which sometimes seem colder than being outdoors). Beijing also has a strong wind from February on, which brings more shivers. Take a nose mask because of the pollution. But most services are more readily available from mid-November through March.

Winter is a good time to visit south China, Guangzhou, Hainan Island, and Yunnan.

Other things to consider when planning dates:

—If you are interested in visiting schools, factories, and offices, avoid vacations and holidays. People wanting to do business should avoid the national holidays.

—If you want to see a festival like the Third Moon Market or the dragon boats, consider those dates. See "Quick Reference."

HOW TO GO?

Take your pick. The group tour is *not* the only way to go, but it could be cheaper and has less hassles for all but the tour guide.

Groups and Individuals

On a prepaid tour This is the easiest way to visit China. Just book with a good travel agent and most of your problems are solved. You can choose one of the set tours offered by a travel agent or you can have one custom-made. The average size of a tour is 20 people or less. Of course, the fewer people you have, the more expensive the rate per person can be.

China prefers prepaid tours. They use scarce staff interpreters more efficiently and are given preference. Even groups of four pay-as-you-go individuals run the risk of being downgraded or having their reservations canceled in favor of a full-scale prepaid tour group.

By ordering and paying in advance, groups, rather than individuals, are more likely to get what they want. For example, a group can book a helicopter in Sichuan to go to Jiuzhaigou, and do the trip in a day. A party of two could also book the helicopter, but if it isn't already going there, the rate for two would be prohibitive to all but the richest tourists. Some of the tours listed in this book, such as cooking and taiqi lessons, are not generally available to one or two individual tourists, but a group can book them, and if there is space left over, then the individuals who happen to be there at the time might be able to pay their share and tag along.

By hiring a professional tour leader, tourists do not have to bother about getting permits for non-open destinations, making reservations, and all the annoying and time-consuming things you will see in the chapter on getting around.

Basically all prepaid tours are treated the same in China except for the quality of the hotel. You can choose between standard or the more expensive "deluxe" rooms. If the price of the same tour still differs from one agency to another, it could be because (1) more restaurant meals are included (rather than hotel meals); (2) there is an orientation session on China, and perhaps a full-time guide, who has more than a superficial knowledge of Chinese history and culture; (3) more than one agency is getting a commission; try to book from the wholesaler; (4) one agent is getting a bigger commission; (5) a luxury tourist ship rather than a ferry is guaranteed on the Yangtze, and that ship's facilities are of the highest quality—lectures, briefings, and side trips. Ask if it has 70 or 180 passengers if you care; (6) the tour operator has better connections in China or flies Air China.

Ask about refunds if you are stuck in an airport for three days. Ask about tipping—will you be asked for tips for guides and drivers in each city? Will you have to spend hours discussing what to give the national guide? Do you have a national guide? (This is important as groups have been abandoned at the airport and their planes have been cancelled. What happens then?)

Prepaid tourists can usually choose what they want to see in each city from a set list. You have to pay extra for any "optional tours." Some tourists complain of the time spent in making group decisions; others are happy to have a choice. If you just want to see China, a general-interest tour is ideal. If you want to visit schools, several factories, or hospitals, better take a special-interest or Friendship association tour. Or you could make sure schools, factories, or hospitals are included in your tour.

Group tours are also flexible insofar as you can choose to avoid most of the group activities. If you want to sleep in a different hotel from the one assigned, you can in some cities. But you might have to pay extra. Just be sure to tell your group leader so no one will look for you.

But you usually have to travel from city to city with the group, or at least in and out of the country with it. Each group has one "group visa" and individual passports are not stamped at the border. The only way you can leave the country without your group is to have a new visa stamped in your passport.

Some group tourists have been able to acquire individual visas once inside China.

Overseas Chinese tour groups are usually given individual visas in the first place so members can visit relatives after the tour is over.

Tour groups can be fun if you have the right people. But a tendency does develop to look inward toward your own group, and to regard the Chinese as "them" as opposed to "us." As soon as group members start joking about the "natives," you've crossed the line and have truly become a group tourist. If you are visiting China to meet Chinese people and learn about the country, you do have to make an effort to break free from your groupiness and dependence. Do venture out into the streets alone. Lounge in parks especially on Sundays. A lot of students are waiting to practice their English on you. You might even be invited to someone's home.

Luggage for C.I.T.S. foreign tour groups is not usually opened by Chinese Customs, but that of Overseas Chinese might be. The total weight of group luggage to be flown is usually added together and averaged.

On a cruise Among the cruise lines that have included China are Holland America Cruises, Lindblad Travel, Inc., P&O Line, and Cunard Line. You usually pay extra if you want a guided tour at ports of call. See also "Yangtze Gorges" and *Fielding's Worldwide Cruises* by Antoinette DeLand.

On a minipackage C.I.T.S. offers prepaid packages that could include travel tickets, hotel accommodations, and breakfast. You sightsee

on your own or, if available, book sightseeing tours locally. It is an
ideal compromise for business people and those who want the flexibility
of scheduling their own time, as well as the assurance of a place to
sleep. Minipackages are available for many cities, including Beijing,
Chengde, Chengdu, Chongqing, Dalian, Fuzhou, Guilin, Guangzhou,
Hangzhou, Harbin, Jinan, Kunming, Nanjing, Nanning, Qingdao, Qufu,
Shanghai, Suzhou, Taiyuan, Tianjin, Wuhan, Wuxi, Xiamen, and Xi'an.

As a pay-as-you-go traveler   Many foreigners, especially those with
time to spare, have traveled China happily and successfully on their
own. Some backpackers have loved it, not minding the dormitory accommodations and delays. Backpackers should take along the Lonely
Planet guidebook and the *Travel China* newsletter. Travelers with bigger budgets have an easier time. Most hotels have travel desks, and
bookings are made with less difficulty now. If a group tour is not scheduled in a city, you can always hire a taxi.

   On-your-own traveling is not, however, as easy in China as in
Europe. If you can't speak Chinese, you can get around with this guidebook. See also "Getting Around."

As a traveler of Chinese ancestry   C.I.T.S. guides do not usually
know anything about places in Fujian or Guangdong, where many Overseas Chinese (O.C.) have relatives. However, C.T.S. doesn't have as
many English-speaking staff members.

   Chinese missions abroad have a quota of individual visas for Overseas Chinese, so we don't have to have documentation from China to
get one. It is possible to get a visa from one within a week or, in Hong
Kong, in one working day.

   An Overseas Chinese is anyone with a Chinese surname, face, or
the address of a relative and/or an ancestral village in China, and either
a foreign or Chinese passport. Those with a Chinese ancestor who have
a Chinese name but do not look Chinese might be able to convince
authorities that they qualify.

   Overseas Chinese are regarded as family and are especially welcome in China. You can take in duty-free many kinds of gifts for relatives.

   It is possible to live with relatives in China or have relatives stay
with you in your hotel. It is also possible to take part in special camps
and seminars offered by the Overseas Chinese Association in some
counties in Guangdong province. Xinhui county gives free room, board,
travel in the county, and courses for two weeks, mostly but not exclusively for young people with roots in the county. Taishan gives courses,
but it charges. These are great introductions to China and the area where
you might have relatives. Courses could be on language, cooking,
painting, medicine, music, dance—and are given in English.

You could write the Overseas Chinese Association in your county for information, or try a Chinatown travel agent, a family association, or a county association. You can probably find these in any large Chinatown, New York City, San Francisco, Los Angeles, Toronto, and Vancouver. A Chinese consulate might have information. See also "Special for Overseas Chinese."

As a Hong Kong, Macao, or Taiwan Compatriot   Hong Kong and Macao Chinese who have reentry permits to Hong Kong or Macao can enter China the same way Americans enter Canada. They can just buy a ticket and get on some means of transportation. Taiwan Compatriots are especially welcome and now have permission from Taiwan authorities to visit. Travel arrangements can be made through China Travel Service or any travel agency that deals with it. In 1988, Taiwan citizens were given privileges like cheaper hotels to make them feel more welcome.

On business   The usual procedure here is to communicate with a trade officer at a Chinese mission abroad, your mission in China, or your own government's department of trade. They will all probably tell you to contact a Chinese trading corporation, some of whom have representatives in North America. If the Chinese are interested in what you want to buy or sell, they will send you an invitation that will give you a visa from a Chinese mission. A travel agent can do all the bookings.

Business people can usually take their spouses and travel individually in China, not just for negotiations, but afterward as tourists. You can discuss the logistics with your host trading corporations or deal with a Chinese travel agency once in China. You should tell your host unit the quality of the hotel you want because your host unit might assume you want to save money. The unit might also automatically book you into a hotel with which they have connections (which may not be up to your standards). It is embarrassing for a unit to make changes after you arrive. You can also take time off from a prepaid tour to visit a trading corporation. See also "Special for Business People."

As a foreign student, scholar, or foreign expert   Foreign exchange students studying in China are usually there as the result of an agreement between governments or educational institutions. Information on these exchanges can be obtained from the United States Information Agency in Washington, DC, or from the Council on International Educational Exchange, New York. In Canada, contact the Awards division of the Association of Universities and Colleges of Canada in Ottawa. Other countries have their own counterparts.

Most exchange students are already university graduates and stay up to two years. The home government pays transportation to and from

China and gives spending money. The Chinese government pays tuition, the cost of accommodations, and a small stipend. It is possible to save money and also to travel around the country during vacations.

Some universities and colleges abroad have bilateral arrangements with their counterparts in China, and information can be obtained from schools in your home country.

"Self-supporting" foreign students are also accepted at an increasing number of schools in China; prospective students can apply directly. These students should be aware that academic credits for courses studied in China may not be equivalent to those studied in their home countries. Tuition is about US$1200 a year, living expenses about US$200 a month.

Foreign students have lived in guesthouses in rooms sometimes described by students at Beijing University as "cold and small" with little if any privacy. Many have hot tap water only two hours a day. Students at some other universities might fare better. Food is usually of higher standard than that of Chinese students, but with less meat than in the foreigner's home country.

Students learn a great deal about China and the Chinese language. Courses and teaching methods in Chinese institutions, however, are not as rigorous as in Western countries. Students do get closer to Chinese people than most other foreigners.

Chinese missions abroad and foreign missions in China should have information on studying in China. The China Education Association for International Exchanges publishes *The China Education Directory* with a list of institutions.

Scholarly visits are also arranged by government agreement, but much is being done privately now, bilaterally between institutions or directly by scholars themselves. In the United States the U.S. Information Agency, for example, sponsors the Fulbright program, which makes it possible for a limited number of American scholars to teach American studies in Chinese universities. U.S.I.A. also finances the National Program, which helps American scholars and professionals lecture and do exploratory research in China for one to three months.

The Committee on Scholarly Communication with the People's Republic of China (C.S.C.P.R.C.) have developed programs with the Chinese Academy of Sciences, the Chinese Academy of Social Sciences, the State Council on Education, and the Chinese Association for Science and Technology.

The C.S.C.P.R.C.'s activities include a program for American graduate students, postdoctoral students, and research scholars to carry out long-term study or research. This is in affiliation with Chinese universities and research institutes. There are also short-term reciprocal exchanges of senior-level Chinese and American scholars, bilateral conferences, and an exchange of joint working groups in selected fields.

In Ottawa, Canada, contact the Social Sciences Research Council and the Humanities Research Council for information.

People who are going to China in other capacities can also make valuable professional contributions in China. Specialists and professionals can give lectures or demonstrations to their Chinese counterparts if invited to do so.

If you're thinking of getting financial compensation, forget it. If you're thinking of helping China in exchange for a deeper insight, as well as business or academic contacts, do offer to lecture—if you have anything worthwhile to say, that is. Don't expect anything more than a "thank you" and, if you're in business, probably a tax write-off for part of your expenses (if you can convince your tax people that you were actually making business contacts in China).

Full-time **foreign experts** and **teachers** have been hired by the Bureau of Foreign Experts of the State Council on Education and other bodies in Beijing and elsewhere. Teachers at this level need at least a Masters and three years' teaching experience. Increasingly, individual universities and colleges have been doing their own recruiting without going through Beijing, a much faster route. One scholar, who was given a contract for a week or so and then asked four days before leaving the United States to postpone his visit, went ahead and taught anyway. He was not reimbursed as promised for travel because the Chinese had not received his money, as hoped, from their own authorities. But the teaching experience, he said, was worth it.

Many teachers hired by China specialize in a foreign language with one- or two-year contracts. The great need is for English language teachers and teachers of middle-level technology and managerial skills. In recent years, there have been more than 9000 foreign teachers working in China.

Long-term experts should receive a contract giving them their transportation paid from home and back, as well as home leave, after the first year and then every other year, for a month or so. The stipend ranges from about ¥500 to ¥1000, with a few getting as much as ¥1,500 a month, depending on qualifications. An M.A., for example, has received ¥700–750. Fifty percent of one's salary can be taken out of China in foreign currency. Certain categories of experts also receive free accommodation, free medical care, transportation to and from work, and a month's vacation in China. The salary for foreign experts is frequently ten times that of local teachers, so no complaints, please.

Foreign *teachers* (as differentiated from *experts*) are usually locally hired and do not get the same benefits as experts. Some money-strapped colleges have hired native English-speakers without any teaching qualifications who just drop by. They give them only room and board, and try to help them find financing through North American religious or government organizations. *Teacher-students* occasionally teach part-time and study part-time.

Foreigners working in China have been advised by one teacher assigned to Nanjing "to know how to say 'no,' since the Chinese will often pile work on them. I would also suggest, if possible, getting advice from someone who has taught in China prior to one's assignment, and bringing as many teaching materials as possible, including textbooks. Warm clothes for winter and a commitment from the university about sufficient heat for housing are essential. . . . Some foreign experts have had a terrible time with the cold." Ask any branch of a China Friendship Association for the names of teachers with experience in China. Another group hiring are the China People's Association for Friendship with Foreign Countries, Beijing. The China Friendship Associations and China desks of national councils of churches or church denominations should be able to tell you of job openings. Christian groups are now getting involved with sending technical and professional experts to China but not missionaries. The International Volunteers Organization of the United Nations has sent a few volunteer teachers to China. Australian teachers should write to the Australia-China Education Co-op Program. Teachers' organizations should have information. Americans are recruited through the Peace Corps. The Great Britain-China Center has a list of organizations. Contact the education officer at a Chinese consulate.

As a consultant   Many foreign and Chinese organizations recruit experts to China in connection with their own projects. The foreign companies offer the most money and usually the best living conditions.

The Canadian Executive Service Overseas (C.E.S.O.), Toronto, sends recently retired Canadians to work as volunteer consultants to industry, institutions, and governments in developing areas such as China. Other countries and some companies probably have similar programs.

Many foreign workers and students get taken on sightseeing tours for free, but more likely at much cheaper rates than regular tourists. Do read *China Bound, A Guide to Academic Life and Work in the PRC* by Karen Turner-Gottschang. For background, there's also the National Academy Press's *A Relationship Restored. Trends in U.S.-China Educational Exchanges, 1978–1984,* and Goede's *Love in Beijing,* a collection of short stories about foreigners and Chinese living in Beijing's Friendship Hotel, home of many foreign teachers.

While some foreigners live without (horrors!) a refrigerator and air conditioning—and the minimal heat gets turned off on March 15 no matter what the weather—many are pleased with the experience. Some are not. Working in a developing country is the best way to learn how most of the world has to live and how very privileged those in the developed world are. In addition to the cheaper travel, foreign residents benefit from learning that perishable foods can be kept on balconies in cold weather and perhaps under a continuously wet rag in summer. They learn that silk jackets can be made for ¥25, and other such secrets, previously known only to the Chinese. They do make some Chinese friends, especially if they live outside of Beijing.

The standard of living of foreign experts and students has risen over the years.

As a casual student   Many provincial travel and tourism offices are now offering courses in cooking, martial arts, acupuncture, and other Chinese arts, but primarily for groups. Several colleges and universities offer six- to eight-week summer Chinese language courses, for students 16 to 45 years of age, 55 for teachers. Some of these schools also give spring and autumn courses. Some of the schools are in Beijing, Shanghai, Tianjin, Nanjing, Wuhan, Jinan, Xiamen, Hefei, and Guangzhou. Information can be obtained from Chinese missions abroad.

The Stone Flower Mountain Inn in Taishan (Guangdong) offers courses in Chinese with academic credit from Zhongshan University in Guangzhou. Individuals can join. The Federation of Canada-China Friendship Associations organizes three-week seminars with sightseeing in China, etc. Many provincial tourism administrations offer courses for groups.

One should not expect to learn Chinese or any other language in eight weeks. Nor can one learn taiqi in a day. It would be better to start learning such skills before you go to China, and expect polishing from the short course.

As a job hunter   Tourists can try to pick up a job while traveling in China, but don't count on it. If you want to live in any particular place and are an experienced teacher, you could start by asking C.I.T.S. or any college or university if teachers are needed locally. If English is your native language and you have any idea about teaching, you could also ask any about-to-be-opened hotel or a tourism school if they want an English teacher. Many places want English teachers but do not have the foreign exchange to pay a ''foreign expert.'' But again, don't expect to earn very much money. If that's not your line, talk with business people about job possibilities. Good English-speaking secretaries are in short supply. But check out work regulations and income tax for foreigners first. Local hires might be paid Chinese-level salaries.

For medical treatment   Some provincial travel and tourism agencies, for example Wuxi, offer tour packages for treatment in Chinese sanitariums, but you can book directly. Just do not expect North American standards. Some hotels have *gigong,* acupuncture, or no-smoking clinics.

As a property buyer Foreigners and Overseas Chinese can now buy resort, residential, and business property in some Chinese cities. Contact a Chinese mission or the municipal office in the city of your choice. Advertisements frequently appear in Hong Kong newspapers. Many Overseas Chinese have retired in China, especially in the south.

On a convention Many cities can now handle hundreds of convention visitors. Some of the new or renovated hotels have simultaneous translation facilities. Contact the China Council for the Promotion of International Trade (C.C.P.I.T.) or any travel agent specializing in China for information.

As a journalist Contact a Chinese mission or Xinhua, the New China News Agency, if it is represented in your country. You could also contact the Information Office of the Foreign Ministry, Beijing.

Special tours The important thing to remember is that C.I.T.S. and C.T.S. tours are set up primarily for tourists. They cannot be expected to understand the needs of travelers primarily interested in meeting Chinese Christians, for example, or doctors wanting to meet their counterparts in China. The needs of doctors and scientists can be met by some of the Chinese travel agents if you tell them exactly what you want, preferably with names and addresses. Give them plenty of time in advance. Or you could contact the Foreign Affairs Department of the Chinese Academy of Sciences yourself. Mountain climbers should contact the Chinese Mountaineering Association, and school groups, China Youth Travel Service. Sports teams wanting to play Chinese teams, or individuals wanting a ski package or parachuting should go through China Sports Service. Unusual requests like the Hong Kong-Beijing Motor Rally have taken several years to arrange. Most, however, can be worked out more quickly. A good travel agent experienced with China knows how. For religious groups, see also "Religion."

If you have any other questions, it might help to consult an experienced travel agent, a Chinese mission, or a China Friendship Association. Yes, you can write an organization in China directly with a good chance of getting a reply—but don't count on it.

In dealing directly with China, the best way to communicate is by Telex or Fax. Letters can take up to three weeks from North America. They do arrive more quickly if addressed in Chinese, and are answered more quickly if written in Chinese. If you telephone China, be sure to have a Mandarin-speaking person with you in case no one understands English at the other end of the line.

For Addresses, see "Important Addresses and Information."

Should You Take Your Children?

I took my five-year-old for a five-week visit in 1973, my seven-year-old to visit relatives in 1978, and my nine-year-old on a group tour in 1979. I even took a reluctant teenager on an eight-destination tour. I was glad I did, but then, this depends on the child. A year later, the teenager went back to China on her own with her school to work on a commune!

I did not use a baby-sitter because the younger children accompanied me to evening movies and theatrical performances. Chinese dance dramas are easy for a child to understand, and acrobats and puppets are fun for all ages. The younger children did find the traditional operas boring, so unless you're sure of lots of action, skip them.

I would not take a child just to be left with a Chinese-speaking baby-sitter unless the child understood Chinese.

At communes and factories, many willing hands kept the children amused while grown-ups talked. The children were interested in seeing how things were made. Guilin, with its caves, mountains, and boat trip was ideal. My nine-year-old found the 2100-year-old cadaver in Changsha fascinating.

The Chinese love children and are intrigued by those different from their own. You may have to protect children with blond hair and blue eyes, for instance, from being overly fondled. Tour-bus drivers bought mine popsicles; cheeks were pinched. In restaurants they disappeared with waiters to be shown off to the cooks.

Two of them became sick with bad colds, but doctors took care of them. They were well in a couple of days, missing only one day of the tour. Two of them lived with relatives. The seven-year-old had a ball learning how to bring up water from an open well, washing his own clothes by hand, and tending a wood cooking fire. It took awhile to adjust to the smelly outhouses, but he managed.

The neighborhoods where we lived with family were full of other children, and in spite of initial shyness and the language barrier, they made friends. Strangers on the street and in buses would stop and try to talk to them. Barriers of formality melted right away, and I'm not the only one who has gotten a room in an overcrowded hotel because "my child is very tired."

Food was a problem. One lived only on scrambled eggs and *char siu bow* (steamed barbecued pork buns). Hamburgers and milk are now easier to find. Baby food in jars for infants and disposable diapers have arrived at Friendship Stores, but may not always be available at the time and place you want them and are very expensive.

Some hotels do not charge for children sharing their parents' room.

Should You Go If Your Health Is Fragile?

Things to consider: A prepaid group tour is usually strenuous, with lots of stairs to climb, and a packed schedule—unless the group agrees to a slower pace. Most hotels but not restaurants have elevators. Chinese guides are very considerate of older people.

Things can be easier for pay-as-you-go individual travelers who can do things at their own pace. But in no circumstances do we recommend traveling alone.

So far we have only heard of a few hotels set up for handicapped people, with wider bathroom doors and bars near toilets. A lot of helpful hands are available, however. And many hotels have ramps.

Chinese hospitals are adequate, and some doctors have Western training and excellent Western standards. But most facilities are at least 30 years behind what you're used to, and communicating with nurses could be difficult.

Could you be left behind alone by your group in a hospital and in a city where you have no friends, no language skills, and at your own expense? How would you feel about that?

Disabled travelers should contact organizations that specialize in travel for people with allergies, diabetes, wheelchairs, epilepsy, etc., like Freedom in Travelling (F.I.T.), 65 Tromley Dr., Etobicoke, Ont., M9B 5Y7; tel. (416) 234–8511; or *Itinerary* Magazine, Box 1084, Bayonne, NJ 07002-1084. See our chapter on local customs and emergencies. And read about Grace Wyatt's experiences in our Appendix.

CHOOSING A TRAVEL AGENT

You can deal directly with any authorized travel agent in Hong Kong or China (time-consuming) or work through a travel agent at home. Do not hesitate about bothering agents. They make their money from commissions. Sometimes a travel agent will discount, especially if you buy packages. And yes, you can save money organizing your own tour group. The more people you have, the cheaper it is, but also the more headaches.

In dealing with a travel agent, consider seriously the following, especially if these apply to your situation.

How experienced is the tour organizer with tours to China? In other words, has the wholesaler established good relationships with tourism officials in China so you will get the best rooms and services for your money? The Chinese do their best for people they know and trust. If a tour organizer sends a lot of tours to China, and has been doing so for several years, then the organizer is in a stronger position than some company organizing only a few groups.

We have found that the cheapet tours from North America are from Canada. We have talked with people who have been pleased with tours booked through Tour East and Conference Travel. These tours are even cheaper than flying to Hong Kong or China and booking tours from there.

The cheapest flights are probably through Chinatown agencies. We suggest you contact Air China, get a quote from its major wholesalers, and see if your own travel agent can match it. For individual travelers, does the agent know enough to advise you what to do in the event of a plane cancellation in a strange city where no hotel rooms are available? Would the agent know the prices and quality of cheaper hotels? Whether or not the city has tour groups you can join on the spot? The cost of taxis?

For prepaid tours with set itineraries especially

How many of your desired destinations are offered? How many days will you have in each place? Does the price include the Dazu sculptures in Chongqing, for example, or do you have to pay extra?

Do the dates fit your own schedule, weather preference, and Chinese holidays?

What is the price? Why is it different from another organizer's with the same cities and same number of days? What are you paying for? Usually the price includes visa fee, group transportation (be sure you establish if this is from your home or from your first point in China), hotel accommodation (double or single occupancy?), three meals and beverages a day, sightseeing, group transfers, transporting one piece of luggage (maximum 20 kg per person?), and admission tickets to tourist attractions and cultural events. Does the price include all the taxes and service charges along the way? Will you be traveling with a guide-interpreter? (Groups of over six people qualify for an escort in China.)

Are the hotel rooms "standard" or "deluxe," and do you get a refund if a deluxe room is not available? Are the trains soft or hard class? Are the airplanes first or economy class?

Price quotes do not usually include passport fees, laundry, hairdressing, taxis, postage, long-distance telephone calls, excess baggage, medical, and other expenses of a personal nature. Nor do they include insurance for expenses for changes in the itinerary, or prolonged tours "due to unforeseen circumstances." Ask about those "unforeseen circumstances." These could include plane cancellations, overbooking, arriving at the airport after the plane leaves, illness, or accident. Who pays for these inconveniences? Tour escorts have been known to pay for minor "extras," but will you be expected to pay on the spot or at the end of the tour for any substantial changes? If not, get it in writing. Ask about these, health insurance and cancelation insurance. Do you need evacuation insurance!! What about compensation for delays!? Evacuation insurance should be considered if you are in questionable health or traveling alone.

What is the minimum group size required before the tour is cancelled? Are promised hotels guaranteed, and what happens if there is a change?

What language will the guides speak? For example, a tour booked in Japan may only have Japanese-speaking guides, while some tours booked in Hong Kong are in English. Or a tour might be in Beijing dialect and you expected Cantonese.

Do you get a group visa or an individual visa? Some tours allow longer time for individuals to visit relatives or negotiate business, etc.

How many people are in the group? How old? Sexes?

How much is the deposit and when do you pay in full? Are departures guaranteed? What refund do you get if the tour is canceled? Should you buy cancelation insurance? What happens if you have to leave partway through the China portion? Will you get a prorated refund? Do you get a refund if a hotel lacks all the services described in its brochure? What hotels do you get? (Check these hotels in "Destinations" to see if that is what you want.) If you want an evaluation, check the *Travel China Newsletter* and *Guide to China's Hotels*.

Will you be able to see everything you want?

Does the tour operator offer the Yangtze Gorges tour on a regular public ship or on a luxury, air-conditioned tourist ship? Which would you prefer? See "Yangtze Gorges" and "On a prepaid tour" earlier in this chapter.

All tours are subject to changes in itinerary by the Chinese, so don't blame your travel agent. These changes should become less frequent as China acquires more hotels, trains, and airplanes. Prices, too, are subject to change.

Travel agents China National Tourist Offices, now in New York City, Los Angeles, Tokyo, Sydney, London, Paris, and Frankfurt should be able to answer travel questions. Some representatives of C.I.T.S. branches are now in North America, and should be able to answer questions and make bookings for their own tours. If you can't find an experienced agent, here are some suggestions. Most of these can also make arrangements for individuals. You can also get a list of U.S. tour operators from China National Tourist Office.

U.S.A. *AFS Intercultural Programs:* Offers six weeks of summer classes in Mandarin, *taiji,* Chinese cooking, and culture and history in a Chinese school dormitory. It also has year-long academic programs in Mandarin at a Chinese university while teaching English; *Arunas Travel Co.:* Mostly professional, semi-professional, and special-interest group tours as well as custom tours for FITs. Scuba-diving tours; *China Edu-*

cational Tours: All tours custom designed and marketed to educational institutions, museums, professional organizations, and community groups. Also administers semesters abroad for colleges, short-term residential programs for secondary schools, colleges, and professional schools; *China International Travel Service Inc. (Guangdong):* Says it can book confirmed domestic flights in China and book Hong Kong-to-China flights. It can set up exhibitions, special tours, and help issue visas for the Trade Fair in Guangzhou; *Chinasmith:* Says it can book Hong Kong charters and Dragonair to China from New York, and trans-Siberian train from Beijing; *Hemphill Harris:* Top-of-the-market luxurious tours; *Indoculture Tours:* Off-the-beaten-path tours from Nepal and Pakistan, Tibetan festivals, and can arrange permits for research, expeditions, filming, etc., in remote regions; *Kuo Feng:* General and special-interest tours, art and archaeology, broadcast studying, wildlife viewing, Karakoram Highway. Knowledgeable about travel for Overseas Chinese; *Lindblad Travel, Inc.:* More comfortable than most tours, since Lindblad has invested capital to improve services in China. General interest and off-beat tours. Uses some of the best hotels; M.S. *Bashan* tourist ship on Yangtze, with Sinologist and guaranteed single accommodations if desired; *Mountain Travel:* Adventure travel, mountaineering and trekking in Northwest China. Mountaineering. Tibet to Nepal, Pakistan-Xinjiang overland; *Pacific Delight Tours:* Special and general interest. Claims to send more people to China than any other agency in the world; *Sino-American Tours:* One of the more aggressive operators. For leisure, business, and independent travelers. Some hotel reservations; special interest, incentive, exhibitions and conventions; *STI* has youth tours; *U.S. China Travel Service* is a branch of China Travel Service (H.K.), and is able to book fixed-schedule air charters between Hong Kong and major cities in China. Specializes in general, deluxe, cruises, and individual tours.

Canada *Blyth & Co.* (for off-beat tours). *Best Way Tours* and *Safaris/Sitara Travel* (for entry from Pakistan and the Silk Road); *Canadian Travel Abroad* (Sino-Soviet tours); *China Travel Service (Canada)* has general, custom, academic, youth, deluxe, and individual tours, and expects to book confirmed domestic flights in 1989; *Conference Tours of Canada* (among the cheapest for general tours); *Cultural Tours* (Vancouver and Toronto); and *Tour East Holidays* (among the cheapest for flights and general tours).

Hong Kong See "Getting There."

Australia *Holidays, Hertz Asia Pacific,* and *China Travel Service* (self-drive holidays to Guilin). *China Travel Service* also has offices in Bangkok, Manila, Singapore, and Britain. *Sitara Travel* has an office in the U.K.

New Zealand *Globe Trotter Tours NZ LTD.*

China Friendship Associations all over the world can give information on travel to China and their own study tours. Some of these associations can organize tours for individuals. They also entertain visiting Chinese delegations and students, teach English, collect books for China, show movies, and provide lecturers on China. They can give you an idea of organizations who send people to China. Addresses can usually be obtained through the Cultural Affairs Officer at a Chinese mission. Among these are the Australia-China Friendship Society, the Federation of Canada-China Friendship Associations, the New Zealand-China Friendship Society and the U.S.-China Peoples Friendship Associations.

See also "Getting Around" and money-saving travel tips in "Budget."

BEFORE YOU GO

BOOKING INTO CHINA

Book as much of your itinerary as possible beforehand. Complex international bookings are not as easy to make in China as in other countries. Trains, buses, and ferries can be booked into China by travel agents in Hong Kong. Buses can be booked from Pakistan; the Kobe-Shanghai ferry from Japan; trains from Mongolia and U.S.S.R. A travel agent should be able to handle everything. You do have options, even when booking a tour.

If you have over three days, you can book in Hong Kong after you arrive (except during the lunar New Year holidays). If possible, get as many visas as you need. Getting a Chinese visa there takes less than one day.

Ask your agent if the international flights are nonstop. Do you care? Is there an extra charge for stopovers? A day in Paris? You've always wanted to see Kyoto! Budget airport taxes, taxis, and a hotel. Is going via Hong Kong really the cheapest? Maybe it's better via Karachi, Singapore, or Bangkok. How about entering China at Urumqi? How about around-the-world fares?

By air Every travel agent has a computer with the current schedules of every major airline in the world. In some cases, you pay less through an agent because a good one should know about cheaper flights like the excursion fares, off-season discounts, and charters of *all* airlines. On the other hand, each airline understandably prefers to sell you space on its own planes. A travel agent can also discount off published fares.

A travel agency can tell you when airlines fly between China and the other places you want to go. It can also tell you which ones have direct flights and which have the shortest flight time. (Finnair claims the shortest time from the east coast to Beijing: less than 16 hours in two shifts.) Airlines do not fly all routes daily; some fly once a week. So you must plan your schedule carefully. Give your agent a list of stops you want to make before and after China, and how long you want to spend in each place. Suggest several options. Your agent should be able to work out a satisfactory itinerary. See also CAAC in "Getting Around" and "Introduction."

China's airlines now fly direct, with no, one, or two stops, from the following cities to China, unless otherwise indicated. Because of reciprocal arrangements, at least one airline of another country also flies the same route.

Addis Ababa to Beijing
Bagdad to Beijing
Bangkok to Guangzhou; Beijing; Kunming and Shantou
Belgrade to Beijing
Berlin to Beijing
Bombay to Beijing
Bucharest to Beijing
Frankfurt to Beijing
Fukuoka to Shanghai; Beijing
Geneva to Beijing
Helsinki to Beijing
Hong Kong to Beijing, Guangzhou, Hangzhou, Kunming, Shanghai, and Tianjin. For regularly scheduled charters from Hong Kong see "Getting There."
Istanbul to Urumqi; Beijing
Karachi to Beijing
Kathmandu to Lhasa (no winter service)
Kuwait to Beijing
Los Angeles to Beijing; Shanghai
London to Beijing
Manila to Guangzhou; Beijing; Xiamen
Melbourne to Guangzhou; to Beijing
Moscow to Beijing
Nagasaki to Shanghai
New York to Beijing; to Shanghai
Osaka to Shanghai; Beijing
Paris to Beijing; Shanghai
Pyongyang to Beijing
Rangoon to Kunming
Rome to Beijing
San Francisco to Shanghai; Beijing
Sharjah to Beijing; Urumqi
Singapore to Guangzhou; Shanghai; Beijing
Stockholm to Beijing
Sydney to Guangzhou; Beijing
Tokyo to Beijing; Dalian; Shanghai
Toronto to Beijing; Shanghai

Vancouver to Shanghai; Beijing
Zurich to Beijing

In addition, international services to some of the other 14 Coastal Cities should commence this year.

By ship: Regular passenger ships sail from Hong Kong. These are not luxurious, but they are adequate. A ferry now plies between Kobe, Japan, and Shanghai, and between Taiwan and China.

By land: The only land routes that have been open to west China are from Nepal and Pakistan, with possible delays due to mountain landslides. Chinese officials have been talking about a railway line through northwestern Xinjiang province linking up with the Soviet railway system across the border, but that won't be for a while! Going overland via the old Silk Road has been done, but is not generally advised, as that route is not developed.

The North Korean border has opened and several Soviet border points will probably be opening soon, if they haven't already.

By train from Moscow and Ulan Bator, Mongolia, to Beijing, from Pyongyang, Korea, to Beijing, and from Hong Kong to Guangzhou. A train line exists from Hanoi, but China is not on good terms with Vietnam.

By bus from Hong Kong and Macao to various points in Guangdong and Fujian provinces.

For travel via Hong Kong, see "Getting There."

BOOKING DOMESTIC TRAVEL

You should try to book domestic flights as early as possible before leaving for a trip to China. If it can't be done, you will have to take a chance and book them after your arrival. You must reconfirm your ticket after arrival in China or you risk being bumped off. Things may have changed for the better by the time you get there, but do keep this in mind.

In most Chinese cities one had to wait until one's arrival to book the next leg of one's flight.

Flight schedules that are a great help in planning trips have been difficult to obtain in China. They do exist in English and it might be easier to get them from CAAC in the U.S. or Hong Kong.

Public buses, trains, and ferries inside China can only be booked in China itself. You could speed the process by contacting a Chinese travel agency or your hotel (at a fee).

FORMALITIES

Passport. If you haven't got a passport valid for your trip and preferably three months afterward, get one. You can't travel without it. Give yourself plenty of time to get a copy of your birth certificate, photos, etc. Contact your closest passport office or consulate, or consult your travel agent.

A **China tourist visa** can be obtained from any Chinese consulate in five working days. During peak season (May, Aug., Sept., and Oct.), a tourist needs a letter or telex from a host organization in China, which can be a travel agency or a hotel. A frequent traveler can obtain a multiple-entry visa. A Chinese passport holder living abroad does not need an entry and exit visa. In the low season, December through March, all you need is your valid passport and photos.

Transit visas are not necessary if you stay less than 24 hours and remain inside the airport. You must have a visa for your next stop, and a confirmed plane reservation out. In an emergency, visas can be obtained at some ports in China. Emergencies include last-minute invitations, invitations to provide scientific or technological consultations, and visits to seriously ill patients or to make funeral arrangements. The ports include Beijing, Dalian, Fuzhou, Guangzhou, Hangzhou, Kunming, Shanghai, Shenzhen, Tianjin, Xiamen, Xi'an, and Zhuhai. Shenzhen and Zhuhai can issue 3-day visas on the spot. Zhongshan can issue regular visas on the spot.

Also, if you go to Hong Kong, travel agents there can usually provide anyone a visa in 24 hours or less (for a service charge). Tourist visas from the Visa Office of China's Foreign Ministry are cheaper. See "Getting There."

Travel agents usually obtain one visa for a prepaid group tour of 9 to 30 people, but you have to enter and leave China with your group unless arrangements are made inside China. You do have to give your travel agent your passport number and other such information.

Overseas Chinese with Chinese passports do not need any visas at all for entry or exit. Nationals of South Africa, the Vatican, Israel, and South Korea are not usually allowed into China but some have entered after getting permission from China.

A **Visa Application Form** requires one photo and the following information: name; nationality; sex; date of birth; place of birth; type and number of passport. Valid until . . . ; occupation; place of work; telephone number.

Also asked are: home address; telephone number; purpose of journey; host unit in China.

The host unit is usually C.I.T.S., but it could be whatever Chinese agency is organizing your trip, the hotel where you have a confirmed reservation, or a friend in China who has invited you.

The form goes on to ask intended date of entry; duration of stay in China; places to visit in China; accompanying persons using the same passport (name, sex, date of birth, relationship to applicant); relatives or friends in China (to be filled in only by persons visiting relatives or friends; you will need their name, nationality, occupation and place of work, and relationship to applicant).

Sometimes, especially if booking by mail, a photocopy of the first four essential pages of your passport is required.

Overseas Chinese will win Brownie points if they add their Chinese name in Chinese. **In case of unexpected delays,** give yourself a few more days in China than you think you need.

Your visa will be almost entirely in Chinese and will admit you to any international airport or seaport in China and to any of the cities currently open to foreign visitors without a travel permit within the time limit mentioned. If you want to stay longer, you can apply in China for an extension.

Other visas may be required for countries in which you will be traveling. They are not necessary for countries where you change planes, as long as you stay in the transit section of the airport. They may be necessary for train travel, such as through the Democratic Republic of Germany, Poland, the U.S.S.R., and Mongolia, all of which have missions in Beijing. It can be difficult getting a Mongolian visa because its embassy keeps irregular hours. But do you want to spend precious time there getting visas? Consult your travel agent, who can obtain visas by mail or courier. Individual visas are processed more quickly and cheaply if you take your passport to a country's mission yourself.

Shots. You will need a certificate of immunization only if you are in a cholera or yellow fever area just prior to visiting China. Otherwise, no shots are required for China for short-term travelers. Long-term travelers should consult their embassies in China especially about Encephalitis B. However, if you are going to be living in the countryside, endemic areas, or any place where hygiene is minimal, consult the health department in your home city. At press time health departments in some North American cities were recommending immunization against typhoid, tetanus, polio, and hepatitis A. A health certificate is required for people residing in China for over a year and includes an AIDS test. Best get one before you leave home. In south China, once-a-week pills against malaria are recommended wherever mosquitos are thick at night. Most tourists do not have to worry about this, but those going off-the-beaten-track should think about it. The health department or your travel agent should know if immunization is required for the other countries you will be visiting.

Plan your budget See "Local Customs and Emergencies" and "Budget."

Chinese customs regulations Check through the customs regulations in "Important Addresses and Information" to see what you can and cannot take into China.

Hotel reservations Your travel agent can take care of reservations in top hotels, but if you want to do it yourself, phone your airline or the relevant hotel reservation system. For example, for the Sheraton Hotel in Beijing, phone the closest Sheraton to you. See "Budget and Hotel Quick Reference." Reservations can be made now at medium-priced hotels through some North American travel agents or directly by telex with those hotels. Reservations are recommended during high tourist season, festivals, or trade fairs. The top hotels and most medium-priced tourist hotels usually telex an answer to a request for a reservation. A few will charge for the telex, or answer only collect. Some medium-priced hotels, however, will telex an answer only if there is no room. Some will not accept reservations at all and will not answer. Hotels for backpackers and some medium-priced hotels do not usually accept reservations.

We have tried to mention the reservation policy along with the hotel where we have the information.

Write ahead to people you want to meet, giving yourself at least 30 days for an answer if by mail. Do ask for their telephone numbers so you can call when you arrive. Most people could arrange their schedules to fit yours. Chinese friends and relatives should also be able to take time off with pay from their jobs to visit and even sightsee with you. If you receive no reply, it could mean they are not interested, or you have the wrong address, or they are terrible letter writers. Sorry, I can't decide for you.

China does go through occasional xenophobic periods and your Chinese friends especially might get into a lot of difficulty explaining your relationship to them. Recent years have been all right. If you get replies welcoming you to China, then you can make plans to meet. If you have only a couple of days in their city and do not know your exact itinerary ahead of time, you could telegraph them after you arrive in China. See "Local Customs" on looking up specific Chinese citizens.

Overseas Chinese in particular may want to write to ask what their relatives would like you to bring them. Don't be surprised if they ask for a refrigerator, video, and motorcycle. Other relatives abroad could help pay for expensive gifts. If you cannot afford these, take a less expensive present and they will (or should) be happy to see you anyway.

Usually, Chinese relatives just want you and your foreign passport for use as a courier. Only Overseas Chinese with foreign passports can import certain desirable goods duty-free. Hong Kong and Macao are set up for such shopping. You can either bring the goods in with you (the store or a travel agency supplying the transport), or you can just pay and carry the receipt and have it stamped by Chinese Customs officials at the border. It depends on the availability of the ''gifts'' in China. Your relatives can pick up the goods later in an Overseas Chinese store in China. I have never had trouble being reimbursed and I have carted sewing machines and bicycles on the train from Hong Kong! **But make sure reimbursement and in what terms are understood.** You have already saved them 30–50%!

At this stage, Overseas Chinese should start collecting the names of relatives, particularly of ancestors, born in China. The name of your ancestral village is essential. Usually you should refer only to your father's family. No one cares about maternal lines! The names should help people in your village place you. The welcome if they can establish a connection is better than if they can't. The names, of course, should be written in Chinese. Take as much documentation as you can: a letter in Chinese from your family association, your father's or grandfather's old passport or head tax receipt, and a map of where they lived in the village.

Overseas Chinese in particular should use both their Chinese and English names on correspondence and refer to themselves by the Chinese one, especially if they travel with C.T.S. The Chinese remember Chinese names more easily. If you don't know how to write your name in Chinese, learn. If you don't have a Chinese name, get one. It doesn't have to be legal, but it will make things easier for you as you travel around China. Just be sure you know how it is pronounced in both your family dialect and *pu tung hua* (standard Chinese).

Overseas Chinese whose families might have property in China should think about registering deeds if they have not already done so. It takes at least three months and lots of red tape to prove ownership, and it can be done through an agent on the spot. You could start proceedings during a visit. With the development especially of Guangdong and Fujian provinces, property values are going up. I discovered that my grandfather's old two-story, black-brick house a few blocks from the main street in Xinhui was worth about Y50,000 to Y60,000 RMB. Village property is probably less. But if you want to use it or sell it, you will be in a better position if you register.

If you sell property, the money will be in RMB, which you cannot repatriate. You could use it on trips to China, or for scholarships, for family, or business investments in China.

In case of emergency, inform people at home how you can be reached in China. Give **copies of your itinerary,** with your tour number and travel agent, to key people. If you are with a C.I.T.S. tour, your friends can telephone the C.I.T.S. branch wherever you are in China and ask that you be told to telephone home. The tour number and itinerary are important to help locate you. Your friends could also try the airline if you took an airline tour. The mission of your country in Beijing, Shanghai, or Guangzhou might also be able to help. If you are traveling on your own without a set itinerary, an advertisement could be placed in *China Daily* asking you to phone home. This means you have to read *China Daily*. Outside of the big cities, it arrives several days late.

If you are not on a prepaid tour, it is best to schedule a **mail, telex, or cable pick-up** at your embassy, or at one of the big hotels (whether or not you are staying there). Ask at the desk or look for a bulletin board. American Express now has client mail service in its Beijing office, the White Swan Hotel (Guangzhou), and c/o C.I.T.S. Shanghai.

Also leave your **passport number** with whomever does your banking, in case money has to be cabled to you through the Bank of China. Photocopy the essentials of your passport in case of loss and carry this copy with you in a separate place as you travel. Take extra **passport pictures** in case you need them on the trip.

Since letters could take up to 15 days to reach you, quicker if by "express" or courier, it is best to tell friends not to write unless your trip is longer than that.

Consider buying **health insurance** in case of serious illness or accident, and **travel insurance** in case you lose anything. Many people already are covered by travel or health insurance if their tickets are bought with certain credit cards or through certain plans at home. Hospitalization in China costs about Y300 a day, which you have to pay before you leave.

Medical evacuation insurance could lend you money for the hospital, bring a relative to stay with you should you be in for a long time, and arrange for your repatriation.

The most active evacuation service in China is SOS, with offices in Beijing and Hong Kong, and branches in or planned for Xi'an, Guangzhou, Shanghai, and Chengdu. It has an emergency center in Beijing and is training Chinese doctors in emergency aero-medical medicine. Air Ambulance International is another evacuation service with a bit of Chinese experience, but we haven't seen either of these in action.

IAMAT is free and has a list of Western-trained, English-speaking doctors in several Chinese cities. Fees for their doctors seem to exceed the going rates, but you pay nothing if you don't have to use them.

Essential up-to-date information If you are wondering before you go if any particular city is unsafe to visit due to floods, earthquakes, war, or civil disturbances, phone the State Department in Washington, (202) 647–6300; the Citizen Emergency Center, (202) 647–5225; or consult the Travel Advisory bulletin, found at every American consulate abroad (American Citizens' Services). You don't have to be American to get information. The State Department's Bureau of Consumer Affairs also has a booklet, "Tips for Travelers to the People's Republic of China" (#9199). Try to get a version newer than 1986.

Learn some Chinese   If nothing else, learn to read numbers. Then at least you will know dates in museums and street numbers.

If you're going to live with friends or relatives and they're Cantonese, Fukienese, or Shanghainese, they probably speak this dialect at home. If you're traveling around China, however, it would be more practical to learn Mandarin, *pu tung hua,* which is understood all over the country.

The same Chinese characters are also understood throughout China. The characters used today have been simplified since 1950, and Chinese people living abroad do not know the revisions unless they have kept up with the changes. Just make sure that whoever teaches you the characters gives you the new script and the pinyin romanization. The new script is used in "Useful Phrases." It might be good to memorize some of these phrases so you can communicate.

As in any country, the more of the local language you learn, the cheaper your expenses will be. In the meantime, use the "Useful Phrases." The standard of English spoken in China is improving daily, but it is still poor.

A great little book is James D. McCawley's *The Eater's Guide to Chinese Characters,* which will get you started on reading menus. (But be aware that menus in English are available at all tourist hotels and restaurants.)

I don't speak much Chinese but traveled alone and had a good time even without an interpreter. Unlike the French, the Chinese try very hard to understand attempts to communicate. Draw pictures and try charades. Point at the characters in this book. At hotels, look for individual travelers, especially in restaurants, many of whom are lonely and delighted to make friends. Some of these speak Chinese and could interpret for you.

The more you try to speak Chinese, the more friends you'll make, and the more you'll enjoy China.

Learn about China   To get the most out of your trip, learn something about China before you go. There is a dizzying list of good books on China. Here are only a few suggestions. See "Bibliography" for details.

The more you know about most countries, the better you will enjoy going there. A statue may be striking, but it becomes more meaningful if you know it's the "warrior woman," made famous in American literature by Maxine Hong Kingston. A building in a park in Lhasa becomes the movie theater built by Heinrich Herrar where the German refugee showed the eager young Dalai Lama his first movies. A peaceful street in Beijing becomes the fortress for terrified foreigners caught in a noisy, life-death siege at the turn of the last century. A tranquil lake is the site of an American missionary compound during the Northern Expedition, its idealistic residents fighting the attempts of the U.S. Navy to take them to "safety."

Armed with background knowledge, you can also be sensitive to internal conflicts and avoid unwise activities like taking sides on human rights issues. You will be able to understand the people you meet—what do they really mean by inviting you to dinner? Are they just being hospitable? Or do they want you to help get the son into a school abroad? And how can you, too, develop your own *guanxi* (connections) so you can get what you want?

Books: If you know nothing about China, start out with a **general history** like Brian Catchpole's *A Map History of Modern China,* which is extremely easy to read (high-school level), half maps and diagrams, the rest text. You can graduate from that to *China, Yesterday and Today,* a paperback that you might want to take with you for background. This covers the history of China, its political life, agricultural policy, etc.

Good bedside reading and very informative are *The Wise Man from the West,* about Matteo Ricci's unsuccessful attempts to convert China to Christianity 400 years ago, and *Son of the Revolution,* an autobiography of a young Chinese who grew up on the wrong side of the political fence and married his American teacher. *Son of the Revolution* is imperative for anyone wanting to get an insider's look at today's system, how the various campaigns since Liberation have affected the kind of people that you will be meeting, and how some Chinese circumvent the rules and stifling bureaucracy.

Fascinating is the *Soong Dynasty,* about the Chinese Christian who was educated in America, and whose children controlled China's economy for several decades. Daughter Soong Ching-ling eloped with Dr. Sun Yat-sen and worked and died (1981) in China. Her sister Soong Mei-ling married Chiang Kai-shek and fled with him to Taiwan.

Also readable, especially if you go to Shanghai, is Noel Barber's *The Fall of Shanghai,* about its 1949 takeover by the Communists.

You might want to read about all the **cities** to which you will be going—in addition to this guide, that is. Write to the C.I.T.S. branch in those cities and hope for an answer and a brochure. If those cities are ancient capitals, then look into dynastic history. Raymond Dawson's *Imperial China* is another book to carry along—a good index and lots of juicy gossip about the likes of Tang Empress Wu and her boy-friends.

If you are going to Hangzhou, the classic is *Daily Life in China* by Jacques Gernet, with a map of the city in 1274—if you want to look for changes.

For Beijing, read any biography of the Ming or Qing emperors and that of Empress Dowager Cixi (Tzu Hsi) and *her* boyfriend. For Tibet, read Heinrich Herrar's two books, his classic *Seven Years in Tibet* and the recent sequel. Behr's *The Last Emperor* gives more background than the movie.

Han Suyin's autobiographical trilogy *The Crippled Tree (1885–1928)*, *A Mortal Flower (1928–1938)*, and *Birdless Summer (1938–48)* are good background for those periods. She grew up in Chengdu. Her earlier *Destination Chungking* is for those who will be going there too. It is set during the Japanese war when Chiang Kai-shek was a hero to her.

People interested in **history** could consider Frank Ching's *Ancestors*, a detailed 900-year history of the author's own family. For **British involvement** in China, there's George Woodcock's *The British in the Far East*, about the bad, old, but interesting imperialists like Captain Charles "Chinese" Gordon. For **U.S. involvement**, there's John Fairbank's *The United States and China*. If you're interested in missionaries, try Pat Barr's *To China with Love* or Alvyn J. Austin's *Saving China—Canadian Missionaries in the Middle Kingdom, 1888–1959*.

For more **recent history**, see Schram's or Hollingworth's biographies of Mao Tse-tung, and especially Edgar Snow's *Red Star Over China*, which not only relates the history of the Long March but has the only autobiography dictated by Mao. Don't let the Chinese tell you that Yang Kai-hui was his first wife. According to Snow, Mao had four—his first was a village girl whom he ignored.

Then there are the **personal accounts** of people who lived in China, notably Chen Yuan-Tsung's *The Dragon's Village*, a good picture of land reform in a poor village in western China in the early 1950s. Jack Chen's *A Year in Upper Felicity* and Ken Ling's *The Revenge of Heaven* are both set during the Cultural Revolution. For more details on that painful period, Jean Daubier has published *A History of the Chinese Cultural Revolution* and Roxanne Witke has written *Comrade Chiang Ching*, one of the best books about Chairman Mao's widow. A recent best-seller has been Nien Cheng's *Life and Death in Shanghai*.

Among the modern **Western novels**, the Communists used to say that Pearl S. Buck romanticized China too much and did not make political analyses, but a lot of the flavor of old China is in *The Good Earth* and *Pavilion of Women*, if you can find them. *The Sand Pebbles* by Richard McKenna was better as a movie, but is worth reading or seeing, for a good story and Northern Expedition background. It tells of an American gunboat engineer and a missionary woman in Changsha and the Yangtze in 1925. (Remember Steve McQueen and Candice Bergen?) Or try a Chinese novel. Gu Hua's *A Small Town Called Hibiscus* is very good.

If you're interested in **Chinese arts and crafts,** I would take along Margaret Medley's *A Handbook of Chinese Art,* Michael Sullivan's *The Arts of China,* or C.A.S. Williams's *Outlines of Chinese Symbolism and Art Motives*. These are all excellent reference books, profusely illustrated, that will help you appreciate the architecture, symbols, mythology, and customs of China. But do keep in mind that Williams's was written before Liberation.

Look up back issues of magazines like *China Reconstructs* and *China Pictorial,* which have articles about many of the places you will be visiting, descriptions of Chinese movies and plays, and Chinese arts and history. The glossy magazines *China Tourism* and *Shanghai Hotels and Tourism* should inspire you. The National Tourism Administration's *China Tourism News* has a lot of good news for travelers. Also helpful and current are the *Travel China Newsletter* and its companion hotel guide with reviews of hotels by recent North American guests.

Chinese **periodicals** can usually be found in bookstores in many Chinatowns. In the United States, the best-stocked store for China books is China Books and Periodicals, Inc. Write for a catalog. In Hong Kong, there's the Joint Publishing Co., Peace Book Co., and Commercial Press.

Many western periodicals now have their own correspondents in Beijing, and you should keep your eyes open for news reports about China before you go. Updated travel information can be found in Hong Kong's *Asia Travel Trade. China Daily,* Beijing's English language newspaper, is printed also in New York City, San Francisco, and Hong Kong. All are available by subscription.

You can pick up the very good Cartographic Department **maps** and China City Guides after you get there. One exists for every major city. They are inexpensive and describe the tourist attractions in some detail. However, you may want to see where you're going before you get there, and China Books and Periodicals, some travel book stores, and Chinese book stores abroad may carry them. Chinese publications are considerably cheaper in China.

Lecturers The China Friendship Associations can recommend lecturers, and some branches have copies of Chinese periodicals in their libraries. Talk also to old China hands, recently returned schoolteachers as well as travelers contacted through these groups.

Videos of tourist attractions can be borrowed from Chinese missions, and film festivals do show Chinese **films** occasionally, some of which are no longer available in China. My favorite is the sentimental *Memories of Old Peking. Red Sorghum* is surprisingly frank, powerful, and fascinating. For good historical background, look for some China-made joint-venture movies. Attempts have been made to depict authentic clothing, architecture, and lifestyles, and some have been photographed at the actual site. Try to find movies like *Power Behind the Throne, The Burning of the Summer Palace* (see "Beijing"), and *Shaolin Temple*. The Lu Xun classic, *The Story of Ah Q* was filmed in Shaoxing. You could try also to find an abridged copy of *Marco Polo,* filmed for television in China. [In the 1980s, Chinese-made movies have been very good technically and no longer drip with propaganda.]

The only foreign-made movies I can recommend about China are *The Sand Pebbles* (although filmed in Taiwan), *The Last Emperor* (with great shots of the Forbidden Palace), and *A Great Wall* (about a Chinese-American family visiting relatives in China). These are entertaining and essential for anyone wanting to see the emotional component behind the relics and scenery.

Learn about your own country   This is indispensable in your preparation for China if you want to see factories and schools there. Visit a factory at home and take notes so you can compare with China's such things as incentives to work, unions, employee benefits, maternity leave, child care for working mothers, job security, automation, and so forth.

When was the last time you were in a school? Find out what subjects are taught at what level, how discipline is maintained, how many students are in a class, and about "open" classrooms. What about teacher qualifications, incentives to learning, and slow learners? Who makes the decisions as to what subjects are taught? How many computers does the school have? Audio-visual equipment? Take your notes with you, and in China, ask similar questions, point by point. With good facts on hand, you can also help to clear up Chinese misconceptions about your country.

Helping out   If you are thinking of inviting **relatives or friends** to join you as immigrants or students, it has been increasingly possible to do so. Check before you go with the China desk in your government's foreign office, or your country's immigration office. You can also ask for information at your country's consulate in China.

Getting permission is a long process and you should not expect all procedures to be completed during a short trip. A new regulation says that local public security bureaus must notify Chinese citizens applying for a passport of their decision within 30 days in cities and 60 days in the countryside.

See also "Gifts" and "Special for Overseas Chinese."

Check your own Customs regulations   Best write for a booklet. Find out what you cannot take back into your own country. Dried mushrooms and dried beef have been confiscated. Some kinds of fruits and plants are forbidden; orchid plants grown without soil are permitted entry only in some instances. Certain animal products are forbidden or restricted; for example, the United States will allow only "a couple of" pieces of ivory, and no crocodile or alligator, leopard, or tiger products, as these are endangered species. China has sable, mink, fox, and wolf fur coats and hats for sale, also. See page 112.

Canada says no elephant ivory whatsoever.

In many countries, coin and stamp collections, antiques (over 100 years old), and "works of art" (one of a kind—not factory-made copies) are duty-free. Be sure to get a certificate of proof at time of purchase. Canada has allowed sculptures duty-free if valued over $75.

Some items may be duty-free but liable to sales tax in Canada. You will need to keep receipts for purchases in China. The red wax seal on an antique is China's proof that the vase or incense burner is over 100 years old, but you have to convince a customs officer.

Before you leave your own country, register valuable items such as cameras and expensive jewelry with Customs, especially if these items look new. This is to avoid a hassle with customs officials on your return. You don't want to pay duty on items you've had for years.

For the United States, obtain a booklet from the U.S. Customs Service. Americans are allowed a duty-free exemption of $400, with payment of 10% on the next $1000 worth of goods, even though items like uncut gems are normally dutiable at 2.3%. If you are planning to do a lot of shopping, it would be wise to consult the Customs regulations and tax rates before you go. For example, the tax rate on carvings from Hong Kong is lower than the tax rate on carvings from China. You can mail gifts worth US$50 or less, but the receiver cannot accept more than one duty-free parcel in one day.

Canada has a duty-free personal exemption on $100 worth of goods after 48 hours absence or more, and a duty-free exemption once every calendar year of Can$300. Beyond that, you pay 20%. These exemptions have to be claimed on separate trips. You may send duty-free gifts from abroad to friends or relatives in Canada, each gift valued at no more than Can$40. These must not be alcoholic beverages, tobacco, or advertising matter. Be sure to enclose a gift card. The cost of shipping, however, may exceed the cost of the duty.

For more detailed information, please contact your local customs office. It is easier to get the information before leaving. Diplomatic missions abroad do not always have the latest regulations.

Comparison shopping   If you are a serious shopper intent on bargains, I suggest doing some research and keeping notes.

First of all, many goods you can buy in China are available abroad, and one traveler sadly related how the painted eggs she bought there were the same price as the ones she found later in a Washington store.

So look around at home, especially in local Chinatowns, where prices are usually cheaper than in fancy curio shops.

On the whole, however, the choice for bargains is really between Hong Kong and China. Serious shoppers should try to spend several days in Hong Kong going and returning. The China-made products available there are frequently priced cheaper than in China in order to attract the foreign exchange. The variety is better too. And so are the antiques.

WHAT TO TAKE

Besides the items mentioned in the last chapter, such as passport, ticket, money, gifts, reference books, etc., here are some more suggestions. But weigh each decision carefully. Do not take anything you're not going to use.

If you're going in a tour group, you're usually allowed one suitcase. You should also have a **carry-on bag** for overnight train rides (your big bag may not be accessible) and airplanes.

If you're not in a tour group, remember that China's domestic airlines are usually very lenient about hand-carried luggage, but strict about their limit on checked bags. (First class 30 kg, economy 20 kg.) Discounted fares have an allowance of 20 kg (first class) and 15 kg (economy). Economy carry-on bags should not exceed a total length, width, and height of 115 cm. (or 45 inches), but in practice this is not usually enforced. A weight limit usually applies on trains.

Also keep in mind the lack of porters. This is usually no problem with tour groups, but independent travelers should be prepared to carry their own luggage in some train stations, perhaps up and down a flight of steps, to a taxi. Porters and trolleys are available in some but not all train stations and airports. Even if you are being met, you may be embarrassed if your guide offers to carry your luggage. Consider a set of **luggage wheels.**

Consider also the strength of your bag. Visitors report that some bags have been damaged in handling or left out in the rain. See also *CAAC* in "Getting Around."

Money Major credit cards are now accepted at all the top hotels, and many of the medium-priced hotels in big cities. In addition, some are accepted in top restaurants, and in many government-designated tourist stores for purchases. For cash advances, the Bank of China charges a 4% surcharge. The following are among those accepted in China: American Express, Visa, MasterCard, Diners, Federal, Great Wall. American Express seems to be the most useful, particularly with its free emergency check-cashing service. One can apply for a MasterCard in China, as MasterCard has satellite communications with North America. A

Chinese can apply for an American Express Gold Card through CITIC Industrial Bank (Beijing), Bank of China, or the Bank of Communications (Shanghai). With an American Express card, one can purchase traveler's checks in a large number of cities at the Bank of China.

Careful travelers might want to also keep valuables in a **money belt** while traveling. **Do not depend entirely on credit cards.** Especially if you are straying off the high-priced tourist track, take traveler's checks. Canadians should note that American Express "can also arrange refund of lost traveler's checks at the three above banks. As most of the branches only stock US$ traveler's checks, the refund will be in US$ traveler's checks. It is always advisable for travelers to China to purchase checks in US dollars," says an American Express official.

At press time, personal checks are not generally accepted. American Express has free emergency check cashing. Checks of companies and embassies established in China are accepted if known to the person cashing the check; it takes five banking days to cable money to you in China, assuming everyone does his job right; you might ask your embassy to help you cash a personal check, but don't count on it. At this writing, aside from the Hongkong Bank, no foreign bank had a branch in China that could cash checks or change money. This is changing, of course, so check with your bank before you go. Most of the foreign bank branches will be in the Special Economic Zones. The International Trade Center in Shenzhen has a money machine. Many banks have representatives for liaison and consultation, but few can do actual banking.

This all means, of course, that you should take enough cash and traveler's checks. You get less Chinese currency for cash than for traveler's checks. We suggest you separate your valuables when traveling. For example, you could put part of your traveler's checks in a briefcase, part in your inside coat pocket. If you lose your briefcase, you still have some of your checks to tide you over.

Clothing   From early November to late March, north China, including Beijing, is bitterly cold, sometimes with snow. I even froze in Beijing one May; two sweaters and a top coat were barely enough. Many of the buildings are not heated and many foreigners complain of the cold even in hotels. A jogging suit is ideal for lounging and sleeping on trains.

The Chinese sometimes lend heavy, padded jackets to visitors who didn't anticipate the cold, but you should take along your own coat plus long thermal underwear and heavy slacks. Thermal socks and underwear, warm boots, and *hot water bottles* are in order too.

I suggest you do as the natives do: plan on layers of warm clothing and a lightweight top layer. This is better than one thick, heavy coat that would only be excess weight in the warmer south. Down coats and jackets, and in some areas, winter-weight wool or silk underwear are on sale in cold weather, sometimes at half the price you would pay at home. They are ideal if you are staying a long time. If you are also traveling to warmer climes or need room in your luggage for purchases, you might consider taking clothes you don't mind discarding when no longer useful.

The rainy season is March to May in the south, with rain or drizzle almost every day. After it starts getting hot, a trench coat or plastic raincoat will feel like a sauna. You could buy a cheap umbrella then. The Chinese sell plastic sandals, which are great for rain, but they may not have big enough sizes for Western feet.

All of lowland China is hot in July. Sundresses on foreign women in tour groups are common now in big cities. In smaller towns, especially if you are alone, please cover your shoulders. The more you deviate from what the Chinese wear, the more they will stare at and surround you, a most oppressive experience on a hot day or when you're tired.

Generally speaking, most Chinese women wear trousers, loose-fitting blouses, sweaters, and jackets in winter, and, increasingly, skirts or long shorts and blouses, always with short sleeves, in summer. For men, slacks and loose-fitting white shirts are worn in the summer even in offices. In winter, they wear layers of sweaters and Mao jackets or Western-style jackets. Everyone wears padded coats. Trench coats for cooler weather are in style for office workers now. Ties are in.

The new, with-it generation is dressing more colorfully, and even men wear high heels. Jeans are fashionable at dance parties. A few younger Chinese tourists have been seen in felt hats, Western suits, and ties—but don't let any fad intimidate you. For the first time in their lives, many people, especially those traveling on vacation, are dressing any way they want to!

At banquets, cocktail parties, embassy receptions, and other formal occasions, Chinese men, particularly high officials, show up in Western suits and ties, or well-tailored Mao jackets. Black-tie occasions are rare. Foreign men should dress equally well, but women should dress modestly, as Chinese women don't usually wear elegant clothes except on the highest levels of society. Please don't upstage your hostess.

If you are invited to dinner, you could ask your host if what you have on is all right. Should men wear ties? How fancy is the restaurant? Your host may be pleased you asked, and dress accordingly himself. Women should not hesitate to wear some makeup, but, again don't overdo it, or you'll have other people at the table wondering if your eyelashes and hair are real. Does everyone in Australia have blue eyelids? Some younger Chinese women are beginning to wear makeup themselves. Go easy on the jewelry too. My mother had shampoos and sets four times, and three were great. The fourth became great after she insisted the hairdresser do it again.

Wearing cosmetics, jewelry, and bright colors (except for children) has been frowned on from Liberation until recently. Doing so led to hours of interrogation and even imprisonment during the Cultural Revolution. People who wore them then were considered self-indulgent, bourgeois, and counter-revolutionary. People in tight trousers then sometimes had them torn off in the streets. Long hair was seized and shorn off. It is understandable why the older generation hesitates about changes.

At less formal banquets, with friends and family, in ordinary restaurants (as opposed to fancy hotels), many Chinese men and women wear loose-fitting short-sleeved shirts and loose-fitting trousers. Some might be coming from work or arriving by bicycle. Going home and coming back to a restaurant on a bicycle after changing into something more dressy just isn't practical. Chinese officials have not been bringing their spouses to banquets, but this is changing.

For business, you should dress as you would in your own country if you want to show respect; otherwise dress casually. Most government offices are dumpy and tacky until you reach near the top. Though this too is changing.

Tourists should dress for comfort, with good walking shoes. You will be on your feet a lot and climbing stairs. You may even climb rough stone paths, treacherous for high heels. Sneakers are ideal. Please, no short-shorts; you might be thought of as sexually promiscuous. The natives are going to stare at you anyway, even if you are Overseas Chinese, so if you want to minimize the attention, wear conservative colors—dark blues and grays. White is the color of mourning, so brighten it up with colored ribbons or something.

Laundry is done in one day at most hotels if in by 8 a.m. Not all hotels have dry cleaning. Don't expect high-class service. The Chinese do an adequate job, but if your dress is special, covered with "pearls" or such, they could ruin it. It would be wise not to take your most expensive clothes to China, and to wash delicate clothes like underwear by hand yourself.

You can take drip-dry clothing if you want to do your own laundry, and in some luxury hotels clothes lines are provided. Take your own. I found that even lightweight clothes took two days to dry in humid Guangzhou, except in air conditioning. In the humid south, too, anything but predominantly cotton mixtures were stifling hot.

One feels compelled to dress up, however, in the new international-class hotels, where the clothes of staff members look better than that of the average Chinese and government official. But some tourists do lounge around the fancy lobbies in shorts and Hawaiian shirts, so wear what you feel most comfortable in.

Toiletries Take your favorite brands of shampoo, toothpaste, shaving cream, soap, sanitary napkins or tampons, if you wish. You will probably be able to buy China's equivalent of all of these in hotels and Friendship Stores in big cities, but not always when you want them in a hurry. The quality is quite good and has been improving. Foreign-brand toiletries are beginning to appear in Friendship Stores even in small towns and especially in the luxury hotels. Some are made in China as the result of joint ventures. Otherwise, prices are higher than in their country of manufacture. If you're adventurous, you might want to experiment with Chinese brands. The lemon shampoo is acceptable. The ginseng toothpaste is weird, but it might improve your sex life. Sandalwood soap smells heavenly. It can be used to make drawers smell nice at home.

Finicky people have taken a disinfectant or scouring powder for the bathtubs, and their own towel. If you care about fine clothes, take a small plastic bag of detergent or a small bottle of Woolite.

There is no need to bring toilet paper. Just pick up a day's supply from your hotel. But individually packaged wipes for cleaning hands are imperative.

Shortwave transistor radios are still needed to get the BBC, Voice of America, or Radio Australia world news. Better hotels have radios in the rooms, but not short-wave. You can receive news hourly from Radio Beijing in English. Check *China Daily* for the news in English on television. In the three largest cities, you can buy the current day's edition of *China Daily* (for market reports, local television schedules, NFL football scores, and some Chinese and world news). About two days late are the *Asian Wall St. Journal* and *International Herald Tribune*. Also available are *Time, Newsweek,* etc.

Some hotels have direct television transmission from the U.S. or Hong Kong, and these are noted in "Destinations."

Photography See "Customs Regulations." You can buy Kodak film, usually Kodacolor, in China, but you have more choice if you import your own supply. Kodak film is available all over the country, but the prices are cheaper if you pay in F.E.C.s. Color print film can be processed in many cities, but the quality may not be as good as at home except in the top cities. If you're going to be in Hong Kong afterward, best have films processed there, as prices are considerably cheaper than in America. Masterprint in Hong Kong does great enlargements and Kodak stores are usually reliable.

Be sure to take extra camera batteries, flash cubes, video tapes, and Polaroid film if needed, since these are not readily available in China. If you run out, Guangzhou and Beijing have some available in special stores, but the button-shaped batteries are hard to find.

Videocassettes might be erased by airport x-ray n
them in lead pouches. If declared, these cassettes mi
to a couple of weeks for screening with a charge of a
Chinese Customs. They are looking for pornography a
terials. You could argue tht your cassettes are for yo _ _.... use, but
you might be fined.

Maps and books   See "Learning about China" in the previous chapter for books to take with you. Some foreign books are available in
China, but titles are limited. Even if you are on an escorted tour, you
may not get a knowledgeable guide. So take out the relevant pages of
this book, stapling each city together for lighter carrying. Take along a
domestic airline timetable (available from Air China in North America)
especially if you're traveling on your own and need to choose the best
flights.

You can usually buy a good tourist map in English in each city. A
Chinese-English dictionary is superfluous if you have a bilingual person
with you most of the time. For wandering around on your own, I have
tried to anticipate most needs in the "Useful Phrases" in this book.

Medicines and vitamins   Take what you will need; exact Chinese
equivalents may be hard to find. The Chinese do have antibiotics, cold
tablets, and cough syrups. Chinese traditional medicines are frequently
effective, so if you're adventurous, you might rely on those after you
arrive. A few Chinese pharmacists can fill basic Western prescriptions,
but don't count on it. You may want to take PeptoBismol tablets (mild)
and Immodium (serious) in case of diarrhea or upset stomach. Do read
the directions. Do not take Immodium as a preventative as some travelers have done. Ask your doctor about Diamox for altitude sickness
medicine for Tibet. If you are bothered by pollution or dust, take a nose
mask (or buy a cheap silk scarf in China) like the Chinese do. I also
take a few sleeping pills to help regulate jetlagged sleep patterns.

Gifts   are not essential, but because of the "no tipping" policy, you
may want to leave an expression of your appreciation or a souvenir of
your visit for friends, or attendants who have given you extra-special
service. See "Tipping" in "Local Customs and Emergencies."

So what should you give? Anything *not* made in China is usually
acceptable. Ties, lipsticks and other cosmetics, and panty-hose are fine.

Many Chinese now collect postage stamps, so start saving them
from your own letters to give away. Some Chinese are saving foreign
coins. Be careful this doesn't look like a tip. A Canadian or U.S. dollar
coin along with a "Do you collect coins?" should be okay. Some people give novelties like those magnetic things you stick on refrigerators,
unusual ball-point pens, or candy.

Trade, commerce, and other officials dealing with Japanese and Hong Kongers have been accepting television sets for several years now, and some are reported asking shamelessly for videos, computers, and mopeds. North Americans do not give such gifts. There is no guarantee that an expensive gift will get you what you want, and the intent could prove counterproductive.

The danger is that from time to time, campaigns rage against corrupt officials who use their positions for personal gain. Don't encourage corruption. Chinese jails aren't as nice as those at home. And Chinese legal rights aren't the same either. Capital punishment has been imposed for corruption.

Usually, inviting an official to a banquet to celebrate a deal, or to thank especially helpful people, is sufficient. Modest corporate gifts like portable metal business card cases, calculators, agenda books, "traveling offices," and lighters are fine. Some, but not all, Chinese appreciate hard liquor.

It is not imperative to take gifts to schools, and certainly not to factories and communes that you visit for a few hours. The factories and communes will make money from your purchases. But schools do not usually receive any material compensation for the disruption caused by visitors. If you want to leave a souvenir of your visit, give **general gifts** like books and pictures that everyone can enjoy. Giving to a few individuals may antagonize the others. One tour group collected ¥20 for a youth palace in Beijing. If you want to do the same, ask your host to buy some treats or equipment for the children.

Since people everywhere are studying English and other foreign language, give **books.** Textbooks, good supplementary reading books, and objective histories of Asia would be great. *The Soong Dynasty* is easily read and enlightening. Agatha Christie is fun. Edgar Snow is popular. Please, no sexy novels! Books from museums are great. C.I.T.S. guides have written to ask for "best-sellers," Chinese-English dictionaries and thesauruses. Books about your country are fine, particularly if you have a sister-city or sister-province relationship with China.

"Talking books" on cassettes are good for learning English and are lighter to carry. Most guides and schools have access to cassette players. Since you may be carrying music tapes anyway for dance parties, you could give some of these as gifts just before you leave.

You could take **posters and educational materials** for schools, novelty toys like Frisbees, and unusual (for China) **sports equipment** like a boomerang, hockey sticks and pucks where there's ice, or a baseball and bat. As football has been seen on television in China, a football would probably be much appreciated. Don't forget to demonstrate their use. The Chinese already have basketball, Ping-Pong, and soccer. China is so short of teaching materials, especially in science, technology, and languages, that the Chinese should appreciate everything you can give them—educational movies (16 mm is okay), taped English lessons and, if possible, tape recorders to match. Books on space and the history of flying come immediately to mind. As souvenirs of a visit, a geological delegation might want to give labeled rock specimens; a solar energy group may want to give a simple model.

Group gifts are difficult to organize on general-interest tours, where you might meet your fellow travelers for the first time on a plane across the Pacific. So don't worry about gifts. But **special-interest** and **Friendship tours** are different. Again, it's up to you. You may want to write ahead to the schools where you will be spending *more* than just an afternoon. Ask what they need. If the gift needs duty-free customs clearance, give the institution your date and point of entry so the papers will be ready for you. Do not be surprised if you get a list of books worth US$50,000. Never mind; take only what you can afford. The Chinese are used to spending very little money for locally printed books; they think books are cheap everywhere. See Chinese Customs in "Important Addresses and Information."

Just don't be turned off by a request for expensive presents. In all fairness, the Chinese really do not know the value of money outside China. When you get there just say something like, "I'm sorry I could only get these. They are just a fraction of what I wanted to bring." That should satisfy them. If it doesn't, don't feel guilty. Don't encourage greed. You did your best. Besides, some cheap pirated foreign textbooks are now available in China.

For **guides,** surprisingly, the best gifts are reference books on *China.* Many get their spiels from old copies of *Nagel's* and you might want to leave behind this guide. Yes, guidebooks with lots of good photos from your own country are also important. C.I.T.S. is eager to improve its services and would like to see what other countries offer tourists.

Officially, tour guides are not allowed to receive gifts, but no one quibbles about inexpensive things. Guides will usually knock themselves out trying to help you anyway. You could pick up a carton of cigarettes (Marlboro Lights is a favorite), and pass packs around to **drivers,** but that would be encouraging cancer, wouldn't it! How about chocolate bars, or wouldn't that rot their teeth! What about cute novelties, oversized pencils, bouncing things for decorating their buses? Ballpoint pens have become too common! You can give lipsticks and other cosmetics to women.

If you are going to Lhasa, Tibetans appreciate photos of the Dalai Lama. But be aware that by passing these out, you may be construed as taking sides in an internal dispute.

If you are visiting **foreign residents** in China, do write and ask what would be best to take them, especially if they are living in isolated communities away from the big cities and fancy hotels. Many are teaching English, so as many relevant books as you can possibly carry would be helpful. They also appreciate hard-to-get snack foods: cheeses, popping corn, Cheese Curls, instant coffee and tea bags, and Mom's homemade cookies. Around your holiday times, take traditional spices, condiments, and treats like cranberry sauce, Christmas spices, Sunkist oranges, delicious apples, the makings for minced meat and pumpkin pies. China has all kinds of fruit, a limited variety of vegetables, and many meats, but there's nothing like goodies from home. If you are flying to the north from the south, pick up some tropical fruit, like litchis, in Guangzhou.

Ice Breakers. I think bringing bags of balloons and passing one each to little children on the street is fine. I am not happy about passing out ball-point pens because sometimes children end up fighting for them.

Museum pieces. The next suggestion is entirely my own, so don't blame anyone else for it. So many things were stolen from China by looting foreigners in the old days that as a gesture of friendship and support for the current policy of openness to foreigners, some visitors may want to return Chinese relics if they have any. These, of course, must have historic value, which could be simply the act of returning them. The British once returned a sword belonging to one of the Taiping princes. It is now in the Taiping museum in Nanjing. I think old photos of foreigners in China (against recognizable Chinese backgrounds), important old documents, and missionary clothes and old military uniforms would be most welcome. A museum official in Zhenjiang said she was eager to get anything like that.

You really should write ahead of time to the Bureau of Historical Relics in Beijing *and* directly to the museum in the city relevant to the relics. Give details and ask if they would be interested in receiving the relics as a gift. Keep in mind that China has a problem of too many historical objects, but something unique and significant would be appreciated.

Your next problem is getting gifts into China without paying duty. See *Customs Regulations* in "Getting There."

Business Cards. These are essential for anyone doing business in China. Best have them printed before you arrive, preferably with the Chinese on the back side. Best also take a one-page introduction in Chinese of your company and business. A few of the top hotels do print cards within 24 hours and rent typewriters and computers by the day or hour (very expensive).

Miscellaneous If you're fussy about coffee and tea, take your favorite brands, powdered cream, sugar, and a spoon. Many imported goods like Nescafe and Listerine are now available in the big cities, but cost considerably more than where they're made. Buying Cup o' Noodles may not save you money, but at least you are assured of cleanliness. Having disposable chopsticks would make washing utensils unnecessary. Most Chinese hotels provide cups and a big thermos of hot water every day. Take prunes if traveling makes you constipated. A jackknife is handy for cutting fruit for snacks and a flashlight imperative for caves, museums, dark houses, and late-night walks. (Drivers of motor vehicles do not always turn headlights on at night, and many streets have ditches and potholes with no warning signs.) Cheap jackknives and flashlights can be bought in China too. You can sometimes borrow a hair dryer or an iron from a hotel. If you take your own, consider "Voltage" below.

Take a money belt to hold valuables if you will be sleeping on boats or trains. If you're fussy about your cigarettes or liquor, take some duty-free in with you. China has some foreign cigarettes and liquor, but they may not be your favorites and are more expensive. Cocktails and beer are not served on airplanes. Visitors are usually pleased with the local beer, but find the wine very sweet. In many hotels you now find ice (made from boiled water, I hope). Chinese brandy and vodka have been described as "outstanding," and of course there's *maotai*. But these are all a matter of taste. Yes, Coca-Cola is available locally, but not all varieties.

Take granola bars, hot chocolate mix, instant cereal, things to munch on, and a can opener, but not too much unless you want to save money. Most hotels have Western-style coffee shops. You may get tired of Chinese food. Carry snacks on domestic flights in case of delay, or no food is available at airports (even in Shanghai, when the restaurant is closed). You can buy crackers, cookies, instant soups, Chinese potato chips, candy, American instant coffee, etc., in China.

During the rainy season you might be bothered by mosquitoes, if, for example, you're staying with a family or in an isolated rural guesthouse. Also take insect repellant then. Hot water bottles are great for hotels that have little or no heat in winter. Hot water from thermoses is easily available.

For people who want to do unusual things, and are not on a whirlwind tour, yes, take your paints, or if you want to be able to say you ice-skated in China, take your skates. Take your alpine skis or at least your boots if you're going to Jilin or Harbin in winter. (You can rent these there, too.) Take cross-country skis if you're staying any length of time in snow country, the northeast. Some trails have been developed. Some hotels have swimming pools, tennis, and squash. For people expecting to rent bicycles, take some old identification cards or anything else with your photo. You are asked to leave a passport as a deposit and anyone can take yours by error; these make good substitutes. The only scuba diving is in Zhanjiang, and Sanya on Hainan Island. Some Hong Kong dive shops are tied in with the sport in China, so you can get information from them before you go. Keep in mind that the Chinese are very concerned about the safety of visitors and your guides may hover around you protectively.

If you're backpacking, the following have been suggested by Louise Lore, a veteran: "Youth hostel sheet, towel, daypack (for biking especially), mouth masks (to keep out dust), folding cup (or buy a cup with cover in China), chopsticks, rain cape, plug for electrical appliances, small water bottle, tea strainer, throat lozenges, cough medicine, flashlight, rucksack, and luggage wheels.

"If you're going to Tibet and staying in cheap hotels, take flea powder, scouring pads, and medicine for altitude sickness. The medicine should be recommended by a doctor as you have to take some precautions with it. If you're going on the bus to Lhasa, take all your own food, long underwear, and winter clothing, even in summer."

If you're big on bicycling and staying any length of time, buy a bicycle in China or take one in with you. Chinese bicycles usually have one gear but a few have three or five. You can sell it when you leave if you want.

If you're staying at cheaper hotels where anyone with a key can go into your room, you may want a rubber wedge to ensure your privacy when you're inside.

For mailing packages in China, take cellulose tape or rope. Packages have to be inspected before mailing.

Take extra passport pictures for visas, other legal documents, or in case your passport is lost. Take photocopies of the essential pages of your passport, including your China visa. Pack these separately.

We suggest you carry essential medicines in more than one container in different bags.

Your luggage should be locked and will probably have to endure a lot of punishment. Some bags have been left out in the rain, some have been slashed. Your bags should have your name, telephone number, and address outside and in. (Take along an extra luggage tag in case yours disappears or you buy another bag that has to be checked.)

Think of everything you need before you go and try to be as self-sufficient as possible. If goods are sent in by mail, a hefty duty may have to be paid at a hard-to-find government office.

Voltage Chinese appliances are 220V and have either two-, or more commonly, three-pronged plugs (with straight or slanted prongs). Many hotels have transformers for electric razors. Some but not all hotels have adapters. No need for electrical kettles. You may want to pick up 220V electronics in Hong Kong.

GETTING THERE (AND BACK)

The prepaid traveler with a human guide does not have to worry about logistics. Read the sections on *Border Formalities, Adjusting Your Watch,* and *Leaving China,* but just glance at the rest of this chapter in case your guide disappears. (It's happened!)

The do-it-yourself traveler does have to read most of it.

Via Hong Kong   While many travelers go directly from their own country into China, many more enter China via Hong Kong. This is because flights from North America and Britain can be cheaper to Hong Kong, and South China is not much farther.

Because hundreds of thousands of Hong Kong Chinese and many foreign residents travel to China yearly from Hong Kong, competing travel agents there have developed a high degree of expertise. They are usually the first to upgrade services. Many have direct connections with individual tourism officials in China with whom they share a common language. Hong Kong is also loaded with professional China watchers, China-related banks, and experienced business people who can give advice. But we are getting close to 1997, when Hong Kong reverts back to China, and some people are thinking of leaving. One does get the feeling that Hong Kong businesses are more concerned with making a buck than with giving service that will bring customers back. So beware!

While its prices have risen over the years, Hong Kong is still one of the bargain cities of the world, with its tax-free and duty-free jewelry, cameras, watches, and radios, and its relatively cheap shoes and clothes. It is a good place to stock up on camera film, video tapes, snacks, down coats, dried-food gifts for relatives, and locally published China guidebooks. Books published abroad and cosmetics are more expensive in Hong Kong. But a good selection of China books is available.

Bargains are also to be found in the stores primarily stocked with goods from China. Some of these stores, like Yue Hwa, China Products, and Chinese Merchandise Emporium, should have up-to-date lists of what Overseas Chinese can take into China duty-free. They will even pack and ship purchases to the railway station or provide a truck into China if you give them a couple of days' notice. You can also purchase coupons for duty-free goods to be picked up in China. (You can buy these coupons in North America at some Chinatown travel agencies too.) These coupons must be stamped later at the Chinese border by Customs officials when you enter China. Prices are "fixed," but they will give you a 10% discount card if you ask. (Try the Overseas Chinese Service Department, usually on the top floor.)

In the smaller owner-clerk stores, you can haggle. Prices will go up automatically because you are a foreigner, so if there's no one else around, try your hand at this fine art. See *Hong Kong Gems and Jewelery*. There are also duty-free stores in China where you can buy televisions and computers for relatives. This saves a lot of carrying.

Avoid money changers. You get better rates at banks.

Hong Kong was taken from China by the British during and after the Opium Wars. It will revert back to China in 1997. Urban areas are extremely crowded because of the refugees from China. You can feel some of the flavor of old China there, especially in isolated island villages or in the New Territories—the tiny temples, colorful incense-smoked festivals, elaborate weddings with brides dressed in red, and funerals with wailing mourners clad in sackcloth and white. It is a good introduction to the contrasts of new China next door, and it might be good for you to talk with refugees from China—why did they risk their lives to leave? Welfare agencies can help you contact them, or just ask around. China is beginning to practice again many of the old Chinese customs you will see here—but not so elaborately.

From Hong Kong to Guangzhou, times subject to change: Three **hovercrafts** daily (8:40, 8:50, 9 a.m. (Zhoutouzui); 9:45 a.m. (Huangpu), and **catamarans** (at 8:20 and 8:45 a.m.) make the 3-hour trip. These are recommended because the maximum 68 passengers each means shorter queues; however, you can't see much of the scenery.

Overnight ferries, either the *Xing Hu* and *Tien Hu,* leave Hong Kong and Guangzhou nightly at 8:30 p.m. No sailings on the 31st of any month. The trip is comfortable in air-conditioned deluxe cabins (2 and 4 passengers), though some people have found the cabins stuffy and the bathrooms badly maintained. No announcements are made in English. A duty-free store is on board. The early morning arrival means you've saved a night in a hotel room and you have a full day in China ahead of you.

Some ships leave Hong Kong at Tai Kok Tsui, near the Yaumati Typhoon Shelter in Kowloon. This is a convenient ferry ride from Blake's Pier in Central. Others leave from the new China Ferry pier on Canton Road near the Star Ferry Terminal in Tsim Sha Tsui. This may change, so be sure to find out exactly where the ferry terminal is. Ferries dock at Zhoutouzui, on Guangzhou's south shore. Customs and immigration sometimes take over an hour to clear if they have 500 or so passengers.

Because the ships are on a river, stability is good except during typhoons. Seasickness is not usually a problem.

Four air-conditioned **through-trains** leave Hunghom Railway Station in Kowloon (near East Tsimshatsui hotels) daily at 8:15 a.m., 9:45 a.m., 12:35 p.m., and 2:35 p.m. for the 3-hour ride to the main railway station. Best buy tickets in advance, but you can also buy them at the train station on the day of departure—if any are left.

Frequent **electric trains** zip to the border at Lo Wu where passengers line up to walk through two customs buildings. This way is cheaper than the express train, but not recommended unless you like waiting in railway stations, or standing on trains or in lines. No toilets are on the Hong Kong trains, which leave Hunghom railway station in Kowloon or Kowloon Tong MTR Station. An electric service all the way to Guangzhou is now operating from Shenzhen to the new Tonghe Railway Station in Guangzhou, closer to the Garden Hotel and Holiday Inn City Center. Be sure to get the name of the railway station so people meeting you will not be confused.

CAAC or Dragonair planes leave for the 35-minute trip to Guangzhou at least three times a day.

A **bus** departs daily.

Other destinations from Hong Kong
By air (Monday is 1, Tuesday is 2, etc.).

Either CAAC regular charter flight, Cathay Pacific, or Dragonair:
Beijing (daily); Chengdu (3, 6); Chongqing (4); Dalian (3); Fuzhou (daily); Guilin (daily); Hefei (5); Haikou (daily); Hangzhou (daily except 6); Kunming (2, 3, 6, 7); Nanjing (daily); Qingdao (3); Shanghai (daily); Shantou (1–6); Shenyang (1, 4); Tianjin (daily); Wuhan (1, 2, 4); Xiamen (daily); Xian (4, 7); Zhanjiang (3, 6); Zhengzhou (7).

In the future, Dragonair also plans to fly from Hong Kong to Chengdu, Fuzhou, Quingdao, Wuhan, Xi'an.

By ferry:
—to **Shanghai,** about every five days on the S.S. *Hai Xing,* S.S. *Shanghai,* or S.S. *Jinjiang,* a 2½-day voyage. See also "Shanghai."

—to **Xiamen,** on the M.S. *Gulangyu* (2, 5)

—to **Zhuhai** (about an hour), **Shekou** (about 30 minutes), **Jiangmen** (about four hours), and to **Wenzhou** and then by bus to **Guilin.**

—to **Hainan Island.**

Ferries also go from Hong Kong to Haikou, Sam Foo, San Wei, Sanya (Hainan), Zhaoqing, Zhongshan, etc. CTS is your best source for ferries to Guangdong province.

Contact the China Merchants Steam Navigation Co., 152–155

Connaught Rd., C.; tel. 5–430945. For Zhuhai, see Zhuhai Tours. For Xiamen, try Yick Gung Shipping and Enterprise Company Ltd.

Depending on the class, going by ship could be the cheapest and most direct way to get to these cities from Hong Kong. Buses could be cheaper, but are not as comfortable. Avoiding Guangzhou saves time and hassle too. Services are basic. Lineups to disembark start early.

On the overnight ships, no regard for sexes is considered in the assignment of cabins, but you might successfully protest. Meals are usually very early. On the bigger ships, the pools may be unswimable.

By express buses: regularly to **Shantou, Xingning, Guangzhou, Xiamen, Haikou, Zhaoqing, Zhenjiang,** and **Fuzhou.** Some routes may have an overnight hotel stop. A double-decker city bus goes between Hong Kong and hotels in Shenzhen, at least twice a day.

Generally:

As services are continually being improved and opened to more cities, it is helpful to ask the Hong Kong Tourist Association for up-to-date information. It has offices conveniently located at the Star Ferry pier in Tsimshatsui, Kowloon, and in the Post Office building beside the Star Ferry on the Hong Kong side.

Most **Hong Kong travel agents** listed here should be able to book some or all of these. Most can get you an individual visa within three working days, or, for a higher service charge, within 3 hours or less. These agents can book you on a variety of prepaid tours to China, and some are content to get you just a visa and a train or ferry ticket.

A few Hong Kong travel agents, but not those listed here, have given the industry a bad name because of unreliable service. Worse are the ones who take your money and disappear. The following have been in business for years, and I have used some of them myself. If any of them fail you, please let me know and I will certainly take them off the list in future editions. Tell us also if you have found others reliable.

If you try a travel agency on your own, make sure it is a member of the Hong Kong Tourist Association. If it does anything questionable, then you have the association to intercede for you. Always telephone first for information and tell the agency where you got its name. Having learned of it through this book, they are answerable for any mistakes to me. They should do their best for you. You in turn are adding to my influence with them. This is a lesson in Chinese *guanxi*.

Since the price of visas, tours, and train tickets can vary from agent to agent, do also ask about prices and services. It would be advisable to book long group tours one to three months in advance, but you still might be able to get a tour after your arrival in Hong Kong. Hong Kong agents need two passport photos, 1 or 2 application forms, and your passport for a China visa. Send a photocopy of the passport if done by mail.

China International Travel Service (H.K.) offers group tours for individuals in English, individual visas, hotel bookings, and ship and CAAC tickets. Other languages are offered if booked for a whole group. C.I.T.S. is primarily for Foreign Friends. Booking by mail is possible. Write for a list of tours and prices if only to compare with what you are being offered elsewhere.

China Merchants International Travel Services Ltd. offers hotel reservations, tours, (relatively cheap) visa service, and a cruise ship on the Yangtze River.

China Travel Service (H.K.), the granddaddy of them all, is primarily for Overseas Chinese and Compatriots, and is cheaper than C.I.T.S. if you qualify. Foreign Friends, children, and spouses can also go. C.T.S. provides the same services as C.I.T.S. and has recently increased its number of English-speaking guides. Bookings by mail accepted. With an office in the railway station, it can help you ship heavy luggage to China.

China Youth Travel arranges tours "of interest to and in conformity with the studiousness and vitality of young people the world over." Special tours are offered for professional groups like medical doctors, lawyers, and teachers to broaden contacts and exchange knowledge/experiences with their Chinese counterparts. For youth, it arranges general sightseeing and visits to schools, communes, and national minorities. It also arranges seminars with university students and scholars, summer camps, cycling expeditions, cultural studies, and performing arts troupes. It can guarantee 14 most popular itineraries for a minimum of two passengers. Can book YMCAs in Hong Kong. Good for budget travelers. Tied with China Youth Travel Service in China.

Hong Kong Student Travel Ltd. offers conventional package tours, but also individual arrangements. Commune living in Taishan, Guangdong (for a minimum of two). Can book Trans-Siberian train, train (coach) tours, and bicycle tours. Budget and deluxe prices.

Rosalind Henwood is a general agent who specializes in cheaper air fares anywhere. Books C.T.S. tours for groups and FITs. One-day businessman's package to Guangzhou.

Time Travel Services has been my own favorite for budget travelers. General agent. Confirmed domestic flights with minipackages, train tickets, all classes of hotels, cheaper flights to Beijing and Xiamen via Manila.

Travel Advisers Ltd.: All kinds of tours and services. In business since 1932. Books through C.I.T.S. and also organizes charter flights. Cargo handling.

Zhuhai Tours (HK) Ltd. Can custom-tailor tours. Can book hotels and golf courses in Zhuhai and Zhongshan. Tickets and hotel vouchers can be picked up at MTR Travel Services Centre and C.T.S. Connections with Hongkong Macao Hydrofoil Co. Ltd.

The Visa Office of the Chinese Ministry of Foreign Affairs issues visas at the cheapest prices. This is not a travel agent, but the equivalent of a Chinese consulate.

Via Macao This Portuguese territory on the other side of the Pearl River delta can be reached after a 50-minute jetfoil ride from Hong Kong. It is also a free port, its prices lower than Hong Kong's because rent and labor costs are less. But its shopping selection is not as vast. Noted for its gambling casinos and good Portuguese food, it might be closer than Hong Kong for some ancestral villages.

The Portuguese traders lived in Macao from the 16th century, but went seasonally to Guangzhou to trade. Macao will revert back to China in 1999.

Travel Agencies in Macao can arrange taxis and air-conditioned bus rides to Guangzhou and other points in the province. They can also arrange trips, such as one to the nearby birthplace of Dr. Sun Yat-sen. See "Zhongshan." Duty-free stores here can even provide you with a truck (at a price) to take large items like refrigerators to relatives in China. C.I.T.S. Zhuhai branch has an office in Macao. China Travel Service (Macao) and Hertz Asia Pacific have self-drive car tours to Guilin.

Via Nepal The most current information comes from the tour agencies active in this area: **Lindblad, Mountain Travel, Indoculture Tours, Arunas Travel,** and C.I.T.S., C.T.S., and C.Y.T.S. of Lhasa. The **Holiday Inn Lhasa** has also sent information. Because of the political situation, only prepaid travelers can enter Tibet. Because of landslides, road travel from Kathmandu to Lhasa has not been easy, with a three-hour walk (early 1989) between Kodari and Zhangmu. One can hire taxis from Kathmandu to Kodari.

Flights from Kathmandu to Lhasa have been Wednesdays and Saturdays, but in 1988–89 were suspended from December to March. **Indoculture** can book these flights.

Via Pakistan The best source of information on this spectacular, Himalayan route has been **Bestway Tours & Safaris** (Vancouver). China visas can be obtained in Islamabad in three working days. The Karakorum Highway and border posts at Sust (Pakistan) and Pirali (China) are open daily May 1 to October 31 for foreign tour groups. After that time nothing is dependable because of snow. Public minibuses and tours are available and individual travel is possible. However, because of the few hotel rooms in Tashurghan, and the paucity of public buses on the Chinese side, we cannot recommend on-your-own travel in this area.

One can fly to Gilgit (Pakistan) from Islamabad. From Gilgit to the Chinese border at Khunjerab takes about eight hours (189 miles by road). From Khunjerab to Pirali is 31 miles.

A modest guest house is at Tashurghan, 53 miles north of Pirali, with 33 rooms (only 20 of them with private bath). From here to Kashgar (175 miles), public buses only budge when full. You could be delayed for days with no bed.

The highest point on the road is about 16,000 ft. at Khunjerab Pass. The temperature ranges from −4° C to 30° C in summer. Rains July–August could mean landslides.

Border Formalities Anywhere in China   Have ready for inspection your passport, Baggage Declaration form in duplicate, Health Declaration, and Entry forms. If you are taking in any duty-free gifts to China, necessitating a stamp on a receipt, have that ready too. You surrender the copy of your Baggage Declaration form when you leave China. The Baggage Declaration form asks what Chinese and foreign currencies you are taking into China. Probably no one will count your money. If you declare only U.S. dollars, you can pay for duty-free goods in China only with U.S. dollars, and you can take only U.S. dollars and F.E.C. legally out of China when you leave.

Everything you mark down—gold and silver ornaments, camera, tape recorder, video and movie camera—should be declared on the way out. Outgoing Customs once asked to see the wedding ring and camera I declared upon entry. If they think you left something in China, you might have to pay duty on it. If something is stolen in China, get a police report.

If you declare recorded videotapes upon entry, you may be delayed as Customs officials screen them. You will also be charged about Y5 for reviewing each tape. If you don't declare recorded videotapes, and they are found on you, you will be fined and the tapes confiscated.

You should declare any large gifts you are going to leave in China. Unless you are Overseas Chinese on your first trip of the year to visit relatives, you will probably have to pay a very heavy duty.

Keep the Baggage Declaration and Departure Card in a safe place. You will need them on the way out.

Immigration   In most cases, you will have to line up to have your passport stamped by immigration officials. If the whole group has one group visa, then that will be stamped, and officials will take a quick look at each passport. If you are considered a VIP, you will be taken into a comfortable waiting room where you can make your own tea while you wait for immigration and health authorities.

Customs regulations   At this writing, Customs searches of foreigners and Overseas Chinese were rare, and of Compatriots occasional. See regulations in ''Important Addresses and Information.''

Money changing Facilities to change money into Chinese currency exist at border points, the Bank of China, and at major hotels. Change only what you think you need for three or four days at a time. Small quantities can be changed back to foreign currency easily.

You will be given **Foreign Exchange Certificates** (F.E.C.s), which are different from *renminbi* (R.M.B.)—people's currency. There is a small service charge for traveler's checks and a lower exchange rate for cash. You will need your passport number and, in some cases, your passport to change money. The F.E.C.s must be used in *some* stores, hotels, taxis, and restaurants. They were introduced to control the illegal exchange of foreign currency. Chinese citizens are allowed to use them. Foreigners are not allowed to buy or sell foreign exchange except at designated exchange agencies at the official exchange rate quoted for the day. This agency will give you an "exchange memo," which you must produce before you can buy back any foreign exchange within six months of selling it.

F.E.C.s can be taken out of China, but not R.M.B.s.

In Guangzhou, and especially in Shenzhen, Hong Kong currency has been accepted in stores or by street peddlers. However, using foreign currency is illegal, and there are periodic crackdowns. Local Chinese value F.E.C.s so they can buy otherwise hard-to-obtain items like bicycles and TVs at Friendship Stores. Some enterprises try to purchase F.E.C.s so they can buy equipment abroad without government red tape.

To avoid getting change in local currency (R.M.B.), keep a lot of small bills on hand. You can spend R.M.B. in most stores and even some tourist hotels, but do not keep too much of this currency as it is not as valuable as the F.E.C.s. Some stores will refuse it from foreigners. In markets and some stores, prices may go up if you offer R.M.B.s. Even some post offices ask for F.E.C.

Foreigners have been arrested and deported for illegally selling F.E.C.s. Foreign Exchange Certificates are labeled as such in English. R.M.B.s are usually dirtier, with no English.

For a list of acceptable traveler's checks and credit cards, see "Budget."

Getting from your arrival point to your hotel Top hotels now have vehicles that can meet you at airports, bus, ship, and railway stations if you let them know you are coming. In most cities now, **taxis** are also available in these places. In some cities, very aggressive touts might compete for your fare. Please don't encourage such uncouth behavior. Usually there is a cheaper taxi stand outside with drivers waiting in line.

Another new development for China is the overcharging taxi driver preying on new arrivals who don't know local prices. If your taxi has no meter, settle on a price for the trip (not per passenger) before you go. Make a point to take down the odometer reading when you get in and when you arrive at your destination. For the per kilometer rate, see "Budget" in "Quick Reference." If the fare seems exorbitant or doesn't tally with your calculations, ask a staff member at the hotel for the price, or take down the license number of the taxi and complain to the police, taxi company, and the local Tourism Administration. If that fails to satisfy you, write to *China Daily* and the governor of the province. For some cities, the distance from the airport to the hotel is listed in this book with the hotel, so you will have a rough idea of the charges.

To be perfectly fair, most taxi drivers are honest, but . . .

There is also an airport bus after every flight to the CAAC office in town. This must be grabbed quickly before it disappears. If you must telephone for a taxi, be aware that it has to come from a taxi station and you will be charged from that point.

If you neglected to make hotel reservations, or otherwise need help, look first to see if there is a C.I.T.S. branch wherever you are. If not, telephone C.I.T.S., C.T.S., or one of the hotels listed in "Destinations." You could also take a chance and go to a hotel directly. Some cities have touts trying to grab customers for inconveniently located hotels. See also "Getting Around."

Your passport   Keep it handy for registering at hotels, buying travel tickets, checking in at airports, applying for an alien travel permit, and sometimes changing money. Otherwise keep it locked up in a safe deposit box or in a suitcase in your hotel room.

Adjust your watch to the local time   All China is in the same time zone, though this may change in Xinjiang. See "Quick Reference" about Daylight Savings Time.

Once settled in your hotel, lie down or go to a coffee shop or bar and relax. You are now in China! Soon you will be ready to tackle the country and make use of the rest of the information in this book!

Leaving China   Reconfirm your flight at least 72 hours before departure. You can telephone your airline yourself unless you are flying CAAC. This Chinese airline has required that you have your ticket stamped. Recently, confirmations have been made by telephone. Get a reservation number so that you can locate your reservation in person later. You can avoid the bother and frustration of going to the CAAC ticket office by asking your hotel or a travel agent to reconfirm for you for a very small fee and if it has time, it might do it. However, if C.I.T.S. or any other travel agency can't confirm it, you'll probably have to go to the CAAC office yourself. Ask what time you should check in at the airport.

Make sure your visa has not expired or you will be detained.

If your flight is very early in the morning, book transport and breakfast the night before. Some airports have restaurants. After you arrive there, be prepared to pay the airport tax required for all international flights, including those to Hong Kong. Have your departure card ready.

You can change your money before or after Customs clearance if you have your foreign exchange receipts. At Customs, complete the blanks in your Baggage Declaration Form and hand it in. If you've lost it, you may be asked to fill out another, pay an "administrative fee," or be waved on. Just put down what you think you brought in and make sure it is less than you've marked on the form previously. Probably no one will check it against your original, especially if you don't look like a smuggler. On flights from Beijing via Shanghai to North America, you go through Customs in Beijing and immigration in Shanghai.

Your next big hurdle is Customs in your own country. Have receipts ready. If you know the rate of duty, list the goods with the highest rate first on your declaration form. The Customs officials might just dismiss the little "souvenirs." Do report unaccompanied luggage so these will be exempted too. Since much depends on the whim of each individual officer, you may not have trouble at all. On the other hand, undeclared dutiable purchases, if found, may be confiscated, and fines imposed.

The onus of proof that an article is an "antique" or "work of art" is on the owner of the goods. A Customs officer might not accept your certificate or receipts. Depending on the country, you probably have the right to appeal any decision

HOTELS

HISTORY

The hotels of China **toward the end of 1978** were run by municipal service bureaus to provide travelers with not much more than a place to bathe, sleep, and eat. Many hotels were subsidized. One of the managers said then that he preferred Chinese guests because foreigners were too fussy: "Americans should learn from the Japanese not to complain!"

In some cities, especially during high tourist seasons, the demand for rooms exceeded supply. In the early 1980s, tour groups for Beijing were put into Tianjin hotels, or 50 km away in Hubei province. Some business people attending the Canton trade fair slept in hotel lobbies in 1979. Yet other cities had a surplus of rooms.

For many hotels, room reservations for groups could not be made very much in advance, and individual bookings could be canceled if Chinese officials wanted the rooms too. In addition, the revolutionary attitude was roughly, "If people are comfortable, they will become counter-revolutionary or revisionist. So don't let them be comfortable." Fortunately, this point of view has almost gone, but keep in mind that not all that much time has passed since this attitude was prevalent.

You can imagine what kinds of hotels resulted. Few, if any, were built during the early and mid-1970s. After the fall of the Gang of Four and the rise of Deng Xiaoping, the situation changed.

TODAY

Chinese tourism officials have been trying to solve these and other problems so they can accommodate the large numbers of foreigners and domestic tourists desiring to visit China. While most hotels are still owned by some government agency or other, the building of many new hotels has resulted in good old-fashioned capitalistic competition. Pleasing the visitors has become important! Standards have risen! Chinese guests sometimes get displaced to make room for foreigners!

Each province or city state has a tourism administration that now regulates hotel prices and standards. While the tourism administration also owns and operates some of these hotels, it does have a mandate to make sure hotels are of good enough quality for foreigners. By the time you get to China, the local tourism administration should have a list of acceptable hotels, some with a plaque to that effect. If you have any complaints, you can take them up with the tourism administration. It is in a position to cancel licenses and help you get satisfaction.

The hotels you will use today are a world apart from the hotels of even the early 1980s. They still are not perfect but are considerably better, the regular hotels very adequate and those of international standard good. By the end of 1990, all hotels should be officially government-rated one to five stars (with five the highest) on architecture, maintenance, service and facilities.

Foreign investment in the form of joint ventures both in the construction and in the management of some hotels has given China several hotels of international deluxe standard. A few hotels are being built solely by foreign interests. The big chains have been getting involved. Hilton, Holiday Inn, Sheraton, Hyatt, Intercontinental, and Nikko are companies that have already appeared on the sides of beautiful new buildings.

Some staff members have been sent on training programs outside China, and regular training programs take place on the job. Many hotels have also imported foreign executives and managers.

This does not mean that all joint ventures are of international standard. Some of the new hotels have deteriorated because of poor management. It does mean that in the early 1990s, foreign tourists are being billeted wherever possible in a standard Chinese hotel, or, if they choose to pay more, in a better hotel, possibly of international "deluxe" standard (if one of these is available). They can also choose, as backpackers will tell you, to live cheaply in a shared dormitory. But C.I.T.S. won't book you into those!

Hotels with standards deemed unacceptable to most foreigners are being phased out as better ones open. Future historians will look on the 1980s as the decade of the new hotels. At the turn of the decade, the rate of construction was still continuing even in small cities and mountain resorts, but it should stop soon. A surplus of deluxe hotel rooms has already become apparent.

New hotels may not yet have their acts together in regard to services, but at least the rooms will be in pristine condition. There is a tendency for Chinese partners to insist on a "soft" opening even before all facilities are ready, and you may find yourself in a hotel with only a restaurant, the lobby, and a block of rooms. A lot of hammering and the hint of better things after the "hard" or "grand" opening may be annoying. The *Travel China Newsletter* will try to keep you informed of hotel quality.

NOTE · · · Many hotels now have Public Relations Departments. Should you have problems, try the "Gong Gong Guan Si" during office hours.

Standard Foreign Tourist Hotels

Generally speaking, prepaid foreign tourists are assigned a regular room in an adequate hotel probably with:

—**porter service.** Yes, it does seem strange not to tip!

—at least one **dining room** for Chinese food and usually another for Western. The Western food may not be what you're used to (especially the greasy fried eggs for breakfast). These restaurants are usually open only from 7 to 9 a.m., 11:30 a.m. to 2 p.m., and 5:30 to 7 p.m. Depending on the quality of the hotel, coffee shops open from 2 hours up to 24-hours a day.

—facilities for **changing money.** If it does not, the service desk can accept your money and several hours later have Chinese currency ready for you.

—**post office facilities.** Be sure you use the glue pot on your stamps. Many are not the licking variety. If no post office exists, the service desk can direct you to one. The post office might also take cables. **Mail distribution** is sent directly to your room or is waiting in a pile at the service desk.

—**retail store(s),** always with souvenirs, but frequently with soap, toothpaste, toilet paper, etc., and sometimes with fresh fruit, Kodak film, flashlights, stationery, maps, books, imported beverages, and cigarettes.

—a **service desk** in the lobby where you should be able to book tours, buy theater tickets, make restaurant reservations, and in some cases book plane and train tickets. Staff here can get you a **taxi** and help with **long-distance telephone calls.** This desk is most frequently busy right after breakfast and before dinner.

—a **barbershop, hairdresser,** and **masseur.** The massage with a shampoo will have your scalp tingling for days. Chinese massages are vigorous and probably much cheaper than in your home country. Best watch how these people treat other customers before you subject yourself to their mercy. Don't be a willing victim.

—attendants on every floor who clean your room and daily provide **hot water** in thermoses and **drinking water** in flasks. The water in the flask is usually what has been in the thermos the day before and can be used for drinking and brushing teeth. **DO NOT DRINK WATER OUT OF THE TAPS.**

Upon request and payment, attendants can usually provide cold beer, ice, soft drinks, and cigarettes. In some hotels, you can borrow adapters (for electric razors), radios, portable electric heaters, hairdryers, and irons, and have photographs developed and excess luggage stored (sometimes for a fee). Attendants have arranged for shoes to be repaired for a pittance. Many hotels have 110/210v outlets for shavers.

—a **television set** in most rooms. Some hotels also have closed-circuit programming in English or with English subtitles. Shown are old reruns of American television shows, not normally available to local Chinese. So feel privileged!

—**hot water** from faucets, but not all the time, and usually in the evening. The plumbing has improved in the last few years, but toilets still make strange noises, sometimes showers do not work, and rusty water still flows from a few taps. See "Useful Phrases." But all bathrooms now have shower curtains, previously unknown!

—**laundry and usually dry cleaning service** in one day if clothes are left at the service desk on your floor before 8 a.m.

—**air conditioning and heat,** depending on the season, but not always adequate.

—**good reading lights.**

—firm comfortable **beds,** but rooms for groups in standard hotels usually have twin-size beds.

—**elevator(s)** if the hotel is over three stories; sometimes these are turned off around midnight, so if you're dependent on them, ask for the hours of service.

—**sports facilities.** Ask the staff about badminton, bicycle rentals, and billiards. Even modest hotels might have imported gym equipment.

—**good security.** You don't usually see anyone but hotel guests and staff on guest room floors. Hotel thefts are rare, but don't leave tempting valuables unlocked and in sight.

—**convenient taxi service.** If no taxi stand is nearby, the service desk can order a taxi for you. If requested, the hotel can pick you up at the airport.

—**telephones** in individual rooms or at least at the service desk on each floor. You can make local calls in most cities by dialing "O" and then the number once you get the dial tone. If it is not a dial phone, tell the operator what number you want. You might be able to get an attendant to translate. To reach an outside line, say *"wai xian"* (why she-an). To ask for the service desk, where there just might be someone who speaks English, say *"fu wu tai"* (foo woo tie). Local calls are usually free. To get other rooms in most hotels, just dial the room number unless otherwise notified.

You can usually telephone abroad from your hotel and even from your room. You might have to book the call at the service desk and, except at luxury hotels, pay a service charge beforehand. At luxury hotels, you get billed for the call. In some hotels, a service charge also exists for collect calls if not completed. You get a long-distance booking form. You could offer to speak to the overseas operator yourself.

Unless International Direct-Dial service is introduced, overseas calls might take 30 minutes to 2 hours to complete from a big city, and at least 2 hours to a couple of days from an isolated town (where connections have first to be made to several larger cities). Except with IDD, overseas calls should not be attempted if you are in a hurry and especially not in the evenings (when many people in the hotel are also trying to telephone abroad).

See also *Communications* in "Getting Around."

Some hotels also:

—have **clinics** with doctors who can fix you up with medicines for a cold or diarrhea. Some hotels will refer you to the closest hospital with facilities for foreigners.

—have **great views** from their roofs, free copies of *China Daily,* bedside TV and light controls, room refrigerators, fire-escape maps in English, second telephones, and computers to keep track of guests.

—have **telex services** and **direct television** from the United States. (You get the evening news in the morning.)

—have **video games, night clubs** and **discos,** but don't expect the latest Western music unless you bring your own cassettes.

—have **mosquito nets.** Shake out mosquitoes before using, and tuck the net under the mattress after you get inside so that none can enter.

—**different room-key systems.** Some rooms are opened and locked by an attendant. While thefts in hotel rooms are comparatively rare, it is best to keep valuables locked in your suitcase to avoid temptation.

—have **key cards or keys** that turn lights off and on.

—have **travel services** on their premises.

—have **joint-venture restaurants** with foreign partners, imported ingredients, and higher prices.

—have **suites,** some of which are impressively serviced (with gold faucets, pianos, Jacuzzis, and private saunas), even though the rest of the hotel might look cruddy. Many have Chinese suites with traditional decor if you want to feel more Chinese ambience. Ask to look at them.

—offer **special regional dishes,** as well as standard fare. These are well advertised near the dining room, and might have to be ordered a day in advance.

—have a **buffet Western breakfast** especially for group tours, with good American coffee.

—have a **swimming pool.**

—have free **toothbrush, toothpaste,** and **shampoo.**

—have **smoke detectors** in every bedroom. The floor desk in a few hotels has smoke-detector monitors. Most hotels have fire extinguishers and well-marked exit signs on every floor, and fire hoses on higher floors.

—have **wake-up** services; the better the hotel, the more reliable.

—can be reserved by cable or telex to the hotel or C.I.T.S. in that city, but you should ask for a confirmation. Sometimes telexes for reservations get ignored in a pile with all other incoming telexes. And a few hotels do not automatically tell you if a room is available or not. A few of the cheaper hotels will charge for telexing you an answer. Expensive hotels can be reserved through an airline or a travel agency.

—will give you a **discount** if you insist, especially in slow periods.

—have a **noon check-out time** with 50% of the room rate charged if you stay until 6 p.m.

—have **bus tours** to scenic sights.

—have **short blankets.** Tall people should ask for extra blankets to cover their feet before attendants disappear for the night.

—will quote prices in U.S. or Hong Kong dollars, the F.E.C. price dependent on that day's exchange rate.

BUT some hotels

—have smelly and clogged **public toilets.** The ones in guest rooms are usually fine.

—have two-inch-long **cockroaches** in warm climates. These do not bite anything but books and food, and tend to ignore people. Call the attendant, who should exterminate them for you.

—have **rats. Please do not leave food lying around to attract the local wildlife.**

—though new, can look dirty. Insist on clean linens and a clean bathtub.

—are finding it difficult to fire incompetent staff.

—have **attendants** who snarl at guests, are reluctant to carry luggage, answer bells, or give any type of service. Some attendants speak no English, while others still barge into a room after only a cursory knock. During earlier times, one guest caught in the buff had to apologize for embarrassing the attendant! Be grateful *those* days are over!

—are **fire traps,** with all but one stairway exit blocked or locked. As you should anywhere in the world, check the various exits before you go to sleep.

—have **very dim reading lamps** and **dirty and badly laid carpets.**

—have **discos** and **nightclubs** blaring noise after 10:30 p.m.

—are badly made, with air conditioners, light switches, and floor drains that don't fit holes, poor caulking around bathtubs, and sloppily applied paint and wallpaper glue.

International Deluxe Hotels

At the time of this writing, we found no hotel in the same league with Hong Kong's Shangri-la, Mandarin, or Regent. A few have world-class Western food. Some hotels came close to five-star American standards. Most of the top luxury-class hotels in China would probably be rated three or four stars.

Lack of fluent English and the inability to anticipate the needs of world-class travelers are the main problems. This should change with time. Poor quality workmanship is another problem. In one top-class joint-venture hotel, the wall in a suite between the bedroom and living room was really a nonsoundproof room divider. When you opened the cupboard in the bedroom, you saw the back of the television set, and the living room.

Chinese hotels of international deluxe standard are basically like good hotels elsewhere, with the best services of the hotels above, and more. Many joint ventures employ foreign or Hong Kong Chinese managers. In Xi'an's Golden Flower, we have had an afternoon nap, showered, and gone out to dinner. Upon our return, the beds were made again and fresh towels supplied. You can reserve them usually with confidence that the reservation will be honored. Most will Telex back if you ask them to. Your reservation could be guaranteed until 6 p.m. that day or, if you give them your credit card number, you can arrive later than that. Sheraton will hold a reservation until 4 p.m. Reservations for international chains can be made through their representatives in North America. See "Budget and Hotel Quick Reference" for toll-free numbers. If they tell you there is no room, you might still get a room by telexing directly to the hotel.

Deluxe hotels have larger rooms and beds, marble bathrooms, imported fixtures, and are stocked with imported soap, bath oil, and shampoo. Rooms greet you with literature explaining hotel services, telephone numbers, and information about shopping and tourism in the city. In a few, the VIPs are also greeted with fruit or flowers.

Luxury hotels now have at least 16 hour-a-day room service, but no hot water in thermoses unless requested. A few have electric kettles that turn themselves off upon boiling. Because this does not give enough time to kill any bacteria in the water, we urge you not to use tap water in these. While some joint-venture hotels do have potable, filtered water in their taps, not all of them do. We repeat, **AS A GENERAL RULE, DO NOT DRINK THE TAP WATER** even in a luxury-class joint-venture hotel. Most have a telephone service in English that can take reliable messages and ring the room of any guest you request by name. (This was impossible in the old days.) Most also have fitness facilities like good gym equipment, sauna, whirlpool, indoor swimming pools (with swimsuits for rent and attendants, but not trained life guards), tennis courts, and health centers. Some have bowling alleys. Almost all have safe-deposit boxes. They have tailored staff uniforms, above-average staff pay, 24-hour-a-day hot tap water, and free daily newspapers.

Some luxury hotels have their own fleet of Mercedes limos or Toyota vans that make regular runs to the airport or city center. At least two hotels have Rolls Royces. A few have offices of airlines and travel agents and a business center with photocopying machine on the premises. You can order a real Western breakfast of fresh orange juice, eggs benedict, and strong Melitta coffee if that is your pleasure. No greasy eggs and weak coffee here! All give a choice of foreign restaurants with imported ingredients, as well as a wide variety of different Chinese cuisines.

Top hotels clean and redecorate whenever necessary, and one hotel said it shampoos carpets in public areas every two or three days. (Some old-style hotels still mop carpets with dirty hot water, painting them a ratty shade of gray!)

A top hotel could also be a state guesthouse where paying guests might rub tour bus to limousine with visiting heads of state. But generally state guest houses lack the services and maintenance of a deluxe hotel.

Miscellaneous

—Some hotels add a tax and a surcharge of 5 to 15% to the bill for practically everything, including telephone calls, laundry, and meals.

—If tips are left behind, they are "shared in a collective way," said one manager. But asking for tips is illegal.

—Some hotels can be paid for by some credit cards.

—If you're unhappy with any room, consult your group leader or guide. Ask the receptionist for another room.

—A few hotels have "No Smoking" areas.

—Chinese visitors no longer have to sign forms and show identification cards before they can visit you in a hotel room in some cities. And no unregistered guests can stay in the rooms after 10 or 11 p.m., depending on the hotel.

—Laundry can be so expensive in the top hotels that you may want to wash your own or buy underwear, dress shirts, and sports clothes instead. These are very inexpensive in free markets and Friendship stores.

—We have found only a few hotels with facilities for wheelchair-confined travelers: no wider bathroom doors with bars beside toilets, no lower sinks, etc. Most hotels have ramps from the street for luggage, but some of these are too steep for wheelchairs. We'll keep you posted.

But hotels and travel agencies have a lot of willing hands. And if you have a companion helping, people in wheelchairs can get around China.

—Some of the new hotels were deliberately engineered to withstand earthquakes.

—The danger of a luxury hotel, in China as elsewhere, is its great economic disparity with the life of the ordinary citizen. The cost of one night in such a hotel could be the equivalent of at least four months' salary for a Chinese in China. The extravagance can be seductive, especially in contrast to the drabness and modesty of life outside. Your attitude to China could become like your attitude to Disneyland, whose purpose is to transport and amuse you in a world different from your own. You could become like the lonely Dalai Lama looking at the masses from the Potala in Lhasa through a telescope.

If you went to China to learn about China, you have to make a much greater effort to do so if you stay in a luxury hotel.

—Up to and including this edition, we have listed hotels mainly because they were places where you could bathe, sleep, and eat. We have attempted to at least give you an idea of price and what to expect. The situation is changing so rapidly, we can do little else. Many hotels are newly opened or newly renovated and working hard to iron out the wrinkles. They could be functioning perfectly by the time you get there; but then again, they might not.

Grading hotels is very difficult. You could help us rate them for future editions by telling us about your experiences and using the form in the back of this book. We hope to send around our own examiners, but we need your suggestions too. Future generations of readers will be grateful. Your opinions should filter back to China.

FOOD

BACKGROUND

The infinite number of Chinese dishes, flavors, textures, and methods of cooking, makes eating Chinese food especially exciting. The most famous cooking styles are Beijing, Cantonese, Shanghai, and Sichuan, but others also exist, including vegetarian.

Chinese food is usually chopped up in thin, bite-size pieces, making knives unnecessary at the dinner table. The thinness is deliberate for quick cooking, using a minimum of fuel. Chinese food can also appear whole, like fish or pork hocks, but these are cooked so they can be easily separated by chopsticks. When poultry is cooked whole, it is chopped up before appearing at the table. Sometimes the bones are splintered, so be careful. This is done purposely so the food inside the bones can be reached.

Chinese ingredients reflect the many periods of famine in Chinese history. Everything possible is eaten; nothing is wasted, not even chicken feet, duck tongues, jellyfish, and sea slugs—all of these famous delicacies.

The Chinese food served to most prepaid groups is usually adequate. It is not the best, but it is usually tasty and filling. If you want to eat better, you have to pay more for specialty restaurants. If food is most important to you, take a gourmet tour.

THINGS TO REMEMBER
ABOUT RESTAURANTS IN CHINA

Restaurants until recently were generally dumpy and tacky, a reflection of revolutionary attitudes. The new economic policies have given China many new or renovated eating places, some very striking joint ventures in the gaudy Hong Kong style, and even a branch of Maxim's de Paris. International-class hotels can import ingredients and executive chefs. Some families and factories have also started restaurants, competing with much better food and service than state-run establishments. The current make-a-profit-or-quit policy has forced improvements everywhere. At the same time, provincial and city-state tourism administrations are now also regulating restaurants. They should have a list of restaurants deemed fit for foreign tourists and should you have a complaint, contact the local tourism administration. Each restaurant should have a plaque that says it's been approved. All of these mean good eating is possible for everyone, especially in the big cities.

Most foreigners will automatically be put into **private dining rooms** in restaurants. These are less colorful and cleaner than eating with the masses, and usually cost a bit more. Sometimes these rooms have to be paid for in F.E.C.s. However, you won't be stared at, can make a reservation, and can enjoy a meal free of smoke, unless your party creates its own.

Many state-run restaurants receive guests until 6 p.m. and then rush them out at 8:30 or 9 p.m. so the staff can go home. If you want to linger, choose a privately owned restaurant or coffee shop in a hotel.

Ordering   Menus in hotels and restaurants for foreign visitors are usually in English and Chinese. Many restaurants have a menu in English, too, so ask for one if you don't get it. Every hotel restaurant has an **a la carte menu** where you choose individual dishes. Some restaurants have a **fixed menu** too. You don't usually get to see the fixed menu. You have to ask about it. The fixed menu is served to prepaid tour groups, who do not need to worry about ordering. Individuals can order this, too, and it is the easy way out.

Food on the fixed menu is relatively inexpensive and you get more variety for one or two people. Just say *feng fan.*

In one hotel, lunch for one, *feng fan*, was steamed meatballs, curry chicken, spicy hot beef, greens and mushrooms, two steamed buns with sweetened black bean filling, egg custard cubes and tomatoes, clear soup with bits of meat and vegetables, white rice, and fresh watermelon. Of this I could only eat one third. While this was the most luxurious of the *feng fan* meals I had, most of the others were varied and filling. Menus change every day.

Gourmets avoid fixed menus because the food is not always freshly cooked. Gourmets also avoid **Chinese food buffets** for the same reason. But buffets, with their large number of different dishes, are good introductions to new foods. If you like something, you can ask the name, and order that dish again.

Every restaurant has its **specialties**—dishes the chefs are especially good at. So ask about these too. They will probably be a little more expensive than most on the menu but are usually worth it. Aim also for **local or regional dishes**—fresh seafoods if you're near an ocean. Seafood reaches Beijing frozen, so try for something else there. Meals in the countryside are usually excellent because the vegetables come right from the garden to the wok.

It is best to eat with a large group of people to get a greater number of different courses. Ten is ideal for a table, and you may even get a private room thrown in. When ordering, choose one poultry, one pork, one beef, one fish, one vegetable dish, one soup, and so on. Calculate one course for each person, then rice, noodles, or buns, and one more course. For example, two people should order three courses plus a starch; five people should order six courses plus a starch or two. This will give you variety and abundance. If you find you are getting too much, order less next time.

If you need more courses, start the rounds again. If you've already chosen chicken, then choose duck or goose. If you've ordered fish, then take shrimp or cuttle fish. Vary the tastes and textures: sweet, pepper-hot, salty, steamed, deep-fried, poached or boiled, roasted, baked in mud—the choice is endless.

Don't feel that every meal should be a banquet. The danger in China is overeating.

For popular restaurants, it is always best to reserve a table and even order meals ahead of time by telephone, especially for **banquets.** Restaurants for the masses won't take reservations. Ask the service desk at your hotel to make reservations for you, telling the restaurant how much you want to pay **but also approving the dishes** suggested. One restaurant suggested bears' paws, a local delicacy and an endangered species, which no one ate. Most of the cost went into that one dish!

Elaborate banquet dishes should be ordered at least 24 hours ahead of time, and a hefty charge is levied if you cancel.

Don't look for **chop suey or chow mein** with crispy noodles, or fortune cookies—those are American dishes. China has fried noodles, but they are not the same as in the United States. But then again, with the new economic policies, anything could show up!

Please be aware that some wild animals used by the Chinese as food are, or may soon be, on the **endangered species** list. Please avoid them. Tell your host in advance that you don't want them and why. See "Local Customs."

Some travelers have felt they were overcharged as items on their bill were higher than on the menu. Sometimes menu prices are quoted in F.E.C. but because of a large local clientele, are translated to R.M.B. on bills. Check out this possibility before calling the manager.

Special diets: If you do have special food preferences, let your guide know.

If you have an upset stomach, order rice congee, which is rice cooked to a gruel consistency and flavored with salted egg, fermented bean curd, or whatever. Congee is easy on the stomach. Avoid fried dishes, spices, and dairy products. Eat dry crackers, arrowroot biscuits, and apple sauce.

If you have cankers in the mouth, try *hung pean* (chrysanthemum

HOW TO USE CHOPSTICKS

The bottom stick is held firmly by the base of the thumb and the knuckle of the ring finger. The top stick is the ONLY one that is moved and is held by the thumb and the index and middle fingers. The tip of the top stick should be brought toward the tip of the bottom one. Keep the tips even.

MARTIN MALLOY

tea). It comes already sweetened with sugar in one-cup packages at Friendship Stores and is an old Chinese remedy.

People on general-interest tours should not expect special diets. Salt-free and diabetic diets are impossible then. Chinese cooking uses more salt than Western cooking. You could, however, go on a tour organized especially for people with the same restrictions. Vegetarians usually manage on a general tour if they don't mind meat sauces. Vegetarian restaurants exist, but these are not on the daily tourist route. Moslem restaurants also exist. So far, we haven't found any kosher restaurants.

Desserts   Foreign Friends will be offered Western-style sweet pastries and fresh or canned fruits. If you're in Guangdong in May or June, ask for fresh lichees—or buy them in markets. Look for pomelo, especially in Guilin or in Sichuan in season. It's a sweet grapefruit with a thick rind. Try Hami melon on the Silk Road. China also has ice cream, sweet red beans, sweet almond paste, and deep-fried crystallized apples and bananas. Aside from fruit, the Chinese do not have much of a tradition for desserts. You might want to try a coffee shop in one of the fancy hotels afterward.

Beverages   Most prepaid meals for Foreign Friends include Chinese soft drinks, beer, and tea. Canned fruit juice, foreign-brand soft drinks, and liquor cost extra. Overseas Chinese pay extra for all drinks except for tea. Coca-Cola and Pepsi have bottling plants in China. The dreaded orange soda is being replaced in some cities by good, fresh or reconstituted juices.

. **Tea** drinking is an art in China. Some springs are famous for their tea-making qualities. If you go to Hangzhou, try *long jing* tea there. A favorite tea in hot weather is *po li*. *Keemun* is good in the wintertime and when you've had greasy food. *Lu an* should help you sleep. *Oolong* is the most common tea in south China, while most foreigners like *jasmine*, the sweet-scented tea with bits of jasmine flower petals in it. Jasmine is said to heat the blood and should be balanced at the same meal with *po li*.

Every Chinese has a personal list of the four most famous green teas. *Long jing* (dragon well), *yun wu* (mist of the clouds), *mao hong* (red straw), and *bi lu chuen* (green spring) are probably among the most popular. The Sheraton in Tianjin gives a course in tea-drinking.

Dairies are beginning to open up, but in most places only UHT or canned **milk** is available. A shortage of refrigerator trucks hampers the distribution of fresh milk.

The Chinese consider the best **liquors** to be: *Mao tai*, made from sorghum and wheat yeast, and aged five or six years in Guizhou province. It is very potent and usually served in tiny goblets; *Fenjiu*, mellow and delicate flavor from Shanxi province: *Wuliangye*, five-grain spirit from southern Sichuan, with a fragrant and invigorating flavor.

The best **wines** are: *Tantai red wine* from Shandong, *Chinese red wine* from Beijing, *Shaoxing red wine* from Zhejiang, and *Longyan rice wine* from Fujian. If you get to any of the above places and have to bring a gift back for a Chinese friend, a bottle would be appropriate.

Qingdao **beer** is the favorite. It is made from barley, spring water, and hops from a German recipe. Five Star Beer has been designated by the government for state banquets. Foreign beers are increasingly available. Laoshan is the most famous **mineral water.** In Moslem restaurants, take your own bottle, as alcohol is not served.

Breakfasts   Most foreign tour groups are given Western breakfasts with greasy eggs. You also usually get toast, coffee, and fruit or canned juice. Tour groups in the 1950s and '60s were given Chinese breakfasts, but requested Western instead. The deluxe hotels now have good Western breakfast buffets

You can opt for Chinese breakfasts if enough people in the group want them. Chinese breakfasts differ regionally: *dim sum* or rice congee with peanuts, pickles, and salted or 1000-year-old eggs in south China. In the north, you could get lots of different buns, or "oil sticks," which are like foot-long doughnuts, deep-fried and delicious but hard to digest. You dip these in hot soy milk. In Shanghai you might get gelatinous rice balls with sugar inside, or baked buns with sweet bean paste inside. They are great.

Western food is now advertised in most *standard* tourist hotels, but I have rarely found it as good as Chinese. Bread is cut thick and is usually white. Sometimes "Western" food is one Chinese meat-and-vegetable course with bread instead of rice. Excellent Western food is more consistently found in the deluxe hotels, international clubs, and some restaurants. Some deluxe hotels also have delicatessens where you can buy cold cuts like salami and pastrami. Some restaurants in Northeast China have Russian food.

Local Chinese seem to prefer Chinese food and have rejected invitations to Western meals "because of too much meat." It could also be because of lack of familiarity with knives, forks, and Western table manners.

Courtesies Group tours in particular should be punctual at meals as the food is usually ready on time, and in family style all dishes may even be sitting at the table getting (ugh!) cold.

Guests of honor are traditionally given seats where they face the door. You might have fun speculating on the reason. Left-handed people have a problem and should sit where clashes with right-handed chopsticks can be avoided.

In many restaurants, damp hot or cold towels are distributed at the beginning of meals to refresh guests as well as to clean. One can wipe faces and backs of necks, as well as hands with them. Sometimes towels are distributed during the meal, too, and always at the end.

If tea or bowls or calling cards are to be passed, to be polite, use both hands.

Chinese food is usually served on large platters, which ideally arrive one at a time. The food comes hot off the wok at the peak of its perfection and should be eaten immediately. Time is allowed before the next course arrives steaming, to take what is desired of the current dish.

In families, diners pick what they want with chopsticks, and should be careful not to spread their germs to food left on the platter. Chopsticks are great for reaching across tables, keeping fingers clean, and hitting naughty children. Outside of families, spoons should be used for serving, and if no convenient "lazy Susan" exists, then the platters on the table are relocated from time to time so that all can reach. Don't be shy about asking for serving spoons.

To begin eating after guests express admiration for the beauty of the food, Chinese hosts put the best morsels on the plates of the people around them. You could do this, too, after the first round if you want. Since you put your own chopsticks into your mouth, you could use the clean other end of your chopsticks for serving. The host usually invites guests to start eating. Or groups of friends could declare a moratorium on such formalities and have everybody dig in. *Hei fai* means "Raise chopsticks!"

Do not be embarrassed about slurping or even burping. This indicates that you are enjoying your meal. If you don't have enough room on your dish for bones and other discards, just leave them neatly on the table itself. Less-polished Chinese will spit them on the floor!

Good restaurants do not make their guests stand up and serve their own beverages. Getting your own rice from a big pot away from your table is only expected in families or very informal restaurants.

In very fancy restaurants, an attendant distributes every course and guests do not help themselves. Individual plates are removed and replaced with clean ones after most courses. The host usually invites guests to start eating.

Giving a banquet is the accepted and most important way to return hospitality or to show gratitude for a favor. If your guide persists in refusing your invitation to eat with you, he may relent and join you the day before you leave as a farewell gesture.

You may want to throw a banquet for some of your Chinese colleagues and people who have been particularly helpful. Discuss your guest list with one of the Chinese involved so you won't offend anybody important by leaving them out. If your guide is invited, be sure he knows. Discuss spouses and times and seating arrangements, but don't be offended if spouses don't show up. The venue is important because some restaurants are more prestigious than others.

Toasting   Chinese people do not like to drink alone. Toasting at banquets is a complicated art, and you are not expected to know the finer points. Just do what you do at home. Stand up, give one or two sentences, make sure everybody else is joining you, and drink. *Gan bei!* means "Empty your glass!"

The first toaster is usually the host, who gets the ball rolling. A frequent toast is to the friendship of the people of your country and China, and the health of friends and comrades present. The next toaster can tell a funny story and then, perhaps, talk about your sadness about leaving China and the new friends you have made, or wishes that you will all meet again in your country.

Toasts might continue all evening, and so might the meal, or at least until the restaurant turns out the lights. If the banquet is extremely large, the host might circulate to all the tables, drinking toasts at each one. On smaller, less formal occasions, the Chinese may want to drink you under the table. Be alert; they may be putting tea in their own glasses. You may want to try that yourself after awhile.

I have been to banquets where I haven't touched a drop of liquor. I can't get *mao tai* past my nose—it's so strong. Chinese hosts are not usually offended, especially if you toast with tea or soft drinks. If you don't want to drink so much liquor, try to divert your fellow diners. Try exchanging songs—but not drinking songs or games. It may be the only occasion when you'll hear the national anthem of China. You could also turn your cup or glass upside down to signal to the waiter that you've had enough.

If you want to stop eating and your host keeps piling food onto your plate, just lay down your chopsticks. Thank him politely but don't eat anymore. They shouldn't feel offended.

Recently, as an austerity measure, the lavishness of top-level state banquets was curtailed officially to four courses and a soup, and one and a half hours. This might be the beginning of a trend, but then again, it might not be. Banquets are part of the culture. This rule didn't seem to apply to government departments.

Eating with the People

You can eat quite well for comparatively little money if you're willing to try food stalls and restaurants and sections of restaurants for the masses. The standard of cleanliness and speed of service, however, are not generally as high as in hotels and restaurants for tourists. The cigarette smoke may be suffocating. It is customary to share tables with other diners in busy restaurants, and if no tables are available, even in tourist hotels.

Payment is made when you order (so you can't stomp out impatiently). Some finicky eaters take their own chopsticks and spoons to places like this, but as far as I can see the dishes are scalded, and if the food is freshly cooked, there should be no problems. The soup sterilizes the utensils (you hope), but you can also scald them yourself with tea. Usually a spittoon waits nearby for the discarded tea. We highly recommend James D. McCauley's *The Eater's Guide to Chinese Characters* if you are eating off the tourist track.

Dumpling and noodle shops are better for speed (if the lineup isn't too long). The food can be good too. Foreigners are frequently pushed to the head of the line. A knowledge of Chinese isn't necessary because you can point.

Fast food stalls, mobile canteens, and cafeterias are recent innovations and are multiplying quickly. Some serve instant noodles.

Outdoor night markets are a new, adventurous attraction for gourmet as well as budget foreigners. Just make sure the food is steaming hot and utensils scalded.

Food Streets first started in Hong Kong, but are also proliferating in China. They seem to be run by hotels so are cleaner and more foreigner-oriented than other restaurants. The food is usually light and prices are reasonable: noodles, fried rice, side orders of barbecued duck, cuttlefish, etc. We paid in RMB.

The Food Street at the Jin Jiang Hotel in Shanghai, however, seems to be more upmarket than the others.

At **restaurants for the masses,** it is best to take a Chinese friend who can help you order and possibly get you cheaper rates. You can also use the "Useful Phrases" or the *Regional and Special Dishes* below if no menu in English appears.

To eat:

—*mantou,* the plain steamed roll, either take bites off while holding with chopsticks or fingers, or break apart and stuff pieces with bits of meat. You can also dip it in the sauces. *Jiao zi* are the small stuffed ravioli-like pastries in soup; *bao zi* are steamed dumplings and may have beans, or meat and vegetables inside. The names get confusing;

—*white rice,* which is served in bowls, put the bowl up to your mouth and shove the rice in with chopsticks. More genteel people might want to pick up chunks with chopsticks;

—*1000-year-old eggs,* you usually have to either acquire a taste or close your eyes and think of something else; they are best eaten with pickles and are delicious;

—*shrimps with shells left on,* take a bite of half, then, with your teeth and chopsticks, squeeze out the meat. You may want to use your fingers to shell them. Cooking shrimps with their shells retains most of the yummy flavor;

—*two- and three-foot-long noodles,* lean over your bowl and pick up a few with chopsticks. Put the noodles in your mouth, biting off pieces and leaving the rest temporarily in your bowl. Don't worry about slurping. The Chinese like long noodles because they symbolize longevity;

—*ice cream,* ask for a spoon.

To avoid an upset stomach and intestinal parasites, do not drink water out of faucets. Steer clear of ice, popsicles, ice cream (except in tourist restaurants), watermelon, and any other fruit with lots of ground water. Don't eat anything raw unless imported, or carefully washed and then peeled. Animal and human manure is used in China as fertilizer. Local people develop immunities. Bottled drinks are fine.

Be careful on ferries and small boats. Dishes are frequently washed in river water and not always scalded carefully afterward. Some people take disinfectants like tincture of iodine. Two drops in a liter of water kill all germs in contact with them in 20 minutes. When cooking your own food as in Mongolian Hot Pot, be careful that the utensils you use on raw meat or fish are not the same utensils you put into your own mouth. Just sterilize your own utensils in the hot pot.

Other tips The secret of eating a Chinese meal is finding out first how many courses you will be getting. Banquet meals usually have a copy of the menu on the table. If there are 12 courses, take no more than one-twelfth of what you would usually eat in a meal from each plate; otherwise, you will be too full to eat any of the later dishes. Also take your time. You can't rush through a big meal. Some famous banquets have taken days.

Fish is usually the last formal course. If you happen to be eating with superstitious fishermen, don't turn a fish over to get at flesh on the other side. It means their boat will turn over!

Do not worry about "Chinese restaurant syndrome." Its symptoms are an increased pulse and a tight feeling around the sinuses. This "syndrome" is a result of the large amount of monosodium glutamate put in Chinese food in America. Cooks in China use a little, but not so much. You can ask them to leave out MSG or salt or chilis or anything.

Among the beauties of a Chinese meal is the variety. If you don't like one thing, you might like something else.

On prepaid tours, you might want to talk with your escort about the overabundance of food when meat for the common man is so limited—if, indeed, this bothers you.

To best enjoy a meal, never ask what a particular morsel is.

Even-numbered days are more auspicious than odd-numbered days. Restaurants may be busier with wedding parties then.

Menus in English are by translators, not public relations people. Some dishes may sound absolutely terrible, but are really very good. Don't let a name like "frog oil soup" throw you.

Preserved fruit is delicious, but do not eat too many at a sitting as they are full of preservatives.

Another new development are the **health restaurants,** with dishes made from Chinese herbal medicines. I've found them in Chengdu and Beijing, but if you look, they should be in other cities too. Lots of ginseng, sea horses, deer antlers, and things best left unmentioned. Some foods to combat high blood pressure; other foods good for pregnant women. These are indeed for the adventurous eater because of their unusual flavors, and they can be very delicious.

If you are invited to a restaurant by nonofficial Chinese friends, don't be surprised if they ask to buy F.E.C.s from you. Most of the top restaurants are paid in foreign exchange.

If you invite average Chinese people to dinner, be sensitive that a meal in a tourist restaurant is a real treat. Normally, they cannot afford it. Since they get little meat, do order more for them. Do encourage them to take the leftovers home. They may be too polite to ask.

See also "Useful Phrases" and "Destinations." For some prices, see "Budget."

SOME REGIONAL AND SPECIAL DISHES

Beijing (a.k.a. Peking or Northern) Dishes 北京

Light, with few sauces; roasts; lots of garlic, leeks, and scallions; flour-made buns, rolls and meat dumplings, baked, steamed, fried, or boiled in soup. Salty.

Smoked chicken/duck	熏鸡／鸭
Crispy duck	香酥鸭
Peking duck	北京烤鸭
Sweet-sour fish/pork	糖醋鱼／肉
Deep-fried shrimp toast	炸虾托
Chicken and cucumber salad	凉拌三丝
Stir-fried pork with bean sprouts (served with pancakes)	京酱肉丝
Chinese cabbage with black mushrooms	冬菇白菜
Pan-fried onion cake	葱油饼
Hot and sour soup	酸辣汤
Pan-fried dumplings with minced pork	生煎小包子
Steamed bread rolls	银丝卷
Assorted meat soup in casserole	什锦砂锅
Shrimp with popped rice	虾仁锅巴
Apple/Banana Fritter	拨丝苹果／香蕉

Cantonese (a.k.a. Guangdong or Southern) Dishes 粤菜

Quickly cooked in peanut oil; crisp vegetables; somewhat sweet; starches in the sauces. Uses a lot of oyster sauce or fish sauce in cooking or poured over boiled vegetables. Many dishes are steamed to preserve natural flavors. Really exotic banquet dishes are dog, monkey, and snake. Please, no pangolin and other endangered species!

Crisp-skinned roasted goose/pork	烧鹅 / 烤乳猪
Steamed chicken with green onion	葱油鸡
Cha-shiu (barbecued) pork	叉烧
Stir-fried diced fish/filet	松子鱼 / 炒鱼片
Shark's fin in chicken and ham soup	鱼翅羹
Steamed live fish	清蒸鱼
Quick-boiled fresh shrimp	白灼虾
Stir-fried beef in oyster sauce	蚝油牛肉
Cantonese stuffed bean curd	酿豆腐
Sauteed fresh Chinese vegetable	炒新鲜蔬菜
Assorted meats in winter melon	冬瓜盅
Bird's nest in coconut milk	椰奶燕窝羹

Dim Sum 点心

These small fried or steamed pastries are for breakfast or lunch and sometimes ordered from a menu (classier), or chosen from a trolley brought to your table. You can ask the trolley attendant to take off any cover to see inside if you want. Your bill is usually calculated from the number of baskets or plates on your table.

The variety of dim sum has been more extensive in Hong Kong than in China except at the famous Panxi Restaurant in Guangzhou. Chicken feet, known as Phoenix feet, are delicious! Honest!

Har gau: smoothly wrapped shrimp dumpling	虾饺
Shui mai: minced pork and shrimp dumpling	烧卖
Cha shiu bau: barbecued pork buns	叉烧包
Tsun guen: deep-fried spring roll with pork, mushrooms, chicken, bamboo shoots, and bean sprouts	春卷
Ho yip fan: steamed fried rice wrapped in lotus leaf	荷叶饭
Pai gwat: steamed pork spareribs	排骨
Gai chuk: steamed chicken in bean curd wrapping	腐竹包鸡
Daan tart: egg custard tart	蛋挞

Fujian Dishes 福建菜

Lots of seafood and light soups, suckling pig, and nonfat spring rolls.
You may recognize Filipino dishes like *lumpia* and *lechon*, originally
from this province.

Five spices roll	五香卷
Fried fish slices	炒鱼片
Fried pig's kidneys	炒腰片
Spareribs in sweet-sour sauce	糖醋排骨
Fish with Brown Sauce	红烧全鱼
Fried straw mushrooms with pork	草菇肉片
Fried shrimps in sweet-sour sauce	糖醋虾
Fried razor clams in sweet-sour sauce	糖醋鲜蚌

Hangzhou Dishes 杭州菜

Shelled shrimp with *long jing* tea leaves	龙井虾仁
Beggar's chicken	叫化鸡
West Lake fish in vinegar sauce	西湖醋鱼
Steamed pork dumplings	小笼包子

(From the Dongya Restaurant in **Xi'an**)

Assorted cold dishes in the shape of a phoenix	凤凰拼饼
Four small cold dishes	四围碟
Sea cucumber in the shape and color of hibiscus	芙蓉海参
Crisp fried duck	香酥鸭
Mushrooms with the Three Delicacies	口蘑三样
Fried fillet of chicken	炸鸡排
Shark's fins with three kinds of slices (pork, bamboo shoots, and chicken)	三丝鱼翅
Fried fish shaped like grapes	鸡丝拉皮
Steamed carp	清蒸鲤鱼
White fungus with pineapple	菠萝银耳
Cakes and pastries	点心
	冰淇淋

Shandong Dishes 山东菜

Abalone with green vegetables on shell	鲍鱼青菜
Fresh scallops with shell	鲜带壳干贝
Roast prawns	烤大虾
Conch with fire	火螺
Steamed sea bream	馒头
Sweet and sour croaker	酸甜黄花鱼
Three Delicacies Soup	三鲜汤
Toffee Apples	拔丝苹果

Shanghai Dishes 沪菜

From central China; Suzhou, Yangzhou, Wuxi, etc. foods are variations. Longer cooking in sesame oil, neither sweet nor salty. Can be very ornamental. Borsch is on the menu of most of Shanghai's restaurants because of all the White Russians who once lived in Shanghai.

Smoked fish	熏鱼
Deep-fried shrimp balls	炸虾球
Vegetarian vegetables	素什锦
Sauteed fresh bamboo shoots	红烧冬笋
West Lake fish	西湖醋鱼
Chicken with cashew nuts	西湖醋鱼
Scallops with turnip balls	干贝萝卜球
Won-ton (dumplings) in soup	虾仁馄饨
Beggar's chicken	叫化鸡
Sauteed egg plant	红烧茄子
Lion's head casserole	红烧狮子头
Sweet sesame dumplings	芝蔴汤园

Sichuan (Szechuan) Dishes 川菜

Some dishes are highly spiced, peppery hot, and oily. Formal banquet cooking is more bland.

Smoked duck with camphor and tea flavor (not spicy hot)	樟茶鸭
Stir-fried chicken with hot pepper	宫爆鸡丁
Spicy stir-fried prawns	干烧明虾
Stir-fried shrimp with peas	碗豆炒虾仁
Stir-fried squid with/without hot pepper	金钓鱿鱼
Bon-bon chicken	棒棒鸡
Dry-fried string beans	干煸四季豆
Steamed spareribs (or pork) coated with rice powder	粉蒸排骨
Steamed fish with fermented black beans	豆豉鱼
Mo-po bean curd	麻婆豆腐

Suzhou Dishes 京菜

Sauteed shrimp meat	清炒虾仁
Squirrel Mandarin fish	松鼠桂鱼
Stewed turtle	清蒸元鱼
Stir-fried eel	生炒鳝贝
Fried crisp duck	香酥肥鸭
Water-shield soup with floating Mandarin duck	鸳鸯莼菜汤
Snow-white crab in shell	白雪蟹斗
Pickled duck	苏州酱鸭

Vegetarian cooking has had a long tradition in China and was first documented 2000 years ago. It developed with Buddhism, which forbids its adherents from killing animals, and restaurants are frequently found near Buddhist temples. Distinctively Chinese are dishes that imitate meat in taste, texture, and looks. While this does not encourage reverence for life as taught by Buddha, it does make it easier for some Buddhists to become vegetarian.

The following are some suggested dishes from the Ju Shi Lih Restaurant near the Lama Temple in Beijing and should give you an idea of what is available. Sorry, no calligraphy available yet.

Hors d'oeuvres

Water chestnuts and bean curd

Mushrooms and bamboo shoots

Shrimps (actually carrots, cucumber, bamboo shoots, mushrooms, radish)

Black and white fungi

Sea crab (actually potato, radish, mushroom, bamboo shoots)

Roast duck (actually bean curd)

Sweet and sour pork (actually locust seed)

Fish ball soup (tomato and celery)

GETTING AROUND

If you have someone taking care of all the logistics, read this only for reference in case your guide doesn't show up. The following is how things were at press time. Since then, the Chinese have probably made improvements.

Note: · · · A cancellation fee is always charged when you make changes in travel arrangements.

It is always best, no matter where and how you go, to have your destination written in Chinese so you can ask for directions. At least carry the name of your hotel in Chinese in case you stray from your tour group.

Always carry a wad of toilet tissue with you.

If you are traveling overnight by hard-class train, or by ferry (not a luxury tourist ship), take your own mug, soap, chopsticks, and towel.

The low tourist season is mid-November to mid-March, at which time many hotel prices are discounted and life is easier for individual travelers. But individual travelers should still expect difficulties, such as missing trains because you can't find the right platform. Few, if any, signs exist in English.

Formalities   You are allowed to go to any of a wide range of cities and counties in China without further formalities. You may have to get an **alien travel permit** to go to other places even if just traveling by road between open cities. Ask a travel agent in China especially if you are going off the main tourist road. But some provinces have no restrictions: among these are Fujian, Guandong, and Shandong. Jilin is 99% open, and Liaong is almost all open.

Foreign travelers who have inadvertently (or deliberately) wandered into a restricted area have been detained by the police, sometimes questioned most impolitely, and put on the next bus out. You might be put in jail and deported. Or nothing might happen. It is a matter of who you are, enforcement, and being caught.

Getting visas and visa extensions: If your visa has expired, you will probably be detained when you try to leave the country. Visa extensions can be acquired from the Foreign Affairs Department of the

Security Police in one or two days. Be sure you take your passport and a few *yuan*.

Information   For information before you leave home, see "Before You Go." You can also contact any China National Tourist Office in North America, Europe, or Australia for brochures and maps, or write directly to the provincial or city Tourism Administration in China. You can also get a wide range of literature from bookstores like China Books and Periodicals.

After arriving in China, please note that China has been producing a large number of maps, guidebooks in English, and a twice-a-month tourism newspaper. The Cartographic Department maps are very helpful as they include maps of important tourist attractions in many cities. Jinan's, for example, also shows Taishan Mountain and Qufu (with diagrams of the Confucian Family Mansion and Confucian temple). These maps list major hotels, tourist attractions, restaurants, stores, and important telephone numbers. The China City Guides series is excellent for background. Like the maps, one exists for most major cities. They are inexpensive and worth buying if you want to wander around on your own. Some cities also have public transportation maps.

The China Travel & Tourism Press has a lot of good information in English. Its main store is across the road from the Beijing Hotel in Beijing (but you might not find anyone speaking English there). Better try its office at Room 304, Chongwenmen Hotel (tel. 757181, X304) and ask for Lu Niangao, deputy chief editor, who speaks excellent English. This company publishes picture books, calendars, maps, cook books, and the excellent little *Old Tales of China.*

Many tourist attractions now have relatively inexpensive, knowledgeable **on-site guides** paid by the hour. A few of the important tourist spots have English-speaking guides, but most speak only Chinese. Some tourist attractions also have freelance guides, who may know very little about the site and speak poor English. Test them and decide on a fair price beforehand if you want to hire them. (Try Y5 an hour first.) You could also eavesdrop on someone else's English-speaking guide.

Diplomatic missions are not travel agencies, but some of them have libraries with books about China. The U.S. consulates have current travel advisories with up-to-date information on health problems, natural disasters, shortages of hotel rooms, and civil disturbances. Consulates should also have important addresses like those of doctors and pharmacies.

Fellow travelers are great. Most love to share their experiences. (Few people at home really care about the little important details.) You can find them on trains, in airport waiting rooms, in hotel elevators, at tourist attractions. They will tell you what they found worthwhile to visit and what was not. Don't be shy about asking.

Foreign residents are also great. Diplomats don't have much time for tourists except for emergencies and unforeseen circumstances, but you could try them. But foreign students and experts frequently meet in good (but cheap) hotels for support. Try the Hangzhou Hotel (Hangzhou) coffee shop or the Jinling Hotel (Nanjing) some evenings. They may look down on tourists, but if you invite them to dinner they should be able to give you a lot of good tips, such as where you can buy Jordache jeans for Y18.

National, provincial and city tourism administrations The National Tourism Administration is the body directly under the State Council responsible for the study, promotion, coordination, and supervision of tourism in China. It has information offices in Frankfurt, London, New York (and soon Los Angeles), Paris, Tokyo and Australia.

National policies get handed down to provincial and city (i.e., Beijing, Shanghai and Tianjin) tourism administrations to handle. So if you want information about tourism in Jiangsu province, for example, you ask the Jiangsu Tourism Administration.

Tourism administrations regulate tourism in their areas, the pricing and quality of hotels, restaurants, travel agencies, taxis, stores, etc., approved for foreign tourists, and the behavior of tour guides. It is to these provincial and city tourism administrations that you can address complaints about the services of establishments approved for foreign tourists. They have the power to punish or take away licenses of these establishments or tour guides if they violate regulations. This authority is a recent development of the late 1980s and may not work perfectly everywhere. I am still waiting for lists of approved establishments in English. But do be aware they can help you. Each one should have a public relations department with English-speaking staff.

Travel agencies in China make traveling easier, but not all services are cheap or available. Commissions are usually added to the ticket price. You will find travel service agencies in many hotels. The main travel agency for foreigners is China International Travel Service. China Travel Service, along with China Youth Travel Service and China Sports Service, are government agencies. Other agencies are frequently arms of government departments. They are all government-regulated and are probably reliable. Many are staffed by former C.I.T.S. guides and are usually found in hotels, with prices not necessarily the same as C.I.T.S.' Addresses are listed under "Destinations."

C.T.S. Dalian can get Overseas Chinese to historic Port Arthur but C.I.T.S. can't. Only C.V.T.S. has tours to a satellite launching station. But generally they all can do the same things, limited to the resources of the service or agency, especially during high season, when groups have top priority. Services and agencies should be able to meet you at airports, buy travel tickets for you, reserve hotel rooms and sightseeing tours, confirm flights, obtain travel permits, etc. They should be able to find guide-interpreters and also book individual travelers on mini-packages and group tours. In practice, some travelers have found that going 2 or 3 to a taxi is cheaper than taking city tours.

Some hotels organize tours for their own guests, so ask at travel or service desks in luxury hotels. Some foreign travel agencies like American Express can also provide services in China, such as purchasing plane tickets and booking trains.

Ticket-buyers should always double-check the number of tickets you are buying, and times and dates. The efficiency of any ticket seller or travel agency depends on its individual representatives. Some clerks have also been rude, especially when harassed and tired; others have been pleasant and polite.

For group tours, in the event arrangements are cancelled, C.I.T.S. has made substitutions, rather than refunds. For example, when CAAC cancelled a flight and passengers had to go by train instead, it made up the difference with another's day's sightseeing and meals. In one case, where a national guide could not be provided, group members were given beautiful tablecloths instead.

We have had no significant feedback yet as to the quality of service of travel agencies other than the ones named in this section. They have smaller staffs and fewer branches, but they might try harder.

China International Travel Service (C.I.T.S.), in Chinese **Zhong Guoji Luxingshe** (pronounced Loo-shing-sheh), organizes prepaid tours around China with a guide who speaks one of several languages besides Chinese. 91% of its clients are on tour packages of more than 10 people. F.I.T.s make up only 9%, but this percentage is growing.

C.I.T.S. isn't always able to give all its services to individual travelers, especially during high tourist seasons when guides are busy with groups. You may have to find someone else to help you then, do some of these annoying and time-consuming essentials yourself, or do without.

But C.I.T.S. is the most experienced and most efficient of the agencies helping foreigners, with the largest number of branches around the country. It usually has an office in or near every tourist center. It also has a booking office in Hong Kong. In a few small cities, notably in Guangdong and Fujian provinces, it is represented by China Travel Service. Some C.I.T.S. branches have joint ventures with foreign tour companies.

For more information on C.I.T.S., see ''The Basics,'' ''Before You Go,'' and ''Getting There.''

China Travel Service (C.T.S.) has 370 branches and over 20,000 staff members, and handles more visitors than C.I.T.S. Many of its clients, however, know Chinese and can manage largely on their own. C.T.S. operates especially in Guangdong and Fujian, the two provinces with the most Overseas Chinese visitors. Its tours also take Foreign Friends, who might be charged less than for a comparable C.I.T.S. tour. The children of Overseas Chinese, but not the spouses, are considered Overseas Chinese. You may have to do some arguing to qualify for O.C. discounts (if any) if you don't look Chinese.

C.T.S. can do all the things C.I.T.S. does for travelers. It can also arrange permission and transportation to one's ancestral village and ship gifts to relatives. It can help you locate long-lost relatives. It does have fewer English-speaking guides than C.I.T.S. It does not appear to be as efficient as C.I.T.S. with individual arrangements.

C.T.S. has booked blocks of rooms in hotels, usually cheaper and less classy than those for Foreign Friends. But C.T.S. can book deluxe hotels too. C.T.S. tours usually take second place to C.I.T.S. tours (except where the tour guide has *guanxi*).

Since Overseas Chinese in groups can sometimes travel on planes and trains more cheaply than Foreign Friends, stay in some hotels at discount prices, and usually have no need for an English-speaking guide, C.T.S. tour prices are cheaper than C.I.T.S. tours. Individual travelers can book through C.T.S.

China Youth Travel Service's main task is to receive groups of young people, but it also takes care of older people. It is currently wooing "young business people" with fancy hotels. It has a total of 50 branches and is represented in every province. Tour prices are a little cheaper than C.I.T.S.'s because of student discounts and less luxurious accommodations. Sometimes young people are put into school dormitories normally used by foreign students, but mostly they are billeted in hotels. C.Y.T.S. also can arrange informal sports competitions with Chinese youth.

C.Y.T.S. has an office in Hong Kong that seems better organized for answering letters than that in Beijing. See "Getting There."

China Sports Service Company handles formal international sports competitions and demonstrations, motorcycle tours, and television rights to international sporting events in China. It is affiliated with the All-China Sports Federation, but you don't have to be a professional or even a serious athlete to go this route. It has over 30 branches, with representation in every province. Among its services are skiing, hunting, and sky diving packages, Ping-Pong and martial arts clinics (the latter in Shaolin Temple itself). If anyone wants to meet China's Olympic gold medalist, C.S.S. should be able to arrange it. See also "The Basics."

Guides The people who escort foreign visitors are guide-interpreters, "guides" for short. Most are graduates of universities or foreign-languages institutes, with three or four years of foreign-language training at this level.

Training has been on the job, usually learned by accompanying an experienced guide for several months. But C.I.T.S. has been so short-handed at times that some guides with little English and training have been used. The Department of Education is now responsible for staff training, and prospective guides are currently spending four years learning a language, Chinese history, geography, and art history.

Guides must now pass an exam before they can wear an official badge with their photo. They could lose their badge (and their job) for accepting commissions from stores. If you are on a group tour of several cities, you might get a national guide who stays with you during your whole stay in China. At each city you also get a different local guide and, at some tourist attractions, an on-the-spot guide.

Because of the shortage you may not get a national guide.

For most visitors, your Chinese escorts will be the only Chinese people you can get to know with any depth. Guides are open about discussing their salaries and their training, especially if they like you. You could ask them questions, like how much money do they make? do they get bonuses? how much is their rent? what happens if a tour group misses a plane? who pays?

You might notice your guide getting kickbacks or gifts from the stores and factories to which they take their tours. This is against regulations, and the guide can be fined and the store can lose its license. In any case, visitors intent more on seeing China than on shopping or eating should make their wishes known.

One important question is, can guides accept gifts? Officially, they are not allowed to ask for gifts or money, nor to accept them, but no one quibbles over little souvenirs. Again, a guide could be fired for accepting a tip. It really would be better if you wrote a letter to the manager of the guide expressing how good (or bad) the guide was. The guide could get a bonus for it. See *Gifts* in "What to Take" and "Tipping."

In over a dozen trips to China, I have only met one guide who was not conscientious. But some travel agents are complaining that guides are getting lazy. You should make them work by asking a lot of questions.

Guides are not allowed to be alone in the hotel room of a visitor of the opposite sex.

Please be patient when a guide is speaking English. If it is painful to listen to, keep muttering to yourself, "This is better than nothing." A confusion over numbers is one of the most common translation problems. The Chinese think in terms of ten thousands rather than thousands. Do not mistake sixteen for sixty, seventeen for seventy, either. Ask your guide to write down big or important figures for you. When you are using an interpreter, speak slowly. Phrase what you want to be translated simply, one sentence at a time.

Also remember that unlike Greek tour guides, Chinese guides are not scholars. Their knowledge of traditional Chinese culture is frequently limited to the few books they read. Studying the old culture and history was strongly discouraged during the Cultural Revolution, when many of these people were students. This lack of knowledge is also being remedied now.

Yes, you should take *Fielding's People's Republic of China* with you, as otherwise you might not get background information. You might want to take only the pages relevant to your trip.

Guides are not usually allowed to eat with you. At mealtimes, they can be found in a staff dining room. They also stay in your hotel overnight. It is good insurance to ask where they can be reached.

TRANSPORTATION

Flying   Buying tickets is not always easy and you may have to resort to flying stand-by, showing up at the airport ticket counter pleading emergency. Because many travelers book more than one flight in order to assure themselves a seat, keep trying if you don't succeed. If you have a choice of flights, choose the shortest flying time. You will more likely get a newer plane with bigger seats and a more comfortable flight. Tickets have to be paid for not later than 12 p.m. (noon) the day before scheduled departure time. Credit cards are still not accepted. All reservations have to be reconfirmed not later than 12 o'clock noon the day before the flight (72 hours prior to departure for international passengers if you stay for more than 72 hours in the city of departure) or you risk being bumped off your flight. But you cannot reconfirm with CAAC in China by telephone. The ticket has to be stamped. Travel agencies should be able to do this for a fee, but are not always able. When you reconfirm, ask for the check-in time. It is best to arrive at the airport early in case of overbooking or planes taking off ahead of schedule. We suggest 1½ hours for domestic flights; 2 hours for international. It is very difficult to get accurate flight departure information over the telephone. Give yourself extra time to get to the airport in rain or snow.

By getting to the airport early, you might avoid being bumped off because of overbooking or missing flights that leave early. Most planes get booked from the front and there may not be room for all the carry-on bags. Planes have left early, but more often late. Some planes have been delayed for days.

Do not expect luggage carts (except at international airports) or porters. Be prepared to carry your own bags.

We suggest you carry some snacks, and a good book. You may

find lots of time to kill and nothing to eat. If you are traveling without a national guide, take along the telephone number of the local branch of a travel agency. If your flight is cancelled, at least you can telephone for help.

In some airports, you have to go through Security before checking in. Then you line up under a sign with your flight number and city in English. Make a note of other people in the line so you can reassure yourself later that you are getting on the same plane. Sometimes there are queue jumpers and shoving.

The clerk should look at your passport and take your checked bags and give you your ticket, baggage stubs, and boarding pass. You then have to go through Security; show your passport, boarding pass, and ticket.

Airport waiting rooms all have an information desk with a clerk who might know some English. Because boarding announcements are not always audible or in English, check frequently with Information. I would look out the window for my plane; the plane number is painted on the fusilage and should be mentioned on the pass. I would also double-check by looking for other people with the same color boarding pass and trying out my few words of Mandarin. Some people take a friendly interest in foreign travelers and will tell you when to board the flight.

Many airport waiting rooms are filled with smokers.

If a flight is late, insist on a progress report; if very late, food. If the plane is postponed overnight, also insist that the airline arrange a hotel room and transportation there and back.

Be prepared to walk to your plane no matter what the weather, and to be pushed by other travelers. Usually no effort is made at orderly boarding.

Until recently, CAAC has been the only airline operating domestically in China since Liberation. In pre-Liberation days, it was originally known as China National Aviation Corporation. In 1949 it became the Civil Aviation Administration of China (CAAC), and now the General Administration of Civil Aviation of China. All of its financing has been government.

The aviation industry in China is currently being restructured. CAAC is overseeing the organization of several new airlines. CAAC will continue to manage civil aviation generally in China, including safety standards and airports, licensing and international relations.

The restructuring will result in: (1) **state airlines,** Air China will carry out international operations. Five others will operate regionally in China; (2) **provincial airlines,** run by provinces and autonomous regions in cooperation with CAAC. Some of these will be totally managed by the provinces; (3) **airlines operating only within the boundaries of a province;** and (4) **general aviation**—for agriculture, exploration, etc. See "Introduction."

The state airlines are regional subsidiaries of CAAC, and will be run by former CAAC personnel with CAAC planes and facilities. With the number referring to the first digit of the flight number, there are: 1 Air China (Beijing), 2 CAAC Lanzhou Regional Administration, 3 CAAC Guangzhou (South China Airlines), 4 China Southwest Airlines (Chengdu), 5 China Eastern (Shanghai), and 6 Shenyang Regional Administration (North China Airlines). Not all of these new airlines have been inaugurated yet, and some names will be changed. While all airlines have to follow strict safety regulations and be under the administration of CAAC, differences in quality of service are apparent.

The most prominent of the other new airlines are China United Airlines (with military planes) and Shanghai Airlines. Their schedules and publicity are only in Chinese. CUA has at least 17 branch offices, among them Chengdu, Fuzhou, Hangzhou, Suzhou, and Wuxi. All have been buying new planes recently.

The first of the non-state airlines has begun service to Beijing, Anyang, Zhengzhou, and Huiyang (Shenzhen). It is named Zhongyuan (Central China) Non-Governmental Air Co. With about 23 new airlines coming into operation in the late 1980s, there might be a bit of confusion. It would help other travelers if you send us the date, flight number, plane number, and route of your flights. We are trying to decide which airline is best, and your input would be helpful.

The schedules of the CAAC affiliates are available. In China, local travel agents should also be able to make bookings for the smaller airlines and regular provincial charters. English-language schedules can now be obtained from CAAC offices in major cities for flights of CAAC and its subsidiaries, but they are not easy to get. One can also write CAAC offices in North America. The schedules are printed twice a year.

At press time it was not possible to confirm a domestic flight from North America (or a return flight while in China, for that matter). If it becomes possible, you should give yourself plenty of time before departure. Making domestic reservations in China should improve soon, especially out of Beijing and Shanghai, as the computerization of the reservation system gets completed. Then you should be able to make reservations 15 days before a flight. Ticket offices are open in some airports but only for that day's flight. You may still have to wait until you arrive at each destination to buy onward domestic tickets.

In the early 1990s, Chinese airlines will fly Tridents, Viscounts, 747s, 707s, 757s, A310-200 airbuses, Shorts 360s, 737s, 767s, MD-80s, Twin Otters, MIG 8s, 146 B Aerospace Chinese-made planes (Yuns and MD-82s), and new and old Soviet planes on **domestic flights.** Announcements are usually made in *pu tung hua* and English. Following a couple of hijackings, security at airports has tightened, with metal detectors and body searches.

Most flights have only economy class, but a growing number also offer first class. The food served is usually cold (and dry) and no alcoholic beverages are available. Some overhead luggage racks are open and allowed to be overstuffed. Call the attendant if you think the goods will fall on your head. Be sure to confirm delays with more than one official before you go back into town or whatever. Flights have taken off without all their original passengers because of conflicting information.

With competition and more and bigger planes, domestic services should continue to improve. Recent travelers on some domestic flights have found stewardesses giving safety spiels, and checking seat belts (but not badly stowed carry-ons). Lights have been dimmed properly on night takeoffs. But the quality of service and safety is uneven. No crew members objected if passengers stood in the aisles during takeoff. Don't expect world-class service yet.

CAAC has already provided booking offices in some hotels.

The following **regulations** have been in effect in China but are subject to change and should apply to all airlines. If any domestic airline loses your luggage, you get RMB Y40 per kg for full fare-paying passengers, and RMB Y25 per kg for discounted passengers, unless you have declared a higher value beforehand.

If any domestic airline is responsible for unscheduled overnight stopovers, hotel accommodation will be arranged by the carrier free of charge. (But you might have to insist.)

If any domestic airline cancels a flight, you get a full refund. If a passenger asks for a refund 24 hours before flight departure, the cancellation fee is 10%; if within 24 and 2 hours before flight departure, the cancellation fee is 20% of the original fare.

If the cancellation is within 2 hours of flight departure, the cancellation fee is 50%. If you fail to cancel before flight time **there is no refund.**

Refunds can only be made at the place of purchase or a place approved by CAAC.

There is no smoking on domestic flights.

The 20 kg (for economy class) and 30 kg (for first class) free baggage allowance for full-fare passengers seem to be *strictly enforced.* (An allowance of 15 kg for economy and 20 kg for first class is allowed on a discounted fare. There is no allowance for infants paying 10% of the adult fare.) Carry-on baggage should not exceed 9″ by 16″ by 20″, but frequently does.

No babies under 10 days of age and no pregnant women almost due are allowed to fly. An infant under two not occupying a separate seat and accompanied by an adult is charged 10% of the adult fare. Children 2–12 are charged 50% of the adult fare.

Helicopter service is available in some cities for sightseeing, sometimes on charter. Regular flights now go on between Zhuai and Taishan, and Zhuhai and Guangzhou.

CAAC (China International Airlines), operates **international flights** almost the same as other international airlines, but again with minimal services. Flights have headsets for music and have alcoholic drinks. On its New York-Beijing run we had two Chinese movies (with English subtitles) and two U.S. movies. The Chinese movies were a good opportunity to see Chinese lifestyles. Reservations will be canceled unless reconfirmed on flights wholly within Europe. Full refunds on international tickets are made if you cancel before check-in time. A 25% cancellation fee is charged for "no shows." The free baggage allowance on flights to China from North America is two pieces each, with size and weight limits dependent on class.

An airport tax is charged on all departing international flights, including those to Hong Kong. Exceptions are diplomats, transit passengers, and children under 12. Passengers holding international tickets with confirmed space on the first connecting flight should get free meals and hotel accommodations provided by CAAC within 24 hours after their arrival at the connecting points.

We suggest that you avoid sitting beside toilets.

If you are trying to make connecting flights in China, give yourself plenty of time. You have to clear Immigration and Customs first, and then from Shanghai international airport to the domestic departure lounge is about one km. But an international passenger connecting with a confirmed domestic flight the next day should get overnight accommodations with meals.

Foreign airlines also fly to China but have no domestic services. Some but not all can sell seats on their own planes in China. Some will accept credit card payments for tickets. Some, like Canadian Airlines, have different dimensions for carry-on luggage (22″ x 14″ x 9″ or 56 x 36 x 23 cm) and are more strict than the Chinese about enforcing them.

Trains   China has a vast network of railways, linking every provincial and regional capital except Lhasa to Beijing. And even that omission is being remedied. Railway lines have been burgeoning in the 1980s.

Tickets can be obtained through hotels or travel agencies (usually for service fee). Since the travel agencies cannot always be counted on to buy tickets for individual travelers, especially during high tourist seasons, you might have to go to the railway station and buy them yourself. In some big cities, special ticket windows are provided for foreigners, but lineups can be long, especially for hard class. Best buy your tickets at least four days in advance. Getting train tickets is now more difficult then ever. Scalpers around train stations and in some coffee shops can buy tickets for you for F.E.C. equivalents of local prices. While this is illegal, everybody does it; but some scalpers might not be seen again.

One pays upon receipt. Travelers have boarded trains using platform tickets and then bought tickets from the conductor on the train. This, however, is risky, as space may not be available.

Except for international trains originating abroad, train tickets can only be booked in China.

Train schedules, comprehended with difficulty in English, for all Chinese trains are now available, sold in foreign counters in railway stations for a small fee. Be sure to give yourself plenty of time to find your train; platforms are not marked in English, but the destination of each coach should be marked on its side.

Like travel on overnight ferries, men and women are assigned berths without regard to sex even in soft class. If this arrangement bothers you, ask for another compartment. The Chinese are used to such travel and are not embarrassed. Tourist groups usually sort themselves out. I have never heard of sexual harassment on a train in China, so don't feel nervous. One can get used to sleeping in one's clothes and washing with strangers of the opposite sex nearby.

If you're *desperate* and can't wait for roommates to leave, change your clothes in the toilet room. You could also ask your roommates to wait outside your compartment for a moment while you change, undress under the covers, or wait until the lights are out. Businessmen wearing suits might look a little wrinkled next day, but who cares? Wrinkles aren't all that important in China.

To protect valuables, do not use your purse as a pillow. Things have been stolen that way. Put your valuables in a money belt around your waist. Tie your camera to your arm.

Toilets look like they've been hosed down and not scrubbed. On coaches reserved for foreign tourists, you can be quite sure of toilet paper and soap (in a common soap dish). Soft-class travelers on some trains now have a choice of a Western toilet seat or a squat.

A washroom in each car offers several sinks with running water. Many prepaid tourists wait until they arrive at their hotels before washing. However, sometimes on arrival early in the morning hotel rooms have not yet been vacated, and tourists are frequently taken sightseeing or to breakfast instead.

Trains are usually hot and dusty in the summer, unless you are lucky and find yourself in one of the new air-conditioned cars. No smoking is allowed in some coaches. Baggage might be checked for inflammable and dangerous articles. Luggage is frequently pushed in and out of train windows. Conductors sometimes check luggage, demanding payment for overweight. On trains slowed by too much weight, people with luggage over their limits have been asked to get rid of some bags, or leave with all of it.

Do not discard your ticket. You are asked for it again at the exit gate of your arrival station.

Trains are special express, express, regular, and suburban. Passengers could have a choice of hard- and soft-class seats and hard- and soft-class berths. The most comfortable are in the middle of a coach, away from noise and wheel vibrations. When you buy your ticket, state your preference.

Prepaid tourists usually travel **soft-class berth,** which can be almost the same price as going by plane. The berths are the height of bourgeois comfort if you have air conditioning. Compartments usually have clean slipcovers with lace doilies, lace curtains, a 16″ by 24″ table with a lamp and potted plant, an overhead fan, four porcelain mugs (for tea), and sleeping spaces with bedding and towels for four people on two uppers and two lowers. An overhead loft stores large suitcases, but you have to rely on strong arms to get them up there and down. Train conductors are usually very helpful and friendly. An attendant keeps refilling the thermos of hot water and sweeping the floors.

It is best to take a small overnight bag if you are sleeping on the train, unless you want to do acrobatics or limit your leg room. Most group luggage is stored at one end of the car and may not be easily accessible.

Compartment doors can be closed for privacy. Do not worry if you cannot lock them from the outside. The conductor usually locks your door when you go to the dining car. The plug for the fan (if you have one) and the switch for the loudspeaker are under the table.

Dining-car food is edible and, on some trains, surprisingly good, but simple. Passengers usually give their orders to a steward beforehand and are notified when their food is ready.

Six people share one compartment of **hard-class berths** in the same amount of space as "soft." Berths are padded, however, and tiered in threes with even less privacy, the middle berth being the best.

Hard class is noisy and dirty, with frequent clearing of throats and spitting on the floor. You also cannot turn off the loudspeaker, which starts at 6 a.m. every morning. The coaches are mopped frequently. Sheets and warm blankets are provided, but if you get on between the two terminals, these may already have been used. Passengers can eat in the dining car, but can also buy food from vendors at train stations or circulating on the train itself. Don't expect gourmet fare! In fact, food from vendors can be downright unappetizing, like a box of rice with pork (including the skin, with hair left on). It might be best to bring your own instant noodles if you're on a tight budget. Steaming hot water is available in each car. Hard-class seats are very crowded and some travelers have ignored "no smoking" signs.

Accommodations can be upgraded after the train is underway if space is available.

China started using luxury-class, double-decker railway cars in 1988 on its Nanjing-Shanghai run. In addition to the Hong Kong-Guangzhou express train, China does have air-conditioned carriages and is introducing more.

Long-distance buses   Air-conditioned buses and mini-buses speed along a few routes, especially from Hong Kong and Macao, and in other parts of the country as well. Ask about the kind of bus you will be taking because some buses are small, hard-seated, and very crowded, with little luggage space except on the roof. They can be uncomfortable for big foreigners, especially if you have to stand or squat. We have also heard horror stories of windows impossible to close in freezing weather, and carbon monoxide poisoning because of bad maintenance. So check your bus before you commit yourself. On some routes, you do have a choice of new Japanese-built buses. Not all highways are paved. Still, buses are good for seeing the countryside and meeting people—but you have to be young in spirit, strong, and adventurous. You usually book ahead of time at a bus station, Overseas Chinese hotels, or ask CITS. We strongly urge you to take your own food. These buses do stop at dumpy restaurants with a busload of travelers, and one can't expect service immediately. As soon as the driver is finished, the bus leaves. Toilets are usually primitive.

Long-distance ferries   Overnight ships between Hong Kong and Chinese ports usually have small, comfortable, but not luxurious cabins. See "Getting There." For boats on the Yangtze, see "Yangtze Gorges." For small one-class ships, see "Jiangmen." Some ferries have good reputations, like those between Shanghai and Ningpo. The ferry between Guangzhou and Haikou is said to be dirty, however. Standards are uneven. Take a supply of seasick pills if you're susceptible. Take your own mug, towel, chopsticks, and soap on overnight trips.

Accidents have occurred because of overcrowding.

By road   Some but not all roads are being opened to foreigners. The problem is military zones. Open for your visit is the road from Shanghai to Beijing. Ask the China Youth Travel Service about others. Tour groups of self-drive jeeps and cars are available in Xi'an. Hertz Asia Pacific and C.T.S. Macao have individual self-drive tours to Guilin (with an escort). Studies are being made that should allow foreigners to bring their own jeeps and boats (for touring the Yellow River).

Some youth travel agencies have tours by bus in Fujian and Guangdong, a great way to see the country. One can take a group tour by motorcycle or bicycle, but these tours are not cheap. A truck carrying spare parts follows behind, picking up tired bikers.

Some adventurous bikers have traveled from town to town on their own. Please be aware of the problems. You might find only substandard hotels, you may not be able to get bicycle parts, in case of accident, you might not be able to communicate, roads might not be paved. No guide books have yet been found for this kind of travel. You might have to get alien travel permits for some areas. Do check for licenses if you want to attempt individual travel by motorcycle. Police in China hassle motorcyclists.

For safety's sake, we urge you not to travel alone. If you do, let us know what happens so we can pass on information to other travelers.

It is possible to hire a **taxi** to take you from city to city, but you have to pay the return fare if you leave it at a city other than its home base. Always ask ahead of time for the approximate fare and distance and if you need an Alien Travel Permit. See "Budget."

Hitchhiking has been and may have to be done. Backpackers have hitched rides with truck drivers. On-your-own tourists in isolated spots like the cave temples near Dunhuang (with only two public buses a day) have been able to get rides on tour buses (sometimes free). It's a matter of luck. If you have connections with foreign experts, etc., you might be able to use staff cars for much lower rates than taxis.

Porters. A big problem is lack of porters at bus and railway stations, ferry quays, and airports. Some places have them, but one never knows. Some freelance porters may be available, but they might also disappear with your luggage or not get you to your train on time. When you notify people you are coming tell them you need a porter or be prepared to carry your own luggage, especially if you arrive by bus or train. You can give your baggage checks to hotel drivers to claim at airports.

LOCAL TRANSPORTATION

Bicycles can be rented from hotels and bicycle-rental shops.

Some rented bicycles have fallen apart. Be sure to check the brakes, tires, bell, lock, etc. You will probably have to leave a deposit or some identification, but try not to leave a passport. Clerks have accepted old student cards, expired driver's licenses, anything with a photo. Guard your receipt carefully. Always park in a supervised parking lot; otherwise your bicycle may disappear, to be found again at a police station, you hope. Make a note of what it looks like, the license number, and the place where you have left it. Finding it quickly again among hundreds of identical bicycles may otherwise be a problem. Most cities have bicycle lanes, and some have streets forbidden to bicycles.

If you are staying any length of time in China, you might want to buy a Chinese bicycle and sell it when you leave. China makes a lot of bicycles, but few locally made ones have more than one speed.

Phoenix has a 10-speed, but I don't know how good it is.

Officially all bicycles should have bicycle licenses, but most foreign riders have had no trouble riding without one. Some people have taken their own bicycles into China hoping to travel around the country, but only a few have been able to do this, and some have had to leave their bicycles behind because of the hassles. (To ship a bicycle by train means having to go to the train station a day ahead of time and, at the other end, spending time finding it.) Spare parts for foreign makes are also a problem.

Motorscooter rickshaws for two or more are cheaper than taxis and could take lots of luggage, but they are not comfortable, with much swerving and bouncing. Prices are often fixed and paid in advance at a stand.

Bicycle rickshaws built for two cost very little or a lot (in tourist areas), but you can only go short distances. Please consider the driver and get off and walk up steep slopes. Bicycle rickshaws are ideal for leisurely sightseeing in places like Hangzhou. Big cities seem to be phasing them out, and please don't ride them in heavy motorized traffic since they can be dangerous. Do agree on a price in advance, especially in tourist towns, where revolutionary morals have given way to market forces. Make sure the price is for the ride, not for each person. If the driver demands something exorbitant, just hand him what is fair and walk away. If the price is right, he won't scream at you.

Taxis are normally found outside most tourist hotels, at railway stations, airports, and passenger-ship quays. Some can be found outside Friendship Stores and places frequented by visitors. If these places don't have taxi stands of their own, their service desks should telephone for a taxi for you, even though you may not be a customer. If you are not near any of these places, you can still ask someone to help you telephone for a taxi. See ''Useful Phrases.'' Taxis can be flagged on the street in only a few cities (notably Guangzhou). In some places, taxi drivers don't want to go short distances.

Taxis are not always easy to find. If you have several stops to make, it is usually better to hire a taxi by the half day or day, and have the driver wait for you. Or you could pay by the meter (or odometer) with a charge for ''waiting time.'' Always check rates before you go. Usually you need not pay for a meal for a driver if you are near his home base, but you might invite the driver to a meal if you are a long way away. Restaurants and hotels have sections for staff if you don't want to eat together.

If you need a taxi early in the morning or for a full or half day, it is best to make a reservation at the taxi stand the night before. Taxi companies also have minibuses for larger groups.

Not all taxis have meters, and drivers have been known to cheat. While most drivers are honest, a few have added unused ''waiting time'' in Chinese to the receipts, or just charged higher rates. Taxi drivers without meters should calculate fares according to the distance per taxi, not per passenger. See ''Budget'' for recent per kilometer rate. (See

Getting from the Airport to Your Hotel in "Getting There" for other tricks.) It would be wise to ask the price before you go and *make a note of the odometer reading before you start.* Ask for a receipt. You can usually pay for taxis in R.M.B., but you stand a better chance of getting one if they know you have F.E.C.s.

If you feel a driver is cheating you, don't pay, and ask *cheerfully* for someone to call a policeman to mediate. Hotel and C.I.T.S. staff members should know the distance from the airport, and between tourist attractions. If you have already paid, get a receipt, take the driver's name and license number, and complain to the manager or dispatcher at his/her taxi stand or to the local tourism administration. Ask your consulate for advice. Some cities have a taxi complaint office. Letters of complaint to *China Daily* have resulted in penalties for the driver and apologies from the taxi company.

Another ploy is to pay what you consider the proper fare, get out, and leave. If the driver follows you, then reconsider your calculations and negotiate a settlement.

Some drivers charge extra because they have to pay the touts who bring them customers. Try to avoid the middle man. Some drivers will give you R.M.B. instead of F.E.C.s in change. Drivers who cheat are a new phenomenon and should be discouraged.

Public tour buses are available in a few cities, notably Beijing and Xi'an, offering relatively cheap transportation to some tourist attractions with a detailed commentary in English. Cheaper still are bus tours for Chinese people, a good bargain if you take along a guide book. Best take your own lunch to save time eating in restaurants, and make sure you know how long your bus is staying at each stop. Write down the bus number so you can find it again.

Shuttle buses are available at a few hotels for free or for a fee. These go to airports, Friendship Stores, and perhaps a few tourist attractions.

Public city buses are usually very crowded, especially during the early-morning and late-afternoon rush hours, and all day Sunday. But they are cheap and are often your only means of transportation. Try them if you are athletic or adventurous. Hotel personnel can tell you which bus to take. Some cities have bus maps in English. Or you can take a map with you and point. Fellow passengers are usually friendly and helpful. Public mini-buses are starting to appear on some routes. They are more expensive than a bus but cheaper than a taxi.

As in all crowded places, beware of pickpockets.

Subways are in Beijing and soon in Shanghai and Guangzhou, and maps are available. Walk down the stairs, pay your money (cheap), and choose your platform.

Public ferries and tour boats. China has some real antiques crossing harbors and rivers. They are cheap, but avoid them if they look too crowded and tippy. (Fatal accidents with tour boats have recently been blamed on overloading and drunken crews.)

Something has to be said about **walking** because of all the bicycles. Crossing streets can be dangerous. Try to let a native upstream run interference. Cross at lights. Some cities have overpasses—use them!

COMMUNICATIONS

Services have greatly improved in the last few years and are still developing.

Postal services are generally reliable, and faster if the addresses are marked in Chinese. China now has express service to a couple of hundred Chinese cities.

Sending parcels is a problem. You have to use a regular post office rather than one at your hotel. All packages are inspected, even those sent inside China. Best take rope or tape along with your partially wrapped parcel. Some post offices sell boxes for a little over ¥1. They are looking for more than two cartons of cigarettes, pornographic literature, used clothing and antiques.

Some small city post offices will accept only airmail packages. In Foshan I tried to mail a 4-kg beaded curtain to Canada. Not only did the clerk ask that it be sewn in cloth, but it would have cost almost ¥200, as no surface post was available.

Surface mail to North America can take six weeks to three months. Registration is cheap. Airmail takes about 7 to 10 days. Post offices are asking for payment in F.E.C. China is starting to be strict about postal codes.

Courier service is available.

Telephones: Local calls from hotels are easy except when everyone else wants to use the few lines available. Some circuits are busier than others. So far, we haven't found any automatic forwarding equipment. If a line is busy, you have to keep dialing.

Many public telephones are in stores. Look for a picture of a telephone outside. Guangzhou and a Canadian company are experimenting with telephone booths and telephones used with a prepaid credit card. These can be used for long distance calls as well.

As a general rule, Chinese citizens do not have private telephones yet (though the situation is improving). Sets are available in most urban neighborhoods, factories, and offices, with a small sign in Chinese about seven feet from the ground by the door. Cheap. Each village usually has at least one telephone in the village office. China is currently putting a lot of effort into improving telecommunications, but in the meantime, one can, for example, leave a message asking your friends to telephone you at your hotel. Be sure to give your room number.

The easiest way to call long distance and overseas is at your hotel.

See "Hotels." These calls can also be made at a Post and Telecommunications office, where reception might be better.

Direct dial between Chinese cities, and international direct dial are usually easy, once you get a direct dial line. Just don't try when every one else is trying to use it. Direct dial is much faster (20 seconds) than operator-assisted calls, which might take from three minutes to a couple of days (in remote towns). Direct dial is available in an increasing number of the biggest cities.

Don't forget the time difference. New York City is 13 hours behind China during the winter months, and 12 or 13 hours during daylight saving months. Thus in winter, 8 p.m. China time is 7 a.m. New York or Toronto standard time, 12 noon Greenwich Mean Time, or 4 a.m. San Francisco time. See "Quick Reference" for time zones and Chinese telephone codes.

Holiday Inn's Teleplan means cheaper hotel service charges for telephone calls. Ask about it.

Telex service is usually instantaneous and reliable, but we suggest you ask for an answer in China because, for example, telexes requesting reservations have been ignored in some hotels. Not all telex services are available 24 hours a day. Many hotels have telex services. You could save money typing your own telexes in some hotels because of service charges.

If you expect a telex in your hotel in China, best give your room number as part of your address. And for double insurance, keep looking for incoming telexes in the telex pile. Ask Reception.

Cable is cheaper and slower and could take over a day. You usually book them through post offices.

Fax is not as efficient as telex, as it is dependent on overused telephone lines.

Travelers on their own aiming for travel without stress (but not backpackers). Hopefully, by the time you read this, you should be able to:

1) book all domestic flights from outside China at least two months before arriving in China. Because new flights are frequently added, try again later if you can't book any particular leg of your trip.

2) make reservations in hotels during high tourist season in the main tourist and business cities. You could take a chance in smaller, less important places, and arrive without one at other times. No. 1 and 2 can be done through a travel agent. High season is June, August, September and October.

3) telex your hotel before you arrive to meet you with transport giving flight number, or train and coach numbers. Someone at your destination should hold up a sign with your name or the hotel's name on it. A few hotels do not charge for picking you up. If you have less

than three days, you could also ask the hotel or travel agency to reconfirm or book the next stage of your travel.

4) consult your hotel travel service or a travel agency about your
next travel plans, reconfirming plane tickets or booking train tickets,
and repeating no. 3.

5) for your day of departure, book a taxi and ask if the driver can
carry your luggage to the train platform or check-in counter. If the driver
cannot and you have loads of luggage, ask the hotel or a travel agency
to help you.

6) avoid much hassle by booking mini-packages along the way
through C.I.T.S. (more expensive). This can also be done through a
travel agent in North America if you pay in advance and send a photocopy of your passport.

Backpackers or anyone else trying to travel on a shoestring and carrying their own luggage:

1) should first and foremost be flexible, assertive, resourceful, polite, and patient. You should expect to do only a percentage of what
you want to do, and make the most of standing in queues.

2) should not expect to make reservations in cheaper hotels, which
usually take people on a first-come basis. Some train stations and airports have hotel-booking offices or C.I.T.S. who can refer you to hotels. And if you arrive at a hotel that is full, the clerks should be able
to refer you to another hotel.

3) can save money sleeping in hotel dormitories, riding public buses,
and eating in open-air food stalls. CAAC has an airport bus downtown
that could go near some of the cheaper hotels. Try to ask fellow passengers to point out a suitable hotel if you don't know of any.

4) should look to China Youth Travel Service or your hotel to
recommend other hotels and make hard-class train or ship bookings. If
they can't or these services are too expensive, you have to do it yourself.

5) should consider taking overnight ships between cities (to save
on paying for a hotel bed).

6) should not expect a high standard of English or service or cleanliness or 24-hour hot water in cheaper hotels.

7) should network with other foreign backpackers.

Yes, you can do it successfully and cheaply.

LOCAL CUSTOMS AND EMERGENCIES

DOES "YES" MEAN "YES"? Well, usually. Cultural differences do create misunderstandings. For example, a memorandum of understanding in trade means there is reason to believe that negotiations can begin in earnest. It does not mean, as many foreigners have sadly discovered, that a contract has been signed. The official dealt with might be overruled by his superior. Also, if a Chinese nods and says "yes, yes," he could be just trying to please you. He may not understand a word you are saying. So be wary. Ask a question that needs a full sentence in reply. For the same reason, a Chinese might give you dates and spellings and swear they are right. But what he means is that it is the best information he has and if you press him, he will check—but if you don't, he won't bother.

Chinese people are very polite in their personal relationships with friends or business acquaintances—people they will see again and again. They try not to hurt feelings, yours or their own. If you make a mistake, the very polite ones will not point it out to you. If you do something they do not like, they might ask someone senior to you to talk to you about it. My aunt was asked to criticize me when my nieces thought my clothes were a little too risque.

But Chinese people may not seem polite at times, especially crowds, or clerks in government stores. But if someone introduces you properly, most Chinese will prove to be extremely hospitable and helpful. The shop girl who ignores you is probably afraid of you or bored and unfulfilled by her job. Don't take it personally.

Once I caught my knee in the door of a crowded bus and got a bruise that lasted for weeks. At the time, my cousins laughed while I felt like crying. It was just their way of reacting—probably embarrassment, not knowing how else to react. Just don't feel offended.

DOES "NO" MEAN "NO"? Well, sometimes. You will have to judge for yourself when a negative decision can be challenged.

You might hear "mei you" often. It means "there isn't any." Some foreigners have challenged it successfully at airline ticket offices by standing firm, smiling, asking for the manager, and refusing to budge until they get a ticket. Basically it means "please disappear," and when you don't disappear, something has to be done.

By protesting to a hotel clerk who said there was no room, I did get a bed in a dorm. This does not mean you should try to argue every time you are told "it is not possible," or that "your safety cannot be guaranteed." It could mean (1) language is a problem and they do not understand your request; (2) they don't want to be bothered trying; (3) they don't want too many people going there, but if you insist, they'll let you go; (4) there is genuine concern for your safety; (5) you really aren't allowed to go.

Arguing is an art too. Do not lose your temper or you've lost the battle. You should argue as much as possible in their terms. For example, one single traveler was put, as is the custom, in a small banquet room in one hotel for meals. There were no other foreign guests and the room was dingy and depressing. Two requests to move into the main dining room with the Chinese guests were refused. Single Traveler decided to go to a restaurant instead, pointing out to her guide that it was her problem. She said she was willing to pay for the hotel meals too, but she just couldn't bear eating alone under the circumstances. She was allowed to eat with the others.

Note: Sometimes no answer is a "no."

ASK QUESTIONS   An official of the Overseas Chinese Travel Service once told me the only advice he had for visitors was, "Ask questions." It is good advice. For some reason, the Chinese do not volunteer much information. It might have something to do with their own lines of communication. So when in doubt, ask!

APPLAUSE   You will frequently be greeted by applause as a sign of welcome or appreciation at institutions and cultural performances. It might even happen on the streets. The usual response is to applaud back.

CRITICISMS AND SUGGESTIONS   You may be asked for these and see many booklets in hotels, train dining cars, and restaurants with this title. If you have any criticisms and suggestions, do give them. But don't go on about how things are done in North America. Much doesn't apply to China. Criticisms should be helpful in the context of a developing country. Criticisms and suggestions are considered seriously, especially now that China is trying to improve her tourist facilities. Yes, mention that the bathroom floor is filthy. Go further than that and ask the attendant to clean it. If an atten-dant has been particularly helpful, write it down. She may get a bonus because of it.

TIPPING is forbidden. Officially it is considered insulting. The attendants themselves may have other feelings, but most are now only allowed very minor gifts. But some attendants and guides do accept tips and make more money than doctors, university professors, and government officials. Is it fair? The turn of the decade is an era of transition and new rules are developing. We suggest you tip only for services above the call of duty. Do not tip the attendant who fixes your broken toilet. That is his duty. Avoid tipping in hotels that add a percentage for service. While staff may not necessarily get the service charge, you have already paid additional for their service. In some hotels, tips are accepted "as a token of friendship" and shared among all the staff. We suggest you ask your tour guide to handle tipping. Miserable hours have been wasted arguing about tips and gifts.

Asking for tips in strictly forbidden. If there is any doubt about tipping, phone the local tourism administration or the manager of C.I.T.S. Some attendants and guides will actually refuse tips. They should be thanked profusely and perhaps given a modest "sourvenir" instead. See *Gifts* in "What to Take."

GOOD MANNERS at home are good manners anywhere. Don't litter. Don't take "souvenirs," especially from historical places, such as a rock from the Great Wall. Don't pick flowers in parks.

In most other Asian countries it is fashionable to be late. Not so in China, where groups of children may be outside in the rain waiting for your car so they can applaud as you arrive.

Traditionally, Chinese conversations, even business conversations, start out with something innocuous: a discussion of the weather, of the calligraphy or a painting on the wall, or whatever. A mood of friendliness is set first. Then comes the business.

It is true that Chinese people themselves may not be polite in crowds. They may surround your bus and stare at you, crowd around when it's hot and ignore your pleas for help. But it is their country and just because you paid a lot of money to visit, it doesn't mean you can be rude.

Also, when you are using an interpreter, don't forget to look at the person with whom you are actually conversing.

JOKING ABOUT POLITICS AND SEX Many visitors are warned not to joke about sex or politics, particularly Chinese politics. To joke about sex is considered crude, and you condemn yourself when you do it. To joke about politics or even to argue about it is to show lack of sensitivity. Politics is taken very seriously in China. People are put into jail because of it, lose their jobs, waste years of schooling, and spend long hours in meetings discussing political implications.

BEGGARS   Yes, there are a few. Use your own discretion. As I would in New York City, I would ask them why they have to beg, and then decide whether or not to give. Or I might take them to the closest restaurant and give them a meal. Or ignore.

FLIRTING   You may be tempted to flirt with a cute Chinese citizen of the opposite sex. Friendliness is appreciated, but anything beyond that used to and still may mean an interview with the Security Police, where you are asked why you insulted a Chinese citizen. It could also mean a fine or deportation. This puritanical attitude is much less strict now, but you will notice that even handholding is not too common especially in smaller towns. Chinese are more likely to socialize with members of their own sex than to pair off in public. Casual dating is certainly frowned on. Friendly embraces common abroad are unusual even upon greeting a Chinese friend of long standing. (Chinese people overseas do it—but not in China.) You will probably be considered uncivilized if you indulge in too much display of affection in public, even with your own spouse. The Chinese will be embarrassed. But things are changing.

It should take a month to get permission for marriages between Chinese and foreigners, if all goes well.

Foreigners are fined heavily (over U.S. $1000 in at least one case) if caught with an unrelated and unregistered Chinese of the opposite sex in a hotel room.

WILL YOU BE FOLLOWED?   Most probably not, unless the Chinese have a special reason to watch you. They might catch some foreigner selling foreign currency illegally to show they mean business. A foreigner is conspicuous. If you do anything wrong, your movements could be easily traced.

PHOTOGRAPHY   China is now like most other countries regarding photographs. At one time I couldn't even take a photo of my five-year-old on a public boat. There are still restrictions: You are not allowed to photograph police stations, for example. In 1978 I allowed my bored child to take a photo of friendly policemen only to be told officiously by the officer in charge who suddenly appeared that "taking photographs in police stations is forbidden, but since he is only seven years old, we will not prosecute." We had been waiting to be registered.

Today you can take pictures out of airplanes, on and off boats—everywhere except military installations and certain museums which, like ours, find they cannot sell their own photos if cameras are allowed.

The Chinese also feel that flash photography damages relics. They charge a fee or confiscate your film.

Out of courtesy, please do ask people for permission to photograph them close up. Would you like someone to stick a camera in your face without permission?

IF YOU GET INTO TROUBLE   Chances are these things won't happen, but just in case . . .

Earthquakes   The main danger here is collapsing buildings. If you don't have time to get outside into the open, away from falling debris, dive under a desk, table, or bed, or take shelter in a doorway. If the building falls down around you, at least you might have some protection. As soon as the shaking stops, which is usually after a few seconds, rush outside by stairway (not elevator).

Typhoons   This Chinese word meaning "big wind" is the Asian word for hurricane or tropical cyclone. These usually originate east of the Philippines and may hit China anywhere along the Pacific coast from April to November. They usually last for a maximum of three days and you should stay inside substantial buildings on high ground. The danger is falling debris, as well as strong winds and rain. Airports will probably be closed.

If you run out of money   Ask your embassy to cable home for some, or telephone collect. It usually takes five banking days. Borrow if you can from fellow travelers. You can get cash advances, with a 4% service charge, or free check cashing from the Bank of China with some credit cards. Some airlines take credit cards. The U.S. embassy gives small emergency loans, but very reluctantly.

If you lose your passport   Talk to your guide about it. Inform the local police and contact your embassy. Diplomatic offices are in Beijing, but some consulates are in Shanghai, Shenyang, and Guangzhou. Be sure you have your passport number somewhere in your luggage. If you're on a group tour, your tour escort should have a note of it and can give you a document so you can travel to other cities in China to get a new passport. C.I.T.S. should be able to help you if you are on your own. You should have extra passport photos on hand, even though some U.S. consulates now have instant passport photo machines. Your embassy could give you a temporary passport; with this document you can get a Chinese visa, without which you cannot leave China.

Losing a passport creates a lot of trouble and additional expense, as it probably means staying a couple of extra days or leaving your tour group. Guard yours carefully.

Hostile crowds The May 1985 soccer riot in Beijing proved that this could happen. Anyone looking like the victorious Hong Kong Chinese was singled out for threats and abuse. But riots by soccer fans of defeated hometown teams can happen anywhere in the world, and did that year. Remember Brussels? This is not a Chinese phenomenon.

If you *think* you're surrounded by hostile people, try smiling. Chances are they're just curious or even jealous. Ignore them or try to make friends. Speak to individuals quietly, in English if you don't know Chinese. Someone may understand. Above all, act friendly and cool. Shouting obscenities is counterproductive.

If you are convinced the crowd is hostile, try to find out why. The Chinese do not get angry at foreigners just because they are foreigners. Even Japanese people, the hated invader for so many years, are received politely here. Hostility could be caused by something you have done. It used to be taking pictures of the wrong places and superstitious people but this is rare now. It could be an argument with a rickshaw or taxi driver. Try not to lose your temper; keep cool, polite, friendly. Call for the police. Apologize if you need to. If someone is drunk, just leave.

Demonstrations Don't be afraid of them. They are usually orderly except in Tibet, where demonstrators and by-standers have been shot without warning by police. Avoid demonstrations there, please. The blond wife of one foreign correspondent used to wave at marching demonstrators with a big, friendly grin on her face during times less friendly to foreigners. Participants used to be so surprised by this, they'd break step, stare, and grin back. If a policeman asks you to move on and not take photos, do as he says, or accept the consequences.

Recent demonstrations against African students should not discourage other Black people from visiting China. I have never heard of any unpleasantness specifically against Blacks in general. Chinese people stare and occasionally titter at all foreigners. Please let me know if you find anything different.

Car and bicycle accidents If your car accidentally injures anyone, do what you should in your own country. Give first aid, and then arrange to get the victim to a doctor or a hospital quickly. Otherwise, stay where you are. Do not get involved in arguments. Wait until the police arrive. The police will take statements, and if you are found to be in any way responsible as the driver or even as a passenger (were you distracting the driver?), you may be liable to a fine or payment for damages. The fine would be to remunerate the family of the injured or deceased for the rest of his productive years. There is a standard formula. If the accident is serious, contact your embassy. There have been cases where a Chinese was found at fault and his work unit paid for a broken windshield. There have also been cases of drunken diplomats causing traffic accidents. Many were asked to leave China. Since most tourists will not be driving, car accidents are not really a problem, but bicycle accidents might be.

Breaking the law If you are accused of breaking a Chinese law, try to contact your embassy as soon as you can. Do not expect the rights that you would have in your own country, like to bail or even to see a lawyer. China has only recently rewritten its civil law, which says that foreigners cannot be arrested without a warrant from the People's Procurate or the People's Court. Minor violations could mean detention and deportation. More serious violations like "burglary of scarce industrial materials" have meant the death penalty for Chinese citizens. Taking bribes worth ¥58,000 has meant life imprisonment. An American who fell asleep while smoking set fire to a hotel, resulting in the deaths of ten people. He was sentenced to 18 months' imprisonment and ordered to pay ¥150,000 compensation. Just don't do anything illegal! China has relations with Interpol.

What if you get hurt or sick? China has been among the healthiest and cleanest countries in Asia. But standards seem to be slipping.

There have been reports of typhoid, malaria, plague, and rabies usually in isolated rural areas far off the tourist routes, though a few cases of rabies have shown up in Shanghai. Venereal diseases are back after being absent for decades, but are still rare compared to other Asian countries. One hears occasionally of encephalitis, hepatitis B, cholera, and intestinal parasites. Avoid wading in lakes and rivers in central China's Yangtze River area because of schistosomiasis.

You can find out about these and about malaria areas from the World Health Organization. If you are bothered by mosquitoes in China, use the net above your bed, or ask for one if there isn't any. You can also burn incense coils that keep mosquitoes away. To keep visitors happy, a lot of insecticide spray is used in rural areas, and even recently, sprayed from planes in Guangzhou. This might create other problems, but never mind.

Chinese medical facilities are good for common ailments. Many Overseas Chinese go to China for acupuncture and even Western medical treatment. If visitors are sick, it is usually the common cold or an upset stomach (see "Food"). Some visitors have also had hernias, heart attacks, and cancer. Your guide or the service desk at your hotel should be able to direct you to a doctor. Hotels frequently have medical clinics on the premises. We have listed a few hospitals that should be able to help foreigners.

If you become ill at night, try the attendant on your floor. Some attendants sleep in a room close to the service desk. If you have a language problem, point to what you need in the "Useful Phrases."

In emergencies, knowledgeable foreign residents say **taxis are quicker to get than ambulances.**

You will probably be given a choice of Western or traditional Chinese medicine, or both. Chinese herbal medicines are frequently effective, but one of my kids had to be bribed with lots of candy to drink his herbal tea, it tasted so awful.

Chinese medical facilities might look grubbier than those in the West. An examination with medicines for an upset stomach at a hotel clinic at this writing costs from ¥5 to about ¥35. The foreign in-patients' section of Capital Hospital in Beijing charges about ¥300 a day. Since the Chinese have recently upgraded some facilities especially for foreigners, prices for foreigners are higher than for local people.

If a foreigner is treated the same way as a local Chinese, the charges are lower, similar to that for a local person.

The Chinese are concerned about the health of their guests. They frequently check whether you have enough clothing on. If you complain about your health too much, you might get a doctor even if you don't request one.

It must be pointed out that most tour organizers state emphatically that tours to China are rugged. They are not for invalids or people with respiratory or heart conditions because of dust and air pollution.

It is true that the Chinese are especially nice to older people, and many people want to see China before they die. A few people of Chinese ancestry want to be buried in China and the easiest way they can do this is to die there.

But for the rest of you, here are some things to consider:

Do take it easy. If you feel tired, cut out excursions and rest instead. You don't have to climb mountains, or if you do climb steps to the cable car, go slowly; or wait at the bus with the bus driver, who is usually very nice. You can teach him English or walk around on level ground and enjoy the view, or develop your own theories about the antics of Chinese tourists. Have someone help you up the Great Wall so you can say that you were on it. You don't have to go out to the theater in the evening. You can stay in your hotel and try to fathom Chinese television. Operas are frequently on television too.

Facilities for treating emergencies in China are not as sophisticated as in many other countries. Do not expect elaborate life-support equipment, or to be up walking the day after a broken hip.

The Chinese do not store O-negative blood in their blood banks because Chinese people do not have it.

Take any essential medicines with you. Do not count on a prescription made out to a pharmacist in the U.S. being filled in China, especially if it uses brand names.

If you do go to the hospital, you might have to take your own mug, plate, towel, soap, and a friend. The staff and other patients may not speak English. Standards are not the same as in America. In one of the best hospitals in China, beds were only changed once a week. One Canadian patient found that even a spilled bed pan didn't change the rules. (She got bed sores.)

In case of very serious ailments, contact your consulate. You may have to be evacuated outside of China for treatment.

In the event of a death? The Chinese contact the relevant embassy, which in turn tries to get in touch with next of kin. An embassy can make arrangements for repatriation if desired. Goods belonging to the deceased and death certificates might be released to next-of-kin *only* after the bills are paid.

SMOKING The smokers in China still hold power, but the handwriting is on the wall. Smoking is now forbidden on domestic flights, in some train coaches, the Beijing subway station, and some railway stations. Some hotels are beginning to have no smoking areas in coffee shops, and on some floors. Smoking is forbidden in elevators, and some hotels have signs forbidding smoking in bed. (A few hotels have smoke alarm monitors at the desk on the floor.)

The Zhuhai Hotel (Zhuhai) has a "Give-Up Smoking Clinic" where patients inhale a concoction of 30 different Chinese herbs for 30 minutes a day for three days. By the end of the third session, patients no longer want a cigarette. But the Zhuhai Hotel itself has no "no smoking" areas.

Some hotels are thinking about no smoking areas and should be encouraged.

SPITTING Campaigns in some cities have taken place from time to time against this unhealthy, disgusting habit many people have of spitting on streets, hard-class trains, etc. It is a reflection of rural society. Fines in Beijing have averaged ¥.42 and have been successful in curtailing spitting for a while, at least. The Chinese believe that swallowing phlegm is unhealthy, but haven't acquired any alternatives yet. Madame Chiang Kai-shek also had a campaign in 1934 against spitting, but with no permanent success. One American successfully hands tissues and plastic bags to people with whom she is traveling.

LOOKING UP SPECIFIC CHINESE CITIZENS Yes, you can usually visit friends and relatives in China, even while on a group tour or business trip. As a courtesy to your hosts or sponsors in China, do inform them if you want to take time off from the schedule planned for you. You might ask when the best time would be. In recent years, local Chinese could go to your hotel, but they may be interrogated by hotel staff. Previously they had to make application outside the building stating the reason for their visit and showing their identification cards.

Some front-office clerks are rude to local Chinese. Some local people may feel uneasy about entering a hotel, particularly a fancy one. Many are glad of the opportunity to see inside and brag to their friends that they ate there or at least had a photograph taken inside. If they are reluctant, however, to go there, you could arrange to meet in a restaurant, a park, or their home. You could take them on sightseeing trips with your tour group (for a fee). This will give you time to visit with friends without missing the attractions.

Your chances of going to the home of a friend will depend on the political climate at the time. It could also depend on how embarrassed some Chinese are about the modesty of their lodgings, and whether or not they can afford a taxi or elaborate meal for you. Previously, anyone who hosted foreigners in their homes was grilled later as to what the relationship was, what was talked about, etc. In the early 1980s, only a few appointed workers in each work unit were allowed to fraternize socially with their resident foreign expert. At the turn of the decade, people seemed very open to receiving foreign guests in their homes, but curious neighbors still wanted to know who they were. So do not insist if local Chinese friends are reluctant to take you home.

Making contact may be a problem until telephones become more common. If you've sent a letter, telegram, or cable earlier and your friend hasn't shown up, you may have to go to the home or work place. If you are worried about making trouble for your friend, ask someone less conspicuous than yourself to go and inquire.

When you do make contact, it is always better to visit friends alone, as they may be uncomfortable about talking openly if anyone else is around. Do not persist in asking questions that a Chinese seems reluctant to answer. Do not expect any spontaneous rap sessions, though you may get some now. I once asked a friend in the early '80s what happened to his family during the Cultural Revolution and was bluntly but politely told it was none of my business. In the mid-'80s, however, new friends quite openly complained about hauling manure on farms and sweeping floors in factories then.

Be sensitive and play along if people whisper to you. Don't say aloud, "Why are you whispering?" They are afraid someone is listening! It is hard to get over the terrors of the Cultural Revolution, and human rights today still are not like those in your own country.

Overseas Chinese have a freer time talking with Chinese citizens. Chinese people generally are not open about discussing their deepest feelings and problems with even close friends. Nor will Chinese people easily discuss their sex life. It once took six months of living together before one Chinese roommate confided to me how unhappy she was about her parents.

CHINESE HOSPITALITY This can be very lavish and people may go into debt to show how happy they are to see you. It is always appropriate to take a gift when you go to a Chinese home. Especially welcome are cigarettes (Marlboro Lights are a current favorite). Unless the family is religious, novelties, souvenirs from abroad, and presents for children.

But don't insult them by being overly generous. It is all right, however, to give their children money (about ¥10 each) if you are a relative or a close friend. Otherwise, it is insulting. If you have time for a return banquet, that would be the easy way out.

If you are accompanied by a Chinese friend or relative, avoid buying anything in a store because he may want to pay for it. The salary range for most people is quite low. Of course, rent is low. A Chinese doesn't have to pay exorbitant medical bills if he is sick, and most pay no income tax. But he has to save a long time to buy what you wouldn't think twice about paying for. Hospitality may demand that you be given a gift. Be gracious and suggest something inexpensive like a poster if you are asked.

I have visited many homes—of peasants, officials, workers, and professional people. By Western standards, most are crowded. One professional couple with two children might have a small apartment with two tiny bedrooms. Poorer families might share a kitchen and bathroom with several other families. In only rare cases will there be room for overnight guests, especially in the cities. Toilets may be the squatting kind. In smaller communities you may find a container of earth or a bucket of water for covering or flushing.

In rural areas, you might have to sightsee on foot or on the hard back ends of bicycles, since there may not be any other means of transportation. It is a real adventure!

IF YOU'RE INVITED TO A WEDDING In old China, a gift of money in a red packet was the accepted thing to give. Money is still much appreciated. But gifts to help set up a new household are most frequently given now; porcelain tea sets, clocks, blankets (preferably red, for happiness). Something imported from a foreigner would give you more *guanxi*. Some Friendship Stores may have gift certificates. Wedding invitations usually mean a banquet, but do ask. You could say something like "I've never been to a Chinese wedding before. Tell me what to expect." Budget ¥20 to ¥30 for casual acquaintances. See *Banquets and Toasting,* in "Food."

GIFT GIVING One usually gives a gift upon first meeting the recipient unless it is inconvenient. For example, if the recipient is in a long reception line, it might be difficult. But you could mention in passing that you have something for him or her, and ask where you can leave it. The most important person receives the best gift, and gets it first. It is important not to give too expensive a gift. Some recipients may feel they have to reciprocate. Officials are forbidden to accept expensive gifts, samples, trial uses, etc.

RELIGION   Chinese people tend to be very pragmatic, worshiping whatever gods might answer their prayers. Religions were encouraged, tolerated, or persecuted depending on the times. In the early Tang, Buddhists were killed. But Buddhism later flourished, with imperial encouragement.

It has not been unusual for the same person to give support to several different temples and churches at the same time, and especially to worship one's ancestors. One owed one's life to ancestors and depended on them for good fortune even after they had passed on. It was one's duty to keep ancestral spirits happy. See Confucianism under "Qufu."

Christianity really suffered because of its relation to the unequal treaties following the end of the first Opium War in 1844. Many Chinese questioned the Christian preaching of only one way to salvation. Some foreign missionaries had to close their eyes to ancestor worship or they wouldn't have made many converts. Because of this backing by the foreign powers, Chinese Christians tended to become an elite group, at times appealing successfully to their foreign protectors even if they got in trouble with Chinese law. This, of course, caused much resentment.

Dr. Sun Yat-sen, the father of the Chinese republic, was a Christian, but as a Chinese nationalist he criticized missionaries as lackeys of foreign imperialists. Missionary motives were sometimes misunderstood, and some of these fears led to such incidents as the Tientsin Massacre (see "Tianjin"). Many missionaries were attacked more because they were foreigners caught in the growing nationalism of the era than because of what they taught.

Some Chinese Communist leaders were influenced by missionary schools. Mao Zedong (Mao Tse-tung) himself once edited the Christian-sponsored *Yale-in-China Review*. Some Christian ideals can be found in his teachings.

In 1950, the hysteria of the Korean War led the Chinese to consider Westerners, including many Christian missionaries, as "enemy aliens." Some were expelled and a few jailed at that time. After all, Americans and Canadians were killing Chinese soldiers in that neighboring country. Americans and Canadians reacted similarly during World War II to Japanese people on our west coasts. Even locally born Japanese people had their property confiscated and were shoved off to internment camps. The Chinese also overreacted against all foreigners and those influenced by them, with accusations of spying and sabotage, jail, executions, or deportations.

The Communists also felt that foreign imperialism would continue as long as Chinese Christians maintained their dependency on foreign missionaries. After Liberation, the Christian churches were encouraged to be independent of their foreign roots, and the Protestants set up the Three-Self Patriotic Movement.

The Catholic church, however, officially opposed the rulers of new China. Most of the Chinese bishops not jailed fled to Taiwan, while foreign bishops left for other assignments. When those Catholic leaders who remained nominated new bishops to meet the pastoral needs of more than 100 vacant dioceses, the nominations were ignored by the Vatican. When Chinese leaders went ahead with consecrations, these new bishops were initially ex-communicated, their consecrations later regarded as irregular and never recognized. This left hurt and resentment in the minds and hearts of Roman Catholic leaders in China seeking to meet the needs of loyal adherents. Chinese Catholics still celebrate mass in Latin, and the Vatican, supporting priests who fled to Taiwan and Hong Kong, does not recognize the current Chinese Catholic leadership.

During the Cultural Revolution, churches and temples were destroyed or closed by the Red Guards as part of the movement against the "Four Olds." The youthful revolutionaries and Mao ignored the constitution, which said that "Citizens enjoy freedom to believe in religion, and freedom not to believe in religion and freedom to propagate atheism." Many church buildings became apartments and factories. The Catholic Cathedral in Guangzhou was used for storage.

In 1978–79, the government encouraged the rebuilding of temples and churches, returning deeds to them and paying overdue rents. People and factories who had taken over the buildings had to be relocated before the buildings could become places of worship or tourism again, a time-consuming process. Some Christians actually continued to tithe even while the churches were closed and later brought these treasures to their newly opened gathering places.

Today the Chinese constitution simply says that all Chinese citizens have freedom of belief. About 1800 churches across China were flourishing at press time, a few having to open Saturdays as well as Sundays to accommodate the many worshipers. Some Christians worship corporately in their homes. While some foreigners have questioned the authenticity of the "state-recognized" versus the "house" Christians, Chinese believers do not regard these as two different categories. It may simply be a matter of convenience or accessibility. Some Christians attend both the small family fellowships and the large general congregations.

Foreigners wanting to contact Protestant groups should ask for the

Three-Self Patriotic Movement 中国基督教三自爱国运动 . Catholics should ask for the Chinese Patriotic Catholic Association 中国
天主教爱国会 . Don't let the word *Patriotic* bother you. It doesn't sound
as chauvinistic in Chinese. This movement and this association are non-
governmental. You should also consult with the national headquarters
of your own church or national church organizations. Some may have
China committees and full-time China-watchers who should have the
addresses of churches in cities you will be visiting and can give you
advice. It is better that you write in advance advising the congregations
that you wish to worship with them. And when you get there, *worship*
with them, even though you do not understand the words. And please
do not disturb the service with a camera, or by being late, or by leaving
early, as many tourists have done. Church services are not tourist attractions.

Chinese Christians, particularly those in isolated places, will probably be delighted to have you join them. At least one foreign church-
goer was asked to sing with the Chinese choir once it was known that
he was a soloist in a choir in Canada. Please restrain yourself from
giving a lot of money to the congregations. To encourage materialistic
values in a spiritual movement could dilute its spiritual strength. The
Chinese want to be self-reliant. Donations can be made to the new service arm of the churches, the Amity Foundation of the China Christian
Council. The foundation is a way of contributing to China's modernization in and beyond the Christian community.

Recently, a group of foreigners were arrested for proselytizing. It
is illegal for foreigners to do so. You could ask Christians in China if
you want foreign missionaries. As for smuggling in Bibles, those days
are over. The United Bible Society has given a modern press to the
Amity Foundation, which will help the churches publish their own literature. Since 1981, the Three-Self Movement has printed over 1.5 million copies of the Bible. The China Christian Council recently said there
are now 4044 Protestant churches and 16,868 family meeting points,
with over 3 million Protestant Christians. In 1988, two Protestant bishops were installed. It was the first such event since 1955.

There are also over 3 million Catholic Christians, 1000 large Catholic churches, and 1000 chapels. Between 1980 and 1985, about 130,000
adults were baptized. Eleven seminars are now open and about 12 con-
vents with 200 women under formation.

There are also now 3600 Buddhist temples open for worship with
over 30,000 monks and nuns.

See also *Religious Buildings* in "What Is There to See and Do."

PEOPLE'S FEELINGS   If you read Chinese history, particularly the
history of imperialist times from 1840 to 1949, you should be struck by
the lack of sensitivity foreigners had for the Chinese people. As a result,

the Chinese started hitting back in whatever way they could. They demonstrated; they stoned churches; they murdered individual foreigners. Of course, they were desperate people then, pushed to extremes, but let's not provoke incidents.

Please dress modestly and save your jokes for the privacy of your own rooms. Someone who speaks English may hear you and be offended. Be aware if your driver is blocking a road, causing people pulling heavy loads to go around your bus. Your driver is trying to please *you*. Tell your driver to move somewhere else.

In 1981 a British student was deported for writing "Long Live the Gang of Four" as a joke.

FORMS OF ADDRESS "Attendant" is the best translation for all service personnel like waiters, room boys, and chambermaids. If you have to get their attention, you can call them "fo wu yuan." Ask your guide what he/she wants to be called. Some are beginning to use English names.

You can call your guide "mister" or "miss," and if you feel comfortable with it, you can call him/her what the Chinese call each other: *lau* (as in "loud") plus surname, or *xiao* (like "show" as in "shower") plus surname, no matter the sex. *Lau* means "old" and *xiao* means "small." *Lau* is not derogatory in China and refers to anyone forty and older.

Relatives are referred to and called by their relationship to you, like "Second Aunt Older Than My Father," or "Fifth Maternal Uncle of My Grandfather's Generation" (two Chinese words for each of these). Your relatives will tell you what to call them.

Chinese names have surnames first. Chou En-lai would be Premier Chou. You rarely address a person by his given name, except children or relatives.

POLITICS Here are some things to remember about the new China:

Guides and officials usually give foreign visitors the accepted current political line, but a few are frank with their own ideas after they get to know you.

Chairman Mao is the Lenin of the Chinese revolution. He will always be considered the father of the People's Republic.

Recently, China has been giving the impression it is shelving Mao's revolutionary struggle (from socialism to communism and to the classless society) in favor of modernization. This does not mean the revolution has stopped. So much in China happens out of the public eye.

Much will depend on events in the 1980s, the success of the modernization program, world markets, relations with bordering countries like Vietnam and the Soviet Union, the struggle between factions within the Communist Party in China, the leadership succession, the reaction of the army, etc.

GOVERNMENT   Communist. Officially at the top is the National People's Congress. (See *Great Hall of the People*, "Beijing.") The State Council is the executive organ accountable to the Congress and is similar in makeup to a cabinet. The Communist Party was once involved in almost every facet of life but has voluntarily diminished some of its own power.

GUANXI   "Relationships," "influence," "pull," "connections." This is an important part of Chinese life. Schoolmates, teachers, relatives, workmates—people who know each other well have a stronger and longer hold on each other than in the West. *Guanxi* is related to merit and to helping each other. Strangers are politely accepted, but with reservation, until they have proved themselves trustworthy, friendly, and useful.

The government has spoken out against the excesses of *guanxi* because it isn't fair to people without connections.

DEMOCRACY WALLS   These were not new. Writing criticisms and complaints in public places has occurred from time to time in China for centuries and was especially popular during the Cultural Revolution, when they were used for political debates and attacks on "capitalist roaders." The institution was protected by the constitution.

Late in 1978 the writing of big character posters on Democracy Walls flourished unhindered. Four months later, the right to "speak out freely, air views fully, hold great debates, and write big-character posters" was restricted. Taboo were criticisms of socialism, the dictatorship of the proletariat, party leadership, and the ideas of Marx, Lenin, and Mao.

In 1979 foreigners could visit Democracy Walls, talk with anyone who wanted to talk to them, and accept any leaflets anyone wanted to give them. But some of the Chinese were arrested and charged with passing state secrets to foreigners. In December 1979, however, wall posters were curtailed. In September 1980, these rights were deleted from the constitution because they were "easily abused by careerists and schemers like the Gang of Four."

If you're thinking of encouraging dissident movements, just because you believe in democracy, please ask yourself a few questions first. Can China afford an American-style opposition? Would political unrest upset China's program of feeding her tremendous population and furthering her goals of modernization? Do the dissidents represent a sizable majority? Has China ever had a Western-style democratic government?

If you want more information on this subject, Amnesty International does have a report on China, and the Western press does watch this carefully, sometimes too carefully.

TRIPLE STANDARDS   It may not seem fair that foreigners are charged more for the same hotel rooms and sometimes the same transportation as Chinese. The point is debatable, and you might want to pass the time on trains in your tour group discussing it. Some points to consider: most Chinese **salaries.** Chinese people would never be able to travel by train or plane if they had to pay the prices you do. Government organizations pay the expenses of workers traveling on company business. The transportation system has been government subsidized. Why should it be subsidized for people who can afford it and are willing to pay? Look around you at living standards. The Chinese need to make money. Foreign tourist prices have not stifled China's growing foreign tourist industry. Up to the mid-'80s, prices, in fact, actually diminished because of the foreign exchange rate.

As for Overseas Chinese, we are considered family, and a discount helps make us feel obligated. If you stay longer to help, you'll get one too.

IF A CHINESE   asks for help to visit, study in, or emigrate abroad, use your own judgment. In some cases it is possible but not easy. If you're willing to go to a lot of trouble, so be it. But don't make empty promises that will cause great disappointment later. Check with your embassy regarding regulations.

If a local Chinese asks for foreign currency in exchange for regular Chinese currency, this is illegal. Do not break a law just because you have been given a lavish meal.

You could say you have no time to find places to spend RMB. They might offer to pay for your purchases or taxis in RMB in return for FEC. This is so borderline, in terms of the law, that I would do it for friends. You might want to do it privately, too, but keep in mind that exchanging money at par is not to your advantage.

Be aware of the status of drivers in China. Until Chinese people do their own driving, keeping a driver happy is very important. You may find drivers sharing your table at mealtimes.

If a Chinese official visits you in North America, even on business, please be sensitive of foreign exchange. Inviting them to dinner might be better than giving a gift, so they can save on their *per diem* and buy exactly what they want to take home. They might ask to use your phone to call China. Don't be afraid to say no if you can't afford such a call.

FIRECRACKERS   are allowed to be exploded in China, but usually in designated places. Many Hong Kong Chinese, forbidden to set them oft at home, go berserk when they celebrate in China. Local Chinese are increasingly setting them off noisily at weddings, birthdays, and grand openings. It is not machine-gun fire!

ENDANGERED SPECIES China and many other countries are parties to the Convention on International Trade in Endangered Species of Wild Fauna and Flora (CITES). Any species or products of a species on its lists could be seized by the Customs Department of any of the signatories, unless you have a permit to carry them. The details of the regulations can be obtained usually from your government wildlife service. See ''Important Addresses.'' The much-publicized Save the Panda campaign is an expression of this concern.

Locally, however, Chinese officials are lax about restricting the sale and eating of many endangered or threatened species, notably wild animals like pangolin (scaly anteater) and giant salamander. Coats of spotted cats have been found for sale in Friendship Stores.

Even while passing through Hong Kong, you risk confiscation of

No! No! You may have trouble taking this spotted cat jacket back to your home. It was on sale in the Guangzhou Friendship Store, and is held by Wu Hsiu-yi of C.I.T.S.

garments and ornaments made of parts of certain animals, like turtles.

The problem is knowing what is or is not on the list. When in doubt, don't eat or buy products made from any **wild animals,** especially spotted cats, alligators, and birds. Some deer, for example, are grown commercially in China, and therefore can be eaten.

Among the other Chinese species listed by the Convention are: Himalayan argali, Tibetan brown bear, golden cat, dhole (wild dog), gibbons, Przewalski's horse, langur, macaque, and wild yak. Among the birds are the relict gull, crested ibis, and some varieties of cranes, storks, pheasants, and egrets. Avoid any elephant parts.

A copy of this photo of a spotted-cat jacket on sale in the Guangzhou Friendship store was sent to the U.S. Federal Wildlife Permit Office. An official replied, "Such an article of clothing cannot be imported into the United States."

The Canadian Wildlife Service replied, "To import a garment made of leopard cat skins, you must be in possession of a CITES export permit issued by the Government of China. On import, the foreign export permit must be surrendered to Canada Customs. Any attempt to enter the coat without the foreign CITES permit could, at the very least, result in seizure."

The authority allowed to issue CITES permits in China is:

The People's Republic of China Endangered Species of Wild Fauna and Flora Import and Export Administrative Office, Ministry of Forestry, Hepingli, Beijing; tel. 464180. Branches also in Guangzhou and Tianjin.

SHOPPING

The most important things to remember about shopping in China are:

—there are stores approved for foreign visitors where goods are "guaranteed," prices reasonable and fixed by the local tourism bureau or administration. These stores should not take commissions from tour guides. If customers have solid evidence of misrepresentations about the merchandise, they should be able to get their money back. Customers can also appeal to the tourism bureau for mediation. Payment is usually in F.E.C. Beijing, for example, has about 72 approved stores.

—there are privately operated stores and peddlers with whom you should haggle as prices are negotiable in R.M.B. or F.E.C. You can usually differentiate these from approved stores because the clerks are more aggressive, and should you start to move away they will ask how much you want to pay.

Haggling is imperative in these stores unless you want to pay three or four times the going rate. Start at one quarter what the clerk is asking. You should haggle in all free markets. Check Friendship Stores for current prices and try to beat them. Don't expect guides to be on your side; some have been scolded or beaten for telling tourists the price is too high. Prices should fall quicker if you show them F.E.C.

—there are fakes and misrepresentations, plastic pearls being passed off as real, substitutes being passed off as jade or pearls. Your "approved" stores should be okay. Be careful in other stores.

—there are stores that accept RMB. You have to figure out which currency is to your advantage as even "40% discount for F.E.C." doesn't match the black market rate.

—an American size 9 doesn't mean a thing in China. If you are buying for yourself, you should try on clothes. If you are buying clothes for someone else, you should have their measurements.

NOTE: · · · Not all stores can crate and ship goods outside of China. Ask before you buy.

Take your own bag or basket for shopping in markets.

Save your sales slips so you can argue with Customs officials if need be in your own country. Receipts will be in Chinese with English numerals, so make a note of what each refers to.

Clothing and other items imported from elsewhere for sale in China are, of course, cheaper in the country of origin. Some of what you see may have been made in Hong Kong, whose quality and styles are usually better than China's.

When comparing Chinese prices with those elsewhere, don't forget to include the sales tax at home, the rate of duty, and the shipping costs if these apply. In China you pay no additions to the asking price.

Several kinds of stores should interest foreign shoppers.

FRIENDSHIP STORES were originally set up so that foreigners wouldn't have to buck curious crowds while shopping. But now anyone with F.E.C.s has been able to shop there. At least one Friendship Store serves every city. Prices are about the same or slightly higher than other Chinese stores, but the goods are of better quality there, and some items are unavailable elsewhere.

In addition to arts and crafts, many larger Friendship Stores have textiles, television sets, radios, watches, bicycles, sewing machines, cosmetics, herbal medicines, food, jewelry, thermos bottles, camera film, jackknives, flashlights, cashmere sweaters, silk blouses and shirts—just about anything needed by visitors and relatives of visitors. Friendship Stores usually have locally made goods for sale. The best stores are in Guangzhou, Beijing, and Shanghai. Be aware that some privately run stores are using the ''Friendship'' name and reputation, but they are not government Friendship Stores.

ARTS, CRAFTS, AND ANTIQUE STORES These may or may not be government-owned, and are usually less crowded than Friendship Stores. The quality of goods is sometimes better than that of Friendship Stores. These can be found in hotels or on shopping streets, some selling only for F.E.C.s and others for R.M.B.

FACTORIES Every arts and crafts factory has a showroom where visitors can buy. Prices are usually lower than elsewhere. Some showrooms are open all the time; others are open by appointment only.

DEPARTMENT STORES sometimes have arts and crafts, too, but of lower quality than the above stores. Visitors might find good buys in clothing, down, furs, novelties, etc. Pay with RMB.

FREE MARKETS are where farmers sell their excess produce, people with connections abroad sell foreign-made clothes, tailors solicit customers, and cottage industries sell handicrafts and baked goods. With no changing rooms, people buying jeans have to try them on over their own trousers. Many markets are in alleys under shelter.

Antiques have been sold in free markets but some antiques are not antique sections in free markets are closed down from time to time because of unauthorized sales of antiques. Look for the red wax seal. Great buys in clothes made for export are at the free market between the Friendship Store and the Jianguo Hotel in Beijing.

OVERSEAS CHINESE STORES are mainly for relatives of Overseas Chinese who receive foreign exchange. In these they can buy normally hard-to-obtain items. Some of these stores are called Duty-Free Stores and sell imported and locally made refrigerators, videos, microwaves, etc.

SPECIALTY STORES are for everyone. They sell a wide variety of one or two items such as furs, watches, jewelry, etc.

SECONDHAND STORES may only have a lot of junk, but treasure hunters with lots of time might find something of interest, like European antiques. Many of these stores have musical instruments and old and new theatrical costumes. But more frequently they might only have used watches and electric fans of recent vintage.

WHAT TO BUY

China is famous for its **arts and crafts,** though your best prices for China-made products are frequently in Hong Kong. But you may find something you like in China that you won't find in Hong Kong. And besides you may not be going to Hong Kong.

Usually your **best prices** in China are at the factories, your next best at stores in the same city or province as the factory. Sometimes demand has something to do with prices. Store managers do not always know how much to charge for an item, and so the same thing may have a different price in another store. Rubbings bought at temples where they were made might cost more than the same thing at the Friendship Stores. The only difference is a red souvenir seal on the temple-bought rubbing, but is it worth extra to you? The seal is important to people who know about things like this.

Compare prices in several stores. Price should not always be the deciding factor, though. You have to know quality to get good buys. Learn it by studying a lot of good art, and try your own hand at carving and painting before you go to China. Read books, talk with dealers like Hanart in Hong Kong, and even take courses. Go to museums in your own country that have displays of Chinese art. Many places in China make reproductions.

If you are a **serious shopper,** plan your trip so you can see how a favorite craft is made. Locally made crafts are listed under each destination in this book. For background reading on Chinese goods, you could try Roberta Stalberg's *Shopping in China—Arts, Crafts and the*

Unusual. It gives histories, lists of recommended crafts and prices, and the names and addresses of stores, for a limited number of crafts.

Telephone the factories first. If you are a "buyer" and have business cards to that effect, just telephone for an appointment. If you are an amateur without *guanxi,* you might have to make arrangements through C.I.T.S. (and pay). Not all factories are open all the time for tourists.

In the factory, you can study how the pieces are made, and ask about the most difficult techniques, the criteria of a good piece, and how to tell a phony from a genuine article. You can find out how to clean a piece and where the best materials are from. Will the wood or lacquer crack in dry, centrally heated homes? You should be allowed to handle some of the best pieces. Feel the weight, the surface texture. Compare these with the ordinary quality. Take notes if you can't remember details. For reproductions, study the originals in nearby museums. Remember also that handmade articles are each different—of course! So before you buy, check carefully, not just for flaws, but for the rendering that you like best.

Generally speaking, **consider** (1) the amount of work involved in the production—the finer, the more intricate something is, the better; (2) good proportions, lines, balance, and color; (3) how closely it represents what it is supposed to represent; (4) the quality of the material— will it chip? (soapstone breaks easily and is almost not worth buying); and (5) whether it will be a joy forever, or will you easily tire of it? Primitive art doesn't have to be well proportioned or intricate.

Remember, too, that government stores have a reputation for honesty. If they know something is better, usually they will tell you. Just ask.

If you are looking for an **investment,** your best bet today is revolutionary art—good art depicting peasants, workers, and revolutionary heroes. Like art labeled "Made in Occupied Japan" now, good revolutionary art is becoming valuable and scarce, for it represents a period in China's history. Very little of it is being made today, while the traditional themes are being made by the containerload. But of course, it has to be artistically good in its own right. And think, twenty years from now collectors will be collecting art showing the different stages of the Long March!

Another investment is good rubbings—not the cheap ¥2.50–¥12 kind made from wooden reproductions of the original stone, but the expensive kind, like the Wing of the Cicada, thin and transparent, or the shiny Black Gold. Someday, the original stones will be too worn to make any more rubbings. Then, if you have picked a famous stone you will have something very valuable. Of course, all this is speculation. China may goof up my predictions by producing a lot more revolutionary art. But you can't buy busts of Chairman Mao today.

Crafts can also be **made-to-order,** but most Chinese factories are not set up for easy ordering. The cross-stitch factory in Yantai can make good replicas of photographs, for example. These of course take a lot of time. The most difficult part of such an exercise is getting the idea of what you want over to the craftsman.

Most general tours include at least one handicraft factory and always one Friendship or Arts and Crafts store. Most factories have a retail outlet. Many cities also have handicraft *institutes* where new crafts are developed and craftspeople are trained. In these, you may not be able to buy; however, these are very important for the education of the serious buyer.

If you are more interested in handicrafts than temples, it is best if you take an individual or special-interest tour. On a regular tour, the average tourist will be back at the bus waiting for you while you're still talking about texture or the iron content in glazes.

The destinations with the largest number of various handicrafts are Beijing, Tianjin, Shanghai, and Guangzhou.

Here is a list of some crafts and where they are made.

Bamboo: Guangdong (especially Huaiji County), Guangxi, Hunan and Hubei provinces

Batiks: Xi'an, Yunnan and Guizhou

Beaded curtains: Zhejiang province

Carpets: Tianjin, Shanghai, Qingdao, Beijing, Changchun, Urumqi, Inner Mongolia

Cashmere sweaters: Hohhot

Clay sculptures, painted: Tianjin, Wuxi

Cloisonne (metal base, wire designs filled in with enamel and baked): Beijing, Tianjin, Xi'an

Dough figurines: Beijing, Guilin, Shanghai. Peddlers used to make these for fascinated children who then promptly ate them. Today a chemical that makes the dough very hard is now added. For fine sculpture, this is your cheapest buy.

Embroidered linens: best buys in Shantou, Guangzhou, and also Shandong

Feather pictures: Shenyang

Furniture: Good quality traditional Chinese furniture: Xi'an. **Miniature furniture:** Suzhou

Furs: Shijiazhuang, Dalian, Tianjin, Beijing, Harbin

Glass, artistic: Chongqing, Dalian, Shanghai, Tianjin, Zibo in Shandong, Beijing

Glass snuff bottles: Beijing

Ivory: Guangzhou, Shanghai, and Beijing

Jewelry: Beijing, Guangzhou

Kites: Weifang, Tianjin

Lacquer: Yangjiang in Guangdong, Shanghai, Beijing, Xi'an, Shantou, Fuzhou, Yangzhou

Metal handicrafts: Jiangdu County in Jiangsu, Hangzhou, Shanghai, Chengdu, Zhangzhu in Jiangsu

Metal—swords and knives: Husaba in Longchuan County, Yunnan, Longquan in Zhejiang

Paintings and calligraphy: everywhere

Paper—wood-block printing: Beijing (Rong Bao Zhai), Tianjin

Paper-cuts: everywhere. Transient peddlers used to make these on the spot and then sell them. Now you can get postcard-type paper-cuts on every theme imaginable. For those mounted on colored paper: Hailun County in Heilongjiang; for multicolored ones: Yuxian County in Hubei; for large ones, about 2 × 3 feet: Foshan.

Paper New Year's pictures: Formerly of the kitchen god and the doorway gods, etc., these are now of cherubs and mythological characters. They are for posting around the house at New Year. Brighter, more cheerful colors than traditional art: Weifang in Shandong, Tianjin

Pearls: Zhejiang and Jiangsu for fresh-water; Hainan Island for cultured.

Porcelain: most famous—Jingdezhen (blue and white, eggshell); Yixing (for purple, unglazed); Foshan (for Shiwan); Shantou (for multicolored and chrysanthemums in high relief); Liling in Hunan south of Changsha; Pengcheng County in Hebei (for the Cizhou kiln's ''iron embroidery'' ware); Longquan in Zhejiang, Hangzhou, and Jingdezhen (for celadon, that porcelain attempt to imitate green jade). The finest porcelain is said to be white as jade, shiny as a mirror, thin as paper, and resonant as a bell.

Reproductions: of ancient porcelains: Jingdezhen; of bronzes: Hangzhou, Luoyang; of three-color Tang: Luoyang and Xi'an

Rubbings: Xi'an (best), Luoyang, Suzhou

Shell art: Qingdao, Xi'an, Dalian

Silk: Guangzhou, Shanghai, Suzhou, Hangzhou, Nanjing, Changzhou in Jiangsu; **brocade:** Shanghai; **double-faced silk paintings:** Zhangzhu in Jiangsu; **embroidery:** most famous schools—*Suzhou, Xiang* (Hunan—Changsha), *Yue* (Guangdong—Shantou), and *Shu* (Sichuan). Also of note: Shanghai, for **embroidered silk blouses; festival lanterns:** Beijing, Shanghai, Foshan, and Jiangsu, Fujian, Zhejiang, and Anhui provinces; **flowers:** Shanghai; **underwear:** Jiangsu and Zhejiang; tie-dyed **kerchiefs:** Xi'an

Stone carvings: Fuzhou in Fujian, Qingtian in Zhejiang, and Liuyang chrysanthemum stone carving in Hunan; **jade:** Shanghai, Beijing, Guilin, Xi'an. Jade can be nephrite (hard as glass, greasy look known as mutton fat, best pure white) or jadeite (wide range of colors, including emerald green; used more in jewelry, the more translucent the better). Since jade is very hard and thus difficult to carve, the most expensive is the most intricately carved and multicolored. The colors are cleverly worked into the design. Serpentine is not true jade but frequently passes as jade. It is softer. The Chinese use the word jade to mean a wide range of hard stones. Soapstone is cheap and breaks easily.

Straw: Fujian, Sichuan, Guangdong, and Shandong (Yantai) provinces

Tribal weaving: the Miao in Guizhou province, and any place where national minorities live.

Wood carvings: Quanzhou and Putian in Fujian, Changchun, Dongyang in Zhejiang (gingko wood), Fuzhou (longan wood), northeast provinces (azalea root), Wenzhou, Shanghai, Beijing. For **gilt camphor wood:** Chaozhou and Shantou. For **sandalwood fans** (smell before buying): Suzhou and Hangzhou

Wool needlepoint: Shanghai Arts and Crafts Studio; Yantai in Shandong.

Favorite mythological and/or historical subjects of arts and crafts:

Poet Shi Yung—late Spring and Autumn Period. Knot on top of head. Sword on back.

Wei Tou—guardian of Buddhism and of the Goddess of Mercy.

Guan Yin—originally a god, but in recent sculpture, always the Goddess of Mercy. Depicted with children, or carrying a cloud duster (like a horsetail whip), or with many heads, or with a vase.

Princess Wen Chen—the Chinese princess who married a Tibetan king and took Buddhism to Tibet.

Scholar Dong Kuo—who was kind even to wolves. He once saved a wolf from a hunter and was admonished by the hunter that a wolf can't change its habits.

Li Shi-zen—Ming dynasty author of the classic book on medicinal herbs. Depicted carrying herbs in a basket, and a hoe.

God of Longevity—old man with peach.

God of Wealth—well-dressed man with scepter.

God of Happiness—man with scroll.

Laughing Buddha—sometimes with five children or standing alone with raised hands.

Eight Taoist Genii—see *Taoist temples* in ''What Is There to See and Do?''

Fa Mu-lan—famous woman general who inspired Maxine Hong Kingston's *The Woman Warrior*.

Characters from classical Chinese novels—Water Margin, Dream of the Red Chamber, Pilgrimage to the West.

Favorite revolutionary subjects of arts and crafts:

Soldier O Yang Hai—usually shown on railway track pushing a horse. He was killed but the horse was saved.

Dr. Norman Bethune—usually the only foreigner depicted. Canadian doctor who worked with the Eighth Route Army until his death from blood poisoning.

Lu Xun—famous modern Chinese writer.

Soldier Lei Feng—PLA truck driver based in Shenyang who was always helping people selflessly and, like the Lone Ranger, anonymously. Killed in accident about 1964.

Antiques: As with such shopping elsewhere, you have to know your goods if you want a bargain. Antiques are not cheap, but Chinese antiques are usually cheaper there than in most stores in your own country. Actually your best buy in Chinese antiques is outside of China, but only if you know your stuff better than the person you're buying from.

So much has been smuggled out to Hong Kong that prices there are good. In China itself, you can get good buys in antiques in smaller communities like Qufu (which has a lot of old, ornately carved beds for sale). Antique stores abound all over.

You have to prove to your own Customs people that what you have bought is a duty-free antique. Get convincing documents.

You can sometimes buy ''antiques'' in free markets, but nothing is guaranteed there. People are clearing out their homes of ''old'' things to sell and they don't know how old or how valuable they are. The usual rule is ''If you like it, and want to pay the price, then buy it.'' See also ''Before You Go.''

Officially, antiques are not allowed out of China unless they have a red wax seal on them and are not older than Qing dynasty. But in practice Customs officials rarely search the bags of departing visitors.

Novelties and miscellaneous: If your speed, like mine, is not in the $3000 carpet class, China does have a good variety of novelties, things distinctively Chinese to take back to your nieces and nephews and bridge buddies. Most of the following are obtainable from Friendship Stores, but some only from big department stores.

Acupuncture dolls: These are about ten inches high with genuine acupuncture needles and an instruction booklet (in Chinese) for do-it-yourselfers. If these are too expensive, try **acupuncture posters,** found in bookstores—cheap. **Health balls** to improve blood circulation and avoid arthritis.

Posters, postcards, and comic books are fun and cheap, and so is a **map** of the world showing China in the center, or of Canada and the U.S. in Chinese characters.

Books: There are some children's books showing Chinese characters with equivalent pictures, like our ABCs. If you're in a foreign-language bookstore, you'll find a great many books in English (cheap), all printed in China. They also make great souvenirs.

Museum reproductions: Some of these are quite good and not too expensive. Check out the retail store in any museum you visit.

T-shirts: marked ''Xi'an,'' ''Shanghai,'' or ''Shaoshan.'' Lots of cheap souvenir pins with the name of a touristy site. Then there are Chinese **kites,** traditional **baby bonnets** of silk or rayon trimmed with fur ears to make baby look like a tiger kitten, **Mao caps, plastic eggs** with chicks inside, **folding scissors.**

Cloisonne: comes in beads, bracelets, vases, thimbles, scissors, jack-knives, nail clippers, and pill boxes. **Silk** comes in ties and cute, cheap panties.

There are fancy gold-trimmed **chopsticks** from Fuzhou, lovely metal-tipped chopsticks from Hangzhou and stone **seals** where you can have a rubber stamp made of your name in Chinese (get a friend to translate) with a fancy, carved stone handle. Hong Kong visitors say these are cheaper in China than Hong Kong.

Some visitors take back Chinese **wines** and **vodka** or Chinese **teas.**

Vests with appliques have been a hit with tourists to Xi'an, where they are cheaper than elsewhere in China. Now that people are free to market their handicrafts, a lot of new designs are being created. A lot of junk is being made too. If you buy the junk, the Chinese will only make more of it.

Those **books** printed in China are cheaper here than elsewhere, if you don't care about the quality of the paper or reproductions of photographs. China, however, is producing some good picture books printed elsewhere, including Hong Kong. A large number of titles in English and other foreign languages are available if you are interested in the art, literature, history, and sciences in China. Of the 30,000-plus new titles a year, 2000 are in foreign languages.

Chinese fiction is not written full of conflict, sex, and violence, the way some popular Western fiction is, but try some of the classics and Lu Xun if you want. Books make good gifts. China pirates Chinese translations of Western textbooks, but foreigners are not allowed to buy in those sections of the book stores. Book lovers must visit Liulichang in Beijing to look at samples of fine Chinese printing. Try China Travel and Tourism Press for picture books.

Tailors are not as good as in other places in Asia, like Hong Kong, and clothes take longer to make. But they are cheap! Don't bother having clothes tailored here unless a tailor is recommended by Western friends and you have a picture or sample of what you want made. Even Shanghai tailors have lost the art. See ''Shanghai.''

Furs, down coats, and jackets are bargains, but please, please, don't buy any endangered species. A Hong Kong furrier said the quality of the tanning of a lot of Chinese furs in general is not very good and the fur will stink. See ''Local Customs.''

Live plants, birds, and animals: Check with your embassy. Usually these are not allowed into your country without specific certificates, not easily obtainable outside your country.

Cassettes: China has some fine musicians, and music lovers might like recordings. For names and titles see "What Is There to See and Do?"

Movies and slides of Chinese tourist attractions are available. The films are in 16 and 35mm and video cassette. The videos may have to be converted for use abroad; this takes a couple of days. Contact China Tourism Audio-Visual Publication Corporation, Ritan Park, Beijing; tel. 502393, 502527; cable 2393.

WHAT IS THERE TO SEE AND DO?

How Observant Are You?

By the time you've been in China a week, you should have some idea: (1) if the Chinese people are happy; (2) if the modernization campaign is succeeding; (3) who the premier is; (4) what the population is; (5) what kind of a government China has and how it functions.

You should also know: (6) the name of the capital; (7) the names of two provinces; (8) the names of two rivers.

And, one hopes, you would have looked at the inside of a Chinese home and chatted with some Chinese people besides your guide.

If you haven't done 80 percent of these, then think about why you came to China in the first place. Visiting China is a great opportunity to learn about another culture, another history, another way of life. It is a chance to speculate if China is going to affect your future: Will there be a war that would involve your country? Will its cheaper labor affect your economy? Will China's solutions to its problems help solve your country's problems? How did it eliminate prostitution? Drug addiction? Crime in the streets? What is it doing about controlling the growth of its population? The energy shortage? Its ethnic minorities? Is there anything China can teach you about arts? Patience?

NOTE: · · · Visitors to China in previous years were given the impression that everything was going well in China. Yet later the Chinese themselves were saying that things were very wrong in several of the previous periods. So do evaluate what you hear critically. The person who briefs you is telling you the truth as he sees it. Do cross-examine pleasantly if he gives you information that just doesn't quite ring true to you. It may also be something you've misunderstood.

Things to Do

Checklist: To help you observe, especially when you have nothing to do on a train or bus, use this list. Make a check if you see any of these things:

148

1. a foot-operated water pump ( )
2. an electric water pump ( )
3. an earthen cone-shaped tomb ( )
4. a funeral ( )
5. a pregnant woman ( )
6. a cat ( )
7. a village watchtower (mainly in south) ( )
8. a woman doing manual labor in high heels ( )
9. a village without electrical wiring ( )
10. a city without a construction crane ( )
11. a mud sled with runners ( )
12. an old woman with tiny bound feet ( )
13. *a qi pao/cheong sam,* the narrow, women's dress with a side-slit (aside from hotels or restaurants) ( )
14. coal-dust bricks drying ( )
15. a brick kiln ( )
16. three kinds of wild birds, ( ), ( ), and ( )
17. a boy carrying a baby ( )
18. a statue of Chairman Mao ( )
19. a city with a no honking horn regulation ( )
20. a road not lined with trees ( )
21. criminals marching to be executed ( )

Walk   Go for a walk by yourself or with *one* friend and a copy of this book. Go early in the morning before breakfast when you are fresh (if you are fresh in the morning). Walk slowly without a camera, for cameras tend to separate people; they keep you from feeling, from savoring the waking of a world that is unlike any other on earth. Walk away from the main streets; explore the alleys.

Life swims around you; a woman brushes her teeth on the street. People line up doing the ethereal *taiji quan* exercises in slow motion. Most are following one leader. Join them and try it yourself. Usually they won't mind.

Look at the tiny houses, the charming paper windows, the carvings on the door hinges, the storefronts open to the street; wait—maybe they're tiny factories or homes with workshops in front. Go to a park; you might even hear some beautiful but very shy singers practicing. You might be asked to help a student practice his English. If the park is a historic monument, savor it slowly. There is no tour guide rushing you from place to place. Imagine how it looked 300 years ago when the common people and you were not allowed here. Think of the centuries of bustling human activity that took place here.

Go back to the street and watch the people riding to work on bicycles, buses, or trucks. Do they look harried, content, blank? Imagine yourself riding with them. Imagine yourself living in one of their apartments. Do you know enough about them to know how they feel?

Look for signs of Westernization. Any Coca-Cola ads yet? Any Western movies? Permanent waves? High heels? Is that bright-red billboard a Four Modernizations slogan? Or is it a poem by Chairman Mao? What are the sounds you hear? Traffic noises? The strains of "The East Is Red" on the loudspeaker or something from *The Sound of Music*? Listen to the language. It is tonal, like singing almost.

Look for old churches (Gothic-type windows) and temples. Was that bicycle cart an ambulance? Is that a woman pulling a heavy cart? Smile back at people who stare at you. Give them a cheery "Ni hao?" You might get a smile back. If you get lost, don't worry. See "Useful Phrases."

Visit a factory, any factory, just as long as it's not a handicraft factory where you'll get involved in discussions of artistic techniques and buying. C.I.T.S. or the service desk in your hotel can arrange the trip and a guide. Tell them you want to visit a worker's home and talk to some workers. You won't need the Chinese in the "Useful Phrases" if you have an interpreter, but these might give you some idea of what questions to ask first.

What is interesting about Chinese workers is mobility (or lack of it), job security, what happens if they don't like their jobs, housing, time off and vacations, medical benefits, travel, work incentives before 1978 and now, what they think of as they bicycle to work, and how did they meet their spouses. How are young people today different from the previous generation? What are the incentives for a planned family? What if someone in the work unit absents himself too often? Workers' schools? Taxes?

Who decides on what products to manufacture? Is the factory privately, collectively, or state owned? What is the difference? Do they have political meetings? How often? What about criticism–self-criticism sessions? What is the extent of recently introduced capitalistic practices? Are workers paid piecemeal or by salary? Will workers follow the Polish example?

Learn about the manufacturing process and how different things are in China from your home country. Find out how the new economic policies have affected labor. Have the best and the brightest left to set up enterprises of their own?

Visit the countryside Rural China has also changed dramatically lately. Formerly, the countryside was divided into "communes" and you might still hear the term used as it is still a political unit. Communes are now "counties" again, and "production brigades" and "teams" are "villages," depending on location.

In addition to name changes, the average per capita income in counties has risen considerably since the early '80s, and living in a village now seems more appealing than living in a city. How have they done this? What percentage of the income is still agricultural? What is happening to the lifestyle? The birth-control program, with the economy based on the family? Since most of China is considered rural, developments here are very important.

Some counties are more interesting to visit than others. The ones around Guangzhou offer shooting galleries, ox-cart rides, lion dances, and bicycle rentals! At harvest time, some villages will allow you to eat all the lichees/litchis and apples you want. You can learn a lot from the villages that preserve fruit, or grow jasmine tea, or silk worms. Around Beijing, you can see how Peking ducks are force-fed. Gardeners should have a field day learning about exotic vegetables. Have you ever seen rice growing before? Water chestnuts? Bamboo shoots, fungi, and *facai*? All are yummy ingredients you find in Chinese restaurants! Why does China have to import grain? Why is there a pork shortage?

But you can also look at the industries. Some counties produce transformers, cement boats, and arts and crafts, like Cabbage Patch clones. Look at the schools and facilities for children. Some counties have built swimming pools, zoos, and merry-go-rounds.

You will probably be given a briefing with the basic statistics. You could also ask: What about old-age pensions? What security is there if not children? What about the people who are not making as much money as the others? Is it a matter of luck, or are they not working as hard? Has anyone from here gone to university? Traveled abroad? Do young people still want to move to the cities? Why are some counties richer than others? Is any of the produce here exported abroad? Who decides what is grown?

Visit a school   Nursery schools are always entertaining. You have to be very hard-hearted if you aren't charmed by them. Count on half a day. In some nursery schools, visitors are involved in some of the children's games. In all nursery schools you will tour the classrooms, have a performance of songs and dances, and get a briefing with an opportunity to ask questions. Nursery-school songs are a good indicator of the current political atmosphere. At one time the children were singing songs about shooting down American planes. In more advanced schools, you may be expected to read an English lesson. Suggest that your reading be recorded so the children can hear it again and memorize your accent and inflections.

Chinese schools were closed during the Cultural Revolution, so that the students could make revolution."¹ After they were opened again, the curriculum placed more emphasis on politics than academics, even as a criterion for university entrance. How was this allowed to happen? What has happened to this generation of academically unprepared students? Is education going too much the other way now? Are students losing touch with peasants and workers? Do they still spend time working in factories? What is happening with the new examination system? Why are only a few people going to university when China needs highly trained people? What kind of teaching aids do they have? How many students in each class? What about the slow learners? The exceptionally bright child? What scientific apparatus do they have? What prospects for graduates? Why have there been student demonstrations?

See also *Gifts* in "What to Take."

Offer to help, but only if the Chinese seem interested. (See also the section on visiting as a scholar in "The Basics.") This is not just for China's sake but also to give you a deeper experience in China. You may make some good professional contacts.

Two hours in a Chinese school will not tell you much about the education system, but struggling with an English class will tell you a lot more. If you are at a university and Chinese scholars start asking probing questions, then grab your chance. If you are in a tour group, make a date to meet them again. If you have brought along slides or pictures, tell them. If you are talking with a museum director and Chinese history is your field, offer to write the English titles on the exhibits or catalog their English-language library.

If you are already successfully helping hotel attendants with their English, and you're not on a tightly scheduled tour, offer to stay a few more days to make tape recordings or give more lessons. Hint that you don't have much money and can't stay too long. If the hotel management is sharp, they should grab the opportunity for a teacher in return for a room and maybe foreign experts' rates on food. This way they don't have to go through the red tape of getting a teacher. Student groups might offer to help plant trees with Chinese student groups if they're in China on tree-planting day in March or April.

Get off the well-beaten tourist track —it's safe. Just don't go anywhere there's a sign that says foreigners are forbidden. If anyone asks what you are doing, tell him. Just don't take photographs in police stations.

Actually, **police stations** are interesting. If you're lost, you might look for one to ask directions back. I once saw three teenagers locked in a cage under the stairs.

Visit a public market The free market is where commune members sell the surplus from their private vegetable plots. You will see some women with three eggs or a couple of pounds of cabbage.

Look for an old map of the city you are in. The museum may have one you can copy. Follow the **old wall** or look for remains of gates. Follow rivers and canals. Figure out how the city was defended.

Learn Chinese No, it's not all that hard to understand. Listen carefully as it is spoken. Some words reoccur frequently. Ask what these mean. You probably know some Chinese already. *Shanghai* means "above the sea." *Shang* is "above." When you get to Beijing, you will hear about Beihai Park, "North Sea Park." *Hai* again is "sea." As for *Bei*, also found in *Beijing*, it means "north." *Beijing* is "Northern Capital." *Jing* is the same "jing" as in *Nanjing*, "Southern Capital."

Learn your numbers and make the elevator operator grin. *Lou* as in "loud" means "floor." Reading numbers will help in museums. You only have to learn ten. The rest are combinations. See "Useful Phrases." Learn the polite things first: "good morning," "please," "thank you," and "good-bye." When someone asks you to help with English, ask him or her to help you with your Chinese. Exchange lessons with people you meet at English Corners, which are found in many cities in a designated park on Sundays. Ask C.I.T.S.

Visit museums These can be deadly dull if you don't do it right. I have seen people hurrying past pieces that set my heart pounding, without batting an eyelash. You will get much more out of a Chinese museum (1) if you read something about Chinese history first; for a quick course see "Milestones in Chinese History"; (2) if you take a knowledgeable guide; and (3) if you are eager to learn things like the date of the earliest pottery, blue and white porcelain, weaving, writing, money, sewer pipes, paper, gun powder, metal implements, etc. It might excite you even more to compare these with the earliest in your civilization. Try to figure out how and why things were made. Trace their development. How did neolithic man get his fire? When did the Chinese first use fertilizer?

China is so rich in archaeology that most cities have good collections. These are lessons in history. The problem for foreigners is that most museums do not have titles in English. If you don't have a guide and have learned your Chinese numbers, at least you could look up the dates in "Milestones" and get a general idea of the period and what the relic might be. There is also a list of dynasties in the "Quick Reference" section with the names in Chinese and English. Each gallery is usually labeled with a dynasty name and/or a date. You could try to figure from this too.

Chinese museums are usually set up chronologically from primitive to revolutionary times. City and provincial museums usually have relics found in the area. Some have exhibits of how things like bronzes were made. Most have excavations from ancient tombs, pottery figures of humans and animals, some of the most lifelike statues in China. Some of the most important pieces may not be original, but will be good reproductions. The originals are too valuable to expose to light and to the possibility of deterioration. You might notice that the lights are dim. It is deliberate. Take a flashlight.

Some museums have booklets in English. Some museums have been built over archaeological sites, a most exciting idea. You stand where you know people stood 6000 years ago and look at the remains of their houses, and where they stored their farm tools and buried their children. The skeletons are still there, excavated and protected by glass so you can see them. If you are at all psychic, you might feel some ancient vibes in a situation like this. Take your time. Meditate. I have a friend who gets visions sometimes if she holds a relic. She believes she sees the culture from which the relic came as if it were a movie.

Bronzes are not as well known abroad as Chinese porcelains or paintings. The museums in China are full of these ceremonial vessels, easily dismissed as uninteresting. They are, in fact, very exciting, the products of a highly developed technology with no peer anywhere else in the world at that time. Where else was there cast 800 kg of molten bronze into a one-piece bell over 3000 years ago? Just think of the logistics of doing it! How many men were accidentally burned to death in the process? Did they use cranes? How many finished bells were discarded when they did not produce the correct tone? Did anyone get beheaded for the mistake?

And then to bury the result! The economy must have been pretty solid to support this kind of extravagance. Or did the masses have to suffer for it? Confucius, who seems to have been sensitive to the needs of common people, looked back to the Zhou dynasty as a golden age of order and prosperity. Something about the bronze era must have been right.

Bronzes are uncensored history books cast in metal, said one enthusiastic scientist. On them have been inscribed the earliest script, like the family Bible of old, recording family names and important dates. Later, historical events were reported on them.

The shapes of the ritual bronzes were based originally on utensils of everyday use like two-level steamers and cooking pots. From bronzes, archaeologists have concluded that weapons and agricultural tools were basically of the same designs. No one seems to know if the bronzes themselves were used in daily life. They were usually found in tombs buried with the dead for the use of the spirits.

The Chinese cast this alloy of tin and copper from molds. Emperor

Gu—Wine goblet

Be—Ewer

Ding—Food vessel

Jue—Wine goblet

̷̶̶ ̶̶̶ ̶̶̶ ̷̶ Xia Dynasty (about 21st–16th Century B.C.) is believed to have ordered some vessels made by vassal states as tribute. Unfortunately, those bronzes were lost by the end of the Zhou dynasty and no solid evidence has since surfaced.

The oldest surviving bronzes are from the Shang dynasty, and one can trace the development of the art in China's well-stocked museums. The shapes of the legs, the decorations, the type of script. Even if you can't read Chinese, at least you can see the differences in style from dynasty to dynasty.

As you study them, note that the early thin-walled Shang pieces were relatively crude, with two-dimensional patterns and stylized boogeyman figures. Look for "ogres," serpents, dragons, and "nipples" (bosses) in bands. Later, the patterns covered the whole vessels in increasingly elaborate ways. Can you recognize cowrie shells, cicadas, birds, and braided rope motifs? Animal heads became three-dimensional and realistic. Animal statues like elephants and tigers started appearing. Bosses became coiled serpents. (Castings of human figures were rare.) Walls became thicker. The shapes of the legs developed from blades to dowels. Then gold or silver inlay came into being. More and different shapes appeared.

Bronzes were fashionable until the Han, after which the art died out. (See also *Provincial Museum* under "Wuhan" in Destinations.)

Some guides are steering tourists away from the revolutionary sections of museums, thinking they may not be interested. Do tell them if you are. It is good to see China's version of historic events. It may differ from what you have always heard. For this reason, Chinese history from 1840 on should be of tremendous interest. Did British soldiers really sack and rape in every city they captured? Was the British ship *Amethyst* acting cowardly or heroically? Did the missionaries deserve to be thrown out of China? Why do the Communists glorify the Christian-inspired Taipings and the fanatical Boxers? Was the Long March a cowardly or heroic act? Was the Great Leap Forward a mistake? Was the Cultural Revolution a mistake without any redeeming features?

Ask political questions Don't be afraid to do this. If it is done in the right spirit, both the Chinese and you can learn a lot. Political discussions can get heated. Please keep the conversation friendly and relaxed. If you succeed in convincing them of your opinions or vice versa, it won't be because of shouting and red faces.

Do ask them why they think Richard Nixon is a hero, what is meant by "democratic centralism," what they think will happen if the Four Modernizations fail, and whether it was right to imprison novelist Ding Ling (Ting Ling) and poet Ai Qing (Ai Ching) after the Hundred Flower Movement. If they look like they're uncomfortable with the question, don't pursue it. They may be under a lot of pressure to give the correct political answer and they may not know it. The better you know a person, the franker an answer you will get. And no answer will also give you an indication of the answer, if you know what I mean.

Go to cultural events   During and after the Cultural Revolution, at the instigation of Jiang Qing, wife of Chairman Mao, only eight operas were allowed to be performed, all with strong revolutionary messages. Since the end of 1976, many of the restrictions on entertainment have been lifted. It no longer has to "serve the revolution." Some of it can be and is frivolous.

One doesn't go to China to see American or European movies. Some theaters are equipped with simultaneous interpretation, but these are only good if the interpreter is good. So bring your own if you can. Most movies are in Chinese. Of the Chinese movies, some are no longer blatantly full of propaganda, depicting pure and good Communists and evil Nationalists. Look for movie versions of operas, set in China, comedies about life in the factories, and cartoons. The *China Daily* has announcements about cultural events in Beijing and on national television.

Chinese **television** consists primarily of documentaries, *kung fu* action thrillers, and tearjerkers. It also has news, sports coverage, commercials, and educational broadcasts, such as language lessons. Occasionally it will have something especially good, like a visiting British ballet company or live coverage of historical events. Your hotel television may have closed-circuit programming with more of the kinds of programs you're used to.

The best **acrobats** are from Shenyang, Shanghai, and Wuhan, and foreigners usually find acrobats very entertaining. Also offered are **song and dance troupes** and **sports competitions.** I highly recommend exhibitions of **wushu,** the traditional martial arts.

Most tour groups will be taken to one or two cultural presentations. If you want to go to more, you can on your own. They are very cheap—usually less than two yuan. Tickets are frequently hard to get at the box office and must be booked in advance. See "Useful Phrases."

In Beijing, anyone can go to good movies, usually with English subtitles, at the International Club or the Great Wall Hotel. In almost every city, batches of seats for various kinds of performances are reserved for foreigners. You might be able to get some of these at your hotel service desk or through C.I.T.S. China has ticket scalpers, too, at sometimes twice the going price.

Chinese traditional opera should be experienced at least once. It is very popular with older people, but not so much with younger ones, since it is sung in its own classical language. Your guide might not understand it except for the subtitles for the songs. The jabbering in the audience is not a result of boredom; it is those who understand it explanning to those who want it. To the uninitiated, traditional Chinese opera can be dull, with its many long monologues, its high-pitched singing, and its sluggish action. The villain is always known at the beginning. The chairs in the theater are frequently hard, and there may not be heat or air conditioning. The performance usually takes three hours, and the percussion instruments, especially, are loud, as if to elevate the audience to a higher level of consciousness—but not as high as at a rock concert.

The stories are usually ancient, so a knowledge of history helps. Or they could be something out of classic literature, *The Dream of the Red Chamber* or *Pilgrimage to the West*. Some are based on modern history. Two books, published in China, should be helpful: Latsch's *Peking Opera as a European Sees It* and Wu's *Peking Opera and Mei Lanfang*.

Mei Lanfang was one of the greatest of the female impersonators. It is common to have a man play the woman's role, and vice versa. One opera company, the Shaoxing, has only female players. The male roles are extraordinarily well done. The makeup might throw you, but much goes into it: the temples taped to slant the eyes, paste-on hair pieces to reshape faces, and many colors to indicate character or specific roles such as the Monkey King, or the red-and-black-faced Zhang Fei. A face painted black is an honest but uncouth character; a white face shows a treacherous, cunning, but dignified person; a white patch on the nose indicates a villain. Red is for loyalty and sincerity; black for honesty and all-around goodness. Yellow is for impulsiveness and gold and silver for demons and gods.

It is always fun to watch the actresses in love scenes expressing themselves with delicate and reserved gestures. Note how they excitedly carry their tune to a higher and higher pitch within one breath.

Usually the staging, the costumes, and the acting are outstanding. The fighting scenes, if any, are breathtaking and graceful, like ballet. Cymbals and hollow wooden knockers punctuate the action, and somewhere in the orchestra is an instrument that sounds like a bagpipe. The audience frequently applauds a musician, especially the one playing the stringed *erhu*. Usually a good opera singer tries to keep his own erhu player for life. The costumes are handmade and artfully embroidered, depending on the character played.

The singing, ah yes, the singing takes some getting used to. It can sound like screeching and whining, and one wonders how long voices can last under that kind of abuse. But it takes many years of training to achieve such perfection.

Settings are usually simple and symbolic. The acting, too, is symbolic, and Chinese audiences know what every gesture, every move of the eyebrow means. Among the symbols: an old man and a girl with an oar are on a boat; a man lifting up his foot as he exits is stepping over the high threshold of a door. Crossed eyes mean anger. Walking with hands extended in front means it's dark. A man holding a riding crop means he's riding a horse, or sometimes he *is* a horse. You should be able to tell the difference! A particularly well-executed swing of long hair (anguish) or prolonged trembling (fear) will elicit gasps of appreciation and applause.

With settings, two bamboo poles with some cloth attached is a city wall or gate. A chariot is two yellow flags with a wheel drawn on each. A couple of poles on either side of an actor is a sedan chair. A hat with two long, dangling pheasant or peacock feathers is worn by a high military officer, usually a marshal; a hat with wobbling wings out to the sides just above the ears belongs to a magistrate. Generals have flags matching their costumes and mounted like wings on their backs. The flags are distributed to identify imperial messengers.

After the performance, you may want to go backstage to see everything up close, and possibly makeup being removed. See "Useful Phrases."

Chinese opera dates from the Yuan, and blossomed into one of the most popular entertainment forms during the Ming for noble and commoner alike. For a largely illiterate population, operas were courses in history. For their entertainment value, they were performed at major festivals, weddings, funerals, births, promotions, etc., for human and ghostly guests.

China has many forms of traditional opera, the distinctions known to fans. The most popular are Beijing and Qunqi. Qunqi has more dancing movements and more melodic, mellow tunes. During a performance, one sees either a whole story or excerpts from several operas.

In the old days, operas were social events. As some went on for weeks, people came and left as they pleased, chatted with friends, ate and drank. The crack of watermelon seeds and the sipping of tea blended with the music, which spectators also sang if the tune was familiar. In approval and clapping, one also growled and swore when actors were less than perfect. The audiences sounded much like Elizabethan ones. In the old days, performers were considered little better than beggars and prostitutes in spite of many years of training and practice. Today, performers are considered cultural workers and are respected as artists.

Listen to music   Music lovers should be interested in hearing classical Western and contemporary Chinese and Western music. Among the best Chinese orchestras are the Shanghai Chinese Orchestra , the Hong Kong Chinese Orchestra , Peking Central Folk Orchestra , Beijing Central Philharmonic Orchestra, , and China Broadcasting Symphony Orchestra .

Among the most famous contemporary Chinese composers are Chou Wen-chung (USA), Luo Jing-jing (Shanghai), Tan Dun (Beijing), Ma Sitson (USA), and Ju Hsiaosong (Beijing).

You might also look for programs or cassettes that include popular compositions like the erhu concerto Manjianghong ; The Butterfly Lovers for orchestra and violin; Reflections of the Moon on Two Lakes , an erhu concerto; Lady General Mu Kweiying , an orchestral work converted from Chinese opera.

Also recommended are: Li Sao (The Lament) , an orchestral work; Willows in the Spring Breeze , light music; Tao Jin Ling , orchestral; The Swaying Plum Blossoms pipa or flute; and Silver Snow in the Early Spring , pipa.

Then there are: The River Suite , erhu solo; Moon and Lanterns , East China Silk and Bamboo Music recording; A Selection of Chinese Melodies on Traditional Instruments ; Autumn Moon on a Calm Lake , for piano or orchestra; and Pastoral Song .

The *erhu* , *banhu, gaohu,* and *zhonghu* are stringed instruments held upright and played with a bow. The *pipa* and *liugin* look and sound like mandolins, the *ruan* more like a banjo. The *yanggin* is like a dulcimer played with bamboo mallets.

Other Chinese instruments are the *kuchin* , *sheng* , bamboo flute , and *tseng* .

Night Life Dance parties and discos are fun, even if you sit on the sidelines and watch. They are more fun if you get up and dance. Some are organized at hotels. The one I saw in a small city (Yantai) took place in a large open courtyard, with a couple of hundred people, mainly men, but also some women and children. With the shortage of women, men were dancing arm-in-arm with other men. Some women, however,

The pearl-border

"T" pattern

Key pattern

These are favorites for the rims of cups and bowls.

The Dragon of Heaven

danced with each other. The music was a melange of fox trots, waltzes, tangos, cha-cha, and rock. It was great to see the Chinese letting loose after so many years of considering such activity bourgeois and frivolous. Many people say they dance for the exercise. The music was live. In some places, you can take your own cassettes. Quick, enjoy it, before dance parties get banned again!

Night markets are opening up all over where weather permits, for clothes and for some great cheap cooking. (See "Food.") Some hotels have started providing microphones for guests in bars, a Japanese tradition. Guests can then perform with music, and some can be surprisingly good. Some can be terrible.

Nightclubs have started, especially in Guangdong province (for Hong Kong visitors) with live entertainment. And many hotels now have gym equipment, bowling alleys, and lighted tennis courts. Hotel coffee shops, bars, and many stores stay open late.

The days of going to bed at 9 p.m. because there's nothing to do are beginning to disappear.

The cloud design

Cloud border

Still water

Sea waves; the little clouds over the angles represent the sea spray.

Decorative compositions of the hieroglyphic form of thunder.

Mountains and crags

Lightning and fire designs

Learn how to identify details of Chinese designs You will see these everywhere in China: in palaces, temples, pagodas, museums, fancy restaurants, gardens, parks, on dishes, windows, and screens. Knowing what they are will help you recognize bits of Chinese culture abroad, too, especially on rugs, in textiles, in Chinese antiques, and in Chinese restaurants.

Illustrated are some of the more common designs. While their origins might be Taoist or Buddhist, Chinese symbols are primarily Chinese, taken over as part of the national culture, and not confined to any particular religion.

The Chinese Dragon is said to have the head of a camel, the horns of a deer, the eyes of a rabbit, the ears of a cow, the neck of a snake, the belly of a frog, the scales of a carp, the claws of a hawk, and the palm of a tiger. It has whiskers and a beard, and is deaf. It is generally regarded as benevolent but is also the source of thunder and lightning. The five-clawed variation was once reserved exclusively for the emperor. The flaming ball is said by some to represent thunder and lightning, by others, to be either the sun, the moon, or the pearl of potentiality. It is frequently surrounded by clouds.

The cloud design is now most frequently seen in blue as the lower border of a rich man's gown either in a traditional opera or a painted antique portrait.

This scepter is frequently about half a meter long and made of metal, stone, bone, or wood. It is like a magic wand and is frequently given as a gift, a symbol of good wishes for the prosperity and longevity of the recipient. The larger ones are found in museums.

The scepter of the supreme heavenly deity

The lion

The phoenix

The lion is not native to China. The design is unique to China because the craftsmen never saw a real one. Lions are frequently seen in front of buildings as protectors either playing with a ball (male) or a kitten (female). They are considered benevolent. The ball is said by some to represent the imperial treasury or peace. Others say it is the sun, a precious stone, or the Yin-Yang. Seen also on festive occasions as a costume for dancers, the lion is sometimes confused with the Fo dog, which is usually blue with longer ears.

The phoenix is said to resemble a swan in front, a unicorn behind, with ''the throat of a swallow, the bill of a fowl, the neck of a snake, the tail of a peacock, the forehead of a crane, the crown of a Mandarin duck, the stripes of a dragon, and the back of a tortoise.'' Its appearance is said to mean an era of peace and prosperity. It was the symbol used by the empresses of China and is often combined in designs with the dragon.

The intellectual elite was associated with these four symbols in ancient times.

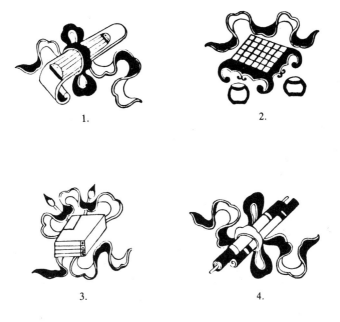

1.

2.

3.

4.

1. The harp
2. The chessboard
3. The books
4. The paintings

a.

b.

c.

d.

e.

f.

g.

h.

The eight precious things

a. The pearl
b. The coin
c. The rhombus (victory)
d. The books
e. The paintings
f. The musical stone of jade (blessing)
g. The rhinoceros-horn cups
h. The artemisia leaf (dignity)

1.

2.

Character sign symbols
1. The round *Shou*
2. The long *Shou*, both meaning "long life"

These are only two of the many variations frequently seen. There is even a teapot in the *shou* design.

This is but one of the many variations of the character for happiness. Sometimes it is circular and doubled, especially prominent at weddings.

The *Fu*, meaning ''happiness''

The word for bat in Chinese is *fu*. So is the word for happiness. A bat is thus a symbol of happiness. These are everywhere: on the walls and ceilings of the Forbidden City, on the ceiling of the restaurant of the Peace Hotel in Shanghai. The peach is a symbol of longevity.

The bat

Bat and peach

Five bats, surrounding the character *Shou*

When five bats are combined with the longevity character, they mean the five great blessings: happiness, wealth, peace, virtue, and longevity.

Scepter, writing brush, and uncoined silver. Together, these are a symbol of success.

The three Fruits

These are fragrant fingers of Buddha, peach, and pomegranate. Together they mean happiness, longevity, and male children.

Prunus

Orchid

Bamboo

Peony

The prunus or plum blossom symbolizes beauty; the orchid, fragrance; bamboo is an emblem of longevity, and the peony means wealth and respectability.

Peach blossom

Lotus flower

Chrysanthemum

Narcissus

These are featured singly or combined in a set of four, since the peach blossom represents spring, the lotus flower is summer, chrysanthemum is autumn, and narcissus is winter. Frequently there are only one of each of these on a four-panel screen.

Among **other common symbols** are the *crane* (longevity), the *stag* (longevity and prosperity), and the *lotus* (purity and perfection). The Buddha is usually seated on a lotus.

Among the many **strange beings** are the two at the top two corners of many temple roofs, tails pointing to the sky. This is a *carp turning into a dragon*. There is also the *unicorn,* known as *qi-lin,* with the "body of the musk deer, the tail of an ox, the forehead of a wolf, and · the hoofs of a horse." The male has a horn, but the female does not. It is a good, gentle, and benevolent creature.

The wooden *"fish,"* a red object found in most Buddhist temples, is a clapper, used for beating time while the monks chant the sutras. Some say that the monks dropped the sutras in water as the holy scriptures were being brought from India. A fish ate the sutras, so it was beaten to force it to regurgitate. Others say if you don't beat the fish, there will be an earthquake.

The *tortoise,* usually seen with a giant stele on its back, is one of the four supernatural animals, the others being the phoenix, the dragon, and the unicorn. Real ones are frequently kept at Buddhist temples, for they are sacred, an emblem of longevity, strength, and endurance.

Visit religious buildings After sampling a few temples, you should be able to identify the various kinds just from a quick glance inside.

Confucian temples were in every sizable community. (For a history of Confucius, see "Qufu" in Destinations.) Everyone who passed by had to stop and bow respectfully before the gate, or be punished. Scholars came here both to worship the sage, for good luck, and to write examinations for the imperial civil service. Confucius was officially worshiped at the spring and autumn equinoxes. Try to imagine the burning of incense and the muffled clang of gongs, as processions of officials in long red gowns and caps arrived. The men kowtowed, their heads to the ground, in deepest reverence. They left offerings of food and wine on the altar. Musicians played ritual bells. Such ceremonies still take place in Qufu (and in Taiwan).

Confucian temples did not usually have statues, but simply tablets with the names of ancestors written on them. The walls were red. The south gate was usually left unbuilt until a son from the town passed the difficult examinations and became a Senior Scholar. Only a Senior Scholar and the Emperor could enter by the south gate. No women were considered for the examinations, but if Chinese opera plots are to be believed, some did successfully take them disguised as men.

Was Confucianism a religion or a philosophy? This question is frequently debated. While Confucius himself skeptically rejected the supernatural, Chinese people did and, in some cases, still do consider him a god. He is among the Taoist deities too. But he was primarily a teacher of ethics, of "right conduct," and good, stable government.

Many Confucian temples now are used as museums because Confucianism no longer has imperial patronage. The largest temples are in Beijing and Qufu.

Buddhist temples come in two basic varieties, of which there are infinite variations.

(1) Buddhist temples, surrounded by windowless walls, frequently have four fierce-looking, larger than life-size, human-type guardians after you enter the first gate. Each temple might have different names for these. Inside the first hall, visitors are greeted by the fat, laughing Buddha, *Maitreya,* or in Chinese, *Mi Lo Fu.* He is the Buddha still-to-come. Behind him is *Wei Tou,* the military bodhisattva, the armed warrior who guards the Buddhist scriptures. Wei Tou is probably comparable to the Indian god Indra.

Central in the main hall is the Buddha, a.k.a. the Enlightened One, Sakyamuni, or Prince Siddhartha Gautama. Also in this hall are usually statues or paintings of *bodhisattvas,* known in Chinese as *pusas.* These are saints who have gained Enlightenment but have come back to the world to help other people attain it too. A favorite bodhisattva is Avalokita, a.k.a. Guanyin (Kwan Yin, Kuan Yin), or the Goddess of Mercy, who may have several heads and arms and may be carrying a vase or a child. She is usually behind Sakyamuni, facing north. Guanyin started out as a male god in China until about the 12th century, when his followers preferred to worship him as a woman. He is still sometimes depicted as male. Said one guide, "Men believe he is male and women believe she is female."

Other bodhisattvas could be *Amitabha,* in charge of the souls of the dead, *Manjusri,* in charge of wisdom, usually with a sword in his right hand and a lotus in his left, and the Bodhisattvas of Pharmacy, Universal Benevolence, and the Earth.

Arhats, known in Chinese as *lohan,* are people who have achieved Nirvana. They are usually depicted in groupings of 16, 18, or 500, and are based on real Indian holy men. These are frequently seen in paintings, or as statues. Devout Buddhists should know each of them by name.

Gautama was the Indian prince, born in the 6th century B.C., who was brought up confined to a palace. One day, upon seeing the suffering of the outside world, he forsook his wealth and family. He was 29 years old then. For six years, he went searching for life's meaning. Finding it, he then preached his ideas for 45 years: the Four Noble Truths and the Noble Eightfold Path to Nirvana. These numbers now correspond to the circles on top of Buddhist stupas and pagodas.

Buddha taught that the source of all suffering is selfish desire, and one must stop all craving for it. Some sects believe in asceticism. The Chinese, Mongolians, and Tibetans follow the Mahayana school of faith and good works, which believes Buddha is divine and can answer prayers. You will see people in temples, smoking incense in hand, nodding to the statues or kowtowing on the floor. All forms of Buddhism aim at stopping the continuous cycle of reincarnation—but some adherents are more serious about this than others. Nirvana is the extinction of existence.

The swastika is a Buddhist symbol of good luck, later inverted and used by the Nazis. Most temples have live fish and turtles. Full-time Buddhists are vegetarians. Some Buddhist monks have pieces of incense burned into their skulls at their initiation.

The swastika, symbol of luck

Swastika border design

The swastika was a Buddhist good luck symbol of Indian origin long before the Nazis existed. You will find it on the bellies of some Buddhist statues and latticed on screens and windows in complicated variations.

An interesting study to make as you sightsee is of the clothing carved on buddhas. Some wear the plain, draped robes of Indian holy men, others the fancy, feminine Chinese court dress with jewelry. Buddhism arrived in China from India, but Buddhist art became distinctly Chinese. Can you date a statue from its clothes? The fatness of its face?

You will probably see many more Buddhist temples than Taoist and Confucian. You can also see and hear robed monks chanting prayers if your timing is right.

(2) **Lama temples** are expressions of the Tibetan and Mongolian form of Buddhism, into which have been injected elements of the early Tibetan religion called Bon. Some sources say that the dalai lama, who is considered both the temporal and religious head of Lamaism, is a reincarnation of Avalokita or Guanyin, or the god Chenrezi. The religion is riddled with superstition, demons, and an incredibly horrifying hell for sinners. All of these are reflected in the murals and statues of Lamaist temples. Lamaism is also divided into sects, the main ones being the meditative Yellow Hats and the sensual Red Hats.

These temples are different from other Chinese Buddhist temples not only in their statues, but also in their architecture. Usually built on mountainsides, they have tall, narrow windows, flatter, less ornate roofs,

The eight Buddhist emblems of happy augury
a. The wheel of the law
b. The conch shell
c. The state umbrella
d. The canopy
e. The lotus flower
f. The covered vase
g. The pair of fishes
h. The endless knot

and are usually decorated over the main door with a gilded wheel of
Buddhist doctrine and two deer. Statues inside are frequently decorated
with turquoise and coral, and many wear pointed caps. The best-known
Lama temples are in Tibet, but important Lama temples are in Beijing,
Chengde, Qinghai, and Inner Mongolia. A Lama temple also stands in
Beijing's Summer Palace. See also ''Lhasa'' and ''Chengde.''

Taoist temples are identified by Taoist gods, among whom are

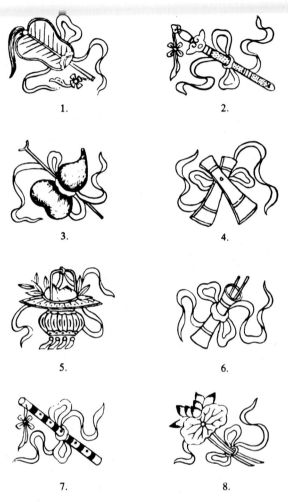

The attributes of the eight Taoistic genii
1. The fan
2. The sword
3. The pilgrim's staff and gourd
4. The castanets
5. The flower basket
6. The tube and rods
7. The flute
8. The lotus flower

Guanyin and Confucius, so don't get confused. Other gods and saints can be identified by the things they carry.

The Eight Taoist Genii or Immortals or Fairies were originally eight humans who discovered the secrets of nature. They lived alone in remote mountains (one of them in a cave at Lushan), had magic powers and could revive the dead. They are usually found together on a vase or in one painting, or as a set of eight porcelain pieces. Chung Li-chuan carries the fan to revive the spirits of the dead, Lu Tung-pin the supernatural sword, Li Tieh-kuai the staff, Tsao Kuo-chiu the castanets, Lan Tsai-ho the flower basket, Chang Kuo the bamboo tube, Han Hsiang-tzu the flute, and Ho Hsien-ku the lotus flower. Two are women.

Daoism (Taoism) was founded 1800 years ago by a sage named Lao Zi (Lao Tzu), whose message was conveyed to the world by a disciple named Mencius. It preaches that everything exists through the interplay of two opposite forces: male-female; positive-negative; hot-cold; light-dark; heaven-earth; yang-yin, etc. One wonders if Chairman Mao's theory of opposites and his emphasis on contradictions is related to this theory.

In the center of the dual Yin-Yang, the principles of being, surrounded by the eight trigrams of divination. The Eight Trigrams represent eight animals and eight directions. At eleven o'clock are the three unbroken lines of heaven; then clockwise, clouds, thunder, mountains, water, fire, earth, and wind. These are used in fortune telling. You may have heard of the I Ching.

Taoists try to achieve harmony out of the conflict of these forces through the Tao or the Way. Taoism is closer to nature than the other religions, its saints finding enlightenment after spending years meditating in caves. Over the years, it also has been diluted by superstition, its adherents believing in charms and spells, ghosts, nature spirits, and the worship of supernatural beings. *Feng-shui* geomancy, where man places his dwelling in harmony with natural forces, is an expression of Taoism.

Taoism was most popular in the Tang and Song, but declined in the Ming. Its most famous monasteries are in Beijing, Chengdu, Shenyang, and Suzhou.

Moslem Mosques are architecturally of two varieties and *visitors always remove their shoes* inside the great halls. The mosques similar to those in western Asia, with rounded, onionlike domes, are mainly in northwest China. Other mosques look like other Chinese temples, with curved roofs and ornate dragons and phoenixes (in spite of the prophet's teachings against making images).

In either style, there is a place for washing hands and feet before prayers. The main building is the Great Hall, which is frequently decarated with Arabic writing, arches, and flower motifs. Moslems pray five times a day, facing the holy city of Mecca in Saudi Arabia. Every mosque has a minaret. You could ask if the *muezzin* or *imam* calls the faithful to prayers from the minaret as is done in other countries.

Moslems can pray anywhere, but the devout usually pray in a mosque if they can. Note the prayer rugs with designs woven into them indicating the direction in which to kneel. Carpets made in Moslem areas deliberately do not have images of animals or objects on them, in keeping with the commandment forbidding "graven images." Note also the disproportionate number of women worshipers, and in some mosques, separate sections for women.

Moslems are followers of the Prophet Mohammed, who was born in A.D. 570. Known as Islam, his religion gives a different emphasis to the god of Judaism and Christianity. Old Testament prophets and Jesus Christ are considered honored prophets, but Mohammed was the last and the greatest. The holy book is the Koran, which teaches a strict code of behavior (no pork, no alcohol, no idols, etc.), and universal brotherhood of all believers. During the holy month of Ramadan, believers fast during the day.

Islam arrived in China in A.D. 652 during the Tang, with Arab and Persian traders who settled in Guangzhou, Quanzhou, Hangzhou, and Yangzhou. During the 13th century, many Moslem soldiers, artisans, and officials were brought to China to fight and work with Kublai Khan. The approximately 10 million Moslems in China are known as Hui, but Uygurs, Kazaks, Kirgiz, Ozbeks, etc., are also Moslem. Most Moslems live in the northwest. Friday is the holy day and mosques, which might otherwise be closed, are always opened Friday afternoons.

Besides those of the major religions, **other religious buildings** exist in China. Many of these are **ancestral temples** (*miao*), frequently one to a village. Many villages are each comprised of people with a common name and ancestor, so they only need one temple. Some of these temples were very elaborate and are used also as the village school. In ancestral temples, tablets with the names of the ancestors were kept in neat rows and worshiped with burning incense, gifts of food, and ceremonial bowing at least twice a year. The ancestors were informed of important family events like births and marriages, both verbally and in writing in a family history book. One worshiped ancestors in gratitude for one's life, but more so because the spirits of departed ancestors had to be kept happy so they could influence one's current fortunes. Many of these tablets were destroyed or hidden during the Cultural Revolution. When you go to a village, ask to see the ancestral temple.

Cave temples with frescoes and Buddhist statues were first built in India and spread with the Silk Road into China. Caves have always been conducive to meditation. There, one gets a feeling of security, like being back in a mother's womb. Dunhuang is the greatest for its paintings. The two at Lanzhou are noted for their strikingly dramatic sites and the richness of their sculpture. Important for carvings are also Datong and Luoyang.

Other cave temples listed as protected historical monuments by the State Council are at Anxi and Linxia in Gansu; Handan in Hebei; Turpan, Baicheng, and Kuqu in Xinjiang; Guangyuan, Leshan, and Dazu in Sichuan; Jianchuan in Yunnan; Gongxian in Henan; Guyuan in Ningxia; and Hangzhou in Zhejiang.

In old China, people worshiped any number of gods. They wanted to cover all possible bases. If a friend prayed successfully to one god for a baby boy, then other barren women tried that god too. It was not unusual for one person to have his children baptized as Christians, burn incense to a deceased grandfather, and then retire to contemplate in a Taoist or Buddhist monastery.

There are temples to the city gods. Fishermen worshiped the Goddess of Heaven, Tian Hou, who bears some resemblance to the goddess Guanyin. See ''Quanzhou'' for Manicheanism and ''Xi'an'' and ''Quanzhou'' for Nestorian.

Christian churches were most frequently built with gothic windows, as in Western architecture. Many Roman Catholic churches look like transplants from Europe. For more on Christianity in China, see *Religion* in ''Local Customs.''

Zoos are usually pathetic, but many have pandas. Beijing's is the largest. Animals do not have much space to roam.

Relax in a Chinese garden This is different from rushing through on a guided tour. Go back to one you especially like and just sit and absorb. A Chinese garden is not just a park or something attached to a building. It is an art form, the world in miniature, with mountains, water, plants, and buildings—a three-dimensional Chinese painting you can enter to try to experience infinity.

Gardens were built for a leisurely lifestyle in which poetry, philosophical contemplation, and the beauty of nature were of the utmost importance. Imagine *living* here! The ugly world of poverty and injustice was kept outside the high walls. ''Above Heaven; below Suzhou and Hangzhou'' probably referred more to the gardens than anything else.

Take your time exploring. Look at the integration of the buildings with nature, the pinpointing of places of particular beauty by unusually shaped windows and moon gates. Absorb the tranquillity of the water. Look at the reflections. Think of poetry. The meaning of life. A garden takes time—infinite time.

Do a study—it is easy to get cultural indigestion. After the third temple, they could all look alike. But they don't! Take notes. Draw diaa.

b.

c.

d.

e.

The shapes of pagodas came from either the Indian temple (b and c) or from the multistoried Chinese pavilion (lou). How many variations of these two basic shapes can you find, and how many pagodas can you accurately date just by looking at them? These are rough sketches of some examples: a—Guangzhou (Ming); b—Zhengzhou (Songshan—6th century); c—Xi'an (Tang); d—any number of dynasties and places. This can be seen even in Chinese-style mosques; e—Xi'an (also Tang) but a different derivation than c.

grams. Link up roof styles to dynasties and regions. Which ones have animals? And which animals? Are the roofs southern or northern?

Study the shapes of **pagodas**—those related to the Chinese *lou* and those related to Indian shapes. Is the shape distinctive to different dynasties? Do they all have an uneven number of stories? Which dynasties' are octagonal? Which pagodas have a different number of stories inside than outside?

Do a study of **tile faces** (wa dang) or eave tiles, for instance. These are the circular pieces of tile at the lower edges of a roof. Some have animal faces on them, some flowers, some Chinese characters. The designs were chosen in some cases as good luck symbols.

Find out details. Why do you have to step so high to get through some doorways and not others? Is it because of flood? Or because it blocks bad luck? What are the bumps on the head of some of the Buddhas? What do the different positions of Buddhist statues mean?

Who was China's most prolific graffiti artist? My vote would go to Qing Emperor Qianlong. Why is "son of a tortoise" one of the worst insults you can give?

Why have the Chinese placed so much emphasis on **calligraphy**? Why is it more than a means of communication, a very sophisticated art? Why is the calligraphy on one tablet better than the calligraphy on another?

Chinese people spend years mastering their written language. They first learn by copying the characters over and over again, an exercise in patience, perseverance, and discipline. For good calligraphy, writing legibly is not enough. One follows one of the four accepted basic styles with individual variations. One's calligraphy has to express one's personality and feelings, in tune with the content of the written message.

Chinese painting developed out of calligraphy, using the same materials and holding the brush in the same vertical way. Ideally, one needs an ink brush made of animal hair, rice paper, ink stick, and ink tablets. Students are taught to keep their backs, upper torsos, heads, and souls(!) in a straight line. The calligraphy you see on buildings, by Emperor Qianlong or whomever, was chiseled by someone else. Chairman Mao also was an excellent calligrapher.

Learn about **feng-shui** and the placement of buildings in harmony with the contours of the earth. Do all temples face south? Do all tombs face south? What role do pagodas play? Why are there screens in front of doorways and gates? How can you improve your own house to insure that good luck doesn't just go out your windows and doors?

Study the **different tomb styles**: Ming, Qing, Song, Han. How are they different?

Learn about Chinese **mythology.** Pick up a copy of *Old Tales of China—a tourist guidebook to better understanding of China's stage, cinema, arts and crafts.* Published by China Travel and Tourism Press, this inexpensive booklet in English relates many of the famous stories, some of which will help you understand Chinese opera plots. Try to figure out why these stories are so popular.

Read. Get immersed in old (and new) China. Read *Romance of the Three Kingdoms* while sitting on a cliff at Zhenjiang, overlooking the Yangtze, at the place where the widow of Liu Pei pined for her husband. Read *A Dream of the Red Chamber* while relaxing in the courtyard of one of the new reproductions of the setting. Read *Pilgrimage to the West* on a trip along the Silk Road. Translations of these books are cheaper in China, and if you have the time, will add immeasurably to your experiences there.

A Dream of the Red Chamber (a.k.a. Dream of Red Mansions) is one of the most popular novels published in China because it paints a vivid and convincing picture of how the rich (and their servants) lived during feudal times. Any Chinese over 35 years of age should know it. It is the story of a wealthy family, connected with the imperial court, who lived and declined during the Qing dynasty. The plot might move too slowly for Western readers, who probably will have trouble also remembering the Chinese names. (Make notes as you read it.) However, for details of lifestyles it is excellent, with descriptions of a funeral, impertinent bond servants, the visit home of daughter and imperial concubine Yuan-chun, etc. The sexual encounters are mentioned, and some are surprising, but they are not fully described.

Favorite among the characters is the bored, spoiled young hero Jia Pao-yu, who is surrounded by servants and is good at writing couplets. Sad to say, as the novel is popular largely because of its poetry, the poetry loses much in translation. Pao-yu is in love with his cousin, the beautiful Lin Tai-yu, but he is forced to marry someone else.

Attendants dressed as the characters inhabit the Red Chamber reproductions, known also as *Daguan Yuan* (Grand View Garden).

Learn about **China's minorities** (or nationalities). China has 56 different ethnic groups, 55 of whom are 6.7% of the population. These 55 million people live in areas totaling half of China. Yunnan province has 26 different nationalities. A nationality doesn't necessarily settle in one location. Often sub-branches are spread over several provinces, with different costumes and dialects. For example, the Miao nationality is found in Guizhou, Hunan, Yunnan, Guangdong, Guangxi, and Sichuan provinces. Miao women in Guizhou wear pleated skirts while those in Hunan wear pants. The color and designs of their turbans are also different.

During festivals and market days, most of the minorities, especially the women, wear their distinctive costumes, which are usually decorated with fine embroidery, and, sometimes, heavy silver jewelry. Their hairstyles could indicate their marital status.

Some minorities are very musical, expressing more liveliness in their dances than the majority Han Chinese. Although the levels of their Chinese education and their economy is generally lower than average, their cultural heritage is rich and meaningful. Unusual courtship rituals are still practiced.

The festivals of the nationalities are usually worth experiencing. The Dai celebrate a watersplashing festival similar to that in neighboring Thailand and Burma. The Kazaks have a Horse Racing Festival, the Bai a Torch Festival, the Tibetans celebrate their New Year, etc. Mongolians have equally colorful sporting meets, with their distinctive wrestling, horses, and motorcycles. Facilities for tourists in minority areas are still modest but not impossible. Collecting minority weaving, jewelry, and musical instruments can be very interesting. Comparing customs can keep anthropologists and folklorists occupied for years.

We suggest booking a tour through a travel agency because festivals attract tens of thousands of people. As one of the crowd, you won't see much unless you're well over six feet tall, but if the travel agencies have organized something, you should be able to get a good seat. The National Tourism Administration has a booklet on folk festivals but alas, no Western dates. Some dates are listed in ''Destinations'' and ''Quick Reference.''

DESTINATIONS

Over 500 destinations are open to foreign visitors now, more than that if you count the smaller tourist sites available from major cities. For these, you do not need any permits to visit beyond your visa to China. For any other places, you need **alien travel permits,** readily available from the Security Police. See "Getting Around."

Listed here are the most important destinations. Mentioned under these headings, especially those of the provincial capitals, are minor destinations. The list here is alphabetical by pinyin, with alternative spellings in parentheses. Where the **Chinese characters** or **pinyin** for tourist sites, hotels, and restaurants have been available, they are printed so you can ask taxi drivers and people on the street to help you find where you want to go. The words *Guesthouse* and *Hotel* are interchangeable and do not imply quality. The words *monastery* and *temple* are also interchangeable.

To locate any of these cities on a **map,** note the tourist region right after the name of the city; for example, "Northwest China." Look for the Northwest China regional map in the back of the book. For **shoppers,** we have listed items produced locally. These are usually cheaper and with more variety at the factory and in the province than elsewhere.

Don't jump to the conclusion that a temple "founded in 1250" means the buildings are over 700 years old. The buildings may have been rebuilt recently. (In a country that has had as many upheavals, air raids, and revolutions as China, it is amazing that so many great monuments have survived to this day.)

No other country has as many historic sites or as varied offerings as China. Chinese governments on all levels have selected some of the more important ones for renovation. This is a good indicator that the buildings are genuine and culturally significant. **An * means the site is protected as a historical or revolutionary monument by the State Council** of the national government.

(And please don't think that old is beautiful. Frequently the older the monument, the less developed and intricate.)

Hours given for stores and tourist sites are approximate, those in summer about an hour later than those in winter. **Schools, villages,** and

factories are basically the same in the whole of China, and these are not mentioned in every destination unless there is something special about them. We do urge you to visit schools, villages, and factories wherever possible.

For those trying to learn Chinese:

ang = nunnery
bingguan = guesthouse
ci = temple
dong = east
ge = small pavilion
hai = sea
hu = lake
jie = street
ling = tomb

lu = road
miao = temple, usually ancestral or Confucian
nan = south
sha = sand
si = temple
tang = temple

xi = west
yuan = garden
zhou = city state (smaller than a province; larger than a city)

bei = north
chan guan = restaurant
da lu = avenue
fan dian = hotel or restaurant
guan = pass
he = river
jiang = river
jing = capital
lou = multistoried pavilion big enough for people to live in
men = gate

quan = spring
shan = mountain
ta = pagoda
ting = tiny pavilion usually in rural surroundings in which people can rest
xian = county
zhong = middle or central

You will note some redundancy in names, such as Lu Shan Mountain, but those are for people who don't know Chinese, since such names are commonly used. It may appear cumbersome to put in the *pin yin,* the English, and the Chinese characters for place names, but in China some people will use the Chinese names and others will use the English, so the Chinese characters should help avoid confusion.

Sources differ sometimes as to historical dates and events, and *English translations* of site names. Please be flexible. Names like Han, Song, Ming, and Qing refer to dynasty, as ''in the Ming,'' with Mongol the same as Yuan, and Manchu the same as Qing.

Correct telephone numbers have also been difficult to obtain. In some places more than one is listed because sources differed. If one doesn't work, try the other. Failing that, ask any English-speaking source like C.I.T.S., a foreign airline, or an embassy for an up-to-date telephone number. To complicate matters, in the late 1980s some revolu-

Telephone numbers of **hotels** and **toll-free North American reservation numbers** are listed with current prices in ''Budget and Hotel Quick Reference.''

The quality of a hotel facility in China frequently depends on the time that has passed since its renovation. It also depends on the room one gets. It is therefore impossible for us to grade Chinese-managed hotels. Recent evaluations by guests and staff surveys are available from the *Travel China Newsletter*.

Although we have been unable to obtain all information about all hotels, the following will give you an idea of what to expect.

Many hotels have singles, suites, and dorms in addition to double rooms. Hotels marked as telexing an answer have promised us they will do so even if no rooms are available. Please let us know of those who don't.

Hotels listed here are up to minimal standards except where noted. In some cases, we have listed the best hotels in a city even though they may not be very good.

The **restaurants** listed are those recommended by C.I.T.S. except in Beijing, Guangzhou, and Shanghai, where we have developed our own lists. Note that population figures for ''cities'' usually include several counties and municipalities. We have tried to give the figures for the main urban area where they were available. And some of the tourist sites offered, especially those away from the main cities, are available only to tour groups booking in advance, not to individuals.

In trying to pack as much information as possible in this book, we have used the following abbreviations:

C.C.	Credit cards—American Express, Visa, Master-Card, and sometimes Diner's
Dist.A.P.	Distance from airport
Dist.R.W.	Distance from main railway station
IDD	International Direct Dial
J.V.	Joint Venture
Ren.	Renovated
T.R.	Hotel promises to telex answer to request for a reservation if requested.
USTV	Direct television transmission from the U.S. Hotels might have one or two channels.

ANSHAN 鞍山

Northeast China. 1½ hours by train, SW of Shenyang and still cold. Minimum in winter—⁻25°C; but maximum in summer is 34°C. Annual precipitation 715 mm, including snow. Urban population 1.2 million. Plane from Beijing Mondays and Thursdays.

Anshan was settled in the Yan State during the Warring States period. Its mines and smelting date back to the second century B.C. In 1395 (Ming), a city was built here; the ruins can still be seen. The Japanese colonized this area in the 1930s until 1945. The Communists took over on Feb. 19, 1948.

Today Anshan mines magnesite, talcum, white and green marble, and graphite, and has China's biggest iron and steel works. It is also known for **Mt. Qianshan** 千山风景区 , 44 square km of wilderness and jagged peaks, the highest 708 meters above sea level. Five Buddhist temples, one founded in the Tang but rebuilt in the Ming, and a Taoist temple add interest. It is 18 km SE of the main hotels.

The other main tourist attraction is **Tanggangzi Hot Spring Sanatorium** 汤岗子温泉 , 15 km south of Anshan, where visitors can relax, drink mineral water, and get physiotherapy, hydrotherapy, and acupuncture treatment. Arthritis, sciatica, and psoriasis are treated here. Hostel and gardens on the premises. A room was built for the Last Emperor, but he seldom used it. At Liaoyang, about 15 km NE, are some *Han and Wei tombs with murals, not yet open.

For fans of **steam locomotives,** tourists can go for a 38-km ride at the big iron and steel complex.

Haicheng silk, ginseng, and Nanguo pears are specialties of the city. Tourism officials recommend the Anshan Roast Duck restaurant (May Rd) and the Lao Zhen Xin (in the center of town).

HOTELS
Anshan Hotel (Ashan Bingguan) 鞍山宾馆 ● *121, First Section, Shengli Rd., Tiedong District, Anshan Dist.A.P.15 km. Dist.R.W.1*

New plumbing. Except for carpets, clean and well-maintained. This is the better hotel.

Victory Hotel (Shengli Bingguan) 胜利宾馆 *● 2 Xinhua St., Tiedong District, Anshan Telex 810032 SLHOT CN. Cable 2163. Walk from free market, park, department store. Near trolley line. Dist.A.P.15 km. Dist.R.W.2 km. ● 1958, ren. 1987. 8 stories. Dorms, big rooms.* Limited hot running water. Some rooms air-conditioned. Four-meter-high ceilings. Limited IDD, no C.C.

C.I.T.S. is in the Anshan Hotel; tel. 24403. Cable 2005. Telex 80005 SARI CN.

China United Airlines, Iron and Steel Complex branch, Tuan Jie St., Dui Lu Shan, Tiedong Dist.

Friendship Store is in the Anshan First Department Store (May 1 Rd., Tiedong District). Open 8:30 a.m. to 6 p.m.

See also ''Shenyang.''

ANYANG 安阳

Northwest China. Northern part of Henan province north of the Yellow River near the Hebei border.

This city of half a million people is one of the oldest in China, founded in the Shang dynasty. For short periods in the 16th century B.C., it was a Shang capital. In the 14th century, the problem of flooding solved, it was made a permanent city, the capital for King Pan Geng (Pan Keng) of the State of Yin, and continued as the royal capital for some 270 years.

It was here that the oracle bones, an ancient means of divination, were later found. Here early writing was inscribed on tortoise shells and shoulder blades of oxen, and then cracked with heat. The direction of the crack foretold the future. Today the city is highly industrial, with an iron and steel works. Tourists might be interested in visiting its jade-carving, plaited-straw, and carpet-weaving factories. But its prime attraction is to students of archaeology and ancient and modern Chinese history (even though important, excavated artifacts are mainly in the provincial museum in Zhengzhou). It is also exciting to people into air sports. Where else in China can you sightsee from a hot-air balloon or glider?

A one-day visit can include: the *Yin Ruins** 殷墟 , 2.5 km from the Anyang Guest House. The ruins include palace foundations, royal tombs, and bronze and jade artifacts. Yin was the last capital of the Xia dynasty in the 11th century B.C. The Anyang Museum and the **Wenfeng Pagoda** 灵谷寺 are also important. The pagoda is unusual, as it appears to be larger at the top, with a dagoba (stupa) at the summit. Some excellent brick carvings of saints are close enough to the ground to be studied. A new museum resembling China's first ancient palace stands on the ruins of the late Shang dynasty capital just outside the city.

The Mausoleum of Yuan Shikai 袁林 (2.5 km from the Anyang Hotel) holds the remains of the ambitious, brilliant official of the Manchu court. Also a warlord, Yuan took over the presidency of republican China from Dr. Sun Yat-sen in 1913, declared himself emperor in 1915, and died of a heart attack in 1916.

Yuefei's Temple 岳飞庙 (22 km from the Anyang Hotel) is a memorial to the maligned national hero.

If you have more time, then you can take in the **Azure-cloud Palace Temple** 碧霞宫和大石佛 (60 km from the hotel) with the oldest and largest Buddha in the province. The **Red Flag Canal** 红旗渠 , one of the Communists' earliest achievements, is 96 km away, a spectacular example of water management.

One of the more exotic things to do in China is hot-air ballooning, sky-diving, or gliding, which can probably be enjoyed at the Gliding School. If any of these are essential to your visit here, do make arrangements with C.I.T.S. before you go.

RESTAURANTS

Jubinlou Restaurant 聚宾楼饭庄 • *north entrance of Baida St.; tel. 3698* • specializes in squid with chicken wing tips, fish with crispy skin, egg pudding, and toffee apples.

Yingchun Garden Roast-duck Restaurant 迎春园烤鸭店 • *Middle section, Hongqi Rd.; tel. 2469* • specializes in roast duck, quick-fried prawns, grilled sharks' fins, quick-fried rolled squid, and sea slugs with egg white.

HOTELS

Anyang Guest House 安阳宾馆 • *1 Youyi (Friendship) Rd., 1 km from railway station* • 1959; renovated 1984. This is the main tourist hotel.

~~Taihang Guest House 飛行其他 • Dengla Dong Roll • 1976r~~

Xiangzhou Guest House 相州宾馆 • *northern section of Huan-cheng Xi Rd.*

The **Xiangzhou Hotel** 相州酒家 , on the same grounds as the Xiangzhou Guest House, will be ready for your visit.

C.I.T.S. 国际旅行社 is in the Anyang Guest House (1 Youyi Rd.; tel. 2145.)

BAOTOU 包头

(Paotow) North China. Western Inner Mongolia. This mining and industrial city is a 14-hour train trip or 1½ hour flight from Beijing, and is not for the weak. Its tourist attractions are mainly out of town. Take a scarf to cover your nose in case you encounter a sandstorm. The maximum temperature is 38°C, the minimum is ⁻30°C in winter! The average altitude is 1000 meters. Annual rainfall is a sparse 312 mm. The local tourist office points out 132 frostfree days a year! Prepare for cold weather except in summer.

The city was founded in the 17th century (Qing) on a neolithic site. At that time, people were encouraged to settle here to open up agriculture and defend the borders. The urban population is now about 870,000, of whom the Han are 90%, the Mongolians 2.5%, and the rest 21 other national minorities.

Of 1000 or so factories, visitors might want to see and shop at those producing leather and furs, porcelain, and arts and crafts. The **Baotou Carpet Factory** 包头地毯厂 is about 25 km from the main hotel.

If you only have one day, C.I.T.S. recommends the Wudangzhao Temple and a quick city tour. The city has over 40 archaeological sites, including the wall of the Zhao Kingdom and a Han dynasty town. The **Wudangzhao Temple** 五当召 is 70 km from the Blue Mountain Hotel and could be a rough trip. It is a massive 2500-room complex established in 1749 (Qing), once home to 1200 monks and covering about 50 acres. The largest lamasery in western Inner Mongolia, it contains statues, murals, and tankas typical of yellow sect Buddhism. More about Tibetan Buddhism under ''Lhasa'' and ''Chengde.''

If you have more time, the **Meidaizhao Temple** was originally built in the Ming. It is also known as the Sanniangzi Temple after the concubine of its Mongolian founder. She is buried here. A Han Chinese, she helped to bridge the differences between the two groups. The ***Tomb of Genghis Khan** 成吉思汗陵墓 was moved south of Baotou to Ejin-horoq (Elinhoro) in 1954. It is in the shape of three yurts and has been restored. It is actually a memorial. No one knows where Genghis Khan is buried.

Two new parks may be open by the time you arrive: the **Kongdu-lung Reservoir** 昆都仑水库风景区 , about 13 km from the hotel, and the **Nanhaizi Water Park** 南海子水上公园 , about 25 km.

In summer ask about the Nadam Fair: Seven days of horse racing, archery, and wrestling.

HOTELS

Qingshan (Blue Mountain) Hotel 青山宾馆 • *Qingshan district, Baotou Dist. A.P.30 km. Dist.R.W.7 km. Near government trade offices, and tourist shopping* • 1958; ren. 1988; Two stories, five buildings. Only Visa C.C. No IDD. Business center. Bicycles.

Baotou Hotel 包头宾馆 • *Kongdulung district* • 1957; renovated 1983.

The hotels serve Chinese, Western, and Moslem food. Local delicacies include camel hump and camel paw and, of course, mutton dishes.

C.I.T.S. 国际旅行社 is in Baotou Hotel (tel. 24615).
CAAC 中国民航 (Donghe district; tel. 41404).

See also ''Hohhot.''

BEIDAIHE 北戴河

(Pehtaiho, Peitaihe; North Dai River) North China, Hebei, is a lovely seaside resort 5 hours by train via Tianjin due east of Beijing, and about 10 km south of Qinhuangdao; 7 trains a day each way serve Beidaihe. The town is 12 km from the railway station. An airport is at Shanhaiguan, 35 km north, for the 50-minute air link with the capital. Air service also with Shijiazhang.

Beidaihe was built after the completion of the Beijing-Shanhaiguan railway in 1893. By 1949, 706 villas and hotel buildings had been completed, many of them for foreign diplomats and missionaries as well as wealthy Chinese. After Liberation, the Chinese government rebuilt some of the old buildings and added new ones as rest and recreation centers for its employees. In 1979, the resort was opened to foreign tourists, who are now served by the Beidaihe Beach Tourist Corporation. The population is around 20,000.

The resort stretches along 12 km of hard, golden sand sloping gently out into the Bohai Sea. Swimming is good though there may be a few jellyfish. The beaches are divided by rock promontories. At the **Pigeon's Nest** 鹰角石 in the east, you can see Qinhuangdao across the bay and the best sunrise. At the **Tiger Stone** 老虎石 in the center, crab fishermen sell their catch in the summer.

Several swimming areas are attached to each of the hotels, manned by life guards and protected by nets. Each hotel has changing rooms on the beach with hot and cold fresh-water showers, open 8 a.m.–10 p.m. The swimming season is from May to September, depending on how cold you like your water. The hottest days are in August (maximum 36°C for a few days), but the high is usually 31°C, sometimes dropping to 24 or 25 at night.

A **Guanyin Temple** 观音祠 built in 1911 is on the grounds of the West Hill Hotel. The buildings were beautifully restored in 1979, the two statues and frescoes inside replaced after being destroyed by the Red Guards. The temple is about 1.5 km behind the hotel's service bureau, a nice morning's walk. The **Xiaobaohezhai Village** is also good to visit. It was one of the first in China to have pensions for its older citizens and one of the first with a birth-control program. It grows apples, peaches and pears for export, so an ideal time to visit is late August September.

A good view of Beidaihe can be enjoyed from **Lianfengshan Park** 莲蓬山公园 . One can also rent bicycles, sailboats, and sailboards. The tourist corporation can arrange summer camping, bicycle tours, bird watching, international conferences, and health care tours too.

EXCURSIONS

Qinhuangdao—see separate listing.

Great Wall at Shanhaiguan—see ''Great Wall'' and ''Shanhaiguan.''

Mengjiangnu Temple and **Yansai Lake**—see ''Shanhaiguan.''

RESTAURANTS

Beihai Restaurant　北海饭庄　• seafood

Kissling Restaurant　起士林餐厅　• mainly European food

International Club　国际俱乐部　• Chinese and Western food

HOTELS

The top hotel is the Jinshan, says the Beidaihe Beach Tourism Corporation.

Xishan (West Hill) Hotel　西山宾馆　• *western sector of the beach* • 148 buildings spread along 3 km of beachfront. Has been and probably still is used also by the Military and the Party Central committees of the central government. On the grounds is also the **Beidaihe Beach Club,** which has a comfortable theater seating about 850, table tennis, billiards, art exhibitions, and a restaurant.

Beidaihe Hotel for Diplomatic Personnel • *1 Baosan Rd., Beidaihe Beach* • Open end of May to mid-September. Book through C.I.T.S. or Beidaihe Beach Tourist Corp. Private Beach.

Jinshan Hotel　金山宾馆　• *No. 4 Jinshanzui Rd. Cable 0518. Dist.R.W.18 km.* • 1986; 400 beds. Closed-circuit TV, radio, air conditioning, conference hall, ballroom, function room, open-air bar, beach, and several dining halls. Bicycles, gym, bowling, sauna, tennis, and pool.

Beidaihe Beach Tourism Corporation and Beidaihe International Travel Service • *No. 4 Jinshanzui Rd. Tel. 41748. Cable 0518. Telex 271053 JSH CN* • Office in Beijing, No. 37 Xiangongfu. (Back building of Beijing Hotel). Tel. 5137766–2837. Book three days in advance.

NOTE: · · · Regular public buses between Beidaihe and the beach operate every 30 minutes from 6 a.m. to 6:30 p.m.

BEIJING

(Peking; Northern Capital) North China, surrounded by Hebei province on the northern fringe of the north China plain; 183 km west of the seacoast, about 44 meters above sea level, has mountains to the north, west, and east; 36 hours by train north of Guangzhou and 19 hours NW of Shanghai, it can also be reached by train from Ulan Bator and, beyond that, from Moscow. On almost the same latitude as Philadelphia, Beijing is about 4 hours west of Tokyo by air, 3 north of Guangzhou or Hong Kong, and 2 NW of Shanghai. The best time to visit is in the autumn. The hottest days are in July and August—up to 38°C for a week or so; the coldest are in January and February—down to ⁻20°C. Dust storms occasionally blow from December to late March, and sometimes into May. The winter air has been heavily polluted with coal dust in the past, and few visitors escaped sore throats and colds then. The government has made a great effort to restrict the burning of coal. Pollution is not as big a problem anymore. Annual precipitation is 683 mm, usually from June to August. Beijing has a chronic water shortage. Population is 9.95 million (5 million urban); 5 million bicycles.

Beijing is the most important place to visit in China, not just because it is the capital but because it has a 3000-year history, from the

Western Zhou, when it was known as Ji (Chi). Its most impressive historical monuments date from the 13th century. The museums here are the best in China, the temples among the most impressive. The palaces are the biggest and most elaborate. For most Chinese people, visiting Beijing has been and still is a lifetime ambition and, fortunately, many are now able to do it. They take a great deal of pride in being here and details are very much sought after by envious neighbors and friends once they get back home.

If you must pick only one city to visit in this country of thousands of outstanding ancient monuments, you, too, should choose Beijing.

The Liao (916–1125) were the first to build a capital here. They called it Nanjing, Southern Capital, as distinct from their old capital farther north in Manchuria. The name was changed again to Yanjing (Yen Ching) in 1013. In 1125, the Jin, a Tartar dynasty, overthrew the Liao and enlarged the city, calling it Zhongdu, Central Capital. The Mongols (Yuan), under Kublai Khan, overthrew the Jin and built a new capital called Dadu (Ta Tu). In 1368 the Ming drove out the Yuan and established their capital at Nanjing with Beijing, then called Peiping Fu, as an auxiliary capital in 1409.

Beijing became the main capital again in 1421 (Ming) and continued as the Qing capital into the early 1900s. In 1860, it was invaded by foreign, mainly English and French, troops. The foreigners completely destroyed the Yuanmingyuan Palace. The Boxers took over in 1900 and laid siege to the Foreign Legation section, but were repelled by an international military force while the Qing Empress Dowager fled temporarily to Xi'an. In 1928, the Nationalist government moved its capital to today's Nanjing, and Beijing became Peiping (Northern Peace). The Japanese held it from 1937 to 1945. When the Communists took over in 1949, it regained its old name and former position as capital of the nation.

Fortunately, the buildings of Beijing escaped the Pacific War relatively intact. During imperial times, no structures taller than the Forbidden City were allowed. In 1959, ten massive buildings were completed for the tenth anniversary of the founding of the People's Republic. Built in the heavy, plain Soviet style, these included the Great Hall of the People, the Museums of History and the Revolution, the Agricultural Exhibition Hall, and the Palace of the Minorities. They are period pieces now.

In 1966, Beijing's Tian Anmen Square was the setting for mass Red Guard rallies of over a million people. In 1976, the square was also the site of a clash between supporters of the Gang of Four and those of Premier Chou Enlai. Beijing usually is peaceful, except for the bustling of bicycles and motor vehicles.

Beijing is centered around the Forbidden City and Tian Anmen Square. The old foreign legation area was SE of these, near the current

Xinqiao Hotel. The few remaining European buildings there reflect that period of its history. The Chinese city was south of the Qianmen Gate on the southern edge of Tian Anmen Square.

Beijing now consists of ten districts and nine counties. Rural villages raise the famous force-fed Beijing ducks. Over 2000 factories, mainly in the suburbs, produce iron and steel, coal mining, machines, basic chemicals and petroleum, electronics, and textiles.

The people of Beijing speak Mandarin or *pu tung hua,* the official national language, but they twirl their tongues more. They are predominantly Han, but you will see many flat, wide Mongolian faces too. Beijing people tend to be reserved compared to other Chinese. Don't be put off by this, for they are warm and friendly once they get to know you.

Beijing needs at least six days to cover its important attractions. Many individual travelers use public transportation successfully if they have plenty of time. Just avoid rush hours. Bus and subway maps are available in many hotels. The east-west subway line is 24 km long, each station in a different color marble. Trains operate every 3–8 minutes from early morning to late evening west from the railway station. Note the stations at the south end of Tian Anmen Square and the Minzu Hotel. The circle subway, a 16-km loop, completes the rectangle around Tian Anmen Square and the Forbidden City and reaches near the Beijing Zoo and Friendship Hotel. A second line opened in 1988 brings the total to 40 km.

A good, inexpensive introduction is the **Beijing City Bus Tour** from the Great Wall, Kunlun, Jinglun, or Jianguo Hotels, or anywhere else along its 16-stop, 45-km-long route. Each bus has an English-speaking guide on board and you can get off or on at any stop, seeing some of the main tourist attractions: the Friendship Store, Wangfujing St. (shopping), Drum Tower, and Lama Temple. Buses also stop at the Forbidden City; we recommend at least a day in that area. The bus schedule is on bright two-meter-high poles outside these tourist attractions. A non-stop trip takes 2½ hours. The last bus leaves the Great Wall at 2:30 p.m.

A relatively inexpensive **tourist bus** service run by the Beijing Motor Bus Company is recommended for those with a good guidebook or map. The human guides only give short introductions. Basically you're on your own. Regular tours go to the Great Wall, Ming Tombs, Fragrant Hills, Summer Palace, Tanzhe Temple, Yunshui Cave, Qing tombs, and Chengde (Jehol). None of these buses tour downtown Beijing itself. These out-of-town tours can be booked south of Tian Anmen Square on the same street as the Kentucky Fried Chicken Restaurant. C.I.T.S. has more expensive day tours booked from the Lido, Great Wall, and Jinglun hotels with English-speaking guides. These are less expensive than booking a tour for just one or two people through a hotel. A **train** goes daily, except Wednesdays, to the Great Wall (but not the Ming Tombs) at about 7:30 a.m., returning at about 12:35 p.m. If you are in a big hurry, this is the way to see both. A Tourist Information Center is inside the baggage-claim area in the international airport.

To help you plan your time so you can cover the most important sights, these groupings are suggested. The days can be interchangeable, depending on weather, train schedules, upset stomachs, traffic jams, and the hours a particular attraction is open.

DAY 1:   Tian Anmen Square, Imperial Palace, and Jing Hill. If you make a reservation a month in advance, you can lunch in the Great Hall of the People (tel. 335484). Failing that, there's the Beijing, Peace, and Palace Hotels and the Wangfujing Beijing Duck Restaurant to the east, and restaurants (including Kentucky Fried Chicken!) at the south end of the Square. Excellent World Showcase Restaurants and a Kentucky Fried Chicken are between the Beijing Hotel and the Forbidden City half a block north of Chang An Ave. on Hua Long Jie, Bei Lou, tel. 5129180. I loved the Tea House. There is a snack stand in the Forbidden City.

DAY 2:   The Museums of Chinese History and the Chinese Revolution, Beihai Park and the Temple of Heaven. Tour of Dazhalan if you make arrangements first, and shopping at Liulichang. Lunch if you make a reservation on time at the Fang Shan (Imperial Kitchen) Restaurant (tel. 442573, Beihai Park). Also any of the ''Day 1'' restaurants.

DAY 3:   Summer Palace, temples of the Western Hills, Fragrant Hill, ruins of the Yuanmingyuan, and Great Bell Temple. The temple is closed once a week, probably Wednesdays, so phone C.I.T.S. first to make sure it is open. Avoid all but the temple if the weather is bad. Lunch at the Summer Palace (reservation needed at the Tingliguan there), or the Fragrant Hills Hotel.

DAY 4:   Great Wall and Ming Tombs, but not on Wednesday if you take the train, or Sundays (traffic jam). Avoid in bad weather. Take your own lunch if you want, especially in pleasant weather. Most tourists visit the Great Wall at Badaling. If you want to get away from the commercialism and crowds, ask for Mutiayu.

DAY 5:   Lama Temple (closed on Mondays), Confucius Temple/Capital Museum, China Art Gallery—half a day. Remainder and **DAY 6:** choice of arts and crafts factories, rural visit, shopping, cultural performances, or repeat visits to places where you wanted to spend more time but couldn't. Choice of other excursions.

As you can see, this is a very heavy schedule and you may have to squeeze your shopping and strolling into the evenings. One really needs more time. You can't enjoy details if you keep looking at your watch.

DAY 1

Tian Anmen (Tien An Men) Square 前门城门 , 98 acres. Great for kite-flying in the spring. Try to imagine 1966 at the beginning of the Cultural Revolution when a million schoolchildren filled this square, chanting slogans and waving the little red book of quotations from Chairman Mao. The father of Communist China stood at the front of the gate to the north and acknowledged the screams and cheers of the youngsters. Besides giving them a vacation from school, he also gave them a mandate to travel around the country on the trains with room and board in each city—all free. Truckloads of shoes were swept away after the rallies. No one was able to retrieve lost shoes as the crowd surged wildly. Protests and rallies are still held here.

This square is bounded on the north by the Tian Anmen gate and on the west by the Great Hall of the People. On the east is the Museum of the Chinese Revolution and the Museum of Chinese History, and on the south one can't miss the imposing Qianmen (Chien Men) gate. In the center, from the north to south, are the Monument to the People's Heroes and the Chairman Mao Memorial Hall. Every May 1 and Oct. 1 the big portraits are displayed. They are, left to right, Marx, Engels, Lenin, and Stalin. Also prominent is Dr. Sun Yat-sen.

The **Great Hall of the People,** a.k.a. People's Congress Hall, built in 1959; 171,800 square meters. Three main sections include a 5000-seat banquet hall, a three-story, 10,000-seat auditorium, and lounges in the style of each of the provinces. This is China's equivalent of a parliament. To some observers, it is merely a rubber-stamp group of representatives. To others, the People's Congress is a forum for the opinions of the masses. Open Tuesdays, Wednesdays, and Saturday mornings for a small fee. Banquets can be booked (tel. 335484). The restaurant entrance is on the north side (Chang'an Xi Ave.).

Qianmen Gate 天安门 is not open, but it is a magnificent, beautiful gate. To the south is Dazalan, a Chinese shopping area (see Day 2). The bus to the Great Wall can also be booked nearby.

Beijing's gates are marvelous. Each had a very specific purpose; for example, night soil could only go through the Andingmen in the north; prisoners to be executed plodded through the west gate, Xuanwumen. Departing soldiers marched through another of the north gates even if they had to fight in the south. The impressive Deshengmen (Victory Gate) can still be visited.

Monument to the People's Heroes 人民英雄纪念碑 : If you had taken my advice and learned your numbers in Chinese, you would know the dates under each sculpture. Then if you looked up "Milestones in Chinese History'' you would know that the sculptures here represent the burning of the opium and the Opium War, 1840–42; the Taiping Heavenly Kingdom, 1851–64; the Revolution of 1911; the May 4, 1919, demonstration against the Versailles Treaty and for the New Cultural Movement (such as literature in plain rather than the generally incomprehensible classical language); the May 30, 1925, Incident in Shanghai, a protest against foreign powers in China after a Chinese worker was killed by a Japanese foreman. Look also for the August 1, 1927, uprising in Nanchang and the Anti-Japanese War, 1937–45.

In April 1976, during the Qingming (Ching Ming) festival, when the dead are honored (in the old days ''worshiped''), attempts by the Gang of Four to remove wreaths brought by private citizens in memory of Premier Chou En-lai were resisted by pro-Chou supporters at this monument. Hundreds were wounded and thousands arrested. This protest is now referred to as the April Fifth Movement against the Gang of Four, and encouraged pro-Chou politicians like Deng Xiaoping to attempt to overthrow them.

The **Chairman Mao Memorial Hall**　毛主席纪念堂　was built in 1977. It has been open on Mondays, Wednesdays, and Friday mornings. Whether it remains open depends on the political climate. In this mausoleum rest the remains of China's great leader. The simple white building, with 44 granite columns and glazed yellow trim, is 33.6 meters high and 105 meters square. The sculptures on the north side were symbolic of the achievements of the Chinese people in the preceding half century under Mao's leadership; those on the south express the people's determination to ''act on his behests and carry the cause of our proletarian revolution through to the end.''

Foreign and Overseas Chinese visitors line up separately from Chinese citizens, and the visit takes less than 30 minutes. As a token of respect, visitors are advised not to wear bright colors, especially red, but no one was stopped when I was there. No cameras or purses are allowed. One enters first the North Hall, where there is a seated, 3-meter-high marble statue of the leader. Then, quietly, two by two, you enter the Central Hall where Chairman Mao (1893–1976) lies in state.

Tian Anmen (Tien An Men; Gate of Heavenly Peace)　天安门　is the most famous structure in China except for the Great Wall. From its high balcony the imperial edicts were read, and this is where, on October 1, 1949, Chairman Mao Zedong (Mao Tse-tung) proclaimed the People's Republic of China. It is therefore a symbol of old and new China. The country's leaders frequently appear here on national days to review the parades and festivities. It was built in 1651 and stands 33.7 meters high. In 1988, the rostrum where Chairman Mao stood was opened to tourists for Y 30.

Through the gate under Chairman Mao's portrait, to the left, is Zhongshan Park, the memorial park to Dr. Sun Yat-sen. To the right is

Working People's Cultural Park. These two parks are great for 6 a.m. walks because of the magnificent walls, towers, gates, moats, and pavilions, and also because of the people limbering up for the day. Some are exercising not just their arms and legs but their vocal chords. You might hear some very beautiful voices resound off the walls from very shy singers hiding behind bushes and screens. Crowded apartments give little opportunity for singers to practice.

In the square between the two parks is a tiny white marble pavilion looking much like a Japanese lantern. In imperial times, if an official made a serious error, his black gauze cap was placed inside and he was taken out to be executed at the Wumen in front of the palace. Commoners were dispatched at the marketplace 7 km SW of here near the Qianmen Hotel.

*Gu Gong (Imperial Palace),** a.k.a. Palace Museum or Forbidden City 故宫 : open 8:30 a.m.–4:30 p.m. (summer). No admittance after 3:30 p.m. Visitors usually enter by the **Wumen (Meridian Gate)** inside the Tian Anmen between the two above-mentioned parks, and head north. Because of the crowds wearing down the Forbidden City, a daily limit of about 25,000 tourists has been imposed. Foreigners might be exempt. An acoustiguide, a recording of Peter Ustinov giving details about a limited area, is recommended if you want a good commentary in English.

The Gu Gong was the home and audience hall of the Ming and Qing emperors. Many buildings here are as the Qing left them, minus relics now in the National Palace Museum in Taiwan. Many of the buildings are exhibition halls for historic treasures from all over China. Relics of the Last Emperor Pu Yi might still be seen, including his queue (which he cut off himself), his bicycle, and his cricket box. To walk at a leisurely pace from one end to the other takes about 30 minutes, but to explore it thoroughly takes at least a full day—some would say a week. And not all parts are open to the public!

The Forbidden City was originally built from 1406 to 1420 as the palace of the Ming emperors. It is on more than 720,000 square meters (178 acres) of land. Over 9000 rooms cover a total floor space of about 150,000 square meters. The surrounding imperial red wall is over 10 meters high. Only imperial palaces were allowed to have yellow ceramic roofs. (Commoners could only use gray.) This massive city was built by 100,000 artisans and a million laborers.

Toward the end of the Qing, 280,000 taels of silver were needed annually to maintain the palace, the money collected in taxes and rents from 658,000 acres of royal estates. During the Ming, 9000 ladies-in-waiting and 100,000 eunuchs (castrated males) served here. Some eunuchs became more powerful than the self-indulgent emperors. Sacked by foreign powers in 1900, the Forbidden City was restored and now maintains a permanent staff of painters and carpenters so that every 20 years all the buildings are renewed.

The city is divided into two major sections: the outer palace (for business) and the inner residential courts. Directly beyond the Meridian Gate are the five marble bridges "like arrows reporting on the emperor to Heaven." The **River of Gold** below is shaped like a bow. Note the gates; red was used only for important places like this. Each has 81 studs—nine times nine, an imperial number. Seven layers of brick line the courtyards, so no one could tunnel in from below. Note the white squares, on each of which a royal guard stood whenever the emperor ventured past.

Throughout the palace, huge caldrons of water stand ready for possible fires. On the north side, beneath the caldrons, are air vents to fan fires set in winter to keep the water inside from freezing. Note the lack of hiding places for possible assassins.

The first building is the **Taihedian** (Tai Ho Tien; Hall of Supreme Harmony) 太和殿, the most stately of all the buildings. It is surrounded by incense burners, 18 bronze ones representing the then 18 provinces, and others in the form of a stork (longevity) and a dragon-headed tortoise (strength and endurance). Note the copy of an ancient sundial and the small openings on the side of the pavilion to allow air to circulate inside. The building was used for major ceremonies like the emperor's birthday, for imperial edicts, and for state affairs. Imagine the area in front of it covered with silk-gowned ministers and officials kneeling in rows. Imagine their heads to the ground in front of the hall while smoke poured from the incense burners and musicians played on the balcony. Can you see the child emperor being carried by palaquin above them to the highly carved throne? If you can't, try to see the Chinese historical movie *Power Behind the Throne* and the American movie *The Last Emperor*. Good books to read are *Inside Stories of the Forbidden City,* published in China, and E. Behr's *The Last Emperor*.

Each of the 18-meter-high cedar pillars was made from one piece of wood. Each of the floor tiles took 136 days to bake, after which it was immersed in oil for a permanent polish. The bricks are solid, about 5″ thick and 18″ square. The base and throne are carved sandalwood.

The **Zonghedian (Hall of Complete Harmony)** 中和殿 was used by the emperor to receive his ministers, to rest, and to dress before he entered the Taihedian. The two Qing sedan chairs here were for traveling within the palace. The braziers were for heat, the four cylindrical burners for sandalwood incense. Note the imperial dragon symbols on the ceiling.

The **Baohedian (Hall of Preserving Harmony)** 保和殿, the most decorative of these halls, was for imperial banquets and, during the Qing, the retesting of the top scorers in the national examinations. Note the village and plains. Behind this hall, between the stairways, is a giant carving of dragons in one piece of marble from Fanshan county, 16.5 meters by 3 meters and weighing about 250 tons. Anyone caught touching this imperial symbol was executed. The carving and the timbers were brought here in winter by sliding them over ice made from water of wells especially sunk for the occasion. Nothing was too extravagant for the representative of Heaven!

Several buildings on both sides of these main halls were used for study, lectures, a library, and even a printing shop. Beyond this third hall are the **Inner Courts,** the three main buildings, similar to the three in the outer palace; the **Qianqingong (Hall of Heavenly Purity)** 乾清, where the emperors used to live and where deceased emperors lay in state. Here also Cixi (Tsu Hsi), the infamous Empress Dowager, received foreign envoys; the **Jiaotaidian (Hall of Union)** 交泰殿, where ceremonies involving empresses took place (women were not allowed in the outer palace!); and the **Kunninggong (Palace of Earthly Tranquillity)** 坤宁宫, which was a residence in the Ming and a shrine in the Qing. One of the Qing emperors used its eastern room as a bridal chamber. East of the Kunninggong is a hall where clocks from all over the world are exhibited, gifts from foreign missions. In the back of the inner court is the **Imperial Garden,** where a snack bar might save thirsty tourists. The imperial family sipped tea, played chess, and meditated in this beautifully designed garden. Can you imagine living here!

Then, continuing northward, one arrives at the back gate, where tour groups usually meet their buses. But you're not finished yet! Retracing your steps to the entrance of the inner court, turn left (east) at the Qianqingong, past the washrooms and the **Nine Dragon Screen,** and then turn left again. Here are several pavilions with exhibitions well worth seeing. One might have a stunning collection of gold artifacts—bells, incense burners, table service (with jade handles), and scepters. There are also precious Buddhist relics and the biggest jade sculpture in China, a 5-ton Ming statue depicting one of the earliest attempts in the Xia Dynasty to control the Yellow River. Look for paintings and antique jewelry, pottery and bronzes. Also notable north of this area is the 12″-diameter well in which the obviously thin Pearl Concubine was drowned by a eunuch after she incurred the wrath of the Empress Dowager in 1900.

A clean toilet is in this area near the jewelry exhibit.

In each building, look at the ceilings and the palace lanterns, the distinctive blue Manchu cloisonne, and the Western clocks. Where were the imperial toilets? the kitchens? Think of the children who grew up within these walls and never set foot outside! Think of the eunuchs who gave up their manhood for a job that would benefit their families.

American Express is placing wooden signboards here with historical information.

Jingshan (Coal) Hill 景山 , outside the north gate of the palace, was originally the site of a Ming coal pile. It was built with earth excavated from the moats and is 43 meters high. It is now a park with a good view of the Forbidden City and the lakes to the west and north. As the Manchus were breaking into the city, the last of the Ming emperors hung himself on a locust tree located at the foot of the hill on the east side.

DAY 2

The exhibits in the **Museum of the Chinese Revolution** 中国革命 博物馆 are good for those who want to learn something about China after 1840, and are divided into the following sections: the Opium War, the Taiping Heavenly Kingdom, the Sino-French War and the Sino-Japanese War, Tsarist Russian Aggression, the Reform Movement of 1898, the Anti-Imperialist Movement of the Yi He Tuan, the Revolution of 1911, and the founding of the Communist Party, Chou En-lai, the civil wars, and the Japanese war. Be sure to pick up a short description in English.

The **Museum of Chinese History** 中国历史博物馆 is China's best. It is divided into four sections: primitive society, slave society, feudal society, and semicolonial, semifeudal society. You can walk through without absorbing much in an hour, it is so large. You need at least a half day to do it justice. Please take it in short doses, especially if your feet tire easily. There is a lot to see! (See also *Visit Museums* in "What Is There to See and Do" and "Milestones in Chinese History.") Both museums are entered opposite the Great Hall of the People. The history museum is to the right. Open 8:30 a.m.–5 p.m. or 9 a.m.–12:30 p.m.; 2–5:30 p.m.

Relics here start from 1.7-million-year-old pre-human teeth to 1911. They include a model of the cave where the Peking Man was found. Also on display are a 14th-century B.C. ivory cup inlaid with jade, a Shang bronze wine vessel with four protruding rams' heads, and a Western Zhou sewer pipe with the head of a tiger. Intriguing, too, are a model of a Warring States irrigation system, tomb figures galore, and a model of a first-century B.C. wheel used to operate a bellows to melt iron. Here, too, is the Flying Horse of Gansu, which people around the world waited many hours to see when it was exhibited abroad. No queues here!

There is also a model of a 1700-year-old drum chariot with a figure of a child on top, always pointing south, and another miniature drum chariot with a figure that beats a drum every 500 meters, a Yuan water clock, and some Yuan rockets attached to spears. I can only whet your appetite. It is best to take a Chinese-reading friend since there have been no signs in English.

The ***Tiantan (Temple of Heaven)** 天坛 is about 5 km south of the Forbidden City. Think of the processions of incense-swinging priests, spear-bearing palace guards, and the palaquin bearers carrying the emperor—all marching from the palace unseen by anyone else. Setting eyes on the emperor was a crime punishable by death.

The temple is set in the middle of a 667-acre park with many pine and cypress trees, some over 500 years old. Give yourself at least 20 minutes for a quick look, an hour for a more thorough tour. The Temple of Heaven was built in the same period as the Forbidden City (1420), and ranks among the most famous structures in China. It was used a couple of times a year when the emperor, bearing all the sins of the Chinese people, humbled himself before Heaven and performed the rituals calculated to bring good harvests. The temple has two concentric walls, both round at the north and straight at the south, heaven being round and earth square, or didn't you know! The raised, 360-meter passage between the main buildings is the **Red Stairway Bridge.** To the north is the **Qiniandian (Hall of Prayer for Good Harvests)** with triple eaves, 38 meters high and 30 meters in diameter. The four central columns represent the four seasons. Around these four are two rings of 12 columns each, the inner symbolizing the 12 months and the outer the 12 divisions of day and night. Here, the emperor performed the rites on the 15th day of the first moon of the lunar calendar. All the columns are wood from Yunnan province.

South of this is the **Imperial Vault of Heaven,** originally built in 1530 and rebuilt in 1752. In this building without horizontal beams were stored the tablets of the God of Heaven, the Wind God, the Rain God, etc. Sacrifices were made on the circular Sacrificial Altar on the winter solstice. The surrounding wall has a strange echo effect. You can hear people talking softly beside it from an unusual distance. Also count the number of stone slabs on the floor, staircases, and balustrades. They are in multiples of nine.

*Beihai (North Sea) Park 北海公园 , open 7:30 a.m.–4 p.m., is only a few blocks west of Coal Hill. (Take bus 103 along Wangfujing St. from the Beijing Hotel if you wish.) If you are short of time, just head for **Baita Shan (White Dagoba Hill)** 白塔山 and then the **Nine Dragon Screen** (1756) on the opposite side of the lake. While the whole area is a historic site protected by the State Council, these are the highlights of a big, 168-acre park full of intriguing old buildings, the recently renovated **Jingxinzhai (Serenity Study),** winding paths, and interesting rocks, that could take a half day to explore. Rowboats are for hire and, in the winter, ice skating on the lake is an exotic experience (but bring your own skates). The Fang Shan Restaurant near the White Dagoba serves the same fancy, delicate dishes (well, almost!) once presented to the Empress Dowager. But you do have to make a reservation or risk going hungry.

In the 10th century (Liao), an imperial residence was built on the site and called Precious Islet Imperial Lodging. In the 12th century (Jin), auxiliary palaces were constructed here and a lake excavated, the earth used to build the artificial hills and the *Round City at the southern edge. Rocks from Kaifeng were also used. During the Yuan, the Qionghua Islet was expanded and the palace of Kublai Khan was made the center of the city. This palace is no longer standing. Also on the islet, the 35.9-meter-high, bell-shaped White Dagoba was first constructed in 1271 in the Tibetan style. The current stupa was built in 1731.

Also noteworthy is Kublai Khan's 3000-liter jade liquor container (1265) and the Jade Buddha in Chengguang Hall in the Round City on the mainland, by the White Dagoba causeway.

The Nine Dragon Screen on the north side of the lake is of glazed brick and is 5 by 27 by 1.2 meters. Successive dynasties added buildings to Beihai, and this park was also looted by the foreign powers in 1900 and, more recently, by the Red Guards.

Zhongnanhai 中南海 , south of Beihai, has not been generally open to the public because it contains the residences and offices of China's leaders. Very special tour groups have successfully requested a visit if nothing else is happening at the time. The Guanxu (Kuang Hsu) emperor, who attempted to make modern reforms, much to the displeasure of the Empress Dowager Cixi, was imprisoned here during the winters when he was not at the Summer Palace. The historically important Pavilion of Purple Light and Fairy Tower were recently repaired. The south gate, brilliant red and fancy, is on Changan Avenue west of the Tian Anmen, too prominent to be overlooked.

Now, if you have more time, the 18-shop antiques, arts and crafts shopping center of **Liulichang** 琉璃厂 is nearby, a pleasant place to poke around. Built during the reign of Qing emperor Qianlong, it has recently been renovated in the old Qing style. See *Shopping*. The shopping area of **Dazalan** 颐和园 , just south of the Qianmen, is the market area for ordinary people. However, a huge, 3000-meter-long underground air-raid shelter (now a well-maintained underground tourist attraction, with arts and crafts store and a hotel) makes this special. The shelter has 90 entrances and can hold 10,000 people. Officials estimate the teeming streets above can be cleared in six minutes in an emergency.

Dazalan's underground is worth visiting, but arrangements must be made in advance by joining a tour. You can enter by a trap door in the floor of a clothing shop.

DAY 3

Summer Palace, Temple of the Azure Clouds, Temple of the Sleeping Buddha, and Fragrant Hill are all within 10 km of each other,

~~JU JU lim PM af the Tian Anmeni Decause of traffic jams, avoid Oun~~ days here. If time permits, you can visit the Yuanmingyuan and Great Bell Temple too.

The **Yiheyuan (Garden of Cultivating Peace)** 仁寿殿 , a.k.a. **Summer Palace** (open 6 a.m.–5:30 p.m.) A visit to this 717-acre garden usually takes half a day. It is three quarters water. Originally built in the 12th century, it was expanded in 1750 for the 60th birthday of the mother of the Qianlong emperor and burned in 1860 by the British-French army. It was rebuilt by the Empress Dowager Cixi (Tzu Hsi) on the occasion of her 60th birthday (1895) and financed with funds meant for building the Chinese navy. It was badly damaged by the foreign powers in 1900. The existing buildings were restored in 1903.

The imperial court lived here every year, when possible, from April 15 to October 15, receiving diplomats and conducting business in the **Renshoudian (Hall of Longevity and Benevolence)** 大戏楼 . Empress Dowager Cixi, who was the power behind the throne from 1861 to 1908, lived in this hall near the **Deheyuan (Grand Stage)** , where she could indulge in her passion for theatricals. The stage floor is hollow so that "ghosts" could emerge from it. The Grand Stage is now a separate museum requiring an additional fee. It contains Cixi's jewelry and dinnerware, and wax figures of Cixi and two imperial concubines. Attendants are in Qing palace costumes, and you can have your photo taken with a live "eunuch" or wax figures. In the exhibition hall behind the stage is the 1898 automobile given to the emperor by General Yuan Shikai.

Twenty-eight ladies-in-waiting, twenty eunuchs, and eight female officials waited on the empress dowager. For lunch, she was offered 128 courses daily.

In the **Hall of Jade Ripples** 玉栏堂 , to the south of the main entrance, she kept the Guangxu (Kuang Hsu) emperor imprisoned every summer from 1898 to 1908 after he tried unsuccessfully to institute reforms to modernize China and to take his rightful power back. Note the walls around the compound. The rooms here and elsewhere are furnished as they were then.

The **Long Corridor** extends 728 meters along the lake to the famous **Qingyan (Marble) Boat.** The 1400 paintings here (count them if you don't believe it!) are a most spectacular display. To the north up the hill are the **Hall of Dispelling Clouds** 排云殿 , the **Tower of Buddhist Incense** 佛香阁 , and the **Temple of the Sea of Wisdom** 智慧海 , where the empress used to hold her birthday celebrations and religious services. The **Xiequeyuan (Garden of Harmonious Interests)** 谐趣园 was designed like the Jichangyuan (Garden) in Wuxi. Also on the hill is a Tibetan-style Lama temple. Crossing Kunming Lake is a 17-arch bridge and, on an island, the **Dragon King Temple** 龙王庙 .

A good restaurant is in the **Tingliguan (Pavilion for Listening to

Orioles) 听鹂馆 ; reservations essential (tel. 283955). Here you can also have your picture taken in elegant imperial dress.

The Summer Palace Hotel is in the garden, near the Hall of Scalloped Clouds, an exotic experience if you don't mind being isolated. It is a long way from downtown. Club Med is also here.

Northwest of the Summer Palace is the **Temple of the Sleeping Buddha,** a.k.a. Temple of Universal Spiritual Awakening 卧佛寺 . This was first built in the Tang and reconstructed and renamed in the Yuan, Ming, and Qing. The lacquered bronze Sakyamuni, which was cast in 1331 (Yuan), is 5.33 meters long and weighs 54 tons. It is the largest bronze statue in China. The Buddha here is giving his last words to his disciples before his earthly death. Because he is barefooted here, successions of emperors have presented the statue with 11 pairs of huge handmade cloth shoes, which are on display in the same room. On either side are the 12 bodhisattvas, his disciples. A long hiking trail extends to the left behind the fish pond up the mountain through a garden. One can also stay in the temple overnight very cheaply.

The **Biyunsi (Temple of Azure Clouds)** 白云寺 is more important than the Sleeping Buddha because of its stunning collection of religious statues and the Diamond Throne Pagoda. The Biyun was first built in the Yuan as a nunnery. During the Ming, it was the burial place for powerful eunuchs. In 1748, Emperor Qian Long (Chien Lung) ordered to be built the **Hall of Five Hundred Arhats** 五百罗汉堂 and the **Diamond Throne (a.k.a. Vajra Throne) Pagoda** 金钢宝座塔 . The 508 gilded, wooden arhats are life-size and strikingly beautiful, each different. How many are not sitting? Which have two heads? Which would you like to talk with? What do you think he'd say? It is good to have a flashlight here too.

In 1925, the body of Dr. Sun Yat-sen lay in state at this temple until the completion of his mausoleum in Nanjing. A tiny museum is at the spot. The unique 34.7-meter Diamond Throne Pagoda consists of five small pagodas in the Indian style and has some excellent carvings and towers, showing a great deal of Indian influence.

Xiang Shan (Fragrant Hill) Park 香山公园 , open 7:30 a.m.–5:30 p.m., was a 150-hectare (384-acre) hunting ground for many emperors. A 20-minute chairlift to the top of the mountain now gives a spectacular view of the area, especially in autumn, when the air is less dusty and some leaves are red. The waiting line is long, but anyone can get preferential treatment if they pay three times the regular fare at another window, which isn't much anyway for tourists. Prepaid tour groups automatically jump the queue because they have already paid the higher fee. The highest peak here is 557 meters above sea level. The lift goes by a small Glazed Pagoda, a Western-style mansion that was presumably the hunting lodge, and a Tibetan-style temple, which you can inspect at closer range later.

Drop in at the **Xiang Shan (Fragrant Hill) Hotel** 香山饭店 for coffee. See *Hotels* below.

If time permits on the way back to town, glimpse the **Yuanmingyuan** 圆明园 ruins. This Garden of Clear Ripples was built in an area full of bubbling springs and was used as an imperial resort beginning in the 11th century. It became the site of a major palace in 1690 and later was rebuilt into a favorite 160-hectare palace garden by Qing Emperor Qianlong, with buildings copied from Suzhou, Hangzhou, and Yangzhou. Sacked by Anglo-French forces in 1860 (after the Qing defeated the foreigners at Taku and tortured their envoys), it was partially repaired only to be destroyed again in 1900. The foreigners wanted to punish the emperor who loved it in revenge for the siege of the legations. The foreigners were also greedy for more power in China. The few remains of this ''Garden of gardens'' and ''Palace of palaces'' can be glimpsed in twenty minutes if you are in a hurry to get to the Great Bell Temple. Much of what was left was taken by scavengers. Enough remains of the marble archways of the Evergreen Palace to show the influence of the European missionaries who helped design it early in the 1750s. Since the imperial families favored the Yuanmingyuan over the Imperial Palace, they kept their most precious treasures and books here. The 1860 burning took two days and is documented in a good Chinese-made movie, *The Burning of the Summer Palace.* One of the best accounts in English is Garnet J. Wolseley's *Narrative of the War with China in 1860.* A small exhibition near the entrance tells the story. The maze and some other buildings have been reconstructed.

You are rushing now to get to the **Jueshengsi (Temple of Awareness of Life),** popularly known as the Temple of the Great Bell大钟寺. This temple houses over 40 different ancient bells. The most spectacular bell was cast in the reign of Emperor Yongle of the Ming (1403–25) in a clay mold, and weighs 46.5 tons. How would *you* have brought the bell here without a crane and truck? In 1733, the Chinese slid it on ice in winter or on wheat shells in summer and put it on a mound. After attaching the bell onto the beams, the mound was dug out and then the hall was built around it. The 220,000 amazingly handsome Chinese characters decorating it are Buddhist scriptures and prayers.

The other bells in the exhibit were for various purposes. In religious ceremonies they drove away worldly worries and attracted the attention of the gods. Some bells here announced the time of day and the closing of the city gates. Some were used in music rituals. (See also ''Wuhan''). A small hall contains an exhibit on how the bells were made, unfortunately labeled only in Chinese.

DAY 4

Some people prefer to take their own box lunch to the Great Wall even though restaurants are available.

Great Wall—see separate listing.

Shisan Ling (Ming Tombs) 十三陵 , open daily 8 a.m.–4 p.m., are usually combined with a trip to the Great Wall at Badaling. They are a 50-km (1¾-hour) drive NW of the Tian Anmen. Avoid Sunday traffic jams.

These 13 imperial tombs were built from 1409 to 1644 and spread over 40 square km. Each tomb consists of a Soul Tower, a Sacrificial Hall, and an Underground Palace, surrounded by a wall. Approaching from the south, one sees a big, carved white marble archway, erected in 1590, beyond which are the Great Red Gate, ornamental pillars, and the Tablet Pavilion. The Sacred Way has 24 stone animals (lions, unicorns, camels, elephants, etc., 12 larger-than-life-size humans (military officers and government officials), and an army of enterprising hawkers (also an old China tradition) selling everything from furs, porcelain, and fruit to junk. The 400-year-old stone animals and figures cannot be mounted.

At least two of the tombs are open to visitors: **Chang Ling** 乾陵 , the biggest and earliest, and **Ding Ling** 定陵 , which has been excavated and can be entered. Ding Ling is the tomb of the 13th Ming Emperor Wanli, who ruled for 48 years, starting at age 10. The tomb was begun when he was 22 years old. It took six years and cost eight million taels of silver to build.

The underground palace consists of three halls, the central one with passages to annex chambers, totaling 1195 square meters. The marble doors each weigh four tons and were closed *from the inside* by propping two large stone poles against them. Note the two triangular depressions in the ground inside the door where the poles rested. Note also the blue and white porcelain jars with the dragons, which were half filled with oil when the tomb was opened. The oil was burned to create an oxygen-free vacuum inside.

In the central hall are three marble altars, two for the empresses, one for the emperor. Note the ''Five Altar Pieces'' and the porcelain lamp. The rear hall has the three coffins and plaster replicas of 26 chests. Don't miss the separate museum which has on display some of the objects found in the tomb, such as the gold crown, headdresses, a jade belt, and a gold bowl. A 20-minute movie about the opening of Ding Ling is shown. Ding Ling Restaurant nearby is okay. Many groups now eat at the exotic Ming Yuan Hotel a few km away.

Enjoy the rural beauty, the vast, open spaces between the tombs, and the peace when you escape the 10,000-a-day tourists and peddlers. If you have time, you should also wander around the other tombs, which are not repaired and are usually free of tourists. These other tombs are not opened because of the high cost of careful archaeological excavation. Besides, no one knows where the entrances are because their builders were executed and no records have survived. The tombs and the Great

Wall are best seen at dusk, when one feels the presence of ghosts. Seeing weeds growing on imperial terraces and birds making nests on once glorious beams is a good time to reflect on life and death. Think of the cracked roofs and fallen walls of the monuments you yourself have built.

But visit here soon. The Beijing Municipal Government and a Japanese firm have started work on a recreation complex with roller coasters, Ferris wheels, hotels, and camel-racing tracks. It is expected to be completed in 1990. An 18-hole golf course has already opened.

DAY 5

*Yonghegong (Lama Temple) 雍和宫 : Count on at least 40 minutes. The Temple of Harmony and Peace was first built in 1694. This Mongolian-Tibetan yellow-sect temple is within walking distance of the No. 2 Overseas Chinese Hotel 第二华侨饭店 . It should not be missed. Beautifully renovated, it reveals pavilion after pavilion of increasingly startling figures, the largest in the back hall 18 meters high. This Buddha was carved from one piece of sandalwood from Tibet and the temple was built around it.

The steles are incised with Han, Manchurian, Mongolian, and Tibetan script. The statues in the main halls resemble those in most Buddhist temples, but some statues do wear the pointed Himalayan caps and white Tibetan scarves, a traditional gift. On either side of the symmetrical structure, however, the more typically Tibetan demons, human skulls, and tankas are displayed. Another admission ticket is required for the exhibition hall that shows many Tibetan silver utensils of very intricate craftsmanship.

The Yonghegong was built in 1694 as an imperial residence for Emperor Yongzheng, then still a prince. It was transformed into a Lama temple in 1744 during Qianlong's reign. Prayer wheels are for sale. Closed Mondays.

This temple was an attempt by Emperor Qianlong to unite the Han, Manchu, Mongol, and Tibetan nationalities into one country. He also took a Uygur princess from what is now Xinjiang into his court as one of his favorite empresses. For more on Lamaism, see also ''Lhasa'' and ''Chengde.''

The **Shudian (Capital Museum)** 首都博物馆 is in the old Yuan dynasty **Confucius Temple** 孔庙 , almost across Yonghegong Avenue from the Lama Temple. It is the second largest Confucian temple in China (the largest is in Qufu, the hometown of the sage). The exhibits on Beijing history, Qing armor, and the stone drums are worth seeing. Look for maps and relics of the old Yuan city too.

If you want to see the work of contemporary artists, the **China Art Gallery** 中国美术馆 is open daily, 9 a.m.–5 p.m. April 30–May 13, closed on Mondays. It is about two blocks east of Jing Hill, itself behind the Forbidden City, and has changing exhibitions.

For *your last day and a half,* assuming you only have six days, you must choose from the following. If you want to do more, then you have to stay longer or come back again.

—**Arts and crafts factories:** favorites are cloisonne and ivory and jade carving. Travel agents can arrange.

—A **rural village or cooperative**

—The **Cultural Palace of the Nationalities** 民族文化宫 (Fuxingmennei Ave.), for those who have been or will be visiting areas where there are many groups of ethnic minorities. Its restaurant in the west wing arranges banquets with the food of the different nationalities. It houses exhibitions of the various ethnic groups. Disco dances of some Western subcultures have been held here three times a week from 8 p.m. to 2 a.m. Books and minority handicrafts for sale.

—Shopping

—**Daguanyuan (Grand View Garden)** is a 100,000 square-meter theme park in southwest Beijing inspired by one of China's greatest novels, the *Dream of the Red Chamber.* The buildings are sometimes staffed by actors dressed in Qing fashions as characters from the beloved novel.

—The **White Dagoba Monastery* 白塔寺 at Miaoyingsi (Temple of Excellent Confirmation) in Xichang is Yuan (1271). During repairs made in 1978 after the Tangshan earthquake, archaeologists found more than ten relics inside dated 1753, from the Qianlong emperor. He was indeed a busy man. These include a pure gold 5.4-centimeter-long gem-studded Buddha and a glazed Goddess of Mercy.

—The **Residence of Mme. Soong Ching-ling** is interesting not only because she was an illustrious humanitarian, the respected widow of Dr. Sun Yat-sen, but next to this house, Emperor Pu-yi (the "Last Emperor") was born. Canadians might be intrigued by a copy of Margaret Trudeau's book in the library. (Read *Soong Dynasty.*)

—**Niujiu Mosque** 牛街回民区 : In the southeast part of the city, where about 10,000 Moslems live on Niujiu Street, this mosque is primarily for visitors with an interest in Islam and religious buildings. You should phone ahead for reservations (tel. 557824), though you might take a chance and just drop in. The mosque was founded in the Liao dynasty (A.D. 996) by the Arabian scholar Nasullindin and rebuilt and enlarged in subsequent dynasties. Although it is in classical Chinese architecture, the interior does have west Asian arches and Arabic writing. Note the curtained-off section for women. Open daily 8 a.m.–10 p.m. (See also "What Is There to See and Do.")

—**Beijing Gu Guanxiangtai* (Ancient astronomical observatory) 古天文台 (Jianguomen Ave., near the Friendship Store and Jianguo

Hotel) was built in 1442 (Ming) and has some instruments dating from 1437 to 1442. Good for a history of Chinese astronomy, with many Qing exhibits as well.

—**Beiyunguan (Temple of White Clouds)** 白云寺 , outside Fuxingmenwai, southwest of Beijing TV, is the largest Taoist Temple in China. Built originally in the Tang, it burned down in the Jin and was rebuilt in the Ming. During the Qing, it was enlarged. It has some striking incense burners and gilded statues, including that of Taishang Laojun, the initiator of Taoism. Open every Tuesday and Friday from 9 a.m. to 10 p.m. Attended by young men in Taoist robes and long hair. A visit takes about two hours. See *Taoism* in ''What Is There to See and Do?''

The only nunnery open is the **Tongjiao Nunnery** (Zhen Xian Lane, Beixiao St., in the Eastern District). Established during the Ming, it now has 30 nuns. Public religious ceremonies are held once a week.

Among the recently opened tourist attractions is **Prince Gong's Mansion** (23 Lu Yin Jie), built from 1776 to 1785 and owned at one time by the great-uncle of the Last Emperor. Open daily.

The **International Club** 国际俱乐部 (Jianguomenwai Ave., near the Friendship Store and Jianguo Hotel) is a place for homesick foreigners. Open 9 a.m.–9:30 p.m. Usually there is no need to show a passport. It has a coffee shop and dining room (12–2:30 p.m. and 6–8:30 p.m) with Western food. Reasonable prices. Movies (U.S., Hong Kong, and Chinese) are shown most evenings (sometimes with English subtitles.) The swimming pool is open in summer. Tennis. Disco dancing.

Bicycle Rentals: A rental shop is opposite the Friendship Store (Jianguomenwai Ave.; tel. 592391). Also see ''Hotels.''

Walks: Around the Xinqiao Hotel for the old European architecture. This foreign legation area was under siege during the Boxer invasion, from June 13, 1900. On June 20, most foreign diplomats and missionaries and 2000 Chinese Christian refugees took shelter in the British Legation until the International Relief Force arrived on August 13. That British Legation building has been torn down to make way for a housing project.

The area around the Minzu Hotel and the Xi Dan Market toward the Forbidden City is full of old houses, antique doors, carvings, grinding stones used as steps, and fancy, carved stone door hinges. The back alleys with tiny houses and crowded courtyards with paper windows, are also fascinating.

The names of the alleys immediately around the Forbidden City are appealing. Nai Zi Hutong (Wet Nurse Lane) was the street where the new mothers who nursed the imperial babies lived. Flower Lane was for those who handmade all the silk flowers for the imperial ladies. There were also Goldsmith Lane, Laundry Lane, and Bowstrings Lane.

NIGHT LIFE AND CULTURAL EVENTS
The best of China is here: opera, ballet, symphony orchestras, movies, acrobats, gymnastics. (See also *Go to Cultural Events* in "What Is There to See and Do?") The main hotels and the International Club frequently offer movies and ballroom and disco dancing. The larger hotels also offer cocktail lounges with live music. The trendy (for China) **Je Je's Cafe** (92 Chaoyang Men Wei) is a modest after-hours coffee shop and bar that accepts RMBs and is genuinely "local."

Beijing also has a Central Conservatory for Music, which gives many excellent concerts of Western and Chinese music. It is located in an alley across the street from the Nationalities Cultural Palace. You could ask these musicians to perform for your "distinguished" group if you want.

DAY TRIPS
The **Tan Zhe Si** 潭拓寺 and **Hui Zhi Si** are only 6 km apart, so can be seen in one day, but they are not very exciting. Southwest of Beijing, they make a pleasant excursion into the mountains. The Tan Zhe Si has its roots in the Tang. During the Yuan, the daughter of Kublai Khan is said to have resided at the Tan Zhe Si to try to atone for her father's sins. In 1888 a Qing prince retired here. After the 1911 Revolution many foreigners used it as a summer resort, and after Liberation it was a workers' health spa. The Ming temple bell here is over 400 years old.

Lugouqiao (Reed Valley Bridge) a.k.a. Marco Polo Bridge 芦沟 is 20 km SW of the city. Primarily of interest to historians, it is not all that beautiful. Built in the 12th century, it is 250 meters long with 11 stone arches and 485 stone lions spaced along its railings, each one different. The bridge is named for Marco Polo because the Venetian explorer described it at length in his book. It is the site of the incident that touched off the Japanese war on July 7, 1937. The bridge was renovated in the late 1980s with the addition of a museum of Chinese resistance to the Japanese invaders.

*Zhoukoudian 周口店 (48 km south of Beijing) is where the Peking Man, who lived 400,000–500,000 years ago, was found in a cave in 1927. At least 44 skulls have been discovered there. A small museum has some relics, but many of the bones were lost during the Japanese war. A model of the area is in the Museum of Chinese History in Beijing.

New scenic tourist spots in the area are Shidu (Tenth Ferry) River Valley, the Long Qing Gorge Reservoir, and White Dragon Pool.

See also "Zunhua" for Qing tombs.

For **overnight trips,** see "Chengde" (3 days), "Tianjin," "Shijiazhuang," "Beidaihe," "Shanhaiguan," and "Datong."

TRAINS TO THE SOVIET UNION

The better train is the Chinese one, leaving on Wednesdays via Datong. The Russian train leaves on Saturdays via Shenyang and Harbin. They take seven days to reach Moscow. Tickets can be bought at C.I.T.S. (Beijing International Hotel). However, give yourself at least two weeks in Beijing to get all the visas. You have to get a visa for your farthest point first, before you can get the others.

FESTIVALS

The week before and after the lunar new year, a temple fair takes place at the Temple of the Earth, the Ditan. Folk shows during tourist season Tuesdays, Thursdays, Saturdays, and Sundays. Ice sculpture shows. Golden Autumn Festival at the Yuanmingyuan. Dragon boat races. Kite-flying contests.

SHOPPING

Beijing has the best shopping after Shanghai. The Beijing Tourism Administration has a list of shops approved for foreign visitors. Most stores are open 8:30 or 9 a.m. to 7 or 8:30 p.m. Available are goods from all over the country (at higher prices, of course). Made locally are cloisonne, lacquerware, jade carving, filigree jewelry, carpets, and woodblock prints. Cheap souvenirs are the yogurt containers that say "Beijing Dairy" in Chinese, available from the supermarket at the Friendship Store. Also made locally are felt hats and track suits.

The main shopping street is **Wangfujing Ave.** 王府井 , along the east side of the Beijing Hotel. Resident foreigners check shopping bags at the desk under the international clocks of this hotel while they go out for more. You might want to do that too. On this street are **Beijing Department Store** 北京百货公司 (on west side; tel. 556761), **Jianhua Fur Store** (#192; tel. 556557), **Beijing Arts and Crafts** 北京工艺美术公司 (on east side; tel. 556806), and the large **Xinhua Book Store** 新华书店, , with books in English as well as Chinese. The **Marco Polo Shop** at 86–88 (tel. 555380) specializes in jewelry. **The Yuan Long Embroidery Silk Co.** (55 Tiantan Rd.) has a good selection of silk textiles as well as jewelry, carpets, embroidery, furs, and silk clothes. Tel. 754059, 753287.

There are art reproductions at Rong Bao Zhai (tel. 333352), but the largest collection of stores selling antiques and arts and crafts is **Liulichang** 兆龙饭店 (on both sides of Nanxinhua), the main street where the buses stop. Open 9 a.m.–5:30 p.m. (winter) or to 6 p.m. (summer). In 1277, glazed tiles were made here. In the Qing, it was a market with 140 shops selling the same sort of arts it does today, including reproductions of paintings, the Dunhuang murals, bronzes, and porcelains. Some frequent shoppers feel prices here are better than at the Friendship Store. It is less crowded too.

Some U.S. name-brand, factory-overrun clothing has been found in **Dazalan** (the area south of the Qian Men, with the air raid shelter) and on Gongren Tiyuchang Road, near Workers' Stadium. Cheaper than in the U.S. A very good market for export-quality goods is between the Jianguo Hotel and Friendship Store on Xiushui East St.

Beijing Huaxia Arts and Crafts Shop (12 Dong Cheng Qu, Chong Nei Da Jia, tel. 541754, 546019; branch at 293 Wangfujing St., tel. 551819) is known also as the **Theater Shop** because of its theatrical costumes. Also secondhand goods (antique clocks, brass, furs, furniture, etc.).

Friendship Store 友谊商店 (Jianguomenwai Ave. near the Jianguo Hotel; tel. 5003311; service dept., tel. 483893): One can buy any crafts made locally, plus furs, down coats, and even fresh flowers, etc. The Friendship Store can reset jewelry. Also has a snack bar and a good supermarket. And a tailor here does a reasonable job in three weeks. Merchandise bought here can be easily customs-cleared and packed for shipping.

Marco Polo Shop 懋隆商店 (Temple of Heaven, near West Gate, Temple of Heaven; tel. 754940): arts, crafts, reproductions.

Marco Polo Carpet Shop: Hall No. 7, Beijing Agricultural Exhibition Hall, tel. 582331 x301, 304.

A large **free market** is at Beitaitingzhan 北太平庄 , beyond the northern moat. Another is along the NE edge of the Temple of Heaven grounds.

RESTAURANTS

(See also *Food* under "Useful Phrases" and "Food.") Beijing food is much like Shandong's, but influenced by the imperial kitchens. It is usually salty (as opposed to sweet), but is not highly spiced. Sauces are less frequently used than in Cantonese cooking. Everyone must try Peking duck at least once! The best part is the crispy skin, which is dipped in sweet, dark brown *hoisin* sauce, seasoned with a green onion, and then wrapped in a thick pancake and eaten by hand. Worth trying, especially on those early morning walks, are the rolls, or the Chinese equivalent of doughnuts—the long, deep-fried "oil sticks" 油条 —dipped in sweetened hot soy milk (cheap). Also famous are the *baozhe* 包子 , meat dumplings either steamed or boiled in soup.

Also local is Mongolian food, especially hot pot and barbecue.

Beijing is a gourmet's delight, with excellent food from all over the country and the world. The current "in" restaurants for foreign business people seem to be **Windows on the World** (28th and 29th floors, CITIC Building, 19 Jianguomenwui; tel. 5005333), and the Shangri-la Hotel. Unique are the previously mentioned **Tingliguan (Pavilion for Listening to Orioles)** in the Summer Palace (tel. 283955) and the **Fang Shan Restaurant** 仿膳 in Beihai Park (along the lake by the White Dagoba; tel. 442573). Their cooks were taught by the Empress Dowager's own cooks. Some popular restaurants, particularly the Fang Shan and the **Wangfujing Beijing Duck Restaurant** 王府井 烤鸭店 (tel. 553310) may require reservations well in advance. Resident foreigners dub this duck restaurant the ''Sick Duck'' because it is near the Capital Hospital. Another exotic experience is lunch or dinner at the **Great Hall of the People.** See *Day 1* above.

Some foreigners have celebrated their weddings with dinner on a boat in Kunming Lake at the Summer Palace, or enjoyed picnic suppers on the night of a full moon at the Ming Tombs. Another special and exotic experience is **Miss Lili's,** a one-table ten-seat restaurant in a private home. In a lane full of tiny old Manchu houses it's across the lake from Soong Ching-ling's residence. Great imperial cooking and classy table settings. A reservation is required months in advance and a party of ten get priority (of course). Set menu. Please do not cancel without notice; the restaurant will have bought food only for you. This restaurant is very difficult to find, with no sign outside the gate. Have your driver telephone 6011915 for directions.

For budget travelers, there's the cafeteria at the Xinqiao Hotel and the International Club. Chinese food is good and reasonably priced at the Beijing Hotel. For good noodles, try the Minzu Hotel and the Overseas Chinese Hotel #2. A favorite of budget travelers is the ''Rosenbec'' shop at the Xinqiao Hotel.

OTHER RECOMMENDED RESTAURANTS:

Dasanyuan Restaurant 大三元饭店 • *Jingshan Xi St.; tel. 44–5376.*

Healthy Restaurant 长寿餐厅 • *16, Taiping Lane, West City* • Recommended mainly because of the novelty, although the food is good too. This restaurant is part of a Chinese medicine factory, and its dishes, a combination of food and tonics, are designed to cure a variety of ailments from high blood pressure to whatever.

Henan Restaurant 河南饭店 • *behind the Minzu Hotel; tel. 86–2178* • Good food, friendly concerned manager, Mrs. Hong. Henan food.

International Club Nakabachi, Cherry Garden • *11 Ritan Rd., Jianguomenwei, tel. 5004275* • Steak House Teppanyaki.

Liyuan Restaurant • *8 Xihuang Chenggen N. St., Xicheng Dist, tel. 6015234* • Thai. Open until 11 p.m. Manager speaks English.

Mongolian Restaurant • *Meng Gu Kao Ru, Qian Men St.*

Peking Roast-Duck Restaurant 北京烤鸭店 • *Hepingmen; tel. 334422* • a.k.a. Wall Street Duck to local foreigners because a wall was once beside it, of course. An old six-story restaurant.

Qianmen Peking Duck Restaurant 前门烤鸭店 • a.k.a. ''Big Duck.'' Tends to mass-produce duck dinners for tourists, but it's good.

Ritan Park Restaurant • *southwest corner of Ritan Park, within sight of sign on top of CITIC Building; tel. 592648* • In a palace. Sichuan, Huiyang, and Imperial food. Not always good.

Sichuan Fan Dian 四川饭店 • *Rongxian Hutong, Xuanwumennei Ave.; tel. 336844* • Sichuan.

For **suggested Beijing dishes,** see ''Food.''

For **Western food,** many of the newer luxury hotels have very good restaurants with a wide variety of food, especially the Jianguo, Shangri-La, Great Wall, and Lido. Good homestyle German food is available, and the Kentucky Fried Chicken restaurant is at the south end of Tiananmen Square, a half block west, at Qianmen Xi Ave., Zheng Yang Market, tel. 541415. The Movenpick has imported Swiss ice cream. The Park has good Korean barbeque.

Maxim's • *2, Qianmen Dong Ave.; tel. 512–1992* • Opened in 1983 by Pierre Cardin himself. Reputation good. Extremely expensive. Also Happy Hours and dancing. Closed Sundays. Minim's, next door, is cheaper.

Snack Bar at Friendship Store • If you're desperate for a cheap hamburger and a Coke. Outdoor patio open in summer.

HOTELS

We couldn't sleep in them all to test the service but the best-looking hotel currently is the Shangri-La, followed closely by the Great Wall and the Lido. The Jianguo and Beijing-Toronto are also near the top. The Palace, Chang Fu Gong, the new Palace Tower of the Beijing, and China World Hotels should also be very good after they get some experience. The Kunlun is good but a little shabby. The Huadu, Guanghua, and the Beijing are good value for the money. The Diaoyutai is in a class by itself, some villas fit for queens but others lacking in some services.

Among the cheaper hotels, the Xiyuan and Zhaolong look good. Even cheaper is the Qianmen, a little scuffy but okay.

In traditional Chinese-style architecture are the Palace, Movenpick, the villa used by Queen Elizabeth in the Diaoyutai, and the two hotels in the Summer Palace. Most other hotels look like you never left home.

We consider the best *location* for tourists the Beijing Hotel, which is the closest hotel to Tian Anmen Square, the Forbidden City, main museums, and the main shopping street. Also within walking distance of these are the Peace and Palace. Due in 1990 are the 350-room Holiday Inn Crowne Plaza, the Tianlun, and the SARA Hotel, all aiming for five stars and all on Wangfujing St. These will also be within walking distance of the Forbidden City. About 4 km east is the next-best area, centered around the Friendship Store, CITIC, Noble Tower, International Club, and near one of the embassy areas. Also in the neighborhood is the China World Trade Center. Here you will find the Chang Fu Gong, Trader's, Guanghua, Jianguo, Beijing-Toronto, and China World Hotel—the best-located for business people. The new Beijing International Hotel is between them and the Beijing Hotel, close to the railway station in the second-best area for tourists. You can walk to the other two from here.

Still central but farther out is the Qianmen. Toward the airport and close to the International Exhibition center and diplomatic areas are the Huadu, the Great Wall, the Lufthansa Center, and the Kunlun (within walking distance of each other). The Zhaolong is between the Kunlun and Beijing-Toronto.

Farther out, side by side, are the Yanxiang, Holiday Inn Lido, and the budget-priced Si Hai Hotel. This area is a meeting place for local foreign residents and is closest to the airport.

Tour buses pick up individual tourists at the Lido, Great Wall, and Jinglun hotels. The China World and Shangri-La hotels are the only ones found with rooms specially made for travelers confined to wheelchairs, though such travelers have told us that the Huadu, with its ramps, is okay.

You could contact any hotel directly or Beijing Tourism Administration, 13 Xia Gong Fu St. Tel. 550490, 551365. Telex 22489 BTTC CN. Cable 8049 for more information.

The Dabei Hotel • *across from the World Trade Center* • has been the best value for budget travelers.

Beijing (Peking) Hotel (Beijing Fandian) • *33 Chang'an East Ave; cable 6531. Telex 22426 BHCTL CN, Fax 5137307 Dist.A.P.30 km. Dist.R.W.2 km* • T.R, C.C. (no Diner's). Middle wing (1915) and west wing (1954), 300 rooms. The east wing (1974, ren. 1989), 600 rooms.

New five-star wing Palace Tower (Gui Bin Lou) due late 1989 with 280 rooms, some overlooking the Forbidden City. IDD. Good shopping. Domestic airline booking desk, post office, bank.

Beijing International Hotel (Beijing Guoji Fandian) • *9 Jianguo-menwai Ave. 100005; Telex 211121 BIH CN, Fax 5129972, Dist.A.P.28 km. Dist.R.W.0.5 km Dist. Forbidden City 1.5 km* • C.C Prefers reservations by EECO system. Mainly for tour groups. Grand opening due mid-1989. 29 stories, 1047 rooms. Business center. IDD. Italian and vegetarian food. Should also have Japanese food, gym, indoor pool, tennis, bowling, USTV, and Air China and Air Iran offices.

Beijing-Toronto Hotel (Jinglun Fandian) • *3 Jianguomenwai; Cable 5650. Telex 210012 JLH CN, Fax 5002022. Dist.A.P.30 km. Dist.R.W.3 km* • T.R., C.C. 1984, ren. 1989. 659-room, 12-story glitzy hotel with over-sized beds. Indoor pool, health club, business center. Aeroflot, Dragonair, United Airlines, Air China and American Express offices. Managed by Nikko Hotels International.

Chang Fu Gong Hotel (Chang Fu Gong Fandian) • *Jianguomen-wai Dajie; Telex 210342 BCFGC CN. Fax 5125346* • Managed by New Otani International. Grand opening due mid-1989. 25 stories, 512 rooms. Japanese food. IDD. JAL office. Pool, tennis, gym, business center.

China World Hotel (Guoji Mao Yi Zhong Xin) • *1 Jianguomen-wai Ave.; Telex 211206 CWHCN. Fax 5005258 In China World Trade Center east of the Beijing-Toronto Hotel* • Office tower and apartments in same complex. Dist.A.P.33 km. Dist.R.W.5 km. Managed by Shangri-La International. 1989. 21 stories, 743 rooms. T.R., C.C. "No Smoking" floor. Gym, squash, tennis, USTV, pool, bowling, fitness and business centers, IDD. Deli, drugstore, 24-hour room service, cake shop. Trader's Hotel here cheaper.

Club Med • *Summer Palace (Yiheyuan)* • Two villas, entrances less than one km north and south of the main Palace entrance. Few services. Hard to get room. Information from Club Med, Hong Kong.

Diaoyutai State Guest House (Diaoyutai Guo Bingguan) • *San-lihe Rd., western Beijing; Telex 22798 DYTSG CN. Fax 8013362. Dist.A.P.35 km. Dist.R.W.10 km.* • T.R., C.C. 1959. Government guest house set on 42 acres of old Imperial gardens. 15 separate villages with individual rooms available. The beautiful temple-like Villa #18, renovated for Queen Elizabeth II, can be booked for US$20,000 per day. IDD, pool, gym, tennis. No travel service.

Beijing-Toronto Hotel (Jing Lun Guan Fandian) • *133 Xi Zhu Men Wai St; Fax 8021450. Cable 1717. Telex 22395 BECH CN. Dist.A.P.40 km. Dist.R.W.14 km.* • Next to Beijing Exhibition Center. T.R., C.C. 1988. 7 stories, 250 rooms. Small tubs.

Fragrant Hills Hotel (Xiangshan Fandian) • *Xiangshan Park, Haidian District. Cable 7391. Telex 222202 FHH CN. Dist.A.P.40 km. Dist.R.W.30 km* • Rural setting near superb temples. Great for hikers. T.R., C.C. 1982, ren. every three years from 1988. Three and four stories, 292 rooms with view of greenery. Beautiful, austere-looking public areas. Grubby carpets, but otherwise fine. Pool, business center, IDD. Architect: I. M. Pei.

Friendship Hotel (Youyi Bingguan) • *Bashiqiao 3 Rd; Fax 8314661. Cable 2222. Telex 222362 BJFH CN. Dist.A.P.33 km. Dist.R.W.16 km. NW of residential suburbs* • Closest large hotel to Beijing and Qinghua Universities. C.C. Five- and six-story buildings of different qualities. 800 rooms for foreign tourists. 1952; #5 Building ren. 1988, #1 Building ren. 1990, #2 Building ren. 1987. No IDD. Subway stop nearby. Free shuttle bus to Tian An Men. Pool, gym, Suzhou garden, vast grounds. Business center. Badly laid carpets, glue on walls. Japanese, Russian, and Arabian-style food. We highly recommend that guests read *Love in Beijing* by William Goede.

Grand Hotel • *Hong Kong Macao Center. 1 Chao Yang Men Bei Da Jie (2nd Ring Road) at North Gong Ren Ti Yu Chang Rd, about 2 km north of CITIC Bldg.* • Partial opening due in early 1990. Managed by Swissotel. 18 stories, 500 rooms, Aiming for five stars. 15-story office and 15-story residential tower in same complex. 24-hour room service, pool, health and recreation centers. IDD, business center, clinic, delicatessen/bakery, nightclub, executive apartments.

Great Wall Sheraton (Changcheng Fandian) • *Donghuan Bei Rd. Chaoyang Dist. 100026. Telex 22002 GWHBJ CN; Fax 5003398. Dist.A.P.25 km. Dist.R.W.9 km. Near Chaoyang Golf Course* • Reservations strongly suggested all year. T.R., C.C. 1985; ren. 1989. 1,004 rooms, 21 stories in central block. No smoking areas in coffee shop. Pool, health club, tennis courts, mini-golf. 24-hour business center with 24-hour printing service, CAAC (international), and C.I.T.S. IDD, USTV, simultaneous translations facilities, shuttle service, French restaurant, bicycles, shuttle bus. Patterned after glitzy Dallas hotel.

Guang Hua Hotel (Guang Hua Fandian) • *38 Donghuan Bei Rd; Cable 5929. Telex 211234 GHHCN. Dist.A.P.33 km. Dist.R.W.6 km.*

Good location • 1967, ren. 1988. Four stories, 100 rooms. Should have C.C., IDD, and bar now. No elevators or business center. Rooms spacious but a little grubby. Handshowers, chipped dishes.

Hilton International Beijing • *Third Ring Rd. in embassy area, adjacent to Oriental Arts Bldg.* • Theatre. 400 rooms. Will have Japanese restaurant, pool, ballroom, sports facilities, health club, and executive floors. Due late 1990.

Holiday Inn Crowne Plaza • *Wangfujing and Dengsikou Dajie* • Partial opening due October 1990. 400 rooms. Health club, indoor pool, C.C.

Holiday Inn Financial Center • *98 Bei Lishi Rd. Xichengqu, in financial district opposite the Bank of China headquarters on Second Ring Rd.* • Partial opening due late 1990. C.C. Health club, indoor pool.

Holiday Inn Grand View Garden • *beside park* • Based on the setting of the famous Qing novel *Dream of the Red Chamber.* Aiming for five stars. Partial opening due October 1990. 500 rooms. Check with Holiday Inn.

Holiday Inn Lido (Lido Fandian) • *Jichang Rd., Jiang Tai Rd. 100004; Telex 22618 LIDOH CN. Fax 5006237. Cable 8333. Dist.A.P.17 km. Dist.R.W.15 km.* • T.R., C.C. 1984–85, ren. (500 rooms) 1989. Total 1029 rooms. World's largest Holiday Inn. IDD, USTV, supermarket. 20-lane bowling center, health club, indoor pool, squash, tennis. Pizzeria, deli, noodle house, pub, German farmhouse food. No smoking area in coffee shop. Apartments, office block, CAAC international booking office. Schools and kindergarten on premises. Free shuttle bus.

Huadu Hotel (Huadu Fandian) • *8 Xinyuan South Rd., Chaoyang Dist; Telex 22028 HUADU CN, Telex reservations 211112 HDRSV. Fax 5001615. Cable 5431* • T.R., C.C. Dist.A.P.25 km. Dist.R.W.9 km. 1982, ren. 1989. Six stories, 71 rooms and suites. Should have IDD by now. Business center. Luggage repairs.

Huaqiao (Huiqiao Fandian) • *Heping Li Dong St., Bei Tu Cheng; Telex 210324 HQH CN. Dist.A.P.30 km. Dist.R.W.13 km* • No. C.C. Near China-Japan Hospital and University of International Business. One block beyond end of 119 bus line (from Ditan Park). 1986. 228 rooms. Not elegant, old plumbing, but good value for money. Budget travelers only.

Jianguo Hotel (Jianguo Fandian) • *Jianguomenwai Dejie; Telex 22439 JGHBJ CN. Fax 5002871. Dist.A.P.30 km. Dist.R.W.3 km* • T.R., C.C. Reservations recommended most of the year. Managed by Swiss-Belhotel. 1982, ren. 1989. Mediterranean style. 4 stories with 9-story tower; 386 rooms, 72 suites. Japanese food, IDD, 24-hour room service, business center. Heated pool, acupuncture, gourmet food/bake shop. Northwest, CAIL, and Cathay Pacific airline offices.

Jing Guang Centre • 452 rooms. Due end of 1989. 51-story bldg. With apartments and offices. New World International management.

Kunlun Hotel (Kunlun Fandian) • *2 Xin Yuan Nan Rd., Chao yang Dist; Cable 2745. Telex 210327, 210328, or 211166 BJKLH CN. Fax 5003228. Dist.A.P.25 km. Dist.R.W.9 km* • C.C. 1986–88. 28 stories, 853 rooms, 74 office suites. C.I.T.S. Pool, tennis, revolving restaurant, rooftop helipad. Japanese and French restaurants, IDD, shuttle bus. Workmanship poor.

Lu Song Yuan Hotel • *22 Ban Chang Hutong (bus #104)* • 120 beds, dorms. Affiliated with the International Youth Hostel Federation. 1992.

Lufthansa Center • *600 rooms. 1990. Lufthansa office, apartments, clinic, and kindergarten.*

Ming Yuan Hotel • *Huzhuang, the Ming Tombs, Changping; Telex 222486 EMYH CN* • Near Ming Tombs, Great Wall, and Beijing International Golf Club. Charming Chinese garden style architecture. 148 rooms, sauna.

Movenpick Hotel Dragon Spring (Long Quan Bingguan) • *Shui Zha Bei Lu, Men Tou Gou Dist., (P.O. Box 9083); Telex 222292 DSHBJ CN. Fax 3014377. Dist.A.P.60 km. Dist.R.W.25 km* • Quiet location, on 16 acres in western suburbs bordering on reservoir. Near factories, far from downtown nightlife. Workmanship poor. C.C. 1987, ren. 1989. 235 rooms, Eight rambling one- and two-story buildings. Can arrange concerts and acrobatic performances. Swiss-style food. 25-meter pool, tennis, gym, IDD, bicycles, free shuttle bus, clinic. Dim reading lamps. Affiliated with Radisson Hotels.

Overseas Chinese Hotel (Huaqiao Fandian) • *5 Beixingqiao 3-Tiao, 100004; cable 8010. Telex 210336 BOCH CN. Fax (01) 4012386. Near Lama Temple* • 1950s, ren. 1987. 174 rooms. Slightly scruffy, poor drapes. Not much English. IDD in office only. For budget travelers only.

Palace Hotel (Wangfu Fandian) • *Jinyu Hutung, off Wangfujing; Telex 222696 PALBJ CN. Fax 5129050. Cable PALACE HOTELBJ. Dist.A.P.35 km* • C.C. Partial opening 1989. 15 stories, 570 rooms. Duplex suites, executive floors. IDD. Managed by the Manila Hotel International. French, Italian, Bavarian, and Japanese cuisine. Indoor pool, fitness and business centers, deli, simultaneous translation facilities. Rolls Royces.

Peace Hotel (Heping Bingguan) • *3 Jinyu Hutung, Wangfujing, Dong Cheng District; Cable 5131 (Reserve by cable)* • Great location. 1952. Partial opening of 500-room tower in 1988. 22 stories. Cafeteria, Qing Imperial food, British and French cuisine. Pool, gym, tennis.

Qianmen Hotel (Qianmen Fandian) • *175 Yongan Rd., Hepingmenwai; Cable 8710. Telex 222382 QMHTL CN. Dist.A.P.36 km. Dist.R.W.6 km. Dist. Liulichang 1 km* • T.R., no C.C. for room. 1956, ren. 1987. 8 stories, 410 rooms, IDD, business center. French and Russian food.

Ramada Asia Hotel • *2 Xinzhong Xi Jie, Gongti Bei Rd; Telex 211138 AHR CN. Fax 5005466. Near Workers Stadium, convenient to embassies* • Due 1990. 300 rooms. IDD, Mediterranean and Korean food, pizza, noodle shop. Pool, health club, business center.

SARA Hotel Beijing • *2 Wangfujing St.* • Due late 1990. Eleven stories, 400 rooms. Continental food, health club, office space. Same management as Golden Flower Hotel (Xi'an).

Shangri-La Hotel (Shangri-La Fandian) • *29 Zizhuyuan Rd. 100081; Telex 222231 SHABJ CN. Fax 8021471. Dist.A.P.35 km. Dist.R.W.15 km* • Inconvenient location but close to Negotiation Bldg. T.R., C.C. Managed by Shangri-La International. 1986–87. 24 stories, 742 rooms, 44 offices. Executive floors and golf-driving range due. Tennis, pool, Qigong, gym. 24-hour business center. ''No smoking'' floor. USTV. Continental and Italian cuisine. The Chinese pronounce the name ''Shang Gorilla.''

Summer Palace Guest House • *Summer Palace (Yiheyuan).*

Trader's Hotel see China World Hotel.

Xiyuan Hotel (Xiyuan Fandian) • *5 Erliguo, Xizhimenwai St; Telex 22831-22835 XYH CN. Fax 8314577. Dist.A.P.30 km. Dist.R.W.13 km. Close to Negotiation Bldg.* • T.R., C.C. 1984–85. 26 stories, 749 beautifully decorated rooms. Conference facilities, pool, gym. IDD. 709 more rooms due. In 1986. Revolving restaurant (tacky with poor carpets), shuttle bus.

Yanxiang Hotel (Fandian) ● *A2 Jiang Tai Rd., Chaoyang Dist; Cable SWALLOW. Telex 210014 YXH CN. Fax 5006231. Dist.A.P.17 km. Dist.R.W.15 km* ● Some guests walk to the Holiday Inn next door for better services. T.R., no C.C. 1985, some ren. 1988. 400 rooms. Pool, IDD. A bit scruffy, dark halls. Mainly groups.

Zhaolong Hotel (Fandian) ● *2 Congtibei, Chaoyang Dist. 100026; Cable 4559. Telex 210079 ZLH CN. Fax 5003319. Dist.A.P.28 km. Dist.R.W.6 km* ● T.R., C.C. 1985. 270 rooms. Pool, IDD. A bit scruffy.

OTHER IMPORTANT ADDRESSES
Airlines:

Air China: tel. 4013331
Aeroflot: tel. 5232181, 5233581.
Air France: tel. 5233487, 5233894.
All Nippon Airways: tel. 5125551.
British Airways: tel. 5124070, 5124075.
CAAC 中国民航 : 117 Dongsi Ave. Information tel. 558861, 557591. International tel. 556720, 554175, 473228. Domestic tel. 553245, 554415. Airport tel. 558341, X2917.
CAAC booking offices: domestic, Beijing Hotel; international, Great Wall and Lido Hotels. The new CAAC ticketing center should be open in the future (at the west side of the telegram office building on West Chang'an Ave.).
Canadian Airlines International Limited: tel. 5001956.
Cathay Pacific: tel. 5002233, X152, 5003339.
Ethiopian Airlines: tel. 5233285.
Finnair: tel. 5127180
Iranair: tel. 5233249, 5233843.
Japan Airlines: tel. 5002221.
LOT: tel. 5002233 X139.
Lufthansa: tel. 5123535.
Northwest: tel. 5002233.
Philippine Air Lines: tel. 5233992.
PIA: tel. 523274, 523989.
Qantas: Hotel Beijing-Toronto, tel. 5002481.
SAS: tel. 5120575.
SIA: tel. 5004138.
Swissair: tel. 5123555, 5123556.
Thai: tel. 5123881-3
United Airlines: tel. 5128888.
Airport 北京机场 **:** Plane inquiries: tel. 552515, 555531, X382.

American Express: Shop D, Lobby, Beijing Toronto (Jinglun) Hotel, tel. 5001841, 5001733; telex: 210172 AMEXB CN; fax: 5001841.

Bank of China 中国银行 : Bank of China Bldg., Fuchengmen Nei Dajie; tel. 6016688. Telex 22254 or 22289 BCHO CN. Cable HO-CHUNGKUO BEIJING. Foreign exchange counters in most major hotels, tourist stores, and some tourist attractions.

Beijing City Bus Tours: tel. 5004488 X411.

Beijing Tourist Bureau: tel. 550490.

China-Canada Trade Council: Suite 27E, CITIC Bldg. 19 Jianguomenwai St.; tel. 500225 X2765, 2766. Telex 22929 CCTC CN. Fax 512–6125.

China Sports Travel Service: tel. 5112859.

China Youth Travel: tel. 546974.

CITIC International Building: 19 Jianguomenwai Dajie; tel. 5002255.

C.I.T.S. National Headquarters 中国国际旅行社全国总社 : 6 Chang'an Dong Ave.; tel. 5125385. Telex 22350 CITSH CN. Cable CITSH. Fax 5122068.

C.I.T.S. Beijing Branch 中国国际旅行社北京分社 : Chongwenmen Xi Ave., ground floor Chongwenmen Hotel; tel. 5122211, 5122443, 5122448.

C.T.S. and Overseas Chinese Travel Service 中国旅行社 : Chongwenmen Xi Ave.; tel. 5122211, 5122245. Also 2 Qianmen Dong Ave. and Xuanwenmen Hotel.

Thomas Cook: Room 803, Chongwenmen Hotel, tel. 5122211, X663, telex: 22032 BCTS CN.

DHL: tel. 486761.

Embassies: See also "Useful Phrases."

Australia 澳大利亚大使馆 : 15 Dongzhimenwai St., Sanlitun; tel. 5322331.

Britain 英国大使馆 : 22 Kuanghua Rd., Jianguomenwai; tel. 5321961.

Canada 加拿大大使馆 : 10 Sanlitun Rd., Chao Yang District; tel. 5323536; Trade Annex, 2–4–1 Tayuan Bldg., 14 Liang Ma He Nan Rd; tel. 523031. Telex 22717 CANAD CN.

France 法国大使馆 : 3 Sanlitun Rd., Chao Yang District; tel. 5321331, 5321332.

Democratic Republic of Germany 德国民主共和国大使馆 . (Open Wed. and Fri. a.m., 9–12 only.) Dong Fourth St., #3 Sanlitun; tel. 5321631.

Federal Republic of Germany, 5 Dong Zhimen Wai St., Chaoyang District; tel. 5322161.

Japan 日本大使馆 : 7 Ritan Rd., Jianguomenwai; tel. 5322361.

Mongolia 蒙古共和国大使馆 : tel. 5321203; 2 Xiushui Bei Jie. (Open Mon., Wed., Fri., 8:30 to 10:30 a.m.) Accepts only US$ for visas.

New Zealand 新西兰大使馆 : 1 Ritan Donger St., Chaoyang District; tel. 5322731.

Philippines 菲律宾大使馆 : 23 Xiu Shui Bei St., Jianguomen-wai; tel. 5322794.

Poland 波兰大使馆 : 2 Ritan Rd.; tel. 5321235. (Open Mon., Tues., Wed., Fri., 8:30 to 11:30 a.m.)

Switzerland 瑞士大使馆 : 3 Dongwu St.; tel. 5322736, 5322637.

U.S. 美国大使馆 : Xiushui Dongjie 1 (Chancery), tel. 5323831. Bruce Bldg., Xiushui Dongjie 2 (American Citizen Services), tel. 5323831, ext. 250. 17 Guanghua Rd. (Press and Culture), tel. 5321161.

U.S.S.R. 俄国大使馆 : Dongzhimen Bei Zhong Jie #4 (Open Mon., Wed., Fri., 9 a.m. to 1 p.m.), tel. 5321267, 5322051.

Embassy office hours are usually 8:30 or 9 a.m. to 12 or 12:30 p.m.; 1:30, 2, or 2:30 p.m. to 5 or 6 p.m., Monday to Friday; Saturday mornings also. Summer hours are even more complicated: some are open only 7 a.m.–noon. Most embassies are north of the Friendship Store and International Club.

English Corner: Purple Bamboo Park near Capital Stadium. Sundays.

Foreign Affairs Section, Public Security Bureau 公安局外事科 : Beichizi.

Foreign Ministry: switchboard, tel. 553831. Information: tel. 555505. Protocol: tel. 552642.

Foreign Trade Ministry: 553031.

Foreign News Agencies

ABC, Inc.: tel. 5322671.

Associated Press: tel. 5323419, 5323743.

Australian Broadcasting Corp.: tel. 5322410, 5322514.

Reuters: tel. 5323517, 5321921.

British Broadcasting Corp.: tel. 5323777, 5323694.

Canadian Broadcasting Corp.: tel. 5321510, 5323754.

CBS: tel. 5322301, 5322472.

Toronto Globe and Mail: tel. 5231661, 5232582, 5233672.

Agence France-Presse: tel. 5231992, 5231409.

NBC, Inc.: tel. 5233153, 5233961.

New York Times: tel. 5233115, 5232658.

Time: tel. 5232669, 5231293.

Wall Street Journal: tel. 5233673.

Washington Post: tel. 5233464, 5232944.

Golf Course: Beijing International Golf Club, Qianmen Fandian, 4021 Yong'an Rd., Xuanwu Dist., Beijing, tel. 3103434; Chaoyang Golf Course, tel. 5001149, 583380.

Hospitals: Most tourist hotels have a clinic or can help you find a doctor. See also "Useful Phrases."

Shoudu/Xiehe (Capital) Hospital 首都医院 : tel. 553731, X217 or X565. Also for dental emergencies.

Beijing Friendship Hospital 北京友谊医院 : tel. 338671, 331631.
Ambulance: tel. 120. Emergency Center at Gi Jou Chong Xin (near Kentucky Fried Chicken).
Hotline to Mayor: 5590206
MasterCard International, Room 4023, Beijing International Hotel, no. 9, Jianguo Mennei Ave.
Ministry of Foreign Economic Relations and Trade (MOFERT): Tel. 5128319. Telex 22560 FICPO CN.
Police 警察 or **Fire** 火警 : tel. 550720, 552725, 553772.
Railway Station 火车站 : Jianguomenwai Ave. Train inquiries: tel. 554866, 755272. Has special room for foreigners to buy tickets; better to buy in advance.
SOS International Assistance: tel. 51200411, 5003388–438.
Taxis: Capital Car Company: tel. 863661, 557461 for buses or mini-buses and 444468 for cars.
China Beijing Car and Limousine Service: tel. 59-4441, 557661. Buses, minibuses, and limousines.
Telephone Operators
information: 114; Long-distance information: 116; Overseas operator: tel. 155 or 336550; Domestic long-distance operator: tel. 330100, 331230.
Tourist Bus Co.: 2 Qianmen Dong Ave.; tel. 755414
Transportation Service for Foreigners: tel. 594375, 592616, 591082, 591813.
Travel Agents other than American Express, C.I.T.S., C.T.S., above: check first with your hotel which may not charge anything for some services. Services are usually less costly in the cheaper hotels.
All-China Youth Federation Travel Dept., 23 Dong Jiao Min Xiang, tel. 551531. Telex 20024 CYTS CN; China Sports Services, tel. 757381, 754250; China Youth Travel Service (Lu Song Yuan Hotel), tel. 440436; Heavenly Steed (east entrance), 6 Changan Ave. East, across from Beijing Hotel; Swan Travel Agency, Beijing Hotel.
YMCA, 21 Dong Dan Bei Da: tel. 555086.

BOOKS ON BEIJING (See "Bibliography" for details)
Behr, Edward: *The Last Emperor*.
Bredon, Juliet: *Peking*. First published in Shanghai, 1919.
Haldane, Charlotte: *The Last Great Empress of China*. A biography of Cixi.
Lin Yutang: *Moment in Peking*. The story of a Peking family beginning in 1900 as the foreign forces are marching on Beijing.
Warner, Marina: *The Dragon Empress. Life and Times of Tz'u-hsi, 1835–1908, Empress Dowager of China*.

CHANGCHUN 长春

Northeast China. This capital of Jilin province (formerly Manchu-ria) is a 1½-hour flight NE of Beijing. It can also be reached by plane from Guangzhou, Shanghai, Dalian, Harbin, and Shenyang; or by train, via Shenyang and Harbin. It is noted mostly as an industrial city manufacturing automobiles (China's first plant), trucks, railway carriages, tractors, and textiles. The urban population is 1.6 million. Changchun is very cold in winter (lowest ⁻30°C) with lots of snow. There are ice carvings in the parks then. The summers are relatively cool with a high of 32°C. Average annual rainfall is 600–700 mm, mainly in the east, in July and August. About 150 frostfree days!

The city was founded in 1800. Invaded by Tsarist Russia in the 1890s, it became a Japanese concession in 1905 and the capital of Japanese-controlled ''Manchukuo'' from 1931 until 1945. It is a highly industrialized city, but it can be very attractive with its lovely broad avenues flanked by beautiful hospital and university buildings.

The province of Jilin borders on Korea and the Soviet Union. Its 24 million people include Koreans, Manchus, Hui, Mongols and Xibes. Settlements have been recorded since the Qin dynasty. It has developed a regional opera based on song-and-dance duets.

If you have only one day in Changchun, you must see the **Jilin Provincial Museum** 吉林省博物馆 , 10 km from the Changbaishan Hotel. From 1932 to 1945, the Last Emperor of China lived and worked in this complex. Pu Yi was head and then Emperor of Manchukuo. The Ton Ge Palace was actually used as one of the sets in the movie *The Last Emperor*. (The movie company put in the chandelier). Only one of Pu Yi's wives lived in this palace which was built for Pu Yi by the Japanese and now holds provincial relics. A good guide can tell you which rooms she lived in. Pu Yi himself lived in a neighboring building; he believed the Ton Ge Palace was bugged and used it only for receptions.

You can see the emperor's throne in the white trim building, the Qian Ming. His living quarters should be restored in 1990. Photographs of the emperor, his wedding, wives, parents, and English teacher are on display. The palace was looted after the Japanese surrender and Pu Yi was taken off to the Soviet Union. After Liberation, an automobile factory used it as an office. A hall was built in 1963 to teach young people of the cruelty of the Japanese invasion, but this museum was neglected again during the Cultural Revolution. (Mao badges were produced here.)

A tunnel goes from here to the railway station, but it is not open to the public yet. This museum is open 8:30 a.m. to 5 p.m. in summer, and 8 a.m. to 4:30 p.m. in winter. Tourism officials say they can make arrangements for visitors to meet one of Pu Yi's widows.

In Changchun, C.I.T.S. recommends: the **Changchun Film Studio** 长春电影制片厂 , (tel. 53900, 53688), one of China's largest, and the **Changchun No. 1 Motor Vehicle Plant** 长春第一汽车制造厂, where you can watch a more labor-intensive manufacturing process than in America or Europe. You won't believe the wages! You can skate in the winter and swim in the summer in **Nanhu Park** 南湖公园 , the largest park in the city.

If you have more time, **Xinlicheng Reservoir** 新立城水库 in the suburbs has some sika deer, ginseng root, and is stocked with fish. The **Changchun Movie City** project has been put on hold because of cutbacks. It is a large theme park with movie sets, musical fountain, exhibition hall of movie props and trick photography, sedan chairs, and the like. The 480-square-km **Songhua Lake** 松花湖 is about 20 km SE of the city. The **Changbaishan Nature Reserve,** with tigers, deer, and sable is in **Antu County** about 300 km SE, with its own mythical monster and at least two hotels.

Jilin has a Korean area and an **ancient Korean capital,** dating back 1400 years, with Korean festivals. It also offers a **white river expedition.**

For fans of **steam locomotives,** tourism officials boast that Jilin has no diesel engines stationed here (which says a lot about the air quality). In one of its forest areas is a narrow-gauge train which tourists can ride. Because it is hilly and engines have to work harder (and thus produce more photogenic steam, especially in wintertime), photos are good at the East Junction (Tong Har Tao Kao), 15 minutes by taxi from the Changbaishan Hotel. Another good site for photos is the South Bridge (Quan Ping Tao Quo—tram 53 or 54).

One of my most moving experiences in China has come at 6 a.m., in front of the palacial **Geological College** here, watching over a thousand people enjoying themselves **dancing** in unison.

FESTIVALS

Sept. 3 to 6, yearly. **Liberation Day.** Holiday celebrating the Japanese surrender.

Lunar third month, third day. **Mongolian Festival** in Daicheng, 100 km from Changchun. For 5 to 6 days. Horse racing, archery, wrestling, dances. C.I.T.S. can arrange a tour. Hotel not very good.

A **Ginseng Festival** is held for three days, usually in August, in Fusong county at the foot of Changbai Mountain.

SHOPPING

Locally produced are: wine, ginseng, sable furs, deer antlers (aphrodisiacs), and frog oil (tonic). Tonghua and Changhaishan wines are made from wild grapes. Changchun produces carpets, embroidery, feather patchwork, mushrooms, azalea, wood carving, and bark pictures. The deer farm also has a retail shop. Please avoid furs from endangered species. I've found a leopard skin coat in this city. Store hours: 9 a.m. to 6 p.m. (winter) or to 7 p.m. (summer). The **Friendship Store** 友谊商店 is at Zhi You Da Rd and Beijing St. See also "Jilin."

Jilin Provincial Antique and Curio Store 吉林省文物店 (7 Xi'an Rd.; tel. 22537); **Changchun Fur Factory** 长春市皮毛厂 (4 Lane 7, North Second Rd., north of railway; tel. 37765). Please, no endangered species! **Changchun Wood Carving Factory** (8 Xiangyang Rd.; tel. 24797).

RESTAURANTS

Chunyi Hotel Restaurant 春谊饭店 (in the hotel; 2 Stalin St.; tel. 38495). **Changchun Restaurant** 长春饭店 (in the center of the city; tel. 25442).

Exotic specialties: houtou (golden orchid monkey head) mushrooms 猴头菇 , ginseng chicken 人参鸡 , thick deer antler soup (with sea cucumber, prawn, egg white, ham, and chicken) 鹿茸羹 , and frog oil soup 哈什蚂油汤 . Frog oil is said to be very nutritious and tastes better than it sounds. Please, no endangered species! And yes, you can get other dishes too!

HOTELS

The top hotel here should be either the Nanhu Guest House (because of its garden setting and big rooms) or the Changbaishan (with better rooms on its top two floors and better location for business people and tourists). Both are good but not exceptional.

Changbaishan Guest House 长白山宾馆 ● *12 Xinmin St.; Telex 83026 BOOTH CN, Cable 1119, 1833. Dist.A.P.26 km. Dist.R.W.8 km* ● In attractive setting near park, hospitals, and university. T.R., no C.C. 1982. 12 stories, 268 rooms. 11th and 12th stories ren. 1987. Elevator old and slow. C.I.T.S. on premises.

Changchun Overseas Chinese Mansion (Huaqiao Da Xia) • *Nanhu Rd.* • Open 1989 or 1990.

Nanhu Guest House 南湖宾馆 • *2 Nanhu Rd. Dist.A.P.15 km. Dist.R.W.10 km. Near small vegetable market. Isolated location on bank of Nanhu Lake* • No. C.C. Indoor pool, bowling. Seven villas on 80 hectares of gardens. #6 villa, with 20 beds, cost Y2000. Villa #7, for foreign tourists, has 160 beds. 1960, ren. 1989. Large rooms, three-meter-high ceilings. Tennis. Poor reading lights, worn and dirty carpets, no air conditioners, old plumbing.

Provincial Chunyi Hotel 省春谊宾馆 • *2 Stalin St., Dist.A.P.16 km. Dist.R.W.100 meters* • Centrally located. Front section built 1904 in two-story tsarist style. (It was known as the Railway Hotel then.) Back section built 1934 in 4-story Japanese style. 80 rooms, some with 4-meter-high ceilings. No IDD, no C.C. Should now have 24-hour hot running water. Standards barely adequate, but the ambiance of the 1930s is charming. Dorms.

CAAC 中国民航 *2 Liaoning Rd.; tel. 39772.*

C.I.T.S. 中国国际旅行社 • *12 Xinmin St.; tel. 885069, 882419, 52401; Telex: 83028 CITSC CN. Cable 1119.*

C.T.S. • *12 Xinmin Ave; tel. 36406. Cable 1195. Telex 83035 JLCTS CN.*

Jilin Overseas Tourism Corporation • *12 Xinmin St.; tel. 882401, 885069. Fax 882419. Cable and telex same as C.I.T.S.*

CHANGSHA (LONG SAND)

South China. Capital of Hunan province south of the Yangtze River. 85-minutes' flight SW of Shanghai, 1 hour NE of Guilin, and 3¼ hours south of Beijing. There may be a direct flight from Hong Kong by now. On the main Beijing-Guangzhou railway line, 726 km north of Guangzhou. Population: 1 million. Coldest temperature is about ⁻8°C in January; hottest about 30°C in July. Rainfall from 1250–1750 mm, mostly late summer or early autumn.

Changsha, in one of China's main rice-growing areas, was a small town 2000 years ago. It was almost completely destroyed during the Japanese War. It is famous because Chairman Mao was born and lived nearby in Shaoshan. He studied for about five years at the Hunan Provincial First Normal School (1912–18). Yale started its mission in about 1904 and eventually established a medical school, hospital, and middle school. The Americans left shortly after Liberation.

Changsha is also known for its important Han excavation. Its embroidery is one of the four most famous in China.

The novel and movie *The Sand Pebbles* was set partly in Changsha during the Northern Expedition in the late 1920s. The hero was an engineer on an American gun boat, which sailed up the Yangtze through

Lake Dongting and along the Xiang River. The movie is one of the few good Hollywood efforts on China.

Changsha is also the setting of a more recent book, Liang Heng and Judith Shapiro's autobiographical *Son of the Revolution,* a refreshing look at growing up in Communist China and beating the system. The excellent novel *A Small Town Called Hibiscus,* is set in the southern part of this province.

Hunan province's nationalities include Han, Tujia, Miao, Dong, Yao, Hui, Uygur, and Zhuang.

If you only have one day in this city, C.I.T.S. suggests the Hunan Provincial Museum and the Ceramic Exhibition in the morning, and the embroidery factory and city tour in the afternoon.

Hunan Provincial Museum   湖南省博物馆   (Dongfeng Rd.; tel. 25123): Because this is the main tourist attraction, skip everything else if you are short on time. The 1972–74 excavations of three 2100-year-old tombs have overshadowed the revolutionary and other ancient collections in this museum. You must see these Han relics, important because of their excellent state of preservation and vast number. You may want to return to see the rest of the museum later.

The Han collection is in the white middle building on the right after you enter the gate. The three tombs were of Li Tsang, chancellor to the Prince of Changsha and Marquis of Dai, his wife, and his son. The son died in 168 B.C. The body of the woman, 1.52 meters long and weighing 34.3 kg, is incredibly well preserved, with flesh, 16 teeth, and internal organs. The lungs, intestines, and stomach were removed after disinterment and preserved in formaldehyde. They are all on display in the basement. An autopsy revealed arteriosclerosis, gallstones, tuberculosis, and parasites. Death came to her suddenly at age 50; there were undigested melon seeds in her stomach. The remarkable state of preservation is attributed to the body's being wrapped in hemp and nine silk ribbons, and sealed from oxygen and water in three coffins surrounded by 5000 kg of charcoal and sticky white clay. She died after her husband; maybe that is why her tomb is the largest and she is the best preserved of all. She probably planned it herself.

The 5000 relics include 1800 pieces of lacquerware, many of which needed only cleaning to appear new. Look for the ear cups for wine and soup, and a makeup box with comb, mirror, powder, and lipstick. She also had for her after-death use incense burners, clothes, silk fabrics, medicinal herbs, and nine musical instruments. Maybe she did use them! An inventory of the relics was written on bamboo strips, paper still being rare then. In the building to the left as you leave the marquess are the three coffins and a model of the tomb site. To the right is an arts and crafts and antiques store. Some reproductions are on sale. Open daily (except Sundays), 8–11 a.m. and 2:30–5 p.m. Exceptions made on request.

The **Han tomb site** 墓址 , only 4 km away in Mawangdui 马王堆 , is now just a large hole in the ground under a roof. One can see the pyramid-shaped hill, the neat, earthen walls, and staircase inside. Geomancy students can figure out the *feng shui*. Was it practiced then? Did the tomb face south?

The **Hunan Provincial Embroidery Factory** 湖南省湘绣厂 (285 Bayi Rd.; tel. 27219) is worthwhile, as you can see this ancient craft being performed and be amazed at the number of workers not wearing eyeglasses. Look for embroidery so fine it can be displayed from either side.

A tour of the city includes **Tianxin Park,** the highest point here, with a small section of the 600-plus-year-old city wall. Open daily, 6 a.m.–8 p.m. **Juzi (Orange) Island** 橘子岛 , 5 km long, is probably the ''long sand'' after which Changsha is named. In the middle of the Xiang River at Changsha, it is 300 meters at its widest. The island is inhabited, cultivated with orange groves, and stacked with reeds for making paper. It has a small sand beach for swimming and a place to change. Good for relaxing evening walks and bicycling. Open daily, 6:30 a.m.–9 p.m.; tel. 82152.

The **Hunan Normal School** (Shuyuan Rd.), outside the south gate of the city, has a small museum. Mao studied and taught here in 1913–18 and 1920–21. The current structure, built in 1968, is a copy of the 1912 school and reflects its European connections. Open daily for visitors, 8 a.m.–noon and 2–6 p.m.; tel. 31786.

Yuelu Hill 岳麓山 , on the western side of the Xiang River, is good for climbing and hiking. The Wangxiang Pavilion has a good view from the top. The **Lushan Temple** 麓山寺 was built in A.D. 268 and reconstructed last in 1681. The **Yuelu Academy** 岳麓书院 was one of the four major institutes of higher learning from A.D. 976 (Song), rebuilt last in 1670. The **Aiwan Pavilion** 爱晚亭 was built in 1792 (Qing). Open daily, from 8:30 a.m.–4:30 p.m.; tel. 82011. These are not very spectacular.

A new tourist attraction, **Zhang Jiajie State Forest Park,** is being prepared 400 km west of Changsha (7 hrs by bus; 22 by train). It is a forest close to Dayon county in the western part of Hunan province, full of beautiful hills, stone pillars, flowers and wild boar, monkeys and lcopards. Six small hotels and several guesthouses should be ready by the time of your visit.

Also in the province are ''Hengshan'' Mountain, ''Shaoshan,'' and ''Yueyang,'' under separate listings.

ENTERTAINMENT
Local Huagu opera originated from provincial folk songs and ditties. The Hunan Provincial Puppet Show Troupe is well known.

SHOPPING

Made in the province are embroideries, porcelain and pottery, chrysanthemum stone and bamboo carvings, fans, firecrackers, lacquer reproductions, smoky quartz and bloodstone carvings, handicrafts from minorities, and duck-down clothing.

Hunan Antique Store 湖南省博物馆文物商店 (3 Dongfeng Rd., inside the Hunan Provincial Museum; tel. 25277); **Hunan Arts and Crafts Shop** 湖南工艺品商店 (Xiangxiu Building, Wuyi Square; tel. 22253); **Zhongshan Rd. Department Stores** 韶山路百货商店 (213 Zhongshan Rd.; tel. 24621); **Shaoshan Rd. Department Store** 中山路百货商店 (Shaoshan Rd.; tel. 24588); **Hunan Foreign-Languages Bookstore** 湖南外文书店 (89 Wuyi Rd., 2nd floor; tel. 24102).

RESTAURANTS

Fire Palace Restaurant 火宫店餐馆 ● *147 Pozi St.; tel. 25391.*

Another Village Restaurant 又一村饭店 ● *111 Zhongshan Rd.; tel. 24257.*

HOTELS

Lotus Hotel ● *Wuyi Dong Rd. Dist.A.P.22 km. Dist.R.W.1.5 km* ● 1984, ren. 1988. No IDD. Business center. 275 rooms. C.C. (no Diner's).

Xiangjiang (Xiang River) Hotel 湘江宾馆 ● *Zhongshan Rd. Telex: 98131 XIANG CN. Cable 6666.* ● Close to shopping and post and cable office. Near the former site of Mao's Teach-Yourself College; Dist.A.P.22 km. Dist.R.W.5 km. 1951, ren. 1988. Nine stories, 300 rooms. C.C. (no Diner's). IDD, USTV. Business center, bicycles.

OTHER IMPORTANT ADDRESSES

Bureau of Tourism Administration: Hunan Province, Wu Dong Rd., tel. 20736, telex: 33410 HPFAO CN.
C.I.T.S. 中国国际旅行社 : 130 Wuyi Dong Rd. (Furong Hotel), tel. 22250, 26448, telex: 98132 HLHCT CN.
C.T.S. 中国旅行社 : 130 Sanxing St., Wuyi Rd.; tel. 25101.
Bank of China 中国银行 : 55 Wuyi Rd.; tel. 23688.
CAAC 中国民航 : 5 Wuyi Dong Rd.; tel. 23820, 22560.
Railway Station 火车站 : Wuyi Rd.; tel. 26326.
Taxi: Hunan Provincial Bureau of Tourism, Xiangjiang Hotel; tel. 26261 X390.

Changsha Taxi Company: Wuyi Rd.; tel. 26495.
Hospital: Check first with your hotel. Otherwise, No. 2 Hospital of Hunan Medical College 湖南医学院第二医院 : Wenyi Rd.; tel. 24608, 25830.

Changsha Medical and First-Aid Station 民沙医疗急救站 : tel.
23636
Fire 火警 : tel. 119
Police 警察 : tel. 110
Foreign Affairs Section, Bureau of Public Security 公安局外事处 :
tel. 26241.

CHANGZHOU 常州

East China, Jiangsu province, halfway between Shanghai and
Nanjing on the Grand Canal. Population about 460,000.

This 2600-year-old city was called Yanling in the Zhou, Piling in
the Han, and Lanling in the Jin. Notable are Hongmei Park, Tianningsi
(Heavenly Tranquillity) Temple, Yizhouting Pavilion, and Wenbita
(Writing Brush) Pagoda. A 1500-year-old comb factory still makes
wooden and bamboo combs. One can buy ''Palace Combs,'' one of the
''eight famous hair decorations worn by imperial women.''

HOTELS
Changzhou Hotel (No. 101) ● *Dongdajie St.; tel. 24886, 24046.
Cable 0057.*

Hotel Jiang Nan Chua ● *Dist.A.P.20 km. Dist.R.W.* ● 1982, ren.
1987. Seven stories, 190 rooms. IDD, business center, bicycles, C.C.
(no Diner's).

CHENGDE 承德

(Chengteh, Chengte, Jehol, Jehe.) North China, Hebei province, 250 km NE of Beijing. Urban population, 130,000. Coldest temperature—⁻19°C; hottest—35°C for a very short time each year. Most rain June and July. An express train leaves Beijing at 7:17 a.m. arriving at 12:12. You can leave Chengde next day at 2:02 p.m. arriving in Beijing at 7:14 p.m. for a very quick trip. You could also ask about taxis if you don't have the time.

The Qing imperial summer resort here was built for Emperor Kangxi (Kang-hsi) from 1703 to 1790, not just to relax in, but to curry favor with the Mongolian nobles in the area. To help win them over, he built 11 Lama temples also. Chengde is well worth seeing, especially if you don't go to Tibet. It is one of the 24 historical cities protected by the State Council.

The **Imperial Summer Resort** 避暑山庄 covers an area of 5.6 million square meters, which is larger than the Summer Palace in Beijing. Most of it is surrounded by a 10-km-long wall. From Beijing, it is a 3-day bus tour, but at the moment the bus is only for Chinese tourists, as the road goes through a couple of restricted areas.

In the last century a one-way trip took the Manchus 3–20 days by horseback, palanquin, or bumpy chariot.

Chengde oozes with history. The Qing court lived here from May to October each year. It was in a yurt here in 1793 that Lord Macartney of Britain refused to kowtow to Qing Emperor Qianlong (Chien Lung) and where the envoy was dismissed as a ''bearer of tribute'' from ''vassal king'' George III, his requests to trade refused. In 1860 the Manchu court fled to Chengde as Anglo-French forces approached Beijing. The death of Emperor Xianfeng (Hsien Feng) here in 1862 led to the rise of Cixi (Tzu Hsi), the empress dowager, as regent. Think of the plotting that went on as he lay on his deathbed. Cixi visited here again, by train, in 1900. In the 1930s, many of the buildings were looted and destroyed by the warlord Tang Yu Liu. The most important buildings have been or are in the process of being repaired. Some of the ruins are intriguing and fascinating in themselves. Sit in the hulk of the "Potala" at dusk and tell ghost stories as darkness falls.

You can see the main palace and garden in one day and five of the outer temples on a second day. If you rush and avoid the climb to the Club Stone, all the open temples and the summer resort can be covered in one full, hurried day.

The Imperial Summer Resort has nine courtyards. It is not as palatial as Beijing's Summer Palace, but it is worth seeing. The building to the right inside the second gate has a painting of the Macartney visit 马戈尔尼来访画片 and a hunting scene 木兰秋狄图 (with officials sporting animal head masks and imitating mating calls to attract the bear, deer, wolves, leopards, and tigers). To the left is the **Hall of No Worldly Lust but True Faith,** which is also called the **Nanmu Hall** 楠木殿 because of the scented wood from which it is made. You might get a whiff of it. The emperor received subjects and envoys in this ceremonial hall. On either side are waiting rooms, one for foreign visitors and one for relatives and tribal leaders. Among the exhibits in these and other halls are Manchu coats with sleeves shaped like horses' hooves, sedan chairs, an elephant dotted with pearls, brilliant blue kingfisher feather ornaments. In a hall displaying fine porcelain are Qing imitations of Ming vases.

The **Refreshing-at-Mist-Veiled-Waters Pavilion** was the imperial bedroom. On either side are the pavilions of the two empresses. The imperial bedroom has a "hollow wall" 夹层墙 (seen from the back) where Cixi listened carefully as the emperor lay dying inside. As a result of her eavesdropping, she was able to seize power from her rival. Cixi lived in the **Pine and Crane Pavilion,** which was originally built for the mother of Emperor Qianlong.

The emperor used the two-story pavilion beyond to enjoy the moon 云山胜地 with his concubines. It has no interior stairs. The Qian Long Emperor studied in the pavilion, which now houses paintings for sale.

The garden is beautiful, and visitors should be able to rent ice skates and bicycles. The trees planted by the Qing are tagged with identification numbers. The two most influential emperors chose 72 scenic spots and wrote poems about each. Kangxi's poems have four characters; Qianlong's have three. Thirty of these places are still marked by pavilions from which you can see the view, including one on the top of the hill to view the snow 南山积雪 . There is even one to view the Club Stone.

Among the buildings counterclockwise around the lake is the **Jinshan Pavilion** 金山亭 , copied from one of the same name in Zhenjiang, and the **Yanyulou (Misty-Rain Tower)** 烟雨楼 , the latter built by Qianlong, a copy of one now destroyed in Zhejiang. It was used to watch the misty rain, of course, and to read.

On the flatland area here, Emperor Qianlong stooped to receive the equally arrogant Lord Macartney, the envoy from Britain. One of the scenes from the television movie *Marco Polo* was filmed in this garden—the one where Polo meets the Yuan emperor.

The walled garden on the **Changlang Islet** 沧浪屿 is a copy of the Changlang Garden in Suzhou. Some people collect postcards when they travel; the Qianlong emperor collected buildings!

Nearby on a side road is a herd of about 40 spotted deer 鹿场. A herd was started here during the Qing because some of the emperors drank deer's blood as a tonic.

The two-story Imperial Library 文津阁 has a pond in front and few trees as a precaution against fire. It is approached through the rockeries. If you see tourists in front of the library staring into the water, it's because they are looking for the reflection of a crescent moon. Look for it yourself. The library is a copy of one in Shaoxing.

As a Chinese garden, this imperial summer resort is one of the best, a microcosm of the whole country with lake, grasslands, and mountains.

The **Outer Temples** 外八庙, outside the walls, are a mixture of Manchu, Mongolian, Tibetan, and Han Chinese architecture with a similiar mix of artifacts inside. Once housing 1000 lamas or monks, they are now all museums. The steles usually have Manchu writing in front, Chinese behind, and Mongolian and Tibetan on the sides. If you are short of time, the Putuozongsheng and Puning are the most important to see. Otherwise, start with the *Pule 普乐寺, which is also known as the Round Pavilion, as it was built in 1766 to resemble the Temple of Heaven. Inside is a statue of two hard-to-see copulating gods from the esoteric sect of Lama Buddhism. From this temple one can climb to the **Club Stone** 磬锤峰, the giant, mallet-shaped stone, for a marvelous view of the palace, the temples, and Chengde city itself.

The small **Anyuan Temple** 安远庙 is patterned after a temple in Xinjiang that no longer exists. Inside is a statue of Lu Du Mo, a female goddess. The **Puren** should be open for your visit.

Near the Puning Temple, one can get a Qing horse cart ride, or a room in a tiny hotel aimed at Chinese tourists. Inside the temple gate is a stele about Qianlong's suppression of a rebellion of the minorities. The *Puning Temple* 普宁寺 contains a copy of the spectacular 1000-headed and 1000-armed Guan Yin, Goddess of Mercy, which should not be missed. Actually he/she has only 42 hands and arms, each representing 25. On each palm is an eye. The statue is 22.28 meters high. It is in the Mahayana Hall 大乘之阁. The warlord stole the original.

The Puning Temple is patterned after the Sumeru temple in Tibet and is known also as the Temple of Universal Peace or Big Buddha Temple. Inside are a drum and a bell tower, a laughing Buddha, and four guardian kings. About 100 larger-than-life-size arhats remain of the original 508; the others were destroyed by fire. Only eight of the arhats are Chinese. The mural of the 18 arhats is 250 years old and original, remarkable for its preservation. Look for the big bronze cooking pot that fed 1000 lamas. The buildings in back are classic Tibetan style, with nothing inside. The number of buildings and stupas are symbolic— the center of the world was Sumeru Mountain, with four great continents around it.

The **Xumifushou (Longevity and Happiness) Temple** 须弥福寿 was inspired by the Xiashelumpo (Zhaxilhunbu) Temple in Shigatse, Tibet, and used as a residence for the sixth panchen lama. Dragons seem to scamper along the edges of the roof, most unusual for a Han temple. Built in 1780, it is the newest of the temples and commemorates Qianlong's 70th birthday, at which point he started to learn Tibetan. In the main building is a statue of the founder of Lamaism and behind him, Sakyamuni. The tentlike pagoda in the back is similar to the one in Fragrant Hill Park in Beijing.

The ***Putuozongcheng Temple** 普陀宗乘之庙 is patterned after the Potala Palace, home of the dalai lama, in Lhasa, Tibet. It was built from 1767 to 1771 for the 60th birthday of Qianlong and for the 80th birthday of his mother. The elephant symbolizes the Mahayana sect. (One elephant equals 500 horses.) The five pagodas on several of the buildings symbolize the five schools of Lamaism. Not to be missed is the **Donggang Zi Dian (East Hall),** where statues unusual for this part of China can be found. Please try not to show your insensitivity as an embarrassed guide explains what is happening under the yellow aprons. These are statues of the Red Hat sect of Lamaism, where sex with a person other than one's spouse was part of the religious ritual. In the opposite hall on the same level are other metal Buddhist statues. Another 164 steps lead up to the main building, which is decorated by Buddhas in niches—the 80 at the top representing Qianlong's mother's age. The six in front each symbolize ten years of Qianlong's life. Some birthday cake!

The temple was built to commemorate the birthdays, as well as a visit by tribal leaders. This temple is the largest, and most of it should be repaired by the time you read this. A great deal of it was still gutted on my recent visit, and it was intriguing to try to figure out what stood where.

The **Shuxiang Temple** 殊象寺 should be open when you visit too.

A 300-meter-long **Qing dynasty-style street** 清朝一条街 should now also be open, with tea houses and souvenir and local product shops. Planned also are Qing horse-drawn carriages and sedan chair rides.

The **Jinshan Ling** 金山岭长城 section of the Great Wall is 110 km away. Officials here say it is better than Badaling, north of Beijing.

SHOPPING

The Friendship Store 友谊商店 is small, near the De Hui Gate. Gardeners of miniature plants might be interested in the cheap water stones, which absorb water and therefore can grow plants on top of them. But they are heavy! The area also produces silk, walnut walking sticks, and wood carvings.

RESTAURANTS

Found at almost every meal are the locally grown apricot kernels, usually sweetened and delicious. The food should improve with the opening of the new hotels.

HOTELS

The best hotel says C.I.T.S. is the Yunshan, and then the Qiwanglou. The Shanzhuang is no. 3. Reservations necessary May through October.

Qiwanglou Hotel 绮望楼宾馆 • *1 East Rd., Bifongmen* • built in ancient Chinese style, inside the palace grounds north of the main gate, used also for heads of state. 1987.

The 33 Yurt Hotel 蒙古包宾馆 • *inside the palace grounds in the shadow of the* **Six Harmonies Pagoda** 六合塔 • 1987. Attendants wear Mongolian dress and the location should give you plenty of time to enjoy the garden in its different moods. 100 beds. Only for the adventurous. Standards not very high.

Yunshan Hotel • *Wu Lie Nan Rd.* • 1988. 12 stories, 230 rooms. Gym, sauna. This hotel has high standards.

Chengde Tourist Hotel 承德旅游饭店 • *South Wulie Rd.* • 1986. 450 beds.

C.I.T.S. 国旅承德支社办公室（中华路北十一号）and **C.T.S.** • *Zhonghua Rd., Dangkou.* • Tel. 3502, 3454.

成 都

CHENGDU

(Chengtu) Southwest China in central Sichuan province, slightly over 2 hours by air SW of Beijing. It can also be reached by a 21-hour train ride from Kunming with about 250 km of tunnels and a view of Mount Emei. Direct flights from elsewhere in China and Hong Kong. Population is 1.6 million, urban. With an altitude of 500 meters, its hottest temperature is 37°C in July and its coldest may be ⁻5°C in January. The tourist season is April to November, with July and August uncomfortably hot. Annual precipitation about 1000 mm, mainly in July and August.

Chengdu has a history of over 2000 years. In the fourth century B.C., the King of Shu moved his capital here and named it Chengdu (Becoming a Capital). In the Han, after brocade weaving became successfully established, it was called ''the Brocade City.'' During the Three Kingdoms, it was the capital of Shu. Many American, Canadian, and British missionaries and teachers lived here before Liberation.

Today it is the provincial capital and an educational and industrial center. Its industries include metallurgy, electronics, and textiles. Its buses run on natural gas. The area grows rice, wheat, rape (for oil), chilis, and sweet potatoes. It also grows medicinal plants and herbs that are sold all over the country.

Chengdu has so much to offer, you need at least 5 days to cover it, preferably more. C.I.T.S. suggests the following grouping based on regions, but you can plan your own schedule:

Day 1: Du Fu's Thatched Cottage, the Temple of Marquis Wu, and the River-Viewing Pavilion.

Day 2: Chengdu Zoo, Tomb of Wang Jian, Divine Light Monastery, bamboo-weaving, brocade, jade-carving, or lacquerware factory.

Day 3: Dujiang Irrigation project.

Day 4 and 5: Meishan, Leshan, and Emei Shan.

Day 6: Jiuzhaigou

*Du Fu (Tu Fu)'s Thatched Roof Cottage 杜甫草堂 is actually a park with a replica of the modest residence of the famous Tang poet who lived here and wrote 240 poems during four years, from A.D. 759. A temple and a garden were first built as a memorial in the Northern Song. These have been replaced periodically, the pavilions here from the Qing. Statues, books, and art exhibitions are also found in the 20-hectare garden. Some translations here of Du Fu's poems in 15 foreign languages might help foreigners understand his importance. Open daily, 8:30 a.m.–6 p.m.; tel. 25258.

The Temple of Marquis Wu 武候祠, in the southern part of the city, was originally built in the sixth century in memory of Zhuge Liang (Chuke Liang), a famous strategist and statesman, prime minister of Shu during the Three Kingdoms (A.D. 220–265). Here are tablets written during the Tang, larger than life-size statues, and the still unexcavated **Tomb of Liu Bei 刘备墓**, the king of Shu, one of the heroes of *The Romance of the Three Kingdoms*. The current buildings are Qing and are open daily, 8:30 a.m.–6 p.m.; tel. 53297. The ***Zhuge Liang Memorial Hall 诸葛亮殿** is also listed as a historical site under State Council protection.

The Wangjianglou (River-Viewing Pavilion) 望江楼, in the southeastern part of the city, was once the residence of a Tang dynasty woman poet, Xue Tao. The park has over 100 varieties of bamboo. Sit in the ''Pavilion for Poem Reciting'' or the ''Chamber to Relieve Your Resentment.'' See if they inspire you, too, to poetry. Sit in them quietly for half an hour and breathe deeply. Open daily, 8:30 a.m.–6 p.m.; tel. 42552.

The 25-hectare **Chengdu Zoo 成都动物园** is 6 km north of the city and boasts about 10 giant pandas, the largest collection of this endangered species in captivity anywhere in the world. It also has rare golden-hair monkeys among 2000 animals of over 200 varieties. Open daily, 8:30 a.m.–6 p.m.; tel. 31951.

Try for the *Tomb of Wang Jian 王建墓 (A.D. 847–918), the emperor of Shu in the 10th century, if you are more interested in history. Wang Jian captured not just Sichuan, but parts of three other provinces, and proclaimed himself emperor in 907. The 23.4-meter-long tomb is elaborate, with double stone arches and carved musicians. Open daily, except Mondays, 8:30 a.m. to 5:30 p.m.; tel. 21245.

The Baoguangsi (Divine Light Monastery) 宝光寺 should not be missed. It is 18 km north of the city at Xindu 新都, and famous. Originally founded during the Eastern Han, about 1900 years ago, it was the site of a palace ordered built by Tang Emperor Li Huan. During the Ming, the monastery was destroyed by war, but it was reconstructed on its original foundation during the Qing in 1671. Pagodas, five halls, and 16 courtyards make it most impressive. The Tang pagoda is 30 meters high, 13 stories with a glazed gold top. The 500 arhats are from the Qing in 1851, each about 2 meters high, unique and vivid. The Stone Carved Stupa is also Qing, 5.5 meters high, in granite. Look for the 175-centimeters-high stone Thousand Buddha Tablet, carved on four sides in A.D. 450. Look also for the Buddhist scriptures written on palm leaves from India. Open daily, 8:30 a.m.–6 p.m.

You may want to skip the factory and go shopping instead. If you are on our 5-day plan, this is your last day in the city. If you dig museums, the Sichuan Provincial Museum 四川省博物馆 (Renmin Nan Rd.) is at your disposal. Learn more about the Long March through Sichuan or local history. Open daily, except Mondays, from 8:30 a.m.– 6 p.m.; tel. 22158.

There's another Buddhist monastery, the Wenshu (God of Wisdom) Monastery 文殊院 (Wenshuyuan St., Beimen; tel. 22378). Founded in the Tang and reconstructed in 1691, this temple has ancient paintings and a white jade statue from Burma, gilded Japanese scripture containers (Tang), and other treasures. Open daily, 8:30 a.m.–8 p.m. The Cultural Park 文化公园 has an old Taoist temple . Open daily, 8 a.m. to 6:30 p.m.; tel. 22378.

The *Dujiangyan Irrigation System 都江堰灌溉系统（灌溉工程） 1½-hours' drive NW (57 km) in Guanxian county 灌县（灌县） usually takes a full day. It was originally built in 256 B.C., the oldest such project in the country. Impressive because of its age and scope, it controlled floods and diverted half of the Minjiang River to the irrigation of the fertile Sichuan plain. This area has old temples, murals, and a swinging bridge. The 240-meter-long swinging bridge over the river was first built before the Song, and most recently rebuilt in 1974, so don't be afraid to walk on it. The Fu Long Kuan (Dragon Subduing Temple) 伏龙观 houses a statue of Li Bing, the mastermind of the project. The **Erwang (Two Kings) Temple** 二王庙 is a memorial to Li Bing and his son.

Near Dujiangyan is a **deer farm** 养鹿场 where you can buy Pilose Antler Juice "for aching back . . . impotence and premature ejaculation." Also near Dujiangyan and 90 km from Chengdu is **Qingcheng (Green City) Mountain** 青城山 , one of the birthplaces of Taoism and still a Taoist center, with 38 buildings left of its 70 original temples, shrines, and grottoes. With some of its cliffs shaped like city walls (hence the name), this strikingly beautiful mountain rises up to 1600 meters. It was also a base for a peasant insurgency led by Zhang Xianzhong (Chang Hsien-chung), who captured Chongqing in 1644 and occupied Chengdu. Visitors can reach the **Jian Fu Temple** (Tang) by road. Guesthouses midway up and on top.

In the Han, one of the founders of Taoism, Zhang Daolin, put up an altar here for preaching. The **Cavern of Taoist Master Temple** was founded in 617–605 B.C.. The building is from the Tang and contains a portrait of Zhang Daolin, stone carvings of the Three Emperors, Ming woodwork, and murals of the Eight Taoist Fairies. The mountain is full of legends.

Sansu Shrine 三苏祠 is in **Meishan County** 眉山县 , 89 km south of the city. It was the residence of three famous literary men of the Northern Song and became a shrine during the Ming (1368–98). The current structures are Qing.

For *Leshan's Giant (Tang) Buddha and *Emei Shan Mountain, see separate listing.

Another excursion possibility is **Jiuzhaigou** 报国寺 , a "fairyland," opened in 1985. Located 800 to 900 km from Chengdu in Nanping county town, this is a 1½-day's drive or an 80-minute helicopter ride each way. The whole helicopter may have to be chartered. An airfield is being built. One can stay in the modest Nuorilang Hotel. A hotel for foreigners should be under construction at the back of the mountain. Three nights and two days are needed, but you can get an idea of this lovely forest in a day if you fly in and out. Trips are usually by bus for two to five days. Current hotels are not yet up to standard.

This is a 60,000-hectare primitive forest with species earlier thought to be extinct. Naturalists should go wild with excitement here. It is the home of many wild, exotic animals like wild pigs, bears and snakes. The setting is full of forested hills, carpets of flowers, lakes and waterfalls, and even some legends.

Jiuzhaigou means "nine stockades canyon," three of which are about 2500 meters above sea level. Tibetan settlers once lived in the area. The best time to visit is August and September.

Wolong Nature Preserve 卧龙自然保护区 , about 150 km from Chengdu, has many pandas in the wild, but tourists might not see any. There are more seen in the Zoo, above. Very rough road. Visitors stay

in the Forestry Bureau hostel. C.I.T.S. can help tourists get permission.
Some wild pandas are also in Mianyang Prefecture, 200 km from
Chengdu. Naturalists estimate that there are now about 1000 pandas in
the wild. Chengdu is building a breeding facility, with help from abroad.

Zigong 240 km from Chengdu is a newly opened city famed for
its Dinosaur Museum (with over 100 unearthed), salt museum, and its
Lantern Festival (with giant dragon lanterns) for about 20 days before
and after the spring festival. It is not easy to get to by public transport,
and tours are arranged by C.I.T.S. in Chengdu only for the festival.
Eight hours drive from Chongqing. Tan Mu Ling Bing Guan (Guest
House). 1985. 50 rooms.

Tours have been leaving from Chengdu by overnight train for the
satellite launching center at **Xichang.** If you are interested, contact
C.Y.T.S.

SHOPPING

Of the factories to which C.I.T.S. can arrange visits, those of interest to visitors make bamboo weavings, brocade, Shu embroidery, filigree crafts, and lacquerware. The main shopping areas are **Renmin
Rd.** 人民路 , **Yanshikou** 盐市口 , and **Chunxi Rd.**

Friendship Store 友谊商店 (519 Dong Da Zhong Rd.; tel. 27067).

Sichuan Antique Store 四川文物商店 (11 Shangyechang; tel.
22787).

Chengdu Arts and Crafts Shop 成都工艺美术品 (10 Chunxi
Rd., Beiduan; tel. 26817). Branches in Jinjiang Hotel and airport.

Chengdu Fine Arts Company (440 Dong Da Xi Rd.; tel. 24184).

RESTAURANTS

Next to Cantonese, Sichuan cuisine is the most famous Chinese
cooking in the world. Not all of it is spicy-hot, and dishes are toned
down for tourists. Flower petals and herbs are used in such specialties
as ''fried lotus flower,'' ''governor's chicken,'' diced chicken with hot
pepper and peanuts, and ''smoked duck with tea fragrance.'' Try also
the dumplings and Dan Dan noodles. See ''Food.'' The restaurants in
the tourist hotels are best.

HOTELS

The Jin Jiang can be good or bad. The quality depends on the floor
and the wing. Flossy tours now also bunk at the **Minshan International**
across the street. No 3 is the Chengdu Hotel and No 4 is probably the
Jing Rong. Chengdu also has an inexpensive college guest house.

China Enterprise Management Training Guest House is also a
cheap and good place to stay because of the long-term Canadian experts
also living here. But only if there is room. Tel. 52273 X 555 and ask
for Mr. Tang. Apartments. It is near the College of Education.

The **Jin Jiang Hotel** • *Ren Min Nan Rd. Cable: 4481, Telex: 60109 JJH CN.* • Across from the Minshan Hotel and close to CAAC and CITS head office and within walking distance of shopping and university. Dist.A.P.18 km. Dist.R.W.7 km. 1962, ren. 1989, 1990. Twelve stories. 437 rooms.

No place to sit in lobby except in bar. Beautiful roof top Garden Restaurant, Chinese and Western food. C.C. IDD in 1989. Rental bicycles. Hong Kong joint venture. Has good business center, lots of stores. Booking offices for CTS, CITS, CYTS, and Lhasa Hotel. Clinic. Long dismal hallways. Some rooms no refrigerators. Generally good but this is not one of China's top hotels.

The **Minshan International Hotel** • *17 Renmin Nan Rd. Cable: 8883, Telex: 60247 MSH CN. Across street from Jin Jiang.* • 1987/1988. 21 stories, 337 rooms. Sichuan and health food restaurants; Western food restaurant joint venture managed by Windows on the World; English pub (with darts) and Food Street (for snacks). T.R. Outdoor swimming pool, sauna, and gym. Rooms tastefully decorated, good reading lights and furniture, stocked refrigerator.

The **Chengdu Hotel** • *Dongyiduan, Shudu; Fax: 441603, Cable: 1015, Telex: 60164 CDHOT CN. Dist.A.P.25 km. Dist.R.W.8 km* • In downtown industrial area. 1984, ren. 1987. 14 stories, 310 rooms, two buildings. T.R., C.C. Swimming pool, barber shop, gym, and clinic. Rooms good decor. Stocked refrigerator.

Foreign Guest House • *Sichuan College of Education, Renmin Nan Rd., Section 3, No 24* • Six stories, 36 rooms. No elevators. Good for budget travelers but inconveniently located.

Jing Rong Hotel • *Beiyiduan, Erhuan Rd. Cable 7110. Telex 60310 JRH CN.* • Partial opening 1988.

OTHER IMPORTANT ADDRESSES

CAAC 中国民航 : Renmin Nan Rd., opposite the Jinjiang Hotel; tel. 23038, 23087.
C.I.T.S.: 180 Renmin Nan Rd.; tel. 25042, 28225. Telex 60154 CITSD CN. Branch in Jin Jiang Hotel.
C.T.S.: Jin Jiang Hotel; tel. 24757; cable 1278; Telex 60154 CITCD CN.
C.Y.T.S.: Room 252, Jin Jiang Hotel; tel. 32021.
Bank of China 中国银行成都分行 : 60 Shuwa Bei 3-St.; tel. 29515.
Hospitals: Check first with your hotel.
Hospitals attached to the West China University of Medical Science (Hua Xi Yi Ko Da Xue) 四川医学院附属医院 : tel. 27905.

Very close to the Jinjiang Hotel on Renmin Nan Rd.

Sichuan Renmin (People's) Hospital 四川省人民医院 : tel. 22712.

Hospital Attached to the Chengdu Institute of Traditional Chinese Medicine 成都中医学院附属医院 : tel. 23902.

Foreign Affairs Department of the Chengdu Public Security Bureau: Wenwu Rd.; tel. 22951 or 29551.

U.S. Consulate: Jinjiang Hotel, tel. 53514, or 24481.

CHONGQING (CHUNGKING)

Southwest China. Southeastern Sichuan province on mountainsides between the Changjiang (Yangtze) and Jialing rivers. A little over 2-hours' flight SW of Beijing or NW of Guangzhou. Overnight train ride from Chengdu. Direct flight from Hong Kong. Population: About 2.6 million urban. Highest temperature in summer, 40°C; lowest in winter, 6°C. Annual precipitation: 1000 mm. Chongqing is one of the "three furnaces" of China. Clear skies only in summer. Fog between November and March. Many flights canceled at this time, so travelers must be flexible.

Chongqing has a history of 3000 years. It was capital of the King-dom of Ba in the 12th century B.C. During the Song, it was named Chongqing, which means "double celebration." During the Qing, a 10-meter-high, 7-km wall was built around the city. Chongqing was one of the treaty ports open to foreigners, and foreign missionaries and teach-ers worked here before Liberation. Innumerable books have been writ-ten in English about this area.

In the late 1930s, during the Sino-Japanese War, the Nationalist government moved its capital here, and Han Suyin's book *Destination Chungking* reflects that period. Unfortunately, Japanese bombs de-stroyed much of the city, and few ancient relics survived the war. Zhou Enlai (Chou En-lai) lived here as he tried to work with the Nationalists against the foreign invader. The American (Stillwell, Hurley, Marshall, Wedmeyer) missions attempted unsuccessfully to get the Nationalists to work with the Communists. Read Theodore H. White's *In Search of History* for that period in the 1940s. The Communists took over the city in November 1949.

Today, Chongqing is smoky, drab, crowded, and industrial, with apparently little regard for city planning. It has very few bicycles be-cause of the narrow, winding, and hilly roads. It is now primarily of interest to students of modern history. It is also the place where you can get a 2-day trip to the Dazu sculptures, 165 km west, and take a ship down the Yangtze through the gorges.

For those who want to pass the time constructively while waiting for boats, you can learn a bit about modern Chinese history at **Hong-yancun Revolutionary Memorial Hall** (a.k.a. Red Crag Village) 红岩村革命纪念馆 (13 Hongyang Village). This was the office of the Communist Party and the Eighth Route Army between 1939 and 1946. It was also residence for Chou En-lai and other revolutionary leaders including, briefly, Mao Zedong (Mao Tse-tung). The opening of this office was greatly influenced by the kidnapping of Nationalist leader Chiang Kai-shek in Xi'an in 1936.

No. 50 Zengjiayan was the residence of some of the people work-ing at Red Crag Village. **Guiyang Garden** was at first the residence of the Nationalist representative but was later used by the Communists. The October 10 Agreement with Chiang Kai-shek was signed here. The prison used by the Nationalists for Communist prisoners is at **Jiatse Cave,** at the base of Gele Mountain in the northwestern suburbs. Today it is an exhibition on the infamous **Sino-American Special Technical Cooperation** 中美合作所集中营展览馆 , responsible for the loss of life of many people who fell afoul of Nationalist government offi-cials. Open daily, 8 a.m.–5:30 p.m.

For less recent history, there's the **Chongqing Museum** 重庆博物馆 (Pipashan Zheng St., near Loquat Park), open daily, 8–11:30 a.m. and 3–6:30 p.m. If you want to go back farther than that, try the

Chongqing Museum of Natural History 重庆自然博物馆 (Beibei District, 43 km NW of the city). Dinosaur bones were found in this region and some are on view here. Open daily, 8:30–11:30 a.m. and 3–6:30 p.m. In the same general vicinity is beautiful **Jinyun Shan,** known also as "Little Emei Shan," with its highest peak 1,030 meters. The **Jinyun Temple** was founded 1500 years ago and has relics from the Six Dynasties and the Ming. **Beiwenquan (North Hot Spring) Park** is below the temple. Its 10 hectares are pleasant and shady, with winding trails for strolling amid ancient Chinese architecture (if you don't care for a hot spring bath). The natural water temperature is 28–35°C. Open daily, 8 a.m.–6 p.m.

As for living animals, the **zoo** 动物园 (at Yangjiaping, in the west of the city) is open daily 6:30 a.m.–8 p.m. For art lovers, the Sichuan Fine Arts Institute in Huang Kuo Ping District is well worth a visit. The institute is one of the best in China, with a teacher-student ratio of 1:2. It has an excellent three-story gallery with art for sale. Open daily, 9–11:30 a.m. and 2–5:30 p.m. (tel. 23423).

For those who just want to pass the time relaxing while waiting for boats, there's **Eling (Goose Neck) Park** 鹅岭公园 , between the two rivers. It has pleasant pavilions, ponds, and gardens. Open daily, 6:30 a.m.–8 p.m. **Pipashan (Loquat Hill) Park** 枇杷山公园 is the highest point in the city and was a former warlord's residence. Good view of the two rivers and the city. Monkeys and birds. Open daily, 6:30 a.m.–10 p.m. Storytellers abound in the evenings!

For real relaxation, try the **Nanwenquan (South Hot Spring) Park** 南温泉公园 , 26 km south of the city. It has a hot water (40°C) swimming pool and baths, and 13 hectares of gardens in which to stroll or jog. Open daily, 8:30 a.m.–6 p.m. **Xiaoquan (Little Spring) Guesthouse** 小泉宾馆 is adjacent, with 168 rooms.

Nanshan (South Mountain) Park 南山公园 , on the south bank of the river, is where George C. Marshall, the American mediator, and Chiang Kai-shek lived. The Nationalist leader lived in "Yun Xiu." Nearby is **Tu Hill**, the site of the residence of King Yu of the Xia, the first ruler to control the rivers (see "Chengdu"). Also close is **Laojun Cave**, where Lao Tzu, the founder of Taoism, lived.

An 800-meter-long **cable car** 缆车 goes across the Jialing River from Cangbailu Station to Jinshajie Station for a bird's-eye view of the area. (6 a.m. to 11 p.m.)

Fengdu, 170 km east of Chongqing on the Yangtze, has a restored seventh-century city based on an ancient legend, a gathering place for ghosts.

For the "Yangtze Gorges" and "Dazu," see separate listings.

SHOPPING

Made in the province are umbrellas, silk, satin, bambooware, glassware, jewelry, knitting wool, and carpets.

Friendship Store 友谊商店 (People's Liberation Monument; tel. 41955); **Chongqing Gallery** 重庆美术馆 (Renmin Guesthouse; tel. 53421), paintings; **Chongqing Arts & Crafts Service** 重庆二艺美术服务 (People's Liberation Monument; tel. 42797); **Chongqing Department Store** 重庆百货公司 (People's Liberation Monument, tel. 41484).

RESTAURANTS

Sichuan food is famous. Not all of it is chili-hot. See *Sichuan Dishes* in "Food."

Chongqing Restaurant 重庆饭店 • *Xiaoshizi, Central District; tel. 43242.*

Weiyuan • *37 Zhouyoon Rd.; tel. 43592* • Sichuan dishes. Cleaner and more pleasant than other local restaurants.

Xiaobinlou • *82 Hsinhau Rd.* • Sichuan dishes and quick snacks.

Yuexiangcun (Old Sichuan) Restaurant • *Bayi Rd., Central District; tel. 41957.*

Yizhishi Restaurant • *People's Liberation Monument, Central District; tel. 42680.*

HOTELS

The top hotel here is the Renmin; No. 2 is the Chongqing (Fan Dian) and Yuzhou. No. 3 is the Chongqing (Bingguan). After it is fully opened, the Holiday Inn should be one of the best too.

Chongqing (Bingguan) Guest House. Built 1930s. Renovated 1985.

Chongqing (Fan Dian) Hotel (a.k.a. Chung King Hotel) • *41–43 Xin Hua Rd. Cable 7315. Telex 62193 CKHCL CN. Near wharf for Yangtze River cruises, Luohan Temple, downtown area, and cableway. Dist.A.P.37 km. Dist.R.W.5 km* • 1988. 9 stories, 200 rooms, 2 buildings. C.C., IDD. Business center, shuttle bus, sauna.

Chongqing Shaping Grand Hotel • *83 New Street, Xiaolongkan, 660030. Telex 62194 SCGH CN. Dist.A.P.15 km. Dist.R.W.10 km. Dist.*

Wharf 15 km • 1988, ren. 1990. 26 stories, 255 rooms. C.C. (no Am. Express). Business center.

Holiday Inn Yangtze Chongqing • *Dian Zi Ping, Nan Ping Xiang, Nan An Dist. Telex 62220 HIYCQ CN. Fax 483388. Dist.A.P.45. Dist.R.W.5 km. In trade zone, on south bank of Yangtze* • 1989. 21 stories, 383 rooms. Hot Pot restaurant. IDD, C.C., business center. Pool. Health club.

Renmin (People's) Hotel • *Renmin Rd.* • Built 1953 as People's Hall. Became hotel in 1978 and renovated 1987. Four stories, over 300 rooms. Now has elevators, bar, shopping center, swimming pool, massage clinic. 4000 seat auditorium. Exotic Chinese architecture.

Yuzhou Guest House • *Yuanjiagang.* • 1950s. Ren. 1987. Four stories, over 200 rooms. Originally a state guest house. 10 km from downtown with garden.

OTHER IMPORTANT ADDRESSES

Bank of China 中国银行 : Money-changing at Renmin, Chongqing, and Yuzhou guesthouses or hotels. Also airport, Friendship Store, railway station 火车站 , and passenger quay 长江客运码头 .

CAAC: 190 Zhongshan San Rd.; tel. 52643, 62970, 52813.

C.I.T.S. 中国国际旅行社 : Renmin Guesthouse, Renmin Rd.; tel. 51556. Telex 62126, CCITS CN. Cable 4015.

C.T.S.: 173 Renmin Rd.; tel. 51449. Cable 4015.

Hospitals: In case of illness, contact your hotel or guide first for a doctor, if convenient.

First Clinic of Chongqing No. 3 People's Hospital 重庆第三人民医院第一诊所 : Feilai Temple; tel. 3786.

Second Clinic of Chongqing No. 3 People's Hospital 重庆第三人民医院第二诊所 : Renmin Rd.; tel. 51228. Near the Renmin Hotel.

First Teaching Hospital of the Chongqing Medical College 重庆医学院第 : Yuanjiagang; tel. 23360.

CONGHUA 从化

(Tsunghua, Chunghua) South China. This is a hot-spring resort about 90 km NE of Guangzhou, in Guangdong province. The sulfurous spring water is said to bring relief for "high blood pressure, rheumatism, enteropathy, stomach and duodenal ulcers, neuralgia, and skin infections." The temperature of the water varies between 30°C and 70°C. The area is also noted for its hot sands, its yellow quartz caves, and a 16-meter-high waterfall.

DALIAN 大连

(Talien, a.k.a. Luda) Northeast China. This ice-free port near the southern tip of Liaoning province is an important industrial center. One of the Fourteen Open Coastal Cities, it can be reached by train or plane from Beijing or Shenyang, and also by plane from Shanghai, Tokyo, Hong Kong, Guangzhou, Xi'an, Urumqi, and Qingdao. It has an international airport. A toll highway joins it to Shenyang. It can also be reached by ship from Shanghai, Tianjin, Qingdao, and Yantai. Ocean cruise ships sometimes stop here. The urban population is 2.2 million. Dalian's hottest temperature (August) is 34°C, its lowest is ⁻21°C. The annual precipitation is 600–800 mm.

Known then as Port Arthur, Dalian was seized briefly by the Japanese in 1894, but was leased as a naval base for 25 years to Russia in 1898 in return for a loan to pay China's indemnity to Japan following the first Sino-Japanese War. Russia was also given the right to build a railroad connecting the base with the Trans-Siberian railroad. As the result of the Russian defeat by Japan in 1905, Japan took over the base until 1945.

Dalian is a very attractive city, with a lot of old tsarist and Japanese architecture and a high percentage of first-rate hotels. It also has 1800 km of coastline and a few beaches. Tourists might be interested in its **ornamental glass factory** 玻璃制品厂 , the centrally located **zoo,** and the harbor and its beautiful beaches. The best swimming beach is at the Bangchuidao Hotel. If the guard at the gate tries to stop you, telephone C.I.T.S. The second best swimming beach seems to be at **Tiger Park Beach** 老虎滩公园 . This beach is rocky and usually very crowded. You might try hiring a sampan to go to an outer island.

The **Natural History Museum** 自然博物馆 (3 Yantai St., in the north of the city), is only open a few days a week from 8 a.m. to 4 p.m.

C.I.T.S. can arrange a visit to a worker's home, a commune, or a genuine wedding if given 20 days' notice. Best between May 1 and Oct. 1. Contact: Foreign Liason Dept. of C.I.T.S. Dalian. It is planning a summer holiday center called **White Clouds Mountain Park** 白云山公园 and bicycle tours, etc.

The old **Port Arthur** has been off-limits to all foreigners except Overseas Chinese. This might change. Check with China Travel Service.

Snake Island, 25 nautical miles away, has an estimated 13,000 pit vipers and is a snake sanctuary. It supplied a research center studying the medical benefits of the venom.

The **Economic and Technical Development Zone** is about 30 km from the city and has its own hotel, the *Silver Sail*. The Trade Fair building is downtown with a 248-room hotel of its own.

FESTIVALS
Temple Fairs: 8th to 18th day of the fourth lunar month.

ENTERTAINMENT
The Dalian Song and Dance Ensemble and the Dalian Acrobatic Troupe have performed internationally. Local foreigners get together once a week at their *Dabizi Julebu* (Big Nose Club), and visitors can join the Hash House Harriers on their weekly run. Contact a foreign resident like the manager at the Furama.

The **English Corner** is every Saturday in Zhongshan Square. There should be a night market in the summer from 7 to 9 p.m. You can rent a tram car for a party.

C.I.T.S. or C.T.S. can arrange for scuba diving (water temp. 16° C to 22° C in summer), fishing, and mountain climbing. Lots of steam locomotives, best seen at Victory Bridge.

SHOPPING

Made here are shell pictures (said to be the best in China), fancy glass ornaments, and dishes.

Arts and Crafts Service Dept. (87 Puzhao St.; tel. 26281); **Antique Store** (229 Tianjin Rd.; tel.24955); **Dalian Department Store** (108 Zhongshan Rd.; tel. 23254) silk on 4th floor; **Dalian Foreign Languages Bookstore** (178 Tianjin St.; tel. 25472); **Friendship Store** (137 Sidalin (Stalin) Rd., tel. 234121); **Tianjinjie Department Store** (199 Tianjin St., tel. 26259).

RESTAURANTS

For seafood, of course:

Bohai Restaurant • *Qingniwa Bridge; tel. 33671.*

Restaurant of Dalian International Seamen's Club • *2/F, Gangwan Bridge; tel. 233181.*

HOTELS

The top hotels are the Regent, Furama, International, and Holiday Inn, but not necessarily in that order. No one seems to agree. All are international luxury standard and only the Regent is outside the city center. The next-best centrally located hotel is the Nanshan (an older hotel with good service and cheaper prices).

Bangchuidao Hotel 棒棰岛宾馆 • *Bangchuidao. Telex 86236 DBCIG CN. Cable 7080. Dist.A.P.22 km. Dist.R.W.10 km. In the southeastern suburbs* • 1961, ren. 1983. Seven villas of differing quality with 10 to 12 beds each, 100 to 500 meters from the beach. 260 rooms. Main building 6 stories. Villa No. 5 has 4-meter-high carved ceilings, gold-plated fixtures in bathrooms, and a jacuzzi. Business center, disco, tennis. Should now have IDD.

The **Dalian International Hotel** • *9 Stalin Rd.; Telex 86363 DIH CN. Fax 860411, 230008. Dist.A.P.25 km. Dist.R.W.3 km* • T.R. 1987. 27 stories, 380 rooms. 24-hour room service. IDD. Business center and business consultation. Chinese herbal medicine clinic, acupuncture to stop smoking. Gym, sauna, Karaoke bar. All-Nippon office. Handy central location.

Furama Hotel Dalian • *74 Stalin Rd. Telex 86441 FRAMA CN. Cable FURAMA. Fax 804455. Dist.Harbor 1 km. Dist.A.P.20 km. Dist.R.W.2 km* • Close to shopping. Will answer request for room only if not available. Book through UTELL. C.C. (no Visa). 1988. 22 stories, 402 rooms. No relation to Furama in Hong Kong. IDD, business center, office suites, free shuttle. Claims best disco and largest ballroom in northeast. Pool, whirlpool, and tennis.

Holiday Inn Dalian • *18 Sheng Li Square, Zhong Shan Ward. Telex 868383. Fax 809704. Dist.A.P.11 km. Dist.Harbor 1 km. Next door to R.W.* • 1989. 24 stories. C.C., IDD., Business center. Japanese food, health club, USTV.

Nanshan Hotel 南山宾馆 • *56, Fenglin St., Cable 5103. Telex 86446 DNSH CN. Fax 804898. Near Nanshan Mountain and children's playground. Dist.A.P.18 km. Dist.R.W.1.5 km.* • 25 villas built 1920 to 1932 with 4 to 6 rooms each. (#25 was headquarters for the Japanese commander of the Sept. 18 Incident.) 1985: 5-story main building, 93 rooms. IDD, health club, sauna, bowling. T.R., C.C. C.I.T.S. office, USTV.

Regent Hotel • *12 Hutan St., Zhongshan Dist. Telex 86352 DLRH CN. Cable 7787. On a hill above souvenir stalls, fishing boats, and Tiger Beach* • Better beach at Bang Chui Island 10 km. away. Dist.A.P.20 km. Dist.R.W.8 km. Japanese J.V. No connection with Hong Kong's Regent. 1988. Nine stories, 220 rooms. IDD, tennis, pool, business center. Rooms 2 to 13, 16 to 27 have seaview. Bicycles. T.R., C.C.

Xu Yue Hotel • *Fujiazhuang Resort, Xia Jia He Zi on beach.* • 1988. 100 rooms, 10 modest two-story villas. Dist.A.P.25 km. Dist.R.W.10 km.

OTHER IMPORTANT TELEPHONE NUMBERS
All Nippon Airways, tel. 239744.
C.I.T.S. 中国国际旅行社 : 1 Chongtong St., Xigang Dist. Tel. 331080. Telex 86485 DCITS CN. Cable 5795. Fax 337831.
C.T.S. 中国旅行社 : 1 Stalin Square. Tel. 335699.
CAAC 中国民航 : tel. 35884, 335884; airport 552071.
Railway Station 火车站 : tel. 203331.
Passenger Quay 客运码头 tel. 229363, 234241.
Cars and buses: Dalian Travel Service; tel. 331831, X514.

Z.M.Li

DATONG

(Tatung) North China. Northern Shanxi. 7 to 8 hours by train from Beijing. From here one can continue by once-a-week train to Ulan Bator and thence onward to Moscow. The population of Datong is 1,040,000, including the rural suburbs. The highest temperature in summer (July–August) is 37.7°C, the lowest (December–February) ⁻29.9°C. Rainfall is a scant 400 mm a year, mainly July–September. The best time to visit is May–October.

Founded during the Warring States, about 2200 years ago, this was a garrison town built between two sections of the Great Wall. The Northern Wei (386–534) declared it their capital and instructed monk Tanyao to supervise the carving of the Yungang Caves. The city wall is Ming.

Datong is basically a coal-mining town, one of the largest open-pit coal producing areas in the world, with a 600-year supply at the current rate of production. The city is industrial and heavily polluted. Outside Datong are visible coal deposits, with all kinds of coal transport equipment blocking up the roads. Some of the equipment is the most advanced in the world. The mining may be ugly but it is worth seeing. Because the mining has unearthed some old burial grounds, Shanxi has all extremely large number of excavated tombs and neolithic sites.

Datong gained considerable publicity recently because Occidental Petroleum of the United States began a joint venture in open-pit coal mining close to the city.

Datong is most famous for the ***Yungang (Yunkang) Grottoes,** said to be the best-preserved, the largest, and the oldest sandstone carvings in China. They can be reached by Bus No. 3 from Datong. Fifty-three caves here contain over 51,000 stone carvings of Buddha, bodhisattvas, apsaras (angels), birds, and animals. These statues range from 17 meters to a few centimeters high, and some of them still retain their original color. They were restored in 1976. The grottoes are at the southern foot of Wuzhou Hills, 16 km west of the city. They were built between A.D. 460 and 494 after a period of persecutions against the Buddhists supposedly led to the illness of Emperor Taiwu. The grottoes extend east-west for a kilometer. The Wei dynasty later moved its capital to Luoyang and built another set of grottoes there.

Although the exposed caves have suffered natural erosion as well as damage by man, they are nicely preserved and well worth visiting. The walking is easy, with no lighting problems. The best are at the Five Caves of Tanyao (Nos. 5, 6, 16–20), which include the largest statues. The large ears, which do make some of them look strange, can be excused because they mean long life. Although Datong was not on the Silk Road, the carvings carry strong Indian, Persian, and even Greek influences. One can expect to spend at least half a day here, strolling from cave to cave. During tourist season, English-speaking guides are available for hire. There is a restaurant in the area for foreign tourists. Open 8:30 a.m. to 4:30 p.m.

If you only have one day to spend in the city, C.I.T.S. recommends the Yungang caves, Huayan Monastery, Shanhua Monastery, and the Nine-Dragon Screen.

The ***Huayan Si (Huayan Monastery)** 华严寺 , a.k.a. Datong Municipal Museum, is the second largest temple in China. One can easily spend from 2 hours to a half day there, there is so much to see. It is in the SW section of the city, 3 km north of the main tourist hotel.

The monastery is well preserved and is separated into the Upper Huayan and the Lower Huayan. You pay two entrance fees. In the upper is the magnificent main hall, Daxiong Bao Dian, built in 1062 and rebuilt in 1140. It is 53.75 meters wide and 29 meters long. The beam structure, murals, five large Ming buddhas, and 26 guardians are most impressive. In the Lower is the main hall, the Bhagavan Stack Hall, built in 1038. Along its walls are 38 two-story wooden cabinets, housing the Buddhist sutras. The temple's exquisite 29 clay statues were made in the Liao. The monastery building also houses the **Datong Mu-**

DESTINATIONS · · · **257**

nicipal Museum's prehistoric fossils and cultural relics.

The *****Shanhua Monastery** 善化寺 , in the SW part of the city, was founded in A.D. 713. Surviving are relics of the Liao and Jin. The **Nine Dragon Screen** 九龙壁 , in the SE section of the old city, is almost 600 years old, and at 45.5 meters, larger than the two in Beijing. The morning is better for taking photographs. Other than a small gate in front of the open yard where the screen stands, there is no other attraction in that general area.

If you have more time or special interest, the 67.3-meter-high *****Sakyamuni Wooden Pagoda at Fogong Temple** 佛宫寺释迦塔 may be worth the 1½-hour drive if you are interested in unusual pagodas. It is the tallest ancient woodframe structure in China. It was constructed in 1056 (Liao), with eight corners and nine stories. From the outside it looks like five stories. Local folklore says that the pagoda only sits on five of its six vertical beams. One of the beams is always "resting," and you can pass a piece of paper underneath it. Each beam takes its turn without having to hold any weight. Bring a piece of paper and test it for yourself. This pagoda is usually locked, but ask for permission to view the interior. It is 75 km from Datong in Yingxian county.

The **Great Wall** 长城 is 40 km away. On **Wutai Mountain** 五台山 , 200 km away, are about 50 temples from the 5th century, three of them historical monuments also protected by the State Council. These are the *Main Hall of the **Nanchan Temple** 南禅寺 (Tang), the *****Foguang Temple** (Tang to Qing), and the *****Xiantong Temple** 佛光寺 (Ming to Qing). The main halls of the Nanchan and Foguang temples are the oldest extant woodframe buildings in the world. Both have histories of over 1200 years and are worth the whiteknuckle trip through the mountains. Ask for the Maopeng Shenzhuang Guest House or the Qixian Pavillion Hotel. The 17 clay statues here are Tang. Wutai is one of the Four Great Buddhist Mountains of China. Hotels have been built in Taihuai. Visitors can hike on a paved path to the summit.

Trips can also be arranged from Datong to **Hengshan Mountain**, 80 km away, for the **Xuankongsi (Temple in Mid-Air)**. See separate listing, "Hengshan Mountain." Visitors should be able to see 11th-century Liao dynasty tombs. For other places of interest in the province, see "Taiyuan."

In Datong there used to be a steam locomotive factory, but now there is only a museum with China's oldest (1882), and a club for enthusiasts. You can also visit a brass products factory 铜器工厂 (hot pots, plates, tea pots). C.I.T.S can arrange visits to both.

A unique **dog corporation** breeds more than 500 kinds of dogs, including sharpei and chows, but the dogs are not for sale. Contact: C.I.T.S., Room 137 Linfen Hotel, Linfen City. Tel. 2951 X561. Cable 2464. Telex 295010 ITSLF CN.

SHOPPING

Made locally are porcelain, brassware, knitting wool, furs, leather, and carpets.

Friendship Store 友谊商店 : 8 West Yingbin Rd.; tel. 32333.
Antique Store 古玩商店 : Huayan Monastery; tel. 33629.

RESTAURANTS

Fenglin Restaurant 枫林饭店 ● *West Rd., Datong; tel. 33680.*

Fengwei Restaurant 风味饭店 ● *East Yingbin Rd.; tel. 32333.*
● Datong style food.

HOTELS

Datong Guest House 大同宾馆 ● *8 West Yingbin Rd. Dist.A.P.50 km. Dist.R.W.13 km.* ● 1958, ren. 1988. Dance hall, bar, and hot pot.

Yungang Hotel 云岗宾馆 ● *21 East Yingbin Rd. Dist.A.P.55 km, Dist.R.W.15 km.* ● 1975. 9 stories, 152 rooms and 8 suites. Business center. Considered the best hotel.

The **Datong Mining Co.** 大同矿物局 has several guesthouses open for tourists.

C.I.T.S. and **Datong Municipal Tourist Bureau:** Yungang Hotel, 21 East Yingbin Rd.; tel. 52265 and 52043. Telex: 28151 CITSD CN. Fax 35044.

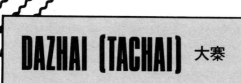

DAZHAI (TACHAI) 大寨

North China. SE of Taiyuan in Shanxi province, Dazhai was a commune famous as a model because of its spirit of hard work and self-sacrifice. Up until 1978, you could frequently hear the slogan ''In agriculture, follow Dazhai.'' In 1979, however, officials pointed out that while this spirit to struggle hard was correct, the slavish copying of Dazhai's example was not. Because every commune had different conditions, every commune had to improve its production in its own way. Dazhai was accused of falsifying its production figures.

DAZU 大足

> Southwest China. About 165 km NW of Chongqing (3 to 4 hours by good winding road) in Sichuan province, this is usually an overnight trip. 280 km SE of Chengdu. Road and plane access from both. Population 780,000. Altitude 380 meters.

The **Dazu Stone Buddhist Sculptures** are considered by some connoisseurs as better preserved and of finer quality than Luoyang, Datong, or Dunhuang. Decide for yourself. About 50,000 of them are located in 43 places in Dazu County, most not readily accessible by car. To see both Beishan and Baodingshan takes about a day and a half. Since the carvings are in hilly surroundings, take time to enjoy the natural scenery and the nearby water reservoir too. Study details. Look for the mother sleeping next to a bed-wetting child, the village girl tending ducks, the funeral rites, the wedding, etc.

The most concentrated numbers are at *Beishan (Northern Hill) 北山 (Tang to Song), 2 km north of the Dazu Guest House. Under State Council protection are **Fowan, Guanyinpo, Foerfeng,** and **Yingpanshan**. From the car park, you have to climb nearly 400 stairs. However, the 25-minute climb is spread out along pleasant, shady trails and is much easier than expected (10 minutes downhill). The sculptures at *Fowan are grouped together like beehives. A couple of chambers are fenced with iron gates and locks. Although some of the sculptures have been damaged, the arrangement and the preservation of some are excellent. Take special note of the enchanting Goddess of Mercy of No. 125, and No. 113. The locked No. 155 and No. 136 are worth careful inspection. The pagoda, about 1 km away, is also full of sculptures and is a popular picnic spot with local students.

The first statue was carved here in A.D. 892 by Wei Junjing. It was then a military camp.

Also worth seeing and accessible in large numbers are the sculptures at *Baodingshan 宝顶山 (Song dynasty), 15 km NE of the Dazu Guest House. The ones here were basically done by one monk, Zhou Zhifeng, from 1179 to 1249, and centered on the theme "Life is Vanity." The daily life of people is well-illustrated with vivid facial expressions and body language. The work here is largely intact and the sculptures are huge. The Sleeping Buddha is 31 meters long, and some of the standing figures are 7 meters high. It is essential that you obtain a tour guide to explain highlights to you. To see this grouping takes only a few minutes.

The sculptures at *Xiaofowan 小佛湾 are in the Shengshao Temple near the entrance of *Dafowan 大佛湾 . Many tourists are only shown Dafowan, but other sculptures are close by. If you want to see more, do insist on it. Another group of sculptures, carved in the Song Dynasty, are at **Shimenshan,** 23 km from the Dazu Hotel.

Also under State Council protection here are *Guangdashan, *Longtan, and *Linsongpo.

An excellent book on Dazu has been published by the Sichuan Provincial Academy of Social Sciences in English and Chinese.

You might be able to tell roughly when the sculptures were created because the Tang figures are simple, smooth, and more alluring. The Five Dynasty statues are meticulously carved with details. The Song statues are rather reserved but distinctive in personality and expression.

The largest statue is the Sleeping Buddha and the most famous a **1000-armed Goddess of Mercy** 千手观音 , both at Baoding Hill. Beautiful is the face of the **Hen wife** here. You may notice that many of the larger statues are bigger at the top and lean forward to make viewing easier from below.

En route, with some detour, visitors can also stop at the **North Hot-Spring Park** 北温泉公园 with its huge swimming pool, 1500-year-old temple, and dinosaurs.

Made locally are stainless steel tableware and bamboo carvings.

HOTELS
Dazu Guest House 旅馆 ● 70 rooms. Expanded in 1984. New air conditioning 1987. 140 beds. Better-suited for business people.

Beishan Hotel ● 100 rooms. Better. Reservations for either from Renmin Guest House (Chongqing) or Jin Jiang Hotel (Chengdu).

C.I.T.S. and **C.T.S.,** 中国国际旅行社 : 47 Gong Long St., tel. 22245. Cable 2464.

DUNHUANG 敦煌

(Tunhuang, Tunhwang) Northwest China. Western Gansu. Noted for one of the biggest art treasures in the world.

Between the fourth and 14th centuries, more than 1000 caves were cut out of the cliffs 25 km SE of the city and filled with Buddhist carvings, gilt and colored frescoes, and murals. Known as the *Mogao Grottoes 莫高窟 or the Thousand Buddha Caves, 492 of these remain today in three or four rows on a 1½-km-long wall. The State Council has renovated murals like the Feitian (Flying Apsaras) fresco (Tang) and repainted over 2000 statues. Some of the statues in about 20 caves were repainted in the Qing. Note the intricately painted ceilings too.

The most important cave is the Cangjing (Preserving Buddhist Scriptures) Cave 藏经洞 , now No. 17. Dating from the Jin to Song, a span of 600 years, this is where 40,000 important old documents were found, including the Diamond Sutra (A.D. 868), said to be the oldest existing dated printed book. It is now in the British Museum in London. Many archaeologists and historians work in a museum at the site, studying not just Mogao but other cave temples in the area.

Many caves have stories. One of the most famous is outlined in a series of pictures about a woman who was badly treated by her husband. While returning to her mother, she encountered a wolf that killed her two children, one of them newly born. After becoming a nun, she learned that her current miseries were a punishment for mistreating her stepsister in a previous incarnation.

Some of the statues are damaged. Signs indicate which museums abroad have stolen the pieces originally here. Some of the colors are still original and vivid. The red might be from pig's blood or cinnabar. One could get a real feeling of history and mysticism here. Caves were used as temples because they were conducive to meditation and secure, like a mother's womb. Perhaps the womb also symbolizes reincarnation.

The caves are a one-day trip at least. In recent years only a couple of enterprising noodle vendors and a seller of sickly sweet orange drink served visitors here, so you would be better off taking your own lunch, which you could eat in the shade of a tree. As there are few Chinese tourists, public buses from Dunhuang city are infrequent, leaving the Dunhuang Guest House at 8 a.m. and 2 p.m., arriving at Mogao 30 minutes later. Make sure you find out what time the last bus leaves if you have to rely on public transport. The caves are open from 8:30 to 11:00 a.m. and 2:30 to 5 p.m. Knowledgeable guides are available for hire on the site to show you around, but unfortunately they only speak Chinese. As with all cave temples, it is crucial to take your own flashlight, and do not expect to see an entire mural as you would in a spacious museum. You have to piece each section together in your own mind. This fragmentation has disappointed some tourists. Much climbing is involved.

Some recent tourists were not allowed to take photos. You must purchase a ticket for a small fee, which includes a guide who opens locks to the designated caves. In the past, plainclothes guards followed tourists to prevent unauthorized picture-taking.

The caves open to visitors are rotated every year. Unless you know in advance which you want to see, ask for samples of the best from the different dynastic periods: Sui, Tang, Song, etc.

Dunhuang can be reached by train (27 hours) plus a bumpy bus ride (3 hours) from Lanzhou. It is not a comfortable trip and is especially dry and dusty. Take your own drinks. This is, after all, a desert. If flying from Beijing, one usually needs to spend the night in Lanzhou. From Lanzhou to Dunhuang is a 4-hour plane ride with an early-morning departure and one stop, arriving before noon. There is also a flight from Urumqi and Jiayuguan once a week. The bus to Qiayuguan takes nine dusty hours.

Summers are hot; winters are very cold. *The caves are closed from late November through April.*

Dunhuang was an important cultural exchange center and oasis on the Silk Road. The old town is 250 meters west of the current one. Dunhuang was founded in 111 B.C. during the Han. From here, the road west splits into northern and southern routes and ended 7000 km away at the Mediterranean Sea. Dunhuang was a military outpost under the Tang. In A.D. 400, it became the capital of the Xiliang kingdom. An enemy army of 20,000 attacked the city and flooded it 21 years later. It changed hands several times. In 1227, Genghis Khan seized it, and in the Ming, it was a military headquarters. The ruins of the walls and a 16-meter-high tower can be seen in the old part of town. The population now is 10,000.

Visitors also can see the **White Horse Pagoda** 白马塔 (only a 12-meter-high dagoba in the desert and a 5-minute stop). It commemorates the horse of the Indian monk Fumoluoshi, which died here. The **Yang-**

guan Pass 阳关 (70 km south of Dunhuang) is just a wall now, of interest to people who like deserts or have a feeling for history. It was a military command post from the Han to the Yang, but the sands of the desert have inundated it.

The **Yumen (Jade Gate) Pass** 玉门关 (80 km NW of the city) has remains of the old wall. Jade used to be carried through here. These three sites are in themselves really not worth the hardship of getting here, but if you think of what went through here, the caravans of camels and merchants supplying the wealthy homes of Europe, and the envoys bringing tribute to the emperor, they can be emotional experiences. A recent Chinese movie *Dunhuang* makes an attempt to recapture the spirit of the era and could help you appreciate the relics here.

Dunhuang also has a carpet factory 地毡厂 , and the **Mingsha (Ringing Sand) Hill** 鸣沙山 (5 km south), where once a whole army was buried during a sandstorm. Their ghosts are still heard from time to time playing military drums and horns!

Dunhuang Hotel 敦煌饭店 ● *Dong Dajie. Tel. 2492, 2195. Cable 2464. Dist.A.P.13 km. Dist.R.W.130 km* ● 1980. 260 beds. Best in town and quite good.

Feitian Hotel. Handy to bus station. Backpackers only. Eat at the Dunhuang.

C.I.T.S.: tel. 26181. Cable 2646.

See also "Silk Road."

EMEI SHAN 峨眉

(Emei or Omei Mountain) Southwest China; 170 km SW of Chengdu in Sichuan, Emei Shan is one of China's four great Buddhist mountains. The base can be reached by train from the North Railway Station in Chengdu, or by bus to Emeishan City. From there one takes a bus to Baoguo Temple.

The climb to the summit and back can be done on foot in one day if you're energetic, or two days for the less agile. Along the 60-km stone path are 23 monasteries, intriguing caves, gushing waterfalls, magnificent views, and birds. Be careful of monkeys. They can steal food, scratch, and bite. Land Rovers can drive to within 6 km of the peak at **Jieyin Hall** 接引殿 at 2670 meters. At that height, the weather can be very chilly, about ⁻20°C at the top in January. Hostels are at the base of and on the 3100-meter-high summit. Restaurants along the way. Guides available.

The best time to climb is from April to June and September to November. It may be too cold and slippery for climbing from December to March, but the mountain is beautiful. The rainy season is July and August.

Baoguo Temple 报国寺 , at the base, has a scale-model map of the mountain with lights. The temple originates from the Ming. **Wannian Monastery** 万年 (a.k.a. Samantabhadra Monastery), on the slope, dates from the 4th century. Its *bronze and iron Buddha images are Song to Ming. The bronze Samantabhadra on a white elephant is 7.4 meters high and weighs 62 tons. The beamless brick hall, roof, and square walls are said to be typically Ming.

HOTELS

Hong Zhu Shan (Red Spider Hill) Hotel 红珠山宾馆 • *near the Baoguo Temple* • *Dist.A.P.160 km. Dist.R.W.10 km* • 1935, ren. 1980, 1989. 140 rooms, ten buildings. Largest in the city. C.C., IDD, business center, bicycle rentals.

The **Southwest Jiotong University Guest House** is open to groups and individual travelers.

Travel Service, Hong Zhu Shan Hotel; tel. 2528, 2430. Cable 4767.

Hospital: The **Red Cross Hospital,** next to Hong Zhu Shan Hotel.

FOSHAN 佛山

(Fushan; Cantonese Fashan) South China, Guangdong province, about 20 km SW of Guangzhou. Population 290,000. China United flies between Foshan and Beijing, Nanjing, and a few other cities.

Named ''Hill of Buddhas'' because a mound of Buddhist statues were excavated here, this is one of the Four Ancient Towns of China.

The city is over 1300 years old and is famous for its handicrafts. In addition, it has factories making machines, electronics, chemicals, textiles, plastics, pharmaceuticals, cement, etc. It is especially famous for pottery, and a 6-km-long street of ceramic and pottery stores is being built. It is a good one-day excursion from Guangzhou. A superhighway should now be open between the two cities.

Foshan Folk Art Institute 佛山民间艺术研究社 produces palace lanterns, T-shirts, and paper cutouts. It is a training institute for master crafts people in all fields. The **Shiwan Artistic Ceramic Factory** 石湾美术陶瓷厂 is one of the most famous porcelain factories in China; some of its works adorn the tops of temples in south China and Hong Kong. Its collection of maroon-robed *lohan,* with expressive, bulging eyes and unglazed faces, is well known.

The **Ancestral Temple,** now the **Foshan Municipal Museum** 祖庙博物馆 was originally erected in the Song (Emperor Yuanfeng, 1078–1085) and rebuilt in 1372 after a disastrous fire. Expanded and rebuilt after Liberation, the temple contains sculptures, ancient relics, and a 2500 kg bronze figure named Northern Emperor. Note the variety of decorations on the bases of the arches and the stone, wood, and brick carvings. Four of the statues are said to be made of paper, the others of wood or clay. The roof, decorated with Shiwan pottery figures, is one of the most elaborate in the country. A little gaudy, but artistically and culturally important.

The **silk factory** 丝织厂 is also open to visitors. (See also nearby ''Xiqiao Mountain.'')

Air-conditioned bus with television goes from the station near the Foshan Hotel to Hai'an (from where you can get a ferry to Haikou on Hainan Island). Takes about 10 hours.

Nightlife: in the works are evening markets, nightclubs, disco halls, and amusement park.

SHOPPING

Locally made are cuttlebone sculptures, brick carvings, silk, lanterns, paper-cuts, etc.

See also nearby ''Xiqiao Mountain.''

HOTELS

Foshan Hotel • *75 South Fenjiang Rd. Cable 2388. Telex: 44773 FSBRA CN. Fax: 0757--22347. Dist. A.P.4 km. Dist.R.W.1. km. Across from free market and ½ km. from amusement park.* • Attractive Chinese-style garden hotel. Business center conference room, swimming pool. New section good, best in the city.

Foshan Overseas Chinese Hotel • *14 Zumiao Rd. Cable: 4428. Across street from folk art store. Dist.A.P.8 km. Dist.R.W.1 km.* • Ma-for credit cards. 5 stories; 152 rooms. Should have IDD now. Rooms have high ceilings and thin drapes. Good. Clean.

Revolving or Rotating Palace Hotel • *Zumiao Rd. Cable REVO 3288. Fax: 85622 X 328. Telex: 44804 RPH CN. Dist.A.P. 5 km. Dist.R.W. less than 1 km.* • Built 1985, ren. 1988. Most complete for business travelers. Major credit cards. Walk to night market, free market, and ancestral temple. Will answer telex for reservation. IDD. 18 stories, 102 rooms. Clean.

New hotel to open by 1990; **Foshan Garden Hotel** with 22 floors and a hotel opposite the Foshan, for business travelers.

C.I.T.S.国际旅行社: 75 Fenjiang Ave. S.; tel. 23338, 87923 X8814, X4421. Telex 44773 FSBRA CN. Cable 2388.
C.T.S.中旅社: 86511 X240. Cable 4428.
Foshan Tourism Bureau, Third floor, 107 Renmin Rd.,; tel. 85901. Cable 1472.

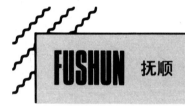

FUSHUN 抚顺

Northeast China. Eastern Liaoning, 50 km NE of Shenyang. It is one of China's biggest coal centers but is becoming best-known for the prison where the Last Emperor spent nine years, from 1950 to 1959. Urban population is 1.24 million. A new airport should be opening soon, between Shenyang and Fushan. Shenyang is one hour away by train. The temperature reaches a high of 36°C in summer and a low of ⁻35°C in winter. Annual precipitation about 800 mm, with 153 frostfree days a year.

Built on a neolithic site, Fushun became a walled city in the Ming. In 1778, the town was rebuilt as a political and economic center. **Xingjing town (Hetuala)** in Yingbin county was built by the founder of the Qing dynasty. Over half of the population are Manchu, and you can see some of the old customs. The first Manchu capital was here in 1616. The last emperors of China were Manchu. **Yongling** (1598) has the oldest Qing tombs, those of the ancestors of the Qing emperors. A pagoda on **Mt. Gaoer** (5 km from the hotel) and a Guanyin temple below it date from the Liao (1088).

Tourists can also visit the 2 by 6.6 km **West Open Cast Coal Mine** 西露天煤矿 (10 km from the hotel) and the **Dahuofang Reservoir** 大伙房水库 (17 km from the hotel). This is a 110-square-km lake. An elaborate 1929-built tomb of a marshal in the Liaoning army is at the foot of Mt. Tiebei on the reservoir. Two hotels are being built here, the 120-bed Hubin and the 40-bed Luo Tai Shan Hotel. C.I.T.S. can also arrange a trip to an old people's home 养老院 (16 km from the hotel).

The real interior of the **Fushun War Criminal Prison** was not seen in the movie *The Last Emperor*. The prison was opened to the public only in 1987, for former Japanese inmates to show their families. It was originally built by the Japanese in 1936. About 900 Japanese prisoners, Emperor Pu Yi, 50 Manchu officials, and over 300 Nationalists were held here. The exhibitions and photos displayed inside are of these three groups, instruments of torture, bacteria warfare experiments, and the Japanese surrender. In 1988, officials were asked to put up signs in English. Please let me know if they have.

A torture chamber, in the basement of the first building, is now used for storage. The building used for prisoners sentenced to death became a clinic in the 1950s. A photo of each prisoner is above his bedspace.

You can see the greenhouse where Pu Yi learned gardening, the room where his last concubine stayed 48 hours with him (and afterwards filed for divorce), and the room where he received his pardon. Arrangements can be made for tourists to sleep in the prison (or the air-conditioned prison guesthouse), and even on Pu Yi's bed. There were 11 other Manchus in his room at first; he was moved in 1952 because he didn't know how to tie his shoelaces. Note the chamberpot. Pu Yi also eventually learned to clean it.

SHOPPING

Amber and jet carvings. Gold and silver filigree, jade carving, artistic candles and artistic glassware are also made here.

RESTAURANTS

Oriental Cherry Restaurant in the hotel.

Chong Le in front of the railway station.

Yan Bin Lou, the largest vegetarian restaurant in the Northeast.

HOTELS

The new section of the **Friendship Hotel** • *Yong'on Square. Dist.R.W.½ km* • should be the best in town. Four-story section built 1958, ren. 1989. Seven story section with dorms should be open now. No C.C. Small TVs, high ceilings.

Fushun Hotel 抚顺宾馆 • *1 Western Rd. Cable 2000. Telex 80388 FSHTL CN. Central. Dist.A.P.40 km. Dist.R.W.½ km.* • No C.C. 1960, expanded 1986. 5 stories, 216 beds for foreigners. No IDD. Small rooms and bathrooms, poor reading lights. CAAC booking office.

Ying Hua (Oriental Cherry) Hotel • *4 Dongsan Rd. Telex 819023. Dist.A.P.33 km. Dist.R.W.one block. Behind department store.* • Built with funds from former Japanese prisoners. 1988. Five stories, 20 medium-sized rooms. Small bathrooms. Japanese restaurant. No elevators. Rents bicycles.

C.I.T.S.: Friendship Hotel, Yong'on Square; tel. 23341. Telex 81914 FSHTL CN Cable 3266.
Fushun Travel & Tourism Section, Foreign Affairs Office, Fushun Municipality, Yong'on Square; tel. 29756.

FUZHOU 福州

(Foochow, Fuchou) East China. Capital of Fujian province on the east coast across from Taiwan, this city is over 2000 years old. Urban pop. 1.3 million. Flights from Hong Kong, Beijing, Shanghai, Guangzhou, and Hangzhou. Buses from Guangzhou (two days) via Shantou, or a 37-hour train ride. Hottest temp. 39°C, July-August; coldest—0.8°C, February.

Opened to foreign trade in 1842, Fuzhou had British and American dockyards, and factories for making tea bricks. Once home to about 10 foreign consulates, its foreign cemetery was dug up and replaced by a school. The old British Community Church, never used by the Chinese, is now a warehouse. Across the street is a women's college looking for native English-speakers willing to teach English in return for room and board.

What you can see are **Gushan (Drum Hill)** 鼓山 , topped by a huge drum-shaped boulder in the eastern suburbs, at least 1004 meters high. The **Yongquan Si (Surging Spring Temple)** 涌泉寺 was founded in A.D. 783 and has a white jade Buddha. Monks chant at 4:30 a.m. and p.m. for one hour. The **Qianfo Taota (Thousand-Buddha Pottery Pagodas)** 千佛陶塔 and the **Shuiyun Ting (Water and Cloud Pavilion)** 水云亭 , east of the Yongquan Si are both from the Song. Views from the 18 caves west of the temple are said to be famous. Several hundred inscriptions on the cliff are near the **Lingyuan Dong (Spirit Source Cave)** 灵源洞 . Over 100 of these writings are from the Song.

The city is also noted for its hot springs, with over a dozen in Fuzhou itself. The most famous temples are the plain-looking **Baita (White Pagoda)** 白塔 , on the west side of Yushan Hill, and the **Wuta (Black Pagoda)** 乌塔 , at the base of Wushi Hill, both in the center of town. The main hall of the *Hualin Temple 华林寺 , from the Song, is worth seeing. The **Jinshan (Gold Mountain) Temple** 金山寺 is snugly perched on an island west of the city.

The **Memorial Hall of Lin Zexu** 林则徐祠堂 , the official who burned the 20,000 chests of opium near Canton in 1839, is a small shrine with a statue of the national hero. Known also as a calligrapher and a poet, Lin was one of the first Qing officials to take an interest in things foreign. Because the British fired on China as a result of Lin's actions, the emperor exiled Lin to Yili in Xinjiang.

Fujian province has only recently been opened to foreign visitors. Most developed for tourists seems to be Xiamen (Amoy), with good hotels. Quanzhou is next, for some interesting things to see. Fuzhou seems to have less to offer. Zhangzhou is worth a few hours. See separate listings.

For outdoor types, **Wuyi Mountain** 武夷山 , in the northwestern part of the province, is a good place to visit, with a native-style hotel and rafting through beautiful Guilin-type scenery. It is a three-day bus trip or a one-hour plane ride (twice a week) from Fuzhou.

Aside from Wuyi, Fujian is mainly for those interested in maritime history, in Koxinga (museums in Xiamen and Quanzhou), and in the relics of Arab traders, Manichaeanism, and Nestorian Christianity. Some of its native sons have returned from Southeast Asia with wealth. They have built monuments, schools, hospitals, and temples. The religious buildings are uniquely flamboyant and show traces of cosmopolitan connections.

The Fujian dialect is distinct, neither Cantonese nor Mandarin. This language is spoken also by the majority on Taiwan, just across the straits. The weather is subtropical, and most of the province is mountainous.

ENTERTAINMENT

Disco at the **Hot Springs** Hotel. Night market near May 1 Square. Festival of Goddess Mazu in April and May.

SHOPPING

Good lacquerware, cork carving, and Shoushan stone carvings are made and sold here.

Friendship Store 友谊商店 (Aug. 17th Rd.; tel. 55406); **Fujian Antique General Store** 省文物总店 (Aug. 17th Rd.; tel. 54792). **Fuzhou Tourist Shopping Center** (May 4th Rd., near Foreign Trade Center, tel. 533491); **Fuzhou Carving Art General Factory** (Tel. 552373); **Bodiless Lacquerware Factory** (North of Wu Yu Rd.; tel. 54411, 50661. For sightseeing as well as buying—no credit cards).

HOTELS

Hotels here are centered around the Foreign Trade Center except the Lakeside and the nearby West Lake Guest House. The best-looking hotel was the classy new Lakeside (if you like modern, glass-walled high-rises) but we don't have a recent evaluation. In any case, its location is lovely and quiet, and its lobby is attractive and bright. The Foreign Trade Center Hotel and the Hot Spring Hotel seem better than the Overseas Chinese Hotel. The Dong Hu was scruffy and had smaller rooms, but handy to C.I.T.S. All the downtown hotels have hot spring water in their rooms and all are convenient for the Foreign Trade Center (FTC) and shopping.

Donghu Hotel ● *44 Dong Da Rd. Cable 9612. Telex 92171 DHHFZ CN. Fax 555519. Dist.A.P.13 km. Dist.R.W.4.* ● Dist.FTC½ km. T.R., C.C. 1984, ren. 1988. Ten stories, over 200 rooms. Standard furnishings. IDD. Business center. Hotel directories in Chinese only.

Fujian Foreign Trade Center Hotel ● *Wusi Rd. Telex 92158 FTC CN. Cable 8612. Fax 550358. Next door to FTC. Dist.A.P.15 km. Dist.R.W.4 km* ● T.R., C.C. 1985, ren. 1988, 1990. 7 stories, 195 rooms. IDD, business center, attractive rooms. Should now have pool, tennis, and conference hall. Preferred by business people, though second best.

Hot Spring Hotel ● *Wusi Rd., middle section. Telex 92180 HSHFZ CN. Cable 8426. Fax 535150. Dist.A.P.13 km. Dist. R.W.4.* ● Dist.FTC ½ km. Reservations through Utell International. 1986, ren. 1989. 15 stories, 311 rooms. IDD. Outdoor pool, gym, tennis, bowling. Business center. Qigong. "Bubble" elevator. Large rooms with balconies, small closets, no drawers. Hair dryers. T.R., C.C.

Lakeside Hotel ● *1 Hubin Rd. Telex 92265 FLHBC CN. Fax 536585* ● T.R., C.C., 1988. 21 stories, 436 rooms. Gym, disco, pool, business center, grill room, IDD. C.I.T.S. in lobby. Rooms for wheelchair guests. Even-numbered rooms have lake view. Good furniture.

Overseas Chinese Hotel 华侨大厦 ● *Wusi Rd. Telex 92123 FJKTS CN. Fax 550648. Dist.A.P.13 km. Dist.R.W.4 km.* ● Across street from FTC. T.R., C.C. 1961, ren. 1988. 8 stories, 273 rooms. C.T.S. office. IDD, florescent lights, thin drapes. Good furniture. Small closets and bathrooms, thin towels. Dorms. Bathrooms have natural hot spring water.

C.I.T.S. 国际旅行社 : 44 Dongda Rd.; tel. 552052. 551950. Cable 8945. Telex 92201 CITS CN.
C.T.S. 中旅社 : Fujian Br., Wusi Rd; tel. 556304, 554215. Cable 8312. Fax 553983. Telex 92123 FJKTS CN. Branch in Guangzhou; tel. 336888 X454.
CAAC 中国民航 : May 1st Rd.; tel. 55113.
Tourism Bureau of Fujian Province: North American Office, #603–1112 West Pender St., Vancouver, B.C., V6E 2S1, Canada; tel. (604) 687–7435. Fax (604) 687–2639.

GEZHOUBA 葛洲坝

Southwest China, in Hubei, is the new town (1970s) where tour boats pass through the locks on the Changjiang (Yangtze) River, 3 km downstream of the Three Gorges and about 1 km upstream of Yichang. The biggest multipurpose water conservancy project on the river, it includes a 2561-meter-long and 70-meter-high dam, two power stations (2.715 million kwh capacity), a silt-discharge gate, a reservoir, a flood-discharge gate, and a channel for migrating fish. Completed in 1988, 21 generators should be able to produce 14.1 billion kwh annually. The difference in water level is about 20 meters.

GRAND CANAL 大运河

The oldest and longest in the world, this canal was built in the Sui dynasty (A.D. 581–618) and originally extended 1794 km from Hangzhou to Beijing.

Today visitors can still take tour boats on parts of the canal, a trip that gives you an intimate look at the life on the water, in waterside houses, villages, and countryside. One can sleep on ferries too between cities to save on paying for a hotel room. But the water is dirty and the trip can be noisy as traffic moves on the canal all night.

At individual cities along the route, you can see parts of the canal. Wuxi has 12 tour boats, including a 36.5-meter-long, two-storied "dragon boat" with flashing eyes and ancient Chinese costumes.

GREAT WALL 长城

(Wanlichangcheng—10,000 li-long wall.) The Great Wall is officially 12,700 Chinese li, or 6350 km, or 3946.55 miles long. The length depends on what you measure, there being many offshoots and parallel walls. It is in various states of repair.

The Great Wall was first built in shorter pieces, starting in the fifth century B.C., as a defensive and boundary wall around the smaller states of Yen, Chao, and Wei. The first Qin emperor (221–206 B.C.), who unified China for the first time, linked up and extended the walls from

Liaoning in the east to Gansu in the NW as protection from the Huns and other nomadic tribes to the north. The wall was subsequently repaired and extended by succeeding dynasties, especially the Ming.

Originally built by slave labor, it has been called the world's longest graveyard because many of its builders were buried where they fell. It was designed to allow five horsemen or ten soldiers to march abreast along the top. It was almost a superhighway, considering the rough mountain terrain. A system of bonfires communicated military information to the emperor at a speed rapid for that period.

The best time to visit is after 2 p.m., when most of the tourists have left. Stay to see the sunset if you can.

The Great Wall is most frequently visited at ***Badaling (Padaling),** about 75 km (two hours) by bus NW of Beijing. Until two other sections near Beijing were opened, it was extremely crowded. You still need to avoid the Sunday traffic jams. Usually the trip can be done by taxi in 4 hours if you don't linger. Most tourists now go from Beijing by tourist bus. Tourist buses leave Beijing daily at 8 a.m. and stop at both the Great Wall and Ming tombs.

A sightseeing helicopter, which can be booked at the Holiday Inn Lido in Beijing, flies over but does not stop at the Wall. See "Beijing."

Badaling is about 1000 meters above sea level. Here the wall averages 7.8 meters high, 6.5 meters wide at the base, and 5.8 meters wide at the top. Watchtowers are located every few hundred meters. Note the giant rocks and bricks of uniform size, the gutters, and the waterspouts. You can walk, and in some places climb, for several hundred feet in either direction. Skateboarding on the wall has been allowed, but is not recommended when it is thick with people, which is most of the time. Try first thing in the morning or late afternoon. A restaurant for eating and usually a shaggy Bactrian camel or pony for photographing are available. Taking a box lunch is recommended, especially in pleasant weather, so you can spend more time at the wall rather than waiting for service in a crowded restaurant. A controversial cableway should be completed by now.

Also of note is the gate in the center of **Juyongguan (Chuyungkuan Pass,** about 10 km south of Badaling. It is built of finely carved marble and called ***Guojie (Cloud Terrace).** Originally the base of a tower built in 1345 (Yuan), the walls are decorated with carvings of Buddhas, four celestial guardians, and the text of a Buddhist sutra in Sanskrit, Tibetan, and four other languages. Currently, tours do not usually stop here except by request.

A recently renovated 2-km-long section of the Great Wall is at **Mutianyu,** 70 km NE of Beijing in Miyun County. It is less crowded and is very beautiful, less commercial, with more rugged hills than Badaling. A 720-meter-long Swiss-built cable car can take you from the parking lot uphill to the base of the wall. You still have to climb the wall, but you can walk 40 minutes down 1100 steps back to the parking lot. Or take the cable car down.

One restaurant open now. All buildings tastefully built in Ming style. A road has been completed so that one can go from here to the Ming tombs. A third section, which should be open now, is at **Simatai,** 140 km from Beijing and also in Miyun County.

The *Great Wall has also been restored and opened to visitors at 3000-year-old Shanhaiguan, over 40 km north from Beidaihe, and about 30 km from Qinhuangdao in the east. See separate listings. There is also a museum in the tower. Note the sign ''The First Pass Under Heaven.'' The gate was built in 1381. Nearby, **Old Dragon Head,** the place where the Great Wall meets the sea, has been repaired, and is now open to visitors.

The Great Wall can also be visited at **Jinshan Ling,** 110 km from Chengde in Hebei, and Huairou County (2 km long), 60 km NE of Beijing. The railway line from Beijing to Chengde crosses it. An 850-meter section is open in Jixian County, north of Tianjin, and another section is open near Datong. In the west, it can be seen in Ningxia at Yinchuan, and in Gansu at *Jiayuguan, its western terminal (Ming). See ''Jiuguan.''

GUANGZHOU
(KWANGCHOW, CANTON)

South China; 125 km NW of Hong Kong in Guangdong province
on the Zhujiang (Pearl River). It can be reached by a nonstop 3-
hour train ride, a 3-hour hydrofoil ride, or a half-hour flight from
Hong Kong. It is also linked by air with Bangkok, Singapore,
Sydney and 48 cities in China. Guangzhou is a 2½-hour flight or
a 36-hour train ride south of Beijing, and a 2-hour drive from
Zhuhai on the Macao border if no traffic jams, otherwise 5 hours.
A double-track electric train is expected to run between Guangzhou and Kowloon before 1990. A super highway is also planned
to link it with Shenzhen, and therefore Hong Kong. Two new
airports are being planned for Shenzhen and Shekou. All these
should relieve the nightmarish situation every time there is a long
Hong Kong holiday, when over 100,000 visitors try to get from
Hong Kong to China and back. Tourists should especially avoid
the lunar new year holiday (late January or early February), trade
fairs, and Qing Ming (early April). Elevated highways and more
bridges have been built to relieve some of the urban traffic
congestion but parking and traffic jams are the price of prosperity.
The weather here is subtropical. Coldest—about 0°C, January–
February; hottest—about 38°C, July–August. Average rainfall: 1680
mm. Extremely humid summers. Best time to visit: October–February. The urban population is over three million.

Guangzhou is also known as the Goat City because five fairies
came here supposedly in 1256 B.C., riding five goats from whose mouths
the fairies drew the first rice seeds. The city was founded over 2000
years ago. In 214 B.C., the first Qin emperor set up the Prefecture of
Nanhai here. It was the capital of the state of Nanyue during the Western Han, a dynasty that lasted 93 years, from 196 B.C. It is best known
as the largest and most prosperous trading city in South China, a role it

has played at least since the Tang dynasty. Arab traders started arriving over 1300 years ago. The Portuguese settled in Macao, 64 km, away in 1557. More recently, it was the site of the Canton Trade Fair, for 23 years China's main foreign trade institution.

Guangzhou is the capital of Guangdong, a province that has three Open Economic Areas (the Pearl River Delta, the Han River Delta—Shantou, and the Jian River Delta—Zhanjiang). Open areas extend along its entire coast and parts of its interior. Guangzhou and Zhanjiang are two of the 14 coastal cities open for economic development. Guangdong is the provincial "home" of many Chinese immigrants to Australia, the United States, Canada, and many parts of Southeast Asia. These people have contributed to the economic development of their adopted lands and have also brought or sent back expertise as well as money to their ancestral home. Many are playing a leading role in China's modernization program, with joint ventures.

In the late 1980s, the province ranked first in revenue growth and exports in the nation. It was called by some journalists the fifth Asian economic "tiger." The Pearl River Delta Economic Zone expanded to include 28 towns and cities with preferential policies encouraging foreign investment and economic cooperation.

Being a long way from the political center of China, the people here developed a rebellious, independent spirit. Guangzhou was the starting point or site of many important historical events:

—the fight against the importation of opium. Chinese officials burned 20,000 chests of it (1839); the struggle against foreign imperialism, at Sanyuanli, for example, during the Opium War in 1841;

—the movement against the Qing dynasty by the Taiping Heavenly Kingdom. Leader Hong Xiuquan (Hung Hsiu-ch'uan) was born about 66 km north of the city and was given the Christian tract that changed his life and China's history in Guangzhou;

—the campaign against the Qing in the early 1900s led by Dr. Sun Yat-sen, who was born south of the city in Zhongshan county near the Macao border. The fight was fueled by the failure of the Qing emperors to repel the encroaching foreign powers;

—the general strike against the unequal foreign treaties, starting in June 1925. It lasted for 16 months and almost closed Hong Kong;

—the Communist Revolution. Mao Zedong taught peasant leaders here in 1926 at the National Peasant Movement Institute;

—the Northern Expedition, whose officers were trained at the nearby Huangpu (Whampoa) Military Academy. Chiang Kai-shek was director; Chou En-lai was in charge of political indoctrination. In June 1926 this expedition to unify China and to assert Chinese nationalism started off from Guangzhou.

—an uprising against the Nationalists led by the Communists in December 1927.

Many foreign missionaries established schools and churches here after the city was opened to foreign trade and residence by the Treaty of Nanking in 1842. From 1938 to 1945, the Japanese occupied Guangzhou. The Communists took over from the Nationalists on October 14, 1948.

In recent years, Guangdong has been one of the main suppliers of food, water, and electricity for neighboring Hong Kong. It is rich in livestock, fruits, and vegetables. Guangdong has 11 institutions of higher learning, including Zhong Shan University, which is on the site of the missionary-founded Ling Nam University. There are 3200 factories producing heavy machinery, textiles (silk and ramie), petrochemicals, sewing machines, ships, and electronics.

Tourists would probably be interested in its **ivory-carving factory,** where about 45 concentric balls within balls have been made from one piece of ivory.

The city is divided by the Zhu (Pearl) River, which is crossed by three bridges and innumerable ferries to be avoided at rush hours. Most of the places of interest to tourists are located on the north side. A subway is due in 1991, two lines totaling 43 km. There are two railway stations, the newer Tianhe near the Garden Hotel serving some Shenzhen trains at presstime.

While *pu tung hua* (Mandarin dialect) is understood by almost everyone, the language spoken in most homes is Cantonese.

If you only have a few hours, see the **Zhen Family Hall,** the **Han Dynasty Mausoleum Museum,** the **Temple of the Six Banyan Trees/ Flower Pagoda** (for exotic Chinese architecture), and the **Qingping Free Market** (for genuine local color). You could also decide on a garden (if you like plants), or an arts and crafts factory. Be sure to eat in one of the **garden restaurants,** have dim sum at the **Banxi Restaurant** or **China Hotel,** and a drink in the riverside coffee shop at the **White Swan Hotel.** If you have more time (at least a day), go to **Foshan** for the ancestral temple and ceramic, silk, and folk art factories. (See "Foshan.")

Guangzhou is not noted as a prime tourist destination, but it has enough to do for two or three days.

Probably the most exciting recent development for Guangzhou has been the discovery in 1983 of a 2100-year-old imperial tomb now officially known as the **Museum of the Western Han Dynasty Mausoleum of the Nanyue King.** The second king of Nanyue ruled this region during the early Western Han (206 B.C.–A.D. 24). More than 1000 burial objects were excavated. Included in the find were a chariot, ritual bronzes, gold and silver vessels, ivory and lacquerware, jades, musical instruments, weapons, and tools. Human sacrifices, concubines, and servants were buried with him also. The relics are beautifully displayed, with English titles, at the actual site. Don't miss the video, in English, at the excavation. The museum is about half a block behind the China Hotel on Renmin Rd. towards the river.

The **Guangdong Provincial Museum** 广东省博物馆 (Wenming Rd.; tel. 332195) displays relics of local primitive society and is not as good generally as the Guangzhou Museum. The **Guangzhou Museum** 广州市博物馆 is in the **Zhenhai (Sea-dominating) Tower** in Yuexiu Park and is better organized (tel. 330627). The original tower itself was built in 1380 to assert the power of the Ming dynasty. It was perhaps more impressive at the time. It has been rebuilt several times since then. Located at one of the highest points in the city, it has been used as a pleasure palace for high-ranking imperial officials and as a Nationalist hospital. Starting with prehistory, on the second floor, to revolutionary history, on the fifth, the exhibits include some interesting old clocks, ceramics, and a painting of the burning of the 20,000 chests of opium. For a city of this size and wealth, however, one would expect a better, larger museum, especially one about Overseas Chinese.

The **Zhen (Chen) Family Temple** 陈氏书院（陈家祠） (7 Zhongshan Rd.; tel. 841559, 885259) is well worth a visit. It was built in the 1890s with nine halls and six courtyards of different sizes and has been used as a school. Its windows, doorframes, and pavilions are all lavishly decorated with intricate carvings and sculptures—almost too much for the mind to absorb at once. Take it in small doses. Because the army occupied these buildings during the Cultural Revolution, the artwork suffered very little damage. The Guangdong Folk Arts and Crafts Museum is located here now, and it is a good place to shop. Just don't let the bargains distract you from the ceramic opera scenes on the roofs and the charming carved mice eating the lichees on the pillars.

Shamian (Shamien, Shameen) Island 沙面, in the Pearl River in central Guangzhou, became a British and French concession in 1859–60. It was then an 80-acre sandbank, later built into a European ghetto, much resented by the Chinese. The architecture reflects its European occupants, but, unfortunately, so many of the old buildings have been destroyed that its overall charm has almost disappeared. The island is joined to the mainland by bridges and now cars are allowed in certain areas. You can still find some of the old buildings, but it isn't the same as it was before the fancy **White Swan Hotel** was built in 1982. At the western tip of the island, this 31-story luxury hotel, built on reclaimed land, is among the top international-standard hotels in China.

The **Mausoleum of the Seventy-two Martyrs at Huanghuagang (Yellow Flower) Hill** 黄花岗七十二烈士墓 (Xianlie Rd.) is past the Garden Hotel and the Friendship Store on the road to the zoo. This commemorates an unsuccessful attempt to overthrow the Qing in 1911, led by Dr. Sun Yat-sen's. Of special interest to visitors of Chinese ancestry, this 260,000-square-meter park was built with donations from Chinese Nationalists' Leagues around the world. The stones in the main monument are inscribed in English with the names of the donors, among these Chicago, Illinois; Moose Jaw, Saskatchewan; and Lima, Peru. The miniature Statue of Liberty on top was replaced in 1987.

The **National Peasant Movement Institute** 广州农民运动讲习厅 (42 Zhongshan 4-Rd.; tel. 331790) was a school for 327 peasant leaders from 20 provinces and regions. It was open only from May to September 1926 in an old temple. Mao Zedong was the director and Zhou Enlai a teacher. The subjects taught were rural education, problems of peasants, and class analysis. The institute was restored after Liberation, including the straw sandals and old rifles used by the students. Mao's office, to the right as you enter, contains rattan trunks and a straw mat on a wooden bed.

The **Dr. Sun Yat-sen Memorial Hall** 中山纪念堂 (tel. 332430, 333432). This is a theater seating over 4500, built in 1931 and expanded and renovated in 1975. This building is architecturally important because its huge hall is supported by four vertical concrete beams that branch out on top to form the octagonal roof. The modern technique and pure Chinese style, with its bright blue circus-tent-shaped ceramic roof, is unique. (For more on the life of Dr. Sun, see ''Nanjing.'')

The *****Guangxiao Temple** 光孝寺 (109 Sheshi Rd. and Guangxiao Rd.; tel. 346775, 885606) has the longest history in the city. It was founded on the site of the residence of the King of the Southern Yue Kingdom. The temple was built in A.D. 397 to commemorate the visit of the Indian monk Dharmayasas, and is the largest temple in South China. An iron pagoda dated A.D. 967 stands inside, historic, well preserved, but not beautiful. The present buildings are from the Five Dynasties to the Ming. A statue of Huineng, who founded the southern sect of Buddhism, meditates peacefully. The attractive Sixth Patriarch's Hair-burying Pagoda is a miniature of the Flower Pagoda. See also ''Shaoguan.''

The **Huaisheng (Remember the Sage) Mosque and Guangta (Smooth) Minaret** 光塔寺 (Guangta Lu; tel. 331878, 333593) is only of historical value. It is not the least bit attractive. Considered the oldest mosque in China, it was built in A.D. 627 by Arab traders. It is open daily. Visitors can climb its minaret, which has also been used as a lighthouse. The 26.3-meter minaret is said to be original. The tomb of the founding Moslem missionary, Sad Ibn Abu Waggas, is in the Orchid Garden.

The **Liu Rong (Six Banyan Trees) Temple** 六榕寺 (Liu Rong Rd.; tel. 887563) was founded 1400 years ago. It was so named because the famous Tang poet Su Dong Po found six luxuriant banyan trees there in 1100. The present buildings were rebuilt in 989. Its nine-story **Flower Pagoda** is 57.6 meters high and originally built in 537. It can be climbed for a good view and the exercise. Monks chant Tuesday and Friday mornings.

The **Shishi (Cathedral of the Sacred Heart)** (Yide Rd.; tel. 336737, 883724) was built in 1863–88. Its 57.95-meter spire was probably built deliberately taller than the pagoda nearby. Shishi means Stone House. It was closed as a church during the Cultural Revolution and used as a storehouse until 1979. Now it has been restored almost to its previous grandeur and is reminiscent of many European cathedrals. Mass has been celebrated weekdays at 6 a.m. and Sundays and festivals at 6, 7:30, and 8:30 a.m. (See *Religion* in "Local Customs.")

The **South China Botanical Garden** (Guangzhou Botanical Garden) 华南植物园 (Longyandong, in the north of the city; tel. 705626, 776604) is a research institute of the Chinese Academy of Science. One of the world's largest botanical gardens, this 300-hectare garden is home to more than 2000 species of tropical and subtropical plants such as palms, bamboos, herbs, and ferns. Depending on the season, bring your own insect repellant.

The **Orchid Garden** 兰圃 (Dabei Rd., west of Yuexiu Park and behind the Foreign Trade Center; tel. 677255) is a delight for orchid lovers. It has more than 100 species and almost 10,000 plants on five hectares.

The **Xi Yuan (West Garden)** 西园 (next to Dongfeng 1-Rd.; tel. 889318, 885867) specializes in *penjing,* miniature trees and landscapes, of the Lingnan School. 25,000 potted plants.

You can go directly to any of the **arts and crafts factories** and **Foshan.** See *Shopping* below. Crafts can also be seen at the Guangzhou Gold and Silver Jewelry Centre. Jewelry is a recently revived craft, having been discouraged since Liberation. The artisans are young. As with gems and jewelry everywhere, you have to know your products to get a good buy, but prices for small freshwater pearls seem to be good in Guangzhou. Our book *Hong Kong Gems and Jewelry* can be helpful here for those intent on serious buying.

The **Pearl River boat ride** 珠江游船 with gourmet dinner can be arranged through hotels from April to October. (7:30 p.m., 39 Pier, Xiti)

Guangzhou Zoo 广州动物园 (Xianli Rd.; tel. 775547) is in the northeastern suburbs. Opened in 1958, it has 200 species, including pandas.

Yuexiu Park 越秀公园 (Jiefang Bei Rd., within walking distance of the China Hotel) is the largest in the city, on 92.8 hectares. There you can find the sculpture of the five goats, symbol of Guangzhou. **Liuhua Park** 流花公园 (Xicun Gong Rd.) was built in 1957–59; it is 800,400 square meters. Both parks are great for early-morning jogging.

Guangzhou Cultural Park 广州文化公园 (near the Nanfang Department Store on Xiti 2-Ma Rd.; tel. 888585) covers 8.3 hectares. More pavement and less sylvan than other parks. Best avoided after 7 p.m. unless you want to see masses of people enjoying Chinese opera, puppet shows, acrobats, exhibit halls, basketball games, and roller-skating. The annual Lantern Festival and flower shows are held here.

A reproduction of a Han dynasty ''city'' has opened with wax figures in imperial period dress. Since most other cities have reproductions of Ming, Qing or Song dynasty streets, this is a good place to compare the architecture and costumes of 206 B.C. to 220 A.D. China.

New areas being developed for tourism are Lotus Flower Hill (30 km. from Guangzhou), and the Yamen Fort (50 km. toward Hong Kong) that made it difficult for the British to attack Canton. The **Huangpu Military Academy** (1924) should be of interest to historians. Changzhou Island, Huangpu; tel. 448083. The **Museum of Hong Xiuquan's Former Residence** (leader of the Taipings) is in Guanglubu Village, Huaxian County, 18 km from the city.

Another escape is a visit to a **village.** Individuals can join cheaper tours organized during the Trade Fairs (advertised in hotel lobbies). Otherwise, individual arrangements can be quite expensive.

Many of the area villages grow and preserve fruit and olives for export, an interesting as well as delicious process to experience, as tourists are frequently given samples. Lucky are those who visit during the lichee season! (April to late June.)

Guangdong tourism officials are offering kung fu, acupuncture, and cooking lessons, plus bicycle tours, mainly for tour groups. Some lessons might be arranged for individuals. **Bicycles** can be rented near the back door of the White Swan Hotel. The **English Corner** is on Shamian Island on Sundays.

Guangdong province has several other places to offer tourists, especially for those who do not want to travel too far from the Hong Kong border: golfing, mountains, rivers, tropics, national minorities, historical sites, arts and crafts and beaches. See also ''Conghua,'' ''Foshan,'' *Hong Kong* (''Getting There''), ''Jiangmen,'' ''Shantou,'' ''Shaoguan,'' ''Shekou,'' ''Shenzhen,'' ''Taishan,'' ''Xiqiao Mountain,'' ''Zhanjiang,'' ''Zhaoqing,'' ''Zhongshan,'' and ''Zhuhai.''

FESTIVALS

Lunar second month, 10th to 13th day. Nanhai God Temple, Miaotou village, Huangpu. Tel. 770927.

SHOPPING

Main shopping area around **Zhongshan 5-Road** 中山五路 and **Beijing Road** 北京路 . Locally made are carvings of ivory, jade, bamboo, and wood, painted porcelain (porcelain from Jingdezhen; hand-painted here), and gold and silver jewelry. Shantou (Swatow) drawnworks and embroidery are famous, and are cheaper here.

Colored Painted Porcelain Factory 广州织金彩瓷工厂 (tel.

001255, 001919), **Daxin Ivory Carving Factory** 广州大新象牙工艺
厂 (Tien Pin Zhar, Saho; tel. 705556); **Daxin Ivory Carving Factory
Sales Dept.** (415 Daxin Rd.; tel. 882870); **Guangzhou Gold and Silver Jewelry Centre** 广州市金银首饰总汇 (199 Dade Rd.; tel.
342320, 337624). Export quality jewelry is at the **Guangdong Jewel-
lery Import and Export Co.**, 54–58 Daxin, tel. 336971. **Nanfang
Jade Factory** a.k.a. Guangzhou South Jade Crafts Factory (15 Xiajiu
Rd.; tel. 889045, 861040).

We haven't been able to check out any of these but for the serious
adventurous shopper, there's the **Guangzhou Arts and Crafts Service
Dept.**, 1/F, 59 Tai Nam Rd., tel. 332258. It has showrooms around the
city.

The **Chung Hwa Artiste-dress Factory** makes opera costumes,
wedding dresses, etc., tel. 330071. For the **Nan Fong Jade Carving
Factory**, tel. 887347, 888040, the **Guangzhou Hand-painted Pottery
and Porcelain Factory**, tel. 330986; **Guangzhou Gold and Silver Wares
Mfy.**, tel. 883540, 883993; **Guangzhou Palace Lamp Factory**, tel.
334366, 331735; **Hwa Nam Wood Carving Furniture Factory**, tel.
330304; **Hung Mein Carving Factory** (screens, rosewood furniture,
etc.), tel. 447368; **Guangzhou Red Wood Furniture Manufacturing**,
tel. 447072.

Needless to say, you need someone who speaks Chinese to follow
up on these leads, and some factories may be wholesale only. Do let us
know how you make out.

One of the free markets here, the **Qing Ping Ziyou Shi Chang**
清平路自由市场 , has been selling antiques like old coins, water
pipes, and old porcelain, with some reproductions. The bargains are
probably the best in China. Qing Ping Free Market is also the largest
herb market in the city (about five blocks), where you can find dehy-
drated lizards, snakes, plants, and weird-looking roots. Some live animals, too, including pangolins, an endangered species and civet cat.
This market is not for the squeamish as they also have skinned barbecued dog dangling in the stalls. The market is not very clean, always
crowded, but fascinating even if you don't want to buy anything. Within
20 minutes' walking distance of the White Swan Hotel, 6 a.m. to 6
p.m. As in all crowded places anywhere in the world, beware of pickpockets!

Huanghua Free Market and the **Xihu Night Market** are good for
clothes, mainly T-shirts, jackets, and trousers. Prices for Hong Kong–
made items can be about three to five times Hong Kong prices, so beware. Some locally made clothes, factory overruns, and seconds are
reasonably priced here.

The Xihu market also has food stalls (mostly dirty and not well
developed) but some foreigners love it. It is open to about midnight,
and is near the White Swan and the Cultural Park.

China Hotel Friendship Store (Liuhua Rd.; tel. 663007) is open 8:30 a.m.–9 p.m. Less crowded than the larger Friendship Store.

Friendship Store 友谊商店 (369 Huanshi Dong Rd.; tel. 776296, 776506) is open 8.30 a.m.–9 p.m. Across from the Garden Hotel and next to the Baiyun. One of the largest in China; well stocked with goods from all over the country and especially Guangdong. It seems to cater more to local Chinese.

Guangdong Antique Store 广东文物商店 (Hongshu Rd.; tel. 345659, 887600); **Guangzhou Antique Store** 广州文物商店 (Wende Rd.; tel. 331241); **Guangzhou Porcelain and Pottery Shop** 广州陶瓷商店 (Zhongshan 5-Rd.; tel. 330328); **Guangdong Arts and Crafts Service** 广东工艺美术服务部 (Dongshanshu Qian Rd.; tel. 773606, 766110); **Nanfang Dept. Store** 南方大厦商店 (49 Yanjiang Xi Rd.; tel. 886022); **Trade Center** 交易中心 (Guangzhou Trade Center, across the street from the Dongfang Hotel; use west entrance); **Yiyuan Art Shop** (Wende Rd.; tel. 336497); **Zhongshan 5-Rd. Department Store** 中山五路百货公司 (tel. 331509, 333154).

Guangzhou Trade Fair is held annually from April 15 to April 29, and October 15 to October 29. Pickpockets as well as traders visit Guangzhou for the event, so be careful.

RESTAURANTS

Guangzhou's **garden restaurants** are among the prettiest in China. The **Nanyuan** and **Beiyuan** are of traditional Qing dynasty China, small dining rooms surrounded by fish ponds, latticed windows, bamboo, and flowers. They rate a visit for the atmosphere as well as for the food. The **Banxi (Pan Hsi) Restaurant** is tops for service and food, specializing in *dim sum*. See "Food." A reservation here is mandatory for the fancy, private banquet rooms, especially the Reception Dining Hall with its traditional, redwood Chinese furniture and beautiful blue glass windows. This restaurant is set around a large pond and we found clean, yes, clean washrooms!

The restaurants in the top hotels are excellent, the Garden, China, Novotel, and White Swan. The Baiyun has a good reputation. Try its "Drunken Prawns." Some opulent Hong Kong-style restaurants have also recently opened here. For lighter, cheaper food like noodles, congee, and dim sum, try China Hotel's **Food Street** and Garden Hotel's **Lai Wan Market** and the Chinese restaurants in the Dong Fang. For hamburgers, try the Friendship Store.

Cantonese food is world famous, but chop suey and fortune cookies are American and haven't been found here yet. For favorite Cantonese dishes, see "Food."

Beiyuan Restaurant 北园酒家 ● *202, Xiao Bei Rd.; tel. 332471, 662471, or 333365* ● One of the garden restaurants.

Guangzhou Restaurant 广州酒家 ● *J Wenchang Nanlu; tel.* *887136, 887840* ● One of the best, but very noisy. A little grubby and no parking.

Moslem Restaurant 回民饭店 ● *325 Zhongshan 6-Rd.; tel.* *888414* ● Mutton dishes. Hot pot in winter.

Mr. Beef ● *A few meters east of Garden Hotel* ● Cantonese hot pot.

Nanyuan Restaurant 南园酒家 ● *120, Qianjin Rd. (south bank of Pearl River); tel. 449211, 448380, 440532, 550532* ● One of the garden restaurants. A little far from the center of things.

Banxi (Pan Hsi) Restaurant 泮溪酒家 ● *151, Long Jun Rd. W.; tel. 815718, 815955* ● Specializes in Dim Sum pastries.

Snake Restaurant 蛇餐馆 ● *4 Jianglan Rd.; tel. 882517, 222517, 883811* ● The cat soup is said to be good. Please, no endangered species!

Tao Tao Ju (Happy, Happy House) ● *No. 20 Dishifu Rd.; tel.* *887501, 862305, 813955.*

HOTELS

Except during the trade fair, *qing ming* festival, and the lunar new year, luxury hotels have caught up with the demand here. During the Trade Fair high season, prices usually go up.

The top hotels are the China, the White Swan and the Garden, each in a different part of the city. The Holiday Inn and Novotel, both new, should be among the top after they get some experience. Also close to the top is the exotic-looking Dong Fang, whose English and service need more work.

Of the less expensive hotels, we also liked the Baiyun International, the Overseas Chinese Mansion, and the Overseas Chinese Hotel. Most hotels can receive Hong Kong television.

Locations: Business people can walk to the Foreign Trade Center from the China, Dong Fang, New Mainland, Huaqiao (Overseas Chinese) Jiu Dian, and Liuhua hotels. The Guangdong is a 20-minute walk away. This area is also good for tourists because it is central and close to the railway station. It has two large parks, the Han Museum, CAAC, C.I.T.S.; and the China Hotel has a good Friendship Store and supermarket.

The second best location is only 20 minutes' drive west and north of the China Hotel, around the Friendship Store. Here are the Garden, Baiyun, and Ocean Hotels, the Holiday Inn City Center, and the International Exhibition Center all within walking distance of each other. Nearby are the zoo and the new Tianhe railway station.

The White Swan is by itself in the southwest part of the city on the Pearl River, its high quality and beauty making up for its rather inconvenient location but an express highway has shortened the time now to the Trade Fair. The Guangzhou Hotel and O.C. Mansion are together, close to the fascinating river, about 20 minutes' drive from the Foreign Trade Center. The hotels by the river are farthest from the airport but are closer to the Hong Kong ferry pier. The Novotel is the closest, and is the only major hotel on the south side of the river. C.T.S. is in the Overseas Chinese Mansion. The Holiday Inn has rooms for wheelchair travelers. Outdoor pools close in November for winter.

Baiyun Hotel (Baiyun Bingguan) • *367 Huanshi Dong Rd. Dist.A.P.6 km, Dist.R.W.4 km. Telex 44698 BYHTL CN. Cable 0682. Fax 336498.* • 1975, ren. 1989. T.R. (will charge for telex), no C.C. 722 rooms, 34 stories. Tunnel to Garden Hotel. 30 minute photo process.

Central Hotel (Zhong Yan Jui Dian) • *38 Guoji Rd., Sanyuanli. Dist.A.P.3 km, Dist.R.W.5 km. Telex 44664 GICSO CN. Fax 678331 X1802* • 1986, 234 rooms, 6 stories. T.R., C.C. Part of International Exhibition Centre. 45 office units and business center. Fast-food center. Two lounges. Pool, gym, IDD.

China Hotel (Zhong Guo Da Qui Dian) • *Liu Hua Rd., telex 44888 CHLGZ CN. Cable 6888. Fax 677014. Dist.A.P.8 km, Dist.R.W.1 km* • 1983, ren. 1988. 18 stories, 1200 rooms, 250 apartments. Reservations mandatory year round. T.R., C.C. (Am. Express, Visa only). During trade fair, deposit paid will be forfeited if reservation canceled and must be booked 60 days prior to arrival. Reservations through UTELL. Ice cream parlor, ballroom, business center, and offices. Tennis, bowling, pool. Managed by New World Hotels International.

Dong Fang Hotel • *120 Liuhua Rd. Dist.A.P.5 km, Dist.R.W.1 km. Telex: 44439 GZDFH CN, Fax 662775. Cable 4221* • 1963, ren. 1987. T.R., C.C. 7 stories, 1200 rooms. Magnificent garden. East wing older, with bigger rooms. Sauna, bar, tea-room, disco, business center, gym, squash, pool. IDD. Tennis and photo-finishing. U.S. Consulate and C.I.T.S. on premises. Karaoke bar, clinic. Convention hall with simultaneous interpretation.

Garden Hotel (Huayuan Jiu Dian) • *368 Huanshi Dong Rd. Dist.A.P.5km, Dist.R.W.2½km. Telex 44788 GDHTL CN. Fax: 338989, X3232* • 1984–1985; renovations 1987. Over 1100 rooms, 30 stories.

I.IL., U.U. Reservations accepted during Trade Fair only if credit card number given, through Peninsula Group. IDD. Classy white Italian marble lobby with gold foil mural. Revolving restaurant, English pub, deli. Pizzeria. Tennis, squash, health club, pool, business center, executive floor. Offices (including some government trade offices) and apartments. No-smoking floor! Group check-in area.

Guangdong Guest House (Guangdong Bingguan) • *603 Jiefang Rd. N. Dist.A.P.7 km, Dist.R.W.3 km. 10-minute jog to China Hotel. Telex 44232 GGGHE CN, 44755 GHEST CN; Fax 332911* • Built 1949 as state guesthouse; became hotel in 1953. C.C., no T.R. Four 4-story buildings set in spacious garden. Limited IDD. 24-hr. room service. Baiyun Bldg. ren. 1988–89. Bihai tower decorated in traditional Chinese style with exotic mother-of-pearl inlaid furniture in lobby. Large rooms. High ceilings. Poor maintenance.

Guangzhou Hotel (Guangzhou Bingguan) • *Haizhu Sq. Dist.A.P.9 km. Dist.R.W.5 km. Telex: 44336 KCHTL CN. Fax 330179. Cable 0520.* • T.R. (only if prepaid), C.C., IDD. 1968, ren. 1989. 27 stories, 510 rooms. Leased to Japanese traders during trade fairs. Outdoor elevator.

Holiday Inn City Center (Jai Re Jiu Dian) • *Huanshi Dong Rd., Overseas Chinese Village. Telex 441045 HICCG CN. Fax 753126. Dist.A.P.12 km, Dist.R.W.5 km* • 1989. T.R., C.C. 24 stories, 431 rooms. Delicatessen, health club. Chui-Chow food, grill room. Exhibition center, health and business centers, cinema, bicycles. Three executive floors. Book through Holiday Inns International. Prefers deposit during Trade Fair.

International Hotel • *96 Xian Lie Zhong Rd. Cable 7524. Telex 441061. Fax 758618* • 1988. 10 stories, 180 rooms. IDD, business center. 1700-seat theater.

Liuhua Hotel (Liuhua Bingguan) • *Huanshi Xi Rd. Cable 0248. Telex 44298 GZLHH CN. Fax 668800 X 2348. Dist.A.P.4 km, Dist.R.W.1/3 km* • Will not answer telex during trade fairs. Otherwise will telex answer collect. Guests usually just show up. 1972. 7 stories, 720 rooms. Chinese food only. South Building renovated 1985; North Building renovated 1989. Cluttered entrance. Luggage storage and telex facilities for guests and non-guests. IDD. C.C. Service poor.

New Mainland Hotel (Xin Da Di Bingguan) • *70 Zhan Qian Rd. Telex 44763 MAINL CN. Dist.A.P.6 km. Dist. R.W.250 meters.* • Old east building not up to our standards. New building 1987.T.R. 9 stories,

180 rooms. Thin drapes, poor plumbing and color scheme, but otherwise adequate. IDD. Business center. Singapore J.V.

Novotel Guangzhou Jiang Nan (Novotel Jiang Nan Da Xia) • *348 Jiang Nan Da Rd.C. Telex 441032 NOVGZ CN. Fax 429645. Cable 7546. Telex 661831. On main street, about 3 km south of Pearl River Bridge, in residential area. Dist.A.P.15 km. Dist.R.W.9 km* • Close to Zhong Shan University. C.C. 1988–89. 28 stories, 450 rooms. IDD. French food, attendants in fast-food restaurant on roller skates. Business center, fitness center, tennis, pool. This hotel is owned by local farmers and managed by Accor.

Ocean Hotel (Yuan Yang Bingguan) • *412 Huanshi Rd. E. Dist.A.P.5 km, Dist.R.W.3 km. Telex 44638 HOHOL CN. Cable 6054.* • Built 1986 with nautical theme. 22 stories (10 for hotel, 10 for offices), 190 rooms. T.R., C.C. IDD. Bar. Business Center.

Overseas Chinese Mansion/Hotel (Huaqiao Da Xia) • *2 Qiao Guang Rd. at Pearl River (Hai Zhu) Bridge. Cable 7045. Dist.A.P.10 km. Dist.R.W.6 km. Dist.Trade Center 4 km.* • No C.C. 1950s, ren. 1987–88. 8 stories, 130 rooms. IDD. By 1990, a 39-story 700-room tower should have pool, bowling, gym, and concert hall.

Overseas Chinese Hotel (Huaqiao Jiu Dian) • *63 Zhan Qian. Cable 3931. Fax 663230. Dist.A.P.5 km, Dist.R.W.½ km, Dist. Hong Kong ship quay 12km* • 1982–83, ren. 1988–89. 9 stories, 391 rooms. 7 restaurants with Meixian, Kegia, Cantonese, and Chaozhou food. C.C. Business center.

Shamian Guest House (Shamian Bingguan) • *Shamian Island at side door of White Swan Hotel.* • 4 floors (no elevators). Hot water evenings only. Aside from no electricity one day a week, adequate for budget travelers.

South Lake Hotel (Nanhu Bingguan) • *Tonghe, Shahe. Cable 0945. Telex 44511 NANHU CN. Dist.A.P.12 km, Dist.R.W.17 km* • In spite of beautiful location and rural resort setting, budget travelers only except for Villas #3, 4, and 5, ren. 1988. Rest not up to standard. Qigong clinic. T.R. by collect telex. (No need for reservations except during Trade Fair.) Only Am. Express C.C.

White Swan Hotel (Baitian E Bingguan) • *1 South St., Shamian Island. Dist.A.P.11 km. Dist.R.W.7 km. Telex 44688 WSH CN. Cable 8888. Fax 861188* • 1982–83. 28 stories, 822 rooms. T.R., C.C. Reservations recommended. Bookings also through the Leading Hotels of the world. Hong Kong joint venture. Beautiful atrium with waterfall and garden. Japanese restaurant, pool, concert hall, business center, adjacent office building. Tennis within walking distance. Health club, massage, sauna. Elizabeth Arden Salon. Golf driving range. Great view of river traffic. Rolls Royces.

Youth Hostel • *Shamian Island near White Swan Hotel.* • Few services. Dorms and double rooms. Backpacker standards.

OTHER IMPORTANT ADDRESSES

Bank of China, Guangzhou Branch 中国银行 : 197 Dong Feng Xi Rd.; tel. 338080.

C.I.T.S. 中国国际旅行社 : Open daily 8:30–12; 2 to 5 p.m. 179 Huanshi Rd. (next to main railway station); tel. 661451, 662948. For tickets, tours and other services, office in Dong Fang Hotel, Room 2366, tel. 669900 X 2366, 662427. Telex 44204 CITS CN. Cable 1954. Fax 678145

C.T.S. 中国旅行社 : 2 Qiaoguang Rd. (Haizhu Square next to Huaqiao Mansion); tel. 336417, 663488, 336888. Cable 3307. Telex 44217 CTS CN.

C.Y.T.S.: 1 Sibeitongjin. Tel. 765112, 776429. Telex 44301 YSYS CN (Attn. CYTS). Fax 765112. Cable 1112.

CAAC: Next to main railway station; tel. 661803 (int.), 662123 X904 (dom.)

Airport Service Desk, Departure Lounge: tel. 678901.
Baiyun Airport: tel. 662794.
Domestic inquiries: tel. 662969.
International inquiries: tel. 661803.

Foreign Affairs Section, **Public Security Bureau** 公安局外事处 : 863 Jiefang Bei Rd.; tel. 331060, 330003.

Foreign Affairs Office, **Guangdong People's Gov't:** 45 Shamian Ave.; tel. 886511.

Foreign Trade Center 外贸中心 : 117 Liuhua Rd.; tel. 677000, 661799. Shopping, supermarket, restaurants, Bank of China, bookstore.

Guangdong Travel & Tourism Bureau: 185 Huanshi Rd., 510010; tel. 661093, 677410. Fax 677426. Cable 4611. Ask for list of stores, restaurants and hotels approved for foreign tourists.

Hospitals (Clinics in Garden and Dong Fang Hotels.)

Guangdong People's Hospital 广东人民医院 : Zhongshan 2-Rd.; tel. 885119.

Guangzhou First People's Hospital 广州第一人民医院 : Panfu Rd., 602 N. Renmin Rd.; tel. 886421. Use if you are near the Dong Fang. Entrance at rear to Pan Song Lou open 6 a.m. to 11 p.m. Use main gate 11 p.m. to 6 a.m.

The First Hospital Attached to Zhongshan Medical College
学院第一附属医院 : Zhongshan 2-Rd.; tel. 778223, 778314.
The Second Hospital Attached to Zhongshan Medical College
医学院第二附属医院 : Yanjiang 1-Rd.; tel. 882012.
Japanese Consulate: Garden Hotel; tel. 338999.
Overseas Chinese Travel Service 华侨旅游服务社 : 2 Qiaoguang Rd.; tel. 332247, 336888.
Passenger Pier for Hong Kong, Zhoutouzui 洲头咀客运码头（往香港）: tel. 446214.
Railway Station 火车站 : tel. 777112, 661789.
Singapore Airlines: Represented by CAAC, tel. 661803.
Thai International 泰国航空公司 : tel. 333684.
U.S. Consulate 澳洲航空公司: Dongfang Hotel; tel. 669900. (If not here, try the White Swan Hotel.)

GUILIN

(Kweilin; City of Cassia Trees) South China. In northern Guangxi, the first "province" west of Guangdong. 55-minute flight NW of Guangzhou and minimum 2-hour flight SW of Beijing. Direct regular charter flights from Hong Kong. Guilin is connected by rail to Beijing, Kunming, Shanghai, Zhanjiang, and Nanning, and by bus to Wuzhou where one can get a boat to Guangzhou and Hong Kong. The weather is subtropical. Hottest—34°C in August; coldest—⁻3°C. Rainy season—February–May. Annual precipitation—1900 mm. The best time to visit is autumn, or late spring, when it is warm enough to ignore the rain. The scenery is best seen in the mist, which inspired centuries of landscape painters, or when the sun and clouds conspire to give you constantly changing pictures. From November until the February rains, the water in the river may be too low for the boat trip all the way to Yangshuo but the deepening of the river should be completed by 1989. Population is 300,000 urban.

Founded in 214 B.C., this prefecture is famous for its vertical limestone mountains rising above tree-lined streets, rice fields, and the meandering Li and Taohua (Peach Blossom) rivers. It is also known for its caves.

Guilin developed with the opening of the Ling Canal in 214 B.C. It was the provincial capital until 1014, and a command post for the Northern Expedition in 1926. During the Japanese war almost all of the city was destroyed, the Seven Star Cave alone sheltering 5000 refugees. Because about one third of the 10 million people living in the province are of Zhuang nationality, Guangxi is an "autonomous region" rather than a "province." National guides may not understand the local dialect.

The city itself, a favorite of honeymooners, is small, full of parks, and ideal for walking. The ground is level except for the sporadic mountains, each of which has a bright-red pavilion complementing nature, an invitation to climb.

You will want to spend a minimum of two days; three would be better. Guilin is one of the 24 cities of historical interest protected by the State Council. Some of its houses are antiques and one should stroll through the past at leisure. Many tame mountains beckon climbers. Unfortunately, Guilin also abounds with tourists, and aspiring young merchants shouting "Hello Hello!" to attract your attention.

For those in a hurry, one morning could be spent at Diecai Hill, Fubo Hill, and Seven Star Park, and the afternoon at Reed Flute Cave and Elephant Hill. The Li River boat trip could be enjoyed on a second day or vice versa. The Ming tomb museum, a handicraft factory, shopping, just walking or cycling and the Ling Canal can fill up your third day.

Diecai (Folded Brocade) Hill 叠彩山 (3.6 km from the Lijiang Hotel) is the tallest in town at 73 meters. The peaks are named Bright Moon, Crane, and Seeing Around the Hill. Partway up past the ornamental arch is the Wind Cave with Ming and Tang poems and memorials on its walls. A good view of the area can be seen from the top.

Fubo (Whirlpool) Hill 伏波山 (2.8 km from the Lijiang Hotel), named after famous Han Marshal Ma Fubo, is 60 meters high. At the base is a 7½-ton iron Qing bell belonging to the temple originally here. To the right is the Cave of the Returned Pearl, where guides might tell you a dragon left a gift of a pearl for a poor family, who returned it: "This illustrates the honesty of working people." Nearby is a rock where Ma Fubo tested his sword, and a cliff with Tang buddhas. Partway up on the right is a pavilion with a view of the river.

Qixing (Seven Star) Park 七星岩 (2.7 km from the Lijiang Hotel) is about 10 square km. It contains a zoo, Camel Hill, and Seven Star Hill, its seven peaks positioned like the stars in the Big Dipper. With lots to see, you may want to return for a more leisurely look. Just think, you will be following in the footsteps of tourists from the Sui (581–618) dynasty! Seven Star Cave, on the west side of Potaraka Hill, has three levels; visitors enter the middle one. It is bigger than Reed Flute Cave, 1 km long, 43 meters at its widest, and 27 meters at its highest. Colored lights highlight the grotesque limestone formations.

The park's pavilions are each constructed of different materials, concrete or bamboo. A forest of cassia trees blossom in spring and a 700-year-old stone replica of the Flower Bridge (Song) spans a stream. Originally built of wood but destroyed in a flood, the bridge was designed so that the water below reflects its arches to form a complete circle.

The "Cave for Hiding a Dragon" 龙隐洞 does look like it could snugly fit a dinosaur. The most famous of the stone Song steles nearby lists people meant for execution. The emperor sent copies around China (although paper was invented by then) and when the verdict was reversed, all but the stele in Guilin were destroyed.

Also on the west side of Putuo (Potaraka) Hill is the Yuanfeng (Deep and Windy) Cave, and on top, the Putuo (Potaraka) Temple (good view) and Guanyin cave.

Ludi (Reed Flute) Cave 芦笛岩 is 8–9 km from the Lijiang Hotel. One km long, this cave takes about 40 minutes to see. The temperature inside is a cool 20°C. The lighting is cleverly placed so that with a bit of imagination, the limestone formations resemble a giant goldfish, a Buddha, a wall of assorted vegetables, etc. The cave is named after the reeds that grow at the entrance.

Xiangbi (Elephant Trunk) Hill 象鼻山 (1.4 km from the Lijiang Hotel), located at the junction of the Li and Yang rivers, really does look like an elephant drinking. Shuiyue (Moon-in-Water) Cave is between the trunk and front legs. Elephant Eye Cave is where you would expect. The Samantabhadra Pagoda tops the hill. Look for a sculpture of the Buddha of Universal Benevolence.

The **Li River boat trip** is the other outstanding attraction in the area. Book at C.I.T.S. or your hotel. The price is about the same. If you want to try for a cheaper trip, you could shop around for boats for Chinese tourists. Ask if the price includes lunch and the bus back to Guilin. Some people stay in Yangshuo to bicycle. The 5-hour, 83-km tour south to Yangshuo usually returns by land about mid-afternoon. The Li River, normally 30–60 meters wide, winds its way between some incredible rock formations, the highest about 80 meters. The boats are self-propelled, or sometimes pulled by a tug because the river is shallow. The middle section of the trip, after the first 2½ hours, is the most beautiful, so do not use up all your film before you get to it.

As you leave Guilin, with a little imagination you will see in succession on the right Elephant Trunk Hill, Fighting Cocks Hill (one on each side), and Reclining Flower Vase Hill on the right. The vase appears as if it were cut in half lengthwise.

At 1½ hours out: Sword-Cut Cliff (as if neatly severed by a giant sword). At 2¼ hours out: left side, Crown Cave (shaped like the British imperial crown). At 2¾ hours: cock with tail up bending down to pick up rice, followed shortly by the U-shaped Ram's Hoof Mountain on the right. At 4 hours out, on the right is Conch Shell Hill, then a temple on a cliff.

On the way, look for large cormorants (real birds, not stone), usually seen sitting on the railings of fishing boats. If you're lucky you might even see them at work, fishing on behalf of people. You might want to also ask about a special tour to see the cormorants fishing at night.

Yangshuo 阳朔 , the tiny town at the end of the boat ride, has a park, museum, and an old temple. If time allows, you might be able to walk along the main street to the right of the landing. Behind Green Lotus Peak on the left of the landing is Jian (Mirror) Hill, so named because some of its cliffs are smooth. The museum is of the famous painter of galloping horses and Li River scenes, Xu Beihong, who lived there between 1935 and 1938. Several hotels are available if you want to stay overnight and bike ride. You can take the bus back the next day.

Chuanyan (Pierced Hill) Village 穿眼村 is 7 km from Yangshuo on the way back to Guilin. Tour buses sometimes stop for the scenery—a giant 1000-year-old banyan tree and the hill, apparently "pierced" by a very big arrow. In the cave are several dwellings reached by a tiny ancient ferry across the Jinbao (Golden Treasure) River.

Duxiu (Unique Beauty) Park was the site of the 1393-built mansion of Zhu Shouqian, grandson of Emperor Hongwu of the Ming. Destroyed during the Qing, and again during the Japanese war, it is now the site of the teachers' college. Today, only the original wall, its gates, and the steps remain.

Recently opened is the **Ancient Tomb Museum,** a good place to bicycle to. You pass old villages, water buffalo herds, mountains, and several intriguing Ming cemeteries, a total of 320 tombs in 100 sq. km. All persons buried there are descendants of the Ming emperor's family. A museum and several guardian statues of animals, servants and officials are at the unexcavated tumulus of the grandson Zhu Shou Qian Chi of the dynasty founder's older brother, who died in 1370 A.D. Much smaller and less elaborate than Ming tombs near Beijing, but worth a visit if you have the time. Open daily 9 a.m. to 5 p.m.

Lingqu (Ling Canal), a.k.a. Xing'an Canal, dug over 2000 years ago (Qin) to connect the Chang (Yangtze) and the Zhu (Pearl) rivers, is also of importance, an inland route to Guangzhou. It was a waterway until the 1930s and is still used for agricultural irrigation. It may be of interest to engineers and history fans. It has 18 locks and sections, and still can be seen starting about 66 km north of Guilin at **Xing'an** or Darongjiang.

The Yuan (1279–1368) **Ling Temple,** in the south section, contains six stone tablets recording successive reconstructions of the canal from the Ming onward. The **Tomb of the Three Generals** contains either the remains of Qin dynasty canal inspectors or three stone masons, depending on which source one believes.

Xishan (West Hill) 西山 , half a kilometer west of Yinshan, was a Buddhist site and has 200 cliffside Buddhist statues from the early Tang; the largest is two meters high.

SHOPPING

Here you can buy locally grown oranges, yellow grapefruitlike pomelo, and mangosteens (luohan guo), all very sweet. The arts and crafts factory makes boxwood, jade, and soapstone carvings, and bamboo chopsticks. Its dough sculptures are very good.

Guilin also produces bamboo and wood carvings, woven and plated handbag, watercolor paintings, embroidery, down jackets, pottery, and porcelain. The main shopping area is along **Zhongshan Zhong Rd.,** where you will find the **Friendship Store** 友谊商店 at 107 (tel. 2743; open 9:30 a.m.–9 p.m.) and the **Arts and Crafts Center** 工艺美术服 at #109 (tel. 2166). For art, there are the **Lishui Chamber** and **Guishanyuan (Garden of Osmanthus Mountain)** 桂山园 .

Also on this street are the **Guilin Antique Store** 桂林文物商店, at 71 (tel. 2594) and the **Guilin Embroidery and Art Crafts** (tel. 2496). The **Yangqiao Department Store** (tel. 2464, 2259) is the largest.

RESTAURANTS

Hotel restaurants are cleaner with better ambiance. Many hotels have Hong Kong chefs.

Chinese food here is usually Guangxi or Guangdong (Cantonese). Food is served with chili sauce and fermented bean curd as condiments. You should like the beancurd if you like blue cheese. Mix a bit with your rice. The local rice wine, Sanhua, is made from a 200-year-old recipe.

Friendship Restaurant 友谊餐厅 • *212 Zhongshan Zhong Rd.; tel. 3741.*

Yueyalou (Crescent) Restaurant 月牙楼餐厅 • *(inside Seven Star Park), tel. 3622* • Vegetarian.

HOTELS

Guilin has many beautiful hotels, but the English needs work. The hotels used most by foreigners seem to be the Gui Shan, Sheraton, and Holiday Inn. The best located hotels, the Ronghu and Holiday Inn Guilin are centered around quiet Ronghu Lake, within walking distance of C.I.T.S., C.T.S., and handicraft shopping. The Li Jiang, Tailien, and Osmanthus are downtown. The Garden, Riverside Resort, Guishan, and Sheraton are very close to the Li River. The Hong Kong, Garland, and Osmanthus are very close to the railway station. The Li Jiang is older but also good, though not as luxurious. The Ronghu is also older with Chinese charm and a fancy villa. A Novotel Hotel should also be open by now.

Gui-shan Hotel • *Chuan Shan Rd. Cable: 3769. Telex: 48443 NWHIL HX. Rural setting between two rivers. Close to 7-Star Park. Dist.A.P.15 km. Dist.R.W.2 km.* • 1987–1988. Managed by New World Hotels International. Five buildings, five stories, 610 rooms. Long-term apartments. C.C., IDD. Business center, pool, tennis, fitness center, bowling. This hotel is pretty spread out.

Guilin Garland (Kaiyue) Hotel: • *84, Zhongshan South Rd. Very conveniently located across the street from the railway station. Dist.A.P.13 km. Near shopping, Elephant Trunk, and Osmanthus Hotel.* • 1987, ren. 1989. 15 stories, 300 rooms. IDD. T.R., C.C. Business center. Managed by Vista International. Beautiful, classy decor with soft pastel colors. Lobby bar for group check in.

Guilin Garden Hotel • *Li Jiang Rd. Telex: 48446 GLGDN CN. South side overlooks Li River* • 1987, ren. 1989. Seven stories, 334 rooms. Waterfall in two-story lobby; beautiful 4-story garden coffee shop. Piano bar. Hair dryer in every room. Solar-heated outlook pool, tennis, business center. C.C. IDD. Bicycles, health spa. Now under O'Phee Group management.

Guilin Osmanthus Hotel • *451 Zhong Shan South Rd. Telex 48455 GLOSH CN. Cable: 0030. Dist.A.P.14 km. Dist.R.W.1 km. On Peach Blossom River near Elephant Hill, CAAC and Reed Flute Cave.* • 1986 west wing 14 stories, 214 deluxe rooms; ren. 1988. 1980 east wing five stories, 157 standard rooms. T.R., C.C. North side view best for mountains and river. Managed by Vista International Hotels. Bowling alley, supermarket, outdoor pool. Good rooms with lots of closet space but no drawers. Business center, bicycles.

Guilin Riverside Resort • *An-Jia-Zhou. Cable: 5031. Telex: 48457 GLRSR. Cable 5031. Dist.A.P.20 km. Dist.R.W.4 km. Beautiful, isolated rural setting close to Pagoda Hill and Penetrating Hill.* • 1986–87. T.R., C.C. 4 stories, 232 rooms, 2 buildings. IDD, bicycles, CIM management. North side rooms look out on real working farmers, rice and vegetable fields, and water buffalo. This hotel targeted for groups. Not much to do in area in evenings.

Holiday Inn Guilin • *14 South Ronghu Rd. Telex: 48456 GLHCL CN. Cable 6333. Reservations through Holiday Inn Holidex. Dist.A.P.14 km. Dist.R.W.3 ½ km* • 1987. T.R., C.C. Small, exquisite and very attractive hotel with Chinese architecture. Shops discreetly hidden. 9 stories, 259 rooms. Courtyard with garden and pond. Top floor rooms have cathedral ceilings. IDD, Visa and MasterCard C.C.

Hong Kong Hotel Guilin • *8 Xihuan Yi Rd. Telex 48454 GLXJH CN. Cable 4359* • 1988–89. 20-story cylindrical building, 300 rooms. C.C. Reservations UTELL. IDD, bowling, health club, revolving restaurant. Managed by Pearl International.

Jia Shan Hotel • *Lees Xia Rd. Cable 0092. Telex 48459 GLJSH CN. On bank of Peach Blossom River. Dist.Reed Flute Cave 3 km in*

*tranquil, pretty setting surrounded by mountains. Dist.A.P.20 km.
Dist.R.W.7 km.* ● 1983. 2 stories. 322 rooms. Dorms. This Australian-built hotel looks like a metal ship container. Renovations planned but any high standards will probably be temporary unless the management itself changes. Budget travelers only.

Li Jiang (River) Hotel 漓江饭店 ● *1 Shanhu N. Road. Cable: 0044. Telex: 48470 GLLIR CN.* ● 1976. American Express card. Will telex collect answer to request for room if requested. 14 stories. 390 rooms. Business office. Rooms good. Building in back with smaller rooms cheaper.

Rong Cheng Hotel/Pine Garden Holiday Resorts ● *Yangguling, Sanlidian. Cable: 1004. Telex 48447 GLRCH CN. Dist.A.P.12 km.; Dist.R.W.8 km. Near Penetrating Hill and 7 Star Park. Near International Trade Exhibition Centre and overlooking lake.* ● 1983–84, ren. 1987. 5 buildings, 259 rooms. 1988 200-room extension. Chinese architecture. Good closet space but no drawers. Very popular disco. Outdoor pool. No business center. Store has good selection of ethnic handicrafts.

Ronghu Hotel 榕湖饭店 ● *17 Ronghu Rd. Cable: 7139. Telex 48461 GLRHU CN. Dist.A.P.15 km. Dist.R.W.3 km. Dist.Fubo Hill 3 km.* ● Chinese architecture. First built 1953 as state guest house and then expanded. 8 buildings, 6 stories, 400 rooms. Became hotel in 1960. T.R. #8 building repaired 1987. #5 is a Hong Kong joint venture called Wintersweet Village. 1988. 156 rooms. Business center. Indoor swimming pool. Scruffy hall carpets. No smoke alarms. Roof garden.

Sheraton Guilin ● *Bing Jiang Nan Rd. Telex 48439 GLMAN CN. Dist.A.P.20 km. Dist.R.W.5 km. Close to Elephant Trunk Hill and shopping* ● 1988–89. Five stories, 490 rooms. Atrium lobby. C.C., IDD. C.I.T.S., Dragonair. Pool, health club, bicycles.

Yangshuo Hotel 阳朔饭店 ● *Yangshuo; tel. 2260* ● Over 120 beds, but only one third of the rooms have private baths.

OTHER IMPORTANT ADDRESSES
Telephone numbers are changing.
Guilin Airport 桂林机场 : tel. 2741.
Bank of China 中国银行 : Zhongshan Zhong Rd.; tel. 3005. (Foreign exchange desks at major hotels.)
CAAC 中国民航 : 144 Zhongshan Zhong Rd.; tel. 3063.

C.I.T.S. 中国国际旅行社 : 14 Ronghu Bei Rd.; tel. 5923. 3870 Telex 48460 GLITS CN.
C.T.S. 中国旅行社 : Ronghu Bei Rd.; tel. 5210, 5395. Cable 3535. Telex 48463 GLERA CN.
Guangxi Guilin Tourism Motor & Boat Company: 1 Yueya Rd.; tel. 5829, 3306; cable: 5307. Sightseeing boats and buses.
Guilin Tourist Company: Ronghu Bei Rd.; tel. 2648 for tickets. Telex 48460 GLITS CN.
Guilin Travel Bureau, Ronghu Bei Rd., tel. 5890.
Hospitals:
  Guilin Renmin Hospital 桂林人民医院 : Binjiang Rd.; tel. 3104.
  Nanxishan Hospital: Zhongshan Nan Rd.; tel. 2001.
Lijiang Navigation Co.: Binjian Rd.; tel. 5878. Boat tours to Yangshuo. Buses and steam ships to Hong Kong. Buses to Guangzhou.
Pedicab Station 三轮车站 : Zhongshan Bei Rd.; tel. 3882.
Public Security Bureau 公安局 : tel. 3202.
Railway Station 火车站 : Zhongshan Nan Rd.; tel. 2904.

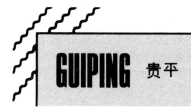

GUIPING 贵平

South China. *Jintian Village, 25 km north of the capital of Guiping County in SE Guangxi, is where the Taiping Revolution (1851–64) broke out. Guiping can be reached from Nanning.

GUIYANG 贵阳

Southwest China, in the central part of Guizhou province, of which it is the capital. It is joined by air with Beijing, Xi'an, Guilin, Changsha, Guangzhou, etc. It is also at the hub of railway lines with Chengdu, Nanning, Kunming, and Changsha. It has an altitude of 1070 meters. The western and central part of the province has an altitude of 1–2000 meters. The terrain is rugged, with karst formations, underground rivers, jagged peaks, dramatic valleys, and terraced rice fields. The annual precipitation is 900–1500 mm. The province is rich in minerals—aluminum, coal, iron, lead, gold, silver, zinc, etc. It has China's largest mercury deposit. It grows rice, corn, tobacco, cork, raw lacquer, and timber. Population about 800,000.

The area has been a part of recorded history since the Shang dynasty, about 3000 years ago. Today, out of a total population of 29.3 million, 26% are minorities: Miao, Bouyei, Dong, Yi, Shui, Hui, Gelo, Zhuang, Yao. They contribute to the fascinating architecture and the over 1000 lively festivals a year, many unlike those in other parts of China. These include bull fights, dragon boats, horse races, antiphonal singing, and Lusheng dancing.

Because this province has only recently been opened to tourists, people looking for the unusual will find it here, especially among the minorities. Be sure to ask about visiting some, but don't expect private baths and hot water everywhere. You'll be lucky to get a clean hotel room. New hotels are currently being built.

Qianling Hill, in the northwestern part of the city, has Qianling Lake with pavilions and the Hongfu Temple (Qing), the center of Buddhism locally. Behind the temple is a good view of Guiyang. **Huaxi Park** is 17 km SW. The **Southern Cave** in Bailongdong in the south suburbs is 587 meters long and full of incredible formations and an underground river.

The only real tourist attraction in the province besides the colorful minorities is **Zhenning,** 45 km from Anshun, with China's most important waterfall. Huangguoshu Falls, 150 km by train or bus from the capital and then a 1-hour bus ride. Part of the Baishui River, the falls are 84 meters wide and 74–90 meters high. The area has 18 falls (some with up to 130-meter drops), a petrified forest, and over 30 caves with interesting formations. Swimming in the area is possible. The pleasant Huangguoshu Guesthouse is near the falls.

Twenty-seven km south of **Anshun** is an intricate set of caverns linked by an underground river. The Dragon King Palace complex has five galleries. The Dragon Gate Falls is in a 50-meter-high, 25-meter-wide cave. From the 10,000-square-meter Dragon Pool, tourists can ride dragon boats into a 1-km-long cave.

The Miao and Dong Autonomous prefecture is 300 km east of Anshun, in the southeastern part of the province. At **Kaili** you will see women laden with silver jewelry and hear the unique Miao antiphonal courtship singing. Dong architecture is unusual; their drum towers especially are a charming mixture of Chinese pagoda styles with flaming eaves.

SHOPPING

Made locally are minority handicrafts, including embroidered vests, silver Miao jewelry, bamboo flutes, lacquerware, and wax printing. Also produced here are Maotai (the most famous and most potent Chinese liquor), pears, oranges, kiwi fruit, and tangerines.

Stores include the **Friendship Store, Arts and Handicrafts Shop,** and the **No. 1 Department Store.**

FOOD

Local delicacies include braised salamander, love bean curd fruit, *bijie* stuffed dumplings, and Eight Delicacies. Please note that the giant salamander, a favorite of the Chinese gourmet, is an endangered species. Roasted bean curd and roasted corn are famous local snack foods.

Huaxi Hotel, Huaxi Dist. Dist.A.P.16 km. Dist.R.W.20 km.

C.I.T.S. and **Guizhou Provincial Tourism Bureau,** Yanan Zhong Rd., Guiyang; tel. 29693, 28388. Telex 66002 GZFAO CN.
C.T.S., tel. 29693, 28388.
CAAC, 170 Zunli Rd.; tel. 22300, 23000.

HAINAN ISLAND 海南岛

South China. China's second largest island, 30 km off its southern coast, became China's 1st province in 1988. Hainan includes the Xisha, Nansha (Spraley), and Zhongsha Islands. It is best reached by a 45-minute flight from Guangzhou or 1-hour flight from Hong Kong or it can also be reached by ship from Guangzhou and Zhanjiang. Flights have started recently between Guangzhou and Sanya, and there is a ferry service between Hong Kong and Haikou. An international airport is due in Sanya in 1992. The island is almost as big as Taiwan, with about the same latitude and climate as southern Cuba. Foreign oil experts have been visiting it for years, but it is only now in the process of being developed for tourists. The few tourists who have been here have raved about unspoiled beaches in the south, 6 hours' drive from Haikou. Hainan is also being developed as a very special economic zone with more flexibility and openness than other SEZs in developing foreign trade. It should become a tax-free zone. Tourist facilities are not well organized and many people seem to be out to make a fast yuan.

Hainan was first colonized by Han dynasty troops. From the Tang, disfavored scholars and officials were sent here to live in exile, a tropical Siberia. During the '30s and '40s, a Communist army detachment fought here, and after Liberation part of the island became an autonomous region because a large percentage of the population are tribal minorities: mainly Li and Miao, but also Hui. Many of these still wear their beautiful, distinctive dress.

It has not been overly developed and is short on electricity, water, and efficiency. The weather is tropical, with 2000 mm of rain a year. Visitors can be admitted to Hainan for 15 days without a visa.

The island produces tea, coffee, rubber, fish, sugar, coconut, and rice. Other industries are being developed. The population is around 6 million.

Haikou 海口 , with a population of 300,000 people, has the **Five Officials Memorial Temple** 五公祠 nearby, which commemorates some of the banished officials. Also to be seen is the **Hai Rui Tomb 海瑞墓.**

Tourists have also visited an Overseas Chinese Farm in **Xinglong** 华侨 , where there is a hot spring and a comfortable hotel. At Sanya, on the south coast (joined by two paved roads to Haikou, the central one shorter), visitors can swim in the Dadonghai Sea. In this area are a pearl cultivation farm and the **Dongshanling Ridge,** with a group of giant boulders. (Beware of tides.) The southernmost point of Hainan Island is the **Ends of the Earth** 天涯海角 . This is not to be confused with the southernmost tip of China. Sanya is linked by rail with Chang-jiang in the western part of the island.

Tourists can also visit the Nanwan Rhesus Monkey Reserve in Lingshui County and eat in the good, nearby Hai Wei Seafood Restaurant with Li waitresses.

SHOPPING

Locally found are rubies and rose quartz. Locally produced are cultured pearls, fruit, and minority handicrafts.

FOOD

Local specialties include Wenchang-style chicken 文昌鸡 , Jiaji duck 加积鸭 , Hele crab 和乐蟹 , and Dongshan mutton 东山羊肉.

HOTELS

There are no luxury hotels on the island, but the Haikou Tower and the Haikou Hotels appear to be the top.

Haikou Hotel • *San Jiaochi. Telex 45084 HHH CN, 45060 HTLHK CN. Fax 22824. Cable 2160 •* Ten stories, 184 rooms. IDD. Exhibition hall. Pool, health club, business center.

Haikou Tower Hotel • *Binhai Rd. Telex 45050, 45051 TOWER CN. Fax 73966. 10 minutes from airport •* 1986. Two stories, 241 rooms. C.C., IDD, business center, bicycles.

International Financial Center Hotel • *Da Tong Rd. Telex 45058. Cable 0582. Fax 23816. Five minutes from airport •* 241 rooms. Pool, business and fitness centers, bowling, conference facilities. C.C.

Outside of Haikou, no luxury-class hotels yet. A fancy 250-room low-rise resort with golf is being built in Lung Ya Bay, 35 km east of Sanya, by Hong Kong interests. It is due about 1992. A hotel run by the high-standard Jinling Hotel (Nanjing) is due in Sanya in 1990 near the beach. A fancy 300-room hotel in Sanya on the waterfront (no beach) run by C.T.S. (HK), is due late 1989.

Hot Spring Hotel • *Xinglong.* • 1989 Villas good. Best hotel on eastern road.

Tongza Resort Hotel • *Hong Kong j.v.* • 1985. Pool open Apr.– Oct. Low season April–June. Set in mountains. C.C.

Da Dong Hai Hotel • *Sanya. Drive is 6 hrs. from Haikou.* • Good location on beach but beware of undertow. Three stories. Rooms big and bright. Balconies overlooking the sea. Best for swimmers.

Lu Hui Tou Hotel • *Sanya.* • Lush, beautiful grounds, but accommodations nothing special. 200 beds. Cheap dorms. For back-packers.

Longhai Hotel • *Ya Long Bay.* • On beautiful 7-km-long beach. Adequate South Korean modules.

C.T.S., 17 Datong Rd., Haikou; tel. 23623. Cable 3307.
C.I.T.S., Da Dong Hai Hotel, Sanya, Haikou, tel. 74640, 72117.
CAAC, 50 Jiefang Rd.; tel. 24614, 72934.

HANDAN 邯郸

North China, south Hebei on the Beijing-Guangzhou railway line.

Handan was the capital of Zhao State during the Warring States, 475–221 B.C. In 198 B.C., it became capital of the prefecture. The *Xiangtangshan Cave Temple from the Wei, northern Qi to Yuan dynasties (about A.D. 500) is in a coal mine. Its nine caves in the north contain 700 buddhas, those in the south more than 3500.

Cizhou pottery, a distinctive traditional style with strong flower patterns, is still made in Pengcheng, near Handan, at eight factories.

HOTELS
Handan Hotel • *Dist.A.P.15 km. Dist.R.W.3 km* • 1958, ren. 1988, 1989. Four stories, 280 rooms, four bldgs. IDD, no C.C. Business center, bicycles.

C.T.S., 66 Zhonghua St.; tel. 5931 X313. Cable 7130.

HANGZHOU (HANGCHOW)

East China. Capital of Zhejiang province, Hangzhou is on the Qiantang River at the southern end of the Grand Canal on the east coast of China. It is 189 km SW of Shanghai and a 2-hour flight SE of Beijing. Direct flights from Hong Kong. Coldest weather is in January, a little below 0°C; hottest in July, with highs of 35°C. Annual precipitation about 1452 mm, mainly May–June. The population is 1.2 million.

Hangzhou is one of the most famous beauty spots of China, with its Xihu (West Lake). It is also of historical importance. Founded over 2200 years ago in the Qin, it began to prosper as a trading center after the completion of the Grand Canal in 610. It was the capital of the tiny state of Wuyueh (893–978), at which time the first dikes forming the lake were built. It was also capital of the Southern Song after 1127. The best source for a detailed picture of the city from 1250 to 1276 is Jacques Gernet's *Daily Life in China on the Eve of the Mongol Invasion,* essential for visitors who want to know a lot of history, to compare life then with today, and to look for old ruins. The city was seized by the Mongols under Kublai Khan in 1279 and visited by Marco Polo the next year when it was known as Kinsai. The Venetian explorer

raved about the city, then the largest and richest in the world, its silks
and handicrafts much in demand in China and abroad.

Hangzhou has been a famous resort for centuries, attracting famous
painters, poets, and retired officials as well as tourists. It is also an
industrial city now, with iron and steel, machine-making, basic chemicals, an oil refinery, and electronics. It also produces generators, machine tools, light trucks, and small tractors. Tourists would probably be
interested in its factories producing silk textiles, satin, brocades, sandalwood fans, scissors, silk parasols, and woven silk ''photographs.''
Villages here grow the famous long jing (Dragon Well) tea and silk
worms. These make a rural excursion especially worthy.

The center of the city is on the east side of **Xi Hu (West Lake)** 西
湖 . The 5.6-square-km lake was originally part of the Qiantang River
until its outlet became silted up. It is now 15 km in circumference, with
an average depth of 1.8 meters. The lake is now linked with the Qiantang River and is usually renewed with fresh water two times a month.
Just strolling around the edge of the lake is worthwhile. Many of the
tourist attractions are close to its shore.

If a visitor only has one day to spend in the city, C.I.T.S. recommends a boat ride on the lake with stops at various famous sites. Then
take in the Pagoda of Six Harmonies, Lingyin Temple, and a silk
factory. Boats are available for hire at four different places around
the lake.

One could also rent a bicycle (faster) from a hotel or the shop at
the intersection north of the Children's Palace, or a pedicab. (See also
''Getting Around''). That way in one day you can ride along Baidi
Causeway with stops at the Autumn Moon on Calm Lake Pavilion,
Wenlan Ge (next to Zhejiang Provincial Museum), Xiling Seal Engraver's Society, Tomb and Temple of Yue Fei, and Jade Spring. After you
park your bicycle at a stand, you could take the cable car up to Lingyin
Temple. Then you can visit the Feilaifeng Grottoes across the stream
from the temple, go back down to pick up your bicycle, and turn back
to the Yue Fei Tomb and then south onto Sudi Causeway. Follow Nan
Shan and then Hubin roads. Stop to enjoy Liulanwenying Park if only
for its name, which means Park to See the Waving Willows and Hear
the Singing of the Birds. Then back to the Children's Palace.

The best times to see the lake itself is in the mist, or in the moonlight, or just at sunrise before the sun makes strong shadows, and when
the birds are singing in the willows. One of the favorite spots for viewing the lake, especially during the harvest moon, is at **Pinghuqiuyue
(Autumn Moon on Calm Lake Pavilion)** 平湖秋月 at the southeastern end of **Gu Shan (Solitary Hill)** 孤山 . But don't expect to be alone.

On the islet also is the **Wenlan Ge (Pavilion for Storing Imperial
Books)** 御书楼 , built in 1699 (Qing), and one of the seven imperial

libraries. This one was especially built to store the Sikuzhunsu, a 33,304-volume Chinese encyclopedia ordered by Emperor Qianlong. Copied by hand, the encyclopedia took 10 years to compile.

The **Xiling Seal Engraver's Society** 西冷印社 was founded in 1903 and has its headquarters on a hillside here full of pavilions, towers, and a pagoda. Seal engraving is a fine art in the Orient, with several different styles. This society meets twice a year, gives many exhibitions, and publishes periodicals. The stone **Chamber to the Three Venerables** *Han San Lao Hui Zi* here was carved in A.D. 52. The island also has a provincial museum and a restaurant, the Louwailou.

Lively **giant golden carp** can be seen at **Huagang Park** 花岗公园 at the SW end of the lake, beyond the Sudi Causeway. A Song official once had a vacation home here. The pavilions were built after Liberation. This 20-hectare park also has a restaurant and a tea house.

The 2.8-km **Sudi Causeway** is the more beautiful of the two causeways here, lined with grass, willows, and peach trees. No motor vehicles are allowed because of its hump-backed bridges. It's a pleasant bicycle or pedicab ride, but please give the driver a break. Get off and walk up those bridges.

The famous **Zig-Zag Bridge** is on the islet **Xiaoyingzhou (Three Pools Mirroring the Moon)** 小瀛州 and can be reached only by boat. It is east of Sudi Causeway. Did you know that bad spirits have to move in straight lines? Stand on the bridge here and nothing can harm you. This islet was first constructed in 1607 (Ming) with mud cleared from the lake. Look for the ''island in a lake and the lake in an island.''

During the Moon Festival, candles light up the small pagodas, thus creating ''Three Pools Mirroring the Moon.'' In June, this is a good place to enjoy water lilies and lotus flowers.

Everywhere around West Lake are exquisite gardens, some with artistically cobbled foot paths. The large mansions on the shore, once owned by the rich, are now hotels or resorts for workers. The 1.8 km **Baidi Causeway** 白堤 in the north was first laid over 1000 years ago and is named after Bai Juyi, the great poet and governor of the Tang.

Visitors can also go by boat to **Ruangongdun Island** on the NW side of West Lake just south of Gushan Hill. **Huanbi Zhuang,** there, is an attempt to reproduce a Song dynasty village with period costumes, sedan chair rides, wine shop, music, and dance. Some tourists have found it fun, but serious students of Chinese history might find it too commercial. At the Mid-lake Pavilion is a 20th-century disco.

The ***Liuhe Ta (Pagoda of Six Harmonies)** 六和塔 is on the north bank of the Qiantang River. Built in A.D. 970 (Song), it is 59.89 meters and 13 stories tall, octagonal, and made of brick and wood. It can be climbed for a good view. West of this temple is the shallow and clear **Nine Creeks and Eighteen Gullies,** which cut through the rugged but tranquil (few tourists) Yangmei Hill. Great for hikers, the paths wind for about 7 km. There are donkeys for rent nearby for the less ambitious.

The **Lingyin (Soul's Retreat) Temple** 灵隐寺 is 9 km from the city, west of West Lake. Founded in A.D. 326 (Jin), its Celestial Kings' Hall and 33.6-meter-high Buddha Hall are all that is left of the original 18 pavilions and 72 halls. Lingyin at one time housed 3000 monks. A friend of mine watched, horrified, in 1966 as Red Guards smashed some of the statues here. The statues have been replaced now. A seated Sakyamuni inside is 19.6 meters high. The temple guardian behind the Four Celestial Kings was carved from camphor wood during the Song. Lingyin is still one of the largest and most magnificent temples in China. Two restaurants serve vegetarian food, the one inside better than the one next to the temple.

Across from Lingyin temple is *****Feilaifeng (Peak that Flew from Afar)** 飞来峰 , named by an Indian monk after a similiar-looking Indian peak that must have flown here. The 380 carvings along the narrow, hilly trails are from the Five Dynasties to the Yuan.

A trip to a silk factory to watch the weaving and designing can be arranged through C.I.T.S. The **Dujinsheng Silk Weaving Factory** (215 Feng Qi Rd.) is about five minutes' walk from the Wanghu Hotel. Silk brocade pictures, cushion covers, fancy tablecloths, silk fabric. Closed on Sunday. The **Hangzhou Silk Printing and Dyeing Complex** 杭州丝织厂 (Gong Zhen Qiao; tel. 87824) is more interesting to see. A 15-minute taxi ride from the Wanghu Hotel, it is next to the Grand Canal on which the cocoons are transported. Here you can see the process of preparing the cocoons, spinning, weaving, printing, and dyeing. To make a shirt requires 500–1000 cocoons, depending on the thickness of the material.

The unpleasant part of a silk factory visit is the deafening noise of the weaving machines, but there are other things to see besides those machines. Do complain about the noise to the management.

It could take three or four days to cover all the important spots in Hangzhou. The 45-meter-high **Baochu (Precious Stone Hill) Pagoda** is on a 200-meter-high hill north of the lake, 2 km from the city. It was first built in 968 (Song) to pray for the safe return of the unjustly arrested Qian Hongchu, a successful effort. The pagoda, last reconstructed in 1933, is now filled with dirt and no one can enter.

The *****Tomb and Temple of Yue Fei** 岳飞庙，岳墳 is at the NW corner of the lake. Yue Fei was a famous Song general who was unjustly executed in 1142 at the age of 39. Public reaction forced a retrial 20 years later that reversed the verdict. A temple was built with statues of his four accusers kneeling for forgiveness before his grave. These four are spat on even today.

Yue Fei was also a calligrapher and poet who came from a family that valued patriotism. His mother tattooed his back with four characters to remind him of his duty to his country. His son was murdered on the day of Yue Fei's death. Their tombs are next to each other, but only contain their clothing. An exhibition hall illustrates Yue Fei's battles and shows his handwritten proposals to the Song emperor.

At the **Hupao (Tiger) Spring** 虎跑 you will find water that will not overflow from a full cup even though many coins are added to it. The high surface tension will also support a carefully placed Chinese coin, a trick that also works in Toronto, so don't be gullible. The spring is near the Hangzhou Zoo, about 6 km from the city SW of the lake on Hupao Road. A handy tea house here serves Dragon Well tea, an exotic experience. The well is named after a tiger in a monk's dream that dug successfully for water here. The monk woke up and excavated this well at the same spot as in his dream.

The **Longjing (Dragon Well)** 龙井, to the NW of Hupao, is another spring. The water here has a curious ripple effect when you stir it, especially on rainy days. This phenomenon is explained by the differences in the specific gravity of the rain water and the spring water, and is a good ploy to encourage business in wet weather.

Two km SW is **Longjingcun (Dragon Well Village)** 龙井村, where you can see the famous tea growing on hillsides. It is usually picked in late March or early April. Connoisseurs of good tea pay fabulously high prices for the best of the harvest, the most tender leaves, hand-picked before the spring rain. The quantity is also limited because only a few villages have the proper soil and water. The best Longjing Tea, when brewed, has a fresh, crystal-green color, a mild and pure fragrance, and a slight sweetness.

At the **Meijiawu Tea Garden** 梅家坞茶园, SW of Longjingcun, you can see the tea production process.

The third of Hangzhou's famous springs is **Jade Spring** 玉泉 (Yugu Rd., off the NW corner of the lake). It is for gold fish and flower lovers, as multicolored ornamental fish are bred here. It is inside the 200-hectare **Hangzhou Botanical Garden** 杭州植物园, which has 3700 species of plants, including 120 varieties of bamboo. Along with the Shanwaishan Restaurant, these are within walking distance of the Hangzhou Hotel.

A **cable car** 缆车 runs from 8 a.m. to 5 p.m. between **Beigao Feng (North Peak)** 北高峰 and near the Lingyin Temple, giving a good view of the lake. Visitors can also drive up **Wushan Hill,** east of the lake, the highest spot in the city. This has an 800-year-old camphor tree and a cave made for the Song emperor. Also accessible is **Yuhuang (Jade Emperor) Mountain** 玉皇山, overlooking the river at a spot where a Song emperor pretended to do manual labor. A **wax museum** on Wushan Hill has paintings and sculptures of local historical figures.

Most temples are open from 7:30 a.m. to 5 p.m. in summer and from 8 a.m. to 4:30 p.m. in winter. Some parks close at 6 p.m.

Excursions can be arranged from Hangzhou. For Ningbo (about 150 km SW) and Shaoxing (about 50 km SE), see separate listings. **Mogan Mountain** 莫干山 , 700 meters high (about 75 km NW), is a well-known summer resort with over 300 hectares of waterfalls, bamboo forests, stone trails, ponds, and caves. Good for hiking and relaxing in beautiful surroundings. **Mogan Shan Hotel** is on Yin Shan Road. **Wuling Guesthouse** 武陵宾馆 . The main town is now known as Wujitu, and Chiang Kai Shek's home was number one. The main town is **Ying Shan** 荫山 .

The large limestone **Yaoling Cave** 瑶琳仙洞 is 120 km SW of the city, close to Tonglu County, and is 25 meters high and 1 km long, with many stairs. As the path is narrow, some visitors have found themselves so afraid of being pushed off the trail by other tourists that they couldn't enjoy the sights. The best time, then, is early afternoon, when most tourists have left. This is usually a one-day bus trip organized daily by C.I.T.S. or local tour companies.

In **Tiantai,** about 100 km from Hangzhou, the **Guoqing Temple** is the home of the Tiantai Buddhist sect.

The **Tidal Bore of the Qiantang River** 钱塘江观潮 is most spectacular on the 18th day of the eighth month (lunar calendar). In 1974 it reached a height of nine meters, but it is not usually that dramatic. Best seen at Yanguan town at Zhan'ao Pagoda 45 km from Hangzhou, or at Hailing. Check with C.T.S., Baochu Rd. tel. 27160 Cable 1954, for dates and bus tours if you are in Hangzhou in late September or early October.

SHOPPING

Produced in the province are silk textiles, woven pictures, Dragon Well tea, umbrellas, lace, Longquan Celedon, fans, woven bambooware, distinctive Tianzhu chopsticks, and stone and wood carvings. Hangzhou makes some fancy scissors that are useful souvenirs. The main shopping area is **Jiefang Rd.** and **Yan'an Rd.** 延安路 . In addition to the above-named silk factory, some important places to shop are:

Hangzhou Antique Store (31 Hubin Rd.; tel. 27141); **Hangzhou Arts and Crafts Service** (220 Yan'an Rd.; tel. 24378); **Hangzhou Department Store** (739 Jiefang Rd.; tel. 22449 20891); **Hangzhou Dragon Well Tea Shop** (33 Yan'an Rd.; tel. 24318); **Hangzhou Friendship Store** 杭州友谊商店 (302 Tiyuchang Rd.; tel. 50317 26480); **Hangzhou Silk Goods Store** (31 Hubin Rd.; tel. 24508); **Wangxingji Fans** (77 Jiefang Rd.; tel. 28255); **Zhang Xiaoquan Scissors Shop** 张小泉 剪刀店 (105 Yan'an Rd.; tel. 21860). The Zhejiang Guest House has a good-sized store.

RESTAURANTS

Food and ambiance in hotels is generally better. The Wanghu top floor is good for Chinese food; the Shangri-La for Western

Kuiyuanguan Restaurant 奎元馆 • *Guanxiangkou, Jiefang Rd.; tel. 25921* • Primarily noodles.

Lingyin Vegetarian Restaurant 灵隐寺素斋馆 • *Lingyin Temple; tel. 21433.*

Louwailou Restaurant 楼外楼饭店 • *30 Waixihu; tel. 21654* • Sweet and sour fish!

Shanwaishan Restaurant 山外山饭店 • *Yuquan Rd.; tel. 26621.*

HOTELS

The top hotel here is the Shangri-La. #2 is the new, partially-opened Dragon. #3 is the Wanghu. #4 the Xin Qiao Hotel. Most hotels are within walking distance of West Lake, the main tourist attraction here. On or almost on the lake are the Overseas Chinese, Hangzhou, and Xihu Hotels. The Wanghu, Xin Qiao, and Friendship are closest to the shopping and business district.

The high tourist season here is August, September, and October. Reservations recommended all year round.

Dragon Hotel • *Shuguang Rd. Telex: 351048 DRAGN CN. Cable: 8083 or 1818. Fax: 558090. Dist.A.P.12 km. Dist.R.W.7 km. Near Bao Chu Hill and Yellow Dragon Cave, but not West Lake.* • 1987–88. 40,000 sq. meter site. Three twin towers, 6, 7 and 9 stories. 555 rooms. Chinese architecture. Courtyard gardens. Largest banquet hall in city. Tennis courts, swimming pool, IDD, C.C. Shuttle service to lake and business district. Designed as hotel for groups. Little drawer space. Pastel colors. Managed by New World Hotels International.

Friendship Hotel • *53 Pinghai Rd. Telex 35068 FRISH CN. Cable 0350. Fax 057173842. Dist.A.P.15 km. Dist.R.W. about 5 km. 300 meters from lake.* • 1986. Will answer telex for reservation within 2 hours. Major credit cards. Good looking hotel. 23 stories, 220 rooms. West side has view of lake. 1988 new wing with tennis, and gymnasium. Japanese joint venture. Business Center. Two discos. Small bathrooms. Little drawer space. IDD.

Huagang Hotel 杭州饭店 • *4 Xishan Rd. Cable: 3263. Telex: 35007 HUAJG CN. Dist.A.P.18 km. Dist.R.W.7.5 km. Near Huagang Park, 5 min. walk to lake.* • Main wing with lobby 1954, renovated

1986. North wing 1980, renovated 1987. Will telex within 48 hours of receipt of request if no room. Set in garden. Chinese architecture. Both garden view. 4 stories; 220 rooms. Beautiful wood carvings. Long dark hallways. Poor decor. Small TVs. Budget travelers only.

Overseas Chinese Hotel • *15 Hubin Rd. Telex: 35070 HOCH CN. Fax 23253. Dist.A.P.15 km. Dist.R.W.5 km. Two blocks from Wanghu Hotel.* • 1983. Must request answer to request for room. Main building 1958, ren. 1987, east building ren. 1989. 5 stories, 308 rooms. C.T.S. on premises. Good rooms and furniture. C.C., IDD, business center, bicycles.

Shangri-La Hotel • *78 Beishan Rd. Telex: 35005/6 HOTCH CN. Fax: 773545. Cable 7391. Dist.A.P.20 km. Dist.R.W.5 km. Walking distance to Solitary Hill Island and wharf for renting boats.* • East building, formerly the Xiling Hotel, renovated 1985. 7 stories. 156 rooms Chinese decor. West building opened 1956, ren. 1987. 6 stories, 199 rooms. More Western decor. The two buildings are joined by a covered walkway cooled by fans. Also three villas with 32 rooms. Total: 387 rooms. One of the top hotels in China. Managed by Shangri-La International. Convention center. 30 acre site. No disco. C.C. Business center. Fast food restaurant on grounds. Old world charm. IDD. May have no smoking floor in 1988. Has brochure with walking and cycling tours. Bicycles. Planning pool and tennis.

Wanghu Hotel 望湖宾馆 • *2 Huanchen Xi Rd. Telex 35003 WHBG CN, 351029 OLWH CN. Fax 71350. Cable 9980 HZWH. Dist.A.P.14 km. Dist.R.W.4 km. Walking distance to branch of Friendship Store, Bank of China and import-export corporation.* • Built 1986. Renovated 1988. Will telex answer to request for reservation. Major credit cards. 8 stories, 360 good rooms. C.I.T.S. and CAAC offices on premises. Business Center. Photo-finishing.

Xihu State Guest House 柳浪宾馆 • *7 Xi Shang Rd. Telex: 35004 BTHXH CN. Set in a 360,000 sq. meter garden. Dist.A.P.20 km. Dist.R.W.15 km. Isolated.* • Renovated and rebuilt 1959, and then 1972. Will telex answer to request for reservation if asked. Built late Qing dynasty. 5 buildings. 2-story villas. 50 beds. Pres. Nixon slept here. Most foreign guests stay in #2 building renovated 1985. Rooms have high ceilings. Grubby. Poorly made drapes don't match decor. Long walk to dining room. For budget travelers.

Xin Qiao Hotel • *176 Jiefang Rd. Cable: 0376. Telex: 351028 XQH CN. Dist.A.P.12 km. Dist.R.W.2 km. 200 meters from lake. Near biggest department store and arts and crafts store.* • 1987. Hong Kong j.v.

20 stories; currently 381 rooms. Italian marble in lobby. Rooms have good furniture but poorly tailored drapes. C.I.T.S. on premises. Mainly Chinese food. Claims biggest disco in city.

Zhejiang Guest House 浙江宾馆 • *San Tai Shan Rd. Cable 6333. Telex 351044 ZIGH CN. Dist.A.P.20 km. Dist.R.W. about 6 km. Near Dragon Well Spring. (Bus 27 to city). Isolated and pretty rural setting.* • Some buildings renovated 1987. Former private villa of Lin Biao, who never lived here. Six buildings on vast grounds, some with own dining rooms. 2 and 5 stories. 400 beds. Dorms with no airconditioning. Basketball. Indoor pool. Large 9 room Friendship Store. American Express card for store only. No disco. Budget travelers only.

OTHER IMPORTANT ADDRESSES

Boats for Hire: Many kinds are available. Hubin (Lakeside) Park 湖滨公园 : tel. 22051; Zhongshan Park 中山公园 : tel. 22336; Huagang Park: tel. 25586; Liulangwenying Park 柳浪闻莺公园 : tel. 23001. Open 7:30 a.m.–5 p.m.
CAAC 中国旅行社: 160 Tiyuchang Rd.; tel. 552575, 554259. Airport: tel. 42160.
C.I.T.S. 中国国际旅行社 : 1 or 2 Shihan Rd.; tel. 23401, 27160. Telex 35031 HZT CN.
C.T.S. 中国民航 : Overseas Chinese Hotel, Hubin Rd.; tel. 57479. Telex 351033 CTSZJ CN.
Hangzhou Railway Station 杭州火车站 : Chengzhan Rd.; tel. 22716.
Hospital: in case of illness, ask for help at your hotel. Otherwise, try the **Zhejiang Hospital** 浙江医院 : Lingyin Rd.; tel. 21357.
Telecommunications Services: Try your hotel first, but 24-hour service at Hangzhou Telegraph Office 杭州电报局 : Qingnian Rd.; tel. 23121, 24017.
Zhejiang China Travel Service: 1 Shihan Rd., tel 57479. Telex 351033 CTSZJ CN. Write for information on provincial attractions.
Zhejiang Tourism Bureau: 1 Shihan Rd., tel. 22478.

HARBIN 哈尔滨

(Haerhpin) Northeast China. This is the capital of China's north-ernmost province of Heilongjiang, formerly part of Manchuria, a 1½-hour flight NE of Beijing or a 5–hour train ride from Jinlin. There is a possibility of flights from Japan, Hong Kong, and Sib-eria. It has a population of over two million and is an industrial city 159 km from the Daqing oil fields, China's biggest. Its high-est summer temperature is 36°C; its lowest in winter is ⁻38°. The winter is six months long, so take your longjohns. Wintertime, however, is brightened by the **Ice Sculpture Festival.** You can also bring skates and skis. Annual precipitation 250–700 mm, mostly June through August.

The area was first settled by people of the Nuzhen nationality in 1097. In the Yuan, the city was renamed Harbin. In 1898 it was opened as a port and became a Russian concession. Tsarist troops and police patrolled the Russian ghetto. From 1932 the Japanese occupied the area until the end of the war. You can see a lot of tsarist and Japanese architecture, although neglected, and cobblestone streets (in Dao Li District). The Northeast is not as developed as other parts of China.

Today, Heilongjiang numbers among its population Han, Manchu, Korean, Hui, Mongolian, Daur, Orogen, Ewenki, Kirgiz, Hezhen, and other nationalities.

If you only have one day here, C.I.T.S. recommends that you tour the harbor and along the Song Hua River, with its 10 km dike. From January 5 to February 5, visit the magical **Ice Sculpture Festival 冰灯 游园会** , about 8 km from the Swan Hotel. The show can take 2 or 3 hours if you can stand the cold. This international competition has at-tracted teams from Canada, Japan, Hong Kong, etc. Full of ice pago-das, bridges, giant lanterns, human figures, mazes, palaces, and children's slides, it is best seen at night with its twinkling lights.

Other attractions include a 2-km-long miniature railway for chil-dren 儿童铁路 (4 km from the Swan); in summer you can rent sail-boats and sampans; in winter you can sail-sled on ice. Among the animals at the **zoo** you can find a Manchurian tiger, a red-crested crane, and a moose. The **Heilongjiang Provincial Museum** is supposed to have one of the best skeletons of a mammoth to be found in China. It should reopen after renovations in 1990.

C.I.T.S. has bird-watching, gold panning, horse riding (Mongolian), and skiing tours. Bicycle tours go from Wuying-Dafeng-Nancha-Dailing to Langxiang. Steam locomotive tours are taken on narrow-gauge mining and logging trains to the railway bridge near the International Hotel. China's biggest bird sanctuary 扎龙自然保护区 , the 210,000-hectare **Zhalong Nature Preserve** is near **Qiqihar,** 280 km away. Its cranes, storks, swans, geese, herons, etc., are best seen from April to September. The famous red-crested cranes are considered a symbol of luck by the Chinese. **C.T.S.** is at 2 Wenhua St., Qiqihar; tel. 72016. **Daqing** is a 6–hour tain ride NW. The best hotel is the Daqing Hotel.

Also in the province is the **Taiyang Island summer resort,** another ice festival in Qiqihar, and **Jingpo Lake** in **Mudanjiang.** 90–minute flights to **Heihe** at the Soviet border are available, or you can make a day trip to **Siberia.**

Skiing here is an experience. It is not for serious skiers. Facilities are not well developed yet, though the province has two resorts with lifts. The China Winter Games (1991) will be at **Yabuli** and ski jumps, lifts, and lodges are being built for athletes and for recreational skiers. Snow late October to late March.

ENTERTAINMENT

Leather-silhouette show. Annual Harbin Summer Music Festival. An unusual sport is sail-sledding on ice.

SHOPPING

Fur hats, jackets, and collars: sable, mink, muskrat. Handicrafts include straw patchwork, horn carving, knitting, and ivory, jade, stone, and wood carving. Good to eat are its pine nuts. Lots of ginseng. Harbin No. 1 Department Store, 146 Diduan St., tel. 49291; Harbin Embroidery Factory, Arts and Crafts Bldg., tel. 225055 (for tablecloths); Tourist Fur Store, 88 Zhongyang St., tel. 49683.

RESTAURANTS

The most famous dishes are served in the International Hotel. There you can try moose nose and hazel grouse. Please, don't eat any endangered species! For those who want something less questionable, try monkey head–shaped mushroom. Russian food in hotels.

International Hotel Restaurant • *124 Dazhi Rd., Nangang District; tel. 31441, 33001.*

Jiangnanqun 江南春饭店 and **Jiangbin Restaurants** 江滨饭 ⑤ for Chinese food, and the **Huamei** for Western. Muslim food is at the **Beilaishun Restaurant**

HOTELS

The top hotel the International or Swan, the former better located for tourists. No. 2 is the Hepingcun Guesthouse. Some business people prefer the Friendship. None are luxury quality.

International Hotel 国际饭店 • *124 Dazhi St. Cable 3001. Telex 87081 GUOLU CN. Dist.A.P.40 km. Dist.R.W.½ km. Walking distance of Friendship Store, antique store, Protestant church on Dazhi St., and museum* • C.C. 1937-built section has bigger rooms. 1980-built section 9 stories. IDD of sorts. 5th-floor lounge should be club for foreigners.

Peace Village (Heping Cun) Hotel 和平邨饭店 • *107 Zhong Shan Rd. Telex 87079 HBHPC CN. Near trade center, arts and crafts factory. Dist.A.P.37 km. Dist. R.W.4 km* • No C.C. 1986. 9 stories, 230 rooms. IDD.

Swan Hotel 天鹅饭店 • *73 Zhongshan Rd. Telex 87080 TIANE CN. Cable 8170. Quiet location. Dist.A.P.35 km. Dist.R.W.5 km* • T.R., C.C. 1983. 15 stories, 258 rooms. 24-hour bar. Soft beds. Near C.I.T.S.

C.I.T.S.: 73 Zhongshan Rd. Cable 1954. Tel. 221088. Telex 87034 HCITS CN. Fax 222579.
CAAC: 85 Zhongshan Rd.; tel. 52334.
C.T.S.: 52 Hongjun St., Nangangju. Tel. 34679, 31476 X330.
Heilongjiang Provincial Tourism Bureau: 124 Dazhi Rd., Nangang Dist. Tel. 35223, 31441. Telex 87081 GUOLU CN. Cable 3001.

HEFEI (HOFEI) 合肥

East China. Capital of Anhui (Anhwei), a province that is about two-thirds north of the Changjiang (Yangtze) River and is separated from the East China Sea by Jiangsu and Zhejiang provinces. Anhui is famous for its dramatic mountains that have inspired poets, mystics, and painters for centuries. In the province live Han, Hui, She, and other nationalities. Flights to Hefei leave from Beijing, Wuhan, Shanghai, and Hong Kong. Train service from Beijing (14½ hours); Nanjing (6 hours); Wuxi, Suzhou, and Shanghai (11 hours). Hefei has a population of 820,000. Its coldest weather in January is a mean temperature of 2.3°C. Its hottest in July and August is a mean temperature of 28.5°C. Because of its strategic location, numerous battles were fought here in the ancient past. Its tourist attractions can be squeezed into one day.

In **Xiaoyaojin** 逍遥津 , near the center of the city, during the Three Kingdoms period 1700 years ago, General Zhang Liao of the State of Wei fought against General Sun Quan (Sun Chuan) of the State of Wu. The site is now a park with three islets, on one of which is the tomb of General Zhang. Near the park is a zoo. Two km south of Xiaoyaojin, the **Lecturing Rostrum/Archery Training Terrace** is where Emperor Caocao trained Wei troops in using crossbows. These sites are marked with pavilions in traditional architecture. The **Mingjiao Temple** is on the terrace. This monastery was founded in the Tang. Destroyed in the 19th century during the Taiping War, its buildings were rebuilt by General Yuan Hongmo of the Taiping Heavenly Kingdom.

The **Temple to Lord Baozheng** 包公祠 , situated in a park in the center of the city, was built in honor of Baozheng, an honest and outstanding official of the Northern Song. He was a magistrate, prefectural head and vice minister of Rites. The **Provincial Museum** has a pleasant dinosaur garden. You might be able to squeeze in the China University of Science and Technology, and local opera too.

SHOPPING

Grown in the province are pears, pomegranates, grapes, kiwi fruit, and herbal medicines. Made are candied dates, tea, bamboo mats, and iron pictures. It is also noted for its four scholarly treasures: Xuan writing brush, Hui ink stick, She ink slab and Xuan paper. Try the Hefei Department Store, Anhui Provincial Arts and Crafts Store, and Gongnongbing Textile Shop. The Chenghuangmiao shopping center was built in the Ming style and surrounds the 900-year-old Town God's Temple. It has department stores, a tea house, and a wine shop.

RESTAURANTS

Anhui specialties are freshwater crabs from Lake Chao nearby and locally produced Gujing Gongjiu wine, once sent as tribute to the Ming emperors. Try cured Mandarin fish 腌鲜桂鱼 , stewed turtle 清炖马蹄鳖 , Fulizi braised chicken 符离集烧鸡 , Xiangzhenshan bamboo shoots and sesame cakes 向政山笋和芝麻糕 . Dishes are somewhat salty and slightly spicy hot, with thick soups.

HOTELS: RESERVATIONS NECESSARY ALL YEAR ROUND

C.I.T.S. considers the Daoxianglou Guest House tops, but don't expect too much. Next is the Jianghuai Hotel and then both the Anhui and Friendship hotels.

Jianghuai Hotel 江淮饭店 • *68 Changjiang Rd.; 13 km from airport* • 1982. 806 beds.

Luyang Hotel 庐阳饭店 • *Yan'an Lu Kou, Jinzhai Rd. Dist.A.P.12 km, Dist.R.W.5 km. 2 km from city center. Telex 90032 LYH CN* • Six stories; 1958, 1985. Should now have extension, tennis, swimming pool. Will answer telex. Accepts American Express cards.

Daoxianglou Hotel 稻香楼宾馆 • *Jinzhai Rd. 400 Yan'an Lu Kou.* • 400 beds.

International Hotel • *Meishan Lu Kou* • H.K.J.V. Before 1990.

C.I.T.S., 43 Tunxi Rd., tel. 61890, X209, telex 90024 AHPBD CN. **CAAC,** Shengli Rd., tel. 37398, 75022.

Overseas Marketing Dept. and C.I.T.S. Reception Dept. of the Anhui Provincial Tourism Corporation (both at 68 Changjiang Rd., Hefei; tel. 76227 X144; telex: 90024 AHPBD CN). These can also arrange study tours around the country. Contact them if you want to go crab- and game-tasting, or look for rare birds and Chinese alligators. The travel agencies can let you also know about Buddhist events on Jiuhua-shan.

OUTSIDE OF HEFEI IN ANHUI

Huangshan (Mount Huangshan) 黄山 is reached from Hefei by bus. The journey takes about 10 hours. See separate listing.

Jiuhuashan (Mt. Jiuhua) 九华山 , one of the Four Buddhist Mountains (alt. 1341 meters), is a day's trip by road. It has 50 Ming and Qing temples, 6000 buddhas, which were untouched by the Red Guards, and 99 peaks. Motor vehicles can drive up to 600 meters. Important are the Roushen Hall and Qiyuan Temple. In the **Baisui Gong (Buddhist Mummy Hall)** is preserved the 400-year-old cadaver of a monk. The Dongyan Hotel has 150 beds. Coldest mean temperature in January is $^-3°C$. Hottest mean temperature is 18°C in July. C.I.T.S. branch.

Wuhu 芜湖 in the southeastern part of the province, is where the Qing-yi River joins the Yangtze. It is slightly warmer than Hefei. On the railway lines from Nanjing and Hefei, it is the main foreign trading river port for the province and the fourth largest port on the Yangtze. It also produces those lovely pictures made of forged iron, usually painted black. It has a silk factory, Alligator Breeding Center, and the Dragon Spring Cave. Yangtze River boat tours. Hotels are the 260-bed Tieshan 铁山宾馆 and the 32-bed Wuhu. C.T.S. at 74 Jinghu Rd., tel. 2674.

Anqing 安庆 , in the SE part of Anhui, on the Yangtze, has the seven-story Zhenfeng Pagoda. Former capital of the province, it has since 1953 been home of the modern Huangmei Opera, the fifth most popular opera form in China. Southwest of here, also on the Yangtze, is a cap-shaped rock, **Xiaogushan (Solitary Hill),** with pavilions on top. C.T.S. at 22 Yicheng Rd., tel. 2215, 2073.

Ma'anshan (Horse Saddle Mountain) 马鞍山 , south of the Yangtze near the eastern provincial border, has impressive stone outcrops into the Yangtze. This large industrial town is on the railway line between Nanjing and Wuhu. Yangtze River Boat tours. The **Taibai Pavilion** was built at Caishiji (Rock of Various Colors) and has relics related to Li Bai, the world-famous Tang poet whose grave is between Ma'anshan and Wuhu near Qingsha. C.T.S. at 22 Hubei Rd., tel. 2944.

The 160–bed **Yushanhu Hotel** 雨山湖饭店 accepts C.C. and has a business center. It rents bicycles, and expects IDD in 1990. Dist.A.P.50 km. Dist.R.W.3 km. C.I.T.S. branch.

In **Fengyang County,** on the railway line between Beijing and Shanghai, is the ancestral home of the first Ming emperor, who proclaimed it a royal city. It contains among its tombs that of Tang He, who was one of the Ming dynasty founders. The *"ruins of the Imperial

City of the Middle Capital and stone inscriptions at the Imperial Mausoleum'' here are now under State Council protection. It also has the Temple of King Yu. One of the first attempts at the ''Responsibility System'' was started here in 1978. Accommodations at the 118-bed **Nanshan Hotel 南山宾馆** . C.T.S. at 128 Zhongshan St., tel. 4150.

　　Tunxi 屯溪 , in the very SE corner of Anhui, has a kiwi fruit cannery, tea processing workshop, ink slab factory, bamboo weaving factory, and Ming and Qing buildings. The kiwi fruit has also been known as the Chinese gooseberry, so you can ask if China or New Zealand had it first. This is a gateway to Huangshan and has an airport. The **Huashan Hotel 华山饭店** here has 100 beds. C.T.S. at 87 Yanan Dong Rd., tel. 2771.

HENGSHAN (MT. HENGSHAN)

There are several of these Hengshans, not all the names written the same in Chinese. Of the two most worthwhile to see is **Hengshan 山西恒山** in Shanxi province, 2 hours' drive on a country road SE of Datong. Along the way are remains of ancient beacon towers (see "Great Wall") and mud cave houses similar to those around Yan'an. Note the windows covered with folk art or paper cuts.

The main attraction here is the very breath-taking ***Temple-in-Mid-Air,** a.k.a. Suspending Temple **悬空寺** . A marvel of cliffside architecture, the temple literally clings to an almost vertical mountainside, some of its 40 small pavilions supported by wooden poles and beams, some by manmade rock foundations, some by natural stone. A trip here is not for people afraid of heights nor for people over 180 lbs., as the walks are narrow and involve many steep stairs.

This temple was first built over 1400 years ago (Northern Wei) and rebuilt in the Tang, Jin, Ming, and Qing dynasties. Its clay statues are not well done so are probably not originals. The bronze and iron castings and stone and wood carvings are older.

Hengshan #2 湖南衡山 is in Hunan province, about 310 km south of Changsha, South China. It is one of the Five Great Mountains of China, with 72 peaks and innumerable Buddhist temples. The most noteworthy of the temples is at Nanyue, occupying 98,000 square meters. First erected in 725 (Tang), it has Song and Ming architecture. A hotel and botanical garden are also on the mountain.

HOHHOT (HUHEHOT) 呼和浩特

North China. The capital of Inner Mongolia (a.k.a. Nei Monggol) Autonomous Region can be reached by train or a 45-minute plane ride from Beijing. It is NW of Beijing in the south central part of the province. But it is *only* for the strong, adventurous traveler who likes to rough it and doesn't mind a mutton diet. The best time to visit is June through Aug. The highest temperature in Hohhot then is 28°C, but the nights are cool. The winters are very cold, with a ⁻32°C low, and you need longjohns even in early May. The spring has sandstorms; the annual precipitation is between a scant 50 and 450 mm, mostly late summer and early autumn. The altitude is 1000 meters above sea level and it has from 90 to 160 frostfree days. The urban population is 500,000.

Inner Mongolia is of historical and religious importance. The Mongols, one of the nationalities living here, united under Genghis Khan in 1206, and their descendents went on to conquer the rest of China and then parts of Europe in the 13th and 14th centuries.

The traditional religion, as reflected now in its monasteries and temples, is a distinctive branch of Buddhism known as Lamaism, and is related to that of Tibet.

Hohhot dates from the Ming, at least 400 years ago. It was called Guisui under the Nationalists. After Liberation it was renamed Hohhot (Green City), the name preferred by the natives. In the past, Nei Mongol has been a home for nomads. Today its population includes Han, Daur, Ewenki, Oroqen, Hui, Manchu, Korean, and, of course, Mongolian nationalities.

In summer, visitors can travel out from here, if they wish, and sleep in a yurt in the grasslands. You can ride camels and camel carts, try Mongolian bows and arrows, and also drink tea laced with milk, butter, and grain, said to be very filling and great for cold winter days. It is too greasy for hot weather. Camel riding is uncomfortable, but at least you can have your picture taken on a two-humped shaggy Bactrian if it's not summer, the season when they shed and look awful. Visitors can go to one of three rural communities located 90–180 km away, usually by jeep on roads cut through the flat grasslands.

A yurt.

Real yurts are made of compressed sheep's wool with no windows. They are shaped somewhat like igloos, and can be folded up and carried by camel. Eight people can put up a large one in 40 minutes. Visitors staying in yurts sleep on padded mattresses described by one tourist as ''hard but comfortable.'' Everything smells of sheep. (Put a bag between you and the wall if the smell keeps you awake.) In some yurt hotels, there is running water and flush toilets (when the pump is working). The people are charming and wear their traditional costumes. The hospitable Mongols will even sing for you in your yurt.

The art in Lamaist monasteries is full of gory scenes of hell and torture. Reincarnation is central, but much superstition has crept into the theology. Monks are frequently lamas, reincarnations of previous monks. Hohhot used to have many temples but they were destroyed during the Cultural Revolution. Among the survivors is the oldest **Dazhao Temple** 大召庙 (Ming) with a rare silver Buddha and many musical instruments, the **Xiaozhao Temple** 小召 and the Wutasi Temple. The **Wutasi (Five Dagoba Temple)** 五塔寺 was founded in the Ming. The tallest of its dagobas is 6.26 meters and they are made of glazed bricks carved with Buddhist symbols and inscribed in three languages: Mongolian, Sanskrit, and Tibetan. Behind the pagodas is a Mongolian astrological chart. The **White Pagoda** 白塔 on the eastern outskirts of the city at the Xilitu Lamasery is from the 10th century and is 40 meters and seven stories high. Inside are native tapestries. Ask also about the **Wudang Lamasery.** For more on Lamaism, see ''Lhasa.''

The **Tomb of Wang Zhaojun** 王昭君坟 is 10 km south of the

city. About 2000 years old, she was an imperial Han concubine, married off to a Xiongnu tribal chief to form an important political alliance. A bit of climbing. The **Great Mosque** 清真大寺 is in Chinese architecture. Hohhot also has the **Provincial Museum** 内蒙古博物馆 , with a good display on Mongolian lifestyle.

ENTERTAINMENT
Folk songs and dances are distinct. Show-jumping, saber fighting, horseback acrobatics, and horse racing. And ask about the Nadam festival during the summer.

SHOPPING
Today, in addition to less exotic goods, Nei Mongol produces woolen textiles, carpets, and tapestries. It also manufactures Mongolian-style riding boots, sabers, saddles, stirrups, and felt stockings. Long-haired goatskin rugs and typical Mongolian silk jackets fancy enough to wear to dinner parties are relatively cheap. Also available are antique bottles of jade or agate. Try the **Hohhot National Commodity Factory,** the **Hohhot Antique Shop,** and the **Hohhot Carpet Factory.**

FOOD
Meat, mainly mutton, but also beef. Notable are barbecued lamb, mutton hot pot, sesame pancakes, braised oxtail, beef kabab, ox tendon in egg white, camel hoof, and *facai* (the edible black hairlike algae that is a favorite in China, especially at New Year's because its name sounds like ''prosperity.'') Delicacies also include braised bear's paw, braised elk's nose, and crisp fried hazel grouse.

HOTELS
Inner Mongolia Hotel 内蒙古旅游馆店 ● *Wulanchabuxi Rd., 15 km from airport* ● 1985. Dance hall, electronic games, stores. Recent guests have found no air-conditioning nor Western food. This is the main hotel. 500 beds; 20 stories; 11 restaurants. Second best hotel.

Xincheng (New City) Hotel 新城宾馆 ● *23 Hulun South Rd., 15 km from airport* ● Western and Chinese food. This is the third best hotel.

Zhuo Jun Hotel. Central. Best hotel. Hong Kong J. V. 500 beds.

C.I.T.S./C.T.S., Inner Mongolia Hotel; tel. 24494, 26241 X8932. Cable 2464. Telex 85016 HTONM CN.
CAAC, Xilin Bei Rd., Minhang Rd.; tel. 24103.
Also in this large province are Xilinhot and Baotou, under separate listings.

HUANGSHAN MOUNTAIN 黄山

East China in southern Anhui province. Huangshan is 120 km in circumference, and is one of China's most spectacular mountains. A climb has been described by one writer as "walking into an unending Chinese landscape painting." Huangshan can be reached by bus from Hefei. The airport at Tunxi, 75 km away, is served from Shanghai, Hefei, or Hangzhou. Tours have been organized by C.T.S. Hangzhou. Visitors can also travel by ship from Shanghai and Nanjing, to Chizhou or Wuhu, and then bus to Huangshan. The coldest time of year is January, with a mean daily temperature of ⁻3.2°C. The warmest is in July, with a mean daily temperature of 17.7°C. Annual precipitation is 2395 mm, mainly from June to September.

The highest of the 72 peaks, **Lian Hua (Lotus Flower)** 莲花峰 rises 1873 meters above sea level. To reach the valley before the final ascent to the top means climbing 800 stone steps cut into an 80° cliff, nose almost to rock.

One section of the second highest, **Tian Du (Heavenly Capital Peak)** 天都峰 (1864 meters), is a ridge less than a meter wide called "Carp's Backbone." Although iron chain railings exist to assure the unsure, some people resort to crawling to get across. This is just to say that Huangshan is for the very strong and adventurous, who will be rewarded by giant vertical peaks, pines (at least one over 1000 years old), hot springs (42°C), lots of streams, mist, magnificent views, and a great feeling of achievement—if you make it.

But there's hope. A **cable car** 缆车 , China's longest, is now operating to the North Sea Hotel from the Cloud Valley Monastery. C.I.T.S. advises no leather or plastic soles, or slippers. The climb is not easy. Take a walking stick, water bottle, and some food, and do not climb alone, here or anywhere else in the world.

If you only have one day, you have a choice. C.I.T.S. suggests taking a bus at 7:30 a.m. to Cloud Valley Monastery and then beginning to climb. Check about the bus the night before. At about 11 a.m. and 3000 stone steps higher, you will arrive at the **Beihai (North Sea) Ho-**

tel. This place is noted for its strangely shaped pines and weathered rocks. The Refreshing Terrace should give you a view of a sea of clouds. Now you have to return the way you came, but if you stay here overnight, this is the best place to see the sunrise. If you do not stay overnight, you can retrace your climb (about 3 hours) and take the bus back to the hotel at the base.

A second descent is via the **Jade Screen Tower 玉屏楼** and the Heavenly Capital Peak. Hostels in each of these places serve Chinese and some Western food.

As with most mountains in China, paths are crowded with hikers during the summer at Huangshan. The end of April is said to be the most beautiful time, and hiking is good to the end of October.

A Ming village with over 100 temples, ancestral halls, pagodas, bridges, pavilions, and other relics collected from that period is planned for the foot of Purple Cloud Peak.

SHOPPING

Paintings of Huangshan, Huangshan tea, bamboo and straw curtains. It is traditional to buy a special stone and find someone to carve your name on it.

HOTELS

Most hotels here are basic; with dirty blankets, dorms, poor service, and no private baths.

Xia Hai Hotel is a Hong Kong J.V.

Yupinglou (Jade Screen) Hotel 玉屏楼 ● Jade Screen Resort, halfway up mountain. 1955; renovated 1984. 24 beds.

Beihai (North Sea) Hotel 北海宾馆 ● North Sea Resort. 1700-meter altitude. 1958; renovated 1984. 112 beds.

Taoyuan (Peach Spring) Hotel 桃源宾馆 ● Hot Spring Scenic Resort. 1979; renovated 1985. 134 beds. Swimming pool, coffee shop, Friendship Store, theater, dance hall, Chinese and Western food. Huangshan specialties available here are stewed chicken with stone mushrooms, shrimps and Maojen tea, and fried stone frog.

OTHER IMPORTANT ADDRESSES

C.I.T.S. 中国国际旅行社 and **C.T.S. 中国民航公司** near Hot Spring, to the left of Peach Spring Hotel in Wenquan; tel. 2206, 2371. Telex 90908 AMTYN CN. Cable 0022. These can arrange a hiking tour with English or Japanese-speaking guide-interpreters.

Arts and Crafts Shop 工艺美术商店 : tel. 2244.
Bus Station 汽车站 : tel. 2210.
Friendship Store 友谊商店 : tel. 2200.
Huangshan Painting Shop 黄山画社 : tel. 2334.

JIANGMEN 江门

(Kiangmen; Cantonese Kongmoon) South China in Guangdong province on the Pearl River Delta, about 100 km south of Guangzhou. This old waterfront city can be reached by public or tourist bus from Guangzhou, but it can also be reached easily by daily nonstop 4-hour ferry from Hong Kong, and Macao. Also ship connections with Guangzhou.

This former foreign treaty port is also a cheap overnight passenger boat ride from Guangzhou, an interesting experience, to say the least. Several ferries leave daily from about 1 km east of the Overseas Chinese Mansion in Guangzhou. The night boat leaves before sunset, so you have a chance to see the never-ending river traffic, the maze of tributaries and canals, many lined with breakwaters, irrigation gates, and factories. If you're lucky, you'll have a full moon—and it's beautiful! You are in another world.

You sleep (if you can—it's somewhat noisy) 12 abreast on wooden platforms, softened only by straw mats and separated from fellow passengers by four-inch-high dividers. Upper and lower platforms line three sides of the room. You could have over 60 to 100 roommates, some of them curious, some friendly, but all discreet. A lot of women travel this way and I've never felt threatened. No privacy exists, not even for bathing, which is from a very public sink (with brown river water). The toilets, however, are in tiny, private cubicles, a hole in the floor through which you can see river water rushing by (and also your pants, if you don't hang on tight!) You can rent pillows and sheets and buy proletarian food. Boiled hot drinking water is available, but you should have had the foresight to carry your own mug and towel, like all the other passengers.

At dawn, or sometimes before, you find the boat entering a canal.

Recent travelers have found a very boisterous group of taxi drivers bidding for their fare at the boat dock. Some travelers have succumbed to several hundreds of yuan worth of transportation but the city bus station is only 5 km away from the pier. From there, mini-buses can take you where you want to go for much less. A public bus can take you to Xinhui in about 20 minutes.

Jiangmen has East Lake Park (with rides), and a small Ming dynasty temple (Chen Bai Sha Temple, in honor of a famous philosopher). It has prospered in the last few years and now has many hotels, one of which has a revolving rooftop restaurant. Two fifths of the people here are Overseas Chinese or have Overseas Chinese relatives and therefore receive remittances from abroad.

Jiangmen City is made up of five counties: Xinhui, Heshan, Kaiping, Enping, and Taishan.

HOTELS

The best hotel is the Dong Hu (East Lake) Hotel in the suburbs. The best hotel in town is the Capital.

Capital Hotel • *2 Xin Li Rd. Cable 0318. Central, near port.*

Dong Hu (East Lake) Hotel • *15 Jiang Kou Rd. Dist. bus station 2 km. Dist. port 5 km. Adjacent to East Lake Park. Business center. Pool. Near shopping and cinema.* • IDD to Hong Kong. Beautiful garden-style architecture. Major credit cards accepted. 1976; renovated 1985. Extension 1986–87. 182 rooms and 13 suites. Pool, disco, sauna. "No-smoking" areas!

C.I.T.S. • *13 Nonglin Rd.; tel. (07682) 56562 or 53384.*
C.T.S. • *15 Gangkou Rd.; tel. 33611. Cable 3307.*

JILIN (KIRIN) 吉林

Northeast China, in the center of Jilin province, 130 km east of the capital Changchun. Population nearly one million. It can be reached by rail from Beijing, Changchun, Shenyang, Harbin, Tianjin, etc. A military airport is 36 km away. Like the rest of the area formerly known as Manchuria, this also is extremely cold, with snow in winter and average minimum temperature December–February of ⁻24°C–⁻15°C.

By Chinese standards, Jilin is young, only about 300 years old. The Japanese took over in 1931, but were forced to leave in 1945. Tourist attractions include the **Deer Farm at Longtan Hill,** which produces antlers (for aphrodisiacs), ginseng, and sable. Also of interest are the ginseng gardens, the **Jilin Exhibition Hall** 吉林展览馆 (with a 1770-kg meteorite, believed to be the largest in the world), and **Jiangnan Park. Songhua Lake** 松花湖 is a 480-square-km manmade lake, and is 20 km from the city center. The Songhua River runs through the city and beautiful hoarfrost forms on the trees lining its banks in winter.

Jilin has alpine skiing but facilities are not good (for example, electricity to run the lifts is not reliable). A 1800-meter-long ski chair lift services its 3.5-square-km "professional" ski area, with runs 3000 meters long. Skis can be rented. It is 16 km from the city at Fengman. Best skiing is December–February.

380 km SE of the city are the **Changbai Mountains,** their highest peak 2691 meters. A 800-meter ski slope is operating here now, but there are no lifts. In this crater is beautiful **Heaven Lake,** and on the other side is Korea. Visitors can also see **Arladi Village,** 70 km from Jilin, where Korean customs are still practiced. In Harbin, look for azalea root carvings, ginseng, and domestic cat fur coats for sale.

FOOD
Local specialties include venison, frog oil soup, steamed whitefish, raw salmon and carp, and chicken and ginseng in earthenware pots.

HOTELS

The major hotels are along the Songhua River, but only the Milky Way comes close to satisfying the fussy. The Xi Guan is interesting because it has a villa once used by the warlord Zhang Zou Xiang. Big rooms and musty smells. Staying there should give you a feel for 1920s history.

Milky Way Hotel • *126 Songjiang Rd. Cable 2214. Telex 84010 BYOOL CN. Dist.R.W.3 km* • T.R., C.C. (not Diner's). Hong Kong J.V. 1988. 15 stories, 200 rooms. Medium-sized rooms, clinic. Should have IDD in 1990.

Xi Guan Hotel • *155 Chuan Ying St. Dist.R.W.7 km* • No C.C. State guest house with several villas on 19 hectares. Huge rooms, 3.3-meter-high ceilings. White villa built 1953, expanding 1989.

C.I.T.S. • *4 Jiangwan Rd.; tel. 57721 X472.*

JINAN (TSINAN) 济南

North China. The capital of Shandong is due south of Beijing, 15 km. from the south shore of the Huanghe (Yellow River), at the junction of the Beijing-Shanghai railway and the Qingdao-Jinan Railway. Jinan can also be reached by plane from Beijing (1¼ hours), Nanjing (1¾ hours), Hefei (1½ hours), and Shanghai. It is on the main Beijing-Guangzhou train line. The climate is temperate. Hottest in late July to early August, is 36°C; coldest in January, ⁻15°C. Annual precipitation is about 700 mm, mainly in July and August. Population is 1.2 million urban.

Jinan dates as a city with a wall from the sixth century B.C., when it was made capital of the State of Qi. However, it was settled here more than 5000 years ago by neolithic cultures, the Dawenkou and the Longshan. It was named Jinan, meaning "south of the Ji River," a name that has been kept even though that river dried up centuries ago.

Jinan was a busy commercial center during the Tang, and Marco Polo wrote favorably of its garden atmosphere and its thriving silk industry after he visited it during the Yuan. It has been the capital since the Ming. It is now an industrial center producing trucks, textiles, and paper, and as a tourist destination, famous primarily for its springs, its Buddhist temples, and its proximity to Taishan Mountain and Qufu.

The excellent quality of the water in this "City of Springs" was first recorded 2500 years ago by a geographer. The Chinese kept records of pretty well everything! During the Jin (1115–1234), someone else listed 72 springs on a tablet. He missed a few. A 1964 survey mentions 108 natural springs.

The "springs" are not just holes in the ground spouting water. They are fountains, wells, and pools, and have been embellished with gardens, rockery, pavilions, and tea houses. The water was forced to the earth's surface here by a subterranean wall of volcanic rock. But unless you have a water fixation, a trip to one or two groupings will suffice. The performance of the water is seasonal because of the lowering water table. The best time seems to be after the rains in August and through the autumn.

The **Baotu Quan (Jet Spring)** 豹突泉 (tel. 23716), in the SW corner of the Old City, is said to be the best, with 16 fountains and the greatest amount of water, and is open from 8 a.m. to 5 p.m. It is in the center of a square pond, three separate sprays of bubbling water gushing almost a foot high.

The **Heihu Quan (Black Tiger Spring Park)** 金线泉 (tel. 20366) is another of the "four most famous springs" of Jinan. It is in the SE corner of the Old City, a 10-minute walk from the east side of Jet Spring. By now you should have learned that "quan" means "spring." In this park the water gushes from the mouths of three stone tigers. Does it sound like the roar of tigers? Nearby is the 11-meters-high Liberation Monument, where the old wall once stood and where the People's Liberation Army forced its way into the city in 1948. The monument can be climbed.

The third famous spring is the **Zhenzhu Quan (Pearl Spring)** 珍珠泉 , tel. 21970. In the courtyard of the Pearl Spring Auditorium. The **Five-Dragon Pool**   completes the list of "four famous springs." It is outside the West Gate.

At this point, especially if you are short of time, head for the outskirts. Take in the **Qianfo (Thousand-Buddha) Hill** 千佛山 (tel. 611792), 2½ km south of the city. The name is misleading since there are fewer than that. Here you find Buddhist images carved into the side of a cliff. Much climbing is involved to see the **Xingguo Si (Revive the Nation Temple)** 兴国寺 , with 60–70 buddhas from 20 centimeters to over three meters tall, ranging from the Sui to the Tang. Look for three caves at the foot of the cliff and in the rooms of the west courtyard of the temple. There you find, yes, more buddhas and historical relics!

In the **Yilan Ting (Pavilion of Panoramic View)** 一览亭 , the tallest building around, you can get a good view of Jinan. An even better view can be had from the top of the hill, especially of Mount Jueshan to the east. On **Jueshan** you can see the 10-meters-high cave inside of which is a buddha head, seven meters tall.

West of Xingguo Temple about 3 km, is the **Yellowstone Cliff** 黄茅岗 a 40-meter-high rock around which were carved more Buddhas, and heavens!—flying devas—some of them nude! These were made during the Northern Wei, about 1600 years ago.

A stimulating time to visit this temple is on the ninth day of the ninth lunar month, when the hill is full of chrysanthemums and market stalls are set up. While some people may find it crowded (beware of pickpockets!), you can experience the excitement of a festival.

If you have a half day left and your own vehicle, you can head to either **Liubu** 柳埠 , 34 km south, or the **Lingyan Temple** 灵岩寺 , which is closer. Both are important. Liubu has even more (210) and better Buddhist statues in five grottoes, most from the Tang, but some from the Song, Yuan, and Ming. In the **Qianfo (Thousand-Buddha) Cliff,** these range from 2.85 meters down to 20 centimeters high. Look for the Buddha called Blessing, ordered for Tang Emperor Taizong by one of his daughters, in much the same spirit as one donates a statue of the Virgin in a Catholic church on someone else's behalf.

The center of Buddhism for the province was at the **Shentong Si (Temple of Magical Power)** at the site of the current Tongtian Yu (Valley that Leads to Heaven). The **Long-hu (Dragon-Tiger) Tower** (Tang) has carvings of dragons, warriors, tigers, and devas. Are these devas (or good spirits) clothed? Look for yourself! The miniature pagodas are tombstones of abbots from the now extinct Temple of Magical Powers. Look for the one-story, 15-meter-high square **Simen* (Four-Door Tower)** 四门塔 . At 1400 years of age, this is the oldest single-story tower of stone in the country. Note the thickness of the walls. A thousand-year-old pine protects its NE corner.

Only 3 km south is the **Jiuding (Temple of the Nine Pagodas)**
Here is the very unusually designed octagonal Nine-Spire Pagoda, probably dating from the Sui. Inside are murals from the Ming and Qing. Can you see the remnants of even older murals these have covered?

The remnants of a 12.6-by-10.7-meter platform, believed to be from the Tang, should be of interest to music and dance lovers, as it is carved with dancers and singers holding musical instruments.

The ***Lingyan Si (Magic Cliff or Intelligent Rock) Temple** in Changqing county is one of the ''four finest temples'' in China. The temple was founded by a famous monk in A.D. 354 who was much moved by the beauty of the surroundings and whose sermons caused birds to listen, animals to stop, and even a rock nearby to nod in agreement. Hence the name. The current temple is from the Tang. The temple expanded in the Song when over 1000 monks studied and worshiped here. Surviving the centuries are the rock grotto from the Northern Wei, the Tang halls and pavilions, the Song clay images, and various rock carvings. Important to see is its **Thousand Buddha Hall,** built in the Tang, and repaired in the Song, Yuan, and Ming. Here are three large statues of Buddha, one of wood and two of bronze. The 40 painted clay arhats are very lively and about 102 centimeters tall. Northwest of this hall is the nine-story, 52.4-meter-high **Pizhi Pagoda** from the Tang, restored in the Song. The iron spire on the top is unusual, with its eight or nine Buddhist wheels chained together.

To the west is another cemetery with tiny dagobas marking the graves of monks, no two dagobas the same. This is the second best graveyard of this nature in the country. (See Shaolin Temple in ''Zhengzhou''). Guess which dagoba belongs to the Tang dynasty temple's founder, Huichong? The most impressive one, of course! This 5.3-meter pagoda is similar to the square Four-Door Tower in Liu Bu; and decorated with dancers, devas (with or without?) and lion heads.

If you have more time in the city, see the **Daming Pool** 大明湖 (pronounced Dah Ming not Damming; tel. 22808, 23800). Here you find 80 hectares of park, of which a little more than half is lake.

The **Shandong Provincial Museum** 山东省博物馆 (Wenhua Xi Rd.; tel. 20486) contains both historical and natural history relics. The history dates from neolithic times and includes Sun Bin's famous treatise on the art of war, written on bamboo about 2000 years ago. Also note the frescoes from Sui dynasty tombs, musical instruments, calligraphy, and paintings from the tomb of the Prince of Lu (Ming), rubbings from a Han tomb showing the aristocratic lifestyle, and musical instruments from the Confucian Family Mansion in Qufu.

You need a couple of days really to see **Taishan,** over 50 km away, and **Qufu,** the hometown of philosopher Confucius, 140 km south. Taishan is listed under ''Tai'an.'' Both are very worthwhile. **Yidu** is near Camel Mountain, with six Buddhist grottoes and a county museum. *****Linzi,** the former capital of Qi, is from the Zhou dynasty. Also convenient by train are Qingdao and Zibo. In the province also are Yantai, Weihai, and Weifang. See separate listings.

SHOPPING
Made in the province are human hair and silk embroidery and lace (Jinan Embroidery Factory); feather pictures (lovely) and dough modeling (yes, they do last!) both from the Jinan Fine Arts Factory. The province also produces Qingdao (Tsingtao) Beer, the most popular Chi-

nese beer. The main shopping area is Quancheng Rd. and also along Jin 2-Rd.

Arts and Crafts Shop (26 Baotu Quan Rd.; tel. 20821–4.); **Daguanyuan Market** (Jing 4-Rd. and Wei 2-Rd.; tel. 21766), this also includes a folk arts theater and a cinema; **Department Store** (Quancheng Rd.; tel. 2610275); **Foreign Languages Bookstore** (Chaoshan St.; tel. 612165); **Friendship Store** (3/F Department Store; tel. 614813); **Jinan Antique Store** (Jing 3-Rd. and Wei 2-Rd.; tel. 22761); **No. 1 Department Store** (Jing 2-Rd. and Wei 4-Rd.; tel. 35429); **Shandong Antique Store** (west of Department Store, Quancheng Rd.; tel. 21185).

RESTAURANTS

Exotic local fare are cattail, lotus roots and lotus seeds from Daming lake, roast duck, winding-thread cakes, and monkey head mushroom.

Huiquan Restaurant • *Quancheng Rd. and Baotuquan Bei Rd.; tel. 20396* • In the Huiquan Hotel. Especially good is the sweet and sour Yellow River carp.

Daming Lake Restaurant • *outside the south gate of the park; tel. 43532* • Its Bapi Guozi is good for breakfast.

HOTELS

The best hotel is the Qilu, then the Shungeng Mountain Villa, and third the Jinan Guest House. The latter is preferred by business people because of its central location.

Foreign Students' Residence, Shandong Teachers' University • *38 Culture Rd. East (No. 18 bus from rwy. station)* • Heat not regular. Some rooms air-conditioned. Budget travelers only.

Jinan Guest House • *Jinan Jing San Wei Rd. Dist.A.P.6 km. Dist.R.W.2 km* • 1920, ren. 1987. Four buildings of 2 and 4 stories, over 70 rooms. Budget travelers.

Qilu Hotel • *Qianfoshan Rd. Cable 3906. Telex 39142 QLHJN CN. Good view to the south of 1000 Buddha Hill in the suburbs. 5-minute walk to C.I.T.S. Dist.A.P.15 km. Dist.R.W.7 km* • C.C. (no Diner's). 1985–86, ren. 1988, 1990. 11 stories, 255 rooms. Tennis, business center. Good standards. Should now have IDD, pool, health center.

Shungeng Mountain Villa • *Shungeng Rd. Telex 39184 MTCTN CN. Near 1000 Buddha Hill, but not the Qilu. Dist.A.P.10 km. Dist.R.W.9 km* • More beautiful than Qilu. C.C. 1987–88. One and two stories, 150 rooms. Bowling, pool.

OTHER IMPORTANT ADDRESSES

C.I.T.S. and **C.T.S.:** 26 Jing Shi Rd.; tel 615858; telex 39144 SDTJN CN. Fax (053) 615870.
CAAC booking, 348 Jing 2 Rd.; tel. 33191; airport 554241.
China United Airlines booking, tel. 47525.
Long Distance: tel. 113.
Directory inquiries: tel. 114.
Foreign Affairs Section of the Jinan Municipal Bureau of Public Security: 54 Wei 5-Rd.; tel. 35778.
Shandong Tourism Bureau, 26 Jing Shi Rd., tel. 615858, 615859. Fax 44679. Cable 7139. Telex 39144 SDTJN CN.
Hospital: In case of illness, if convenient, try the clinic in your hotel. Otherwise, the **Hospital of the Shandong Medical College:** Wenhua Xi Rd. (tel. 21681); the **Shandong People's Hospital:** Jing 5-Rd. and Wei 7-Rd. (tel. 35521); **Qianfoshan Hospital,** Jing 10-Rd. (tel. 44731).

JINGDEZHEN (CHINGTECHEN) 景德镇

South China. Northeast Jiangxi province NE of Nanchang. A must for porcelain lovers. It was from here that some of the best was shipped to Europe centuries ago, including the famous blue-and-white. Today Jingdezhen is still producing some of the best porcelain in China, a combination of the right clay, abundant pine wood for fuel, and easy transport (on the Yangtze). The city was founded in the Han and is considered one of China's Three Ancient Cities.

Jingdezhen has been reached by small plane in 70 minutes from Nanchang daily except Sundays, or by road, usually leaving Nanchang after breakfast and arriving about 4 p.m. It can be reached via Jiujiang, or by rail from Nanchang or Nanjing.

Visitors are usually taken to their choice of different factories, each with its own specialty: the *site of the Hutian Porcelain Kiln, dating from the Five Dynasties (white glazed) to the Song (celadon) and Ming (blue-and-white).

Nanshi, on Pearl Hill, is the site of the Ming and Qing imperial kilns. The town itself is surrounded by mountains and the Yangtze. The town also has a Pottery and Porcelain Exhibition Hall, the Ceramic Institute, and the Pottery and Porcelain College.

The **Jingdezhen Hotel** is on the outskirts of the city, with 200 beds, a porcelain shop, and a dining room. It is the main hotel and is 4 km from the railway station and 8 km from the airport.

C.T.S.: 8 Lianhuatang St., tel. 2293.

JINGGANG SHAN (CHINGKANG MOUNTAINS) 井冈山

South China. Mao Zedong (Mao Tze-tung) led his forces after the Autumn Harvest Uprising in 1927 to this 275-square-km mountain range in Jiangxi province near the Hunan border. Here the Communists established a base, carrying out land reform among the peasants. Forced to flee by the scorched-earth campaign of the Nationalists, the Communists embarked on the now legendary Long March to Yan'an in October 1934.

Mao's former residence, the **Jinggang Shan Revolutionary Museum** 井冈山革命历史博物馆 , and other revolutionary sites are open to the public. These are mainly centered around the town of Ciping (Tseping) 茨坪 . The battles against the Nationalists, who were trying to rid the country of the Communists, took place mainly in the five major mountain passes. These are Bamianshan, Huangyangjie, Shuangmashi, Tongmuling, and Zhushachong. A visit to any of these will show you how difficult it was to destroy the base.

The mountains are now being promoted as a tourist resort rather than a revolutionary monument. They are very beautiful, with steep cliffs and deep valleys in the south. One of many caves, the **Feilong Dong (Flying Dragon) Cave** 飞龙洞 can hold several hundred people. Its height ranges from 1 to 60 meters. Also of note are the **Youji Dong (Guerrillas Cave)** 游击洞 and **Shuilian Dong (Water Curtain Cave)**

水帘洞 . Waterfalls are at Ciping, Liujiaping, Changping (130 meters high), and Longtan (Dragon Pool). The highest mountain is 1428 meters.

Larger in area than Lushan (also in Jiangxi province), Jinggang Shan has guesthouses, hotels, and reception houses, the latter for Chinese workers, operated by their work units. A modern paper mill and bamboo handicraft factory are located here.

In Ciping 茨坪 are also a cinema, restaurants, and library. At press time, it could be reached by a 2-day drive (about 300 km) from Nanchang in the north (overnight stop in Ji An) or by road from the south.

C.T.S.: tel. 504. Cable 0064.

JIUJIANG 九江

(Kiukiang, Chiuchiang, a.k.a. Xunyang) South China. Northern Jiangxi province on the south bank of the Yangtze River, where it bends south between Wuhan and Nanjing. It is bounded on the east by Poyang Lake and Mt. Lushan on the south. Accessible by train from Nanchang and Huangzhou, by plane from Beijing and Huiyang, or by passenger boat along the Yangtze, this 2000-year-old city has been used as a port for the porcelain city of Jingdezhen since ancient times. It was also a treaty port and currently is comprised of two urban districts, ten rural counties, and Mt. Lushan. The population is 200,000.

Of interest to visitors are the **Yanshui Pavilion 烟水亭** in the middle of Lake Gantang, an 1840-square-meter island covered with gardens, hall, and pavilions; and the **causeway between Lake Gantang and Lake Nanmen** 甘棠湖和南门湖之间的长堤 built in A.D. 821. Also important to see are the **Dasheng Pagoda 大胜塔** in Nengren Temple and the **Xunyanglou and Suojianglou Pagoda.** Important also is the **Donglin Temple,** the birthplace of the "Pure Earth" sect of Buddhism (founded 1,500 years ago), and the **Boyang Lake Migrant Birds Preserve,** said to be the largest in the world.

The **Nanhu Hotel** is on the side of South Lake, with villas and is the top hotel. The **Bailu Hotel** on Xunyang Ave. should open late 1989.

C.I.T.S., 28 Nan Hu Rd.; tel. 3390. Telex 95063 IPTXB CN (ATTN: C.I.T.S.) Cable 7139.
C.T.S., 77 Nanci Rd.; tel. 4015.

JIUQUAN 酒泉

Northwest China. Western part of Gansu province, on the southern edge of the Gobi desert, Jiuquan can be reached by plane from Dunhuang, and from Lanzhou in almost 2 hours. Trains also from Beijing, Shanghai, and Urumqi.

Jiuquan is best known because it is only 30 km from the western end of the Great Wall, but it has an identity of its own. About 1650 years ago, government officials and high-ranking military officers were sent here to develop the region and to protect commerce on the Silk Road.

Its imposing **Bell and Drum Tower 鼓楼** was originally built in A.D. 343 and was renovated in the Qing. The **Jiuquan County Museum 酒泉博物馆** is also in the city, with relics from the ancient tombs, including painted bricks. The ''wine spring,'' the Western Han relic after which the city is named, is in the east of the city in **Jiuquan Park 酒泉公园**. A legend relates how the famous Han General Ho Qubing (illegitimate son of the sister of the empress) once poured a victory gift of wine into this spring in order to share the wine with his soldiers.

The other city attraction is the **Luminous Jade Cup Factory 玉杯厂**, where eggshell thin goblets of ''jade'' are made. These four attractions are within walking distance of the Jiuquan Hotel (½ km to 1½ km).

Twenty-one km north, on the way to the Great Wall, are the **Wei-Jin Tombs 魏晋墓群** and tombs from the Sixteen States period. These are in an area 20 km north-south and 3 km wide. The Eastern Jin murals, predating those of Dunhuang, show people at work and reveal a great deal about life 1600 years ago.

Jiayuguan Pass 嘉峪关 is between the Qilian Mountains and the Mazong Mountains, at the western end of the *Great Wall. The wall here has been restored. The city, which was also on the Silk Road, was built in 1372 when the first Ming emperor had the wall repaired and strengthened to keep out the defeated Mongols.

The end of the Great Wall is marked by a magnificent castle and three-story east and west gates. The tower can be climbed.

The **Jiuquan Hotel** 酒泉宾馆 , the only one in Jiuquan, is located at the main traffic circle a 20-minute bicycle ride away from the Great Wall. It was first built in 1958 and renovated in 1982 (2 Changmen St.; 30 km from the airport).

The **C.I.T.S.** 中国国际旅行社 branch is in the hotel (tel. 2943). **C.T.S.** is at 2 Cangmen St. (tel. 2943, 2641. Telex 2646). **CAAC** 中国民航 is across the street (tel. 2136).

See also ''Great Wall'' and ''Silk Road.''

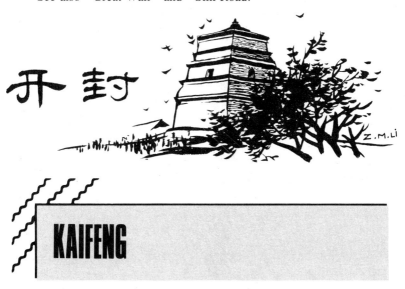

KAIFENG

Northwest China. Northern Henan on the Shanghai-Xi'an railway line, about 75 km east of the provincial capital Zhengzhou. Daily flight from Guangzhou. It is on the southern bank of the Huanghe (Yellow River).

With a history of 2600 years, Kaifeng was the capital of several dynasties, including the Wei, Liang, Later Jin, Han, Later Zhou, Northern Song, and Jin. During the Song it was an important commercial and communications center, producing textiles, metalwork, porcelain, and printing. It was sacked by Jurched tribesmen in 1126 and never recovered its previous glory.

With 120 recorded Yellow River floods due to dams breaking near Kaifeng between 1194 and 1948, one wonders why Kaifeng exists at all. In 1642, during a peasant uprising led by Li Tzu-cheng, the Yellow River dike was destroyed by Ming forces so that the city was completely inundated and 372,000 people were killed. In 1938, the Nationalists destroyed the dam upriver near Zhengzhou in an attempt to stop the Japanese and 840,000 people died. Today, the riverbed, raised by centuries of silt deposits, is about 10 meters higher than ground level near Kaifeng.

Since Liberation, the Chinese have given top priority to controlling the Yellow River, and since 1984 the Chinese government and the United Nations World Grain Planning Program have worked together on an irrigation and warping project here.

Kaifeng is one of the 24 cities of historical importance protected by the State Council. It is laid out in the classic Chinese plan, and has a well-preserved city wall.

The 13-story *Tie Ta ("Iron Pagoda") 铁塔 was built over 900 years ago (Song) leaning towards the wind but it is now standing straight. At a height of 54.6 meters, it is actually of glazed brick. The Xiangguo Temple 相国寺 , built in A.D. 555, was rebuilt in 1766 after the flood. It has a famous thousand-armed, thousand-eyed Buddha of gingko wood. The Longting (Dragon Pavilion) 龙亭 is at the site of the Northern Song palace. The existing buildings here are from the Qing, the stone lions in front from the Song. Also worth seeing are the Yanqing Taoist Temple 延庆观 and the Guild Hall of Three Provinces 山陕甘会馆 . The Yuwang Miao (King Yu's Temple) 禹王台 was built in the Ming in honor of Emperor Yu, who tried to control the floods. The bottom of the Pota Pagoda 繁塔 was built in 977, the top in the Qing, after the original was destroyed because of superstition.

Kaifeng is also famous for its embroidery, and its Jewish community, the remnants of which still remain today. A famous painting of the ancient city, "Qing Ming Festival at the Riverside," inspired the design of the Song Dynasty Village in Hong Kong. A Song dynasty city may be ready for your visit.

Because of its size and compactness, Kaifeng can be seen in a hurried 1-day visit, but better in two. Great for bicycling. It has a city museum. A charming Song dynasty street and a very unusual night food market should be of interest. Kaifeng's Acrobatic Troupe and its Circus with performing monkeys, bears.

Canadians in particular might be interested in the grave of Canadian Dr. Tillson Lever Harrison who died in Changqiu in 1947 after delivering three box cars of medical supplies under horrendous conditions through the Nationalists' areas to the Communists. It is in the Revolutionary Martyrs Cemetery with a stone almost 2 meters high. There is also a Tillson Lever Harrison Memorial School in the city, probably on the site of the old Anglican church where he was first buried.

Restaurants include the **Youyixin Restaurant** and the **Diyilou Steam Dumpling Restaurant. Shopping** is at **Xiangguo Temple Market's** 3000 stalls.

Dongjing Hotel • *14 Yingbin Rd. Dist.A.P.70km, Dist.R.W.2 km* • Three stories. Attractive traditional-style garden.

Kaifeng Guest House 开封宾馆 • *64 Ziyou St., through the South Gate. Dist.R.W.3 km, Dist.A.P.70 km* • Three stories, 119 rooms.

C.I.T.S. : 64 Ziyou Rd.; tel. 23737. Telex: 46110 KFFAO CN. Cable 2464.

KASHI (KASHGAR) 喀什（喀什噶尔）

Northwest China at the farwestern tip of Xinjiang province, about 100 km from the Soviet border. It can be reached by air (1500 km in 4 hours) from Urumqi for a 3-day excursion. It is also accessible by road, but not without a long, tiring, and sometimes spectacular journey from Pakistan.

Government officials here keep office hours by Beijing time, but some shops keep ''Kashgar time,'' and others keep ''Pakistan time''—which could mean a three-hour difference. Kashi is over 2000 years old and has been fought over by many contenders. In the mid-10th century, a Uygur-Turkish coalition, the Karahanids (Qurakhanid) Dynasty took over the area. Its leaders later converted to Islam and made Kashi their capital. Today it grows rice, wheat, fruit, and cotton. Like other cities of Xinjiang, it gives one a feeling more of west Asia than of China.

Kashi was on the Silk Road and is a center of Uygur culture. It is exotic, with many people wearing traditional national dress.

Visitors can see the huge **Abakh Hoja Tomb** 阿巴克和加麻扎尔 (Ming and Qing), the final resting place of 70 descendents of Muhatum Ajam, an Islamic missionary. The **Idkah Mosque** 艾提朵尔清

具寺 , with its blue onion dome, is over 400 years old, one of the most important of the many mosques in the city. The **San Xian (Three Immortals) Buddhist Caves** 三仙洞 are north of the city and difficult to reach. Three rectangular holes high in the side of a cliff beckon the fit and curious. Unless they have been recently repaired, the frescoes inside are not in good condition.

Visitors can also tour the bazaar and a handicrafts workshop and local orchard.

Thirty km east of Kashi is the town of **Hanoi** 罕诺依 , abandoned after the 11th century and now just a ruin. In the area, one can also cruise **South Lake** 南湖 , but it is only a respite from all the dryness. South of the city and east of the Sino-Pakistan Highway toward Afghanistan are 7719-meter-high **Mt. Kongur** 公格尔冰山 and 7546-meter-high **Mt. Muztagta** 穆士塔格山 , part of the Pamirs. If you keep in mind that Hunza in Pakistan and Kashmir in India are also to the south, you will get an idea of the magnificence and isolation of the area here. Think Himalayas! You can see these snow-covered peaks from Kashi. Mountaineers can climb them.

Kashi produces handicrafts: gold and silver ornaments, rugs, jade carving, embroidered caps, daggers, and musical instruments. Its Sunday Bazaar is famous for its horse trading, and you will probably also find a lot of imported goods there in addition to the arts and crafts. The Silk Road has become the Electronics Road.

C.I.T.S. says the top hotel is the **Kashgar,** and then the **Semar.**

C.I.T.S. at Qiriwak Hotel, Semar Rd. (tel. 3156, 3087). **C.T.S.** at Jiefang Bei Rd. (tel. 2217).

See also ''Silk Road.''

KUNMING (A.K.A. KUNNANFU)

Southwest China. The capital of Yunnan province, which borders Vietnam, can be reached by train from Chengdu and by nonstop plane 2 hours each from Guangzhou and Changsha, and from Hong Kong and Rangoon. It is beautifully situated on the 330-sq.-km Dianchi Lake, China's sixth largest. Because of its altitude of 1894 meters and its subtropical location, it is blessed with the best weather in China, spring all year round. The hottest temperature is 29°C in July and the coldest ⁻1°C in January. Most rain falls from May to October. One of the loveliest times to visit is February, when the camellias are in bloom. Population: about 2 million rural and 1 million urban.

Kunming is important to see because of its mountain scenery, the colorfulness of its national minorities, the artistry and history of its temples and architecture, and the Stone Forest. The weather is a big attraction.

In the province also are several unusual sights. These range from almost year-round snow-capped mountains to tropical jungles where elephants and monkeys roam. One third of its over 34 million people belong to national minorities. Many of the groups, especially the women, still wear their distinctive clothes, even while working in the fields. Many still practice old customs—like the Dai **Water-Splashing Festival.** Kunming ranks in my books as the third most desirable tourist destination in China, after Beijing and Xi'an. One could easily spend two weeks in the province.

Kunming itself has a history of 2400 years. The region has always been considered remote and resistent to the central government. The Xiaguan area was part of the Nanzhou empire, which refused to submit to the Tang but was subdued by the Mongols in the 13th century and visited by Marco Polo. The railway from Hanoi was built by the French in 1895, and Kunming was a French concession with a Catholic cathedral, convent, and French Club. The French wanted the province's tin, tungsten, and opium. It was also rich in hard wood, rubber, and rice.

When Yuan Shih-kai proclaimed himself emperor in 1915, Yunnan rebelled. The Japanese wanted it as part of the first phase of their ambitious campaign to capture the whole of southeast Asia, a conflict in which the Vichy French tried not to be involved. The province was ruled during the Japanese War by warlord governors, one of whom, Lung Yun, an ex-bandit and opium king, was later overthrown with American help.

Kunming was one of the terminals of the famous Burma Road during World War II, but, unfortunately, only a small percentage of the supplies reached here, due to thieves, Nationalist incompetence and corruption, and Japanese interference. Today, Kunming has many industries, including steel, machine tools, textiles, chemicals, plastics, marble, and soft coal.

The city is completely surrounded by mountains. Sightseeing here can be a little rugged in spots. The **Dragon Gate** necessitates a climb of 200 stairs, but the effort is well worth it.

If you only have one day, you have to choose between a tour of the city or going to the Stone Forest. It is better that you stay at least two days, preferably more. Important in the city are the Western Hills, Golden Temple, Black Dragon Pool, Bamboo Temple, Yuantong Temple, Daguan Park, and Green Lake.

Xishan (Western Hills) 西山 are about 26 km from the hotels. They have the 14th-century **Huating Temple** 华亭寺 , the largest in the city. South of here is the **Taihua Temple** 太华寺 (Yuan), with the best view of the sunrise over the lake. The **Sanqing Tower**, 2 km farther south, was the summer resort of Emperor Liang of the Yuan. It has nine tiers, each about 30 meters above the other. On the top is the **Long Men (Dragon Gate)** 龙门 , with another great view of the lake. The stone corridors, chambers, paths, and intricate carving of the Dragon Gate were cut from 1609 to 1681.

The coppercast *Golden Temple* 金殿 , NE of the city (11 km away), is 300 years old, 6.5 meters high, and weighs 200 tons. The **Qiong Zhu (Bamboo) Temple** 筇竹寺 18 km NW of the Kunming Hotel, has 500 carved life-size arhats in addition to the usual Buddhist statues, carved in the Qing. These are very expressive and are worth a visit, especially if you've never seen collections of saints before. Here, also, you might find an artist to make paper cuts of your profile, cheaply. The temple was founded in 1280.

The **Daguan Lou Pavilion** 大观楼 , across the lake from Xishan Hill (7 km from the Kunming Hotel), has a 180-character couplet at its entrance, the longest ever found in China. Composed by a Qing scholar, the first half praises the landscape while the second deals with Yunnan history. Also important is the **Black Dragon Pool** 黑龙潭 , with its Ming temple and tomb. The Heishui Shrine here may be from the Han. Nearby are the Botanical Gardens.

Yuan Tong Ji 园通寺 , the only Tang temple in town, is on the same street as the Green Lake Hotel, a little over a kilometer away.

The **Stone Forest of Lunan** 路南石林 , one of the highlights of a Kunming visit, is 126 km SE of the city, and tourists usually stay in the adjacent Stone Forest Hotel 石林宾馆 . About 200 million years ago the area was covered with water. The limestone pushed its way out of the receding sea and rain continued to corrode the stone into these incredible formations. One fifth of the 64,000 acres is open to visitors. Here, too, are many steps and safety fences. The shortest of the two routes is 2½ hours long, and in this maze it's easy to get lost.

Near the hotel is a Sani nationality 撒尼族 village, and minority handicrafts are for sale. You can buy direct from the weavers. Prices here have been better than elsewhere, but be sure to haggle, especially if you're alone. Groups of local dancers in national costume have entertained hotel guests in the evening with songs and dances.

The trip between Kunming and the Stone Forest itself is remarkable because of the hilly scenery, the eucalyptus trees, and the occasional native, brightly costumed.

If you have more time, a 2-hour boat cruise on 340-sq.-km **Lake Dianchi** can be arranged, but go only for the rest, as not much can be seen (except for Daguan Lou and people fishing with large triangular nets). The Provincial Museum 博物馆 is excellent for minority artifacts, and an Institute for Nationalities 少数民族学院 is good for visitors wanting to find out more about these interesting people. At the institute, students perform minority dances on special occasions and carry out field studies to document the history and culture.

Along the west shore of the lake is Sleeping Beauty Hill and a series of swordlike hills. The villas there, formerly of the wealthy, are now sanitoriums for workers. On the southern tip of the lake is **Jinning** county town, the birthplace of the famous Ming navigator Zheng He, who sailed to East Africa half a century before Vasco da Gama. The Memorial Hall to Zheng He 郑和纪念馆 is on a hill above the town.

The **Anning (Emerald) Spa** 安宁温泉 , 47 km SW of Kunming, has comfortable accommodations and hot springs. The water contains calcium, magnesium, potassium, and sodium, and no sulfur dioxide. Two km north is the **Caoxi Temple,** built in the Song, with Song relics inside, including a bronze Buddha. Every 60 years the mid-autumn moon is reflected in a mirror on the Buddha's forehead. The plum trees date from the Yuan.

About 4 hours by car north of Kunming is **Chuxiong,** where many Yi people frequently sing and dance from 9 p.m. to dawn in the center of town, conversing socially through music. The rhythms of the dance and the energy level are just amazing.

Also in the province is **Xishuang Banna** 西双版纳 (pronounced She-Schwan-Ban-Na), a tropical autonomous prefecture 742 km SW (1-

hour flight) of the capital, near the Laotian and Burmese borders. Elevation 550 to 2300 meters. Rain 1200 to 2000 mm annually. Direct flight to **Jinghong (Yunjinghong)** (main city) from Kunming. In Xishuang Banna, the Dai people have a water-splashing festival mid-April, their new year, so if you go at that time, be prepared (with your camera in a plastic bag) for a fun time getting wet, dragon-boat races, and firecrackers. The temples here are similar to those of Thailand, with their intricate flaming roofs and snake designs. Near the border are 300 wild elephants in a nature preserve. Thirteen minorities live in these lush tropics.

Another region to visit is around **Lijiang** 思茅 in northwest Yunnan, about 700 km from Kunming, where the **Yu Long (Jade Dragon) Mountain** 玉龙山 rises spectacularly 6000 meters above sea level. Here the Naxi people still use hieroglyphic writing and wear sheepskin capes on their backs for warmth and to cushion heavy baskets. On the sheepskin are seven small embroidered moons to show how hard they work (until the moon and stars appear). The Naxi have produced writers, musicians, and artists famous in the rest of China. Also important to see are the **Dabaoji Palace, Liuli Temple,** and **Dading Temple,** all in Ming architecture. The **Liiang Guesthouse** (60 rooms) is in Naxi style.

Farther north of Lijiang, toward the Tibet border, is **Zhongdian,** considerably off the tourist path, with an altitude of 3000 meters. **Guihua Si,** on a hilltop there, was once a very prosperous Lama temple. During the Cultural Revolution it was totally destroyed except for the ruins of walls now standing, still an astounding sight. The main hall has been reconstructed and should soon make a visit to this remote area rewarding for those eager to be among the first. The scenery from Zhongdian to Xiaguan is especially great for bird watchers, and is full of lakes, forests, and mountain views. No good hotel here.

Festivals worth experiencing, in addition to the water-splashing, include the **Yi Torch Festival,** in late July or early August in the Stone Forest, the **Third Moon Market** (usually April, sometimes May) in Dali, and the **Horse and Mule Market Meeting,** around early April in Lijiang. C.I.T.S. knows exact dates.

For Dali, see ''Xiaguan.''

C.I.T.S. says it can also plan bird-watching tours, visits to the camellia and rhododendron research center, mountain climbing, and camping in the Stone Forest.

SHOPPING

Blue and white batik, feather products, and tribal handicrafts (especially shoulderbags and clothes), tin and spotted copperware.

FOOD

Specialties include ''Rice Noodles Crossing the Bridge''
米泉 , Yunnan ham, and goat's cheese. The adventurous could try snake, elephant trunk, bear's paw, and deer tendon.

HOTELS

The top hotel is the Golden Dragon, then the Green Lake, and thirdly the Kunming (which is best for business people). The Green Lake is building a new 264-room Singapore J.V., due 1991.

Camellia Hotel • *Tiny hard-to-find hotel. Facing the Kunming Hotel, it is two alleys to the right.* • Favorite of budget travelers who also advise eating in the nearby Cooking School.

Golden Dragon Hotel • *575 Beijing Rd. Cable 4456. Telex 64060 GDHKM CN. Fax 31082. Dist.A.P.7 km. Dist.R.W.1 km* • 1987. 17 stories, 302 rooms, C.C., IDD probably 1989. Business center, bicycles, tennis, hot-spring swimming pool, gym.

Green Lake (Cuihu) Hotel 翠湖宾馆 • *6 South Cuihu Rd. Telex 64073 GLHTL CN. Cable 5046. Dist.A.P.15 km. Dist.R.W.8 km. Across street from park* • 1956, ren. 1990. 5 stories, 160 rooms. C.C., business center, bicycles.

Kunming Hotel 昆明宾馆 • *122–145 East Dongfeng Rd. Telex 64058 KMHTL CN. Dist.A.P.7 km. Dist.R.W.4 km* • 1958 sect. and 1982 sect. both ren. 1989. 450 rooms. C.C., IDD, business center, bicycles. Good food.

C.I.T.S.: 8 Heping Xincun Huancheng Nan Rd.; tel. 36109, 34019. Telex 64027 KMITS CN. Cable 3266. Fax 29240.
C.T.S.: 145 Dongfeng Rd.; tel. 24992, 23922; cable 3266; telex. 64027 KMITS CN.
CAAC中国民航**:** 146 Dongfeng Dong Rd.; tel. 24270.

LANZHOU (LANCHOW) 兰州

Northwest China. Western Gansu province, of which it is the capital. Almost in the center of China, on the Yellow River, it can be reached by air from several cities, including Beijing (2 hours by Trident), Shanghai (2¼ hours by Trident), and Guangzhou. These routes are considerably longer by smaller planes. Lanzhou is also serviced by train.

Lanzhou is important as a stop on the Silk Road and as a gateway to two cave temples, the *Bingling Temple Caves and the *Maijishan Caves. Do not stop here unless you're interested in cave temples and are willing to go out into the desert to look at them. Visitors react to the city itself in different ways. One seasoned tour guide said it was not all that interesting and described it as a "city of poverty." Another visitor said it was his "favorite city." In any case, the infamous pollution here has been reduced by the growing use of electricity instead of coal for cooking. Guides used to hand out masks to visitors to protect lungs and throats.

Founded about 2200 years ago, Lanzhou was called the "Gold City" after gold was found here. At an altitude of 1510 meters, Lanzhou is very cold in winter. The coldest winter temperature is ⁻23°C in January; the hottest, 39.1°C, both some time ago. Annual precipitation in the province is between 30 and 600 mm, the rain mainly in the SE.

With a population of over one million, the city is industrial, with petrochemicals, machine building, and smelting. It is near the oldest oilfields in China.

Gansu province today has a population of 20 million, including Han, Hui, Tibetan, Dongxiang, Yugur, Bonan, Mongolian, Kazak, Tu, Salar, and Manchu nationalities. The area was settled 200,000 years ago; 3000 years ago, the inhabitants started farming the eastern part of Gansu. The province is the setting for Yuan-tsung Chen's excellent autobiographical novel *The Dragon's Village,* a book based on her own experiences with land reform shortly after Liberation.

In Lanzhou, tourists can visit the university, factories, a white pagoda, and a fountain. The **Baita (White Pagoda Park)** 白塔 is on a hill on the north bank of the Yellow River. The buildings here are the Sanxing (Three-Star) Hall, Yingxu (Greet the Sunrise) Pavilion, Yun-yue (Cloudy Moon) Temple, and the White Pagoda Temple. The White Pagoda was first built in the Yuan, then rebuilt and expanded in the Ming and Qing. It has seven stories and eight sides and is about 70 meters high.

The **Wuquan (Five-Fountain) Hill** 五泉山 is south of the old city. Legend credits General Ho Qubing (Huo Chu-ping), in 120 B.C., with stabbing the ground with his sword after finding no water for his horses. Five streams of water appeared and have been flowing ever since. Most of the old buildings here were destroyed in war. Existing still are the Jingang (Buddha's Warrior Attendants) Shrine (Ming), the Qianfo (Thousand Buddhas) Hall, the Mani Temple, the Dizang Temple, and the Sanjiao Cave. The two most important relics to see are the Taihe Iron Bell, 3 meters high, weighing 5 tons, cast in 1202; and the Tong-jieyinfo Buddha, cast in copper in 1370 and weighing nearly 5 tons.

The elaborate fifth-century ***Bingling Temple Caves** (Pinglinghsi) 炳灵寺石窟 are 120 km SW of the city, near **Linxi.** Here are 183 caves and shrines with 694 stone Buddhist statues and 82 clay ones, the biggest Buddha 27 cm high, the smallest only 25. Like some other cave temples, this involves a lot of stairs. The statues range from Northern Wei to Ming, the youngest, at least 350 years old.

The ***Maiji Grottoes** 麦积山石窟 , also Northern Wei to Ming, are 45 km SE of the city of **Tianshui** 天水 , itself 350 km SE of Lan-zhou. Tianshui was a trade distributing center on the Silk Road and has two temples, the Fuxi and the Nanguo, and should now be reached by air.

At Maiji, there are 194 caves full of thousands of stone and clay Buddhist statues, and 1300 square meters of murals dating from the end of the 4th century to the 19th, a period of 1500 years. These caves are on a mountain, which rises almost vertically, and are reached by wooden staircases and protected by doors and windows. Some of the statues are completely unsheltered. One statue 15.28 meters high is from the Sui. The work on the mountain was done by craftsmen who piled blocks of wood up to the top and started carving while standing on them. As the artisans worked their way down, they gradually removed the blocks. The Maiji is better than Bingling.

Also near Tianshui, at **Dadiwan** in Qin'an County, is an on-the-site museum similar to that at Banpo in Xi'an, which should be open in time for your trip. Its 1154-sq.-meter hall covers a 7000-year-old prim-itive village with painted pottery tripods, stone and bone artifacts, and ground paintings. Of the 200 houses so far discovered, one covers 600 square meters, the largest such building found so far in China.

If you have a chance, do see the authentic **Chinese dances** per-formed by the Gansu School of Dance in Lanzhou. The principal, Mme.

Gao, studied the dancing figures in the caves and personally selected 12 girls for five years of training. Now their performance is considered the best in the nation and they have toured many Asian countries.

Also in the province are Dunhuang, Jiayuguan, and Jiuquan. See separate listings.

SHOPPING

Lanzhou produces a kind of honeydew melon, carved ink slabs, ''jade'' cups and bottle gourds. It also manufactures paper cuts, lanterns, and reproductions of ancient paintings based on the Silk Road murals. Some of its replicas of the famous Flying Horse of Gansu are made from molds directly from the original.

Try the **Provincial Arts and Crafts Shop** (West Donggang Rd.) and the **Nanguan Department Store,** with its Friendship Store branch.

FOOD

Roast piglet (delicious!), sweet and sour Yellow River carp, *facai,* steamed chicken, fried camel hoof (ugh), and fried sheep's tail. For snacks, try toffee potatoes and toffee melon. In addition to the hotel restaurants, try the **Yuebinlou Restaurant,** which has Beijing food, and the **Jingyanglou Restaurant,** which specializes in Yangzhou food.

HOTELS

Jincheng Hotel • *363 Tianshui Ave., in the center of town. Cable 6333. Telex BTHJC CN* • 307 rooms. Tea house. Air-conditioned cars for hire. Seems to be the best but don't expect too much.

Lanzhou Hotel　兰州宾馆 • *204 Donggang Rd. W. Telex 72131. Cable 7391. Dist.A.P.80 km. Dist.R.W.1 km* • 1956; renovated. 1425 beds. Chinese and Moslem dining rooms.

CAAC: 46 Donggang Xi Rd.; tel. 23432, 23421.
C.T.S.: 209 Tianshui Rd.; tel. 26181, 26798. Cable 7139. Telex 72103 CTSLB CN.

See also ''Silk Road.''

LESHAN (LE MOUNTAIN) 乐山

Southwest China, about 170 km SW of Chengdu. This can be included in an overnight trip with the base of Emei Mountain (see separate listing) and Sansu Shrine (see ''Chengdu''). It could also be done in a one-day excursion by hovercraft from Chongqing. The long trip by road is preferable if you have the time and want to see the Sichuan countryside, the architecture of the farmhouses, and the most obnoxious truck drivers in the country.

Formerly known as Jiading or Jiazhou, Leshan is a small 1300-year-old town. Warm rain from April through June adds to the mystical atmosphere.

Leshan is the home of the ***Dafu (Great Buddha) Temple** 大佛 . Here sits a 58.7 or 70 meters (depending on sources) Buddha, started in A.D. 713 and completed 90 years later, believed to be the largest in the world. From Leshan city, visitors could take a public bus to the front gate, or arrive by ferry at the foot. The view from the water is better; otherwise you can't see the temple guardians. At the confluence of three rivers (Min, Dadu, and Qingyi), the monastery buildings stand at Buddha's eye level.

This huge statue was built to offset the large number of serious accidents on the river. Since statistics were probably kept before and after, it would be enlightening to know if, indeed, the statue was worth it.

Two guest houses fringe the head of the Buddha. Caves, bare floors, and Chinese beds. Being able to stay at the temple provides a great opportunity for photographers, who can shoot to their hearts' content at dusk and sunrise (when the mist rises on the river). The other statues, all recent reproductions, look better in dim light.

The **Wuyou (Black) Temple** 乌尤寺 can be reached in 15 minutes by footpath from the Dafu Temple, or by 336 steps from where the tour buses stop. It has a good museum for its tiny size.

HOTELS

C.I.T.S. says the Jia Zhou is tops, followed by the Hongzhushan and Xiongxiu. A new three-star hoel, the Nushen (Haitang Rd.), should open 1989–90.

Jia Zhou Hotel 嘉州宾馆 ● *Bai Ta St. Cable 6333. Good location across river from the Great Buddha.* ● 1953, second bldg. 1987, ren. 1992. 13 stories, 307 rooms. C.C., business center, bicycles. Planning pool and sauna. Originally a Canadian mission before Liberation. Near shopping, park, and boat to Great Buddha Temple.

Jiu Ri Feng Hotel 就日峰宾馆 , At Buddha's head. 140 beds. Dorms.

Lan Lou Guest House ● *East side of Buddha's head.* ● Reconstructed 1985. 15 rooms.

C.I.T.S. and **C.T.S.** 国际旅行社 : Leshan city; tel. 2154. Cable 2464.

LHASA 拉萨

Northwest China. The fabled capital of Xizang (Tibet) is currently only open to travelers (except during times of civil unrest) on prepaid tours that can be arranged by Holiday Inn Lhasa or any travel agency. Because tourists have complained of guides with little knowledge and poor English, please take this guide book with you or get something more detailed, like Elisabeth B. Booz's *Tibet*. Contact American tour organizers like Lindblad, Indoculture, Arunas, Mountain Travel, etc. for current information and tours. On-your-own travelers have managed to get in, but you do risk expulsion and maybe prison. Lhasa is north of Bhutan and Bangladesh and almost due south of Urumqi. It is reached by daily flights from Chengdu; flights from Beijing Sundays and Guangzhou Wednesdays; flights from Kathmandu Saturdays and Wednesdays but not in the winter. (These can be booked through Indoculture Tours in the U.S.) You can also go by bus from Golmud, with an overnight stop in Amdo or wherever the driver wants to sleep. About 30 hours' driving time (and the possibility of snow in the passes, even in June. Wear warm clothing and take motion sickness pills, and your own food. No toilets on bus.) Travelers have been going to Lhasa from Kathmandu by land, but you should expect delays due to landslides and bumpy roads most of the year round. Recently, landslides have meant at least a three-hour hike. The whole trip could take three to five days. It is also possible to travel overland from Pakistan to Lhasa, and perhaps soon from India via Darjeeling. The altitude is about 3607 meters.

Tibet is generally safe for visitors except in the vicinity of street demonstrations. Some foreigners (as well as demonstrators) have been shot without warning by police. We also suggest you avoid getting close to the many stray dogs here.

Tibet is one of the more exotic places to visit in China, virtually a country in itself, with an area about the size of France, Spain, and Greece combined. It is isolated by the highest mountains in the world.

It is important to see because of its unique culture, its celebrated mon-asteries, and its magnificent scenery.

This is colorful National Geographic land: you can see prostrating pilgrims, fierce-looking tribesmen, people spinning prayer wheels on the street, a great variety of tribal dress, yaks, maroon-robed monks, unusual handicrafts and architecture, great mountains, and smiling, friendly natives most of whom don't mind having their photo taken when asked. Best take a long lens. The essentials of Lhasa can be cov-ered in two hurried or three less hurried days if you are in good shape.

While visiting Tibet is no longer an experience just for the adven-turous few, it is still not for the weak. The average altitude in Tibet is over 5000 meters (very hard on the skin, so take some good sunscreen). Usually it takes about two days to decide whether or not you'll be sick, and two weeks to feel at home. Bottled oxygen is available in the hotel rooms and on some tour buses. Just don't push yourself too hard. Tak-ing it easy is difficult, as a lot of climbing is involved just to sightsee. Do not go if you have asthma or other pulmonary problems. In addition to the altitude and dust, the temples are full of incense smoke and are lit by butter lamps—all of which might make breathing difficult. Qual-ified doctors may not be available. See section on Altitude Sickness later on.

Since all food, energy, and most building materials have to be imported by truck or plane, the cost of accommodations and sightseeing is higher than in other parts of China for the same quality. You should bring your own flashlight, drinking flask, medicine for altitude sickness, and alarm clock.

Spring and summer days can be very dry with lots of dust blowing. A nose mask and goggles are helpful. Only light clothing needed in summer for Lhasa, but warmer clothes are needed for higher altitudes. Winter days can be warm with highs of 20–25°C and you can get a sunburn. But the nights can be cold. The best time is September to November.

The hottest temperature in Lhasa is 27°C in July and August; the coldest, −15°C in December and January. The annual precipitation is about 500 mm, mainly from June to September. Lhasa is in the Zangpo Valley at over 3000 meters. Some of the hotels are not well heated in winter. (Take a hot-water bottle!)

Tibetans are nomads, or farmers raising barley, yak, and sheep. Tho-tho-ri Nyantsen, 28th king of Tibet, introduced Buddhism into the country in A.D. 233.

In the seventh century, the king of Tubo, conquered the other tribes and made Lhasa his capital. He also invaded neighboring Sichuan, and although he was repulsed, his request for a Chinese wife was granted. His marriage with Tang princess Wen Cheng and his interest in Tang culture introduced much Chinese culture into Tibet. Among the innovations were silk, paper, and the architecture of the palace he built for her. His marriage to a Nepalese princess also meant Indian influences. Tibetan script is basically Indian. Both princesses promoted their own brands of Buddhism. The Tibetan kingdom subsequently expanded to include parts of Yunnan and northern India.

In 779, Buddhism became the state religion. The Mongols invaded Tibet in 1252 and adopted Tibetan Lamaism for themselves and propagated it to help control their subject tribes in other parts of China. Some lamas became very powerful during the Yuan. Kublai Khan appointed a lama as king, but maintained overall power himself. This system has continued with varying degrees of Chinese enforcement ever since. Qing emperor Qianlong (Chien Lung) was one who especially asserted his authority.

The Jesuits were the first western missionaries to arrive in Tibet in 1624. During the lifetime of the fifth Dalai Lama, the office of Dalai Lama became political as well as religious. The first British mission arrived in 1774 and a British military expedition (Younghusband) forced the Dalai Lama to flee to Mongolia from 1904 until 1909. In 1910, the Chinese again asserted their control and the Dalai Lama retreated for a time to India. In 1911, the Tibetans repelled the Chinese. The British tried to maintain some control here, but gave up in 1947 after India became independent.

The Chinese People's Liberation Army arrived in 1951. An abortive uprising by some Tibetans in 1959 forced a large number of Tibetans to flee to India. The current Dalai Lama, the 14th, has been there ever since. In 1964, Tibet was made an Autonomous Region within China. In the last few years, the Chinese have made attempts to train Tibetans to replace Han administrators. The 1.78 million Tibetans here are over 94% of the population.

Recently, some Tibetans demonstrated for independence and several people were killed. China accused the U.S. Congress of interfering in internal affairs. Foreign tourists were again restricted.

As you move around the region, be sensitive to the feelings of people. I have been appalled by the loud talking of my Chinese guide during Tibetan prayers. Walk clockwise around temples. If you hand a picture of the Dalai Lama to a Tibetan, make sure no Han Chinese is around because this could bother him or her. Hold the photo (postcards are great) in both hands, put it to your forehead and then bow your head as you hand it over.

The Dalai Lama is god, and you will be asked "Dalai Lama picture?" in every monastery. One could have given out 40 in the Potala alone. However, having pictures of the Dalai Lama in your possession could be interpreted as support for Tibetan independence. Some foreigners have been arrested for getting involved in this dispute.

Tibet's Buddhism is different from that of the rest of Asia, aside from Mongolia and northern China. It believes strongly in reincarnation and a vicious, torturous hell for sinners, which is reflected in its art. It is full of demons and human skulls, witchcraft and magic, much influenced by the pre-Buddhist polytheism of the Tibetans. It has also many pre-Hindu influences and much recitation of spells. You might hear the chant *Om Mani Padme Hum,* which means "Hail to the Jewel in the Lotus," a mantra that helps the individual communicate with the eternal.

At the same time, Lamaism has many mystical elements, the chanting in chords by each monk, and a highly developed theology.

The goal of Buddhism is the end of continuous reincarnations.

At one time, a quarter of the male population of Tibet were monks, and the theocracy was such that no matter how cold it was, on whatever day spring was proclaimed by the Dalai Lama, everybody had to change into summer clothes!

Like other religions, Lamaism is divided into sects: the two main ones here are the Red Hats, where sex with a person other than one's spouse was part of the ritual, and the Yellow Hats, which is more strict about celibacy and other traditional Buddhist monastic practices. The Dalai Lama is head of the Yellow Hats.

Fascinating are the stories of how the successive dalai lamas were chosen—babies recognizing objects used by themselves in their previous incarnations. The current incumbent is from a peasant family from Amdo, at that time in Qinghai province. The Dalai Lamas are earthly incarnations of the four-armed God Chenrezi, and when each incarnation dies, his spirit takes on the body of another Tibetan child at birth. Disputes have arisen over who is the real reincarnated Dalai Lama, and the issue is politically very sensitive. Lamas are very learned monks or recognized reincarnations of previous lamas or monks.

Among traditional Tibetan customs is the giving of a *hada,* a long silk scarf, as a token of esteem and good luck. The sticking out of the tongue is a sign of respect. At one time, Tibetans practiced polyandry, brothers sharing one wife because of poverty. Every summer a festival celebrates the annual washing and cleaning.

Tea is drunk with yak butter and salt and tastes more like beef broth. It does seem to give much needed energy for survival and is said to be good for colds. The proper way to drink it is to lightly blow the top cream away from you and allow it to settle on the sides of your tea cup. The thicker the cream, the more generous the host. Fresh, hot yak milk has been described as sweet and "heavenly" and has a higher fat content than cow's milk. Often barleylike flour is added to the milk or tea to form a dough. Chang (tsang), a barley wine, is another favorite drink offered to guests.

The remains of the dead are frequently cut up by funeral workers at dawn to feed vultures, in the belief that these birds take the spirits to heaven. Those who cannot afford this expensive rite, like beggars or victims of serious illnesses, are fed to fish—which is why Tibetans don't eat fish. Burial in the ground is for the very poor and unfortunate, such as criminals or victims of murder. High lamas are covered in butter and cremated.

Tourists are discouraged from seeing the birds at work, because the families of the deceased fear the tourists will scare the birds away.

Look for the *tangkas* hung on monastery walls. These are the scrolls used by itinerant preachers to illustrate the teachings of the Buddha. Look for prayer wheels, with a written prayer inside, which adherents spin in the belief that each rotation sends a prayer to Buddha.

Tibet has 50 monasteries open, including seven for nuns, with 3000 men in residence and 138 women. Forty-three more religious buildings are under repair and another 80 will be restored. All this work is being done by the central and local governments, which also maintain the monasteries and the monks. At Liberation, Tibet had 2770 monasteries.

The most important of the buildings are the Jokhang Temple, Potala Palace, Sera Monastery, and Drepung Monastery.

Getting Around. Group tourists need not worry but in your spare time you may want to go out on your own. This small city is flat and most hotels rent out bicycles. Public buses are infrequent; jeep-type vehicles are expensive (almost three times the taxi-rate in any other Chinese city). The Holiday Inn has been operating a shuttle bus free to its guests, with a reasonable fare for others. Monastery hours keep changing so check at your hotel, but the Potala was open mornings 9 a.m. to 12:30 p.m., Wed. & Sat. full day to 5:30 p.m.

To travel to other parts of Tibet, ask your hotel, C.I.T.S. or other travelers. Most hotels have bulletin boards with notices.

Transfers. CAAC's bus from the airport has been meeting people on the runway and can stop at the Holiday Inn before it arrives at the Tibetan city and walking distance to the inns there. The Holiday Inn has been meeting planes with its own bus. Its staff can pick up bags, but baggage on the afternoon flight can't get to you until the next day. (Best take overnight supplies in your carry-on.)

The *Potala Palace 布达拉宫 cannot be missed. It is 3.5 km from the Holiday Inn and 1 km from the Jokhang. It dominates the city from its lofty cliff. Groups get driven up to the entrance. Individual travelers climb 300 meters. The only toilet is near the east entrance. In spite of its 13 stories, there are no elevators. If you follow the crowds and go into every open doorway, you should be able to see everything worth seeing in three hours. No signs in English or arrows. And there are a lot of stairs.

Originally built in the seventh century by Songsten Gampo, the Potala was the official residence of the Dalai Lama, the religious and secular head of Tibet. The first Dalai Lama lived from 1391–1474. The

Potala has 1000 rooms, 10,000 chapels, and the tombs of eight Dalai Lamas, some gold-plated and studded with diamonds, turquoises, corals, and pearls. The largest tomb is 14.85 meters high. More than 200,000 pearls cover the Pearl Pagoda. The tombs are not always open so ask about them. Additional payment is worth it. Every room has a helpful monk-guide. And the discerning have been able to take photos without payment.

The building was destroyed and rebuilt several times, the latest structure dating from 1642. Among its 200,000 statues are those of King Songsten Gampo and his Chinese wife.

Every wall is covered with murals. Noteworthy are those in the Sishiphuntsok Hall. In the West Big Hall, the murals record the life of the Fifth Dalai Lama, including his meeting with Qing Emperor Shunzhi in Beijing in 1652.

The palace is 400 meters by 350 meters, and is made of stone and wood, its walls between three and five meters thick. The White Palace was built during the time of the Fifth Dalai Lama (1617–1682) and the Red Palace afterward. From the 18th century, with the construction of the Norbulinka (Summer Palace), the Potala was used only in winter. Can you imagine a child growing up here? The current dalai lama was brought here at the age of two. Think of him flying his kite from the Potala's roof and exploring the city and its people with a telescope!

The *Jokhang Temple 大昭寺 , a.k.a. Juglakang, is the most important Buddhist temple in Tibet. It is 4.5 km from the Holiday Inn and is the heart of the city. It was built in the mid-seventh century, also during King Songsten Gampo's time. It has been expanded several times since. Note the Nepalese and Chinese features. Princess Wen Cheng brought with her from China the seated statue of the child Sakyamuni. The Tibetans believe that the statue was made by the Buddha himself. The Great Prayer Festival is held annually here from the 3rd to 25th of the first month of the Tibetan calendar.

The temples here are full of worshipers, some prostrating themselves 500 times a day and donating yak butter to feed the lamps.

The *Sera Monastery 色拉寺 in the northern suburbs 10 km from the Holiday Inn and 4 km from downtown, was built in 1419. It was extended in the early 18th century, and is one of the four major monasteries in Tibet, at its height housing 10,000 lamas and monks. The 18 sandalwood arhats and four Heavenly Kings here were gifts from the Ming emperor. Look also for a gold statue of an 11-faced Guan Yin, the Goddess of Mercy.

The *Drepung Monastery 哲蚌寺 , a.k.a. Daipung, is in the western suburbs 6 km from the Holiday Inn and 10 km from the Jokhang. One can climb to the roof for the view of the valley. Financed by the same nobleman who built the Sera, the Drepung was founded in

1416 and extended several times. It is one of the four major monasteries. Among its treasures is a white conch and a gilded Buddha. Inside the abdomen of the statue in the main hall are the remains of a master translator named Dorjidak. At one time, this monastery also had a population of over 10,000 monks and lamas.

If you have more time, **Norbulingka Park** 罗布林卡 was the summer residence of the dalai lamas, with 370 rooms. It is 4 km from the Potala and set in a 100-acre garden. Kalsang Podang, the first building, was originally erected in 1755. The New Palace for the 14th dalai lama was built in 1954–56. It is also full of statues and murals. The murals are of Princess Wen Cheng and her marriage to the king, the three worlds, and Buddha preaching under a banyan tree. The bedroom is as the current dalai lama left it to flee to India. In the 1940s, the German mountain climber Heinrich Harrer set up a movie theater for the dalai lama in this park.

An exhibition of tangkas is usually in one of the temples in the back. If you don't like the toilets, go over to the Holiday Inn nearby.

The *Ganden Monastery** is also protected by the State Council as a historical monument. It is listed as early Ming to Qing. This is a one-day trip as is that to Lake Yamdrok Yamsto. The **Royal Tibetan Tombs,** from the seventh century, are at Chong-gye/Qonggyai in Lhoka/Shannan prefecture, about 180 km SE.

Shigatse/Xigaze is about 225 km (9 hours) west of Lhasa over a 3000-meter-high pass. The *Tashilhunpo (Zhaxilhunbu) Monastery**扎什伦布寺 there is the most important of the religious buildings in that city. It was founded in 1447 and was the home of the Panchen Lamas, the reincarnations of the Buddha of Eternal Light. Only religiously have the Panchen Lamas been equal to the politically superior Dalai Lamas. However, the Chinese consider the Panchen Lama a political equal. This is also a very sensitive and controversial point.

At one time, the Tashilhunpo had a population of 3800 monks. Today there are about 600. This monastery also has many halls and chapels, and statues of the 18 arhats. The Hall of the Buddha Maitreya Champa/Qiangba was built from 1914–18 with a 26.7-meter statue of the Buddha in gold and copper inside. The gold-plated reliquary of the fourth Panchen Lama is 11 meters high and is decorated with precious stones. The tenth Panchan Lama died here in 1989.

You can probably hear the lamas chanting in the Grand Chanting Hall from 8 a.m. to 11 a.m., from 1 p.m. until 3 p.m., and 6 p.m. to 9 p.m. Don't be surprised if you find a 20-inch color television set.

Zhangmu, on the Tibet side of the Nepal border, is now open to tourists, with a 100-bed guesthouse. The trip takes three days. Probably open for your visit are Damshung/Damxung (pastoral area) and Nyingtri/Nyingchi (forest areas). In all of these, yak-hair tents will house tour-

ists. Tingri/Dingri County at the foot of Mount Qomolangma (Everest)
and all mountains in Tibet are expected to be opened gradually to foreigners.

Several Lhasa tour agencies now offer **treks** in Tibet, and prices
for these are higher than similar treks in other countries. Mountaineering can be organized through the Chinese Mountaineering Association.

Highly recommended is Heinrich Harrer's *Seven Years in Tibet,*
about his adventures there in the 1940s, a good picture to compare with
today's Tibet. Harrer, a German, taught the Dalai Lama English and
was his cameraman. A sequel tells of Harrer's recent return trip. Also
recommended are the classic *Tibet and Its History* by Hugh E. Richardson, and Peter Fleming's *Bayonets to Lhasa.*

ALTITUDE SICKNESS

If you only have two days, it may not be worth visiting Lhasa
because of the altitude. About 60% of new arrivals get a headache. If
you are one of the small minority afflicted with severe altitude sickness,
you could spend much of your time in bed.

You won't know you are susceptible until you get to about 8–
9,000 ft. One can travel successfully in high altitudes 20 times and get
it on the 21st. It seems to hit the young and strong more than the old
and weak. Young people have passed out checking into hotels. Jumping
onto a bicycle upon arrival is a no-no.

The symptoms are severe headache, dizziness, insomnia, nausea,
vomiting, and difficulty in breathing. People who make a gradual ascent
by road rarely get it, if at all. People who fly in are prone. So are people
with colds, breathing difficulties, poor health, and heart disease. Pregnant women should stay below 3,600 meters says the Himalayan Rescue
Association in "Hints on High Altitude" circulated by the Holiday Inn.

It is better to let your body adjust naturally. Avoid smoking, alcohol, and sleeping pills. Move about in slow motion. **Drink over three
liters of liquid a day.** Get plenty of bed rest especially if you feel any
of the symptoms. Open your windows. Breathe deeply. Relax. Do not
panic.

Some hotels have oxygen in the rooms. This will give relief but
will retard the time it takes the body to adjust. Some people have found
aspirins helpful. Some have successfully taken the diuretic Diamox
available in North America by prescription only. Most doctors will not
prescribe it because they don't know its effect at high altitudes. With a
few people Diamox has caused vomiting, confusion, and of course uri-
nation. Discuss it with a mountaineering club or travel agency doctor
before you go. You have to start taking it a day before you arrive.

In very severe cases of altitude sickness, the only recourse is evacuation to a lower altitude and you may not get a plane out for days.

FESTIVALS

October–November the Gods Descending Festival. November–December the Fairy Maiden Festival (Jokhang Temple). December Tsong Khapa's Festival. January–February Tibetan New Year. February–March Great Prayer Festival (Jokhang). February–March Butter Lamp Festival. July Giant Tangka Festival (Shigatse). August Shoton (Tibetan Opera) Festival.

SHOPPING

Tibetan boots, rugs, saddle blankets, jewelry, temple bells, prayer wheels, woolen blankets, etc. Look for the market around the Jokhang Temple, the Barkhor (bazaar). There one can also buy Nepalese made Tibetan tangkas which are finer than Tibetan ones, at several times the price of those in Nepal but cheaper than in North America, at Syamukapu International, tel. 214327. (Using the front gate of the Jokhang as 6 o'clock, this up-market store is at about 10 o'clock.) Tangkas and original art can also be bought at the Tibet Art Gallery at the foot of the Potala (bus stop). Not cheap, but cheaper than North America. Unmounted prints of Tibetan tangkas are a great buy for about Y 12 and have been found in the Holiday Inn and at the Potala.

FOOD

Except for the main hotels, restaurants here are generally dirty and the food not good. Few vegetables. If you are going outside of Lhasa, we suggest you stock up on cup noodles, granola bars, peanut butter and crackers, etc. before you arrive.

Tibetan (Yak meat and cheese), Moslem (mutton or lamb), or Chinese.

HOTELS

No hotel has IDD. Telex is faster.

The best hotel is the Holiday Inn Lhasa Hotel (with the best English), then the Tibet Hotel. These two are within walking distance of each other and the Norbulinka. The third best is the Sunlight in the old city.

The cheaper Tibetan inns are within walking distance of each other and the central Jokhang Monastery in the old Tibetan city. The best of these are the **Kirey** and **Banak Shol.** No Tibetan inn has western toilets. Few rooms have private baths and most have cheap dorms too. The **Snowland** has no showers and does not charge for booking plane tickets. Most had concrete floors and lots of flies. Some offered free laundry service. Usually only one telephone and one television for everyone. The clientele (mainly young people) necessitated the sign in one inn, "Do not shit in the shower."

Other inns and hotels are the **Yak**, and the **Plateau.** Some hotels outside of Lhasa can be downright crude.

Banak Shol • *11 Beijing Dong Rd. Dist.A.P.90 km* • 1984. 3 stories, 106 rooms. Bicycles, dorms, no C.C. Western-style toilets. Has good level of English. Two washing machines. Iron. Offers good map of city. Largest bulletin board.

Holiday Inn Lhasa • *1 Minzu Rd. Western suburbs. Cable 7391. Dist.A.P. 90 km. Telex 68010 HILSA CN* • 1985. 468 rooms and suites in five and seven story buildings. Sichuan restaurant. Western coffee shop. CAAC, C.I.T.S., and office of Tibet International Sports Travel (for mountaineers). C.C., clinic, gift shop, massage, live music. City and out-of-town tours one can join if enough demand. Book through any Holiday Inn, or in Chengdu at the Jinjiang Hotel, tel. 24481 X 594. Also known as Lhasa Hotel or Lhasa Guest House.

Tibet Hotel • *Behind the Holiday Inn. Cable 6333. Telex 68013 TGSIH CN.* • This exotic hotel has more upmarket Tibetan flavor in its lobby and its Tibetan rooms and suites than any other hotel. 1986. Can arrange tours for guests. Coffee shop and teahouse. Clinic. Beauty parlor. Swimming pool with cold water, bathing suits for sale.

C.I.T.S. 中国国际旅行社 : West Beijing Rd.; tel. 22980. Cable 8848. Telex 68009 ZMLAS CN or 68012 ITSLT CN; write to ask the dates of festivals so you can plan your trip to include them.
CAAC 中国民航 : Jiefang Rd., No. 12, Lhasa; tel. 22417, 23772. Office also in Holiday Inn.
C.T.S.: tel. 23877, 23633.
China Youth Travel Service: tel. 23329, 24173. Cable 7230. Telex 68017 CYTST CN.
Nepalese Consulate: 13 Norbulingka Rd., tel. 22880.
Tibet Tourism Administration Bureau: tel. 23857. Cable 2466. Telex 68012 ITSLT CN.

LIUZHOU 柳州

South China. Central Guangxi Zhuang Autonomous Region, immediately west of Guangdong province. Both urban and rural population, 585,000 with Zhuang, Han, Miao, Yao, Dong, and Hui nationalities. Weather: hottest 39°C in August; coldest ⁻3.8°C in January. Annual precipitation about 1500 mm, mainly in late spring, early summer.

Liuzhou (a.k.a. Longcheng—City of Dragons) was founded in 111 B.C. (Han) and has been a tourist destination since the Tang. Blessed by colorful minorities, a winding river, karst caves, and hills, among its attractions is the **Liuhou Temple and Tomb** 柳侯公园 . Liu Zongyuan was the famous Tang writer, and for four years provincial governor, who worked to free women from being bond slaves. Women's libbers, take note! His tomb is 1.5 km from the hotel. For natural scenery see **Yufeng (Carp) Hill** 鱼峰山 (shaped like a standing fish, 3 km from the hotel) and the **Dule Caves** 都乐岩 (18 km from the hotel). Also noteworthy are the **Giant Dragon Pond** 大龙潭 and **Horse Saddle Hill** 马鞍山 . Like a miniature, less-developed Guilin, Liuzhou should be a very pleasant, out-of-the-way place to unwind. If you want to kill some time, explore the free market with its dried frogs and delicious fried pasteries.

Only 16 km SE is the **Tongtian Cave** 通天洞 , where Liujiang (Liuchiang) Man lived 20,000–30,000 years ago, a few hundred thousand years younger than Peking Man. Liuzhou produces stone carvings and porcelain.

Liuzhou Hotel 柳州饭店 • *1 Youyi Rd.* • 1956; renovated 1985. 6 km from airport.

Liujiang Hotel 柳江饭店 • *72 Gonyun Rd.*

Dragon City Hotel 龙城大酒家 • 1988.

C.I.T.S.: Liuzhou Hotel; tel. 23009, 23329. Cable 2404.
CAAC bookings only: W. Tongfeng Rd.; tel. 22702.

LUOYANG 洛阳

(Loyang; North Bank of Luo River) Northwest China. 2 hours by train west of the Henan provincial capital and infrequent air connections with Beijing, Guangzhou and Shanghai. An 8-hour train ride east from Xi'an. About 25 km south of the Yellow River. Hottest temperatures: July–August—39°C; coldest: January–February—⁻12°C. Generally mild. Altitude: 145 meters above sea level. Population: over 5 million, of whom over 1 million are urban.

Luoyang is important because of the Longmen Grottoes, the White Horse Temple, the Ancient Tomb Museum, and because it was an imperial capital for many centuries. It is one of the 24 cities of historical importance protected by the State Council.

Luoyang was first built in the 11th century B.C. From 770 B.C. it was the capital at one time or another of the Eastern Zhou, Eastern Han, Wei, Western Jin, Northern Wei, Sui, Tang, Later Liang, and Later Tang dynasties. Moves were frequently made here because of drought in Xi'an, a city that was preferred. Because there are hills on three sides, it was relatively easy to defend, and whoever wanted to control western Henan had to take Luoyang. Consequently, many battles were fought in this area and many treasures were buried to save them from the soldiers. Luoyang was one of the earliest centers of Buddhism, from the first century A.D. During the Tang, it was the biggest city in China. It declined later because the capital, and therefore the whole court, moved away.

Luoyang people will proudly tell you that the Silk Road actually started from Luoyang and not from Xi'an, as is commonly supposed. ''Knowledgeable merchants always came here for silks,'' they say. ''It was cheaper.''

The architecture in the older, eastern part of Luoyang is more interesting than the more substantial and more livable newer buildings.

Today, there are over 400 factories manufacturing everything from truck cranes to ball bearings. Tourists might be interested in its arts and crafts factory, which makes palace lanterns and reproductions of three-color Tang porcelains and Shang bronzes.

Area farms grow cotton, corn, winter wheat, a little rice, sesame, sorghum, sweet potatoes, apples, pears, and grapes. They also raise yellow oxen, goats, and donkeys. The city is also noted for its peonies, first grown in the Sui! Flower lovers should aim for late April in Wangcheng Park. At press time, hotel rooms are in short supply here during the high tourist season.

The following can be covered in one day if you don't dawdle.

The *Baima Si (White Horse) Temple 白马寺 , 13 km east of the Old City and 25 km from the Friendship Hotel, was founded in A.D. 68 after second Han Emperor Mingdi dreamed that a spirit with a halo entered his palace. His ministers convinced him that the spirit was the Buddha, so he sent scholars to India to bring back the sutras. After three years, the famous Indian monks Shemeteng and Zhufalan arrived here with the scriptures on a white horse. The emperor put the monks up in his resort, the Cold Terrace, at the back of what is now this, the first Buddhist temple in China. There they translated the scriptures into Chinese. Both monks died in China and were buried in the east and west corners of the grounds beyond the moon gates.

None of the buildings here are original, though the red brick foundation of the Cold Terrace is Han; none of the others are earlier than Ming. The State Council lists them as Jin to Qing. Tang Empress Wu made one of her favorites the abbot here. The **Celestial Guardians' Hall** has a Maitreya (Laughing) Buddha made of hemp and lacquer with a beautifully carved frame. Here the four guardians are in charge of rain (with parasol), the wind (holding a pagoda), the amount of rain and wind (with musical instrument), and good harvest (with spider).

In the main hall to the right of Sakyamuni is Manjusri, the Bodhisattva of Wisdom, carrying the sutras, and at Sakyamuni's left, Samantabhara, Bodhisattva of Universal Benevolence. In the next hall are 18 clay arhats, each with a magic weapon, the oldest statues here (Yuan). One is Ceylonese, one Chinese (the Tang monk Xuan Zang who went to India), and the rest Indian. Inside the back halls are statues of the two monks, the Pilu Buddha (Sakyamuni), and drawers where the sutras are kept. A stele with characters written horizontally here is most unusual.

The **Qiyun (Cloud Touching) Pagoda** 齐云塔 nearby is in the Tang style, first built in 1175. Only the base with the darker brick is original. It was repaired in the Northern Song and Jin dynasties and has 13 stories. You get a strange echo effect if you stand either north or south of the pagoda and clap your hands.

The **Luoyang Municipal Museum** 洛阳博物馆 has 2000 pieces

On display and roughly 50,000 in its collection. Relics include (1) historical maps of the city. The first imperial city is where Royal City (formerly Laboring People's Park) is now. The *Han and Wei city was east of the White Horse Temple; the Sui and Tang cities were on both sides of the Luo River; (2) two mammoth tusks found right in town in 1960; (3) double boilers used 3700 years before the British used double boilers; (4) cowry shell money; (5) a sword made from an elephant tooth; (6) a crossbow with a trigger (476–221 B.C.); (7) iron farming tools (Han); (8) figures from the tomb of a Northern Wei prince, including a band with one musician falling asleep; (9) *original* three-color Tang horses and camels from which the copies are made. Study these carefully for comparison if you want to buy reproductions.

*Longmen (Lungmen) Grottoes 龙门石窟 : Large statues carved on cliffs or in caves are symbols of permanence. China has 19 important "cave temples" and Longmen is among the top three. Although predating these caves and built also by the Wei, those at Datong are said to be better preserved, more elaborately colored, and bigger. The stone at Longmen, however, is better. The grottoes are 20 km south of the city from the Friendship Hotel and extend north along the Yi River for about 1000 meters. They were not touched by the Red Guards, but the heads and hands of some were damaged at the beginning of this century. The buses stop by a 303-meter copy of a famous Sui bridge built of only stone and cement in 1962.

Work on the caves began about A.D. 494, when Emperor Hsaio Wen of the Northern Wei moved his capital from Datong to here. Work continued at a great pace from then until the Tang. A few statues were added during the Five Dynasties and Northern Song. There are 1352 grottoes, over 750 niches, and about 40 pagodas of various sizes. They contain more than 100,000 Buddhist images, ranging in size from 2 centimeters to 17.14 meters.

Compare the dress of the statues. Some are clothed in the plain robes of Indian holy men; others wear female Chinese court dress, sometimes with jewelry, a later development. One can guess that wealthy, devout worshipers wanted to clothe their gods in the best fashions of the day. This practice is much like that of medieval European religious art, which also ignored the mystical preachings of its teachers. The narrow, regular pleats are characteristic of the Northern Wei. The Tang statues tend to have rounder faces. While it is said that the gods could change their sex at will, the feminine faces are because, as one adherent said, "We want people to look at the face of Buddha. Since women's faces are more attractive than men's, the statues are made to look more feminine."

The **Wan Fo (10,000 Buddhas) Cave** actually has 15,000 Buddhas on the north and south walls. It was completed in A.D. 680 (Tang). Note the musicians and dancers at the base. The back wall has 54 bodhisattvas, each sitting on a lotus flower. Outside the cave is a Guanyin with a water vessel in her left hand and a whisk in her right. There used to be two lions here, but they are now said to be in the Boston Museum of Fine Arts.

The **Guyang Cave** was the earliest, built around A.D. 494 (Northern Wei). The cornlike design represents a string of pearls. The ceiling is covered with Buddhas, lions, and tablets.

Fengxian Temple 奉先寺 , the largest and most spectacular, was completed in A.D. 675. The main statue (17.14 meters) is the Vairocana Buddha (i.e. Sakyamuni). If you look carefully, on the left side of the face are traces of a five-centimeter crack extending from the hairline to the chin. This was repaired recently at a cost of ￥20,000. The square holes around the statues were used to hold the roof structure that was taken down when it was found that sunlight was good for limestone. Behind the smaller disciple to Sakyamuni's right is an imperceptible cave large enough to hold 400 people and from which climbers used to negotiate the top of the head. Fortunately, this is now blocked. On Sakyamuni's far left is Dvarapala, whose ankles are worn black and smooth by individuals trying to embrace them in return for happiness.

Some of the Buddhas in Longmen were commissioned by wealthy people wanting special favors, or generals hoping for victory. Some caves are mixtures of dynastic styles. During imperial times, the common people had to look at them from afar, and in later periods, peasants broke pieces off the statues to make lime fertilizer.

Other attractions include the **Tomb of Guan Yu (Kuan Yu)** 关林庙 —or at least that of his head. Guan Yu was one of the heroes of *The Romance of the Three Kingdoms,* and he is also known as the Chinese god of war. His tomb, between the grottoes and the city, was built in the Ming.

Outside of the city is the **Tomb of Liu Xiu.** He was first emperor of the Eastern Han 1900 years ago. A visit could be combined with a trip to see the bridge across the Yellow River. **Mang Shan Hill** 邙山 , north of the city, is full of the ruins of old palaces, tombs, and ancient summer resorts. The **Luoyang Ancient Tombs Museum,** with 22 Han and Song tombs, is 7 km from the city, near the airport and is worth a visit.

If you have more time, ask about the school for traditional Chinese opera. You might learn to enjoy it!

SHOPPING

Store Hours: 7:30 a.m.–7 p.m.; some 9 a.m.–7:30 p.m.

Friendship Store 友谊商店 : Reproductions, along with brushes, chopsticks, artificial flowers and inkstones, all made locally; **Guangzhou Market** 广州市场 ; **Shanghai Market** 上海市场 ; **State Secondhand Store** 旧货店 : Old city. Had theatrical costumes cheaper

than in Beijing. Also new theatrical caps; **Arts and Crafts Store** 美术
／工艺商店　: Sells palace lanterns and reproductions of Shang bronzes,
Tang horses and camels, made upstairs.

RESTAURANTS
Guangzhou Market Restaurant 广州酒家 ·

Friendship Hotel Restaurant • serves yancai (turnip) soup, mu-
dan (peony soup), fried yellow river carp in wine, and monkey-head
mushrooms.

HOTELS
C.I.T.S. says the best rooms are in the east wing of the Friendship
Hotel. The next best are the glitzy Garden Hotel (a good deal for backpackers) and the Orient. In 1990 the Peony Hotel should open and be a
rival for the top.

Garden Hotel • *Nanchang Rd., near Friendship Hotel* • 1989. C.C.

Orient (Dongfang) Hotel • 1989. 9 stories, 70 small rooms. Low
ceilings in hallways.

Peony Hotel • *Zhong Zhou Xi Rd.* • H.K. J.V. 17 stories, 206
rooms. Closer to government offices.

Youyi (Friendship) Hotel 友谊宾馆 • *6 Xiyuan Rd., western part
of Luoyang. Telex 47011; cable 0645* • 157 rooms in 4-story east wing,
1956; ren. 1987. 168 rooms in west wing, 1984; ren. 1990. • 7 km
from railway station, 10 from Old City, 3 from museum. In residential
district. Park in front. Guangzhou Free Market 2 blocks behind. Swimming pool.

OTHER IMPORTANT ADDRESSES
C.T.S. and **C.I.T.S.:** Friendship Hotel. 6 Xiyuan Rd.; tel. 23701. Telex
47011 CITSL CN. Cable 2463.

Lushan Mountain in Jiangxi Province.

Yu Garden in Shanghai.

Mogao Grottoes in Dunhuang.

Five Pagodas Temple in Hohhot.

Lunan Stone Forest, Kunming.

Great Buddha in Leshan, Sichuan Province.

East Lake in Shaoxing, Zhejiang Province.

The Great Wall.

The Potala Palace, Lhasa.

Qin Army Vault Museum, Xian.

Temple of Heaven in Beijing.

Li Garden in Wuxi.

LUSHAN 庐山

(Mountain of Straw Huts) Part of Jiujiang City, South China. 210 km NW of Nanchang in Jiangxi, the closest airport. Overlooking Poyang Lake and the Yangtze River. 36 km by bus south of the port of Jiujiang. Weather: Hottest—32°C (rare) at noon in July; coldest—⁻16°C in January. Snow from the end of November through February. Best time to visit is June–October. Lots of mist and rain, especially April and May—great for mood photographs but not for view. Altitude: 1094–1400 meters. Annual precipitation: 1916 mm. Population: About 9000 in Gulin. About 10,000 summer tourists in one day. The mountaintop tourist belt is about 8 by 4 km.

Primarily an old mountain resort, highly recommended as an escape from the heat or as a rest stop near the end of a tour. It is great for hiking and is a beautiful place to visit, with enough religious, historical, and folkloric aspects to make it interesting.

Legend says that the seven Kuan brothers lived on the mountain as recluses during the Western Zhou (11th century–771 B.C.). Because they were worthy men, the emperor sent an emissary to invite them to the capital to help govern the country. When the agent arrived, he found only empty straw huts. Hence, the name. The mountain was visited by the Jin poet Tao Yuan-ming (365–427). Its peach blossoms inspired Tang poet Bai Ju-yi. The first Ming emperor is supposed to have escaped an enemy here with supernatural help.

But it was not until after the last half of the 1800s that a resort was developed. About 100 hotel buildings and villas were completed and used by wealthy Chinese, government officials, and foreign missionaries. Most of these people were carried by sedan chair up a steep, 9-km path. People still climb this path from the base in about 2 hours from Lianhuadeng (Lotus Flower Hole). Chiang Kai-shek also visited Lushan when he wasn't campaigning against Mao Zedong at nearby Jinggang Shan. He lived in Building No. 180 in the East Valley.

During the Cultural Revolution, Lushan was closed, and parts were destroyed by the Red Guards. Foreign tourists were first encouraged to come in 1978, and now it is also a stop for some of the Yangtze boat tours. Lushan's views of the plains and the Yangtze are breathtaking. It is full of lovely trees, hills, pavilions, and old Tang pagodas and temples, many still untouched by tourists. Guides can rattle off incredible legends by the hour. It has a printing plant, a hydroelectric power station, and a few small factories.

Lushan is divided into an East Valley and a West Valley, with a tunnel at Gulin. Taxis are available. A tourist bus leaves downtown Gulin near the entrance to the city park whenever full.

Flower Path Park 花径公园 has a flower and Chinese *bonsai* exhibit. The miniature trees that inspired the Tang poet are here. Nearby, in what looks like a well, are two large characters meaning Flower Path, believed to be the calligraphy of the poet Bai Ju-yi. A natural rock formation beside the lake and the highway looks like two ends of a bridge over a ravine, with a little imagination. The story goes that before he became the first Ming emperor in 1368, Zhu Yuanzhang escaped from his rival at this spot. A dragonfly completed the bridge, making it possible for Zhu, but not his enemy, to cross. The lake here was made in 1961 and is shaped like a violin.

Grotto of Taoist Immortal 仙人洞 : Beyond the moon gate to the right is a cave about 30 feet wide, deep, and high, where Lu Tung-pin, a famous monk, studied Taoism so successfully that he became one of the Eight Taoist Immortals, the one with the supernatural sword. Note the formation over the mouth of the cave, shaped like Buddha's hand.

To the right is the Path for Visiting Fairies where, on the right of the pavilion, the three red characters mean ''Bamboo Forest Temple.'' This refers to a temple in the vicinity that rose bodily to heaven because an enchanted boy did not want to grant the gift of immortality to the heads of neighboring temples. To the left inside the moon gate is a stone pavilion with a stele outlining the career of a famous monk who at one point helped the first Ming emperor and his army to cross a stormy river to victory. It was built by Zhu Yuanzhang.

Big Heavenly Pond 大天池 : The water in this pool maintains the same height (it is said) through rain or drought, and is thus said to be ''made in Heaven.'' The pavilion behind the pond is on the site of a temple, built to commemorate the spider who saved Zhu Yuanzhang's life by spinning a web to cover him while Zhu was hiding in a well from his rival. These folk myths about great leaders would make a good study.

The monks who lived in this temple were Taoists who tried to achieve immortality through study and meditation. As a test, they jumped off Dragon Head Cliff. If you look down, you can probably guess why they were never seen again. The climb down to Dragon Head Cliff (by no means the bottom) is about 170 steps, but the view is worth it. On the way, look for a carved step that was probably part of the old temple.

Hanpokou (the Mouth that Holds Poyang Lake) 含鄱口 , named after the shape of this pass in relation to the lake, is the best place to see the rising sun. The lake is one of China's largest and is 20 km away.

The **Lushan Botanical Garden** 庐山植物园 is a short walk from Hanpokou. Belonging to the Academy of Science, this garden has exchange programs with Britain's Royal Botanical Gardens and the National Arboretum in Washington, DC. Here are 3700 varieties, including trees, flowers, grasses, and medicinal herbs on 740 acres of land. Started in 1934, it is the only subalpine garden of the ten botanical gardens in China. Tourists are free to wander through the greenhouses (tropical and subtropical plants), which are open daily from 7:30 a.m. to 6 p.m. Groups can get a guide. The most exotic plant here is the metasequoia tree, a species thought to be extinct and seen only in fossils until one was found in a primitive forest in west China and propagated here. A large specimen stands labeled by the driveway near the parking lot.

The **Three Treasure Trees** 三宝树 are said to be 1500 years old, but botanists say 500. They are nevertheless very impressive, the highest being 40 meters tall. One is a gingko and two are cryptomeria. A few meters away are the Yellow Dragon Pool and the Black Dragon Pool with waterfalls.

Pavilion for Viewing the Yangtze 望江亭 has another stunning view of the countryside below. At this point, the Yangtze River is about 15 km away. To the right, you can see the historic path up which vacationers used to be carried.

At the base of Lushan are the **Donglin Temple** 东林寺 , where Hui Yuan (334–416), a famous Buddhist monk of the Eastern Jin, paraphrased Buddhist canons, and the **White Deer Academy** 白鹿洞书院 where Zhu Xi (1130–1200) of the Song once taught.

SHOPPING

Gulin 牯岭 , the only shopping area, was destroyed by fire in 1947 and then rebuilt. The arts and crafts stores sell porcelain dishes and statues made in Jingdezhen, 180 km away. Other good buys are cloud-mist green tea and watercolors of the mountain scenery. Locally made handicrafts are walking sticks and bamboo brush or pencil holders.

FOOD

Local delicacy—the Three Stones: stone frog, stone fish, and stone fungus.

HOTELS

Some of the buildings here are over 100 years old. Most are made of stone, with lots of space and high ceilings. The best hotel for business people is the Villa Village Hotel, says C.I.T.S.

Lushan Hotel 庐山宾馆 ● *From Gulin, go through the tunnel and turn right for 2 km to 454 Hexi Rd.* ● British-built 1920s; renovated since. The main building has three stories. Villas. Heated.

Lulin Hotel 芦林饭店 ● *Hunan Rd. Dit.A.P.40 km. Dist.R.W.40 km* ● 1958; part renovated 1985. 240 beds for foreigners. Four stories. Farthest hotel from bus station (5 km); 3-minute walk to lake, 15-minute walk to botanical garden, and 20-minute walk to Hanpokou. From Gulin, go through tunnel and turn right. IDD, business center, no C.C. This is the best hotel.

Lushan Mansion 庐山大厦 ● *20-minute walk from bus station* ● 1935; reconstructed 1985. This is No. 3.

Yunzong (Amidst the Clouds) Hotel (云中宾馆)● *Henan Rd. and Hsiang Shan Rd.* ● Built 1930s. Spacious villas (with sitting and reading rooms!) reminiscent of Indian or Burmese hill stations. 10-minute walk to Flower Path Park, and 20-minute walk to the Taoist Grotto. About 3 km to bus station.

C.I.T.S. and **C.T.S.**: Lushan Hotel, Xiong Shu-nan, 454 Hexi Rd., 332900; tel. 282497. Cable 3266.

NANCHANG 南昌

(Southern Prosperity) South China. By air, 2 hours north of Guangzhou, 2 hours SE of Shanghai and 3 hours, 20 minutes south of Beijing. Capital of Jiangxi province. Because it is bounded by mountains on the east, south, and west, it is like a furnace in summer. With no northern mountains, it is very cold in winter. Coldest—⁻10°C in January–February; hottest—40°C, July–September. Provincial annual precipitation, 1200 to 1900 mm, mainly late April and May. Population: 800,000.

Nanchang's principal attractions are its revolutionary museums, primarily of interest to students of modern history.

Nanchang was founded over 2000 years ago on the east bank of the Gan River. It is best known today as the site of the first independent armed effort by the Communists, on August 1, 1927, considered now the founding date of the People's Liberation Army.

August 1st Museum 八一起义纪念馆 : The galleries are numbered and labeled in Chinese. On the second floor: (1) the background of the uprising, planned during the Northern Expedition when the Communists realized there could be no cooperation with the Nationalists (and vice versa), especially after the slaughter of the Communists in several cities in April 1927; (2) preparations for the uprising in Nanchang. Chou En-lai was one of the leaders. Thirty thousand troops took part. Third floor: (3) the uprising. Map with lights shows enemy headquarters in black and insurgent headquarters in red. Five-hour battle ended in victory for the Communists, who held the city until August 5; (4) withdrawal to Jinggang Shan, where in October Mao Tse-tung established a base in the mountains.

Exhibition Hall of Jiangxi Revolutionary History 江西革命历史博物馆 is on the main square, along with the Jiangxi Provincial Museum. It concerns the Anyuan Coal Miners' Strike led by Mao Tse-tung, and Jinggang Shan.

Jiangxi Provincial Museum 江西省博物馆 : This small museum contains some neolithic pieces, Shang bronzes, Song porcelain, an ancient implement for ironing clothes (look for picture demonstrating use), mirrors, and some tomb figures. On the second floor is a model of a Ming tomb, that of the governor of Jiangxi who was the 16th son of the first Ming emperor. Tomb pieces here are from a site about 15 km north in Xinjian. They include a jade belt, hair decorations, an army of servants, sedan chairs, and orchestra. Quite delightful!

Badashanren Museum 八大山人纪念馆 is of the famous landscape painter who lived here during the late Ming and early Qing dynasties.

For other points of interest in Jiangxi, please see separate listings: **Lushan** mountain resort 180 km north; **Jingdezhen,** ancient porcelain city 250 km NE; **Jinggang Shan,** mountain resort and revolutionary base; **Jiujiang,** 34 km north of Lushan on the Yangtze.

HOTELS

Jiangxi Guest House 江西宾馆 *August 1 Ave.* ● 1961. 182 rooms, eight stories. Basketball. Three restaurants. 34 km from airport. Walking distance to biggest department store and main square.

Qingshanhu (Green Mountain Lake) Hotel 青山湖宾馆 ● 1986. 500 beds, 15 stories. Swimming pool.

C.I.T.S. 国际旅行社 : Jiangxi Guest House; tel. 65180; telex 95005 JXH CN.
C.T.S.: 4 Changjiang Rd.; tel. 62571, 65180; cable 7139.
CAAC 中国民航 : 26 Zhanqian Rd.; tel. 62368.

NANJING

(Nanking; Southern Capital) East China. SW part of Jiangsu province on the Changjiang (Yangtze) River, 5 hours by train or 1 hour by air (300 km) NW of Shanghai, or 16 hours by train (2¼ hours by air) SE of Beijing. Direct 2-hour flight from Hong Kong and aiming for international flights in 1990. The 12 meter-wide Nanjing-Shanghai highway should be finished in 1990. One can also go by ship from Shanghai. Nanjing is the capital of Jiangsu. Weather: Hottest: 40°C (rare)—August; coldest: ¯15°C—January. Annual precipitation more than 1000 mm. Rain in summer. Population: over 4 million. A good time to visit is late October to mid-November when the streets are lined with chrysanthemums.

Nanjing is important because of its historical relics and its beauty. It was settled 6000 years ago and was a walled city 2400 years ago. From A.D. 229 to 1421, it was intermittently the capital of the Eastern Wu (229–280 A.D.), Eastern Jin (317–420), Song (420–479), Qi (479–

502), Liang (502–557), Chen (557–589), Southern Tang (937–975), Ming (1368–1421) and Taiping Heavenly Kingdom (1853–64). Jianye, Jiankang, Jinling, and Jingshi are its former names. Many of the ancient relics in the present city are Ming, built by Zhu Yuanzhang (Chu Yuanchang), first emperor of the dynasty (1368–99) whose reign name was Hongwu. After him, the capital was moved to Beijing, where his successors built the Forbidden City and were buried in elaborate tombs north of it.

In 1842, the Treaty of Nanking with England was signed here ending the First Opium War, and the city was declared an open port. In 1853, the Taiping Heavenly Kingdom made Nanjing its capital for 11 years. On January 1, 1912, it became the capital of the Sun Yat-sen government and remained the Nationalist capital until April 5, 1912, when the capital was moved to Beijing. After a period of much confusion, Chiang Kai-shek unilaterally declared Nanjing the capital on April 18, 1927.

The Japanese captured Nanjing on Dec. 12, 1937, and massacred over 200,000 civilians in what is referred to as the Rape of Nanking. A museum was recently opened to commemorate this tragic event. The Nationalists moved their capital to Chongqing but returned to Nanjing after the Japanese surrender in 1945. Most buildings survived the war. The Communists took the city on April 23, 1949, and the capital was moved to Beijing. Nanjing is still the provincial capital.

Nanjing today is a beautiful city of broad avenues thickly lined with 240,000 sycamore trees. Central is the Drum Tower, with Zhongshan Road, the main shopping street, running south, northwest, and east, intersecting in the center of town. Part of Zhongshan South Road was roughly the old Imperial Way, open only for the emperor. The earlier dynasties were centered in this section of town. Xuanwu Lake dominates the northeastern sector. Above it to the east looms 450-meter Zijin (Purple Gold) Mountain. The magnificent Ming city wall snakes around most of the urban area.

Two thousand factories make metallurgical and chemical equipment, ships, telecommunication instruments, and synthetic fibers. The Zhong Xin Yuen silk factory manufactures brocade, and the Arts and Crafts Carving Factory works in ivory and wood.

Tourism officials here have been among the best in the country. They have organized a Grand Canal Tour (Suzhou to Yangzhou), honeymoon tours, bicycle tours, and an all-Jiangsu chartered bus tour.

Nanjing takes two days to see, but if you only have one day in the city itself, most important are the Sun Yat-sen Mausoleum, Linggu Temple, and Ming Tomb in the southeast part of the city, usually combined in a half-day tour. In the afternoon, you can choose from the Observatory (for the view), the museum, the Drum Tower, the Yangtze River Bridge or whatever you want from the following menu. The

Zhonghua Gate and city wall, the Confucian Temple, and the Taiping Museum are close together.

*Sun Yixian (Sun Yat-sen) Mausoleum 中山陵 (open daily) is on an 80,000-square-meter site. The building was built to be better than those of the emperors whom the father of the Chinese republic overthrew. Eight km from the Jinling Hotel, it is on the south side of Purple Gold Mountain, its *feng-shui* ideal. Dr. Sun (1866–1925) was buried here in 1929 in the rear of the hall (see "Milestones in Chinese History"). The mausoleum, 158 meters above sea level, has 392 steps and a 5-meter-high statue, and is well worth visiting.

Sun Yat-sen was born of peasant stock in Guangdong province, near Macao, in what is now called Zhongshan county, renamed after its most distinguished son. Zhongshan was Dr. Sun's honorific name.

Dr. Sun actually spent most of his life outside China, leaving home at the age of 12 to study at an Anglican school in Hawaii, where his older brother had settled. He studied medicine in Hong Kong and for a short time set up practice in Macao. He spent much of his life traveling in Europe and America, and living in Japan, writing and plotting against the Manchus and planning a government for China. His teachings have been slavishly followed in Taiwan, where he is almost worshiped. He is highly respected on the mainland, too.

An intriguing, complex man, Dr. Sun became a Christian early in life and, although he attacked missionaries as being imperialists, he admitted on his death bed to being a Christian still. He fought the Manchus because they could not rid the country of the foreign imperialists. After becoming president, he did make it a point to inform the first Ming emperor of what had happened!

Dr. Sun did not remain president for long. Because of the problems in uniting the country, he abdicated in 1912. The north was not willing to accept a southerner as head of state, he reasoned. He later accepted a post as director of railways for the country. At the same time, he flirted with socialism, coming under the influence of Russian advisers.

He was married first to a peasant woman and later to Soong Ching-ling, much against her father's wishes. The second marriage shocked the Christians but not most Chinese, who were used to the idea of several wives. Mme. Sun was the sister of Mme. Chiang Kai-shek of Taiwan. See also "Shanghai" and "Zhongshan."

Linggu (Valley of the Soul) Temple (open daily) is just an empty building, the only survivor of a whole complex of Buddhist structures, its statues destroyed during the Taiping war, when the Qing army slept here. Eight km from the Jinling Hotel, it was built originally in A.D. 513 by a Liang princess in memory of a famous monk. It was moved to its current location at the eastern foot of Zijin Mountain because the first Ming emperor wanted the original site for his own tomb.

Without beams, it is reminiscent of medieval Europe because of its arches. Its eastern and western walls curve outward. Nearby is a nine-story pagoda built in the 1920s to complement the area around the mausoleum, 2 km to the NE. The pagoda can be climbed for a good view of this beautiful, wooded area.

The **Xiaoling Mausoleum (Ming Tomb)** 明陵 is open daily; tel. 642990. This mausoleum of the first Ming emperor, Zhu Yuanzhang, and his empress (1398 and 1382 respectively) is not as impressive as those north of Beijing, but is worth a visit. The Sacred Way has over a dozen well-proportioned, larger-than-life-size mythical animals, four generals, and four ministers. The stone statues are beautiful. Most of the buildings were destroyed in the early days of the Qing, who overthrew the Ming dynasty, but visitors can get an idea of its past glory from the ruins. The mausoleum is 6 km from the Jinling Hotel.

Zhu Yuanzhang was an unemployed peasant and former Buddhist monk and beggar who fought his way to the throne and was a brilliant emperor.

The **Botanical Garden** 植物园 , with tropical and subtropical plants, is on one side of the Sacred Way.

Zijinshan (Purple Gold Mountain), a.k.a. Bell Mountain 紫金山 dominates the northeastern skyline. The **Observatory** (tel. 642270) is on the west side and can be combined with a visit to Xuanwu Lake. This major research center of the Chinese Academy of Science was built in 1934 and is involved with space research such as manmade satellites. Tourists usually go there for the magnificent view of the city and surrounding countryside and to see the copies of ancient instruments outside.

The armillary sphere (four dragons and spheres) was invented 2000 years ago in the Western Han and was used to locate constellations. The abridged armillary sphere (three dragons) was invented in the Yuan for the same purpose. Both these 500-year-old replicas were stolen by the Germans and French respectively in 1900. They were later returned. The gnomon column next to the abridged sphere was invented 3000 years ago and was used to survey the seasons and calculate the days of the year. It faces due south and north. In the large column is a small hole through which the sun shines at noon, casting an oval of light on the gauge below. Because of this instrument, the Chinese decided very early that there were 365¼ days a year.

Xuanwu Lake 玄武湖 is outside Xuanwu Gate, NE of the city (tel. 633154), 5 km from the Jinling Hotel. Twenty-five km in circumference, this lake is now used for recreation and fish farming. 1–2 meters deep, it was originally built in the fifth century, and several emperors have used it to train or review their navies and for private recreation. A black dragon was spotted here in the fifth century, so if you visit it on a dark and stormy night, you might want to look for it. Today there is a famous pick-your-own-live fish restaurant called the White Garden, a zoo, theater, playground, swimming pool, roller-skating area, boats-for-hire kiosk, and exhibition halls. You can walk from the railway station and take a ferry.

Jiangsu Provincial Museum (a.k.a. Nanjing Museum) 江苏省博物馆 (Zhongshan East Rd; tel. 641554. Closed Mondays) contains exhibits ranging from the era of Peking Man to revolutionary times. This traditional Chinese-style building was begun in the 1930s, and completed in 1949. It was opened as a museum in March 1953. Three thousand items are on display. Among these are a 3000-year-old duck egg—genuine; the jade burial suit that was exhibited in America in 1973 (Eastern Han, from Xuzhou City, Jiangsu); a sixth-century Soul Pot covered with many birds, placed in a tomb so the birds could fly the soul of the deceased to paradise; a small bronze model of a stove (Ming) with five woks; maps of the early capitals in Nanjing from 229 to 589, so you can try to locate ancient landmarks in the modern city; a 20-meter scroll showing the inspection tour by Qing Emperor Kangxi (Kang-hsi) from Nanjing to Zhenjiang; the anchor from a British merchant ship lost in Zhenjiang; a photograph of a Britishbuilt electric company in 1882; a list of institutions set up by the United States in China, with numbers of Chinese students and teachers and of foreign teachers. Located 4 km from Jinling Hotel.

The **Gulou (Drum Tower)** 鼓楼 is at the intersection of Zhongshan North, South, and East roads and Zhongyang and Beijing roads, in the center of the city. Built in 1382, it holds a 6-foot-diameter drum and an ancient giant stone tortoise carrying a stele added in the Qing, a report on the inspection tour of Qing Emperor Kangxi. (See *Drum Towers* in ''What to See and Do.'') Nearby is the Big Bell Pavilion.

Nanjing City Wall 南京城墙 is 12 meters high, 33.4 km in circumference, and from 7.62 to 12 meters thick. Built from 1368 to 1387, it once had 13,616 cannons on top. Roughly 10 km north-south by 5.62 km east-west, it is said to be the longest city wall in the world. The bricks were made in five provinces, and each is inscribed with the name of the superintendent and the brickmaster, plus the date made. The mortar was lime, tung oil, and glutinous rice water. It was originally built with 13 gates, and 11 more were added. Cannot be missed.

The **Zhonghua Gate** 中华门 , on the south side, is the best gate to see. It has four two-story gates in succession (in case the enemy breaks through one), 12 tunnels, and room to garrison 3000 soldiers. One can walk along the top of the wall here.

Jiu Hua Hill (Monk Tang Pagoda) was originally built in the Song, about 1000 years ago, to keep the skull of Xuanzang (Hsuan-tsang), the monk who traveled to India in search of the Buddhist sutras and was immortalized in the novel *Pilgrimage to the Western World*.

The skull of Xuan Zhuang was buried in the southern part of the city, and was moved to Jiu Hua in 1962.

If you have more time or specialized interests:

Inside the city wall: **Qingliang Shan Park** was a lovely gathering place for painters and writers of old, on a hill overlooking the northern part of Nanjing near the university. It is on the main road to the Yangtze River Bridge. Among the writers was the author of the Nanjing-based classic novel *The Scholars*. A crematorium used to be in the area, and as a result few Chinese come here. It is a good place to get away from crowds.

The **Confucius Temple (Fuzimiao),** adjacent shopping center, and free market, are major tourist attractions, featuring Ming and Qing architecture and worth a visit. The Temple was originally built in 1034 A.D. as a place of sacrifice. Wars destroyed it many times and the current building is a post-Liberation reproduction. Birds, fish and clothes sales.

Zhanyuan Garden (Garden for Viewing) 瞻园 (Zhanyuan Rd.) is in the southern part of the city, near the Zhonghua Gate. Open daily; tel. 625262. A good classical Chinese garden, given as a gift to a general of the Ming army.

Originally built in the Ming dynasty, 600 years ago, the palace that now houses the **Taiping Museum** 太平天国历史博物馆 was rebuilt for Yang Xiuqing (Yang Hsin-ching), eastern prince of the Taiping Heavenly Kingdom in the mid-19th century (tel. 623024). It now contains 1000 square meters of exhibits reflecting the: (1) background of the revolution; (2) uprising at Jintian village; (3) Nanjing as capital; (4) regulations and policies; (5) insistence on armed struggle; (6) resisting aggression; (7) safeguarding the capital; (8) continuing the revolution. Prominent inside is a plaque ''in memory of the organizer and leader of the Ever Victorious Army, erected by Frederick Ward Post, American Legion, May 27, 1923.'' Frederick Ward was an American mercenary who fought against the Taiping and died in 1862.

Another relic of the Taipings well worth seeing is the **Tianwang Mansion (The Heavenly King's Mansion)** (292 Changjiang Rd. in the eastern part of the city). Open daily; tel. 641131. The palace was made for Hong Xiuquan (Hung Hsiu-chuan), the head of the Taipings, with materials from the Ming palace. After the 1911 Revolution, the Tianwang Mansion was used as the Presidential Residence.

The Ming Palace 明宫遗址 : These ruins are in the eastern part of Nanjing and can be seen in about five minutes. Built for the first Ming emperor from 1368 to 1386, this palace was copied in Beijing for the Ming palace there. The Forbidden City is about the same size. The palace was partially destroyed in 1645 by Qing troops, and what was left was pulled down to build the Taiping palaces. In 1911 only a gate was left standing, but in 1958 some of the relics were restored. From these you can get an idea of the original. A museum of the Ming palace is being built across from the ruins and should be ready in 1990.

Meiyuan Xincun (Plum Blossom Villa) 梅园新村 : No. 30. Open daily, except Mondays; tel. 644743. Furniture, office, clothing, and photographs are as they were when Premier Chou En-lai headed the Communist delegation in its negotiations with the Nationalists (1946–47).

Shitoucheng (Stone City) of the Wu Dynasty (north of the Hanzhong Gate, inside the western edge of the city wall) is open daily. After the Wu capital was moved here from Zhenjiang, this city, almost 2000 years old, was started by General Sun Chuan on what was then the banks of the Changjiang River. The deep red rock in the area is natural.

An appointment is needed to visit the **Chaotian (Worshiping Heaven) Palace** (east of Mochou Lake, inside the city wall at Yeshan (Smelting) Hill). Permission can be obtained from Nanjing Municipal Museum; tel. 641983. It is said that Fu Chai (Fu Tsai), king of Wu in mid-fifth century B.C. (see also ''Suzhou''), created a special town for making steel swords here. In this city in A.D. 318, a prime minister of the Jin was urged by a geomancer to move the town because the energy emanating from the fire and metal was making the prime minister sick. Wang Dao moved the smelter and used the site as a garden. The smelter was put at its current site, SE of the Stone City.

The first emperor of the Ming dynasty had no such problems with fire and metal, and built a palace at Yeshan Hill for receiving homage from his subjects. In the 19th century, the palace was converted to a Confucian temple, currently the largest Confucian temple complex south of the Yangtze, and the home of the **Nanjing Municipal Museum**南京市博物馆 . (Chongtiangong Jianye. Tel. 641983) Wax figures with costumes from six dynasties should be ready in 1989. Also in the city is a memorial hall to Zheng He, the Moslem eunuch who became one of China's most famous maritime commanders, making seven voyages to 30 countries of Asia and Africa from 1405 to 1433. His tomb is 10 km south of Nanjing. The English Corner is at the foot of Drum Tower Park, every Sunday at 2 p.m.

Dr. Sun Yat-sen's Office in the same compound as Chiang Kai-shek's old headquarters is open to visitors.

Outside the city wall The imposing **Nanjing Yangtze River Bridge** 南京长江大桥 is the second longest in China. Including approaches, it is 4589 meters long, of which 1577 meters are directly over the Changjiang River. The bridge was built in 1960–68 and is 10 km from the Jinling Hotel.

Meiling Palace. About 3 km. outside the Zhongshan Gate. Also for fans of modern Chinese history, this 1930s building was the weekend home of Gen. Chiang Kai-shek and his wife from 1945 to 1949. Church services were held here, sometimes with the American ambassador. The ground floor is now a restaurant.

Yuhuatai (Rain-Flower) People's Revolutionary Martyr's Memorial Park 雨花台烈士陵园 is just south of the Zhonghua Gate, 5 km from the Jinling Hotel. Open daily; tel. 624003. This ancient battleground was later an execution grounds used by the Japanese and warlords. Here the Nationalists killed 100,000 Communists and sympathizers from 1927 to 1949. Now a memorial park with exhibit hall and flower garden, it is known also for its multicolored agate pebbles.

Mochou (Sorrow-Free) Lake Park 莫愁湖 (outside the wall, SW of the city) contains several buildings from the Qing and a small 47-hectare lake. The white marble statue of Mochou is a local landmark. She was the good-hearted wife but submissive daughter-in-law who ended up killing herself, alas, because of her oppressive father-in-law. Open daily; tel. 623243.

Qixia (Lingering Sunset Clouds) Temple 栖霞寺 , 25 km. NE of the city, is open daily, except Mondays; tel. 644470. Originally built in the Qi dynasty (A.D. 479–480) as a monastery. During the Tang, it was one of the four largest temples in China. The years have taken their toll, however, and the buildings were destroyed. The current buildings are from 1908.

Behind the temple is the **Thousand Buddhas Cliff** 千佛岩 , started in A.D. 484 and including three 10.5–11-meter-high Buddhist statues. The carving of these 515 saints ended in A.D. 511 and began again in the Ming. Unfortunately, the heads of the buddhas have been damaged. A finely carved 18.04-meter-high dagoba dates from A.D. 601, with renovations in A.D. 943.

The **Stone Engravings of the Southern Dynasties** 六朝石刻 can be seen any time. Scattered around the suburbs of Nanjing are relics of the Six Dynasties (222–589). Some of the 31 tomb sites (11 emperors and 20 nobles) are in the middle of a field off the main road. Many of the tombs are protected by distinctive pairs of stone mythical animals, pillars, or tablets, symbols of authority and dignity.

The **Southern Tang Tombs** 南唐二陵 are more than 30 km south of the city. Visitors can enter two to see old murals, reliefs, and coffins of the first two emperors of the Tang dynasty, Li Bian and Li Jing, who ruled over 1300 years ago. The tomb of the founder of that glorious dynasty is 21 meters long by 10 meters wide and at least five meters high. The highly decorated coffins of the imperial couple are in the rear under a chart of the stars and planets.

Day trips from Nanjing can be made to Zhenjiang and Yangzhou. Also in the province are Changzhou, Suzhou, Wuxi, Xuzhou, and Yixing. See separate listings. Also promoted is **Huai'an**—Zhou Enlai's birthplace, where there is also a Han pagoda, the Zhen Huai Tower, and a 70-bed hotel. Of note too is **Lianyungang,** on the Yellow Sea, one of the 14 Open Coastal Cities. It has the Ayuwang Pagoda, Water Curtain Cave, a shell carving factory, and a hot spring. The better hotel is the 1987-built **Shenzhou Hotel** with 300 beds.

In **Nantong** the best is the Nantong Hotel, then the Tian Nan and thirdly the Wen Feng. The **Tian Nan Hotel,** at 76 Ren Min R. West, was built in 1987 with 17 stories, 236 rooms. Ren. 1990. IDD, business center, C.C. Dist.A.P.18 km. Dist.R.W.1.5 km. Telex 36537 or 365037 TNHTL CN. Fax (0513) 513519. **C.T.S.** is at 42 Taowu Rd., tel. 519129. Cable 0101.

You can get more information from the Foreign Liaison Office, Jiangsu Travel and Tourism Bureau, especially on bicycling tours, honeymoon and silver or golden anniversary tours, and *taijiquan* lessons.

For background on Nanjing, read Barry Till's *In Search of Old Nanking.*

CULTURAL PERFORMANCES:
The Nanjing Acrobatic Troupe has won international prizes.

SHOPPING
Made in Nanjing are "Yunjin (Figured) Satin" brocade, velvet tapestry and carpets, imitations of ancient wood and ivory carvings, and paper cuts. Made in the province are inlaid lacquer (Yangzhou), purple sand pottery (Yixing), Huishan clay figures, fresh water pearls, silk underwear, and Suzhou embroidery. Store hours: 7 or 7:30 a.m.–7:30 or 8 p.m.; some open 24 hours.

Around the Confucian temple is a lively free market (jeans, fish, birds, back scratchers, etc.) with a good Bao Zi (see "Food") restaurant. On the nearby river, the flower girls used to solicit customers.

Friendship Store 友谊商店 (86 Zhongyang Rd. across from the Jinling; tel. 632802) can package and ship. One of the best in China. 8:30 a.m. to 5:30 (winter); to 6:30 (summer). Lots of shopping also in the **Jinling Hotel** and next door.

Antique Store 古物商店 (5–13 Hanzhong Rd.; tel. 644550); **Sales Department of the Nanjing Handicraft Cooperative** (Zhongshan South Rd.; tel. 642613); **Arts & Crafts Service** 工艺美术服务部 31 Beijing East Rd.; tel. 634193, 634197); **Xinjiekou Department Store** (3 Zhongshan South Rd.; tel. 641300); **Renmin (People's) Market** (79 Zhongshan South Rd.; tel. 642766); **Changjianglu S.&N. China Native Produce Grocery** (west entrance of Changjiang Rd.; tel. 642344) food only; **Overseas Chinese Store** 华侨商店 (86 Zhongyang Rd.; tel. 633883); **Foreign Languages Bookstore** 外文书店 (137 Zhongshan East Rd.; tel. 641887).

RESTAURANTS

Nanjing people say the recipe for Beijing roast duck originally was from Nanjing, so you might want to try the Nanjing version. Among the other local specialties are: salted duck, especially August Sweet-Osmanthus duck, salted duck gizzard, roast chicken with coriander, salted shrimps, casserole cabbage heart, Big Flat Pork Croquette (outside crisp, inside soft), chrysanthemum-shaped herring, long-tailed shrimp and squirrel-like mandarin fish. Restaurants in the top hotels are good.

Maxiangxing Moslem Restaurant 马祥兴菜馆 • *Gulou (Drum Tower), Zhongshan North Rd.; tel. 633807.*

Baiyuan Restaurant • *Liangzhou Isle, Xuanwu Lake; tel. 632903* • Seafood.

Dasanyuan Restaurant 大三元 • *38 Zhongshan Rd.; tel. 641027* • Guangdong.

Sichuan Restaurant 四川饭店 • *171 Taiping South Rd.; tel. 642243, 643651.*

Quyuan Restaurant 奎元菜馆 • *20, Beiting Lane, Zhongshan East Rd.; tel. 641824* • Hunan.

Tongqinglou Restaurant 同庆楼菜馆 • *10 Zhongshan East Rd.; tel. 642880* • Beijing.

Luliuju Vegetarian Restaurant • *Taiping Lu; tel. 643644* • The vegetarian Bao Zi are superb.
For good Western food: the Jinling and Nanjing hotels, especially the first.

HOTELS

The top hotel here is the Jinling, which is also one of the better medium-priced hotels in China. Number 2 are the Nanjing (for its central location) and the Dingshan for its airy, hilltop location and cleanliness. Third is the Sheungmenlou. Reservations essential April to November.

Dingshan Hotel • *90 Cha Ha Er Rd. Cable 6333. Telex 34103 DSHNJ CN. Dist.A.P.16 km. Dist.R.W.7 km.* • 1975. Ren. 1986. If room, will not answer request for reservation. If no room, will answer. Main building. 8 stories. 132 rooms. IDD expected. Business office. C.C.

Bldgs. #5 to 10. Australian-built pre-fab. 220 rooms renovated 1987–88. Budget travelers only this section.

Jinling Hotel • *Xinjiekou Square. Cable 6855. Telex 34110 JLHNJ CN. Fax 643396. Dist.A.P.10 km. Dist.R.W.10 km. 1983. In central commercial district.* • C.C., T.R. Some renovations 1987. Group tour entrance 1988. May renovate rooms 1989. Good maintenance. 37 stories. 818 rooms. 24-hour World Trade Center business center. Gym. Pool. Exhibition hall of Jiangsu products. Revolving restaurant. Lots of shopping.

Nanjing Hotel • *259 North Zhongshan Rd. Cable 6008. Telex 34102 NKHNK CN. Fax in 1988. Dist.A.P.14 km. Dist.R.W.5 km. Dist.Port 5 km.* • Reservations in U.S. at 1–800–221–7982. 1954 ren. 1984. Three buildings 6 and 3 stories. 230 rooms. IDD.

1980-built South Bldg. Smaller rooms. The best now is the Middle Bldg. 1954. Ren. 1984. 206 large rooms with high ceilings. Clean. Has 3 to 5 no-smoking rooms. Planning Japanese j.v. restaurant.

Shuangmenlou Hotel • *135 Huiun Rd. Cable 7175. Telex 34118 SMLNJ CN. Dist.15 km. Dist.R.W.5 km. Dist. Yangtze River Bridge 1/2 km. Near free market.* • 1979. Renovated 1988. T.R. 7 buildings (Nos. 1, 3 and 9 used to be British Embassy). Main building 4 stories. 115 rooms. Small televisions.

IMPORTANT ADDRESSES

C.I.T.S.: 202-1 Zhongshan Bei Rd.; tel. 631782, 639013, 648889. Telex 34024 ITSNJ CN. Fax 631667. Can book all hotels in China.
CAAC 中国民航 : 52 Ruijin Rd. Tel. 649151.
Jiangsu Travel and Tourism Bureau, 259 North Zhongshan Rd. Tel. 685921, 635271; telex 34119. JTTBN CN. Fax 632754. Handles the second highest number of foreign tourists in China. Regulates restaurants, hotels, taxis, stores for foreign visitors, etc.

NANNING 南宁

South China. Capital of Guangxi Zhuang Autonomous Region, in the southwestern part of Guangxi, near the northeastern border of Vietnam. It is on the railway line between Hanoi and Guilin. Can also be reached by air from Guangzhou (1 hour), Guilin (40 minutes), Kunming (1¼ hours) and Beijing. Some tours here have been canceled because of periodic clashes between China and Vietnam. Nanning is on the Yong River. Urban population is 500,000. Nanning has a subtropical climate, meaning great fruit, flowering trees, and mild, humid weather. Hottest—38°C; coldest—5°C. Annual precipitation 1300 mm, mostly May to September. It is worth visiting because of its national minorities, its karst caves, and medicinal herb garden.

Founded in 214 B.C. Nanning was the provincial capital from 1912 to 1936, and after 1949. It has a few industries. In 1988, Guangxi celebrated the 30th anniversary of its founding as an autonomous region.

The **Guangxi Museum** 广西博物馆 (Qiyi Rd.) is open daily, except Mondays and Fridays, 2:30–5:30 p.m. Botanical and zoological specimens, historical relics, and Taiping history. It also boasts the largest collection of bronze drums (over 300) in China. The 126.5-hectare **Nanhu (South Lake) Park** 南湖公园 in the SE has 1200 varieties of medicinal herbs, plus orchids and bonsai. The **Guangxi Botanical Garden of Medicinal Plants** 广西药用植物园 , 8 km from the city in the eastern suburbs, has 2100 kinds on 200 hectares. It also raises animals for medicinal purposes.

The **Yiling cave** 伊岭岩 , 32 km north in Wuming County, is much like a Guilin cave, with colored lights to highlight weird rock formations that here look like lions, a hen, and vegetables. Visitors usually walk 1100 meters. Outside is a pavilion built in the elaborate style of the Dong people.

For those interested in the customs of national minorities, visit a commune of the Zhuang people in Wuming County, and in Nanning, the **Institute of Nationalities** 广西民族学院 or Guangxi Minority Nationality College, 10 km from the Yongzhou Hotel. The **Guangxi Art College** 广西艺术学院 teaches the art, music, and dances of the minorities.

Twelve nationalities live in the region, of which the Zhuang form one third. They are somewhat similar to the people of Thailand. The colorful Miao and Yao live here also. This makes Nanning a good place to look for handicrafts to study and buy.

The Taiping Heavenly Kingdom originated from *Jintian village 272 km NE of the city. This was the most extensive peasant uprising in Chinese history. It started in 1851 and took over a large portion of the country with a capital in Nanjing. Its disruptions were largely responsible for the emigration of Chinese people from south China to America, Australia, and other parts of Asia. At the home of Wei Changhui, one of the leaders, weapons were made and hidden in a nearby trench and pond.

Other public places are the **White Dragon Park** with what looks like a WWII cannon, the **Xijiao (West Suburbs) Park** 西郊公园 (with zoo), and **Lingshui** 灵水 in Wuming County, 46 km north of the city, with its relaxing 23°C lake in a hilly setting. **Guiping Xishan Hill** 桂平西山 , 248 km NE, has a marvelous view of the area.

Newly opened to visitors are the **Mount Hua Rock Paintings** 花山壁昼 along the Ming River, 180 km away. Here one can take a boat trip to see primitive riverside rock paintings. Dances inspired by the paintings can be arranged. One can also pan for gold and visit the Longrui Nature Reserve, the only place in the world inhabited by rare whiteheaded langur monkeys and golden camellias. This is part of the Zhojianghua Shan Tourist Area.

Trips can also be made to hospitals, factories, a kindergarten, local minorities' products center, and a pineapple-growing farm. **Beihai** is Guangxi's sea port, and one of the 14 Open Coastal Cities. In the Dong Autonomous Sanjiang County is the recently restored multi-pagodaed 64-m-long Yongji Bridge in Dong architecture. For other destinations in Guangxi, see also Liuzhou and Guilin under separate listing.

A good time to visit is during the Dragon Boat Festival (5th day of the 5th month), the Zhuang Song Festival (3rd day of the 3rd month), Lantern Festival (15th day of the 1st month), and Mid-Autumn Festival (15th day of the 8th month)—all on the lunar calendar. At the Song Festival, small groups of male and small groups of female singers compete with each other in wit, knowledge, and vocal quality. Then the boys chase the girls they like in order to continue the contest with more privacy. The festival also includes throwing embroidered balls and participating in dragon and buffalo dances. On the Western calendar, it's March 29, 1990.

Other festivals on the Western calendar include:

Song Festival (during Moon Festival). Lingsui Spring in Wuming County. Oct. 3, 1990.

Pan-wang Festival (Yao Nationality). Jingxiu Yao Autonomous Region, Nov. 24, 1988, Nov. 13, 1989, Dec. 1, 1990.

Lu-sheng Festival (Miao Nationality). Rongsui Miao Autonomous Region. Feb. 8, 11, 1990.

Hua-pao (Firecracker) Festival (Dong Nationality). Shanjiang Dong Autonomous Region. March 25, 1990.

Dragon Boat races in Nanning, same dates as rest of China.

SHOPPING

Locally made are Zhuang brocade, bamboo, and pottery ware. The province also makes artistic shell, horn, and feather products, and stone carvings. Also produced are Xishan tea and Milky Spring Wine. Tourists can visit the silk factory. Locally grown are jack fruit, mango, almond, and longan.

Arts and Crafts Service (Xinhua Rd.; tel. 22779); **Bamboo and Wood Handicrafts Store** (Chaoyang Rd.; tel. 25474); **Chaoyang Department Store** (Chaoyang and Xinhua rds.); **Foreign Languages Bookstore** (Minsheng Rd.; tel. 27033); **Friendship Store** (Renmin Rd.; tel. 23480); **Nanning Antique Store** (Guangxi Museum, Gucheng Rd.; tel. 27810).

RESTAURANTS

The food here is much like neighboring Guangdong's: Cantonese. Please avoid eating endangered species.

Bailong Restaurant • *White Dragon Park.*

Fish Restaurant • *Nanhu Park; tel. 22477.*

Snake Restaurant • *Xijiao Park; tel. 26433* • Besides snake, there's also dog and turtle.

HOTELS

C.I.T.S. says the top hotel is the Ming Yuan, then the Xi Yuan, and thirdly the Yongzhou.

Yongzhou Hotel • *Xinmin Rd.* • 860 beds in three buildings: 1957; 1958, and 1980. 32 km from airport.

Xi Yuan Hotel • *Jiang Nan Rd.* • 15 villas built from 1958 to 1985. No. 12 renovated 1984.

Ming Yuan Hotel 明园饭店 • *Xinmin Rd.* • 11 villas built from 1952 to 1985. New building 1985 with over 200 beds.

OTHER IMPORTANT ADDRESSES
Bank of China 中国银行 : tel. 25584, 24247.
CAAC 中国民航 : 64 Chaoyang Rd.; tel. 23333.
C.I.T.S. 中旅社 and **C.T.S.:** 40 Xinmin Rd.; tel. 24793, 22042. Cable 1954. Telex 48142 CITSN CN. Write for list of interesting tour possibilities including forest preserves, Zhuang Nationality traditional medicine, hot sand treatment, and dates of other festivals.
Foreign Affairs Office of the Guangxi Zhuang Autonomous Region 广西壮族自治区外事处 : Minzhu Rd.; tel. 23636.
Hospitals: If convenient, try your guide or hotel attendant first. Otherwise **Guangxi People's Hospital** 广西人民医院 : Taoyuan Rd. (tel. 23237); **Hospital of Guangxi Medical College** 广西医学院附属医院: Taoyuan Rd. (tel. 23014).

NINGBO (NINGPO) 宁波

East China. On the Zhejiang coast south of Shanghai, it can be reached by road from Hangzhou (4 hours), by thrice-weekly plane from Beijing, Guangzhou, Xiamen, and Shanghai (25 minutes), and by daily 11-hour ship from Shanghai (overnight best to save time). A hovercraft from Shanghai can make it in 5½ hours. Ningbo is on the Shanghai-Hangzhou railway line (slow).

A community of 600,000 people, Ningbo is known because some of the world's great ship builders and business people are from this area. It is also noteworthy for the oldest extant library in China and the home of the Goddess of Mercy.

The Ningbo area has been settled at least since 4800 B.C. Archaeologists found evidence of an advanced culture in the village of Hemudu in Yuyao County in 1973, and some scholars now claim the cradle of Chinese civilization was farther east than Henan and not confined to the Yellow River. The 6000–7000-year-old bone flute found in Hemudu is still playable. Inlaid-bone and wood-carving skills were known then.

Ningbo has been recorded since the Spring and Autumn period (700–476 B.C.). It has been a major port since the Tang, trading with Korea, Japan, and Southeast Asia. It was made a treaty port, open to foreign trade and residence, in 1842. After 1860, a French military detachment was stationed here. Ningbo was reopened as a port for foreign trade in 1979 for the first time in 30 years. This icefree port is now one of the 14 Open Coastal Cities.

If you have only one day, see the library, one or two of the temples, and an arts and crafts factory.

The A.D. 1561 (Ming to Qing) *Tianyige Library 天一阁 is ½ km from the Overseas Chinese Hotel in the city. It still has more than 300,000 books. It started as a private library and now has in its more modern extension next door over 80,000 rare books, mostly from the Ming, plus numerous stone tablets. Scholars can see these books upon request. The library is worth visiting for its simple elegance and its peaceful, tastefully designed gardens. This library was the blueprint for the other seven imperial libraries built during the Qing.

At the entrance to the library is a sign that says something like ''This is not an amusement park. No fun inside. Keep out.'' Don't be intimidated by the blunt Ningbo manner. Note also the conversations of the man-in-the-street, which might sound like intense, bitter arguing.

The *Bao Guo Temple 保国寺 , built in 1013 (Northern Song), is the oldest extant wooden structure south of the Yangtze, and is in Yuyao, 20 km north of the Overseas Chinese Hotel. Unlike other temples, which have large beams for support, this one uses many small ones. The Tianfeng Pagoda, built in A.D. 695, was traditionally a place for scholars to gather to compose poems and enjoy the scenery. It is hexagonal, seven stories high, but not as beautiful as younger pagodas.

Both the Tiantong Temples 天童寺 , 35 km from the Overseas Chinese Hotel, and the Ayuwang (King Asoka) Temple 育王寺 , 30 km away, are east of the city. They were founded in the third century. The Tiantong is one of the largest temples south of the Yangtze, with over 700 halls, and some people feel it is more worth seeing than Hangzhou's Lingyin Temple. The Tiantong has sent many teachers to Japan and consequently attracts many Japanese visitors. It is the second holiest shrine of the Zen sect. Zen Buddhist statues are supposed to have deepset eyes looking at their noses as the nose safekeeps one's heart to avoid temptation. See if you can find any. Better still, try crossing your eyes when you feel tempted to sin.

The Ayuwang Temple has relics of Sakyamuni. The famous Buddhist monk Jianzhen (see ''Yangzhou'') once lived here after he failed in his third attempt to reach Japan in the Tang dynasty.

Visitors can also go to an arts and crafts factory (tel. 64617), 4 km from the Overseas Chinese Hotel. Also, the village of **Sanshiliu Wan,** 15 km from Xikou, specializes in *penjing,* the growing and selling of miniature trees.

Putuo Shan 普陀山 is the home of Guanyin (Kuan Yin), the Goddess of Mercy, and is one of the Four Sacred Buddhist Mountains. This 12.5-square-km island is reached by ship from Ningbo, a 4-hour trip offered twice a day. On the way one passes the famous Zhaoshan-Qundao fishing ground with triangular fish nets, a most picturesque view, especially at sunset.

Putuo Shan once had over 200 temples and nunneries, but the years and the Red Guards have done their worst, and only three are now open, the **Puji** 普济寺 , **Fayu** 法雨寺 , and the **Huiji** 慧济寺 **temples.** Those who remember hiking from innumerable nunneries to innumerable temples may be disappointed. No more tiny Buddhist statues inscribed with religious poems to help keep one single-mindedly devout line the narrow mountain paths. But one can still climb thousands of steps and hike through bamboo groves and along the rocky shore and beaches. Enough of the religious atmosphere remains for first-time visitors to enjoy, especially if you avoid the now-paved road, the buses and few taxis and have time for the hospitable and warm-hearted villagers. Many of these villagers now occupy the old temples and rent out rooms to visitors. The vegetables and seafoods they serve are delicious because of the freshness. Just don't expect private baths or running water!

Especially exotic (and noisy) is the **guesthouse** next to the Puji Temple, over a kilometer uphill from the ferry pier, where guests have been awakened early by chanting Buddhists. Rituals at 3 p.m. can also be seen from the upstairs windows. A Japanese j.v. hotel, the Putuo-shan International (200 rooms) is being built. Until it is finished, the Xishan Hotel should be the best. Reservations through C.I.T.S. in Ningbo.

Visitors can also see the kowtowing pilgrims, forehead to ground every three steps, as they pay homage or ask special favors of this favorite deity. Especially touching are the sick and handicapped, carried on the backs of friends or family, who come to pray for healing. Devout Buddhists try to make a trip to Putuo at least once in a lifetime.

It is customary to purchase a yellow sack from one of the temples and, for a fee, have each temple rubber-stamp its seal on the sack to prove you've been there.

Putuo Shan is especially famous because repeated storms kept some Japanese worshipers from carrying away a statue of Guanyin from China. Near a cliff is the "Won't Go Temple," to commemorate the goddess's desire to remain in China. Unfortunately, this spot has become a favorite of would-be suicides, and a sign nearby points out that Buddhism does not approve.

SHOPPING

Made in the area are Mandarin coats, embroidery, bone and wood inlaid articles, bamboo articles, Ming-style furniture, colored clay models, handwoven carpets, blue porcelain, and straw mats.

Sesame seed and glutinous rice balls are served for breakfast. Also try dried longan fruit soup. Both are sweet.

RESTAURANTS

Dong Fu Yuan Restaurant • *5 Zhongshan Rd.. East/Dongmenkou; tel. 32669* • Serves traditional Anhui and Ningbo food.

HOTELS

C.I.T.S. says Asia Garden is best, then Ningbo Hotel, and thirdly the Overseas Chinese Hotel.

Ningbo Asia Garden Hotel • *72 Mayuan Rd. Telex 37020 AGHZJ CN. Cable 3234. Fax 66888 X120, 62138. Dist.A.P.5 km. Dist.R.W.1 km.* • 1987. 10 stories, 180 rooms. C.C., IDD, business center. H.K.J.V.

Ningbo Hotel 宁波饭店 • *65 Mayuan Rd. Dist.A.P.5 km Dist.R.W.1.5 km* • 1982; renovated 1987. Six stories. About 200 rooms.

Overseas Chinese Hotel 华侨饭店 • *130 Liuting St. Telex 37001 NPHCM CN. Cable 3579. Dist.A.P.11 km, Dist.R.W.7/10 km* • 1962; renovated 1989. 5 stories, 132 rooms. Hong Kong J.V. IDD, C.C., business center.

C.I.T.S., 65 Mayuan Rd., tel. 68690, 42391, 42351. Telex 37019 NBHOT CN. Cable 2231. Fax (0574) 68690.
C.T.S., 139 Liuding Rd.; tel. 61181. Cable 3579. Telex 35085 NPHCM CN.

青島

Z.M·Li

QINGDAO (TSINGTAO)

North China. On a peninsula on the southern coast of Shandong province, 393 km east of the provincial capital Jinan by rail. 2-hour flight south from Beijing or north of Shanghai. An international airport should be opened soon connecting the city with Japan. It is on the Huanghai (Yellow Sea) and can also be reached by ship from Shanghai (26 hours) and Yantai, Guangzhou, and Dalian. The climate is temperate. Highest August average, 25°C; coldest January average, ⁻1.2°C. Annual precipitation, 702.4 mm. Population is 1–1.5 million.

Qingdao is an icefree port and summer resort, famous for its beer and mineral water. It should be put at the end of a hectic, tight schedule in summer.

Starting as a fishing village, Qingdao (pronounced Ching Dow) has been an important trading port since the seventh century. During the Ming, it was fortified against pirates. The Germans seized the area in 1897 in retaliation for the assassination of two German missionaries. Here they built a naval base and trading port, and protected them with at least 2000 men. The large number of Germans accounted for most of its architecture and its beer recipe.

In 1919, the Versailles Peace Conference confirmed Japan's 1915 seizing of the German territories in Shandong, including Qingdao. The Japanese stayed long enough to build huge cotton mills before they were forced to withdraw in 1937. During this period, the British built cigarette factories. The Japanese navy regained the city early in 1938, but not before a Chinese mob smashed the breweries, sending rivers of beer into the streets!

Qingdao's breweries were rebuilt, of course, and still produce the most popular Tsingtao Beer. Qingdao also bottles Laoshan mineral water from the mountains behind the city. Full of hills and trees and red-tiled roofs, the city is very pretty.

Qingdao is now the largest city and industrial center in Shandong. Its factories make diesel locomotives, automobiles, TV sets, textiles, and cameras. Its oceanic research institute is internationally famous. Huangdao District, on the west coast of Jiaozhou Bay, is the site of the new economic and technical development zone. Qingdao is one of the 14 Open Coastal Cities.

All of Qingdao's urban attractions can be covered in a day. A second day or two is needed for Laoshan Mountain if you enjoy hiking in exotic settings and want to see it all. Qingdao's 4 km of city beaches slope gently into the sea and are protected by four large bays east from **The Pier** 栈桥 (1891). The 440-meter pier is a good place to see the sunrise, and its Huilan Pavilion is Qingdao's most famous landmark. Southeast of the Pier and linked with the shore by a 700-meter-long dyke is **Xiaoqingdao (Little Qingdao Island)** 小青岛 . This rocky island, with the tall, white lighthouse flashing red at night, will be developed for tourists, having been used by the military for many years.

Each **public beach** has marked swimming areas protected with shark nets, lifeguards, and medical stations. There are changing facilities and freshwater showers. The largest and best of the six city beaches is the **No. 1 Huiquan (Pearl Spring) Beach** 汇泉第一海水浴场 . Be prepared to share any city beach with 100,000 other people in summer. They are open from early July to the end of September.

Two new beaches have been opened in the suburbs. **Xuejiadao** 薛家岛海滩 , SW across the mouth of the harbor, also has fishing, golf, and tennis. **Shilaoren** 石老人海滩 is 5 km east and should be less crowded.

Zhongshan Park 中山公园 is best seen when its 700 cherry trees bloom in April. It also has osmanthus, roses, and peonies. A Seaside Lantern Festival is held here in July and August. Open daily, from 5:30 a.m. to 5:30 p.m. in summer, 8 a.m.–4:30 p.m. in winter.

Luxun Park 鲁迅公园 , with its many hilly paths, rocky hills, and old pine trees, has an excellent view of No. 1 beach, Xiaoqingdao, and the European buildings. The castlelike Museum of Marine Products is in this park. A good view can also be had from **Xiaoyu Shan (Little**

Fish Hill) 小鱼山 , a tastefully designed park with a recent three-story pavilion, and three large ceramic screens showing the eight Taoist ferries crossing the sea, Pu Songlin's Universe, and the logo of Xiaoyu Shan respectively. Qingdao's nine other major peaks are being developed similarly.

The **Qingdao Museum of Marine Products** 青岛水族馆 (tel. 84949) consists of a marine aquarium and an exhibition hall of specimens. The aquarium has 40 tanks with live marine animals, and an outdoor pond for seals. No seals could be seen in the mid-1980s, however. The badly designed exhibition hall has over 900 specimens and poor lighting.

If you can rent or borrow a bicycle, ride through the **Badaguan** area 八达关 , where the streets are named after the eight passes of the 'Great Wall and each street is lined with a different kind of blossoming tree: cherry, peach, or crape myrtle. Behind the streets are individually designed houses with spacious gardens, each one-of-a-kind with interesting features. You can walk through this bit of old Europe. Some of these houses can be rented by the month with cooks and housekeepers. One of the most famous is at 18 Huanghai Road. Built in 1903 in the shape of a castle, with large blocks of granite, it was originally a hunting lodge for the German governor and later used by Chiang Kai-shek as his summer resort. Protected by Qingdao as a historical monument, it is not open to the public yet, but ask about it.

The **Laoshan Mountains** 崂山 are roughly 40 km east of the city and can be reached by land or sea. The boat trip gives an excellent view of the city, but until a pier is built passengers have to be transported to shore by small motorboat. This could be a frightening experience in rough seas.

You may have to choose one of three routes to tour Laoshan. On the South Route you cover the upper and lower Taiqing temples, Longtan Water Fall, and Dragon Well Falls. The North Route covers Shuilienbi (Water Fall Screen), Camel Head Rock, Fishscale Gorge, and Tsaoying Water Fall. The East Route covers Lion Peak (to see the sunrise), Fairy Bridge, Yuelong Cave, and Sheep Rock. A leisurely three-day trip would be ideal.

Do not expect large temples. Many of the temples here are Taoist, with small buildings, small doorways, and small courtyards. The mystical Taoists apparently didn't want to be distracted in their meditative search for eternal peace, their communion with nature.

Laoshan is famous for the masculine shape of its mountains and its rushing waterfalls. It is full of legends. The highest peak, Mt. Laoding, is 1333 meters above sea level. The mountains extend over 386 square km and are full of granite canyons, grotesque crags, old temples, rivers, streams, and the Laoshan reservoir. The **Taiping (Great Peace) Taoist**

Temple 太平宫 was founded in the Song. The biggest **Taiqing Taoist Temple** 太清宫 has over 150 buildings.

The **home of Qing writer Pu Songling** (1640–1715) 蒲松龄旧址 is open to the public. He lived in a very modest corner of the Taiping Temple. Pu wrote his famous *Strange Tales from a Lonely Studio* here. The trees he described are still standing.

An inscription about the visit of the first Qin emperor in 219 B.C. is also on the mountain. The builder of the Xi'an ceramic army searched for pills of immortality in this area.

Qingdao also has the **Qingdao Museum** 青岛博物馆 (Daxue Rd.; tel. 83762) open daily, except Mondays, 8:30 a.m.–5:30 p.m. in summer; 8:30 a.m.–4:30 p.m. in winter. The **Jimo Hot Spring** 即墨温泉 is 75 km NE, with water 90°C tempered to 38°C, said to be good for rheumatoid arthritis.

Other cities easily reached by train or ship are Weifang, Yantai, Weihai, Zibo, and Jinan. See separate listings.

SHOPPING

Shops are along Zhongshan 中山路 and Jiaozhou 胶州路 roads. Made locally are beautiful shell pictures, feather pictures, carpets, weaving, embroidery, and knitting. The shell products and embroidery are especially good buys. One of the largest free markets in China is on **Jimo St.** with clothes, handicrafts and bicycles for sale.

Friendship Store 友谊商店 (Xinjiang Rd.; tel. 27021, 27778); **Qingdao Antique Store** 青岛文物商店 (40 Zhongshan Rd.; tel. 84436); **Qingdao Arts and Crafts Shop** 工艺美术商店 (40 Zhongshan Rd.; tel. 25116); **Qingdao Department Store** 百货公司 (Zhongshan Rd.; tel. 24916).

RESTAURANTS

Seafood, of course! Abalone and prawns. Lots of sea cucumbers and scallops too.

Chunhelou Restaurant 春和楼餐厅 • *Zhongshan Rd.; tel. 227371.*

Qingdao Restaurant 八达关宾馆 • *Qufu Rd.; tel. 283771, 26747.*

HOTELS

The top hotel is the Huiquan, then the Badaguan and thirdly the Huanghai. The new Hai Tian should be open the end of 1988 and become number one. Reservations suggested all year round.

Badaguan Guesthouse 青岛餐厅 • *19 Shan Hai Guan Rd. 266071. Telex 32137 BDGHL CN. Fax 336920. Dist.A.P.35 km. Dist.R.W.4 km. Near beach* • 1949. Became hotel in 1977. 18 villas. 1987 Five-story main building. 237 rooms. Indoor pool, C.C., business center, IDD.

Hai Tian Hotel • Zhanshanda St. Joint venture. 1988.

Huanghai Hotel 黄海饭店 • *75 Yan'an I Rd. Telex 32151 BOOTH CN. Cable 4225. Fax 279795. Near beach* • 21 stories. Foreign tourists on the top floors.

Huaqiao (Overseas Chinese) Hotel 华侨饭店 • *Hunan Rd. Dist.A.P.11 km. Dist.R.W.⁷/10 km* • 1963; ren. 1986, 1989. 5 stories, 132 rooms. C.C., IDD, business center, bicycles.

Huiquan Guesthouse 汇泉宾馆 • *9 Nanhai Rd. Telex 32272 BOOTH CN* • 11 stories, 340 beds. Recreation hall, coffee shop, three restaurants serving Chinese and Western food.
   A Canadian J.V. is expected to open in 1991.

OTHER IMPORTANT ADDRESSES

Bank of China 中国银行 : Zhongshan Rd. Tel. 270648. Currency can be exchanged at some of the major hotels and stores above.
CAAC 中国民航 : 29 Zhongshan Rd.; tel. 283057.
C.I.T.S. 国际旅行社 : 9 Nanhai Rd. (tel. 279215) or Service Center, Huiquan Hotel (tel. 270830, 270691. Telex 32202 QCITS CN).
C.T.S. 中旅社 : 72 Hunan Rd.; tel. 362021. Cable 2464.
Hospitals: If ill, you might find it more convenient to ask at your hotel for help. Failing that, try the **Qingdao People's Hospital** 青岛人民医院 (Dexian Rd.; tel. 26722) or the **Qingdao Municipal Hospital** 青岛市立医院 (Jiaozhou Rd.; tel. 26433, 24133).
Passenger Quay 客运码头 : Xinjiang Rd.; tel. 228002.
Railway Station 火车站 : Tai'an Rd.; tel. 284934.

QINHUANGDAO 秦皇岛

(Chinwangtao) North China, northeastern tip of Hebei province on the Bohai Sea; probably China's second busiest harbor. It is icefree and is the port for a nearby oil field to which it is joined by a pipeline. The closest airport is at Shanhaiguan, 15 km away, with flights from Shanghai, Beijing, Guangzhou, and maybe Xi'an. It should soon be 4.5 hours by train from Beijing.

Originally a small village, Qinhuangdao was opened as a seaport in 1898 and became a base for foreign (especially British) shipping. In 1902 the British army also built a small pier. In 1904, contract workers from nearby East Mountain were recruited for South Africa. The railway was built in 1916. The current population is about 450,000. It is one of the 14 Open Coastal Cities, and includes Beidahe. The aquatic events of the 1990 Asian Games will be held here.

The city is named after a legend. The Qin emperor is believed to have passed through here about 2200 years ago looking for pills of longevity. Suddenly he recognized a special tree described by his teacher. Surprised and afraid, he bowed to the tree and a branch bowed back.

Dong Shan (East Mountain) 东山 is where the Qin emperor searched for the pills and boarded his ships. There's a good view of the sea and the sunrise from here. Walk along the waterfront at night. A cruise boat goes to a fishing village at the mouth of the Xin Kai River and sometimes visitors can see the teams of fishing boats going out together, dragging the big nets between boats. In the old days, the fishermen used to sing to each other.

One can visit a shell-carving factory, the Sea God Temple, and the Qin Emperor's temple. Swimming beaches are at Dong Shan. Swimming also in the solar-energy swimming pool. For excursions from here, see "Great Wall" and "Beidaihe," the resort about 15 km south, and "Shanhaiguan," close to the place where the Great Wall meets the sea.

SHOPPING

Grown locally are peaches, pears, sea cucumbers, and crabs (biggest in September–October). Made locally are pictures, lamps, ashtrays, etc., of shell. Also manufactured are mirrors, magnifying glasses, painted eggs, painted stones, butterfly and insect specimens, bird feather crafts, and necklaces of red beans (symbol of longing between lovers).

RESTAURANTS

Fresh seafood is a specialty here.

Bohai Chun Fan Dian 渤海春饭店 • *Haiyang Rd.; tel.31826* • Tangshan cooking.

Lao Er Restaurant • *Haiyang Rd.; tel. 31525* • Moslem, Jiao Zi.

Wen Hua Lu Fan Dian 文化路饭店 • *tel. 34602* • Tianjin-style buns.

HOTELS

C.I.T.S. says the best hotel here is the Cindic, but you can stay in nearby Beidaihe at the better Jinshan Hotel.
C.T.S.; 13 Guangming Rd., tel. 31426, 31634.
C.I.T.S.; 41 Gangzhuan Rd., tel. (0335) 35974. Telex 271042 QHCHL CN. Cable 2464.

QUANZHOU 泉州

(Chuangchou) East China, 300 km north of Xiamen in Fujian, this ancient city was considered one of the two largest ports in the world by Marco Polo, who knew it as Zaiton or Citong when it exported silks and porcelain as far away as Africa. In the Song it had a population of 500,000. It declined because maritime trade was forbidden. Today, it is one of the 24 cities protected by the State Council as a historical monument. Its downtown area still has a great deal of slow-paced old China flavor plus charming touches of Moslem architecture. It also has the largest number of bicycle rickshaws I've seen in China (with sideseats) and the largest collection of Nestorian Christian and Manichaeist relics. Weather: the hottest in July has been 32°C. Mild winters (no snow). Precipitation is 1400 mm, from July to September.

If you only have one day, C.I.T.S. recommends the Kaiyuan Temple, East and West Pagoda, Overseas Communication Museum, and Old God Rock in the morning. In the afternoon, the Grand Mosque, Wind-Shaken Rock, Holy Islamic Tombs, and Luoyang Bridge.

The **Kaiyuan Temple** 开元寺 is 1 km NW of the Overseas Chinese Hotel and dates from the Tang. The main hall has 100 heavy stone Greek-type columns. On top of 24 of these are gaudy part women/part birds, whose crowns appear to support the beams. These flying musicians are of gilded clay and are most unusual. Indian figures and Chinese dragons and tigers also decorate the temple. Look also for the 1000-armed, 1000-eyed Guanyin. Note the corners of the roof, the curled swallow tails, and the lively dragons that are distinctive aspects of Southern Fujian temple architecture.

Two large pagodas, the trademarks of the city, are on the temple grounds. These are the **East and West Pagodas** 东西塔 . The 48-meter-high **Zhenguo Pagoda** is east. Originally built of wood in 865, it was rebuilt of stone in 1238. The west **Renshou Pagoda,** 44 meters high, was originally built in 916 and rebuilt in 1228.

In the Song dynasty, this temple was home to over 1000 monks.

Near this temple is the **Overseas Communication Museum** 海外交通历史博物馆   , with the remains of a 12th- or 13th-century ship, 24.2 meters long and 9.15 meters wide, found in 1974 in Quanzhou Bay. The museum also outlines Chinese maritime and local Arab history. Religious relics are here in a separate building (with some descriptions in English). Many are tombstones with crosses, one of a Franciscan. Some Moslem tombstones are beside the main gate. Ask for archaeologist Yang Qinzhang.

Old God Rock 老君岩 is 4 km from the city. This stone statue of Laotze/Laotzu, the founder of Taoism, is beautiful. 600 years old, he is about 5 meters high and grandfatherly, with a long beard.

At one time, 10,000 foreigners from Persia, Syria, and Southeast Asia lived in the southern part of the city. Most of them were Moslem. The ***Qingjing (Grand Mosque)** 清净寺 (Tushan St., ½ km from the O.C. Hotel), open daily, was built by local Moslems in 1009. One of the earliest mosques in China, it was copied from a mosque in Damascus and was renovated in 1310. It is one of the few mosques in eastern China with west Asian architecture, but unfortunately much of it is in ruins. But it is lovingly maintained. Arabic writing and west Asian arches point to its former glory. Inside is a small museum with text in English pointing out such events as Moslems fighting alongside Zheng Chenggong (Koxinga) and the continuing observance of customs like Ramadan, weddings officiated by an imam, and abstinence from eating pork. Three thousand Moslems still live on Tushan Street.

The **Islamic Tombs** 圣墓 are on Ling Shan Hill, outside the East Gate, 4 km from the city. They are protected by a Chinese-style pavilion. They could belong to two trader-missionaries who arrived in the city during the Tang. Koxinga prayed here before his fifth voyage to Southeast Asia. If you can read Arabic, you can learn about their lives from their tombstones. Otherwise, these are not all that interesting unless you think of those romantic-sounding times—Cathay, Marco Polo, pirates, and giant Chinese junks sailing to Mozambique.

A few steps away is the 50-ton **Wind-shaking Rock** 风动石 , an elephant-sized boulder that anybody can wobble. Honest!

In the neighborhood of the Luoyang Bridge is a stone-carving factory that makes Japanese lanterns, balustrades, temple pagodas, and photograph-like pictures. The stone columns of Chairman Mao's mausoleum in Beijing were cut here.

If you have more time, **Wanshan Peak** has some rare Manicheist relics. This religion, brought to China in the seventh century from Persia, is a combination of Zoroastrianism, Christianity, and paganism. At one time, St. Augustine was an adherent. On a stone tablet near the site of the monastery are inscribed the activities of the cult during the Song. Behind the ruins is a circular Manichean statue of a man.

Outside the south gate of Quanzhou about 4 km is the **Caoan Temple,** the only Manichean temple left in China. There used to be temples in Xi'an and Luoyang as well, but the religion was persecuted in A.D. 843 and its leaders fled to Quanzhou. From here it spread along the east coast.

The **Heavenly Princess Palace** 天妃宫 and **Confucian Temple** are ½ km from the hotel. One hour by car from the city at the shore is the 1162-built five-story octagonal stone **Tower of the Two Sisters-in-law** 姑嫂塔 . The 21-meter-high structure was originally built as a navigational aid, but its name symbolizes the loneliness of the women left behind by the sailors and emigrating Chinese workmen. The 161-acre **Overseas Chinese University** 华侨大学 is in the mountains east of the city. Its students are drawn from Southeast Asia, Hong Kong, and Macao.

The **Tomb of Zheng Chenggong (Koxinga)** 郑成功墓 is at Nan'an, about 25 km NW of Quanzhou. He was a pirate who allied himself with the defeated Ming forces in the mid-1600s, fighting the Manchus. With his fleet of 800 warships, this national hero successfully rid Taiwan of the Dutch.

SHOPPING

Embroidered blouses at the Friendship Store. Life-like artificial flowers. Also locally produced are stone carvings, woven bamboo, Dehua porcelain, Anxi Guanyin tea.

HOTELS

The two main downtown hotels are adequate and are neighbors. The Overseas Chinese Hotel should now be renovated and looking better than the Golden Fountain. A new hotel is being built at the northern edge of the city.

Golden Fountain Hotel   金泉酒店 • *Baiyuan Qingchipan. Cable 8888. Fax 24388.* • 1965, ren. 1985. Lobby dark. Bit scruffy.

Overseas Chinese Building 中国旅行社 • *Baiyuan Qingchipan.* • 1951, ren. 1989. 12 stories, 221 rooms. C.C., IDD, limited hot running water.

C.I.T.S. 中国国防旅行社 and **C.T.S.** 中国旅行 : Overseas Chinese Building, Baiyuan Rd.; tel. 22192; cable 5132.

QUFU 曲阜

(Chufu) North China. Southwestern Shandong province about 100 km south of Jinan. No airport. Reached by train to Yanzhou on the Beijing-Shanghai line and then by road for 18 km. It can also be reached by road from Jinan. It was believed that a railway would disturb Confucius' grave and its *feng shui*. Population: 40,000.

Two days are minimal for this small, charming city, one day for the ''three Kongs'' (mansion, temple and forest), and one day for the tomb of Mencius, the birthplace cave of Confucius, and the Temple of Shao Hao. This is a good place for bicycling as it is relatively flat and has many interesting things to explore. At least a week for adventurous bicyclists.

The old city is centered around the Confucian monuments; the new city surrounds the old one.

The hometown and grave of Kong Fuzi (Master Kong), known to the west as Confucius, is one of the places to visit if you want to be immersed in old China. Take your time. Stay overnight in the family mansion (if you don't mind the plumbing). Meditate in these beautiful, exotic surroundings. Read the *Analects of Confucius*. The discipline he advocates might be just what your hectic life lacks. Go back to the 17th century.

Confucius lived from 551 to 479 B.C. during the Spring and Autumn Period, a time of small warring kingdoms and political chaos. He was an itinerant teacher who preached that stability could be achieved by a return to the classics and the old Zhou dynasty rituals. He defined and promoted an already existing system of interpersonal relationships with its emphasis on responsibility and obedience.

His teachings were much like the rules of polite society anywhere: The virtuous or benevolent man does not lose his temper; the virtuous man thinks ill of people who criticize others in their absence, who talk badly of other people to make themselves look better, or who persist in promoting deceptions they know are false.

Confucius's virtuous man also did not concern himself with insignificant things, material gain, fame, or ambition. He was moderate in all things.

Confucius's ideas on government were far from democratic. People who do not hold office in a state should not discuss its policies, he said. He advocated that subjects be unquestionably subordinated to rulers, sons to fathers, younger brothers to older brothers, wives to husbands, younger friend to older friend. He was male chauvinism incarnate.

His philosophy was the official ideology in China for over 2000 years, promoted because it supported the oligarchical power structure. Filial piety was essential to the system, and its enforcement was supported by the state. If a child failed to care for his aged parents or was rude to them, the authorities would punish the child. Children owed their lives to their ancestors. They were obligated to respect and worship these people.

The philosophy deteriorated into a religion where descendents performed rituals to keep ancestral spirits happy, so the dead would influence the fortunes of the living.

Much Confucian influence is still felt in 20th-century Asia. One finds elements of his theories still stifling Chinese people everywhere. Confucius was behind the famous civil service system, which was based on the memorization of the classics and his analects. The imperial examinations and the arrogant, insular thinking did, however, outlive their usefulness. These stunted the development of modern China and were largely responsible for its poor defense against the 19th- and 20th-century imperialists. The civil service examination system was abolished in the early 1900s, and Confucius is now being studied dispassionately again.

In some family temples, food is still shared with ancestors, heads bowed and incense burned in worship especially during the Qing Ming Festival in spring, and the autumn equinox. And vestiges of the traditions surrounding the cult remain to this day, in spite of governmental discouragement—arranged marriages, marriages between two deceased people, or between one living and one deceased person, etc. This is not, however, as common as it was before Liberation. Rote memory is still the basis of much education, but hopefully this is changing today.

Confucius was born in Nishan, 35 km. southeast from his temple. He moved with his mother to Qufu after the death of his father, when he was three. His father was a general of the State of Lu. Qufu then was already old. It was the capital of a minor kingdom during the Shang (14th–11 century B.C.). The city is named "Winding City Wall" after the old wall built 3000 years ago. The current wall is Ming.

One fifth of the people in the city are descendents of the philosopher, and those in a direct line have been receiving state pensions for centuries (with no need to earn their living otherwise). Currently living are the 73th–76th generations.

The Confucian monuments have been repaired and are now opened to tourists. They are in one part of the city and can be seen in a day.

The *Confucian Temple 孔庙 , occupying more than 20 hectares (about 50 acres), is the most important one in China and the largest in the world. First built in A.D. 478, it was rebuilt and enlarged to its present size during the Ming and Qing. Its gold-tiled roofs, its arches, red doors, and carved tile dragons are Ming. The two stone soldiers/generals over two meters tall near the gate are from the Han Dynasty (917–971). They once guarded a noble's tomb in another part of the city. Live egrets and cranes nest in the gardens here.

The **Dacheng Hall** is the main hall for paying homage to Confucius. Only the emperor could be carried over the carved tile dragons up to its door. The hall is over 31 meters tall and 54 meters wide, with the same general appearance of some of the buildings in Beijing's Forbidden City which was copied from this temple. Important are the ten carved stone columns, two dragons and a pearl on each, slithering between clouds and a pearl. Note the set of ritual bronze bells, which are played on ceremonial occasions. (See also *Provincial Museum*, "Wuhan.")

The **Life of the Sage Exhibition Hall** contains 120 hard-to-see pictures of the life of Confucius carved in the Ming. A picture book of his life should be available at the Friendship Store.

The *Kong Family Mansion 孔府 , has nine courtyards, over 400 rooms, and a garden, on 14 hectares. The gate in front is Ming. The Main Hall, Second Hall, and Third Hall were offices of the duke of Yansheng, the 46th generation grandson who was made a noble by Emperor Renzong of the Song. These offices, with his desk under a yellow canopy and painted beamed ceiling, give authenticity to opera stage sets of the period. Ancient weapons, banners, and drums line the walls. The mansion was started in 1038.

Gifts to the family from emperors and high-ranking visitors include

Zhou and Shang dynasty bronzes. Visitors would do well to read *In the Mansion of Confucius' Descendants* by Kong Demao and Ke Lan before arriving. From it you can get a feel for the human drama that took place here. Kong Demao, who is still living, was the daughter of the second wife of the Duke of Yansheng, her mother believed poisoned by the first wife. Her tale of being confined behind these walls is pathetic, but she was also party to great events as well as family misfortunes. Some photographs of the family are on display. The current Duke of Yansheng is said to be living in California.

The **Confucian Forest,** 200,000 family tombs, reputedly the oldest and largest cemetary in the world. The trees were collected by disciples from all over the country. It is about 3 x 4 km. and has over 30,000 trees. Elaborately crafted gates, stone lions, and a stone-arched bridge punctuate the lovely greenness. Tall stone nobles and animals guard the gate to the ***Tomb of Confucius** 孔林 , a tumulus marked with stone tablets and fancy incense burners.

A small brick house, **Zi Gong's Hut,** stands nearby, originally built by one of the master's disciples, who lived in it for six years after Confucius's death, to show respect. **Lady Yu's Arch** was named after a daughter of Qing Emperor Qianlong, who was married to the then duke of Yansheng. The title was hereditary.

Also in Qufu is a Sacred Way with stone animals and steles, the Temple of Yan Hui, the Temple of the Duke of Zhou, and the remains of the former capital of the State of Lu.

The tomb of Shao Hao, one of the five legendary rulers, is about 8 km. away. The Temple of Mencius, the later disciple who spread the teachings of Confucius to the rest of China, is 27 km. south of the city. Here is also a small museum, a temple to the mother of Mencius, and a hall for the wife of Mencius.

SHOPPING

Locally produced are wood carvings, stone rubbings, carpets and Nishan inkstones.

The Antique Store in the Mansion (tel. 757) sells beautiful carved wooden beds and can ship them. A souvenir market is between the Queli Hotel and the Confucius Temple, and a market in Ming architecture is one block to the left as you leave the Queli Hotel. A small Friendship Store is on the same street as the Mansion.

HOTELS

The best hotel is the charming Queli which has Western food. The Kong Family Mansion is said to have the best Confucian food, but we didn't think it was any different from the Queli's.

Both the Kong Family Mansion and the Queli are within walking distance of the Mansion and the Temple in the old city, and 10 minutes by pedicab from the Forest.

The medium-priced **Apricot Terrace Hotel** should be open now in the new city.

Kong Family Mansion Hotel. ● *On the grounds of the Kong Family Mansion but with a separate entrance.* ● First built 1038 A.D., repaired and partially air-conditioned in 1986. One story with courtyards, and traditional Chinese architecture. 70 rooms, better at the back than the front. Some two-room suites. Busy season June to Sept. No Western food. Can be reached through back door of Queli.

Queli Hotel ● *1 Queli St. Cable 5287. Telex 39105 BTHQF CN. Almost adjacent to the Temple of Confucius.* ● 1986. Exquisite Chinese architecture with courtyards and ponds. Two stories. 164 rooms. Striking murals and sculptures. Good furniture. Concerts of classical Chinese music if enough interested guests. Video of Confucian ceremonies on request. Business Center.

Confucius Foundation, a research institute, is located in the Kong Family Mansion.

C.I.T.S. and **C.T.S.** 国际旅行社 : 374 Donghuamen Ave. Tel. 491.

上海

Z.M.Li

SHANGHAI (ABOVE THE SEA)

East China, on the north bank of the Huangpu River, 28 km from the (Changjiang) Yangtze River, on the east coast of China due west of the southern tip of Japan. Bordering on Jiangsu and Zhejiang provinces, it is about a 2-hour flight NE of Guangzhou and Hong Kong, and SE of Beijing. It is linked by air with Hong Kong, Japan, the United States and Singapore, and by sea with Hong Kong and Kobe. From Shanghai are many land, river, and air services to other parts of China. Train to Hangzhou 3 to 4 hours; to Suzhou 1 hour. Sharing about the same latitude as Jacksonville, Florida, Shanghai's hottest temperature is 35°C in July–August; its coldest is ⁻5°C in January–February. Most rain arrives in June. Population: 12 million, of whom seven million are in urban Shanghai.

This municipality, directly under the control of the central government, started out 5000 years ago as a tiny fishing village. It became a port in the 17th century. In 1840 its population was 500,000. In 1842 it was captured by the British, and although the Chinese paid a $300,000 ransom to keep it from being sacked, British soldiers and Chinese thieves looted it severely. The Treaty of Nanking of that year opened Shanghai to foreign trade and settlement. This led to its partition into British, French, and, later, Japanese concessions, which is still reflected in its downtown architecture. The British concession eventually became the

International Concession, and all continued until the 1940s. Each of the concessions had its own tax system, police, courts, buses, and electrical wattage. A criminal could escape justice just by going from one concession to another.

Shanghai thrived as a port, trading principally in silk, tea, and opium. Most of the foreign trade was British and one fifth of all the opium reached China in fast American ships.

From 1853 to 1855, the walled section of Shanghai was seized by the Small Sword Society, a Cantonese-Fukinese secret society that wanted to restore the Ming dynasty and prohibit opium. It was helped in its struggle by some foreign seamen, but many other foreigners helped the Manchus regain the city. In 1860, the Taiping Heavenly Kingdom tried unsuccessfully to take Shanghai. In 1915 students and workers demonstrated here against the Twenty-One Demands of Japan. And in July 1921, the first Congress of the Communist Party of China was held here secretly.

In 1925, a worker striking for higher wages was killed at a Japanese factory. This led to a demonstration by workers and students in the International Settlement, during which the British police killed several demonstrators. A rash of nationwide anti-imperialist protests followed. In April 1927, Chiang Kai-shek ordered a massacre of the Communists here, and Chou En-lai barely escaped with his life. This period was the setting of Andre Malraux's famous novel *Man's Fate*.

In 1932, Shanghai resisted a Japanese attack for two months and made a truce. China appealed to the League of Nations and the United States, who did little to help. Japan attacked again in August 1937. The Nationalists fought back for three months before retreating to Nanjing and later to Chongqing. The American movie *Empire of the Sun* is set in this period and parts were shot in Shanghai. The Japanese stayed until 1945. In May 1949, the Communists took the city. During the Cultural Revolution, it was the scene of many intense political struggles, especially in January 1966.

Shanghai is now one of the 14 Open Coastal Cities, especially chosen for intensive economic development.

Shanghai's cosmopolitan heritage is still reflected in its architecture and in the relative sophistication of many of its citizens. Its fashions and standards of products and services are more international than other Chinese cities, a result of its longer, more concentrated period of dealing with fussy foreigners. Its shopping is the best in the country.

Shanghai is one of the biggest ports and the largest city in China. Cruise ships dock almost at the foot of Nanjing Road. It is also still an important trading city and one of the biggest industrial cities. Among its products are trucks and cars, bicycles, television sets, cameras, textiles, watches, electronics, and ships. Its scientific institutions conduct research into lasers, atomic energy, satellite technology, and computers.

As an agricultural area, it is highly developed. Its rural counties are among the richest in the country, completely supplying the city. It grows two crops of rice and one of wheat each year.

Roughly, Shanghai's streets running east-west are named after cities and those running north-south after provinces. Its natives speak a dialect unlike that of Beijing and more akin to that of Hangzhou and Suzhou—only faster.

Not everybody likes Shanghai. It is a big, very crowded city that smells more of trade, commerce, and industry than ancient Chinese culture. The population density is 41,000 per square km, the highest in China. Its ancient relics are mainly outside the city. But it is exciting because its unique history is still reflected in its foreign buildings: the grandeur of the Bank of China lobby, the Greek columns of the customs house, the hybrid flavor of Sun Yat-sen's home. Do a lot of walking through this museum of 19th-century European and Japanese architecture. Look into the lobbies of the buildings along the Bund: Smile at the guard innocently and say "Just looking."

Shanghai is pleasant because the people are outgoing and lively. They are less reserved than those in Beijing. Making friends is easier here. Every Sunday morning in Renmin Park there is an English-speaking corner. Someone is sure to approach you to practice English. Shanghainese have been known for centuries for their quick wit, business talents, and efficiency.

Five days in Shanghai is sufficient to cover the important sights for you, but you have to make choices as there is enough for more. The following is a suggested itinerary.

Day 1: In the morning, the Yuyuan Garden, Huangpu Park, and a walk along the Bund, with lunch at the Peace Hotel; the Municipal Museum and the Arts and Crafts Research Institute in the afternoon.

Day 2: The Jade Buddha Temple, with vegetarian lunch, Children's Palace, any of the modern history sites, and/or a workers' residential district.

On either of these days, you could substitute or try to squeeze in shopping, the zoo, a boat trip, an arts and crafts factory, the Shanghai Industrial Exhibition Hall, People's Square, and the tomb of Soong Qingling. If you want to swim, try one of the clubs.

Day 3: The Botanical Gardens, Longhua Pagoda, Square Pagoda, and Zuibai Ci Pond. Take a picnic lunch with you if you want.

Day 4: Grand View Garden (*Dream of the Red Chamber*). Restaurants there.

Day 5: Jiading County and the Confucian Temple museum, Wuyi Garden (lunch), and Qiuxiapu.

On these last three days, you could also try to squeeze in a production brigade or other rural enterprise. In the evening, try to see the Shanghai Acrobats or Shanghai Kunqu Opera (more melodic and graceful than Beijing Opera). Because tickets for the acrobats are booked by tour groups, individual travelers could try to book tickets through an agency or wait hopefully at the door and approach a tour guide who might have extras.

Huangpu Park 黄浦公园 is the oldest and smallest park in the city (Zhongshan Dong-1 Rd., across the bridge from Shanghai Mansions). Opened in 1868 by the British, next to the Suzhou and Huangpu rivers, this once displayed the infamous sign "No Dogs and Chinese Allowed." Now open from 5 a.m. to 10 p.m., even for foreign tourists.

*Yu Yuan Garden** 豫园 (Yu Yuan Rd.; tel. 260830, 283251) is in the old Chinese part of Shanghai. Open 9–11:30; 1:30–5:30. I can't decide whether or not to recommend it if you are also going to see the gardens of Suzhou. It depends on how much time you have and how much you like gardens. This one is pretty good, but it is crowded. It was originally laid out between 1559 and 1577 by a financial official from Sichuan and now covers 20,000 square meters. About 100 years ago, a part was sold to merchants, and that is now the 98-shop **Yu Yuan Market,** once the busiest in the city. Here you can buy dressmaking patterns (six sizes in one pattern) and novelties, and watch *Jiao Zi* and other Chinese dumplings and pastries being made. The large new Old Shanghai Restaurant (at the parking lot) is famous. Some visitors have found the market fascinating. The area was the old Chinese district and the houses are pretty much the way they used to be.

From 1853 to 1854, the Yu Garden was used as the headquarters of the Small Sword Society, which staged an armed uprising and held part of Shanghai for 18 months. The pavilion opposite the exquisite stage is now a mini-museum.

Other points of interest: the top of Rockery Hill, which is an artificial mountain made with rocks carried from Jiangxi province. Until it was dwarfed by Shanghai's skyscrapers, this was the highest point in the city from which you could see and hear the Huangpu River nearby. The five dragon walls wind concentrically around the garden. Look for their heads. Note the unusually shaped doors, some like vases, and, of course, the lovely moon gate. Look for the **Pavilion to See the Reflection of the Water on the Opposite Side** (these names are really something!) and don't trip over the step-over doorways. The south side of the garden was for women; aristocratic women were usually kept out of sight of all but family members. Snack bar and antique store. (See also *Chinese Gardens* in "What Is There to Do and See?")

Shanghai does have an excellent museum: the **Shanghai Munici-**

pal Museum 上海市博物馆 (Henan Nan Rd.; tel. 280160). Open daily, 9 a.m. to 3:30 p.m. Closed holidays. Opened 1952. Includes (on the ground floor) a demonstration of how the Shang bronzes were cast and what they looked like new (did you really think they drank out of those yucky green things?); a knife for beheading; a model of a 2000-year-old tomb, with skeletons of slaves buried alive so they could serve the departed master in the other world; a water vat used for refrigeration; 2000-year-old gilding on bronze; giant Ka drums. A revealing picture of ancient life can be seen on a bronze cowrie shell (money) container decorated with tigers climbing up the sides, a slave being bound for sacrifice, pigs being slaughtered, and two dead cows. On the second floor, a demonstration of how pottery was made from wicker baskets; an A.D. 618 polo game, three-color Tang camels, and other tomb pieces. A well-designed display of ancient and contemporary porcelain arranged according to regional kilns helps the viewer understand the differences in clay, patterns, glazes, etc., of the various types. The collection of stone sculptures here is not as good as the one at New York's Metropolitan Museum.

On the third floor are murals of *fat* Tang ladies (fat was very fashionable then!); a horizontal scroll of life in 11th-century Kaifeng—look for the bride being carried in the sedan chair; and a collection of ancient calligraphy and paintings including a painting done by fingernail.

Shanghai Arts and Handicrafts Research Institute 上海工艺美术研究所 (79 Fen Yang Rd.) is more interesting than most factories of the same nature because top artisans develop new crafts here, such as wool and silk embroidery, wood carving, ivory, jade, ink stones, kites, porcelain and bamboo carving, lacquer, silk flowers, and colored lanterns. Paper cutting and dough figure making have been demonstrated. Under its wing are over 40 factories.

While the work of the institute is fascinating, its French-style mansion is rather spectacular, too, especially with its two white marble staircases leading to the main entrance. The front lawn with its willow-lined ponds is well maintained. Does the building look familiar? From *Gone with the Wind*, maybe? A retail store next to the main building has reasonable prices. No appointment necessary.

Jade Buddha Temple 玉佛寺 (170 Anyuan Rd., Puto District; tel. 535745, or 538805) is open daily, 8 a.m.–5 p.m., but closed for lunch. A good introduction to Buddhist temples, but nearby Suzhou has better and older ones.

The Jade Buddha Temple was founded in 1882 in the southern outskirts of Shanghai. The temple was bodily moved to Shanghai in 1918 and now occupies about two acres in the western part of the city.

Many monks live in this temple, and you will probably hear them singing or reading the scriptures. At your request and donation, monks will chant prayers for the well-being of your soul, or recite from Buddhist scriptures to enrich the spirits of deceased friends.

In the first hall, a 2.6-meter-high, gold-faced Wei Tuo, the military protector of the Buddhist scriptures, menacingly greets visitors. On each side are two temple guardians about five meters high: the Eastern King, with a mandolinlike instrument, using music to defend and praise Buddha; the Southern King, with his dark, angry face, and sword; the Northern King, with a Chinese parasol; and the Western King, who "looks after the whole world with penetrating eyes and carries a snake which is actually a net to catch converts." Behind Wei Tuo is a 1.6-meter-high Laughing Buddha.

In the courtyard the incense burner made of iron and bronze, cast in 1922, is inscribed with the names of donors and honored deceased relatives. The three largest figures inside the next parallel building are Sakyamuni (center), to his right the Amitaba Buddha (with lotus), and the Yuese Buddha, carrying the Buddhist wheel of law. Along the sides are the 20 guardians of heaven. Guanyin is centered behind the three main Buddhas. Note the very thin Sakyamuni, above, paying homage, and the 18 arhats.

On the second floor of the building, with the Jade Buddha, one changes into slippers. The seated Buddha, 1.9 meters high and carved from one piece of white jade in Burma, was brought to China in 1882. The shelves on both sides of the room contain 7240 volumes of Buddhist scriptures, printed in the Qing 200 years ago. They are similar to the book under the glass.

In another building is a Reclining Buddha, also of white jade, depicting Sakyamuni breathing his last. In the temple complex, too, are a retail store of religious relics. A small museum contains ancient relics. A good vegetarian restaurant, small antique store, and a newly founded Buddhist Academy with 100 students are also in this temple. See also *Buddhist Temples* in "What Is There to See and Do?"

Many group tours include a visit to a **Children's Palace.** These are after-school programs for 7–16-year-olds, much like community centers. Specially chosen children get extra opportunities to learn and practice art, sciences, music, sports, etc. Some of the 23 palaces in the city are in old mansions built by wealthy capitalists. A visit to one will not only give you a chance to learn something of the education of children but also to explore the buildings themselves.

Best set up for tourists is the Children's Palace at 64 Yan'an Road, tel. 581850 (open Tuesday and Saturday afternoons after school hours for visitors but not all summer).

Children's Palaces were a project of Soong Ching-ling, the widow of Dr. Sun Yat-sen. Money is being solicited internationally for the Soong Ching-ling Foundation to continue and expand this work with children.

Modern Chinese history sites offer an opportunity to see the inside of some of those European houses. In addition, you can experience important facets of recent history. My favorite is the **former residence of Dr. Sun Yat-sen** (7 Xiangshan Rd., tel. 372954). It is in the old French Concession, a large house by today's Chinese standards. Not open daily.

Once inside, you find that you have stepped back into the 1920s. The house was bought by Chinese-Canadians for the father of republican China for 16,000 pieces of silver. He lived here with his wife intermittently from 1920 to 1924, just before his death of cancer in 1925. His widow, Soong Ching-ling, lived in the house until 1937, when the war forced her to move to Chongqing. In October 1949 Madame Sun gave the building to the state. It was opened to the public in 1952.

Here, in 1924, Dr. Sun met Communist leader Li Dazhao (Li Tachao) publicly for the first time to work out Nationalist-Communist cooperation. Dr. Sun was much influenced by Marx and Lenin.

Besides the antiques, there are some old photographs, a 1920 China train map, Sun's medical instruments, clothes, and glasses. The railway map is significant because Dr. Sun was in charge of railways for a short time after he resigned as president. The house contains his library: a 1911 *Encyclopedia Britannica,* biographies of Bismarck, Cicero, Lincoln, and Napoleon in English, books in Japanese, and ancient works in Chinese. Because this is a shrine, no photos are allowed. (See also ''Nanjing'' for more about Dr. Sun.)

Museum and Tomb of Lu Xun (Lu Hsun) 鲁迅纪念馆和鲁迅墓 (Hongkou Park; tel. 661181): museum open daily, except Sundays, 8:30 a.m.–4 p.m., except for lunch, and Tuesday and Thursday mornings. Tomb building opens daily, 8 a.m.–7 p.m. These are quite close to each other in the northern part of the city. Lu Xun (1881–1936) was an author of short stories who wrote in the colloquial language about poor people, impoverished literati, and oppressed women. Chinese literature until then had primarily been about the wealthy elite, written in a snobbish literary style, too difficult for the masses to grasp. Although he was not a Communist, Lu Xun is considered a national hero. He died of tuberculosis in Shanghai.

The site of the First National Congress of the Communist Party of China 中国共产党第一次全国代表大会会址 (76 Xingye Rd.; tel. 281177, 285494) was the living room of a small rented house in the former French Concession. There, 12 representatives of the Party from all over China, including Mao Zedong, met secretly for four days starting on July 1, 1921. On July 5, after a stranger burst into the room ''looking for a friend,'' the suspicious delegates immediately left the house. Ten minutes later, the French police arrived, while the delegates went on to Jia Xing county, 98 km west, to complete their work in a rented boat on Nan Hu (lake).

The Congress adopted the first constitution and proclaimed the founding date of the Party. After Liberation, the house was restored to its modest 1921 condition.

Residence of Chou En-lai 周恩来故居 (73 Sinan Rd., tel. 371775) was the Shanghai agency of the Communist Party in 1946 when efforts were being made at peace talks with the Nationalists.

Another relic from a previous era and still in use is the **Shanghai Industrial Exhibition Hall** 上海工业展览馆 (1000 Yan'an Zhong Rd.; tel. 563037). Open daily, except Mondays, 8:30 a.m.–5 p.m., except for lunch breaks. Over 58,000 square meters of floor space with a display area of 20,000. Completed in 1955, with Soviet help, in the massive Soviet style, for trade exhibitions. Large handicraft stores with folk arts and upmarket jewelry.

The **Shanghai Zoo** 上海动物园 (Hongqiao Rd.; tel. 329775) is open daily, 7 a.m.–5 p.m. One of the better zoos in China. 70 hectares, 280 species. Pandas, rare Chinese birds, and Yangtze crocodiles.

If you wish to pay your respects to a very distinguished humanitarian and revolutionist, visit the beautiful white statue and **Tomb of Song Qingling (Soong Ching-ling)** 宋庆龄墓 in Wang Guo (International) Cemetery 万国公墓 (21 Lingyuan Rd.; Changning District near Hongqiao Rd.; tel. 329034). The widow of the founder of republican China died in May 1981. Her parents, and the maid who served her for 52 years, are buried nearby. Do read *The Soong Dynasty*.

Soong Ching-ling was the sister of Mme. Chiang Kai-shek. She eloped with the already married Sun Yat-sen and was virtually disowned by her wealthy Christian father, up to that point a strong supporter of Dr. Sun. She was tolerated by her family and her powerful in-laws, although she was outspoken in her opposition to their exploitation of China. She was, after all, the widow of the widely respected father of the country. She chose to remain in China after Liberation, and worked to promote the welfare of the Chinese people.

The **Huangpu River boat trip** 黄浦江游船 is booked from the wharf near Huangpu Park at the foot of Beijing East Road. Tel. 231662, 211720. This 3½-hour, 60-km trip is usually offered as an option for prepaid tourists for additional payment and is available to individual travelers. It sails to the Changjiang (Yangtze) River at Wusong Kou, and back at 8:30 a.m. and 1:15 p.m. daily, with a 1½-hour night cruise at 7 p.m. during the summer. Important if you want to relax and see sailing junks and ships from all over the world on a muddy river with industries along its shores. On the return trip, however, are a magician and acrobatic show.

Renmin (People's) Square 人民广场 : 467 by 100 meters, 1951. Used for parades, ceremonial occasions, people-watching, and ball-playing. Also has a daily free market with flowers, *penjing* (miniature landscapes) and goldfish of many varieties. Open 7 a.m.–5 p.m.

The **Botanical Gardens** 植物园 (Longhua Rd.; tel. 389413) is in the southern suburbs. Open daily, 8:30 a.m.–4:30 p.m. 70 hectares, 1954. Specializes in rock gardens and potted miniature trees, some several hundred years old.

Longhua Pagoda and Temple 龙华塔，寺 (tel. 389997) is in the southern suburbs and can be combined with the Botanical Gardens and Song Jiang County for a one-day trip. It is a noted scenic spot, the park formerly an execution grounds. The date of the temple's original construction is controversial. Some sources say A.D. 247, some 687, and others 977. It was rebuilt several times, the latest in the early 1980s. It is considered the oldest temple in Shanghai district. Note the fine brick carvings on its walls. It has a small museum.

The brick and wood Song dynasty pagoda stands about 40 meters high, with seven stories. Festival days have attracted 50,000 visitors.

Shanghai has China's first **Museum of Aviation.**

OUTSIDE OF SHANGHAI

Songjiang County 松江 has a history of 2500 years. It is about 40 km SW of the city and usually takes a full day to see. The rare **Square Pagoda** 方塔 in the Xingsheng Monastery (Sangong St., Songjiang) is 48.5 meters high. It was first erected in 1086–94 in the basic Song-dynasty style, with the tetragonal shape of the Tang. It still has some original brick and wooden brackets. During renovations in the late 1970s two Song murals of Buddha were uncovered, and from the pagoda's base, Song and Tang coins, bronze buddhas, and animal skeletons—offerings to atone for the sins of the deceased wife, probably of a nobleman. Its nine stories lean slightly seaward to compensate for prevailing winds.

The screen in front is the oldest brick carving in the area, erected in 1370 to keep evil spirits out of the Temple of the City Gods, which no longer exists. Very well preserved, the mythical animal on it is a *tuan,* greedily eating everything in sight. Note money in mouth. Other ancient relics have been assembled here from different parts of the county.

Also in Songjiang County is the **Zuibai Ci (Pond for Enjoying Bai's Drunkenness) Garden** 醉白池 , outside the West Gate of Songjiang town. First built in 1652 and expanded in 1958. The lotus flowers in the pond are said to date from the 17th century. Highlights include a stone engraving of 91 leading Songjiang citizens from the Ming and early Qing and a small museum. This can be skipped if your time is short, as can the oldest relic in Shanghai, the **Tang stone pillar** 唐朝石柱 (A.D. 859). This 9.3-meter-tall carving, with some Buddhist inscriptions and carvings, just barely visible, is currently in the playground of the Zhongshan Primary School and subject to the carelessness of children at play. Songjiang is also noted for its fine embroidery and Moslem hats.

If you have an extra day, consider **Jiading County** 嘉定. It is 45 km NW of Shanghai and linked by a new superhighway. This should give you some time to also drop in at some prosperous production brigades along the way. At Nanxiang is the 6-hectare **Gu-Yi Garden,** tel. 661246 where you can sample the famous steamed Nanxiang meat buns. First built in 1566 and renovated in 1746, it has two stone pillars inside over 1000 years old. The highly recommended **Qiuxiapu** is a 450-year-old classical garden, once belonging to a Ming officer. It gives *yin-yang* contrasts of stillness and liveliness, reality and dream, with 20 scenic spots in a small space.

The **Confucius Temple** 孔子庙 (Nan Da St., Chenxiangzhen, tel. 952604) is one of the largest in South China. A major part of it is an interesting museum of local history, with maps showing how people migrated, an old fishing boat, and famous stone tablets relating to important events from the Ming. The temple itself was founded in 1219 and enlarged in the Yuan and Ming. Imperial examinations for government administrators used to be held there.

Another full day's excursion is to **Dingshan Lake,** tel. 228228 X6071. 65 km north of Shanghai. The county itself dates from the Song and has many cultural relics, as well as a goldfish breeding farm and a pearl cultivation farm. Over 100 hectares of former farmland have been developed into a huge recreation complex with kite-flying contests in spring, boat rides, 4000 plum trees (mostly for mid-March blossoms, not fruit), 6 hectares of autumn-blossoming osmanthus trees, fishing and swimming areas, restaurants, hotels, vacation village, convalescent homes, and theme park. All the buildings are in traditional southern Chinese architecture. If you look closely at the 47-meter-high pagoda here, you might discern that it is really a water tower. You can still climb five of its seven stories, the top two holding the water.

The prime reason to go to the Dingshan Lake Scenic Area is to see the 11-hectare **Daguanyuan (Grand View Garden),** Shanghai's version of the setting of the popular Qing novel *The Dream of the Red Chamber*. Even if you haven't read this 1886-page novel, a visit is well worthwhile just to see this beautiful complex of pavilions, very tastefully decorated, some with genuine antique and/or real mahogany furniture. Each room is related to a scene from the tragic love story: the sickly heroine Lin Tai-yu's bedroom with medicine bottles, her harp, and her basket for burying flowers; spoiled, rich, but sensitive young hero Pao-yu's stunningly exquisite Happy Red Court, his books left in boxes because he didn't like to read; the Grand View Chamber, the living quarters for a visit home of the daughter who became an imperial concubine.

Reading this novel, with its many plots and subplots, will certainly give you a good picture of aristocratic life a couple of hundred years

A scene from *Dream of the Red Chamber.*

ago and help you appreciate the great effort made here to be as authentic as possible. See also *Dream of the Red Chamber* under "What is There to See and Do?"

On the way back to Shanghai, you may want to visit **Zhujiajiao,** an obscure old village of white plaster row houses and narrow slate-paved streets along the ancient canal, where the masses seem to be living still in Red Chamber times. They are as curious about you as you are about them. Also in Songjiang County, high on a hill beside the Academy of Science's Observatory, is a **Roman Catholic cathedral,** looking most impressive but intriguingly and incongruously European.

Two- and three-day **excursions** can be easily made from Shanghai to Hangzhou (about a 6-hour drive), Ningbo, Suzhou (about a 1½-hour drive), and Wuxi on your own, or arranged by C.I.T.S. See Shanghai in less busy seasons, like mid-winter. The least crowded is very charming Ningbo. See separate listings.

Cultural Events: **Shanghai Acrobatic and Magic Troupe** (tel. 564051): magicians, sword-swallowing, sometimes performing pandas, and juggling. Shanghai has high standards of music, art, and drama. It is a good place to sample the cultural life. **Shanghai Art Theatre** (tel. 565544); **Shanghai Concert Hall** (tel. 281714); **Grand Theatre** (tel. 534260); **Beijing Theatre** (tel. 581197); **Cathay Theatre** (tel. 372549); **Renmin (People's) Theatre** (663 Jiujiang Rd.; tel. 224473). There is also the **Shanghai English Drama Troupe.**

Factories: Tourists might be interested in seeing and shopping in factories for jade carving, embroidery, woolen carpets, and tapestries.

SHOPPING

Produced in the city are jade, ivory, and whitewood carvings, lacquerware, needlepoint tapestries, silks, carpets, embroideries, gold and silver jewelry (especially filigree), artificial flowers, painted eggs, reproductions of antique bronzes, and cheap jogging suits. Big department and book stores along Nanjing Road between the Peace and the Park Hotels, and along Huaihai Road. Antique and jewelry prices here are generally the best in China.

Tailors are again available, but they take about two weeks to make anything and are not aware of the latest Western fashions.

Shanghai Friendship Store 上海友谊商店 , one of the largest in China is east of the Peace Hotel at 40 Beijing Rd. East. Tel. 234600. Open 9 a.m. to at least 9 p.m. Purchases can be crated and shipped. This store is on the grounds of the former British Consulate.

Selling antiques are the **Friendship Store (Antique and Curio Branch)** 友谊商店古玩部 (694 Nanjing Xi Rd.; tel. 534437) and the **Shanghai Antique Store** 上海古玩商店 (194–226 Guangdong Rd.; tel. 232144, 212864. Good reproductions).

Largest free market is at Shi Luo Pu. Be sure to haggle.

Shanghai Arts and Crafts Store 上海工艺美术商店 (190–208 Nanjing Xi Rd.; tel. 276530).

Duoyunxuan (422 Nanjing Dong Rd.; tel. 223410) is a highly specialized Chinese painting supplies store, where one can have scrolls mounted and buy top paintings and calligraphy.

The Overseas Chinese Store 华侨商店 (627 Nanjing Dong Rd.; tel. 225424) is also a travel agency with tickets to cultural performances.

Caitongde Drugstore (320 Nanjing Dong Rd.; tel. 221160): traditional Chinese medicines; **Beijing Chinese Pharmacy** (760 Nanjing Dong Rd.; tel. 222393); **Shanghai Jewelry and Jadeware Store** 上海珠宝玉器店 438 Nanjing Dong Rd.); **Shanghai Arts and Crafts Trade Fair** 上海工艺美术交易所 (1000 Yan'an Zhong Rd. 8:30 to 6 p.m. tel. 533918, 563037, 533781); **139 Longmen Rd.** (between Xizang and Huaihai Rd.) is a tiny shop selling a small selection of good quality silk at half price. Check for flaws.

See also Yu Yuan Market, above, for more proletarian souvenirs like folding scissors, chopsticks, wigs, fans, and crafts, and local snacks.

Foreign Languages Book Stores 外文书店 (390 Fuzhou Rd.; tel. 224109, 223200) will mail books; **Shanghai #1 Department Store** 上海第一百货公司 (830 Nanjing Dong Rd.; tel. 223344): city's largest; **Shanghai #10 Department Store** 上海第十百货公司 (635 Nanjing Dong Rd.; tel. 224466) second largest; **Shanghai Silk Shop** (592 Nanjing Dong Rd.; tel. 224830) has silk from Shanghai, Jiangsu, Zhejiang, and other provinces.

Guan Long, on Nanjing Rd. near Jiangxi Rd. two blocks west of the Peace Hotel should be able to fix some broken cameras.

GETTING AROUND

Buses are incredibly crowded and the subway won't be finished for a while yet. Regular taxis have been very difficult to get in Shanghai, and people have to fight for them on the streets. Until more taxis are available, we strongly advise you to book taxis early at hotels and if you have more than one stop, have the taxi wait for you. The cost of waiting time is usually worth it. You may also have to share taxis with other passengers, and it seems each group of passengers pays the fare from the point of departure. Shanghai also has mini-buses, and tiny Fiat taxis. Any complaints should be addressed to Shanghai Tourism Corporation and to the taxi company.

The first stage of the 14.4 km. subway will go from the railway station to Caohejin. Seven lines are planned to reach a total of 176 km.

Shanghai floods when it rains, so give yourself extra time to get around then, such as an extra hour to get to the airport from downtown.

RESTAURANTS

Shanghai food is sweeter, lighter, and prettier than other Chinese foods, with a delicate consistency. Every big hotel should be able to lay on a great banquet here. The hotel restaurants we've heard recommended are the 12th floor of the Jin Jiang for Sichuan, the Sheraton for both Chinese and Western food, the Peace Hotel 8th floor, Hilton, Nikko, and the Floating Restaurant in the Xi Jiao. I like the Chinese food at the Shanghai, the Jing An, and the Park. Budget travelers get a good view and good food at the Seagull's 2nd floor restaurant. Other restaurants visitors might like:

Dahongyu Restaurant • *556 Fuzhou Rd.; tel. 223176, 223475* • Wuxi food.

Yangzhou Restaurant 扬州饭店 • *308 Nanjing Dong Rd., tel. 222779, 225826.*

De Da Restaurant 德大西菜社 • *Corner Sichuan and Nanjing Rd.; tel. 213810* • Western. Cheaper, but more crowded.

Exhibition Centre • *5th floor* • Cantonese. Hong Kong J.V.

Fang Sang-ting • *Dahua Hotel; tel. 523079* • Qing dynasty imperial food. Waitresses dress in Qing costume. History of dishes outlined.

Shangri-La Restaurant ● *2nd F, Union Bldg. Yanan East Rd., tel. 265230, 265381* ● Reasonably priced Hong Kong standard Western food. Dancing.

Meilongzhen Restaurant ● *1081 Nanjing Xi Rd., Lane 1081, No. 22.* ● Tel. 562718, 551157.

Meixin Restaurant 美心餐厅 ● *314 Shaanxi Nan Rd.; tel. 373991, 377845* ● Cantonese.

Satay House ● *Huashan Rd.; tel. 312211* ● Indonesian.

Sichuan Restaurant 四川饭店 ● *457 Nanjing Dong Rd.; tel. 222246, 222247* ● Sichuan.

Windows on the World ● *Ruijin Bldg. 3rd Floor. 205 Maoming Rd.* ● Tel. 336309.

Xin Ya Restaurant 新雅餐厅 ● *719 Nanjing Dong Rd.; tel. 223636* ● Cantonese.

Yanyunlou Restaurant ● *755 Nanjing Dong Rd.; tel. 223293, 223298* ● Beijing.

HOTELS

With the opening of several new hotels, getting a room downtown is a lot easier if you can afford the top prices. The Sheraton in the outskirts has lowered its prices. No one should arrive here without a confirmed reservation, especially during high season, May–June, Sept.– October.

The top established hotels of luxury quality are the Sheraton, Hilton, and Nikko. New (or about to be opened) in the luxury category are the Garden, Holiday Inn, Hyatt, Jin Jiang Tower, Mandrin, Portman, Westin, and Yangtze. The best of the lovely old hotels (big rooms and high ceilings) from the 1920s are the Peace and Jin Jiang, their services adequate.

The best location for tourists and some business people is the Bund. The Peace is the best here, but Shanghai Mansions and the Seagull (budget only) are all right. Along with the Park and Overseas Chinese Hotels, these are also convenient to Nanjing Road and Friendship Store shopping and C.I.T.S.

The hotel ghettos are:

1) Immediately clustered around the Shanghai Exhibition Center, CAAC, and China Travel Service, (about 5 km from the Bund): the Portman, City, and Mandarin Hotels. These are more for business people

who do not need to see the ''real China.'' Within 2 km of these are the Jin Jiang, Jiang Tower, and Garden. The Hilton, Jing An, and Shanghai are close by. These areas are within walking distance of each other.

2) The Hongqiao Economic area has at least three large hotels (Rainbow, Pacific, and Yangtze), the International Trade Center (due mid-1990), new diplomatic area, international school, and international club. Not as convenient for tourists but less crowded than area 1).

3) the Nikko-Cypress-International Airport Hotels area is within 2 km of the airport. The closest is the Airport Hotel, the best is the Nikko. All have shuttle buses.

If you want to be surrounded by Chinese people rather than other foreigners or office buildings, we suggest you look for isolated hotels like the more modest Jin Sha and Tian Ma, or the fancier Sheraton.

If you're looking for an exquisite hotel, the Nikko does give the impression of intimacy, with good service. Less impersonal than most seem to be the Jin Sha and Tian Ma. For tranquil privacy, there's the Xijiao. For backpackers, we recommend the dorms of the Seagull and the YMCA.

Most hotels here look like clones of American hotels. If you want a feeling of old Shanghai, try the Peace, or the Chinese suites in any hotel.

Cherry Holiday Villa • *77 Hong Gong Rd. Telex 33908 BTHYN CN. Cable SCHV. Dist.A.P.5 km. Dist.R.W.14 km* • Relatively close to Hongqiao Economic area. Set in garden off main road.

Cypress Hotel • *2419 Hongqiao Rd. Cable 9921. Telex 33288 CYH CN. Fax 329323. Set in garden. Dist.A.P.2 km. Dist.R.W.19 km.* • T.R., C.C. 1982, ren. 1988. 160 rooms. CAAC. Book Store, business center, tennis, IDD. Claims biggest recreation center. Clinic, USTV.

Dragon Gate Hotel (Hongmen Bingguan) • *immediately west of railway station at subway stop* • 1989. 25 stories. Aiming for three stars. C.I.T.S.

Garden Hotel (Huayuan Fandian) • *58 Maoming Nan Rd. Fax 338866. Dist.A.P.13 km. Dist.R.W.10 km. On site of old Jinjiang Club* • 1989. 34 stories, 500 rooms. Business center, pool, gym, tennis, IDD. Management by Hotel Okura.

Holiday Inn Yinxing • *338 Panyu Rd.* • Late 1990. 510 rooms. Health club, pool. C.C.

Hua Ting Guest House (Hua Ting Bingguan #2) • *2525 Zhong Shan Xi Rd. Cable 9985. Telex 30192 HTCHS CN. Fax 390322* • T.R.,

C.C. Not to be confused with classier neighbor, the Hua Ting Sheraton. Dist.A.P.10 km. Dist.R.W.10 km. 1987, ren. 1988. 17 stories, 216 rooms. Only Chinese food. IDD,

Hua Ting Sheraton (Hua Ting Bingguan #1) • *1200 Cao Xi Bei Rd. Telex 33589 SHHTH CN. Cable 0703. Fax 550830. Dist.A.P.10 km. Dist.R.W.10 km* • Closer to Hong Qiao Economic area than the Hilton. Walk to park and food market. Across from the biggest sports stadium. T.R., C.C. 1986–87. 28 stories, 1,000 rooms. IDD. Gym, 24-hour business center, pool, tennis, USTV, shuttle bus, bicycles, jogging.

Hyatt Shanghai • *Dist.A.P.22 km. Dist.R.W.4 km. In northern part of the city beyond Lu Xun's tomb. Closest major hotel to Fudan University* • 1990. 26 stories, 420 rooms, part of office complex. T.R., C.C. Two floors of Regency Club. Bistro, business and fitness centers, jogging track, pool, health spa.

Jin Jiang Hotel (Jing Jiang Fan Dian) • *59 Mao Ming Nan Rd. Cable 7777. Telex 33380 GRJJH CN. Fax 582582 X4567. Dist.A.P.13 km. Dist.R.W.5 km* • T.R., C.C. 1929, ren. 1987. 18 stories. four buildings, 730 units. Good shopping, IDD, business center. Offices of Singapore, Northwest, Canadian, and Cathay Pacific airlines. A little grubby.

Jin Jiang Tower (Xin Jin Jiang) • *161 Changle Road, Telex 33380 GRJJH CN. Cable 7777. Fax 582582 X4567. Dist.A.P.14 km. Dist.R.W.2 km* • C.C. 1988–89. 43 stories, 728 rooms. Business center, IDD, health club (gym, pool). Two-level revolving restaurant. Executive floors.

Jing An Guest House (Jing An Bingguan) • *370 Huashan Rd., west wing at 425 Wulumuqi Rd. N. Telex 30022 BTHJA CN. Cable 3304. Fax 552657. Dist.A.P.11 km. Dist.R.W.6 km* • Reserve through C.I.T.S. 1929, ren. 1988. 217 rooms, larger rooms in old section. Business center, IDD, bakery, C.C. Bit rundown and grubby.

Jin Sha Hotel (Jin Sha Jiang Da Jiu Dian) • *801 Jin Sha Jiang Rd. Cable 4650. Telex 33454 BTHJD CN. Dist.A.P. and R.W.5 km. Inconveniently located in northwest part of city in residential area. Close to Changfeng Park, Huadong University, vegetable market, and department store.* • T.R.(collect), C.C. 1987. 12 stories, 300 rooms. Book stall, IDD.

Nikko Longbai Hotel (Re Hong Longbai) • *2451 Hongqiao Rd. Telex 30138 NHISH CN. Fax 593012. Cable NIKKOHTL 9923.*

Dist.R.W.19 km. • 1987. 11 stories, 417 rooms. IDD, business center, Karaoke bar. Tennis, fitness center, pool, clinic. Quiet ambience, plastic bathroom. Good service except for two-day laundry.

Overseas Chinese Hotel (Huaqiao Fandian) • *104 Nanjing Xi Rd. Telex 33909 BTHHF CN. Cable 4321. Fax 269620. Dist.A.P.15 km. Dist.R.W.4 km* • Visa and MasterCard C.C. only. T.R. 1924, ren. 1987. 10 stories, 120 rooms. IDD, small TVs. C.T.S. Bit grubby.

Park Hotel (Guoji Fandian) • *170 Nanjing Xi Rd. Closest to Shanghai Acrobats. Cable 1445. Dist.A.P.15 km. Dist.R.W.4 km. Across from park* • C.C. 1934, ren. 1989. Business center. 24 stories, 200 beds. IDD, Japanese and Hong Kong television reception.

Peace Hotel (Heping Fandian) • *20 Nanjing Dong Rd. Telex 33914 BTHPH CN. Cable 3266. Fax 290300. Dist.A.P.19 km. Dist.R.W.2 km* • C.C. 1929, ren. 1987–89. North Building (with 1920s jazz band in coffee shop) only section recommended. 11 stories, 279 rooms. IDD. Rooms large and good. Walk-in closets.

Portman Hotel • *Shanghai Center, 1376 Nanjing West Rd., on north side of Shanghai Exhibition Center. Telex 33272 CPTCS CN. Fax 332813* • Businesss center, executive floors. IDD, tennis, health club, pool. (Center also has apartments, offices, theater, shopping, helipad.) 1989. 48 stories, 700 rooms. Peninsula Group.

Rainbow Hotel (Hongqiao Bingguan) • *2000 Yanan Xi Rd. Cable 0729. Telex 30330 SRHF CN. Fax 517244. Dist.A.P.7 km. Dist.R.W.10 km. 100 m from International Trade Center* • 1988–89. 31 stories, 661 rooms. C.C. IDD, business center, shuttle bus. Simultaneous translation facilities, gym, pool. Mainly groups. Narrow hallways, fireproof bedspreads and curtains, small bathrooms, hair dryers. Poor workmanship.

Seagull Hotel (Hai Ou Fandian) • *60 Huangpu Rd. Dist.A.P.20 km. Dist.R.W.2 km. Telex 33603 SISC CN. Fax 251500 X128* • T.R. 1985, ren. 1987. 12 stories, 110 rooms. No C.C. for rooms. Modest. Business center has IDD.

Shanghai City Hotel (Cheng Shi Fandian) • *5–7 Shan Xi Rd. South. Telex 30031 SCH CN. Cable 1168. Fax 550211* • 1988–89. C.C., IDD, clinic, business center. Managed by Chains International.

Shanghai Hilton International (Jing An Hilton) • *250 Hua Shan R. Telex 33612 HILTL CN. Fax 553848. Cable HILTELS SHANGHAI*

• 1988. 43 stories, 800 rooms. Business center, health club, IDD, pool, tennis, squash, clinic. Business studios, executive floor.

Shanghai Hotel (Shanghai Bingguan) • *505 Wulumuqi Rd. Telex 33002 BTHSG CN. Reservations 33295 SHR CN. Cable 0244. Fax 331310. Dist.A.P.11 km. Dist.R.W.5 km* • 1983, ren. 1989. 25 stories, 600 rooms. Only Federal C.C. Should have IDD and business center now. C.I.T.S.

Shanghai International Airport Hotel • *2550 Hongqiao Rd. Cable 9918. Fax 518393. Telex 30033 SIAH A CN. Dist.A.P.0.4 km. Dist.R.W.15 km* • 1988. 8 stories, 308 rooms. C.C., CAAC counter, shuttle bus.

Shanghai J.C. Mandarin (Jiang Chang Wen Hua) • *1225 Nanjing West Rd. Dist.A.P.10 km. Dist.R.W.5 km* • C.C. Res. tel. N.Y.(212)838-7874. L.A.(213)627-0185. 1989. 28 stories, 600 rooms. Health club, drug store, clinic, pool, tennis, business center. Mandarin Singapore management.

Shanghai Mansions (Shanghai Da Xia) • *20 North Soochow Rd. Cable 1111. Telex 33007 BTHSM CN, Res. telex 30173 SMH CN. Dist.A.P.18 km, Dist.R.W.5* • T.R. Business center. 1934, ren. 1984. 22 stories, 250 large rooms. Sound-proof windows, C.C., IDD to US but not Canada. Soft beds. Mostly groups.

Tian Ma Hotel (Tian Ma Da Jiu Dian) • *471 Wu Zhong Rd. Telex 30901 BTHTM CN. Cable 89002. Dist.A.P.5 km. Dist.R.W.15 km* • T.R., C.C. Staffed by students of Shanghai Tourism Institute. 1987. 7 stories, 200 rooms. Should have IDD now. Business center. Health club, bowling, gym. Poor reading lamps.

Westin Pacific • *2260 Hongqiao Rd. Fax 332258. Telex 33345. Next to International Trade Center* • 1989. 580 rooms.

Xiqiao Guest House (Xiqiao Bingguan) • *1921 Hong Qiao Rd. Cable 9919. Telex 33004 BTHHQ CN. Fax 336641. Dist.A.P.7 km. Dist.R.W.13 km. 2 km from International Trade Center* • T.R., C.C. 1984. #2 and #3 Villas ren. 1989. 7 buildings of 1 to 3 stories, 150 rooms. Huge beautiful garden. Should now have USTV. IDD. Queen Elizabeth slept in #7 villa (two king-sized beds and his-and-her jacuzzis for US$1,000). Villa #1 built in 1950s (formerly Chairman Mao's); Y4,888. Otherwise, dark hallways, large worn-looking rooms, limited services.

Yangtze New World Hotel (Yangtze Jiang Da Jiu Dian • *2099 Yanan Xi Rd. Fax 518790, 517851. Cable 59960. 50 meters from International Trade Center* • Partial opening 1989. 34 stories, 577 rooms. Business center, Dynasty Club, Pool, health club, vegetarian restaurant. New Worlds Hotels.

YMCA Hotel • *123 Xizang Nan Rd.*

OTHER IMPORTANT ADDRESSES

(Telephone numbers will expand to seven digits in 1989.)

Bank of China 中国银行 : tel. 217466.

CAAC 中国民航 : 789 Yan'an Zhong Rd.; tel. 532255 (international), 535953 (domestic). Also Cypress Jin Jiang, Overseas Chinese, Hua Ting Sheraton, Peace, and Shanghai Hotels, and Ruijin Bldg.

Canadian Airlines International Ltd., #3, Jin Jiang Office Bldg., Room 58239; tel. 376422, 582582, X58239.

Cathay Pacific 国泰航空公司 : Jinjiang Hotel; tel. 336435, 582582 X123.

China Eastern Airlines (see CAAC)

C.I.T.S. 中国国际旅行社 : 33 Zhongshan Rd. E.; tel. 324960, 217200 and 66 Nanjing Rd. E. Cable LUXINGSHE. Telex 33277 SCITS CN. Fax 219305. Tel. for train tickets 217117, 211244 X 278; for plane tickets 211244 X 279; travel arrangements 210032; luggage 232872; in lobby of Shanghai Hotel, tel. 312312 X4141; airport, tel. 329327; railway station, tel. 240319.

Consulate-General of Australia 澳大利亚领事馆 : 17 Fuxing W. Rd., tel. 374580, 334604.

Consulate General of Britain, 244 Yongfu Rd., tel. 374569.

Consulate-General of Canada: 4th Floor, Union Bldg., 100 Yan'an Rd. East, tel. 202822. telex 33608 CANAD CN.

Consulate-General of France 法国领事馆 : 1431 Huaihai Zhong Rd.; tel. 377414.

Consulate General of the Federal Republic of Germany, 181 Yongfu Rd., tel. 379953.

Consulate General of Italy: 121 Wuyi Rd., tel. 524373-4.

Consulate-General of Japan 日本领事馆 : 1517 Huaihai Zhong Rd.; tel. 362073, 372073.

Consulate-General of Poland: 618 Jianguo W. Rd.; tel. 370952.

Consulate-General of the United States 美国领事馆 : 1469 Huaihai Zhong Rd.; tel. 379880, 378511.

A diplomatic enclave is being built on the highway to the airport, and most consulates will probably move there when it is ready.

C.T.S. 中国旅行社 : 104 Nanjing Xi Rd.; tel. 226606, 226226. Telex 30183 CTSIR CHI. Head office: 881 Yanan Rd., tel. 373139, 376490. Telex 33301 COTOS CN. Cable SCTS. Fax 376490.

C.Y.T.S.: 2 Heng Shan Rd.; tel. 330733, 333417. Telex 30241 CYTS CN. Cable 7327. Fax 330507.

Community Church: Hengshan Rd.; tel. 376576.

Duty Free Shop: 881 Yenan Zhong Rd., tel. 378521.

Hong Qiao Airport 虹桥机场 : tel. 537664.

Hospital for Foreigners: Huan Dong Yuen, 221 Yan'an Xi Lu, 6th floor; tel. 563180. Near Shanghai Hotel.

Information: 115.

International Club 国际俱乐部 : 65 Yan'an Xi Lu; tel. 538455. Has an outdoor pool and tennis courts.

International Seamen's Club 国际海员俱乐部 : 33 Zhongshan Dong Ye Rd.; tel. 216149. Regular cultural performances in theater.

Japan Airlines: Room 201, Rui Jin Bldg., 205 Mao Min Nan St.; tel. 336337, 336339.

Northwest Airlines 西北航空公司 : tel. 377387, 582582.

Huangpu River Sightseeing Service Station, Beijing Dong Rd. Wharf; tel. 211098.

Passenger Quay for Hong Kong: Book through C.I.T.S., C.T.S., or China Ocean Shipping Agency, Huangpu Hotel, 255 Jiangxi Rd.; tel. 216327 X79, 455200, and 1, Taiping Rd.; tel. 216327. Leaves 6 times a month from Wai Hong Qiao harbor (at Tai Pin Rd.). 400 berths each, 2½ days each way. Cheaper than flying, depending on class. See "Getting There."

Passenger Quay for Dalian, Qingdao, Ningbo, Chongqing, Wenzhou, and Hankou (Wuhan) 旅客码头往大连，青岛，宁波，重庆，温州，汉口（武汉）.

Passenger Quay for Japan : Shanghai-Kobe ferry. 8500-ton ship; 600 passenger capacity. China Ocean Shipping Agency. See above. Leaves every 7 days. Trip 23 hours to Kobe, 47 hours to Osaka.

Railway Station 火车站 : tel. 242299.

Shanghai Airlines, tel. 582582 X 58421, 587405. Telex 33536 SAL CN or contact Shanghai Crane Travel Service. Flights between Shanghai and Guangzhou and Beijing.

Shanghai Crane Travel Service: 4th Floor, Bldg. 2, Jingjiang Club, 191 Chang Le Rd., Shanshai; tel. 587063, 533527, 582582, X58425; telex 33536 SAL CN. Connections with Shanghai Airlines.

Shanghai Tourism Corporation 上海旅游局 : 2525 Zhongshan Xi Rd. (Hua Ting Guest House); tel. 391869, 391818 X2416. Fax 391519. Cable TOURISM. Telex 33022 TRMCO CN.

Singapore Airlines: Jin Jiang Hotel, tel. 334309, 330517.

Soong Ching Ling Foundation, China Welfare Institute, 157 Changzhu Rd., tel 3768.

Taxi Complaints, tel. 232150.

Tourist Hot Line (for help with problems); tel. 390630, 391818.

United Airlines: tel. 553333.
Specialized Reading (see also "Bibliography")
Barber, Noel. *The Fall of Shanghai.*
Pan Lin, *In Search of Old Shanghai.*
Seagrave, Sterling. *The Soong Dynasty.* Very readable and revealing book about the Soongs, sons-in-law Gen. Chiang Kai-shek and Dr. Sun Yat-sen, son T.V. Soong, reluctant premier and finance minister, and their Soviet, gangster, and wealthy Christian, American, and Chinese friends.

SHANHAIGUAN

North China. Northeastern Hebei province 40 km north of Beidaihe, this small town is one of the places to see the Great Wall. It can be reached by air from Shijiazhuang, Beijing and Guangzhou, and is a three-hour train ride from the capital.

Six km north is the **Meng Jiang-nu Temple,** which was built in memory of another of China's chaste, almost supernatural heroines. Lady Meng traveled on foot during severe winter months in search of her husband, one of the hundreds of thousands of workers building the Great Wall. Her deep sorrow and tears moved Heaven so much that the Great Wall collapsed to reveal her husband's bones.

The temple was originally built in the Song dynasty, but the statues were destroyed during the Cultural Revolution. They were restored in the late 1970s in gaudy, crudely painted clay. But the view of the hills to the north is interesting.

Six km from Shanhaiguan and about 40 km NE of Qinhuangdao is **Yansai Lake,** a.k.a. Shihe Reservoir, at the foot of Yanshan Mountain. Created in 1974, 36 km by 200 meters and 30 meters deep, the lake is formed by a dam (367 km by 60.6 meters) controlling the Shihe River. From the reservoir run 75 km of irrigation ditches, an impressive network along the side of the mountain. A 1-hour boat ride on the lake is breezy and restful. Take a hat if it is sunny.

Laolongtou (Old Dragon Head), the place where the Great Wall meets the sea, is also 4 km south of Shanhaiguan and was recently restored. Chenghai Tower on the seashore was built in 1579, and parts of the wall here are ruins in the sea.

Beijie Restaurant is 200 meters from the Great Wall at Shanhaiguan. Reservations are recommended.

In mid-1990, the **Sheraton Old Dragon Head Resort** should be completed, 100 meters from the beginning of the Great Wall. 300 rooms. Tennis, health club, indoor pool, squash, bowling alley, business center. IDD. Guests will be able to walk or jog along the first 12 km. of the Great Wall.

See also ''Beidaihe,'' ''Qinhuangdao'' and the ''Great Wall.''

SHANTOU 汕头

(a.k.a. Swatow and Chaoshan). South China. Northeastern Guangdong province. This port city and Special Economic Zone is 350 km by air north of Guangzhou, 10 hours by bus. It can also be reached by bus and ship from Hong Kong, ship from Shanghai, and road from Fujian. Flights currently from Hong Kong, Singapore, and Bangkok. Helicopter service from Shenzhen and Zhuhai. Planned air connections with Japan. Shantou is the ancestral home of innumerable Chinese emigrants to South and Southeast Asia, Japan, and Africa. Many Chinese were also kidnapped from here and sent to Cuba in the late 1800s. Today about 15% of the population receives remittances from overseas. With the two municipal areas of Shantou and Chaozhou, and 11 counties, it has a population of about 10 million. The weather is mild, with an annual rainfall of 1400 to 2000 mm, mainly in the summer.

Shantou is famous for its port, which at one time was used by Europeans for the importation of opium to China. The district is also famous for its handicrafts. The Shantou Special Economic Zone is along the east and southeast coast of Shantou on both sides of Shantou harbor.

Among the attractions in **Chaozhou City** 潮州市 are: the **Kaiyuan Temple** 开元寺 , from the Tang dynasty (with its rare set of Buddhist sutras presented by a Qing emperor), **West Lake Park** 西湖 , the **arts and crafts factory,** and the **embroidery factory** 潮绣厂 . Across the **Xiangzi Bridge** is the **Han Wen-gong Temple** 韩祠 .

Chaozhou is a 2000-year-old town to which disgraced officers of the Tang were exiled, notably Yan Hu, who objected to his emperor spending so much money on Buddhist structures. **Ling Shan Temple** (Tang) in Chaoyang County has a record of his dispute with the founder of the temple. Chaozhou is one of the Four Famous Ancient Towns, and still has Tang and Song architecture.

In **Shantou City** 汕头市 , 30 km south of Chaozhou, are: the **Arts and Crafts Exhibition** 工艺展览馆 and **Zhong Shan Park** 中山公园 , with its ''gardens within gardens.'' To the east of Shantou is tiny **Maya Islet** 妈屿海滨浴场 7 km by ferry (2 or 3 times a day) with a temple to Sea Goddess Mazhu and the old British Customs House (now a hostel). Nanho here is the best beach in the area. Across the harbor is the **Jiaoshi Scenic Spot** 岩石风景区 . There are plans to develop Nanho Island with its good beaches, three hours away by boat and near Taiwan's Jinmen (Quemoy).

Chaoyang County 潮阳县 , about 30 km south of Shantou, has two hills with Tang Taoist and Buddhist temples. In addition to the **Ling Shan Temple** 灵山寺 , there is the pagoda of **Wenguang Tower** 葫芦山 and much historical graffiti on **Gourd Hill** 文尖塔 by **West Lake.**

A globe on a tower at Shantou University marks the Tropic of Cancer. From Shantou, one can tour nearby Fujian province.

SHOPPING

The area produces carpets, painted porcelain, jewelry, bamboo carvings, lacquer, lots of lace, and embroidery. It is also noted for its stone, shell, and gilded wood carvings.

HOTELS

The Shantou International seemed classier than the Longhu but both are good. The Overseas Chinese Hotel was basic and drab. By the end of 1989 a new 16-story waterfront hotel should be open.

Longhu Hotel • *Chaozhou. Near the Bank of China, Customs House, and Longhu Park. Telex 45458 LHHTL CN. Fax 60708. Cable 2160. Dist.A.P.10 km. In S.E.Z.* • T.R., C.C. (no Diner's), 1984 three stories, 1987 seven stories; 237 rooms. IDD, gym, clinic. Small bathrooms. Business center.

Overseas Chinese Hotel • *Shantou* • An extension with 300 rooms was completed in 1983.

Shantou International Hotel • *Jin Sha Rd. Telex 45475 STIH CN. Fax 52250. Cable 9909. Dist.A.P.15 km. Dist.S.E.Z.3 km* • T.R., C.C. 1988. 26 stories, 400 rooms. Pool, IDD, business center, revolving restaurant. Lee Gardens International (H.K.) North American reservations at (415)326-0333.

CAAC 中国民航 ● *Shantou.*

C.I.T.S. ● *1st Floor, Peninsula Hotel. 27 Shanzhang Rd., tel. 32355. Cable 3100. Fax 50033.*

C.T.S. 中旅社. ● *Shan Zhang Rd., tel. 33966, 52649. Fax: 52649;* 34 Huancheng Xi Rd., Chaozhou. Cable 3307.

SHAOGUAN 韶山

South China. In northern Guangdong near the Hunan, Jiangxi, and Guangxi borders. This city of over 360,000 people is on the Beijing-Guangzhou railway, with trains from Guangzhou, 220 km away. (By road, it is 320 km, by flight, 40 min.) Only recently opened to foreign tourism, this area might be for people wanting to get off the beaten path, especially in winter, when other parts of China are too cold. It does have 310 frostfree days, with an annual rainfall of up to 2200 mm, mainly in the summer. Hottest temperature in summer could be 40°C; coldest in winter is an occasional ⁻4°C.

Shaoguan is an industrial and mining center, producing 60% of Guangdong's coal and 90% of its nonferrous metals. Although it is set on three rivers, the city itself is not pretty enough to be worth the tedious trip by hard-class train (no soft class available). The surrounding countryside however is a nice mix of anthropology and unusual mountain scenery. One can visit with some of the 130,000 Yao and Zhuang minority peoples.

The area was settled 120,000 years ago! Skull fossils have been found in Maba District, Qujiang County, dating from that period. Other artifacts from 8000 and 5000 years ago have also been discovered in caves in nearby Yingde and Shixing counties. The **Museum of Maba Man** can be visited 19 km south of Shaoguan, 2 km from Maba town. You can also tour the 1-km-long cave where the bones were found. Tel. (0751) 66955. Or you can take a white-water rafting trip at Pinshi.

Gufo (Ancient Buddha) Cave 占佛洞 is 5 km SW of Lechang Town, 56 km north of Shaoguan City. It covers 10,000 square feet and has seven large "palaces," the widest related to the novel *Journey to the West*. Tea room and restaurant in vicinity. Both caves have grotesquely interesting rock formations.

The area has other scenic spots as well. Important is **Danxiashan (Red Cloud Hill)** 丹霞山 , 54 km NE of the city, with a good view of the neighboring countryside and the Jinjiang River. It is a hard climb, with peaks shaped like horses, elephants, and a monk's hat. Halfway up the hill is the newly renovated Buddhist Sutra Hall in the **Biezhuan Temple.**

Tourists can also visit the 1400-year-old **Nanhua (South China) Temple** in Qujiang County, 24 km south of Shaoguan. This recently restored temple has a pagoda dating from the Ming and a statue of the Priest Huineng, the abbott in A.D. 677 who developed the Dhyana sect. During the Cultural Revolution, his bones were found inside the statue. Also in the temple are wooden arhats (Song) and a 5000-kg bronze bell (Song). The largest temple in South China is on 12,000 square meters of land.

HOTELS

Shaoguan city's Shaoguan Hotel is a centrally located high-rise while the Greenlake (a little better) is on the outskirts. All hotels here are just adequate.

Green Lake Villa Hotel • *Shahu Rd. 512028. Telex 45809 CITSG CN. Dist.A.P.35 km. Dist.R.W.6 km.* • Attractive, isolated setting. T.R. Hong Kong J.V. 1987–88. Two stories, 128 rooms. Limited IDD. C.C.(no MasterCard), bicycles.

Jin Yuan Villa • *Danxia Mountain Resort. Cable 2518. Dist.A.P.60 km. Dist.R.W.56 km* • 1980, ren. 1987. Eleven buildings, 128 rooms, across suspension bridge in pretty resort. Swimming. boating. Should have IDD now.

Reception Center Hostel • *Biebi City, Ruyuan County. Dist.R.W.50 km. In fascinating mountain village, home of Yao people* • About 21 beds. No air-conditioning, fans and mosquito nets. Modest dorms, restaurant. No C.C., used by bicycle tours.

Shaoguan Hotel • *162 Jie Fang Rd. Cable 0241. Near shopping and park. Dist.A.P.30 km* • No C.C. Hong Kong J.V. 1988. 16 stories, 150 rooms. No IDD.

C.I.T.S.: Green Lake Hotel, Shahu Rd.; tel. 6231. Cable 6009. Guangzhou office, New Mainland Hotel; tel. 678638 X1736.

C.T.S.: 5/F, Shaoguan Hotel; tel. 3108, 4323. Guangzhou office; tel. 663488 X921.
Shaoguan Tourist Corporation: Fengdu Rd. North; tel. 84718.

SHAOSHAN

South China, 104 km SW of Changsha in Hunan province, the first province north of Guangdong. Shaoshan is a worthwhile 2½-hour trip by road. It can also be reached by train. The countryside is lovely, and if you haven't had a chance before to drive through tea plantations, or orange groves, and rice fields, take it.

The bonus is the ***Birthplace of Chairman Mao,** a simple mud-brick farmhouse where the founder of the People's Republic was born on December 26, 1893. He lived here in this charming and apparently tranquil village until 1910, when he left for studies in Changsha. He returned briefly several times, holding meetings and conducting revolutionary activities. The original house was confiscated and destroyed by the Nationalists in 1929, but after Liberation, it was rebuilt along the original lines. The house was shared by two families, the section on the left as you enter being the Maos'. It is very sparsely furnished. The dining room still has the original small table, typical even for large families. The master bedroom has portraits of his parents and the bed in which he was born. Another room holds original farm tools.

The **museum,** with ten large galleries, is a 10-minute walk from the farmhouse. It is full of exhibits depicting events in the life of the leader, although Mao's deposed wife Jiang Qing (Chiang Ching) and Lin Piao don't appear at all.

Shaoshan Hotel ● *Dist.R.W.5km, 5 minutes' walk from the museum* ● 1967. 3 stories. 70 rooms and 10 suites.

C.T.S.: tel. 2444.

SHAOXING 绍兴

> (Shaohsing) East China, in Zhejiang province. 60 km from Hangzhou by train or road, 3 hours from Ningbo.

This 2000- to 3000-year-old town is best known for its wine, but it was also the birthplace of China's most famous pre-Liberation writer, Luxun (Lu Hsun). His home and school, and a museum can be visited. Some of his famous stories, notably *The Story of Ah Q,* were set in this town, and a highly recommended but very sad 1982 movie was made of the Ah Q novella here. Literary types should pay a visit to his former residence and the **Luxun Memorial Hall** 鲁迅纪念馆 .

Shaoxing is also known for its lovely canals and **East Lake** 东湖 , alive with boats of all descriptions. Especially striking are its distinctive foot boats, the oars worked by feet. Highly recommended is a trip by these boats onto the lake and into the caves cut out of the lake's quarried cliffs to see the hanging gardens, and go under arched bridges to old temples—a good way to see what Shaoxing has to offer.

Shaoxing is famous throughout China for its distinctive opera. It is less formal, full of emotion, action, and audience—pleasing lyrics, gorgeous costumes, and flashy sets. All parts played by women.

Shaoxing is an ancient city. The tomb of the Xia dynasty founder is in the south suburbs at the base of Mt. Kuaiji. Whether or not the third century B.C. pioneer in irrigation and flood control was/is in **Yu-wang Miao** is anyone's guess. In any case, he died in Shaoxing during a visit. The name *Shaoxing* means "gathering place"; for example, of the people celebrating the miraculous engineering feats of Emperor Yu.

Also of interest are the **Orchid Pavilion** 兰亭 , dating back to the fourth century, and the **Shen Family Garden** 沈园 , which commemorates the meeting between Song dynasty lovers. **Jianhu Lake** 鉴湖 , first dredged in the second century, covers more than 200 square km. The home of the early 20th century female revolutionist **Qiu Jin** is open as a museum. **Premier Chou En-lai,** though born in Jiangsu province, was brought up in this city and you can visit his home.

If you want to visit East Lake, Yuwang Miao, Lan Ding (Orchid

Pavilion), Luxun's home and museum, Qiu Jin's home, and stroll about the town, you need at least two full days. You could also ask about the story of the scholar writing with a brush made of mouse whiskers.

Shaoxing is attractive because it still has many houses, streets, canals, and boats hardly changed from centuries ago. Much time can be spent walking around in this time warp.

Changes have been made, however, like the addition of a local television station, and the lovely sycamore and plane trees lining the streets. The **Second Hospital** 第二医院 was the former mission hospital. Near it was an old pagoda.

Writes one former missionary child of his early life in Shaoxing, "I used to play among the ruins of an old temple there and with a child's carelessness and disdain for the familiar, pretend it was something seemingly far more exotic and romantic: a Mayan temple!"

Ted Stannard, now a teacher at Western Washington State College, also says, "In my childhood, Shaoxing's streets and lanes were almost all paved with great rough-hewn but well-worn flagstones. Where they balanced unevenly across hidden drains beneath the thoroughfares, they would sometimes tip and sound hollowly underfoot or rickshaw wheel. Only a few blocks of the midtown shopping area had asphalt paving before World War II. I can still remember the sensation of silent floating when my bicycle reached that stretch . . . I never saw a car in Shaoxing until the Japanese occupation brought in charcoal-burning army trucks, and in the late forties after the war, the mayor installed barrier posts at all the principle entry-ways to the city to keep out all cars except his own.

"Today the main arterials are asphalt-paved, and many streets widened by filling in canals or tearing out the shops or homes that had lined them. Trucks, cars, and those uniquely Chinese farm tractors ply the streets side-by-side with man-hauled carts, cycles, and pedestrians. But step off into any side-street or lane and you are back in timeless China, threading your way between high-walled compounds and across algae-clogged canals on flagstones worn by centuries of footsteps.

"Marco Polo walked these streets, along the lacework of canals that led him, in his journals, to liken Shaoxing (and Suzhou) to Venice. The canals drain a lowland area reclaimed from the sea centuries ago by a hydraulic engineer who succeeded where his father had failed (at the cost of his head, thanks to a popular imperial theory of incentives), and went on to become the Emperor Yu. A local saying credits him with saving the people of Shaoxing from being fishes.

"The **Yuwang Temple** is in moderately good repair, despite some damage during the Cultural Revolution. It has a series of courtyards and steep stairways to the main temple where a gigantic figure of the emperor peers down benignly upon those who visit. Off to one side outside this temple is a pavilion sheltering an ancient stone linga, taller than any man, with a small hole piercing its tip. Traditionally, I recall from childhood visits, childless women would try to toss a pebble or coin through the needle's eye as a fertility charm.''

SHOPPING

Buy Shaoxing wine, of course, brewed with 2000 years' experience. Visitors frequently stop in at the **Xian Heng Wine Shop,** named after a Luxun short story. Also locally made are lace, felt hats, paper fans, silk, porcelain, and ink stones.

HOTEL

Shaoxing Hotel 沼兴宾馆 • *9 Huanshan Rd. Dist.A.P.67km, Dist.R.W.3km* • 1950s. 2 and 3 stories. 115 rooms. Renovated 1988; 85 additional rooms and pool. The dining hall is an old family temple. This is the best hotel.

Longshan Guest House

C.I.T.S. 国际旅行社 : 9 Huanshan Rd.; tel. 33252; cable 2388.

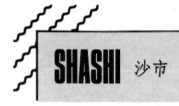

SHASHI 沙市

(Shashih, Shasi) Southwest China. On the north side of the Yangtze River, west of Wuhan in Hubei, Shashi is sometimes a stop on a Yangtze Gorges boat trip. It is an industrial city of 289,000 people making refrigerators, electronics, etc. Shashi is a centuries-old trans-shipment port. In 1895 it was opened to foreign trade under the Treaty of Shimonoseki. Over 2000 years old, the city has such relics as *Zhanghua Temple* (Ming) and a Ming longevity pagoda. There is also a gate built by Guanyu (Kuan Yu) of the Three Kingdom's period. Eight km away is *Jingzhou.* The best hotel is the Zhong Hua. C.I.T.S. tel. 2325. Flights from Guangzhou, Shanghai, Changsha, and Wuhan.

SHEKOU 蛇口

> South China. Guangdong province, 30 km SW of Shenzhen and 40 minutes by hoverferry from Hong Kong on the Chinese side of Deep Bay. It is part of the Shenzhen Special Economic Zone. In addition to its industries, which include off-shore oil support, it is being developed as a resort area, apparently aimed at Hong Kong tourists.

The **tomb of Song Emperor Shao Di** 宋帝昺陵墓 , the **Ancient Battery** 古炮台 , and an exhibit of the **Qin dynasty terracotta warriors and horses** 秦俑展览 can all be visited. The last of the Song emperors fled the Mongols here toward the end of the 13th century.

Minghua/Sea-World is a retired cruise ship moored in Shekou Bay. 239 small rooms.

Other places of interest include **Green Lake Park** 松湖公园 ; **Friendship Store** 友谊商场 ; **Du Le Bookhouse** 都乐书屋 ; and **Mingyuan Restaurant** 茗园 .

Nanhai Hotel • *Dist.R.W.30km, Dist.Hong Kong 50 min. by hoverferry four times a day. Telex 42879 NHHTL CN. Fax 92440* • 1985. 4-story lobby. 395 rooms and suites. Rooms have mini-bars and individual safety deposit boxes. Suites have unique blow-dry toilets with heated toilet seats. Business center. Tennis, mini-golf, pool, disco, Cantonese and Western food. Managed by Hong Kong's Miramar Hotel Group. Excellent setting for honeymooners as well as business people, and those trying to get away from Hong Kong. Beautiful location on bay. C.C. (no Diner's), bicycles. Packages for golfers.

Seaview Restaurant 海景餐厅 ; **Shanghai Restaurant** 上海餐厅 ; **Taizi Hotel** 太子宾馆 ; **Bank of China** 中国银行 ; and **Passenger Wharf** 客运码头 .

See also ''Shenzhen.''

SHENYANG 沈阳

(Formerly Mukden) Northeast China. Capital of Liaoning province, which borders on Korea. 1¼ hours by air NE of Beijing. Regular charter flights from Hong Kong. Also reached by train. An international airport is planned for 1989. Weather: Hottest in August, averaging 23.8°C: coldest in January, ⁻30°C. Rain mainly June to August. A lot of air pollution. Population: urban about 4.3 million, with Manchus the largest group.

With a recorded history of over 2000 years, Shenyang was the Manchu capital from 1625 until 1644. After that, the Qing capital moved to Beijing. Shenyang is the biggest industrial city in this region, which was formerly Japanese-held Manchuria. The Mukden Incident on September 18, 1931, a surprise attack on the Chinese army stationed here, marked the beginning of Japanese aggression in China.

Shenyang today is a cultural center also, with institutions of higher learning and research. It is the home base of the Shenyang Acrobats, among China's best. This troupe was the first cultural mission from the People's Republic of China to tour the United States and Canada in 1972–73.

If you only have one day, C.I.T.S. suggests the Imperial Palace, North Tomb, East Tomb, Zoo, and open market.

The 19-year reigns of Nurhachi/Nulhachi and Huangtaiji (Huang Tai Chi) were enough to build the very impressive ***Imperial Palace** , from 1625 to 1636, now restored to its original gaudy splendor. In an area of almost 60,000 square meters, it is also one of the best museums in China. Unlike the palace in Beijing, which was built by the Ming, this palace is Manchu and reflects more their taste in architecture. Although this palace has a lot of Han influence, look for Mongolian and Manchu-style touches.

The most impressive section is the eastern one, with its octagonal Dazheng Dian (Hall of Great Affairs) and Shiwang Ting (Pavilions of Ten Princes). Does the Beijing Palace have such dragons on its pillars, and the yurtlike design? The hall was used for important ceremonies and meetings with top officials. Huangtaiji commanded his military forces and political business from the Chongzheng Dian (Hall of Supreme Administration). At the back of this hall is a road to the Fenghuang Lou (Phoenix Tower) and the Qingning Gong (Palace of Pure Tranquillity) The Manchu leaders lived in the Qingning Gong, which is the most distinctively Manchu.

In the western section is the Wenshuo Ge (Hall of Literary Source), especially constructed for the *Complete Library of the Four Treasures* of Qing Emperor Qianlong. No signs in English.

The *Beiling (North) Tombs 北陵 (a.k.a. Zhaoling), north of the city, are of Huangtaiji and his wife Borjigid (Poerhchichiteh). Huangtaiji was the son of Nurhachi. Begun in 1643, the tombs were completed in 1651. Hours are from 8:30 a.m. to 4:00 p.m. (summer) and from 10 a.m. to 3 p.m.. (winter). The **Dongling (East) Tombs** 东陵 (a.k.a. Fuling), are of Nurhachi and his wife Yihnaran. During the Ming, Nurhachi unified the tribes, became "khan" in 1616, and made Shenyang his capital in 1625. Also of interest is the **Shenyang Railway Locomotives Museum** 沈阳火车博物馆 Sujiatun Jiwuduan, Sujiatun District (8 a.m. to 4 p.m. in summer and 10 a.m. to 3 p.m. in winter), and an overnight in **Xisheng Village** 西山村 with a peasant family. C.I.T.S. also organizes cycling tours, model plane flying, and visits to criminal trials and prisons. It might offer two free tours for every 15 passengers on a group tour.

The 40-square km **Qianshan Mountain Park** 千山公园 is 20 km south. At Yixiang, about 150 km west of the city is *Fengguo Temple, dating from the Liao and said to be the second largest temple in China. Does anyone dispute that? Also of interest in the province are Anshan and Dalian. See separate listings. Ask also about the Xin Le Neolithic museum on the site, near the entrance to the Friendship Hotel. One can also visit the border area at **Dandong** where you can boat on the Yalu River (famous for those who know about the Korean War), and visit the King of Medicine Temple on Feng Huang (Phoenix) Hill, a visit to which should cure you of all ills.

In Dandong is the Yalu Jiang (River) Hotel. Built 1987. 500 beds. New hotels plan to open in 1990.

SHOPPING

Produced in the province are ginseng, sable, and carvings of jade, agate, jet, and amber. Also produced are ceramics, feather patchwork, the musical instrument *zheng,* shell carvings and pictures.

RESTAURANTS

Local delicacies include monkey head mushrooms, available at the **Lumingchun Restaurant.** (We found a dirty washroom here.) One of the best restaurants is in the Huasha Hotel for Shandong and northeast food.

Laobian Dumpling Restaurant　辽宁大厦　● Dumplings with various fillings.

HOTELS

The best hotel for tourists is the Phoenix. The Liaoning (Bingguan) is a favorite of business travelers because of its central location. The Zhongshan opened recently downtown but we don't have an evaluation yet. (17, Section 2, Zhongshan Rd., Heping Dist.) The Friendship Hotel is mainly for government guests.

The Youyi, Phoenix, Youyuan, and Liaoning Mansions are close together, and 10 to 15 minutes walk to the tomb which is open from 6 p.m. until 10 p.m. The Hua Sha, Zhongshan, and Liaoning Hotel are near the railway station.

Liaoning Hotel (a.k.a. China Liaoning Hotel, or Liaoning Guesthouse) ● *No. 27, section 2, Zhongshan Rd., Dist.A.P. 27 km. Dist. R.W. 1 km. Next to giant statue of Chairman Mao in center of city* ● 1927, Ren. 1983. Four stories. 77 rooms. Lots of charming 1920s ambience. Plan to restore old style with original furniture. T.R.

Phoenix Hotel　凤凰饭店　● *No. 3, Section 6, Huanghe St., Huanggu District. Telex 80045 FHFD CN. Dist. A.P. 18 km* ● 1984. 15 stories. Sauna. Best for shopping of the four. No reply to your telex for a room means room available. Will reply if no room. C.C.

Youyi (Friendship) Hotel (a.k.a. Liaoning Friendship Guesthouse) ● *1, Section 7, Huanghi St., Huanggu Dist. Telex 80082. Dist. A.P. 18 km. Dist. R.W. 8 km.* ● First part built 1920s as palace for local warlord. 1954, four buildings. 1959, five more buildings. 6-meter-high ceilings and two-stories; each villa with own restaurant. Renovations 1986. 24 hr. coffee shop. No air conditioning in main building. #9 is best building, with 11 beds for Y3000. Guarded by company of PLA. No business center. Pool. Also state guest house. Will reply to telex requesting reservation. Major credit cards.

Youyuan Hotel　友园饭店　● *1985.* ● Five stories. Popular with business people. Japanese j.v.

CAAC: 31 Zhonghua Rd., Section 3; tel. 34089, 33705.
C.I.T.S.　中国国际旅行社　: No. 3, Section 6, Huanghe St., Huanggu Dist.; tel. 66037, 66953 Telex 80045 FHFD CN. Cable 6954.
C.T.S.: same compound as Phoenix Hotel; tel. 66697. Cable 6079.
U.S. Consulate: 41 Lane 4, Section 5, Sanjing St., Heping District; tel. 290038, 290000. Shenyang also has a Korean and a Japanese consulate.

Liaoning Tourism Administration: same address as C.I.T.S.; tel. 460636.

SHENZHEN 深圳

> (Shumchun) South China. On the Hong Kong border, this is a Special Economic Zone. Hong Kong currency is freely used, and hotel prices are quoted in it. You can obtain a 5-day visa at the Hong Kong border or a longer one for all of China. "Hong Kong time" is used here, which could be different fr⌐m the rest of China.

Urban Shenzhen (pop. 600,000) is about 7 km by 10 km, spreading mainly east and west from the railway station and its 1987-built Customs House, which touches the border. Only travelers on the through-express trains now cross the famous old covered bridge.

Fast electric trains zip between Kowloon Station and Lowu on the Hong Kong border. The section from Shenzhen to Guangzhou is electrified and takes 2 hours, although you might end up at the wrong railway station in Guangzhou. Shenzhen is building an international airport.

Tourists who must get a tour package to satisfy visa requirements should consider getting one to Shenzhen, and going from there on their own.

At press time, no Hong Kong taxis were allowed into Shenzhen, but city buses ran at least twice a day. Trains are the fastest and most convenient transport. Hong Kong buses take tourists on day trips, or connect with Shenzhen buses for other destinations in Guangdong or Fujian.

The main resorts are in the suburbs, or toward Shekou, which is 29 km west. Two resorts have amusement park rides, the biggest at the Honey Lake Country Club (Dist.R.W.8 km), boasting the longest roller coaster ride (2km) in the world. Its monorail is 4.5 km long. See also "Shekou."

The day trippers see China's largest, wealthiest Special Economic Zone, and its greatest concentration of skyscrapers. They also see a kindergarten, and might see the reservoir that supplies half of Hong

Kong's water supply. Greater Shenzhen has no historical monuments save the modest grave of the last Song emperor, who fled here to escape the Mongols (in Shekou).

During the summertime *litchi (lichee)* season, tourists also come here to pick this sweet fruit. The tour price usually includes all-you-can eat and 2.5 kg to take home. A Lichee and Fine Food Festival takes place the end of June and early July.

From the summit of the 53-story Shenzhen International Trade Building, one should be able to see Hong Kong's Sheung Shui, a neat switch after the decades of tourists getting a peek at China from Hong Kong.

Until Shenzhen can provide other attractions such as a bargain market for its factory overruns, we have to recommend the alternative one-day trips from Hong Kong to Zhongshan (Dr. Sun Yat-sen's home), or to Guangzhou. It is however developing a "miniature China," about 100 models of the main scenic attractions, to woo tourists.

Shenzhen has 90 hotels and resorts suitable for foreigners. In the city itself, the most convenient for business people seemed to be the flashy Century Plaza (close to the International Trade Center—ITC) and the Shenzhen International (further out and less luxurious). After it gets some experience, the Overseas Forum Hotel should be near the top as it is next to the Customs House and run by Inter-Continental. The Bamboo Garden looked good.

Other hotels seen were in outlying areas. The Nanhai in Shekou has maintained its high standards and beautiful seaside surroundings. The Silver Lake looked classier than the Xili Lake (which needed lots of work).

Bamboo Garden Hotel • *Dong Men North Rd. Telex 420390 BGH CN. Dist.R.W.4 km. Dist.ITC 1 km* • Attractive suburban setting. T.R. (collect), C.C. 1981, ren. 1987; addition 1989. Four stories, 170 rooms. Bowling, clinic, Business center. Large rooms, no drawers, soft beds, small bathrooms.

Century Plaza Hotel • *Kin Chit Rd. Fax 234060. Walk to ITC* • C.C. 1987–88. 24 stories, 427 rooms. Executive floor, business center. Pool, health club. Citibank on premises. IDD, soft beds, large bathrooms. Managed by Pacifica International.

Huaqiao (Overseas Chinese) Hotel • *68 Heping Rd.* • 1957; replaced 1983; redecorated 1987. Best location—within walking distance of the Customs House and railway station. 5 stories, 80 rooms. Two sections, one with private baths. Few services. Good Chinese restaurant. Upmarket Arts & Crafts Center with jewelry for sale. Otherwise dumpy.

Shenzhen International Hotel • *Tung Moon Rd. Dist.R.W.7 km. Telex 42299 SIHTL CN or 30067 SIHTL HX. Fax 230702* • C.C. 1983–84, ren. 1988. Five stories, 96 rooms. IDD, business center. No travel service. Two-day laundry service. Medium-sized rooms with garden view.

Shenzhen Overseas Forum Hotel • *68 Heping Rd. Reservations U.S.1-800-33-AGAIN* • 1989. 666 rooms. Pool, health club, business center. Delicatessen, IDD, translation services.

Silver Lake Hotel • *Parker Shan. Dist.R.W.8km. Telex: 420280 SSLRH CN. Dist.R.W.7 km* • C.C. 1983, ren. 1988–89. Eight buildings, one to three stories; 132 rooms. IDD. No travel service nor business center. Large rooms, garden. Poor reading lamps, little rundown, musty. Very pretty, isolated, rural setting on small lake, ideal for conferences. Swimming, gym, boating, disco, horseback riding trails.

C.T.S.: Overseas Chinese Hotel; tel. 23811, 22811. Cable 3307.
Citibank: 4th floor, Century Plaza Hotel.
Hongkong Bank: Shenzhen International Trade Center, Renmin South Rd.; tel. 238016.
Shenzhen International Travel Service: 2/F, Block A, Nanyang Mansion, Kin Chit Rd.; tel. 227511, 227510, 236903. Telex 420306 SZTGC CN. Cable 0595. Fax 36903.
World Trade Center: 3/F, International Trade Center Building, Renmin S. Rd.; tel. 24991-24995. Telex 420296 ITC CN. Fax 24991, 24995 X2645.
See also "Shekou."

SHIHEZI 石河子

(Shihhotzu) Northwest China. In the far-western autonomous region of Xinjiang, this city was reclaimed from the Gobi Desert in 1949 and stands at the northern base of Tianshan Mountain, 150 km NW of the capital, Urumqi. It has an urban population of 130,000 and many industries. The area grows grain and cotton. Among its various nationalities are horse-riding Kazaks.

Important to see are the **Tianshan Dazi Temple,** the desert, the wild Mongolian gazelles, and the **Dachuangou Reservoir** (for boating, swimming, and fishing).

Shihezi Guest House • *Dist.R.W.3 km* • 1978; renovated 1984. 5 stories. Reservations mandatory July to September.

C.I.T.S.: tel. 2414, 2587.
See also "Urumqi."

SHIJIAZHUANG 石家庄

(Shihchiachuang, Shihkiachwang) North China. The capital of Hebei province, a few hours by train south of Beijing, Shijiazhuang is on the main line to Guangzhou, east of the Taihang Mountains on the Hebei Plain. It is linked by air with Beijing, Guangzhou, Hohhot, Shanghai, Wuhan, and other cities in Hebei province. With a population of over 900,000, it is primarily an industrial city.

Shijiazhuang is of importance to Chinese revolutionary history as the burial place of the Canadian who became a Chinese hero. Dr. Norman Bethune　石求恩医生　, the son of a Gravenhurst, Ontario, clergyman, arrived in China in 1938 to help the Communist Eighth Route Army in its fight against the Japanese. Working almost in the front lines, he died of blood poisoning on November 12, 1939, in Huangshikou village, Tangxian county, in Hebei. That year, Chairman Mao wrote a much publicized article, pointing him out as an example of "utter devotion to others without any thought of self." He became known to every schoolchild, and statues were made of him all over the country.

In Shijiazhuang is the **Bethune International Peace Hospital**　白求恩国际和平医院　, first set up in 1937 in the Shanxi-Chahar-Hebei Military Area and moved here in 1948. Dr. Bethune is buried in the western part of the **North China Revolutionary Martyrs' Cemetery**华北军区烈士陵园　, where there is also the Bethune Exhibition Hall and the Memorial Hall for Revolutionary Martyrs. The city also has the **Hebei Provincial Exhibition Hall and Museum** 省展览馆 .

Visitors can see a cotton mill and a free market. Foreign professionals dealing with criminals have visited a prison and a court here.

Shijiazhuang is also known for the ***Zhaozhou (Anji) Bridge** 赵州 安济桥 , still serviceable, although it was built between A.D. 605 and 610. About 2000 meters north is the ***Yongtong (Smaller Stone Bridge)** built between 1190 and 1195, and 32 meters long. In the town of Zhengding, is the ***Longxing Buddhist Temple** 隆兴寺 (Song dynasty), with a bronze 20-meter-high Buddha.

Spectacular is **Cangyan Hill** 苍岩山 , 70 km SW, full of pointed peaks and dramatic cliffs up to which snuggles Fuqing Buddhist temple.

Ninety km from the city is ***Xibaipo Village** 西柏坡 , Pingshan County, the now relocated site of the 1948 headquarters of the Communist Party Central Committee.

An unusual pagoda is at the ***Kaiyuan Temple** in **Dingxian,** about 75 km NW of Shijiazhuang. Dating from the Song, this 11-story, 84-meter-high structure has eight sides, two overlapping squares.

Also in the province are Beidaihe, Chengde, Handan, Qinhuangdao, Shanhaiguan, Tangshan, and Zunhua. See separate listings.

SHOPPING

Locally made are painted-on-the-inside snuff bottles, white marble carvings from Quyang County, and Liuling wine. Elsewhere in the province are made golden-thread tapestry (Zhuoxian), shell crafts (Qinhuangdao), horse saddles (Zhangjiakou), ink slabs (Yishui), woven straw (Chengde), Handan ceramics, and Tangshan porcelain.

HOTELS

Hebei Guest House 河北宾馆 ● *Yucai Rd., 20 km from airport.*

Shijiazhuang Hotel 石家庄市宾馆 ● *Qingyuan St.*

Overseas Chinese Hotel 华侨饭店 ● *1987.*

C.I.T.S. 国际旅行社 : 1 Fuqiang St.; tel. 44319.
CAAC 中国民航 : tel. 45084.

Information about Hebei province and hotel reservations: tel. Beijing 55243.
C.T.S.: 1 Fuqiang Rd.

SILK ROAD

This term was first used by a German author in the 19th century and is still used because it is so apt. Silk was the main commodity carried along the caravan routes between Cathay and Europe. It dazzled the eyes of Marco Polo, who traveled here in 1275. Bales of silk have been found in ancient tombs along the way: it was that highly valued.

Informal trade between China and West Asia goes back over 2000 years. In 138 B.C. (Han), Emperor Wudi sent his emissary Zhang Qian (Chang Ch'ien) on missions westward to get help to fight the Huns. Zhang returned 13 years later, having been imprisoned most of that time by hostile tribes, but he fired the emperor's interest in trade. The Han emperors encouraged trading caravans with imperial protection and the building of beacon signal towers. From then on, the routes flourished periodically until the 14th century, especially in the Tang. It declined because sea-going ships were able to trade more efficiently and because of hostilities along the land routes.

Trade was mainly in high-value or easily transported goods. The Chinese exchanged silk, tea, and seeds for peach and pear trees. They also exchanged skills, such as iron-, steel-, and paper-making. They received grapes, pomegranate and walnut trees, sesame, coriander, spinach, the Fergana horse, alfalfa, Buddhism, Nestorianism, and Islam.

Goods were exchanged along the route especially with India and West Asia. A few items even reached Rome. The road went west from Xi'an along the Weihe River valley, Hexi Corridor, Tarim Basin, Parmirs (in Soviet Asia), Afghanistan, Iran, Iraq, and Syria. It was about 7000 km long. Northern and southern routes divided at Dunhuang.

Many Arab and Persian merchants settled in Xi'an and even as far east as Yangzhou. Some of the cities on the Silk Road are open to foreigners, and tourists find themselves in a world of onion-domed mosques, bazaars, oasis, grapes, Soviet and Turkish faces, embroidered caps, and languages their national guides cannot understand. Spontaneous dancing and singing, uncontrolled by Han reserve, make people here delightful. Visitors are frequently asked to join in and contribute to the festivities.

Tourists find giant rock carvings and murals, some of the best in the world. They can explore earthen-walled ghost cities, the western end of the Great Wall, old tombs, Lama temples, and look for mummies. They can figure out how and what the beacon towers communicated. They can learn how water is channeled to make this desert flourish. They can buy carpets, jade goblets, and musical instruments.

But the Silk Road is not Turkey, Pakistan, or Afghanistan. It is China, an ingredient that makes this area of mixed cultures special and worth the hardships.

Tourists in this area must be fit and adventurous. It is not for the finicky and inflexible. The area is extremely dry and cold even on summer nights. Long train and bus rides through the desert are not comfortable. Tourist buses, but not trains, are air-conditioned. But buses have broken down in the desert and the coolest retreat has been the shade of a rock or a sand dune—if you're lucky. You should be prepared for delays and be pleasantly surprised if they don't happen. While waiting, think about the peasants and herdsmen who struggled to raise crops and animals here while the spring or autumn sandstorms howled mercilessly. Think of the sand smothering the wheat. Think of the caravans passing through. What did the camels and traders do when they couldn't see a foot ahead of them?

You should have the foresight to carry your own liquid refreshments and something to protect your nose and eyes.

The government is in the process of upgrading transportation in this area. By the time you go, planes may be flying into most of the cities on the route. Paved roads might reach the cave temples.

As you travel around, try to pick out the characteristics of the different nationalities. See if you can identify people from their facial features and their distinctive dress. Among the groups along the Silk Road are the Kergez, Han, Huns, Huis (Moslems), Kazaks (not related to Cossacks), Kirghiz, Manchus, Mongols, Russians, Tarjiks (Tajiks), Tartars, Turfans, Uzbeks, Uygurs (Uighurs), and Xibos.

If you don't want to risk spoiling your trip with diarrhea, read about how to avoid upset stomachs in "Food." Do not eat anything from the local market. The meat beyond Xi'an is mainly mutton. Wise is the traveler who says something like "I would love to try it, but it doesn't agree with me. Thank you anyway," when handed a glass of mare's milk buzzing with flies. The well-meaning tribesman in his yurt is not going to appreciate the pain you will go through later. Don't drink it because you "don't want to hurt his feelings." You are the one who will suffer!

Urumqi is the best for shopping. Tourism officials are hoping to open the whole Silk Road by road from Xi'an to Xinjiang to foreign tourists soon.

See "Xi'an," "Dunhuang," "Jiuquan," "Kashi," "Lanzhou," "Shihezi," "Turpan," and "Urumqi."

苏 州

Z.M.Li

SUZHOU (SOOCHOW)

East China. Yangtze basin, Jiangsu province, about 1 hour (86 km) west by train from Shanghai and 219 km SE of Nanjing, on the Beijing-Shanghai railway line. Air connections with Beijing, boat from Hangzhou (30 hours). Weather: Hottest—36°C (usually 1 or 2 days late July, early August); coldest—end of January, averaging 0° to 7°C. Snow once or twice a year. Rush out and take beautiful exotic photos then. Rain: May–July. Population: almost 700,000 in the old city.

Suzhou was founded by He Lu, king of Wu, as his capital in 514 B.C. It is one of China's oldest cities. Iron was smelted here more than 2500 years ago and silk weaving was well developed in the Tang and Song. Marco Polo visited in the latter half of the 13th century. During the Ming, textile manufacturing flourished. From 1860 to 1863, 40,000 troops of the Taiping Heavenly Kingdom controlled the area. During the Japanese occupation, the Jiangsu provincial puppet government headquartered in the Humble Administrator's Garden.

The people here speak the Wu dialect, which is similar to that of Shanghai, only with softer tones and more adjectives. Industries include the manufacturing of TV sets, wristwatches, chemicals, electronics, and instruments. Tourists would probably want to see the **factories** where artisans weave and print silk, make sandalwood and silk fans, and create one of the four most famous embroideries in China. Musical instruments are also made here. The **villages** raise silkworms, jasmine flowers for tea, shrimp, and tangerines, and are therefore particularly good to visit. The old city proper is under state protection as a historic and cultural treasure. No new factories can be built in the old city, and existing factories that pollute are being moved out to the suburbs.

The walled city is about 3 by 5 km and is crisscrossed by many canals. The western and southern moats are actually part of the famous Grand Canal (A.D. 610). The city wall was built in 514 B.C. and remnants, including three gates, remain. Also remaining is one of the eight water gates. These used to be closed at night.

Suzhou is one of the prettiest towns in China, its streets thickly lined with plane trees and its tiny whitewashed houses of uniform design. Unlike many other Chinese communities, the Japanese war inflicted little damage here. It is known primarily as a cultural and scenic city, similar in this respect to Japan's Kyoto. Its classical gardens are among the best in China.

The main street, Renmin (People's) Road, runs north-south; Jingde and Guanqian roads (actually linking) run east-west, meeting with Renmin almost in the center of the city. Many of the buildings were redecorated for Suzhou's 2500th birthday in 1986.

If you only have one day, C.I.T.S. suggests two of the gardens, Tiger Hill, one handicraft factory, and a boat trip.

Shizilin (Shih Tzu Lin; Lion Forest) Garden 狮子林 Dong Bei (Northeast) St., 4 km from the Nanlin Hotel, was built in 1350 during the Yuan and so named because the teacher of the monk who built it lived on Lion Rock Mountain. Some of the rockeries are shaped like lions. Six acres: compact. Guides say that it was once owned by the granduncle of the American architect I. M. Pei. Notable are the maze inside the rockeries at the entrance and the rocks, some carved and then weathered in Lake Tai (Taihu) for scores of years. The rock structure above the stone boat was a waterfall, which in the early days was hand-poured.

Exquisite is the Standing-in-Snow Study, so named because a student once went to visit his teacher there and, too polite to awaken him, stood patiently in the snow. Moved by his spirit, the teacher renamed the pavilion.

Changlang Ting (Gentle Wave or Surging Wave) Pavilion 沧浪 (Renmin Rd.) is 1 km from the Nanlin Hotel. About two acres, it is the only garden that is not surrounded completely by a view-blocking wall. A pond lies outside and can be enjoyed from a View-Borrowing Pavilion. The stones in the rockeries here are also from Lake Tai. A hall houses 125 steles with the images of 500 sages, dating from the kingdom of Wu to the Qing. Carved in relief in 1840, the deeds of each one are confined to 16 poetic characters. The garden, one of the oldest in the city, was founded in 1044 (Song) by the poet Su Tzu-mei. In the Yuan and early Ming, it was a Buddhist nunnery.

Look for the set of dark brown furniture made from mahogany tree roots that look like chocolate-covered peanuts. This garden is not as spectacular as the others, so if you're short on time, skip it.

Yi (Joyous) Garden 怡园 (Renmin Rd.) was built by a Qing official and, at 100 years, it is the newest. It has taken the best of all the gardens, concentrating them into about an acre. The rockeries are from other older gardens. The dry boat is an imitation of the one in the Humble Administrator's.

*Liu (Lingering) Garden 留园 (Liuyuan Rd., 6 km from the Nanlin Hotel) was originally built in 1525 (Ming). The 8-acre garden consists of halls and studios in the east sector, ponds and hills in the central, and woods and hills in the western section. In late autumn, these woods are red. Look through some of the 200 different flower windows at the scene beyond. You are in a living picture gallery. A huge 5-ton, 6-meter-high rock from Lake Tai stands in the eastern section.

Wangshi (Master of Nets) Garden 网师园 (Shiquan St., ½ km from the Nanlin Hotel), originally built in 1140 (Southern Song), is one of the best. The Metropolitan Museum of Art in New York City has reproduced the Peony courtyard as the Astor Chinese Garden Court. This garden is very pretty, especially when decorated with colorful palace lanterns. It is open some summer evenings for this exotic experience.

*Zhuozheng (Humble Administrator's) Garden 拙政园 (Dong Bei St., 5 km from the Nanlin Hotel) is the largest in Suzhou. It was laid out in 1522 (Ming) by a humble administrator (a dismissed official) and later split into three after the owner lost it gambling. It was restored in 1953. The largest and most open of the gardens, three-fifths water, is reminiscent of the water country south of the Yangtze. Almost all buildings are close to water, much of it filled with shore-to-shore lotus flowers in summer. If you only have a short time, visit the central part. Fragrant Island there is a two-story stone "dry boat" complete with gangplank, "deck," and "cabin." The Mandarin Duck Hall has blue windows and classical furniture, with live ducks in a cage at the side of the hall. A garden blooms within a garden. A covered walkway in the western section follows the natural contours of the land. Look also for the Little Flying Rainbow Bridge, the Pavilion of Expecting Frost, and the Pavilion of Fragrant Snow and Azure Clouds.

Note also the Lingering and Listening Hall for listening (of course) to the raindrops on the lotus leaves. Who else but the aristocratic Chinese constructed buildings just for something like that! Ramps instead of stairs make one wonder about wheelchairs back then. Look for the wood carving and the cloud designs on the glass. A 200-year-old miniature pomegranate tree is included in the excellent collection of *penjing* (Chinese miniature gardening).

*Ilu Qiu (Tiger) Hill 虎丘 (9 km from the Nanlin Hotel) is important. The 45-acre site is NW of the city outside the moat. The grounds were an island many years ago, but now they are about 100 km from the East China Sea. It was originally called Hill of Emergence from the Sea. Named Tiger Hill because a white tiger appeared here at one time, the entrance (the head), the pagoda (the tail), and what is in between considered the back of the tiger. On the right after entering is the Sword Testing Rock which He Lu, king of Wu, was supposed to have broken in the sixth century B.C. On the left is a large magic rock. If the stone you throw stays on top, you will give birth to sons—so beware! On the right is a pavilion with red characters, the Tomb of the Good Wife. It commemorates a widow sold by the wicked brothers of her deceased husband to another man. Forced to be a courtesan, she committed suicide.

Here is also where Fu Chai, king of Wu, is said to have built a tomb for his father, He Lu, in the early fifth century B.C., after which the tomb builders were slaughtered to keep the location a secret. Hence, no one is sure if this is indeed the right place. If you look carefully, you can still see the red of the blood on the large flat rock. Oh, come on!

The tomb of He Lu is believed to be beyond the moon gate. In 1956, unsuccessful attempts were made to enter it. The foundation of the pagoda started to protest. Inside are supposed to be 3000 iron and steel swords. You can see the cave, blocked by large, cut stones, from the bridge to the pagoda. Is it or isn't it the 2500-year-old tomb? The two holes on the bridge were for hauling up buckets of water.

The Tiger Hill Pagoda known also as Leaning Tower of Suzhou was built originally in the 10th century A.D. (Northern Song). It caught fire three times, and its wooden eaves burned up. The latest repairs were made in 1981, when its foundation was strengthened. At 47.5 meters high, it tends to tilt to the northwest. Pilgrims used to climb the 53 steps here on their knees. Note the Indian arches.

The **Grand Canal Boat Tours** 大运河游船 go from (1) the Panmen Water Gates, the Wumen Arch Bridge and Ruiguang Pagoda eastward along the city wall, and to the Precious Belt Bridge with its 53 arches: 60 minutes; (2) Suzhou to Wuxi, 45 km in 3 hours.

If you have more time: The **Beisi (North Temple) Pagoda** at the north end of Renmin Road, is nine stories and 76 meters high, the tallest pagoda south of the Changjiang River, first built in the 10th century.

Han Shan (Cold Mountain) Temple 寒山寺 , 10 km west of the Nanlin Hotel, was the home of two Tang monks, Han Shan and Shih Te. To the right of the central, gold Sakyamuni Buddha is Wu Nan, the young disciple who wrote the sutras; the older man is disciple Ja Yeh. The original bell was stolen by Japanese pirates but replaced with a bell cast about 100 years ago as a gift from Japan. Originally built in the Liang dynasty (sixth century), the current buildings were rebuilt at the end of the Qing.

C.I.T.S. organizes special excursions to hear the bronze bells here on midnight Dec. 31, New Year's eve. If one hears the bells chime 108 times on this night, one should have few troubles in life! Monks chant and pray for guests. Young men perform the lion and dragon lantern dances.

Xiyuan (West Garden) Temple 西园 (Liuyuan Rd.) is also very beautiful. Near the Han Shan Temple, it is the largest group of Buddhist buildings in Suzhou. It was originally built in the 16th century but was destroyed by fire, and rebuilt in 1892.

The ceiling in the main building is magnificent—bats (happiness) and cranes (long life) as in Beijing's Forbidden City. The central Buddhas are seven meters tall, including base and mandala. On both sides are 20 devas, gods in charge of natural phenomena such as the sun, moon, and rain. Behind the Buddhas to the right is the Bodhisattva of Wisdom, with a crown on his head. To the left is the Bodhisattva of Universal Benevolence.

The 500 arhats here are worth studying, each face so real, expressive, profound, individual. Outstanding is the crazy monk, who can look sad, happy, or wry, depending on the angle at which you see him. Gilded on modeled clay, each statue is larger than life. But can you find any women? Enjoy those incense burners. At the time of the Great Leap Forward (1958–60) and backyard furnaces, they were supposed to be smelted. But the C.I.T.S. director said no!

Look also for the five-colored carp and giant soft-shelled turtles in the pond in the back garden.

Dongdongtingshan Isle (Eastern Hill Peninsula), 40 km SW of the city jutting into Lake Tai, is worth a visit if you have the time. It is charming. The 16 colored arhats in the **Zijin (Purple Gold) Nunnery** are older (Song) and said to be better than those in the West Garden Temple.

The **Twin Pagodas** 双塔寺 , almost in the middle of Suzhou, are known as the big and small "brushes" (used by Confucius for writing). They were built in the Song in honor of the sage.

The **Xuan Miao Guan (Mysterious Wonder Taoist Temple)** in the middle of the city has been described as the tallest, most magnificent temple in the area and probably in China. Do you agree? Three giant, gilded sculptures of the founders of Taoism dominate. Originating in the Jin (A.D. 265–420), the temple's current central Sanqing Hall was built in the Southern Song.

The **Confucius Temple** 孔庙 looks very big and impressive and is now the Stele Museum of Suzhou. Inside are hundreds of steles.

Lingyan (Divine Cliff) Hill 灵岩, 14 km west of the city, is very important to Buddhists. It is topped by a seven-story pagoda, probably Qing. The pagoda is at the site of the palace built by Fu Chai, king of Wu, for his beautiful queen, Xi Shi. A Buddhist college is in the 25-meter-high Lingyan Temple. At the foot of the hill is the ancient town of Mu Tu, founded during the Wu.

The **Suzhou Embroidery Research Institute** 苏州刺绣研究所 is not a factory. It trains young people to do embroidery, develops new embroideries (new stitches, new materials, for example, human hair), and creates masterpieces in thread for places like Beijing's Great Hall of the People.

The **Suzhou Museum** (Dongbei St.) was the site of the official residence of a Royal Prince of the Taiping troops. First built in 1860.

Music lovers should be fascinated by the **First Ethnic Music Instrument Factory** (15 Vanmanqiao; tel. 24238, 23456). Not only will you see how 400 different Chinese instruments are made, but demonstrations are given by some of the craftspeople, who are renowned musicians themselves. You have to make an appointment (closed on Fridays) and bring your own translator.

Yushan Hill in Changshu city is 45 km NE of the city, with a 12th-century monastery (the Xingfu), and 2000-year-old tombs.

Ancient Opera, Embroidery, and Folk Custom Museums have opened. A Silk Museum will be open soon.

SHOPPING

Inkstones, brushes, jewelry, embroideries, silks, antiques, iron reproductions of ancient relics, excellent prints of Suzhou, and reproductions of some of the arhats are available. This is one of the best places to buy sandalwood fans (always smell them to be sure) and rubbings.

Friendship Store 友谊商店 : 504 Renmin Rd., tel. 25370. Cable 0645. 9:30 a.m. to 8 p.m. Other stores, 7:30 or 8:30 a.m.–6 or 7 p.m.

RESTAURANTS

For recommended local dishes, see "Food."

Songhelou Restaurant ● *Guanqian St.; tel. 3270.*

Deyuelou Restaurant ● *Guanqian St.; tel. 6969.*

HOTELS

The top hotel has been the new wing of the Nanlin, then the Suzhou. We haven't had a chance to look at the two new hotels. The Aster is better for business people, west of the old city. The Bamboo Grove sounds like it's better quality than the Nanlin. The Nanlin, Suzhou and

Gusu are neighbors in northeast Suzhou inside the wall and close to the Master of Nets Garden. They are set in beautiful gardens themselves.

Bamboo Grove (Zhu Hui) Hotel • *Telex 36302 SZTLX CN. Southeast part of old city inside wall. Dist.R.W.7 km. Dist.ferry pier 2 km* • C.C. 1989. Three and five stories. 392 rooms. Garden, IDD, shuttle bus, health club, gym, business center. Lee Gardens International management.

Gusu Hotel 古苏饭店 • *115 Shiquan St. Cable 1196. On grounds of Suzhou Hotel* • 1980 pre-fab. Budget travelers only.

Nanlin Hotel 南林饭店 • *20 Gun Xiu Fang. Cable 4641. Telex 363033 SZCC CN. Dist.R.W.5.5 km. Beside tiny canal and antique stores* • Only Visa and MasterCard C.C. No answer to telex means room; if no room, will send telex. 1950, ren. 1987, 1990. 7 stories, 266 rooms. IDD due 1990. Clinic, business center.

New World Aster • *156 San Xiang Rd. Cable 3138. Telex 363023 ASTER CN. Fax 731838. In the new city. Dist.R.W.6 km. Dist. port 4 km.* • Walk to Suzhou Trade Fair Center and Industrial Exhibition Center (due 1992). Near China Eastern Airlines. 1989. 30 stories, 423 rooms. Gym, pool, C.C., business center. New World International management.

Suzhou Hotel 南园宾馆 • *115 Shiquan St. Telex 363002 SZTLX CN* • C.C. T.R. (collect). C.I.T.S. IDD in hotel post office. Business center. Budget travelers only.

OTHER IMPORTANT ADDRESSES

C.I.T.S. 国际旅行社 : Suzhou Hotel, 115 Shiquan Rd.; tel. 22593. Telex 36302 SZTL CN. Cable 36302.
CAAC 中国民航 : 192 Renmin Rd.; tel. 22788.
Railway Booking Office: 203 Guanqian St.; tel. 26462, 24646.
Railway Station Information Service: tel. 2831, 772831.
Telephone Information: tel. 114
    Long distance: tel. 113
    Correct time: tel. 117

TAI'AN 泰安

North China. About 80 km south of Jinan, the capital of Shandong, the closest airport. You can reach Tai'an by road or rail. The hottest time (36–37°C) is briefly in July and August; the coldest is December and January, when the temperature can fall to minus 10°C. The annual precipitation is 700 mm, mainly from July to September. It is about 10°C colder at the top of the mountain. The best time to climb is from April to October, but one can climb all year round except in inclement weather. Urban population 200,000.

Tai'an is where you go to ascend **Mt. Tai (Taishan)** 泰山 , one of China's Five Sacred Mountains. It is a 2 billion year old mountain, one of the oldest in the world. In ancient times, emperors came here to offer sacrifices to Earth and to Heaven. If they went up the mountain, they were probably carried up, and visitors today have the same choice by bus or taxi. If you have only one day, you can be driven halfway up to the **Zhongtian (Middle Celestial) Gate** 中天门 . Then you can take the 2078-meter-long suspended cable car almost to the top at **Nantian (Southern Celestial) Gate** 南天门 between 7 a.m. and 7 or 8 p.m. (no service during high winds.) From the top of the cable car to the summit at an altitude of 1,500 meters are 500 more steps. You can lunch at the hotel near the summit and then return to see the **Daimiao (Temple)** and a free market.

The longer, more satisfying way is to climb (at least one way) because the mountain has 30 old temples and 66 well-documented scenic spots, including beautifully carved memorial arches, Han dynasty cypress trees, white water, breathtaking views of forests and crags, and a stone pillar that looks suspiciously like a lingam. If you do it the hard way, you are following in the footsteps of Confucius!

The top can be reached in 5 hours on foot through the Path of Eighteen Bends. Important to note are the 7000-plus stone stairs, each carefully placed by human labor! Like an almost vertical Great Wall! And they are not narrow! It is difficult to get lost. The stairs are very steep and in some places difficult to climb. The **Temple of Azure Clouds** is over 970 years old (Song). Note the bronze or iron roof ornaments, rafters, bells, and tiles of the main hall, made of metal to endure the severe mountain storms. Inside are nine huge gilt statues. Can you imagine having to carry these and the bronze Ming tablets up here! The summit is at **Tianzhu Feng (Heavenly Pillar Peak)** 天柱峰 , a.k.a. Yuhuang Ding (Jade Emperor Peak)

The **Tomb of Feng Yuxiang (Feng Yu-hsiang)** 冯玉祥墓 may be of interest to students of modern Chinese history. This was the famous "Christian General" who fought with the Nationalists against the Japanese and baptized his men with water hoses. His tomb is at the east end of the Dazhong Bridge, downhill from the Dragon Pool Reservoir. He is known more for his eccentricity than his military successes.

The visiting emperors used to offer their sacrifices at the **Daimiao (Temple to the God of Taishan)** 岱庙 , close to the Taishan Guest House at the base. This is a very impressive complex of religious buildings. The **Tian Kuang Hall** 天贶殿 , which is the main hall, has a mural 3.3 by 62 meters, painted in the Song, showing the pilgrimage of Song Emperor Zhenzong here. It includes 570 to 657 figures. (Count them!) This hall was built in A.D. 1009 and is considered one of the three eminent halls of China. It and the guesthouse are about 4 km from the railway station.

FESTIVALS
During the third or four lunar month, there is a festival on the summit. In September is a mountain climbing competition.

SHOPPING
There is an antique shop in the Dai Temple. Carpets are made locally. Arts and crafts in Taixin Market.

HOTELS
The best hotel here is the Taishan Grand Hotel at the foot of the mountain. The best on the mountain is the Summit Hotel.

Taishan Grand Hotel • *Around the corner from the Taishan Guest House, ½ block from the arch that marks the beginning of the climb. Walking distance to Daimiao Temple.* • 1987. 200 rooms.

Taishan Guest House 泰山宾馆 • *Daizong Fang, at the southern base of Taishan Mountain* • Ren. 1988–89.

Zhong Tian (Half-Way Gate to Heaven) Guest House 中天门宾 a.k.a. Middle Celestial Guest House • *800 meters above sea level* • 1972. Has about 100 beds.

Daiding Guest House 岱顶宾馆 a.k.a. Summit Guest House •
almost at the summit • 1957. About 100 beds and a restaurant. Climbers
should spend the night in the hotel here so they can get up to see the
sunrise (best in September) and the Yellow River.

Until the Summit Guest House is renovated, there are 1000 cheap,
barely adequate hostel beds on the mountain. Tai'an has many other
hotels.

Antique Store: Dai Temple, tel. 3491.
C.I.T.S. 中国国际旅行社 : Dai Zong Fang, above Dai Temple and
the Taishan Arch; tel. 3259.
Taxi: tel. 2342.

TAISHAN 台山

(Cantonese, Toishan; Toishanese, Hoishan) South China. This place
should not be confused with Taishan, the mountain in Shandong
farther north, listed under Tai'an. Taishan is a county on the
southern coast of Guangdong province, about 100 km SW of
Guangzhou and about 80 km, as the crow flies, west of Aomen
(Macao). The fastest way to get to Taichen, the county seat, is by
helicopter from Guangzhou or Zhuhai. Taichen can be reached by
road from Guangzhou in over 3 hours. It will take less time after
the third bridge is finished in 1988. A fast way to go there from
Hong Kong is the 4-hour ferry to Sam Fou, Kaiping or maybe
Guanghoi, and then bus or taxi. Weather: Subtropical. August is
the hottest month, with a mean temperature of 28°C; January is
the coldest, with a mean of 14°C. The annual precipitation is about
2000 mm, mostly from April to August. It can be very humid in
summer. From this county many Chinese left their families for the
Chinatowns of the United States and Canada. Many families here
live off remittances. See ''Special for Overseas Chinese.''

Visitors can go to a local market, visit cottage industries like embroidery, artistic ceramics, bamboo weaving, etc., or explore a village.
Next to the Overseas Chinese Hotel is a park with a small zoo and a

lake. Also nearby is a statue of Chen Yu Hi, a Chinese-American who returned to China to start in 1906 the first railway line by a private company in China; 100 km. long, it was used from 1912 to 1942 when it was destroyed by the Japanese. The old railway station still standing nearby is patterned after one in Seattle at the time.

Taishan is too far from Macao and Hong Kong to feel much of their influence in its architecture. It still retains a lot of its old over-the-sidewalk architecture and charm. But things are changing.

On the outskirts of town is a 7-story Ming pagoda. **Stone Flower Mountain** 石花山 , one of Taishan's eight scenic attractions, is about 2 km NE of the town, with an artificial lake and rock formations that look like furniture and animals.

Tourists can also visit tractor and porcelain factories.

Shang Chuan Island's **Fei Sa Beach** 飞沙里 is about 64 km south of Taichen, plus a 40-minute boat ride. It has 4 km of beach and clear water. The inns there are not yet up to standard, the best now being the 100-room Fei Sa Beach Center. Taishan is hoping to get permission for a direct ferry from Hong Kong to Fei Sa. Nearby are the St. Francis Xavier Church where the Jesuit died in 1552. (He was buried in Goa.) and a primaeval forest inhabited by 3000 monkeys. To the east is **Zhongshan County,** birthplace of Dr. Sun Yixian (Sun Yat-sen).

Basically, the attractions are rural, of interest mainly to Overseas Chinese looking for their roots, and other visitors wanting a restful exposure to south China. It does not have magnificent temples and palaces.

FESTIVALS

Taichen has a unique festival on the 9th day of the 9th month. During the Qing, a young scholar, angry that he could not get a state post, buried his poems and articles in a tomb on one of the mountains. Then he became successful. Ever since, people have been visiting the tomb for luck.

RESTAURANTS

Taishan food is basically the same as Cantonese, but there are some dishes that are unique, like mud fish, steamed minced pork with salted egg, and peanuts fried with water chestnuts.

The **Boston Seafood Restaurant,** next to the Taishan Bureau of Travel and Tourism, is not as American as it seems. It was financed by Boston Chinese for a cousin who described the food as "fair".

HOTELS

The top hotel is the Garden, #2 is the Overseas Chinese or Mei Li Hua (but neither is exceptional). Hopefully IDD and telex will come soon. The new 13-story Taishan Mansion should open soon and be near the top.

Huaqiao (Overseas Chinese) Mansion • *1, Tong Ji Rd., Taichen. Cable 3307. Dist. bus station 1 km. Central near shops, sports field, and man-made lake.* • 1975; ren. 1988, 1990. Four stories, 66 rooms. C.C., C.T.S. Budget travelers only.

Stone Flower Mountain Inn 石花山旅馆 • *Stone Flower Mountain, northeast edge of Taichen, in garden, beside mountain reservoir. Dist. bus station 1 km.* • No credit cards. 7 buildings. 24 rooms. No meals except for groups. No carpets or room telephones. Slow if any laundry service. Local rural architecture. Mosquito nets. Fans.

In spite of crude facilities, many foreigners like this charming hotel because of its setting and closeness to the Chinese people. Living conditions here are actually better than in most Chinese homes where hot water never comes out of a tap. The Inn has classes for foreigners and local people, and free use of bicycles. Some Chinese language classes get credit from Zhongshan University. Foreign students can teach English at the Inn to save money on expenses. Write Mr. Feng Yuan Chao.

Taishan Yuan Lin (Garden) Hotel • *Taichen. Cable 0954. Dist. bus 1 km. Attractive garden-style hotel on edge of man-made lake at base of mountain.* • Helicopter pad. 108 rooms. Hong Kong j.v. Hot spring water in all rooms. C.I.T.S. office.

C.T.S. 中旅社 Overseas Chinese Hotel. Tel. 24768, 22241, 23562. Cable 3307.
Taishan Bureau of Travel and Tourism • 19 Stone Flower Overseas Chinese Village, Huan Bei St. Tel. 25847.

An inexpensive minibus leaves Taichen's O.C. Hotel for Guangzhou early in the morning. See "Getting There."

太 原

TAIYUAN

North China. In the center of Shanxi province, of which it is the capital, Taiyuan is an hour's flight SW of Beijing. It can be reached by air from such places as Xi'an, Lanzhou, Chengdu, and Xining, and by train from Beijing, Xi'an, Zhengzhou, Hohhot, and Datong, etc. The hottest temperature is 35°C for a few days in August. The coldest is ⁻14°C in January. Annual precipitation is 400 mm from July to September. Altitude: 800 meters. Population is 1.74 million.

The city was founded in the Western Zhou (1066–771 B.C.) Because of its strategic location, it was the site of many wars, changing hands five times between A.D. 396 and 618. It was a silk center under the Sui and has been growing grapes for a thousand years. Although it used to be a highly cultured city with many architectural wonders, the wars and modern industry have changed its complexion.

Taiyuan is most famous for the **Jinci Temple** 晋祠, 25 km SW of the city at the foot of Xuanweng Mountain. Started in the Northern Wei (386–534) in memory of the second son of King Wu of the Western Zhou, the Jin Temple was renovated, with additions, in 1102 (Northern Song). Female statues in temples, aside from goddesses, are very rare in China. Was this second son a lush? A son much pampered by women? Are the women here to continue indulging him in the after-life?

Alas, no! Centuries ago, Shanxi was very short of water. Sea and water deities have usually been female. In Shanxi a spring was found near Jinci, so people started worshiping Shuimu (Mother of Water). The maids-in-waiting and the mermaids were her retinue. This is the only temple in Shanxi to Shuimu.

The temple is the oldest wooden structure in the area and is charming. In the **Shengmu (Sacred Lady Hall)** 圣母殿 are 43 dusty, life-size clay figures, 30 of these court maids-in-waiting, all lithesome, each different in expression, and still retaining much color. This hall is not open to the general public; permission must be obtained. Try C.I.T.S. before you go, or look for an attendant at the site.

Uphill from the Jinci about 40 minutes by road, the Tianlong Shan (Mountain of Celestial Dragon) has a little temple with four *lohan*. The 24 small caves above the temple contain many old Buddhist statues, mostly damaged. They are Eastern Wei, Northern Qi, Sui, and Tang dynasties. It is a beautiful, though hilly walk.

The **Chongshan Monastery** 崇善寺 in the city itself is believed to have been a Sui palace once. Only part of the original (Tang) monastery is standing, and part of that is the Shanxi Provincial Museum. The monastery is famous for its ancient 1000-handed, 1000-eyed Goddess of Mercy. It, along with the two other bodhisattvas are eight meters tall. The beams and ceiling are quite remarkable. During the Sino-Japanese War, a bomb went through the ceiling without exploding, and the repair work is still visible. It is 3 km from the Yingze Hotel.

Next door is the **Shanxi Provincial Museum** 山西省博物馆 . Museum #1 has a vast collection of neolithic artifacts. So far, 200 paleolithic and 500 neolithic sites have been unearthed in the province, plus over 500 tombs and other ancient ruins. The museum is closed on Mondays.

Provincial Museum #2 is considered more important than Museum #1. It is at the site of the Chunyang Palace on the west side of May 1 Square. The palace itself was built between 1573 and 1619, and renovated in the Qing. It contains 20 exhibition halls with ceramics, bronzes, carvings, lacquer, calligraphy, embroidery, books, and other documents unearthed around the province.

The **Shuangta Temple** 菁导寺 , a.k.a. the Yongzuo Monastery, has twin pagodas, symbols of Taiyuan, 8 km from the Yingze Hotel. The pagodas were built in the Ming and are over 50 meters high. They are octagonal and built of carved bricks. Inside the monastery are exhibitions of old coins, pottery, etc., and a corridor with 207 stone tablets of Ming calligraphy.

In Shanxi province are also a great number of important historical monuments. In the southern tip is ***Yong Le Palace** 永乐宫 in **Ruicheng County,** with 400-meter-long Yuan dynasty murals, artistically beautiful. From it, one can also study social and architectural history. Nearby in **Yuncheng County** is the **Guan Di Temple,** founded in the Sui and completely renovated in the Qing. **Pingyao** 平遥 , about 100 km SW of Taiyuan, is a well-preserved ancient city with 6.7 km of city walls, and shops, homes, and streets untouched since the Ming and Qing.

At **Hongdong,** about 200-km SW of Taiyuan, is the ***Guangsheng Temple,** listed as Yuan and Ming. It has excellent colored ceramic figures and frescoes. An intricate, stunning collection of about 1000 lively Buddhist and animal figures over 300 years old is at the **Xiaoxitian (Miniature Western Paradise),** NW of Guangsheng Temple and north of Xixian county town. These are also worth a visit. Be prepared to climb and crane your neck. Take a flashlight and binoculars.

*Dingcun 丁村 paleolithic ruins are in Xianfen county, roughly 25 km SW of Hongdong. Also in this area is a Han (nationality) folk museum, with 19 Ming and Qing courtyards, the oldest built in 1593. **Houma,** another 50 km SW of Linfen, is a Jin site from the Eastern Zhou. A low but spectacular (depending on the season) waterfall is at **Hukou** on the Yellow River, northeast of Dingcun. Guesthouses are at Yuncheng City and **Linfen** 临汾 . See ''Datong'' for the dog corporation here. One could spend a fruitful month exploring this province alone!

See ''Datong'' for the Yungang Grottoes, the Great Wall, Wutai Mountain, Sakyamuni Pagoda, and the Huayan and Shanhua Monasteries. See ''Hengshan'' for the Mid-Air Temple.

SHOPPING

Locally made are fur coats, including rabbit and wild rat(!) skin, gold and lacquer inlaid crafts, reproductions of ancient ironware, black-glazed porcelain, Junco brand carpets, Fen Chiew wines, vinegar, fine glassware, lacquerware, jade carving, and brass and copperware (especially fancy charcoal-burning hot pots). Grown locally are dates, pears, persimmons, walnuts, and wild jujubes.

There is a **Friendship Store** (tel. 28731); Taiyuan also has an antique shop, arts and crafts shop, bazaars, and department stores.

RESTAURANTS

Shanxi people love noodles and vinegar-flavored dishes. The **Jia Yang Restaurant** is known for Shanxi food, especially noodles and Shanxi duck. **Cooks' Training Centre** has special cakes. **Qingheyuan Restaurant** has Mongolian hot pot and mutton. Five hundred-meter-long Food Street, in the southern part of the city, has 46 food shops and restaurants.

HOTELS

Bingzhou Hotel 晋词宾馆 • *Yingze St., SW side of May 1st Square* • 1958; renovated 1985. Six restaurants, one bar. Beijing, Yangzhou, British, Japanese, French, and Korean dishes.

Jinci Hotel 并州旅馆 • *near Jin Temple* • 1957; renovated 1982. Eight villas.

San Jin Mansions • *Yingze St.* • 1982. Small rooms.

Shanxi Hotel • *close to Yingze St.* • 1986. This should become the best hotel in the province, with all kinds of services.

Yingze Hotel • *Yingze St., 17 km from airport* • 1976; renovated 1984. 596 beds. One of the top, but don't expect much. Chinese and foreign food, telex room, dance hall, coffee shop, bar.

C.I.T.S. 中国国际旅行社 : Yingze Hotel; tel. 229155; telex 28009 ITSTY CN.
CAAC 中国民航 : 38 Yingze St.; tel. 229903.
Taxi: Yingze Hotel; tel. 223211 X395.

TANGSHAN 唐山

North China, NE of Tianjin in Hebei province. Tangshan was almost completely destroyed by an earthquake in 1976; 800,000 people were killed. Much has since been rebuilt, and it is back in business as an industrial center, open to foreign visitors. It is not a tourism center.

TIANJIN 天津

(Tientsin; Ferry to the Imperial Capital) North China. Over 2 hours (137 km) by train SE of Beijing, 70 km from the Bohai Sea. On the Beijing-Shanghai and the Beijing-Harbin railway lines. Direct flights (3 hours) from Hong Kong. It can be reached by ship from Dalian (218 nautical miles), Yantai, Qingdao, and Shanghai (708 nautical miles). Coldest: January, ⁻22°C; hottest: July, 40°C. Annual precipitation averaging 600 mm, mostly June–August. Urban Population: 3.34 million.

Tianjin is more of a gateway to elsewhere than a tourist destination in itself. It is a port city, the largest commercial seaport in North China. One of the treaty ports open to foreign trade by the Opium Wars, it is now one of China's biggest industrial centers and one of the 14 Open Coastal Cities. It was also the home of the Last Emperor from 1925 to 1931.

It is mainly for business travelers but in between appointments, there are things to do in addition to golf. For tourists, it is worth a two-day stop, one for city attractions and one for excursions outside. Resident foreigners say it is a good place to live because the people are friendlier and more polite than in Shanghai and Beijing, and the sightseeing is less crowded. Many of Beijing's foreign residents drive the two hours to Tianjin on weekends for a change of pace.

Tianjin was a trading post in the 12th century during the Jin. It developed as a port in the Yuan. During the Ming (1404), city walls were built and the city was called Tianjinwei by the duke of Yen, who crossed the Haihe River here on a military expedition. After the Grand Canal opened in 1412, inland commerce and Tianjin's fortunes improved. A city wall was built about this time, and an imposing old fort once stood at the confluence of the three rivers.

Tianjin was invaded by the British and French in 1858. In June of that year the Treaty of Tientsin was signed, forcing 10 more treaty ports to be opened to foreign trade. Christian missionaries were given freedom of movement, and the Chinese were forced to guarantee the protection of missionaries because ''the Christian religion as professed by Protestants and Roman Catholics inculcates the practices of virtue, and teaches man to do as he would be done by.'' In 1860 British and French troops from Tianjin marched on Beijing. They forced the Qing rulers to ratify the Treaty of Tientsin and burned down the Summer Palace. The resulting Treaty of Peking opened Tianjin and nine other ports to foreign trade.

Nine countries eventually controlled over 3500 acres of this city: Britain (with over 1000 acres), France, Germany, Japan, Russia, Italy, Belgium, Austria, and the United States. The concessions lasted from 20 to 80 years and, as in Shanghai, left the Chinese some very interesting old European architecture as well as bitter memories. The Treaty of Peking also forced the Chinese to permit French missionaries to own or rent property anywhere, and further helped to inflame smoldering anti-Christian and anti-foreign resentment.

Many of these feelings resulted from what the Chinese saw as Christian arrogance, which insisted that the Christian God was the only true God. Added to this were cultural misunderstandings. Quite a few Chinese actually believed that the children in Catholic orphanages were either eaten by nuns or ground up for medicine. The French Catholics did pay money for female babies (to keep them from being killed). By

1870 the atmosphere was so tense that after the French consul fired at a minor Chinese official, the consul was immediately hacked to death. Ten nuns, two priests, and another French official were also brutally killed in what is now known as the Tientsin Massacre, or what the Chinese prefer to call the Tientsin Revolt. The tragedy might not have happened if all Christian missionaries had refused to become arms of western imperialism.

On January 15, 1949, Tianjin was taken by the Communists. In 1976 it was severely damaged by an earthquake centered in nearby Tangshan.

Tianjin today, like Beijing and Shanghai, is a municipality directly under the central government. It has eight urban and four rural districts and five suburban counties. Its factories make Flying Pigeon bicycles, Seagull watches, petrochemicals, textiles, diesel engines, etc. The Dagang Oil Field is 60 km away. Tourists would probably be interested in seeing its arts and crafts factories. Its counties grow walnuts, chestnuts, dates, Xiaozhan rice, and prawns. Cultural presentations here sometimes include traditional opera, Beijing Opera, Tianjin ballet, acrobats, and puppets.

The city proper sprawls on both sides of the Hai River. The area immediately SW of Jiefang (Liberation) Bridge was formerly French. The section south of that, around the Astor Hotel, was formerly British. Liberation Road was Victoria Road. It is smoggy with industries, of interest primarily to fans of old European architecture, modern history, and handicrafts. Cruise ships berth in its harbor, and their passengers sleep in its hotels and commute to Beijing. Like many other Chinese cities in the 1980s, it is serious about tourism and is in the process of upgrading its attractions, roads, services, and air quality.

There is enough in the city for over 2 days depending on your interest. The **Dabei (Grand Mercy) Temple** (Tianwei Rd., near the Grand Canal) is the city's biggest Buddhist temple, founded in 1656 (Qing). The **Grand Mosque** (Dafeng Rd., near the Grand Canal) was built in 1644 (Qing). The **Tianjin History Museum** 天津厂史博物馆 (4 Guanghua Rd.; tel. 41354, 42949) contains exhibits on the ancient and revolutionary histories of Tianjin, and has some bronzes, jade, paintings, and calligraphy.

The **Tianjin Arts Museum** (77 Jiefang Bei Rd.; tel. 32484) has sculptures and other traditional works of art from ancient times. The **Tianjin Museum of Natural History** 自然博物馆 (Machangdao, Hexi Dist.; tel. 30504) has fossils of mammoths and dinosaurs.

The **Friendship Club** 友谊俱乐部 (268 Machang Dao; tel. 30329, 32465, 34904, 36425) was built in 1925. It is open to both Chinese and foreigners. Formerly the Tientsin Club, it reeks of Britain in the early 1900s, with beautiful, high mahogany paneling and a drab, dismal interior. There are billiards, badminton, tennis, four bowling lanes, a 1300-

seat theater, a 600-seat banquet hall, and a ballroom with an "elastic" wooden floor. (Real springs are beneath it.) Swimming is in a 33°C mineral-water pool.

Pleasant, but not very exciting is the **Shuishang (Water) Park** 水 上公园 , about 200 hectares of lake, islets, arch bridges, fish farm, zoo, library, swimming pool, and roller-skating rink. The Dengyinglou Restaurant is here. **Ningyuan Park** is in the classic Chinese style. Originally built for Cixi, the Qing empress dowager, it is on 54 hectares. Its Beijing Restaurant specializes in roast pork with sesame seeds.

The **Zhou Enlai (Chou En-lai) Museum** 周恩来纪念馆 is in the western part of the city, south of the Grand Mosque. The former premier studied at Nankai Middle School here from 1913 to 1917, and briefly at Nankai University (1919), where he led student uprisings before going to France in 1920.

Near **Food Street** is **Ancient Culture Street** in Qing dynasty style, and an A.D. 1326 **Temple of the Sea Goddess.** But it is nothing like Beijing's Liulichang or Nanjing's Confucian Temple area. We found nothing much to buy (except in its well-stocked antique shop). Do let us know if this has changed. But festivals are held on Ancient Culture St., with stilt and dragon dances and special exhibits: ask C.I.T.S. for the dates of the Spring Festival, the Folk Art Show Competition, the Harvest Celebration, and the Workers' Cultural Season.

On the last Sunday of October every year is the International Marathon.

The **Theater Museum** is a "must" for theatre lovers. The building itself is a gem in the gaudy south China style, a guild hall for Guangdong merchants built in 1907. 31 Nanmennei St., Nankai Dist. Tel. 253443, 255017.

The **Catholic Cathedral** is next to the International Market. We found a French-speaking person inside who showed us around. Well worth the effort.

The Last Emperor Pu Yi lived in the **Zhang Yuan Garden** and the **Jing Yuan Garden,** and was an honorary member of the **Tientsin Club** (now the Friendship Club). No other Chinese were allowed to be members then.

Factories

Tianjin is a good place to visit arts and crafts factories.

The **No. 2 Carpet Factory** (Jie Fang South Rd., He Xi District. Tel. 82113, 83321. Cable 9522) is one of the biggest carpet factories here, and makes Junco-brand carpets. Carpets have been made for more than 100 years in Tianjin, thick carpets of pure wool, with no synthetics. Knots are made by hand, either 70 rows per square foot (ordinary) or 120 rows (refined). Embossing is also done by hand. Washing in a chemical solution adds gloss.

Visitors allergic to dust or wool should avoid carpet factories.

No. 1 Metal Handicrafts Factory (Jinggangshandao, Hong-xinglu, Hedong Dist.; tel. 43354, 42172) cloisonne; **Tianjin Painted Sculpture Workshop** (270 Machangdao, Hexi Dist.; tel. 36203); **Tianjin Special Handicrafts Factory** (16 Liuweilu, Hedong Dist.; tel. 42137, 43475); **Yangliuqing New Year Picture Society** (111 Sanheli, Tonglou, Hexi District; tel. 331531): New year's pictures of deities, like the Kitchen God, who informed Heaven of what happened during the year in the family were put up traditionally each lunar new year. These pictures are much brighter and more cheerful than traditional Chinese art.

Silk carpets are made in Wuqing county, about 28 km north.

EXCURSIONS FROM TIANJIN

Beidaihe seaside resort, 3½ hours NE by train—see separate listing.

Beijing—see separate listing.

Chengde, a.k.a. Jehol, Qing Imperial Mountain Resort—see separate listing.

Qing Tombs, about 3 hours' drive NE. See "Zunhua."

*****Dule (Temple of Solitary Joy)**   , 120 km north, about 2 hours' drive, is in the western part of **Jixian city** and can be combined with a trip to Panshan Mountain and the Great Wall in one day. It was founded in the Tang. Its Guanyin (Goddess of Mercy) Hall and the Gate to the Temple were rebuilt in A.D. 984 (Liao). The magnificent Guanyin Hall, 23 meters high, is the oldest existing multistoried wooden structure in China. The 16-meter-high, 11-headed goddess is one of the largest clay sculptures in China. The mythical animals at the gate are the oldest extant *chiweis* in China!

The **Yuyang Guesthouse** 渔阳宾馆 is a 104-room hotel in Jixian. 1980. Chinese food, but Western breakfasts. Fourteen courtyards.

The **Panshan (Screen of Green) Mountain** 盘山 (about 100 km north of Jixian County City in Tianjin Municipality) has been a mountain resort since the Tang. Highest peak is 1000 meters above sea level, on top of which is a pagoda said to contain a tooth of Buddha. Famous for its scenery, unusual rocks, and pines. It also has a lake. Its 70 Buddhist temples were burned by the Japanese during World War II. Some of the buildings have been replaced or renovated.

The **Great Wall** in Jixian County should have a museum by now and a hotel. See also "Great Wall."

SHOPPING

The main shopping streets are Binjiang Dao and Heping Road, with the three largest department stores. Made in Tianjin are wool carpets, painted clay figurines by Master Zhang, New Year pictures, porcelain vases, tablecloths, accordians, cloisonne pens, soccer balls, basketballs, kites, and inlaid, lacquered furniture.

Arts and Crafts Service (234 Heping Rd., tel. 24516); **Friendship Store** 友谊商店 (2 Zhangde Dao; tel. 32513): All of the above, plus jewelry, jade, ivory, fur coats, and hats, suede coats, padded silk jackets, men's suiting, shell work, cloisonne, carved lacquer, screens, inlaid chests, cork and boxwood carvings. Shipments can be made internationally; **Tianjin First Friendship Store** (21 Youyi Rd., Hexi Dist.; tel. 333003, 334505; cable: TFFS) This store has almost everything imaginable on four stories but it is not exceptional. Also ships purchases, tailors, arranges certificates of origin, mail orders, and books tickets for trains, ships, and airplanes; **Painted Sculpture Studio** (270 Machang Dao; tel. 36203); **Quanyechang Emporium** (352 Heping Rd.; tel. 23771); **Tianjin Department Store** (226 Heping Rd.; tel. 24195); **Wenyuange Antique Store** (263 Heping Rd.; tel. 23450); **Yangliuching New Year's Picture Studio:** Good prices for scrolls, reproductions, and prints. See factory, above; **Yilinge Antique Store** (175 Liaoning Rd.; tel. 20308) Branches in Friendship Hotel, and Astor Hotel.

We found the **International Market** too crowded, confusing, and its goods badly displayed. But some shoppers might thrive in it.

RESTAURANTS

The Nanshi Food Street has three stories of shops, restaurants, wine shops, and tea houses. The food here is from all over China and abroad, and includes typical Tianjin snacks such as *goubuli* (steamed meat dumpling), *erduoyan* (fried cake), and *shibajie* (deep-fried dough twist). We found it too dirty to be appetizing. Please let us know if they clean things up as the concept is great.

Friendship Club ● *268 Machang Dao; tel. 36425* ● Chinese and Western food.

Tianjin Baozi Restaurant 红桥饭庄   ● *near the Friendship Hotel* ● Famous for dumplings.

Tianjin Roast Duck Restaurant 天津包子铺 ● *142 Liaoning Rd.; tel. 22660, 22664* ● Tianjin's roast duck is like Beijing's.

Qishilin (Kiessling) Restaurant 起士林餐厅 ● *33 Zhejiang Rd.; tel. 32020, 32561* ● European.

HOTELS

The top luxury-class hotels here are the Hyatt, Sheraton, and Crystal Palace with the cheaper, older Friendship Hotel still popular with business people on a budget.

DESTINATIONS · · · 465

The Hyatt and the Friendship have good locations for business people within walking distance of government offices and foreign trade corporations. The Astor and Tianjin First are almost adjacent to the Hyatt and are also a cheaper, less luxurious alternative.

The Sheraton, Crystal Palace and InterTech are close together with the state guest house in the south suburbs, with more space and greenery, and nearer the International Exhibition Centre, C.I.T.S., and Friendship Store. These are also closer to the development zone and harbor.

In Tanggu, next to the Economic and Technology Development Region, the best hotel appears to be the Victory.

Astor Hotel • *33 Taier Zhuang Rd. Telex 23266, 23268 ASHTL CN. Dist.A.P.30 km. Dist.R.W.4 km. On Haihe River.* • T.R., C.C. Hong Kong management, British built. 1900, Expanded in 1924, ren. 1985. Old wing, where Dr. Sun Yat-sen and President Hoover slept, has 93 big rooms. Old flavor. 1987 wing looks good. 7 stories, 120 rooms. IDD. Business center. For budget travelers.

Crystal Palace Hotel • *Youyi and Binshui Rd. Telex 23277 TCPPH CN. By East Lake. Dist. A.P.35 km. Dist. R.W.8 km.* • 1987–88. 7 stories, 346 rooms. 7-story lobby. Striking, ultra modern palacial architecture deserves a visit. Built in five sections to withstand earthquakes. Beautifully set coffee shop. IDD, C.I.T.S. Health club. Pool. Skates for rent. No smoking floor and areas in restaurant. Art deco decor in rooms. C.C., bicycles, business center.

Friendship Hotel • *94 Nanjing Rd. Telex 23264, 23269 FRHTL CN, 23265 TFH CN. Dist.A.P.22 km. Dist.R.W.4 km.* • No credit cards. No reservations by telex. 1977. Restaurant and lobby redecorated 1987–88. No plans to renovate rooms (now old fashioned but well maintained). 9 stories, 209 rooms. Should have IDD now. Business center.

Hyatt Tianjin • *Jiefang Rd. N. Telex 23270 HYTJN CN. Fax 310021. Dist.A.P.23 km. Dist.R.W.5 km. On bank of Haihe River.* • Free airport pickup if requested and room booked directly with hotel. Primarily business travelers. T.R., C.C., bicycles. USTV. 1986, 19 stories, 450 rooms. IDD. Business center. Jazz band. Very small shop. Health center. Good rooms. No smoking area in coffee shop. Regency Club.

InterTech Corporation • *25 Youyi Rd., He Xi District. Telex 23332 ISTCC CN. Cable TISTCC. Fax 319391.* • The guest house here seems to be ideal for budget business travelers, tourists, or conferences. Soft opening 1987. 8 stories, 62 small but adequate rooms.

InterTech is a business consulting agency currently with 25 mainly American staff (lawyers, engineers, etc.). After the foreigners leave, 27 apartments will also be available. Many of the staff are Christians but this hasn't stopped the smoking and the bar. IDD. American doctor available for consultations.

Sheraton Tianjin Hotel • *Zi Jin Shan Rd., He Xi Dist. Telex 23354 SHTJH CN. Fax 318741. Dist.A.P. 15 km. Dist.R.W. 8 km. Near free market, Yanyuan Gardens, Friendship Club* • T.R., C.C. 1987. 6 stories, 282 rooms. Appears to be trying very hard to please guests. Offering home-style Western dishes like chicken pot pie as well as fancy food. Stores sell locally made goods specifically designed by the hotel for foreigners. Free use of bicycles. 6-story atrium lobby. Business center. Unlike other hotels, reservations held only until 4 p.m. Gym, pool.

Tianjin First Hotel • *158 Jie Fang Rd. Telex 23265 TFH CN. Fax 313341. Dist.A.P.14 km. Dist.R.W.4 km.* • No credit cards. Will answer telex for reservations. Built 1924 as Talati Hotel and still has original elevator alongside new Otis. New 1987 section better rooms. 6 stories, 98 rooms and 20 suites. Mainly for budget travelers. IDD.

Victory Hotel • *11 Jin Tang Rd., Tanggu Dist. Cable 5833. Telex 23375 TJYH CN. Fax 984470, 984270. Dist.A.P.30 km. Dist.R.W. 1 km* • 1987. 15 stories, 298 rooms. C.C. (no Diner's), IDD, business center. Hong Kong J.V. Pool, tennis, bowling, gym, sauna.

Yingbin Guesthouse, a.k.a. Garden Hotel • *337 Machang Dao, He Xi Dist.* • A posh state guesthouse with 93 beds, mostly in suites. Four villas. Near Friendship Club and across lake from Crystal Palace.

OTHER IMPORTANT ADDRESSES
Airport 飞机场
Bank of China: 80 Jiefang Bei Rd.; tel. 32559.
CAAC 中国民航售票处 : 290 Heping Rd.; tel. 704545.
C.I.T.S.: 20 Youyi Rd. Tel. 312619, 314831. Telex 23281 TJITS CN. Fax 312619. Cable 1954. Phone for sub-branches in hotels.
C.T.S.: 20 Youyi Rd. Tel. 318449. Telex 23281 TJITC CN. Fax 312619. Cable 1954. 198 Jiefang Rd.; tel. 318974. Telex 23265 TFH CN.
Hospitals: In case of emergency, if convenient, contact your guide or hotel attendant. Otherwise: No. 1 Central Hospital (at entrance to Munan Dao), Heping Dist.; tel. 34646.
International Seamen's Club: Xingang; tel. 3897.
Taxis: Check first with a hotel. Otherwise the **Tianjin General Tourist Corporation** (Friendship Guesthouse, Shengli Rd., tel. 35647, 35664) provides chartered vehicles or sells individual tickets for sightseeing in the area.

Tianjin Taxi Co.: 383 Heping Rd.; tel. 35221 (for charters), 35771 (for taxis).

Tianjin Tourism Car Hire Company: Youyi Rd., Hexi Dist.; tel. 37175.

Tianjin International Golf Club: Northwest, Tianjin Airport, tel. 249391.

Tianjin Municipal Tourism Bureau, 18 Youyi Rd. Tel. 318718. Cable 3266. Telex 23281 TJITS CN.

Tianjin Railway Station 火车站 : The new railway station should be open late 1988.

Xingang (New Harbor) 新港 : 50 km from Tianjin. Has Friendship Store, hotel, and Seamen's Club. Accessible by train or road.

TURPAN 吐鲁番

(Turfan). Northwest China. Northeast Xinjiang province, roughly 198 km SE of the capital Urumqi. It can be a 2-day trip by road or train from the capital, which should include Gaochang, Jiaohe, the Baziklic Caves, Astana Tombs, Imin Minaret, Karez Wells, and Valley of Grapes. It can also be reached from Lanzhou by road or rail. Weather: The hottest in China! Turpan is in the Turpan Basin, which is known as "the oven." Temperatures reach over 40°C in summer. Rainfall averages 16.6 mm a year, and in very dry years, it has been 4 mm. Strong winds blow more than 30 days a year. The hot air from the basin and cold air from the north create violent storms. In winter, people could wear fur coats in the morning, light clothes at noon, and dine in the evenings around hot stoves. For summer nights, one needs a sweater. It is an area of extremes. Weather people and geographers would love it. The lowest point of the basin is Aydingkol Lake, its water surface 154 meters below sea level. It is second only to the Dead Sea as the lowest body of water in the world. Nearby is Bogda Mountain with an altitude of 5445 meters. **But wait! Don't stop reading!** Some of the people who have been there say the dust and the bumpy roads are worth it!

Turpan was once an oasis on the Silk Route. An oasis? Yes, an oasis! It existed then and now because of subterranean water from the 2000-year-old **Karez wells** 坎儿井 . During the Western Han (206 B.C.– A.D. 24), soldiers were sent to develop agriculture here. Some sources say the technology for the wells came from Shaanxi province. Other historians say farther west. In any case, the wells are most common in Turpan and nearby Hami, to the east.

In spring, snow from the Tianshan Mountain melts, and this water flows into the Turpan Basin. While a lot of this evaporates, some water does soak into the ground and is stored in vast natural underground reservoirs reached by sloping channels tapped in turn by the wells.

Modern irrigation methods based on these wells have transformed Turpan into an agricultural area. Californians, and anyone else who has made deserts produce food, should be fascinated. Cultivated here are grain, grapes, cotton, and the famous Hami melons. Grapes have grown here for 2000 years. The vineyards are north of the city. The wooden huts with the holes are for drying the September-harvested seedless raisins in the hot, dry air. Ask to see the drying process. Hami melons are much in demand. They have a sweet perfume somewhat like face powder, with the texture of cantaloupe and taste of honeydew.

Turpan is also a good place to experience the different cultural minorities. **Uygur (Uighur)** 维吾尔族 and **Hui** 回族 nationalities live here with the Han.

The dry climate has meant the preservation of historical monuments. The area has many ancient tombs, Buddhist grottoes, and the ruins of ancient cities. The best grottoes in the area are in Dunhuang, so you may want to wait until you go there.

The ghost city of *Gaochang 高昌故城 , 40 km SE of Turpan, was capital of the State of Gaochang (500–640) and reached its peak in the ninth century, with a population of more than 30,000. Try to imagine it then. It was on the Silk Road and flourished for 1500 years, from the first century B.C. Here were once 30 to 40 monasteries! The buildings were made of mud bricks and are now without roofs. The town covers 2 million square meters and a stop here takes about 30 minutes. Did it only decline with the Silk Road?

Close to Gaochang are the **Astana Tombs** 阿斯塔娜古墓 , dating from the third century to about the eighth A.D. This is where 500 mummies, plus their belongings, were found, along with 2100 documents and books. Take a flashlight. Visitors routinely see only a couple of mummies in a dark room. Where are the others? The dry weather preserved the bodies with still discernable eye lashes and eyeballs. Was Astana the Uygur capital? Astana means capital in Uygur.

*Jiaohe (a.k.a. Yarkhoto, and possibly Yaerhu) 交河故城 , 10 km west of Turpan, existed from the second century B.C. to the 14th A.D. Its mud brick buildings are better preserved than Gaochang's and were encompassed in an area 1 km by 300 meters. In the northwestern part are temple ruins with the remains of Buddhist images. There is also a rare brick Buddhist temple.

The 44-meter-high **Imim Minaret** 额敏塔 , 200 years old, stands 2 km east of Turpan, its geometric patterns in the Uygur style. However, its smooth inverted-cone shape with rounded top is reminiscent of those towers south of New Delhi on the road to Agra. The ***Pazikelik (Baizeklik) Thousand-Buddha Caves** 柏孜克里克千佛洞 are 50 km NE of Turpan by dusty road on a cliff of the Flaming Mountains. About 60 of the grottoes are still intact. They were built over a period of 1400 years, starting in the Southern and Northern Dynasties (A.D. 420–550). Dunhuang's are more interesting and younger, but it is good to compare the two. The **Flaming Mountains** 火焰山 themselves are historical, so named because the incessant sun is supposed to make the red rocks seem on fire from a distance. Perhaps this happens at sunset just in the classic tale *Pilgrimage to the West.* In that story, the monkey king pushes a hot brick from the furnace of one of the Taoist immortals to stop Monk Xuanzhang from going to India. The mountains are 100 km long and 10 km wide, their highest peak 800 meters above sea level. Unless you know the story, this is just another set of hills and may not be worth a special visit.

Turpan grows grapes with a 15 to 20% sugar content, among the best in China. Grapes grow almost everywhere, along streets and beside private homes. A 2.5-km grape corridor is between the center of the city and the Imam Minaret.

Turpan Tourist Hotel • *Dist.A.P. 30 min.* • 1986. 5 stories. Uygur staff.
China Travel Service: tel. 2907.

URUMQI 乌鲁木齐

(Urumchi) Pronounced Oo-roo-*moo*-chi. Northwest China. This capital of Xinjiang (Sinkiang) Uygur Autonomous Region, an area one sixth of China's total, borders on the Soviet Union and Mongolia. It can be reached by plane from Beijing (over 3 hours), Lanzhou (3 hours), Shanghai (4½ hours), and Guangzhou. Flights also from Istanbul and Sharjah. It can be reached by train from Xining and Lanzhou, but from the Qinghai capital, it is about 1600 km. The Beijing-Urumqi express covers almost 4000 km, the longest train ride in China. Urumqi is at an altitude of 650 to 910 meters and is surrounded by mountains. Weather: Hottest in August, 40.9°C. Coldest in December, ⁻41.5°C. However, the coldest in August has been .5°C. Pack for cold summer nights. In May and June, the coldest has been ⁻8.9°C and ⁻4.2°C! Consider yourself warned. Maybe you can use the weather as an excuse to buy a fur jacket! The annual precipitation is 200 mm. There is snow between mid-November and March. The best time to visit is May–September. Population: 950,000 urban, mainly Uygurs (Uighurs), but also Hans, Kazaks, Mongolians, and Huis. The city has 13 nationalities, the province 47.

Urumqi dates from the Han, but its attractions are its people and the scenery. It has been described as an ugly Russian-looking city. **Tianshan (Heaven Mountain)** 天山 and **Lake Tianzi (Heavenly Lake)** , 115 km south of the city, is about 1950 meters above sea level and colder than Urumqi. Count on half a day at least at these, and take something extra for warmth, especially if you want to climb. Tianzi is worth the trip for the scenery. The lake is 5 square km and 100 meters deep, and can be reached by horseback if you wish. Most visitors, however, go by bus or taxi. An ancient **glacier** 冰山 , about 100 meters thick, 5000 meters by 2000 meters, sprawls near ice caves and valleys. But visitors are frequently too cold to stay to explore. It is interesting to compare this area with the Rockies or Switzerland. But did you ever see a yurt and prancing camels at Lake Louise?

About 65 km south of Urumqi is the **Nanshan Pasture** 南山草原 —mountains, valleys, fountains, waterfalls, and cypress and pine trees. Why do you think the pasture is a symbol of longevity? The pasture is in Kazak country (not related to Cossacks). Horseback riding, mountaineering, and digging for valuable ginseng roots are listed among the attractions. Here, if you are lucky—or unlucky—you might find a game of polo played with an initially live goat instead of a ball! Shades of Afghanistan! You might be able to dine and/or sleep in a yurt. Barbecued mutton drowned by tea with mare's milk has been offered to some groups. Here it is impolite to show the soles of your feet.

In the city itself, one usually visits the nine-story **Hong Ding Shan Ta (Red Hill Pagoda)** 江顶山塔 , founded in the Tang, the current building finished in 1788. From the design of the pagoda here, you should be able to see a resemblance to Indian stupas. This is about a 5-minute stop. The excellent **Xinjiang Museum** 新疆博物馆 has a collection of historical relics of the various nationalities living in the region, and has documented for regional protection 119 historical sites. Exhibits include gold Roman coins, silver Persian coins, and other relics of the Silk Road. One hall contains murals; another displays 3200-year-old mummies. A special new exhibition hall displays ancient artifacts and the customs of 12 minorities in Xinjiang. The museum is good for 2 hours and is close enough to the hotel for visitors to go there on their own. Titles are in Chinese and English!

The **National Minorities Palace** 少数民族宫 is a good place to visit, as it has a museum with costumes of the different groups, as well as a shop.

One of the highlights of Urumqi is the **Free Market/Bazaar** 自由市场 , which is near the hotel. You should find handicrafts there. Don't forget to haggle over prices! And close your eyes to the tempting fruit, "bing" pancakes, and spicy and delicious shish-kebobs there, unless you can see them being cooked. Tourists before you have gotten sick from eating from these stalls.

The different minority groups make for an interesting city. The Uygurs controlled NW China during the Tang. In A.D. 788, a Tang princess married a Uygur khan, by no means a love match. In subsequent years, Chinese silk and sugar were exchanged for Uygur horses and furs. Uygur cavalry often helped the Tang. Strangely enough, the Uygurs were the main supporters of the Manichaean religion (see "Quanzhou"). The power of the Uygurs declined after their capital was sacked by the Kirghiz of Western Siberia. In 842, a food shortage turned the Uygurs into very aggressive raiders and China retaliated with force and the execution of Uygurs in Xi'an.

Other Important Destinations in Xinjiang: This is a huge region, the largest in China. It is much less populated than other parts of China, as a great deal of it is desert and mountain. Two cave temples, not otherwise described in this book, are listed as historical monuments under State Council protection. They may not be open yet for tourism, but you can ask about them. They are at **Baicheng** and **Kuqa,** almost halfway in between Kashi and Urumqi, and are said to be from the third century. Kuqa already has an airport.

For other caves and tourist attractions in the region, see "Silk Road," "Turpan," and "Kashgar." Ask about the Corban Festival, the Moslem New Year, with its songs, dances, horse races, courtship rituals on horseback, wrestling, and lamb snatching.

SHOPPING

Urumqi is just about the best place on the Silk Road to shop for minority handicrafts. These include carpets, jade carving, embroidery, musical instruments, and fur and leather articles. Embroidered caps and hand-knotted wool carpets in Persian designs are especially good buys.

Urumqi Rug Factory 乌鲁木齐地毡厂 (64 Jinger Rd.; tel. 25825); the **National Minorities Palace** also sells costumes, hats, and vests.

FOOD

Local specialties include roast whole sheep, kebabs, thin-skinned steamed buns with stuffing, fried rice (eaten with bare hands), deep-fried *nang,* mare's milk, and dried sour cheese. Local fruits include seedless white grapes, pears, Hami melons, apples, and raisins. The meat in Xinjiang is mainly mutton, because Moslems do not eat pork.

HOTELS

Hotels here, especially the Friendship, might have parties for visitors in the evenings, with guests and staff performing.

Friendship Guesthouse 新疆友谊宾馆 • *Yan'an Rd., Urumqi, 28 km from airport* • One of the main hotels.

Kunlun Hotel • *Youhao Rd. 83000. Dist.A.P.16 km. Dist.R.W.12 km. Near government trade offices.* • 1959 8 stories, 1984 11 stories; ren. 1988. 426 rooms. IDD, no C.C. Xinjiang carpets, electric fans. One of the main hotels.

World Plaza Hotel • 400 rooms, 24 stories. Joint venture. Open soon.

Xinjiang Guest House • *Yan'an Rd.* • 1986. Striking ethnic architecture.

C.I.T.S. 中国国际旅行社 : People's Square; tel. 25794, 25913; cable 2464.

C.T.S.: 47 Xinhua Nan Rd.; tel. 24406, 27238. Cable 0022. Telex 79164 HOOTH. CN.
CAAC 中国民航 : 206 Youhao Rd.; tel. 42942.
See also ''Silk Road.''

WEIFANG 潍坊

North China. Almost in the center of Shandong province, it is noted for its international kite festival (the first 10 days in April) every year and its unique kite museum.

In the city is the small **Shihuyuan Garden** 十笏园 and in the outskirts the **Tuoshan Grotto** 驼山石窟 and the **Yunmenshan Grotto** 云门山石窟 with 638 Buddhist sculptures from the Sui and Tang dynasties. Yunmenshan Grotto is also known for its 7.5 meter high carved stone ''Longevity'' character, the biggest such character in China, carved over 500 years ago. In **Shanwang** 山旺, southwest of the city, 18-million-year-old prehistoric fossils are still being found. The **Shanwang Paleontological Museum** there has 10,000 specimens. **Mount Yimeng** has high cliffs and waterfalls; **Laolongwan Bay** boasts hot spring baths. Tourists can live with farming families.

Students of modern history might be interested in the Second Middle School, a little over a kilometer from the Weifang Hotel. This was once the Weihsien Concentration Camp. British, Canadian, and American prisoners of the Japanese there in the 1940s included Eric Liddell, the hero of the movie *Chariots of Fire*. A gold medalist in the 1924 Olympics for winning the 400 meters, this Scottish athlete refused to race on Sundays. He later became a Congregational missionary in China and died of a brain tumor in 1945. He was buried near the prison camp six months before the end of the war. The site is now covered by a housing development. Some of the original prison-missionary buildings are still standing.

SHOPPING

Made locally are woodblock prints, kites, lacquer inlaid with silver, cotton toys and bronze imitations.

The top hotel is the **Yuanfei** (35 Shengli St.), then the **Weifang Guest House** (33 Shengli St.) and thirdly the **Bohai Guest House.**

C.I.T.S. and **C.T.S.:** 33 Shengli St. Tel. 223854, 222981 X24. (C.T.S. tel. 222981 X61). Cable 0082. Telex 39503 FAOWF CN.

WEIHAI 威海卫

A.k.a. Wei-hai-wei North China. Northern Shandong province on the Bohai Sea east of Yantai and NE of Qingdao.

Weihai was developed in the Ming because of its excellent harbor. Some of the funds to strengthen the navy base here were squandered by Empress Dowager Cixi on her Summer Palace in Beijing. In 1894, the Japanese won a naval battle here and occupied the city. In 1898, it became a British naval base on a 25-year lease, and was used to keep an eye on the Russians at Port Arthur (now Dalian), 100 km north. For the American navy and other imperialists, it was a summer resort with good beaches.

Weihai has one of the three most famous **hot springs** in China. It is not as developed as Japanese hot springs, but the yellowish, 85°C water can be cooled, and is said to be good for skin diseases, rheumatism, etc.

Liugong Island has a museum with the wreck of a warship from the 1890 Sino-Japanese war. Wax figures of the men who fought the Japanese in 1895 are in the former headquarters. In Weihai you can also find factories that produce carpets, leather goods, embroidery, artificial fur, etc.

HOTELS

Dongshan Hotel, on the beach, and the **Shandong Accountants' House,** overlooking the beach, are both good.

WUHAN

Southwest China, almost halfway on the main railway line, 18 hours by train south of Beijing and 18 hours north of Guangzhou. The capital of Hubei province can also be reached by ship, or by air from many cities including Hong Kong. Weather: Hottest— 39°C (July and August); coldest—⁻5°C (January and February). Annual precipitation 1200 mm, mainly February to May. Population: 6.3 million, the fifth largest in China.

Wuhan, the capital of Hubei, is really three cities **Hankou (Hankow)** 汉口 , **Hanyang** 汉阳 , **and Wuchang** 武昌 , separated from each other by the Changjiang (Yangtze) and Han rivers, and joined by bridges. It is the most important site of the republican revolution, and is noted for its industries, its ancient chime bells, and as a gateway to the Wudang Mountains and Yangtze Gorges.

The city itself dates from the 11th century B.C. (Shang). The city wall in Hanyang, no longer standing, was first built in the Han, almost 2000 years ago. The Wuchang wall was built during the Three Kingdoms (220–265), by Sun Chuan, king of Wu, and can still be seen at the **Small East Gate** 小东门 . Hankou and Hanyang were originally one city, but in the 15th century, the Han River changed its course. It has been an important port for at least 2000 years.

Several foreign nations forced concessions here after the Opium War, and some of the architecture still reflects old Europe. Wuchang is especially famous because on October 10, 1911, the first victory of the Sun Yat-sen revolution against the Manchus took place here, although Sun himself was absent. Wuhan became the headquarters of the left wing of the Nationalist party. In 1923, the Communists led a successful railway workers' strike; in 1927, Mao Zedong set up a Peasant Movement Institute in Wuchang.

The city was liberated in May 1949. The three cities merged administratively shortly afterward. During the Cultural Revolution, it experienced some of the heaviest fighting between factions.

Wuhan is the home of the huge Wuhan Iron and Steel Works. Other industries include metallurgy, machine building, and electronics.

The **Museum of Hubei Province**　湖北省博物馆　displays some of the world's most exciting recent archaeological discoveries. In 1978, 7000 articles were excavated from the **Zenghouyi Tomb,** located just outside of Suizhou city. Dating from the Warring States period 2400 years ago, the tomb of Marquis Yi of Zeng contained bronzes, weapons, lacquer, musical instruments, gold, and jade. The contents were found in water in which oxidized copper was accidentally dissolved. This saved most of the pieces from decay. Some of the lacquer is still preserved in water that shows the original brilliant red at its best.

Most important in the find is a complete set of 65 ritual bells of different sizes. When struck, they emit a perfect 12-tone system covering five octaves. Each bell also has two tones depending on where it is struck, a quality that has not yet been found in any other bell anywhere else in the world. In addition, the name of the tone and the date were inscribed on each bell in both the Zeng and Chu scripts. The two languages side by side here are as valuable to linguists as the Rosetta stone.

The bells were a gift from the king of Chu. Since their reigns overlapped by only a few years, the technology to produce them must have been at an astoundingly high level. Not only are their tones precise, they were probably cast in a short length of time. The heaviest is 203.6 kg and 1½ meters high. Imagine pouring hot metal into a mold that size! And of the exact amount to produce the prescribed tone!

Ritual bells were only played for ceremonies, not for pleasure. Only aristocrats and royalty were allowed to possess them, and only in certain numbers. Reproductions have been played for visitors, who have heard *Jingle Bells* as well as ancient Chinese music. They sound crisper than other bells because of the bosses.

Students of modern Chinese history must visit the site of the first victory of the republican revolution, on Shouyi Road in Wuchang. There, revolutionists accidentally exploded some ammunition, and this point of no return started the lightning that led to the takeover of the city. A statue of Dr. Sun Yat-sen dominates the front of the **Hubei Military Government Building** 武昌起义军政府旧址（红楼）, now a museum. Republican troops broke through the **Qiyi Men (Uprising Gate)** 起义门 and seized Wuchang. Originally named Zhonghe Gate, the Qiyi Gate is one of the 10 original gates of Wuchang.

If you have more time the **Guqing Tai (Platform of the Ancient Lute)** 古琴台 in Hanyang dates from at least the fifth century, a monument to a deep friendship between a woodcutter and a musician. **Baotongsi Temple** 宝通禅寺 on Hongshan Hill was originally built in A.D. 630. Important is the **Iron Buddhas' Hall,** with six iron buddhas said to be from the Tang. The temple of the **Xingfusi Pagoda** 兴福寺塔 on the western base of Hongshan Hill in Wuchang was originally built in A.D. 554, the 11.5-meter-high pagoda in 1270.

The 45-meter-high, seven-story **Hongshan Pagoda** 洪山宝塔 in Wuchang dates from the Yuan (1279). The **Guiyang Temple (of Original Purity)** 归元禅寺, started at the end of the Ming over 300 years ago, is the most important Buddhist temple in the city, and one of the 10 biggest in China. It contains 500 clay arhats, each life-size, distinctive, and 250 years old.

The five-story, 51-meter-high, **Huang He Lu (Yellow Crane Tower)** 黄鹤楼, first built in A.D. 223 on top of the Yellow Swan riverside rock, inspired many famous poets, including Li Bai. It was destroyed by nature or war and rebuilt several times. It was reconstructed and expanded on its present site on Snake Hill starting in 1981. The design is based largely on the Qing version that lasted from 1868–84, but is 20 meters taller. It also has elements of the previous versions, pictures of which are inside. The tower gives a good view of the Yangtze and the city.

The poets were inspired by the legend of the wine shop on the original site. Here, the owner used to give free wine to an old man who drew a picture of a yellow crane on the wall in gratitude. After the old man left, the crane came to life and danced for the customers, and the owner became rich. When the old man returned decades later, he mounted the crane and flew off into the sky.

Nearby are the White Tower, the Tablet Corridor, and gardens. Wuhan will be rebuilding 20 historical buildings in the vicinity.

Chibi 赤壁 is the site of a famous Three Kingdom's battle.

The **Bridge over the Yangtze** 长江大桥 is smaller than Nanjing's. Completed in 1957, it is 1670 meters long.

Outside the city are the **Wuzu Temple** 五祖 in Huangmei county, originally built in the seventh century, and **Jingzhou City** 荆州城, whose 1187 city wall was rebuilt in 1646, nine meters high and nine km in circumference, with six gates. The museum here contains a 2100-

year-old male cadaver. **Jinan City** 纪南城 is 5 km north of Jing-ling County and was the capital of the Kingdom of Chu from 689 to 278 B.C.

Yuquan Temple 玉泉寺 , at the eastern base of Yuquan Moun-tain, near Dangyang county city, was built in the Eastern Han. It has an iron pagoda dating from 1061 and a temple from the Southern Song.

The **Wudang Mountain** 武当山 is important as a Taoist center, with an impressive collection of religious buildings. Mostly built in the Ming, it includes eight palaces, two temples, 36 nunneries, and 62 grotto temples, all along a 30-km-or-so mountain path. The highest of its 72 peaks, Tianzhu, is over 1600 meters. On top is the ***Golden Hall** (Yuan and Ming) of gilded copper. Wudang needs 5 days and is not as stren-uous as other mountains. New hotels are at the foot.

The museum at the ***Ancient Copper Mine in Tonglushan** 古铜 矿 , Daye county, has been described by a Canadian metallur-gist as "incredible." One hour by road from Wuhan, it takes another half hour to explore. It is now an open pit with mining tools, shaft, ropes, and baskets, started in the Zhou about 3000 years ago. Nowhere else in the world at the time was mining technology so far advanced.

Wuhan is also planning a 200 meter-long street halfway up She-shan Hill, with old-style shops and attendants in period dress selling souvenirs and local products.

For other destinations in the province see "Gezhouba" and "Yangtze Gorges." From Wuhan, one can take a regular ferry or one of the lux-ury tourist ships through the Yangtze Gorges to Chongqing. See sepa-rate listings.

CULTURAL EVENTS

Noteworthy are the Wuhan Acrobatic Troupe, Beijing Opera Troupe of Wuhan, the Wuhan Song and Dance Drama Troupe, and, of course, the Zenghouyi Chime Bells. All of these have performed abroad.

SHOPPING

Made locally are gold and silver jewelry, lacquerware, carpets, shell carvings, carved turquoise, boxwood carving, feather fans, colored pot-tery, and paintings.

Hubei Antique Shop 武汉古玩店 (Provincial Museum, East Lake Scenic Spot Area; tel. 75336); **Wuhan Antiques and Curios Store** 汉古玩店 (1039 Zhongshan Ave., Hankou; tel. 21453); **Wuhan Car-pet Weaving Mill** (14 Hankou Ruixiang Rd.; tel. 22803, 22003): this factory can be visited; **Wuhan Emporium** (208 Liberation Thorough-fare; tel. 52991); **Wuhan Friendship Store** 友谊商店 (Liberation Thoroughfare, Hankou; tel. 25781 and 25794); **Wuhan Service De-partment of Arts and Crafts** 工艺美术店 (Minshen Rd., Zhongshan Ave., Hankou; tel. 53478).

RESTAURANTS

Among the well-known Hubei dishes are: mianyang three steamings of fish, pork, and chicken; grilled meats of five kinds of poultry; fish balls soup with egg white in the shape of the Three Gorges; stir-fried sliced pork kidney in phoenix-tail shape; fried boneless eel; braised wild duck in brown sauce; steamed catfish; lotus seeds with white fungus in sweet soup.

Guanshengyuan Restaurant • *115 Jianghan No. 1 Rd., Hankou; tel. 23575* • Cantonese.

Laohuibin Restaurant • *50 Sanmin Rd., Hankou; tel. 51971* • Hubei food.

Laotongcheng Restaurant • *Dazhi Rd., Zhongshan Ave., Hankou; tel. 21562.*

Sijimei (Good in All Seasons) Restaurant • *Jianghan Rd., Zhongshan Ave., Hankou; tel. 22842.*

HOTELS

C.I.T.S. says the top hotel is the Qingchuan, then the Jianghan, and thirdly the Yangtze (which is tops for business travelers).

Holiday Inn Wuhan • *Jie Fang Ave.* • 1990, 407 rooms. Bowling, pool, health center, C.C.

Jianghan Hotel • *211 Shengli St., Hankou.* • Old European architecture.

Qingchuan Hotel • *88 Ximachangjie, Hanyang. Cable 8550. Telex 40134 HBQC CN. Dist.Wuchang A.P.15 km. Dist.Hankou A.P.10 km* • 1983. 24 stories. On hill above Yangtze.

Xuangong Hotel • *45 Jianghan No. 1 Rd., Hankou* • Close to shopping.

Yangtze Hotel • *Jie Fang Da Dao, Hankou. Telex 40204 YGHTE CN. Cable 2700. Fax 353759. Dist.A.P.18 km. Dist.R.W.16 km. Near government trading offices.* • C.C. 1987, ren. 1990. Eight stories, 205 rooms. IDD. Should have business and health centers now. Hong Kong J.V.

IMPORTANT ADDRESSES
CAAC 中国民航 : 209 North Liji Rd., Hankou; tel. 51248.
C.I.T.S. 国际旅行社 : 48 Jianghan Yi Lu, Hankou; tel. 25018 and 24109. Cable 1954. Telex 40211 CITWH CN.
C.T.S. 中旅社 : 1365 Zhongshan Ave., Hankou; tel. 21666. Cable 1962.
Hubei Tourism Administrative Bureau 湖北省旅游局 : 1365 Zhongshan Ave., Hankou; tel. 512657, 25552. Telex 40133 HBHTY CN. Cable 1962.
Hospitals: In case of emergency, try your hotel first if convenient. Otherwise: **No. 1 Hospital, Wuhan Medical College** 武汉医学院附一院 389 Liberation Thoroughfare; tel. 51171.
 No. 2 Hospital, Wuhan Medical College 武汉医学院附二院 : 130 Liberation Thoroughfare; tel. 54191.
Wuhan Port Passenger Transport Station 武汉港客运站 : Yianjiang Ave., Hankou; tel. 53875.
Yangtze River cruise ships (S.S. Yangtze): 88 Ximachang St., Hanyang; tel. 444627, 442404. Telex 40133 HBHTY CN.

WUXI 无锡

(Wusih) East China. Between the northern shore of Lake Taihu and the Yangtze River, in southern Jiangsu province, this industrial and resort city also straddles the ancient Grand Canal. It is less than an hour by train from Suzhou, and just west of Shanghai. It is a 2-hour flight south of Beijing. The urban population is 840,000. Weather: Hottest—in July, 38°C; coldest—in January, ⁻4°C. Annual precipitation 1056 mm, mainly in June.

Wuxi is one of the oldest cities in China, founded over 3000 years ago, during the Zhou. After deposits of tin became depleted, its name was changed to Wuxi, meaning ''no tin.'' Contrary to its image of a placid, sail-filled lake, Wuxi has the fifth highest industrial output in China. But it is known as a beauty spot, with classical Chinese gardens and a famous lake from which many of the best gardens get their rockery. Notable are the **Liyuan (Li Garden)** 蠡园 and **Meiyuan (Plum Garden)** 梅园 . The Liyuan has a "thousand-steps veranda," with 89 windows on the inside wall. At the Meiyuan, the plum blossoms are best seen in the early spring. In 2213-square-km **Lake Tai** 太湖 is the **Yuantouzhu (Turtle Head) Islet** 鼋头渚 , with a bridge, temple, and pavilions.

The Liyuan is close to the Shuixiu and Hubin hotels; the Taihu Hotel is close to Meiyuan and Yuantouzhu.

Historical sites include **Xihui Park** 锡惠公园 , west of the city, with its **Tianxia Di'er Quan (Heavenly Second Spring)** 天下第二泉 (Tang), **Jichang (Relaxing the Mind) Garden** 寄畅园 , and the **Longguang (Dragon Light) Pagoda** 龙光塔 (great view), both from the Ming. Jichang Garden is one of the best-known South China gardens, uniting the distant hills with the intimacies within the walls. A copy of this garden is in the Summer Palace in Beijing.

Wuxi is also a silk-producing center, the hills around it filled with mulberry trees. Tourists can see the local **silk industry,** from silkworm-rearing through the printing and dyeing process at a silk factory . There are the **Hui Shan Clay Figures Factory** 惠山泥人厂 boat trips with lunch on Lake Tai and trips on the **Grand Canal** 大运河 (3½ hours to Suzhou, for example, or seven days, also visiting Suzhou, Changzhou, and Zhenjiang). A trip across Lake Tai can also involve a tour of **Huzhou** 湖州 (ancient writing brush factory) before you go to Hangzhou.

Visits can be arranged to **Huaxi Village** less than one hour away for demonstrations of ancient farming and village life. A good time to visit is the Mid-Autumn festival, with lots of colored lanterns, moon cakes, an evening cruise on the lake and, one hopes, a full moon. New is the Artist Palace from the classic novel *Pilgrimage to the West*.

Excursions can be made to nearby (69 km) Yixing purple sandware porcelain factory and caves, and to **Jiangyin** 江阴 (home of Ming dynasty scientist and traveler Xu Xiake). Trips also can be arranged to Changzhou, Zhenjiang, Yangzhou, Suzhou, Nanjing, and Shanghai. See separate listing.

SHOPPING

Locally made and good are clay figurines, embroidery, freshwater pearls, and silk. Made in the province are porcelain and Yixing pottery.

The Friendship Store here is good and has an antique store beside it.

Festivals in May of odd years 1989, 1991, etc., the Lake Tai Arts Festival takes place for one week with folk dancing, singing, Wuxi dialect and Shaoxing opera, etc. In early November of even years, 1988, 1990, etc., Wuxi has an international tourism film festival.

RESTAURANTS

Local specialties include freshwater fish, crabs, and shrimp.

Zhongguo (China) Restaurant 中国饭店 • *Hanchang Rd.; tel. 23438.*

Jiang Nan Restaurant 江南菜馆 • *435 Zhongshan Rd.; tel. 27483.*

Ying Bin Lou (Greeting Guests) Restaurant 迎宾楼

HOTELS

C.I.T.S. says the top hotels are the Grand, then the Hubin, and thirdly the Taihu. C.T.S. says the top is the Grand, then the Milido, and thirdly the Hubin. Both agree that the Grand is best for business people. It and the Milido are in town. The Hubin is best for tourists; it is beside Lake Taihu and standards are good.

Hubin Hotel 湖滨饭店 • *Liyuan. Cable 5080, 4423. Telex 362002 WXHB CN. Dist.A.P. 23 km. Dist.R.W. 12 km.* • 1976–78 Ren. 1987. Restful, beautiful garden setting beside Lake Taihu and Li Garden. If room available, will not telex answer to request for reservation. If room not available, will telex answer. 10 stories. 187 modest, comfortable rooms. Business center. No C.C. Should have IDD by now.

Milido • *2 Liangxi Rd. Telex 36229 WMLD CN. Fax 668660. Cable 6969* • 1987–88. Walk to canal. Three min. drive to Friendship Store. 4 km. from Lake Tai. T.R.(collect). Managed by Yanxiang Hotel (Beijing). 9 stories, 251 rooms. Very attractive decor. Pool. Gym. Should have IDD by now.

Shuixiu Hotel 水秀饭店 • *on the same grounds and with the same management as the Hubin* • 1980. Three small two-story Australian prefabs. 110 rooms. Badly maintained.

State Guest House 国宾馆 • *on Lake Tai.* • 1958. Ren. 1987. Reserve through Wuxi Taihu Hotel. Most travelers stay in No. 1 bldg. Very small hotel. No IDD. Few facilities. Badly maintained.

Taihu Hotel 太湖饭店 • *Meiyuan. Cable 8043. Telex 36302 WXTUH CN. Cable 8043. Dist.A.P.38 km. Dist.R.W.14 km. 20 minute walk to Lake Tai.* • T.R.(collect), no C.C. New building 1987, about 160 rooms. Badly maintained. Older buildings ren. 1988.

Wuxi Grand Hotel • *1 Liangqing Rd. Dist.A.P. over 30 km. Dist. R.W.4 km.* • 1988–89. 22 stories, 342 rooms. Pool, gym, business center. Pan Pacific management.

OTHER IMPORTANT ADDRESSES

C.I.T.S.   7 Xin Sheng Rd.; tel. 200416, 200585. Cable 1954. Telex 362025 WCITS CN.
C.T.S. 59 Chezhang Rd.; tel. 223613, 221030. Cable 0294. Telex 362038 WXCTS CN.
China United Airlines tel. 221323.
Wuxi Municipal Tourism Bureau No. 1 Qing Yang Rd. Tel. 226618.
Wuxi Taxi Company 52 Jiefang Xincun. Dispatcher Tel. 223763. Manager, tel. 228402.
Wuxi Tourist Boat Company Xiao Ji Shan, Jinyuan Garden, West Suburb. Tel. 667934.
Flight to Beijing Ticket office—Bureau of Communications, Renmin Rd.; tel. 29326. From Beijing, ticket office, West Building, Beijing Hotel; tel. 507766 X596. Nanyuan Airport. Flights every Tuesday, Thursday, Saturday.

XIAGUAN 下关

Southwest China. At an altitude of 1000 meters, this is the capital of Dali Bai Autonomous Prefecture, Yunnan province, with most of the population of the Bai nationality. Located at the southern tip of 41-km-long Lake Erhai, it is a 12-hour, 400-km drive (with rest and lunch stops), west and slightly north of Kunming. Part of it lies on the famed Burma Road. The Dali Prefecture merits a visit because of its colorful national minorities, old cities, historical monuments, and views of snow-capped mountains, most of the year round.

Northwest Yunnan is a lovely off-the-beaten path experience discovered mainly by foreign backpackers and social scientists. The government is making a special effort to control drug abuse by foreigners in this area.

The history goes back over 2000 years. In the eighth century, this area was part of the vast Nanzhou empire, which refused to submit to the Tang. It was later subdued by the Mongols, though. Before you go, read C. P. Fitzgerald's *Tower of Five Glories,* about his experiences in this area in the 1930s. One recent visitor didn't think much had changed since then. Public buses stop running after 7:00 p.m., but you can usually hitch a ride on a horse cart. There is a tendency to confuse the names Dali and Xiaguan. Xiaguan was the old term for greater Dali, and the name is still used.

The city has a tea brick factory worth visiting and a temple to the Tang general who failed to conquer Xiaguan.

The hotels in this area are just adequate—no luxuries like 24-hour hot water, heat, or air-conditioning. But they are adequate. The Erhai Hotel is in Xiaguan. Boat trips on the lake can be boarded nearby for great views of 3800-meter-high Cangshan Mountain. **Erhai Lake** was believed to be manmade in the Han, over 2000 years ago. The islands here are inhabited by Bai fisherfolk.

Besides the lake is a cultural museum of the Bai.

Among the day trips, **Dali** 大理 is 10 km north, an old walled town with marble factories and some of the best marble in China. Some houses are made with marble. Look for a large obelisk erected by conquerer Kublai Khan in the 13th century. Dali is also on the lake and appears to be connected with Xiaguan.

Dali has the **Sanyuejie (Third-Month market)** 三月街 , the 15th to 20th day of the third lunar month, with caravans of horses and mules arriving to be traded. It is also an important market for traditional medicines. About 100,000 people take part in the market, from all provinces. Enlivened by races and, perhaps, gambling, the site west of Dali at the foot of the mountain is a former Nationalist execution grounds. The best hotel inside the wall is the Dali Guest House. No. 2 Guest House and the La La Cafe are popular with backpackers.

Xizhou, just north of Dali, has especially remarkable Bai architecture, incorporating marble. Bai architecture is characterized with whitewashed walls and black trim. The much-decorated houses have courtyards in the middle and living quarters on three sides, with the entrance in a painted wall. The women's dress is basically white with red or black vests and a colorful bonnet. The women sing easily on request here. In addition to courtship rituals, the songs also relate local history, and are sung at work and during ceremonies such as weddings and funerals. The Tian Zhuan Bingguan (hotel) here in Bai style is charming.

Shizhong Shan 石钟山 石窟 , near Jianchuan (a long, one-day excursion north), has a unique Buddhist grotto reached by a steep 45-minute climb. It has a 1-meter-high female genitalia, which women rub for fertility and boys for courage. It also has some of the earliest Buddhist carvings in China—several styles, including some humans pictured with long curly hair, probably ancient foreigners. Indians, perhaps? At the base of this mountain lies an exotic old monastery.

Shibao Shan 石宝山 , nearby, also has temples and an annual singing contest in late August or early September by young people of many minorities. During the festival, thousands sleep under the trees or in temples, talents are discovered, and friendships and romances blossom. The singing is a courtship ritual. Currently, public transportation exists in this area, but roads are unpaved. Fish is the local specialty, but the cooking is not outstanding.

San Ta Si (Three Pagoda Temple) 三塔寺 , on the west shore of Lake Erhai, outside the NW gate of Dali, was built in the Nanzhao/Tang period, over a 1000 years ago, and recently renovated. The view of the lake, the three towers (70 meters and 43 meters high), and the mountains behind are famous.

Butterfly Pool 蝴蝶泉 on the northern tip of the lake, is a natural spring with one huge tree covering it. In May strings of different kinds of butterflies appear.

Check with C.I.T.S. in Kunming for dates. See also "Kunming" for **Lijiang** and **Zhongdian,** in other prefectures farther north toward the Tibetan border.

XIAMEN

(Hsiamen, Amoy) East China. SE coast of Fujian (Fukien) province, over 200 km across the straits from Taiwan, but 2½ km from Quemoy (Jinmen/Kinmen), the Nationalist-held island. Xiamen can be reached by air, sea or air-conditioned bus from Guangzhou and Hong Kong. The passenger ships *Gulangyu* and *Jimei* sail every Tuesday and Friday between Hong Kong and Xiamen, a journey of 17 hours. Direct trains from Nanjing and Shanghai. Weekly ship from Taiwan. It is a 1½-hour flight SW of Shanghai and 1 hour flight NE of Guangzhou. It is also linked with Fuzhou, Singapore, Manila, and Hong Kong by air. Weather: hottest—38°C, July–Aug.; coldest—minus 4°C, Feb. Annual precipitation is 1206 mm, mainly from May to July. Population: urban 370,000.

Xiamen was the homebase of General Zheng Chenggong (Cheng Cheng-kung), a.k.a. Koxinga, who repelled the Manchu invaders for a while and then rid Taiwan of the Dutch in 1662. Xiamen was a relatively minor trading port until it was seized by the British in 1839. In 1842, the Treaty of Nanking allowed foreigners to build residences and warehouses here. For many years, especially in the late 1950s, both explosives and propaganda shells have been lobbed to China from Quemoy, off the SE coast of Xiamen.

Xiamen is part of a 131-square-km. Special Economic Zone.

While the national language is also spoken, local people here speak the Xiamen Dialect/Fukienese, which is different from both Cantonese and Mandarin. Fukienese is also spoken by the majority of people on Taiwan.

If you only have one day for sightseeing, take in Gulangyu, South Putuo Temple, and hurry through Jimei.

The southeastern part of the 123-square-km island contains the downtown shopping area, the **botanical gardens** 万石植物园 (where among the tropical and subtropical plants is a redwood tree brought by then U.S. President Richard Nixon). Also in this area are the South Putuo temple, Xiamen University (built by Tan Kah Kee in 1921), and the ferry pier to Gulangyu. Staying at the Lujiang Hotel is convenient to these places.

The 1000-year-old **Nan Putuo (South Putuo) Temple** 南普院 is named after Putuo Island, the home of the Goddess of Mercy. Most of the current buildings are from the 1920s and 1930s, but the tablets, scrolls, sculptures, bells, etc., were made in the Song and Ming. On the lotus base of the statue of Buddha is carved the biography of Sakyamuni, and the story of the monk Xuanzang who went to India. The eight 3-meter-high "imperial tablets" in Mahavira Hall tell about the Qing suppression of an uprising and are written in Manchu and Chinese. Most famous is the stunning, three-faced, multiarmed statue of Guanyin. A festival is held here New Year's Eve.

Behind the temple is **Five Old Men Peaks,** which can be climbed for a good view of the Taiwan Straits. The famous Chinese writer Lu Xun taught at **Xiamen University** 厦门大学 in 1926–27 and a five-room memorial hall on his life is here. He helped to found the **Museum of Anthropology** 人类博物馆, with exhibits from prehistoric man to the Qing, and relics from the national minorities. Look also for the Australian boomerang and the 700-year-old Japanese sword.

At the foot of Five Old Men Peaks is the **Overseas Chinese Museum** 华侨博物馆 , outlining the contributions of natives who emigrated overseas. It also has souvenirs from Thailand, Burma, Cambodia, Malaysia, etc.

One can charter a tour boat around the islands.

Gulangyu (Drum Wave) Island 鼓浪屿 is 1.7 hilly square km, seven minutes across the "Egret River" by ferry. Pop. 25,000. Formerly the foreign ghetto, it is good for another half day unless you want to hike or go swimming too. It has the best beach (Gangzi Hou), frangipani, flame trees, magnolias, and other heavily scented trees, and tiny shops. A very charming collection of old mansions built for foreigners have now been converted into guesthouses. Gulangyu is a car- and bicycle-free resort area, great for children and relaxing. It is cleaner and more prosperous-looking than the fishing villages of Hong Kong's outlying islands, to which it bears some resemblance. Staying here, however, makes it difficult for hectic sightseeing and shopping unless a special ferry to the guesthouses is laid on. The dominating new statue is of Koxinga.

A high percentage of music lovers live here and you will probably hear strains of Bach and Verdi floating on the breeze. The island has a concert hall, which is especially good for chamber music groups.

Everyone *must* climb 90-meter-high **Riguang Yan (Sunlight Rock)** 日光岩 , the highest peak here, for the view and the story of the two devoted egrets, the male killed by a greedy, unromantic goshawk. Also here is the **Lotus Flower Nunnery** (a.k.a. Sunshine Temple), the camp where Koxinga stationed his men, and **Zheng Chenggong Memorial**

Hall 郑成功纪念馆 , with souvenirs of his life, including a history written by a Dutchman about the fall of Taiwan/Formosa. The city museum is nearby. The **Shuzhuang Garden** was built by a Taiwan resident who moved here after the Japanese took over that island in the late 1890s. Unlike most gardens of China, it incorporates the sea into its design. "The garden is in the sea and the sea is in the garden." One can rent sailboards near the ferry pier.

Jimei, 2.83 square km, is worth an hour and is over 10 km north of downtown. It is reached by a 2.8-km granite causeway from Xiamen Island, built in 1953–55, and is on the road to Quanzhou. Eighty percent of the 23,000 people here have relatives abroad. On Jimei is a most interesting monument built by an Overseas Chinese philanthropist, Tan Kah Kee, who made his money from rubber, rice, and pineapples in Singapore. **Turtle Garden** 鳌园 , built in 1950, is an encyclopedia in stone, full of pictures of the things Mr. Tan wanted to teach people: factories, machinery, exotic animals, Chinese literature, history, and culture. How many scenes can you identify? His elaborate tomb is typically horseshoe-shaped. His biography is in pictures around the tomb.

Nearby is the huge **Jimei Middle School,** which he also financed. Here, mainly Overseas Chinese students from all over the world come to study. It is one of the many schools Mr. Tan built in Jimei. For those curious about the man, a tiny museum nearby also shows pictures of his life.

EXCURSIONS

In the vicinity of Xiamen, closer to Fuzhou, is the tomb of Koxinga. Reached by road is also the town of Zhangzhou and the historical city of Quanzhou. See separate listings.

SHOPPING

Locally made are Caiza silk figures, lacquer thread–decorated vases, colored clay figures, and bead embroidery. You may want to try the *Yupi* peanuts, the *gongtang* crisp peanut cakes, dried longan fruit, and preserved olives. Locally grown are longan, litchis, peanuts, sugarcane, and, of course, rice. The main shopping street is Zhongshan Road.

Lujiang Emporium (Xiahe Rd.; tel. 23810); **Huaqiao Shangdian (Overseas Chinese Store)** (7 Zhongshan Rd.; tel. 24163); **Xiamen Antiques and Curios Store** 厦门文物店 (211 Zhongshan Rd.; tel. 23363);

Friendship Store 友谊商店 (tel. 23817, 24385); **Tourist Shopping Center** (103 Si Ming Bei Rd.; tel. 20133); **Lacquer Thread Sculpture Factory** 漆绒雕厂 (tel. 20329); **Arts and Crafts Factory** 工艺美术厂(tel. 24784).

Also open is the Donghai Shopping Center, Zhongshan Bei Rd. (tel. 21094).

RESTAURANTS

Fujian food is much like Cantonese, and heavy on seafoods, of course, with some distinctive dishes. See "Food" for recommended local dishes.

Lu Dao Restaurant 绿岛饭店 • *230–232 Zhong Shan Rd.; tel. 21281, 22264* • Xiamen food.

Moslem Restaurant 清真牛肉店 • *205 Zhong Shan Rd.; tel. 24348.*

Regal Seafood Restaurant • *14 Hu Yuan Rd., tel. 24127.*

Vegetarian Food Restaurant 南普陀寺素菜部 • *South Putuo Temple; tel. 22908.*

HOTELS

Fujian is particularly busy with Taiwan visitors. Reservations are recommended. The top hotel is the Xiamen Mandarin, then the Xiamen Hotel, and thirdly the Lujiang.

The Park is new and is probably second to the Mandarin for business people. Though run-down, the Lujiang is best for tourists, located in old Amoy on the harborfront. The Xiamen is isolated on a hilltop downtown and provides privacy and peace. The Xin Qiao Hotel should open near the O.C. Building in 1989. A Holiday Inn is expected to open here in 1990, and the Hai Jing the end of 1991.

On Gulangyu, the Seaview is ideal for families, but it is dirty and has poor service. Villas No. 4 and No. 5 are best. The Gulangyu might be barely okay too. Both are next to the soccer field.

New hotels for backpackers near railway station.

Lujiang Hotel • *54 Lujiang Rd. Cable 1230. Fax 24644. Telex 93024 LUTEL CN. Dist.A.P.12 km. Dist.R.W.5 km. Walk to Hong Kong ferry pier, ferry to Gulangyu, and shopping* • 1961, some ren. 1989. 6 stories. Will telex answer to request for reservation only if no room available. C.C. Hong Kong management. IDD. No sports facilities. Large rooms. Pleasant but shabby.

Overseas Chinese Building • *70–74 Xinhua Rd. Cable 3330. Telex 93029 CTSXM CN. Fax 31862. Dist.A.P.12 km. Dist.R.W. 3 km* • T.R., C.C. 1956, ren. 1988. 14 stories, 236 rooms. Business center, IDD. Philippine Airlines and C.T.S. No sports facilities. Clinic, medium-sized rooms, Directory in Chinese only. Good furniture, 11th floor best. Handshower, chipped dishes.

Park (Xindeco) Hotel • *Xing Rong, Huli Dist. Telex 93027 INFRM CN. Fax 41814. Dist.A.P.5 km. Dist.R.W.6 km* • Government trade offices. T.R., C.C. Hong Kong/C.Y.T.S. J.V. 1988 12 stories, 128 large rooms. IDD, Business center, gym, pool. USTV and business newswire due in 1989. Some rooms should have direct computer hookup to business satellite.

Xiamen Hotel/Guest House • *16 Hu Yuan Rd. Cable 6333. Telex 93065 GUEST CN. Dist.A.P.11 km. Dist.R.W.3 km. 500 meters to botanical garden* • 1986. 6 stories. #5 Bldg. for foreigners. Pool, IDD, clinic, business center. Large rooms, chipped dishes.

Xiamen Jinbao • *Xin Gang Rd. Cable 2888. Telex 93034 JINBO CN. Fax 43122. Dist.A.P.5 km. Dist.R.W.5 km. Next to Friendship Store* • T.R. (collect). Hong Kong J.V. 1983 Building, ren. 1988, 1990. 6 stories, 100 rooms. IDD, C.C., business center. Medium-sized rooms, soft beds. Badly maintained.

Xiamen Mandarin Hotel 厦门悦华酒店 • *Huli District, Dist.A.P.7 km, Dist.R.W.11 km. Telex 93028 MANDA CN Cable 0385. Fax 41431.* • Upon a hill, surrounded by factories. T.R. (collect), C.C. 1984; 3 stories, 74 rooms. 1988; 7 stories, 133 rooms, 22 two-story villas. Conference hall, sauna, jacuzzi, health club, French restaurant, pool, billiards, tennis, shuttle bus to city. Hong Kong J.V., but no connections with Mandarin International Hotels Ltd.

OTHER IMPORTANT ADDRESSES
C.I.T.S. 中国国际旅行社 : 7 Hai Hou Rd., 3/F; tel. 25277, 20848. Fax 31832. Telex 93063 XMITS CN. Cable 8381. Head office: Zheng Xing Mansion, 15th floor, Hubin Bei Rd.; tel. 51825. Fax 51819. Telex 93148 ITSXM CN, or for FITs 93063 XMITS CN. Service Counter at Lujiang Hotel: tel. 25277, 20846, 31832.
C.T.S. 中旅社 : Overseas Chinese Bldg., 70–74 Xin Hua Rd.; tel. 24286, 25602 X2791. Cable 3330. Telex 93029 CTSXM. Fax 31862.
C.Y.T.S.: 4 Bai Jia Cun Rd.; tel. 20017, 20019. Fax 20024. Cable 2274. Telex 93077 XCYTS CN.
CAAC 中国民航 and **Xiamen Airlines:** Hubin South Road; tel. 25942, 25902 X394, 25802 (airport).
Ferry Quay 轮渡码头 : Lujiang Rd.; tel. 21336. Ferries to Gulangyu every 5–15 minutes.
Foreign Affairs Dept. of Public Security Bureau 公安局外事处 : Xinhua Rd.; tel. 24941, X2545.
International Seamen's Club of Xiamen 厦门国际海员俱乐部 : Dongdu Xingang Rd.; tel. 25763, 24456.
No. 1 Hospital of Xiamen 厦门第一医院 : Zhen Hai Rd.; tel. 22280.

Ticket Office for Ships to Hong Kong 客运轮船售票处 :
Dongwen Rd.; tel. 22517.
Xiamen International Airport 厦门国际机场 : Gao Qi; tel. 20630
(for flight times).
Xiamen Railway Station 火车站 : Wuchun; tel. 22812.
Xiamen Tourism Bureau: 7, 3/F, Haihou Rd.; tel. 25557, 25355; cable
6031.
Zhongshan Hospital South Hubin Rd., tel. 26596, 25468.

XI'AN

(Sian; Western Peace) Northwest China. 1¾-hour flight or about
22-hour train ride SW (1165 km) of Beijing; 8-hour train ride west
of Luoyang. Air routes with many cities now include Hong Kong
and in the future with Dunhuang, Jiayuguan and Xining. New
international airport, Xianyang, should open 1989. Capital of
Shaanxi province on the Guanzhong Plain, it borders on the Loess
Plateau to the north and the Qinling Mountains to the south. Altitude: 400 meters. Weather: Hottest—40°C—July; coldest—
⁻10°C—two weeks in January. Rain all year round, but especially
July through early September. Annual precipitation 550–770 mm.
Fog in winter might affect plane flights. Population: inside wall
2.2 million.

Next to Beijing, Xi'an is the best city to visit in China, especially if you are interested in ancient Chinese history, traditional culture, and archaeology. It is one of the 24 historical cities protected by the State Council.

Just to glimpse all it has to offer takes a full week. To savor Xi'an slowly, to study it deeply, reading about Empress Wu and her lover-protector-henchman while sitting in the shadow of a Tang pagoda—or even reading about that crafty fictional Tang detective Judge Dee, two giant silk-flower petals sticking sideways out of the back of his magisterial cap—even that kind of depth could take months.

Ancient Xi'an is the setting for many Chinese operas, their sweet young heroines waving flowing ribbon sleeves and their flag-pierced generals galloping away to battle amid the clash of cymbals. Here the real camels, caravans, and traders were involved in the exchange of silver, furs, horses, and sesame for Chinese silk and porcelain. Here that egomaniac of an emperor ordered the burning of all books except those he liked, and demanded that his subjects create an army of life-size soldiers so he could maintain his empire after his earthly death.

Xi'an was the capital intermittently for 1087 years and 11 dynasties, including the Zhou (of the ritual bronzes), the Qin (of the Great Wall and ceramic army), the Han (of the jade burial suits), the Sui (of the Grand Canal), and the Tang—ah, the Tang! This city was the center of China's world from the 11th century B.C. to the early 10th A.D. Commerce on the Silk Road thrived west of here to the Mediterranean and beyond. (See "Silk Road.") Thousands of foreigners lived in the Western Market then.

In spite of the occasional invasions and sackings by rebels and tribesmen, Xi'an, then named Chang'an (Everlasting Peace), reached its highest peak in the Tang, the population then almost two million. It was one of the largest cities in the world, with walls measuring 36 km in circumference. It declined because of late Tang debauchery and corruption, the eunuchs ruling the court and increasingly powerful governors-general controlling the provinces. In 906, the last of the Tang emperors allowed one of his generals to take complete charge while he enjoyed his lady love. Xi'an rolled downhill from there on, following the fortunes, also, of the Silk Road.

A short-lived peasant regime made Xi'an a capital again in the 17th century, but it never regained its past glory. Xi'an did, however, continue to be a tourist resort and destination for religious pilgrimages because of its Buddhist roots. In 1900, when the Empress Dowager fled the international force sent to rescue the foreign legation from the Boxers, she went to Xi'an.

During the Xi'an Incident, Generalissimo Chiang Kai-shek was kidnapped. One of Chiang's own officers thus forced him to cooperate with the Communists against the Japanese. (See 1936 in "Milestones in Chinese History.'') After Chiang agreed to his captors' demands, the Communists set up a liaison office here, which is now the *Museum of the Eighth Route Army 八路军西安办事处博物馆. On May 20, 1949, the Communists took over the city.

Today, Xi'an is a textile and manufacturing center. It also produces Chinese and Western medicines, and watches. It is an educational center, with about 20 colleges, universities, and research institutes. Xi'an Jiaotung (Communications) University is the best known, and one of the 11 ''super-key'' universities in the country.

Xi'an's agricultural areas grow cotton, maize, wheat, vegetables, pomegranates, and persimmons. Many houses and walls have been made of loess soil mixed with straw. If cared for properly and protected with bricks on top, mud walls can last 100 years. Cheap too! But today many farmers are rebuilding in brick.

The walled city is laid out in the classic Chinese style in a rectangle, most streets parallel, the bell tower almost in the center. If you only have one day, try to see the Qin Army Vault Museum, Bronze Chariots, Banpo Village, the Big Wild Goose Pagoda, the Provincial Museum, the Bell Tower, and the City Wall and gates. If you've never seen a Chinese-style mosque, try to fit in the Great Mosque too. This is a very rushed itinerary.

The standard 3-day tour is:

—Qin Tomb and Terracotta Warriors, Bronze Chariots, Huaqing Hot Spring, and Banpo Neolithic Village.

—Qianlong Tomb, 75 km west of Xi'an.

—Shaanxi Provincial Museum, Big Wild Goose Pagoda, Bell and Drum Towers, and the Great Mosque.

If you have more than three days, you might want to sightsee according to geographical groupings.

In Xi'an and its immediate vicinity: Wild Goose Pagodas, Bell Tower, Drum Tower, City Wall, Great Mosque, Shaanxi Provincial Museum, Xianqing Palace Park, Banpo Museum, remains of Daming Palace, Memorial Museum of the 8th Route Army.

West and South of Xi'an: Chariot and Horse Pits, Xiangjiao Temple, Xiangji Temple, Qinglong Temple, Temple of Du Fu, Cao Tang Temple, Peasant Painting of Hu County.

East of Xi'an: Huaqing Hot Springs, Qinshihuang's Tomb, Bronze Chariots and Horses.

North and Northwest of Xi'an: Xianyang Museum, Maoling Tomb, Zhaoling Tomb, Qianling Tomb. New international airport.

THE ESSENTIALS

*The Museum of Emperor Qin's Terracotta Army 秦俑坑博物馆 (40 km NE of the city) is the most spectacular and important place to visit here because of its 2180-year-old painted-ceramic army of more than 8000 soldiers buried to "protect" the tomb of the first Qin emperor. **If you take a photo here, you pay a high fee, or have your film confiscated!** (Like Y 800 for 10 minutes shooting!) Slides of reasonable quality can be purchased at the souvenir shops.

The relics were discovered in 1974 by local peasants digging a well. A sign near the entrance shows where the well was dug. The terracotta army is a puzzle because the emperor left no record of its existence. It would be hard to hide a project of this magnitude! Excavation started in 1976. A permanent building protects the army and tourists from most of the elements, and visitors are able to walk around the periphery of the once-buried relics. If you look carefully, you might see signs of oxidation and the loss of original colors.

There are three vaults. **No. 1,** opened to the public in 1979, is 62 by 230 by 5 meters deep. Most of the army was found facing east, toward the tomb, 1½ km away. The soldiers were in lines of roughly 70 across and 150 deep, separated by 10 partition walls and 11 corridors.

The men are hollow from the thigh up and made in two parts; they are 1.78–1.87 meters tall. The soldiers in front hold crossbows; also in front were bells and drums. Charioteers hold their hands out before them as if clutching reins. The horses originally wore harnesses with brass ornaments and have been identified as a breed from Hechu in Gansu. Officers can be distinguished from soldiers by their clothing and armor. Are every one of the 2,000 faces here different? Judge for yourself.

Researchers believe that kilns were built around the molded figures (probably two horses at a time) and destroyed after firing. There are remains of 30 wooden chariots.

Vault No. 2, 20 meters north of No. 1, contains about 1400 cavalrymen, archers, charioteers and infantrymen. **Vault No. 3** has 64 officers and was probably the "command post."

Near the main museum are one of the **two bronze chariots,** one with four horses and one charioteer, the earliest such chariots found so far in China. These are also outstanding and can be seen at closer range. Work on a new museum for the second chariot is in progress and all projects should be completed in 1989.

*Tomb of Emperor Qinshihuang (Chin Shih Huang-ti) 秦陵 is in Lintong County. The first emperor of the Qin Dynasty, the builder of the Great Wall, and first unifier of the Chinese nation, lived from 259 to 210 B.C. and became king of Qin at age 13. What he achieved in so short a reign is incredible, and it is no wonder that he searched his empire for pills of longevity. Over 700,000 people worked on his tomb recorded through history as a deep and magnificent underground palace begun in 246 B.C.

Preliminary explorations at this site have started, and so far archaeologists believe that the tomb has not been robbed, and that the ancient records are correct. "Rivers of mercury" probably flow through it. Lack of money and technology has postponed the excavation of this extremely important tomb. At press time, all that can be seen is a tumulus 6 km in circumference and 40 meters high, covered with pomegranate trees.

The **Huaqing Hot Springs** 华清池 , the *site of the Xi'an Incident, have been so overshadowed by modern events that their ancient history is frequently overlooked. They are at the base of Lishan Hill, 30 km NE of Xi'an. A stop here can be combined with the Qin Army Vault, the Tomb of Qinshihuang, and Banpo village, in a quick half-day excursion. Huaqing has been an imperial resort for the last 3000 years, its most famous tenants Emperor Xuanzong (Hsuan-tsung), the last Tang emperor, and the woman blamed for his downfall, his favorite concubine Yang Guifei (Kuei-fei). The influence of Yang Guifei and her relatives at court caused much dissatisfaction. In 755, an adopted son of hers rebelled, and the emperor's troops refused to fight as long as she remained alive. She had to hang herself. The troops rode out to victory over her dead body. The emperor lived on even though they had vowed to die together. Promises! Promises!

The imperial couple used to winter here because it was warmer than Xi'an. They bathed in the Jiulong (Nine Dragons) Hot Spring and the Guifei Hot Spring. And now, so can you! You pay very little for a 40-minute soak in 43°C mineral water (sodium, sulfur, and magnesium), said to be good for rheumatism and skin disorders. The original buildings were all destroyed, and most of the current ones were built since Liberation in the old Tang style.

You can also trace the flight from his bedroom of Chiang Kai-shek, the Chinese Nationalist leader, as he panicked at the sound of gunfire at 5 a.m. on a cold December morning in 1936. He left behind his false teeth and wore only one shoe. A pavilion today marks the spot up the hill where he was captured.

The *Dayan (Big Wild Goose) Pagoda** 大雁塔 of the Da Chi Eng Temple, along with the Little Wild Goose Pagoda in Jianfu Temple, are the most famous pagodas in China because of their age and their important historical connections. They are not, however, the most beautiful or spectacular. The bigger pagoda was built to house the sutras brought back from India in A.D. 652 (Tang) by the famous monk Xuanzang (Hsuan-Tsang). It was probably named in memory of the temple in India where the monk lived, on a goose-shaped hill. Or it could have acquired its name because some monks were starving and Buddha, in the form of a wild goose, dropped down close to them. The monks, being vegetarians, refused to eat it.

The pagoda has seven stories, 248 steps, and a great view from the top. In adjoining Da Cien Temple (A.D. 647) are painted-clay statues of 18 lohan (Ming), most with strong Indian rather than Chinese features. One gets the impression that the painter must have been playing a joke, the faces are so funny. The Japanese lantern was presented in 1974 in honor of the first Chinese monk who went to Japan in the eighth century. While both pagodas are historical monuments protected by the State Council, only a stop at one is really necessary.

The **Shaanxi Provincial Historical Museums**　省历史博物馆 are in an old (Qing and Ming) Confucian temple and its extensions. The collection is one of the best in China and covers the period from the Zhou to the end of the Tang. It has some outstanding pieces, all labeled in English and Chinese. Among them: (1) an eighth-century B.C. stone drum, believed to be the earliest stone tablet in China, with writing (about a hunting expedition); (2) a bronze gate hinge from the Qin; (3) the standardizations of weights, measures, and currency by the first Qin emperor; (4) a wooden model of a bronze seismograph (eight dragons) from the first or second century B.C.; (5) giant stone carvings, the largest from the eastern Han, including a life-size rhinoceros and ostrich (inspired by live animals given as tribute). Four of the bas-reliefs of horses from the Zhaoling tombs are on one of the walls. Two others are are said to be in Philadelphia. (6) Gold- and silver-inlaid dishes and ancient Byzantine and Persian coins found in the Western Market. A most recent and very celebrated find is the 62 cm-high Gilded Bronze Horse, from the 2000-year-old tomb of Han Emperor Wu Di. Artistically, it is not as beautiful as the Flying Horse of Gansu, but it is one of the largest, oldest, and best-preserved art objects found so far in China.

The museum also has the most important *collection of steles in China, with over 1000 from the Han through the Qing, including 12 Tang engravings of the Confucian classics. These have been used by centuries of scholars to copy and study for content as well as calligraphy.

Important here is the seventh-century Nestorian stele, written in Syriac with a cross at the top. You really have to search for it in this forest, but it is a rare piece of Christian history, the commemoration of the establishment of the church in Xi'an. In the late 1980s before the opening of the new provincial museum, the stele was in the second pavilion of steles at the back of the museum, the first stele on the left. Look for the cross at the top. Rubbings of this and other steles can be obtained in the souvenir shop. The Nestorian sect started in the fifth century but was declared heretical by Rome in A.D. 431. The sect flourished in west Asia, but relics have also been found in Quanzhou.

The City Wall and South Gate can be seen near the museum.

The *Bell Tower 钟楼 was first built in 1384 (Ming) in another location, and moved here 200 years later. It has been renovated several times. Three sets of eaves weaken "the force of the rainfall," and actually only two stories are here. The tower is 36 meters tall. The furniture is gorgeous (Qing) and the very fancy traditional ceiling is Ming. From the second story you can see all four gates of Xi'an. Parking is difficult especially here.

The nearby **Drum Tower** 鼓楼 is also impressive and contains a large antique store, where paintings, porcelain, and jade can be purchased. The tower was built in 1384 and is original. Drums were beaten about 800 times in 10 minutes before the city gates were closed for the night.

The *Great Mosque 大清真寺 , the largest in Xi'an, is on a back street north of the Drum Tower. It was founded as a mosque in 742 (Tang), but the present buildings are mainly Ming, with some subsequent construction. The buildings are a good example of the Sinification of foreign architecture right down to the bats, dragons, unicorns, marbletop tables, and mother-of-pearl-inlaid furniture. The Great Hall (Ming) is, however, more west Asian, the writing Arabic, the arches and flowers more like Istanbul or Baghdad. Shoes must be removed. Prayers are said five times a day. Moslems first came here from Xinjiang and Guangzhou, and they founded this mosque with encouragement from the Tang emperors. Today in Xi'an, 14 other mosques and this one serve 30,000 or so Moslems here. See also "What Is There to See and Do?"

Banpo (Panpo) Museum 半坡博物馆 , in the eastern suburbs of the city, is the actual archaeological site of a 6000-year-old neolithic village. The site covers 50,000 square meters, of which the museum encloses 3000. There you see living quarters, one of the oldest pottery kilns in the country, and a graveyard.

The museum was opened in 1958, encompassing a communal storage area, moat, graveyard (skeletons under glass), and fireplaces. In the museum are also a bow drill, barbed fish hook, clay pots, and pottery whistle believed to be the earliest musical instrument in China. Among its other artifacts are hairpins, stone axes, and a pot with holes in the bottom, probably used as a steamer. Its narrow-necked, narrow-based water jugs, with two handles, look surprisingly like amphoras also used by the ancient Greeks and Romans! Is there a connection? The exhibits are labeled in Chinese and English.

This culture is believed to be matrilineal (1) because of the burial customs. Most of the 174 graves had one skeleton each; the few graves that contained more than one skeleton had no male-female couples; (2) the women gathered wild food at first while the men hunted. After the women discovered how to plant seeds, land became valuable and it was passed on from mother to daughter; (3) because of the burial system (with no couples), scientists concluded that there were no fixed marriages. Besides, did neolithic people know where babies came from? (4) the village consisted of one big house in the center for old and young, and smaller houses for visiting males. The men kept their belongings in their native villages, where they were later buried.

As agriculture developed, men started pursuing it too. As surpluses grew (and probably the basic principles of physiology were discovered), fixed families started. In a later neolithic grave site in Gansu, a male skeleton was found lying straight and a female kneeling in the same grave. In another, a male was in the middle and two females were kneeling toward him. Since the women were bound, they were probably buried alive with him. So much for early women's lib!

Now, what is *your* theory?

*Maoling 茂陵 , on a plateau north of the Wei River, 40 km NW of Xi'an, has more than ten tombs, small grassy pyramids, about 46.5 meters high. The main tomb is that of the fifth Han emperor, built 139–87 B.C. According to records, it contains a jade suit with gold threads (seems to be a Han fad), and, in a gold box, more than 190 different birds and animals, jade, gold, silver, pearls, and rubies. The other identified tombs are of the emperor's favorite concubine Madame Li; ***General Ho Qubing,** who fought the Xiongnus/Huns, and strengthened the dynasty from the age of 18 until he died of disease at 24!; General Wei Qing; his horse breeder Jing Min Ji, who remained faithful even after Jing's tribe was defeated by the emperor; and General Ho Guang.

Some of the earliest and, therefore, most primitive massive stone carvings, originally placed in front of the tombs, can be studied here. Look for the horse stomping a Hun aristocrat. Each stone has a few lines added to the natural shape of the rock. Also in the museum are Han artifacts found by local peasants, including an irrigation pipe and ceramic animal figures. Near Maoling is the **Xianyang Museum,** containing 3000 painted terracotta warriors and horse figures from the Western Han (206 B.C.–A.D 24). They are each between 55 and 68 cm high.

Also near Maoling is the **Tomb of Yang Guifei,** 杨贵妃墓 , the beautiful, tragic imperial concubine.

*Xingjiao Temple (a.k.a. Xiangjiao Temple), about 25 km east of the Renmin Hotel, is on a sylvan hillside, which, with a little mist, could look like the lonely setting of the famous Japanese movie *Rashomon*. The place oozes with atmosphere, although the buildings are recent. It was founded by Tang Emperor Gaozong in A.D. 669, but destroyed and rebuilt several times. The remains (at least some of them) of monk Xuanzang, who first walked to India "day and night" and brought back the sutras, are buried in the small, five-story pagoda here. A map shows his route.

The *City Wall was built from 137· to 1378 (Ming), probably with material from the old Tang wall, which by then had decayed: 3.4 (north-south) by 2.6 km (east-west); 12 meters high. The walls follow the boundaries of the Tang imperial city. The gates open to the public are the imposing **Ximen (West) Gate** 西城门 and the **South Gate.** The wall, gates, and moat are being restored. Six new gates have been added to the original four to facilitate the flow of traffic. A small section of the south wall can be seen in its original Tang dynasty state.

IF YOU HAVE MORE TIME OR SPECIALIZED INTEREST:

*Qianling   Tomb of Tang Emperor Gaozong (Kao-tsung) and the Empress Wu: She was as ruthless and outrageous as Qing Empress Dowager Cixi, but a more successful ruler. He died in A.D. 683 and she in 705. This unexcavated tomb is 85 km NW of the city, a worthwhile full day's excursion that can include other tombs as well. While earlier tombs were built to create their own artificial hills on the plains, the Tang tombs were built into existing hills. This one is 400 meters high, 1049 meters above sea level.

Approaching the hill, one passes statues of horses and ostriches, and 10 large guardian figures holding swords. Then on the left are the life-size statues of guards, tribal heads, and foreign diplomats who paid their respects at the funeral. The statues are now without heads, alas; look for names on their backs. One is labeled Afghanistan. The wall around the tomb is 4470 meters. Some of the minor tombs are excavated, and visitors can go underground to see the coffin and fine murals of court scenes in the tombs of **Princess Yong-tai** and **Prince Yide.**

Although many of the structures at Qianling were destroyed in the war at the end of the Tang, the museum here contains about 4000 pieces.

*Zhaoling 昭陵, 70 km NW of Xi'an, is the tomb of the second Tang Emperor Taizong. It is built against a mountain near Lichuan. The 20,000-hectare cemetery contains 167 minor tombs (children, wives, generals) and took 13 years to build. A small museum with Tang pottery, stone tablets, and murals can be visited. This tomb is not worth visiting unless you can read classical Chinese. The six famous bas-reliefs of the emperor's favorite horses in the Provincial Museum came from here.

If you're tired of tombs by now, head SW of Xi'an to **Huxian County Town**   Here you can visit the Huxian Peasant Painting Exhibition Hall. Some of the 2000 painters in the county have also exhibited abroad these recordings of their everyday lives and achievements in gay colors.

About 15 km away is the thatched-cottage **Caotang Temple** 草堂室 (Tang), where Indian monk Kumarajiva (Chi Mo Lo Shi) translated the sutras into Chinese. He died in A.D. 413 and was buried here in 855. The current buildings are recent, with a fine rose garden. Japanese

Buddhists have presented a modern wooden statue of the monk.

The 2-meter-high stupa has some elaborate carvings and, from a well in the ground, a cloud used to come out at dawn, travel to Xi'an, and return at evening, said the guide. But this hasn't happened since the Cultural Revolution!

The **Horse and Chariot Pit** 车马坑 , Zhangjiapo, Chang'an county, can be combined with Huxian county for a half-day tour. It is the burial site of two chariots, six horses, and one slave (11th century B.C.— Western Zhou) and is the best of seven such pits found. It is of special interest to archaeologists.

Back around town, the ***Small Wild Goose Pagoda** 小雁塔 , outside the south wall, is 45 meters high and was constructed of brick in A.D. 684. Thirteen stories high, it is minus two of its original stories, destroyed during earthquakes in 1444. This is all that remains of the great Da Jianfu Temple, so important in the Tang.

The ruins of ***Daming Palace,** built in A.D. 634 (Tang), are for those people who prefer to figure out for themselves just where the vast banquets were held and where the throne room was. Clue: The hall was large enough to seat 2000 officials in A.D. 819. The foundation of the throne room, where the emperor consulted with officials and granted audiences, can still be seen; 164 pillars held up its roof.

One visitor described the Buddhist **Xiangji Temple** as ''not very interesting,'' but people who like to compare temples may want to include it if time permits. With its 33-meter-high pagoda, the temple honors a famous monk, Shandao. It is 20 km SW of Xi'an in Xiangji Temple village.

Other sights include the **Qinglong Temple,** in the Tang-dynasty Chang'an city in the southern suburbs at Tian Lumiao. Six famous Japanese monks were initiated into Buddhism here between A.D. 794 and 1192, and links with Japan still exist. The modest **Temple of Du Fu** is a memorial to the famous Tang poet, built in 1526, and is east of Weiqu Zhen in Chang'an county.

The **Louguan Taoist Temple** has now been restored. It is beyond Huxian, about 70 km west of Xi'an. It is said to be the place where Lao Tzu, founder of Taoism, taught. The temple has resident monks and makes traditional medicines. The setting and especially the entrance gate are very fine. A big yearly fair is held here.

Binxian County 彬县 is about 130 km NW of the city, and is a two-day trip. It is famous for its caves of Tang Buddhist statues, the largest about 25 meters tall.

***Huangling County:** Tomb of the Yellow Emperor. See ''Yan'an.''

Huashan Mountain 华山 , 150 km east of Xi'an, peaks to 2100 meters. Cable cars and a small hotel are being built. Until then, it is mainly for serious climbers because of its 80-degree cliffs (there *are* iron chains to hang on to) and a ''1000-foot-long Flight of Stone Steps.''

One also squeezes through the "100-foot-long Gorge." Famous as one of the Five Sacred Mountains, it is dotted with old temples.

Also in Shaanxi is "Yan'an." See separate listing.

Several new sites are being or have been opened. **Hanzhong,** 45 minutes by air from Xi'an or 14 hours by train, dates from the Three Kingdoms' period. It has the earliest tunnel in China (40 meters long) and the tomb of Zhuge Liang, Prime Minister of Shu (See also Chengdu.)

Famen Temple, 75 km. from Xi'an, can be included in a one-day trip along with the Qianling Tomb, and a Zhou dynasty bronzeware factory (5 km. from Famen). These are near **Baoji,** a city of 350,000 surrounded by mountains, on the old Silk Road. It also has a 7,000 year old neolithic site, older than Banpo, the municipal museum in the Jintai Monastery, Zhugong's Temple, and a temple to Zhuge Liang. Also nearby are the site of the Jiou Chen Palace (an imperial Tang summer resort), the Longmen Caves from which the Long sect of Taoism came, Mt. Jifeng and Mt. Tiantai. Mt. Taibai is a forest reserve, the home of the rare golden-haired monkies, pandas and ibises.

Famen Temple is extremely important because it houses a finger bone of Prince Gautama, the founder of Buddhism whose statue is in every Buddhist temple in China and who lived in the 5th century B.C. While tourists will not normally be shown this rare relic, they can see some of the treasures that were buried with it. Among the over 900 pieces are well preserved gold-inlaid ceremonial vessels, ancient glass and jade, gilt Buddhas, jewelry, gold walking stick, gold chain basket, fake "bones" of jade—the largest group of Tang artifacts found since 1950. They were gifts from Tang Emperors Yi Zong and Xi Zong. Empress Wu donated gilded embroidery with threads finer than those made today.

The temple was founded in the Han Dynasty, 2000 years ago. The bone and the treasures found with them were re-discovered in the 1980s during repairs to one of the pagodas here. Excavation began in 1987. A video of the excavations exists.

In **Tongchuan City,** Yao Xian county, 200 km. north of Xi'an are the ruins of ancient celadon kilns and workshops. A museum should be open there now. Yao Xian county also has a grotto with 40 Ming statues, the largest 11 meters tall.

Xi'an is the gateway to the Silk Road and road tours west have started.

SHOPPING

The main shopping area is east of the Bell Tower on Dong Ave. Most stores are open 7 or 9 a.m.–8 or 9 p.m. Made locally or in the province are: rubbings, reproductions of three-color Tang camels and horses, Qin Army soldiers, and murals. Also made are inlaid lacquer, cloisonne, stone and jade carvings, gold and silver jewelry, new year's pictures, paper cuts, and celadon.

C.I.T.S. suggests you start haggling at 1/5th the first asking price with all private merchants.

You will also find cheap reproductions of the Terracotta Warriors. Some of these are not kiln-dried and are extremely breakable. The better quality is usually found in government-approved stores.

200 meter long Tang Dynasty style street with food and souvenirs can be found near the Big Wild Goose Pagoda.

At stalls outside many tourist attractions, you will find red felt vests with appliqued snakes, scorpions, lizards, and pandas. These are very popular with tourists. At about ten yuan, they are the cheapest in China here. The yucky bugs are to frighten away the evil spirits.

Xi'an Friendship Store 友谊商店 (Nanxin St., near Dong Da St.; tel 28301); **Xi'an Arts and Crafts** (almost opposite the Friendship Store on Nanxin St.); **Xi'an Art Ceramics Factory** (Puzi Cun; tel. 39942) and **Qianxian Art Handicraft Workshop** (Qianxian) make Tang and Buddhist art reproductions; **Xi'an Antique Store** (Drum Tower; tel. 17187); **Xi'an Jade Carving Workshop** (173 Xi-1 Rd.; tel. 22570); **Xi'an Special Arts and Crafts Factory** (138 Huancheng Xi Rd.; tel. 28891). **Arts and Crafts Factory** (90 km. outside Xi'an near Qianling).

Also **Xi'an Luxury Friendship Store** (No. 5 Building, South St.; tel. 21450, 24789), and **Xi'an Studio Shop of Chinese Cultural Treasures** (No. 19 Yan Ta Rd.; tel. 51212, 53415).

RESTAURANTS

Xi'an food is similar to that of Beijing: somewhat bland. Its famous local dishes are crisp fried chicken or duck, and dried fish shaped like grapes. Much of its food has been inspired by imperial tastes. Two celebrated wines are made here—one thick and sweet with the appearance of milk. Served hot, Chou Jiu wine inspired Tang poet Li Po, who drank 1000 cups and wrote more than 100 poems. The other wine is Xifeng Jiu (55% alcohol), a blend of sour, sweet, bitter, and spicy. It is one of the Eight Most Famous Wines in China. For some local dishes, see ''Food.''

The popular *jiaotze* dumpling restaurant De Fachong near the Bell Tower serves over a hundred different kinds of dumplings. In season, try the persimmons, which are not stringent like American ones.

Dongya Restaurant 东亚饭店 ● *46 Luoma Shi; tel. 27396, 28410* ● Suzhou.

Sichuan Restaurant ● *151 Jiefang Rd.; tel. 24736.*

Night Life Tang Dynasty Theatre Restaurant. Dances. Different programs include classical Tang Dynasty dances, the opera Spirit of the Terracotta Warriors, and provincial folk dances. Elegant theater. Dances by the Shaanxi Provincial Song and Dance Troupe with Tang imperial food. Hong Kong management. The Tang Dynasty, Chang' An Rd. Book through C.I.T.S.

HOTELS

So many new hotels and extensions have opened recently that it is impossible to decide the top three, but you should have no problem getting a room. In the luxury class, the Golden Flower and the Garden have the most experience. We have only tried the Golden Flower and it is very good. In 1989 Holiday Inn, Dynasty, Sheraton, Ramada, Efang Palace, Novotel, and Jianguo were due to open. Some will be late.

In the medium-priced range, the Concord, Xi'an, and Tang Cheng have been good but not perfect. The Concord, Scarlet Bird, Tang Cheng, and the New World Hotel are opening new buildings, quality unknown.

The hotels inside the wall are the Bell Tower Hotel (closest to the Bell Tower) and only a few meters away, the cheaper New World Hotel. Both are convenient to the Friendship Store, mosque, and bell and drum towers. Further away to the northeast are the Renmin, Novotel and Sofitel, convenient to the Friendship Store and city square. All are ideal for walkers, the Bell Tower a little better located than the others. One gets more of a feeling for old China inside the wall, but it has traffic jams and parking problems.

To the east, outside the wall and closest to the zoo and Banpo Museum, are the Golden Flower, Holiday Inn, and Jianguo. To the south are the Dynasty, Garden, Ramada, Scarlet Bird, Shaanxi Sports, Tang Cheng, and Xian. Some of these are close to Wild Goose Pagodas. To the west towards the airport are the Concord and Dynasty (closest to the fancy West Gate).

The Holiday Inn has rooms for wheelchair travelers.

C.I.T.S. office at the rwy. station and airport has a list of vacant rooms.

Bell Tower Hotel • *Southwest corner of Bell Tower. Cable 6988. Telex 70124 XABTH CN. Dist.A.P.5 km. Dist.R.W.5 km* • 1983, ren. 1986–1988 with Holiday Inn management. 7 stories, 321 rooms. Odd numbers have best view of Bell Tower. IDD, C.C. Business center, bicycles.

Concord Hotel Xian • *12 Feng Hao Rd. Cable 4460. Telex 70024 CONHL CN. Set in garden between city wall (2 km.) and airport (2 km). Dist.R.W. 5 km. Near biggest free market.* • T.R., C.C. 1986–

1987. 6 stories, 167 rooms. 1988, 300 more rooms. No IDD. Few services. CAAC office.

Golden Flower • *8 Chang Le Xi Rd. Telex 70145 GFH CN. Fax 32327. Dist. A.P.11 km. Dist.R.W. 3 km. 15 min. walk to Xingqing Park. 10 min. to Zoo (with only brown giant panda in China). Near free market and antique shop.* • 1985; 7 stories, 210 rooms. 1989; 11 stories, 300 rooms. T.R., C.C. Book through SARA or UTELL. Pool, gym, apartments, business center. IDD. Large rooms and beds.

Holiday Inn Xian • *8 South Section, Huang Cheng East Rd. Telex 70043. Fax 721962. Dist.A.P.10 km* • 1989. 14 stories, 372 rooms. Health club, pool, business center.

Hotel Scarlet Bird • *Xiaozhai Rd. West. Cable 7404. Telex 70186 TSBHL CN. Dist.A.P.10 km. Dist.R.W.15 km.* • T.R., AmExpress and MasterCard C.C. 1985, ren. 1988; 4 stories, 110 rooms. 1988; 22 stories, 370 rooms. IDD, business center, bicycles.

Jianguo Hotel • *20 Jin Hua Nan Rd. Fax (029)721688* • C.C. 1989. 6 and 13 stories. 700 rooms. IDD, business center, pool, bicycles. Reservations UTELL. Swiss-Belhotel Management.

Jiaolong University Guest House • Budget travelers only.

New World Hotel • *5 Nan Da Jie. Telex 70042 NWH CN. Fax 716688* • Managed by Chains International.

New World Dynasty Hotel • *Junction of Lian Hu Rd. and Sa Jin Qiao. Part of Xi'an Art and Cultural Center. Dist.A.P.3 km. Dist. R.W.4 km* • C.C. 1989. 14 stories, 502 rooms. Non-smoking floor. Conference facilities, theatre, pool, tennis, IDD. Fitness center, clinic, business center, bicycles. New World International management.

Northwest University Guest House • Budget travelers only.

People's (Renmin) Hotel • *319 Dongxin St. Telex 70176 RMHTA. Cable 0633. Dist.A.P.12 km. Dist.R.W.4 km* • Will telex answer to reservation request only if room available. No C.C. Should have IDD now. Different buildings, different qualities. #2 has small rooms.

Shaanxi Sports Hotel • *Inside the Shaanxi Sports Stadium near Xi'an Hotel* • 1984. 3 stories. 66 rooms. Soft beds. Am Express and Diner's C.C. Bicycles, IDD. Budget travelers only.

Tang Cheng Hotel • *7 South Lingyuan Rd. Cable 3266. Telex 70013 TCH CN. Next to Ramada Hotel and near Northwest University* • T.R., C.C. Dist.A.P.5 km. Dist.R.W.7 km. 1986–87; 11 stories, 406 rooms. 1989; 300 more rooms. Pool, bowling. Should now have IDD. C.I.T.S.

Xi'an Garden Hotel • *Tanghua, No. 4 Dong Yan Yin Rd., Da Yan Ta. Telex 711998 GAHTL CN. Next to Tang Culture and Arts Museum. Dist.R.W.14 km* • T.R. 1988. 4 stories, 301 rooms. Exotic Tang architecture. Japanese management.

Xi'an Hotel • *36 N. Section, Chang'an Rd. Cable 6333. Telex 70135 XAHTL CN. Fax 711796. Dist.A.P.7 km. Dist.R.W.10 km. Near C.I.T.S.* • T.R., C.C. 1982. 14 stories, 286 rooms; ren. 1988. New building (1987) 14 stories, 264 rooms. IDD, business center, bicycles, pool, gym.

OTHER IMPORTANT ADDRESSES

Airport 飞机场 : Xishaomen; tel. 42264, 42402.
Bank of China: 833 Jiefang Rd.; tel. 716931, 22312. Foreign exchange counters at major hotels, Friendship Store, and Xi'an Antique Store, etc.
China International Travel Service: Changan Rd., Cao Chang Po. Tel. 51414, 51419, 53201. Telex 70115 CITSX CN. Fax 711453. Also books charter flights to Hong Kong.
C.I.T.S. Ancient Capital Branch, Chang An Rd. Tel. 54611. Telex 70011 CITSA CN.
China Travel Service and Overseas Chinese Travel Service: 272 Jiefang Rd. Tel. 711309, 711191, 712957. Telex 70148 CTSSP CN.
China Youth Travel Service 48 Hong Ying Rd. Tel. 27296.
CAAC, Xi Shao Men. Tel. 42264. Airport. Tel. 42362.
Hospitals:
    C.I.T.S., above, has a clinic.
    Fourth Army Hospital
    Shaanxi Provincial People's Hospital: Huangyancun; tel. 25991.
Post Offices: at major hotels. The main post office is on NE side of Bell Tower circle.
Railway Station 火车站 : Jiefang Rd.; tel. 26911. (Traditional Chinese architecture, built in 1933 and extended in 1958.)
Travel and Tourism Bureau of Shaanxi Province: Caochangpo, Chang'an Rd.; tel. 53201 53202; cable: 2464. Can organize tours for bring your-own-hot-air balloonist, jeeps along the Silk Road, self-drive cars, and do-it-yourself archeologists. Write for other ideas.

XINHUI 新会

(Hsinhui; Cantonese, Sunwai) South China. This county, about 130 km SW of Guangzhou in Guangdong province, is in the heart of fan-palm country, from which many Chinese emigrated to America and Australia. Every spare inch seems to have these trees, whose leaves are woven into baskets, fans, and mats. The county seat, **Huicheng,** has a population of about 110,000. The city is sometimes combined with Jiangmen in a two- or three-day tour. Both are about a three-hour air-conditioned bus ride from Guangzhou, or a four-hour boat ride from Hong Kong or an overnight boat ride from Guangzhou, both to Jiangmen, and then a half-hour bus ride to Xinhui. The easiest way of all is the 4-hour ferry from Hong Kong, which brings you directly into this part of the province.

Visitors can see the fan-palm factory or relax on very pretty Guifeng Mountain on top of which is Yuhu (Jade) Lake. This artificial lake has a changing room for swimming, the usual pavilions, and a restaurant. A Tang dynasty temple, destroyed during the Japanese war, is being rebuilt on the mountain. In another direction from the city and 7 km away, a magnificent old tree called **Birds' Paradise** is home at night to thousands of cranes and egrets and is best seen at dusk. A small museum is across from the Guifeng Guest House.

In the area also is the **Yutai Temple** (Tang), and the **Zhenshan Pagoda.** In the southeastern part of the county 40 km. away is the **Yamen Fort,** a modest building used by the Qing administrators, and the remains of **Ciyuan Temple,** recently renovated, first built in the Ming by a famous poet. It commemorates some Song generals who fought heroically to the death.

The Overseas Chinese Association in Xinhui organizes free 20 day summer camps for people with roots in the county. Classes in calligraphy, history, traditional medicine, etc.

Aside from the woven palm products, this county is noted for its dried Mandarin orange peel used in soups and congee. (The best smell strongly of oranges.)

HOTELS

The Xinhui Hotel appears to be the best followed closely by the Kui Yuan but neither is outstanding. Both are centrally located and about 10 km. from the port in Jiangmen.

Kui Yuan Hotel • *15 Zhong Xin Rd. Cable 2156. On main street near shopping.* • 1987–88. 15 stories, 198 rooms. Hong Kong j.v. Should have IDD and telex now. Major credit cards.

Xinhui Hotel a.k.a. Guangdong Xinhui Hotel • *Zhi Zheng Bei Rd. Central.* • Major credit cards. 21 stories, 150 rooms. Revolving restaurant on top wobbles.
C.T.S. and C.I.T.S. tel. 63297, 63419. Cable 3307.
Overseas Chinese Association, tel. 63589.

XINING 西宁

Northwest China. Capital of Qinghai (Tsinghai) province. A little over 6 hours by small plane from Beijing (three stops), or 55 minutes NW from Lanzhou. The highway to Lhasa is now asphalted, the highest highway in the world. The railway joins Xining with Golmud in the western part of the province and also with Lanzhou and Xi'an, eastward. Currently being built is a 1200-km line from Golmud to Lhasa. When it is finished, it should be one of the most spectacular train rides in the world. Qinghai is the source of both the Yellow and Yangtze rivers and has a lot of hydroelectric power. It is rich in aluminum, coal, and oil. Weather: Hottest—less than 32°C in July and August; coldest—⁻16°C in January and December. Annual precipitation is 450 mm in July and August. There is a possibility that the Soviet border 92 km away will soon be accessible to visitors.

This province has only recently opened to tourists. A one-day visit to Xining can include the Taer Lamasery, Dongguan Mosque, and North Mountain Temple. The *****Taer Monastery** 塔尔寺 (Ming), the center of the yellow-hat sect of Tibetan Buddhism, is at Huangzhong, about 30 km from the Xining Guest House and the Qinghai Hotel. Built in 1397 (or 1577, depending on the source), it is worth a visit. Its kitchen has three bronze cauldrons that are said to cook 13 cattle at one time to serve 3600 people. Ask why meat is served in this Buddhist monastery! In the winter, frozen butter, two meters high by 26 meters long, is sculptured into Buddhist scenes and displayed on the 15th day of the lunar New Year. It also has 20,000 religious paintings and embroideries. C.T.S. has a branch in the monastery.

The **Dongguan Mosque** 东关，清真寺 , one of the biggest in Northwest China, was built in 1380 and is 2 km from the Xining Guest House. The **North Mountain Temple** 北禅寺 is also 2 km from the hotel.

Qinghai Lake 青海湖 (China's largest saltwater lake) is 3196 meters above sea level and is 130 km from the capital. A bird sanctuary, **Bird Island** 鸟岛 , is about 350 km away from Xining. The 8-square-km island attracts 100,000 migrating geese and gulls each summer and autumn, and has bird-watching pavilions and Tibetan-style hotels.

About 60 km east is another temple also under State Council protection, the *****Qutan Temple** (Ming). Also in the vicinity is the 6282-meter Ma Qing Gang Re Mountain.

The province has wild antelope, yak, donkeys, camels, lynx, deer, and pheasant, all protected.

Golmud 格尔木市 is a new industrial city in the Gobi Desert, in the west of the province. It has a population of 130,000, is 800 km from Xining, and is a trans-shipment point for Tibet. Between Xining and Golmud is the Salt Bridge and Salt Pond.

The province is huge, covering one thirteenth of China, and is in the Qinghai-Tibet Plateau. It has less than four million people, mainly Han (60%), the rest Tibetan, Hui, Mongolian, Kazak, Sala, and Tu. Many of these are nomadic herdsmen. Ninety-six percent of its land is pasture for 22 million horses, yak, and sheep. Livestock breeding has been practiced here for 4000 years, and cow dung is used for fuel. Half of China's yak and one third of all the world's yak are in Qinghai.

Times are changing however: recently, a 3500 gm gold nugget was found, and a gold rush is on. The national government is focusing its economic development on the NW region. Pastureland is now contracted to herdsmen for 30 years, thus encouraging the users to manage it more wisely. Bonuses are given in some counties for families who send children to school, not an easy task for nomads. The government is building railways and highways.

Golmud Hotel primitive but adequate. See ''Lhasa.''

SHOPPING

Good buys are handicrafts made by the minorities.

RESTAURANTS

Rong Yuan Restaurant 蓉苑餐厅 • *1 Xiao Qiao (Small Bridge) Ave., Xining; tel. 54725* • Sichuan and local dishes.

HOTELS

Qinghai Hotel 青海宾馆 • *20 Huang He Rd. 810001. Cable 0524. Dist.A.P.30 km. Dist.R.W.3 km. Near government trade offices and tourist shopping* • 1989. 23 stories, 270 rooms. Clinic, sports center, business and conference centers.

Xining Guest Hotel 西宁宾馆 • *Qiyi Rd.* • 1957; renovated 1985. 12 km from airport. Main tourist hotel.

C.I.T.S. and **C.T.S.** 国际旅行社 : 215 Qiyi Rd.; tel. 23901. Cable 2464.
CAAC 中国民航 : 74 Xining East Ave.; tel. 77434.

XIQIAO MOUNTAIN 西樵山

South China, 70 km SW of Guangzhou via Foshan in Guangdong province. About 25 km. from the airport in Foshan. A good place for a leisurely family vacation relatively close to Hong Kong. With two resort areas, one at the base and the other on top of a 400-meter-high mountain, hikers have an area 10 km in circumference to explore. The mountaintop has three lakes (one in an extinct volcanic crater) with bicycle paddle boats, 44 caves and grottoes, 72 peaks, 207 springs, and innumerable waterfalls. The eight villages are home to 600 people, their houses very traditional. Partway up the mountain is a layer of clam shells near which archaeologists have found 2000-year-old pottery shards. The weather at the base of the mountain is hottest, 32°C, from July to September; it is coldest, 7°C, in January and February. Precipitation is 1150 mm, mainly March to June.

The resort at the base of Xiqiao Mountain seems noisy partly because the area makes firecrackers that are frequently set off by firecracker-deprived Hong Kong tourists. Guangzhou swingers have come here to learn dancing, and schoolchildren come on excursions to visit the three-story Ming tower and the Qing Taoist temple. Also at the base is a 1-km-long artificial lake, horses, shooting gallery (machine guns!), waterfalls, electronic games, basketball court, badminton, roller-skating rink, and amusement park.

A 1-km-long cable car goes up the mountain starting about 200 meters from the Xiqiao Hotel.

HOTELS

Baiyun Lou Guest Hotel 白云楼宾馆 • 1959. Renovated 1986. Restaurant. On top of the mountain. 26 air-conditioned rooms. Hot water, but no heat. Near one of the villages.

Sanhu (Three Lakes) Guest House 国旅商场 • is the main tourist hotel. 1978; renovated 1986. Coffee shop, restaurant, dance hall. Spanish style.

Xiqiao Great Hotel 西樵山大酒店 • 1987. Coffee shop, dance hall, Chinese and Western food. Aiming for four stars. This is the best hotel here.

C.I.T.S. 国际旅行社 : White Cloud Cave, Xiqiao Mountain, Nanhai County; tel. 230 or 56799. It can arrange for taxis to meet you anywhere in the area, such as the Guangzhou airport or railway station.
C.I.T.S. Market : tel. 582.
Taxi: tel. 661.

XUZHOU 徐州

East China. Northwest Jiangsu province, conveniently located on two railway lines and accessible by plane from Shanghai and Guangzhou. Three pits containing 3000 terracotta horses and warriors 27–54-cm-high were recently unearthed here, believed connected with the tomb of a Western Han duke. The Han Dynasty Museum is at the site of the discovery, the mausoleum of Prince Chu, ruler of Xuzhou, during the reign of Emperor Wu Di (156–87 B.C.)

The Han jade burial suit that toured North America came from here. A recently opened imperial tomb possibly built between 201 and 154 B.C. can be explored. A gigantic 11-meter-high bust of Buddha is on Yunlong Mountain. Xuzhou also offers martial arts exhibits and tours on Weishan Lake.

C.I.T.S. says the top hotel is the **South Suburb Guest House,** followed by the **Xuzhou,** and thirdly the **Huaihai.**

HOTELS

South Suburb Guesthouse • *55 Heping Rd. Dist.A.P.10 km, Dist.R.W.5 km* • 1956, ren. 1988. 4 stories, 100 rooms. Am Express C.C. only. IDD. Telex 34077 XZSG CN. Cable 6333.
C.I.T.S. No. 1 Pengcheng Rd. Tel. 24842. Telex 368009 PMXZ CN. Cable 2464.

YAN'AN 延安

(Yenan) Northwest China. 2½ hours by air SW of Beijing (with one stop); 1 hour by air or 8½ hours by road north of Xi'an. No rail connection. Northern Shaanxi in the Loess Plateau. Weather: Hottest—35°C in July; coldest—¯25°C in January. Rainy season: August–September. The altitude in the city is 800–1000 meters. During the rainy season, planes may be postponed or canceled. Urban population: 50,000.

Yan'an was a small administrative town 1000 years ago. In 1936 it had a population of 3000. It became the most important Communist revolutionary site in China in January 1937 after the end of the Long March. The Communists chose to settle here because of the rugged mountain terrain, a wise choice because the Nationalists failed to dislodge them for 10 years. Here, the Communists trained leaders, developed policies, organized the peasants, and planned strategy against the Nationalists and Japanese. In 1945 the population was 100,000. Chiang Kai-shek finally succeeded in capturing the city without a fight in March 1947 and held it until April 1948, while Mao Zedong (Mao Tse-tung) went on to take the whole of China.

Today Yan'an is primarily of interest to revolutionists and students of modern history and architecture. For others it has only a Tang pagoda famous primarily because of the revolution, and a tiny cave of 10,000 Buddhas. This is an interesting off-the-beaten-path destination now.

The city, clinging to the mountainside, stretches along both sides of the Yan River and the South and Dufu streams. The soil is loess, excellent for construction. Most of the area houses are quonset-hut-shape "caves," either freestanding or dug into a mountain. They are said to be cozy and dry in the winter and cool in the summer. Even the university was built in this style, and the villages are fascinating. Many buildings have been converted to brick as income increases.

The city is now largely industrial. Nearby are oil wells and coal mines. Meter-high mounds of huge black chunks of coal piled haphazardly in the streets are a little startling.

The middle school rates a visit insofar as it was started after the

Long March, whose leaders visited often to oversee the curriculum. Now it is like any other school. See also "Milestones in Chinese History."

Yan'an Revolutionary Memorial Hall 延安革命纪念馆: This excellent museum has a giant map outlining the route of the Long March in neon. Titles are in English and Chinese. Exhibits also include a fascinating model of tunnel warfare, Communist bank notes, and Chairman Mao's horse (stuffed).

Residences of Chairman Mao 毛主席旧居 are also museums, furnished as simply as they were then, all of them "caves":

(1) Foot of Fenghuang (Phoenix) Hill 凤凰山麓 January 1937–November 1938. Here Mao wrote his important articles on "contradiction" and "protracted war." The photo in front of the cave was taken in 1937, just after Zhou Enlai (Chou En-lai), who lived nearby, returned from settling the Xi'an Incident. Mao left this cave because of Japanese bombing.

(2) Yangjialing 杨家岭: November 1938–January 1943. The auditorium was the site of several party Central Committee meetings and a national congress (1945), delegates risking their lives to come from and return to Nationalist-held areas. Here also was the site of the Yenan Forum on Arts and Literature to encourage musicians, writers, and painters to "make art and literature serve the workers and peasants better."

(3) Zaoyuan (Date Orchard) 枣园: January 1943–end of 1945. The Secretariat was close by. The lilac tree in front was planted by Mao. On his desk is the first iron bar made in the local foundry. He exercised his hand with the bar to avoid writer's cramp. From here Zhou Enlai flew to Chongqing to negotiate with Chiang, an American-instigated effort to avoid civil war.

(4) Wangjiaping 王家坪: January 1946–March 1947. Headquarters of the Eighth Route Army. Dances were held in the garden. The civil war resumed, and here Mao argued with his military commanders about withdrawing from Yan'an in the face of an enormous Nationalist campaign in March 1947. While his commanders wanted to defend the city, Mao argued, "We must not concentrate on hanging on to places. Our main purpose is to wipe out the enemy's effective forces . . . there are only a few caves here. If they destroy the caves, it is good. We can build high buildings when we come back." The Communists regained the city on April 22, 1948, but Mao did not return then.

Baota (Precious Pagoda) 宝塔 (延安宝塔) a.k.a. Yan'an Pagoda: 44 meters, nine stories; 1300-year-old (Tang) building. Can be climbed.

Wangfo Dong (Cave of the 10,000 Buddhas) 万佛洞 is right in town below the pagoda and relatively close to Wangjiaping. It dates from the Song and Jin. Most of the Buddhas are tiny; some are in good condition. The cave was used to house the printing presses of the Central Committee. Up the hill is a Laughing Buddha carved on the hillside, now the back wall of a house. The god can be seen through the front window. During the Cultural Revolution, it was hidden by a cloth, which saved it from the Red Guards.

If you have more time: **Nanniwan** 南泥湾 , 45 km south, was turned from a wasteland into a productive area in 1941–43 by the 359 Brigade of the revolutionary army. It is now a village with a small museum.

Liu Lin Village has been documented by visitors as far back as the '60s. Read Jan Myrdal's *Report from a Chinese Village* if you want to compare progress then and now.

Huangling County 黄陵 , just about halfway on the road between Xi'an and Yan'an, 4 hours' drive from each. Huangling makes an interesting break and, for ancient Chinese history buffs, is a very important stop. There is a hotel, built 1978.

The *Tomb of the Yellow Emperor Xuan Yuan: 3.6 meters high and 50 meters in circumference, originally built in the Han but moved here to its present site in the Song. The Yellow Emperor is the legendary ancestor of the Chinese people believed to have lived about 2000 B.C. The tomb is at the top of Qiaoshan (hill), 1 km north of Huangling town. At the base is Xuan Yuan temple. Of its 63,000 cypress trees, one is said to have been planted by the Yellow Emperor himself. It is the largest known ancient cypress in China. In front of the tomb is the Platform of Immortality built by Emperor Han Wu (156–87 B.C.) to announce his victory over his enemy and to pray for longevity. The temple of Xuan Yuan was built in the Han, the many steles here recording the sacrifices offered, memorials about repair work, etc. The throne stands in the middle with information about Xuan's life on both sides. In ancient times, travelers had to dismount from their horses and pay respect to their First Ancestor as they passed by.

The **Cave Temple of a Thousand Buddhas** (Tang) is halfway up Ziwu Hill in the western part of Huangling county.

In **Luochuan County,** 120 km south of Yan'an, one can sleep in a guesthouse made of 40 "caves" and see local folk arts—embroidery, animal-head slippers and hats for children, cloth articles, paper cuts, and paintings (based on paper-cut designs). Embroidered aprons are for men to keep bellies warm, not for cooking or cleaning.

See "Food" for local dishes.

HOTELS

Yan'an Guest House 延安宾馆 • 1965. 110 beds, three stories. Expanded 1980 with 250 additional beds. 10 km from airport. Short walk to shopping, downtown, cinema, pagoda. Next door to No. 1 Mao Residence. The hotel has some documentary films showing Mao giving a lecture, available on request.

Being constructed are the 200-bed **Jialing Hotel** and 500-bed **Feng-huang.**
CAAC: Dong-guan Airport; tel. 3854.
C.T.S.: 106 Yanan Ave.; tel. 2589. Cable 6333.
See also ''Jinggang Shan'' and ''Shijiazhuang.''

YANGTZE GORGES 长江三峡

(a.k.a. Yangzi or Changjiang River Gorges) The boat trip through the gorges and on the great river itself to or from Chongqing is highly recommended not just for its relaxed sightseeing of spectacular scenery but also for its history. Do bring binoculars, a telephoto lens if you're a camera bug, and reading material. The scenery includes sheer cliffs rising up to 400 meters on either side of narrow, rushing water, mountains up to 1000 meters, old towns cut by slender lines of stone steps, and a mountain lined from top to bottom with a pagoda. The Yangtze River is also a busy highway now being harnessed even more for flood control, irrigation, and hydroelectric power.

A controversial dam, planned with Canadian help, has been considered. If built, it would displace up to a million people, raise the water level about 175 meters, and destroy the dramatic effect of the gorges. In 1989, the decision was postponed for five years.

Guides will tell you stories of the Three Kingdoms, but do bring your own history books along, or a copy of *The Sand Pebbles* or John Hersey's *A Single Pebble*. The *Romance of the Three Kingdoms* has been translated into English, and the names of the heroes of this great military story will keep coming up almost anywhere you go in central China. If you don't have a guide with you, maybe the steward or cook can point out landmarks. The Yangtze was also central to the foreign merchants, gunboats, and missionaries in the late 1800s and early 1900s, but guides will not give you much information about this embarrassing period.

There are several ways of sailing the Gorges. The cheapest are the **passenger ferries,** where tour groups get first crack at the top second-class accommodations with a lounge and the best view. Second-class has two bunks. No one gets private toilets, baths, or air conditioners. Individual travelers with second-class tickets might even get downgraded to third, fourth, or fifth class, where you share a room with an increasing number of people, or sleep in hallways. You might get bumped off the boat entirely by tour groups. Try for an outside cabin. The inside ones can get pretty stuffy in summer, and you might find other passengers gambling noisily on the floor outside your room.

Stops are prescheduled and not necessarily at tourist sites like Shibaozhou (Shibao Block), nor can you be sure your ship will get close enough to get a photo of that lovely 11-story pagoda unless you have a lens at least 200 mm long. But you only pay for passage to where you want to get off. And, by ferry, you can get closer to Chinese people, and experience with them the loudspeakers blaring announcements at 6 a.m. and queues for showers. After all, didn't you come here to meet the people?

Ferries can be booked through C.I.T.S. in Chongqing and Wuhan, or directly at the pier a couple of days ahead of time.

Currently, air-conditioned ships for tourists ply the Yangtze from April 1 to Dec. 1, and can be booked through tour agents. On these you are isolated from Chinese people, but **tourist ships** are more comfortable.

Itineraries differ depending on which way you are going—up- or downriver, and which ship you book. The most luxurious ship, the *Bashan*, is chartered by Lindblad.

Other ships include the *Goddess, Great Wall, Kunlun, Long Zhong (Merchant Prince), Three Gorges, Xiling,* and *Yangtze River*. These tourist ships stop for sightseeing at some but not all of the following: Lake Dongting, Fengjie, Jingzhou, Jiujiang, Nanjing, Lushan, Shashi, Shibao Block, Wanxian, Wuhan, Yangzhou, Yueyang, Yichang, and Zhenjiang. The highlight for many tourists is the day trip up the three little gorges on the Daning River, where they can see wild monkeys and suspended coffins.

The services of these tourist ships include guide-interpreter, double rooms with private baths, laundry, doctor, currency exchange, post and telegraph, beauty salon, library, lounge (with evening movies), a bar, Western food, and a store—none of which the public ferries have. Depending on class, you would be lucky to get a seat for eating on a passenger ferry.

The quality of the ships differ; they are owned by different companies. Do not expect the *Love Boat* with a social convener. Lindblad says it alone can guarantee single accommodations and a sinologist. There is usually a captain's dinner, and a final dance (to ancient music, so bring your own cassettes). Some ships have smelly toilets. Most have picture windows so you can enjoy the view from your cabin.

Meanwhile back at the **public ferry,** which operates all year round, going downstream from Chongqing to Wuhan, which is the best way to go—faster—the trip takes two nights on board ship and three days on the water. The ferries stop at towns along the way for a few minutes up to several hours. Take your own soap and towel. Each ferry has about 24 second-class cabins. The third class has four to eight to a room, no curtains. None have much privacy. It is better, if you are on a ferry, to ride only to Chenglingji (Yueyang) because the stretch between Yichang and Wuhan, a whole day's ride, isn't all that interesting. After a day of sightseeing around Dongting Lake (Candice Bergen was a missionary there in *The Sand Pebbles*—see "Yueyang"), you can go on to Changsha or Wuhan by train.

Ferry Downstream   —Day 1: Leave Chongqing early (about 7 a.m.). Note white pagoda on north bank at Changshou. At about 3 hours out, Fuling. At 8½ hours out, Zhongxian. At 10 hours out, look for **Shibaozhai (Precious Stone Village),** a.k.a. Shibao Block, on the north bank, with its 11-story Qing pagoda. It is built on a limestone rock hill, Yuyin Shan (Jade Seal Hill), that rises to 160 meters above the river. In the main temple are statues of Liu Bei, Zhuge Liang, Guan Yu, and Zhang Fei, historical personages. Three of these swore oaths in a peach orchard to support each other. They are immortalized in *The Romance of the Three Kingdoms.* Emperor Liu Bei, who led an unsuccessful army to avenge the death of Guan Yu, retreated here and died of sorrow.

At 12½ hours, overnight stop at 2000-year-old **Wanxian,** the site of one of the first successful assertions of Chinese power against the imperialist gunboats during the Northern Expedition. There was a lot of shooting here in the late 1920s. Tourists climb about 85 steps to the 700,000-population town for a tour of a silk factory. There is a Friendship Store.

Day 2: The ship leaves early (about 2:30 a.m.), depending on the current, to reach the first gorge 4½ hours later, at daylight. Near the entrance on the north bank is a two-story pavilion with red lacquer columns, which marks the beginning of the gorges. On the south side of Kui Men Gate are two stone towers and five Chinese characters, which mean "The Kui Men Gate is an unmatched pass."

The **Qutang (Chutang) Gorge** is 8 km long and takes about an hour to pass through. It is the "most imposing" of the gorges, only 100–150 meters wide. Prepare for a very windy passage, as the wind as well as the water is funneled between the cliffs.

The **Wuxia (Wuhsia),** or just Wu Gorge, starts 30 minutes after you leave the Qutang. It is 44 km long and takes about 1½ hours to pass through. Look for the Twelve Peaks Enshrouded in Rain and Mist, of which you can see six on the north bank and three on the south. Of these, the Peak of the Goddess is the highest, at over 1000 meters. It has a tall stone column on top that looks like "a strongly built young woman gazing from high up in the sky at the waterway down below." Look for a tablet-shaped rock with six Chinese characters meaning "The Wu Gorge boasts craggy cliffs," said to be written by a prime minister of the Shu Kingdom in the third century. Ask also about Xiang Xi (Fragrant Stream), where a lady-in-waiting of a Han emperor dropped her pearls accidentally. The water here is said to be "limpid and fragrant" as a result.

About 20 minutes after leaving the Wuxia Gorge at the town of Badong, pomelos, oranges, and persimmons are for sale on shore, if in season. Look for a temple high on a hill. You are now in Hubei province. At this border is being built the largest dam in the world, which will also raise the water level in the gorges 150 meters.

About 1 hour from Badong is the 75-km-long **Xiling (Hsiling) Gorge,** which takes about 1½ hours to pass through. It is the longest and most treacherous of the three. Oranges grow on some of the hillsides. Thirty minutes beyond the entrance, on the south side, is Kuang Ming village, with a large temple, Huang Ling Miao. Then comes Five Sisters Peaks, Three Brothers Rocks, and the Needle. Toward the end of this gorge are unsightly sandstone quarries, and then the locks at Gezhouba dam. After that is Yichang, an industrial city in the plains. This is the end of the spectacular scenery. From here read or get to know some of the 500 other passengers. If you stay on board, you arrive late afternoon the next day in Wuhan.

See also "Gezhouba."

Jingzhou has a well-preserved 2000-year-old mummy, an ancient gate, walls from the Three Kingdoms period (A.D. 220–265), Ka Yuan Taoist Temple from the Tang (now also a museum), and Tai Hui Temple from 1393 A.D., factory for thermos bottles and bedspreads, and a museum.

Fengjie was the capital of the state of Kwei during the Spring and Autumn Period (722–481 B.C.), the time of Confucius. The tomb of Liu Bei's wife is here. See *Romance of the Three Kingdoms*. The ancient wall and gate still stand. Fengjie is near the western entrance to the gorges.

If you miss the boat at any of your stops, C.I.T.S. can arrange transport for you to catch up.

YANGZHOU 揚州

(Yangchow) East China. 20 km north of the Yangtze on the Grand Canal in Jiangsu province, Yangzhou is 2400 years old and famous for its gardens and pavilions. Because of its location, it was a very prosperous port after the Sui emperors had the canal built. In the Tang dynasty, it was the residence of over 5,000 foreigners. One of Prophet Mohammed's descendants is buried here, and in 1282 Marco Polo is said to have spent three years as governor-general. Yangzhou's wealth declined with that of the canal, and by the Qing, it was famous only as an imperial resort city. It is one of the 24 historical and cultural cities protected by the State Council. It is one of the nicest oldest cities, with lots of old Chinese architecture and a relaxed atmosphere. It can now be reached by ferry and bus from Zhenjiang on the south shore, 2 hours by road from Nanjing, or by boat along the Yangtze or the Grand Canal. Its population is 370,000. Its hottest temperature is 38.6°C in July–August; its coldest is ⁻5°C in January–February. Annual precipitation is about 1000 mm, mainly from June to September.

If you only have one day in Yangzhou, C.I.T.S. recommends hurrying through Shouxi Lake, Daming Temple, Geyuan Garden (the best and most typical), Heyuan Garden, and the city museum. You have to choose between a lacquerware, jade-carving or paper-cutting factory. If time permits, there's shopping and the Free Market.

The **Shouxi (Slender West) Lake** 瘦西湖 , in the NW suburbs, is 4.3 km long and surrounded by lovely, peaceful scenes: curled-roof pavilions, the Five Pavilion Bridge, and the imposing White Dagoba (Qing), all packaged in the South China garden style. At the Diaoyutai (Fishing Terrace), Qing Emperor Qianlong is supposed to have fished once. He sounds like a good politician. The Five Pavilion Bridge was built on the occasion of his visit. It is best seen on the night of a full moon, when 15 moons are supposed to reflect from the water under the arches, a Chinese puzzle that must be seen.

The **Daming Temple** 大明寺 , in the northwestern suburbs, was founded in the fifth century. An impressive arch commemorates a famous nine-story pagoda that used to be here but was destroyed by fire in 843. The Daming has 18 three-meter-high carved Buddhist statues.

The **Jian Zhen Memorial Hall** 鉴真纪念堂 , near Daming Temple, was built in 1973 to commemorate the 1200th anniversary of the death of Monk Jian Zhen. It, too, is lovely in spite of its youth; it is a copy of the Toshodai Temple in Nara, Japan. This abbot of Daming Temple persisted in going to Japan to teach Buddhism in spite of five unsuccessful efforts and his blindness. He succeeded at age 66. Because he and his disciples also introduced Tang literature, medicine, architecture, sculpture, and other arts to Japan, he is highly honored in that country, where he died and is buried. An over-1000-year-old statue of Jian Zhen, now a national Japanese treasure, was brought back for a visit "because it looked homesick."

The **Yangzhou Museum** 扬州博物馆 is small, informal, and pleasant. The Marco Polo Hall was opened recently. The Italians sent a bronze lion, the symbol of Venice. Curiously, there are two Italian tombstones on display, one possibly a woman's, dated 1342 and 1344.

The **Geyuan Garden** 个园 (Qing) was started as a private garden and later became the home of the Ye Chun Poet's Society in the Qing. It is full of gnarled rockeries, moon gates, bamboo, latticed doorways, wavy walls, and real picture windows. The rockeries are built around a spring-summer-autumn-winter theme. Do these inspire you, too, to poetry?

The **Heyuan Garden** 何园 (Qing), in the SE part of the city close to the Geyuan, is typical of Yangzhou's gardens. The Arabic-styled **Tomb of Puhaddin** is on the east bank of the Grand Canal, near the Heyuan. Built in the 13th century, it contains the remains of this 16th-generation descendant of Mohammed, the founder of Islam. Puhaddin (Burhdn Al-Dan) came to China as a missionary in the Southern Song. The 700-year-old **Xianhe (Crane) Mosque** is one of the four most famous in China, and was built between 1265 and 1275. It is worth a visit. Open daily except Fridays; tel. 44963.

If you can squeeze in time between the factories, just walking the back alleys and looking into houses is fun. People are friendly and relaxed.

If you have more time, Yangzhou has enough tombs, pagodas, a miniature-tree nursery, and the very interesting Grand Canal to keep you busy another day. The most impressive pagoda is the seven-story **Wen Fang Pagoda** 文峰塔 by the Grand Canal, first built in the Ming and can be climbed. The **Wen Chang (Flourishing Culture) Pavilion** 文昌阁 has a roof like the Temple of Heaven, but that's as far as the resemblance goes. A small, five-story stone Tang pagoda may be of interest, with carvings of Buddhas on each of its sides and layers.

Guang Ling, a classic book publishing house, is the only place in China where you can see the Song dynasty printing process.

Festivals: Jade Flower Festival in May. Food Festival.

Day trips can be arranged to go from here to Zhenjiang and Nanjing; there are longer excursions along the canal to Suzhou.

SHOPPING

Locally made are lacquerware, red lacquer carving, jade carving, paper cuts, and silk lanterns. At the paper-cutting factory, a master craftsman can cut lacy paper chrysanthemums for you. Yangzhou also exports potted landscapes, miniature trees and mountains.

Antique Shop 文物商店 (1 West Yanhe Rd.; tel. 24987); **Friendship Store** 友谊商店 (454 Guoqing Rd. North; tel. 43715, 43032. Cable 0645. **Yangzhou Antique and Curio Store** (1 Yanfu Rd; tel. 24987.) Antiques, arts, and crafts.

RESTAURANTS

Thousand-layer oily cake may sound awful, but it is delicious. People also go to Yangzhou from Nanjing just for the dumplings. The Xiyuan Hotel can reproduce a banquet from the novel *Dream of the Red Chamber.* (The author's father lived here.) The Yangzhou Hotel can prepare a fancy vegetarian Jade Flower Banquet.

Fuchuan Garden Tea House 富春花园茶社 • *15 Yanhe Rd.; at Geyuan; tel. 24326.*

Fuchuang Tea House 富春茶社 • *35 Desheng Bridge, downtown; tel. 24326* • Air-conditioned.

HOTELS

The Yangzhou (Bingguan) Hotel, in a garden, is the best for tourists. It is next to the museum, a couple of parks, and tourist shops in the suburbs. The new Yangzhou (Da Jiu Dian) Hotel downtown might be better located for business people.

Yangzhou Hotel 扬州饭店 • *5 Upper Fengle St., Telex 364001 YZHTL CN. C.C. Dist.A.P. (Nanjing) 20 km. Dist.R.W. (Zhenjiang) 30 km* • 1985, ren. 1988. 9 stories, 150 rooms. Business center, IDD. Set in large garden on the other side of the museum from the Yangzhou. Within 5 km of important tourist attractions.

Xiyuan Hotel 西园饭店 • *1 Upper Fengle St.* • 1976; renovated 1984.

C.I.T.S. 中国国际旅行社 : 1 Upper Fengle St. or Qiong Hua Rd.;
tel. 41925. Telex 364001 YZTLR CN.
C.T.S.: tel. 24804, 42611 X377. Cable 2464.
CAAC 中国民航 : Zhenyuan Hotel, Sanyuan Rd.; tel. 24619.
Taxi: 1 Upper Fengle St.; tel. 22611 X371 and X372.

YANTAI 烟台

A.k.a. Zhifu (Chefoo, Cheefoo) North China. On the northern
coast of Shandong province, about 235 km NE of Qingdao by
train. It can be reached by plane from Beijing, Shanghai, Jinan,
and Dalian. It can also be reached by ship, and by direct 20-hour
train from Beijing and Shanghai. An international airport should
be open by the end of 1988. Weather: Coldest—⁻10°C in January; hottest—28.3°C in July and August. Annual precipitation about
700 mm in June.

Inhabited almost 2200 years ago, this fishing village was visited
by the first Qin emperor early in its existence. That egomaniac really
got around! In 1398, during the Ming, a military post was set up, and
beacon towers built for transmitting messages. Yantai means ''smoke
tower.''

Yantai was opened to foreign trade in 1862. It was a summer resort
for the U.S. Navy's Yangtze Patrol (with White Russian bar girls). The
China Inland Mission operated a school here for missionary children;
the buildings now are used by the Chinese Navy. Yantai's harborside
area and Chaoyang Street still reflect the old architecture. Yantai Hill
once housed 10 foreign consulates.

Yantai is one of the 14 Coastal Cities recently opened to trading
and accelerated industrial development. The urban population is now
over 700,000.

Today, Yantai is an important icefree port that has received international cruise ships like the *Pearl of Scandinavia, Sagafjord,* and *World
Discoverer*. It also claims one third of China's prawn catch, and one
tenth of its total aquatic harvest. It farms prawns, abalone, scallops, and
jelly fish. It grows peanuts (one fifth of China's crop), cherries, grapes,

and apples, and grows and cans white asparagus. It mines one quarter of China's gold. The closest mine is about 80 km from the city.

Yantai is one of the prettiest little cities in China, nestled between the sea and, on three sides, gentle hills. Many of its buildings are topped with orange tiles, and some are of rose-colored stone. It does not have the depressing look of neglected structures that many Chinese cities unfortunately have. It has a cheerful atmosphere of vitality and prosperity. Off the main tourist track, it is more for relaxed family sightseeing and swimming than hectic tourism.

Penglai Pavilion 蓬莱阁 is the most important tourist attraction here and is 83 km NW of the city, past the Yantai Economic and Technology Development Zone. A visit to Penglai can take half a day. Chinese-speaking guides are available on site.

Penglai Pavilion was a favorite place for centuries of scholars and poets, for it was from here, legend says, that the Eight Taoists Immortals flew across the seas. After getting drunk, each tried to compete with the other using his-her own treasure. (See *Attributes of the Eight Taoist Genii* in "What Is There to See and Do?") Some people say they flew to Japan, fighting on the way with the dragon king of the sea. A Japanese legend speaks of seven ferries. But some people say these ferries achieved immortality or arrived in paradise. Myths vary. The pavilion was first built in the Northern Song (1056–63) and extended in 1589. The buildings themselves cover 19,000 square meters.

From the Penglai Pavilion, mirages have been seen on the calm summer surface of the sea by many people. A recent one was in 1987. Natives have conflicting opinions about the ideal conditions for mirages, but they seem to be spring and summer with the east wind blowing shortly after a gentle rain, between 2 and 3 p.m. The mirage is of a high mountain, or old city, which some people believe to be Dalian across the straits. But sometimes, it is of another city!

The pavilion with the tables and chairs has a chair of longevity. If people sit on it, they will live a long time. It was in this room that the immortals had their party! Oh, come on!

Movies about the Taoist ferries have been shown regularly on television. Ask about them, but remember, the ferries were each from different periods of history—but legend says they did get together during the Song! Ferries can do anything!

Among the other buildings nearby are the Temple of the Sea Goddess Tian Hou, a Taoist temple, and the Wind Protection Hall, where lighted matches will not blow out even if the wind is from the north. Important is the room full of calligraphy by a famous Ming calligraphist who lived here for three years waiting unsuccessfully to see a mirage. Let that be a lesson to you!

The ***Penglai Water Town** (a.k.a. Beiwocheng), immediately to the south of the pavilion, was built as a fortress, particularly against

Japanese pirates. The Song and Ming navies trained here, and the Ming expanded the defenses. Intriguing is the water gate. In the old days, pirates were lured inside and the gate closed behind them. Then, after the water level rose, the gate was opened and the dead pirates flushed out. Originally built in 1376, the gate was rebuilt in 1596.

A replica of the Ming town **Dengzhou** 登州 , including an old-style bazaar, is on the way from the bus stop to the pavilion. Staff members wear ancient costumes in summer. Penglai has a small hotel. Two recently built warships take visitors for rides.

Also important to see in Yantai is the **Museum** 烟台博物馆 (2 Yulan St.; tel. 2814, 2877). Open daily, except Mondays, in the middle of town. It is in a gaudy Fujian-style guild hall with a temple dedicated to the sea goddess. The beautifully restored building was constructed from 1884 to 1906 in Fujian, and brought in three sections here. Note the jawbone of a whale and the remains of a giant sea turtle. A statue of the goddess, destroyed during the Cultural Revolution, has not yet been replaced. The museum has a few relics from 8000 B.C. to more recent times, with labels in English. It can be seen in 30 minutes. Antique store on premises.

Pleasant to visit is the 600-year old white **Yuhuang (Jade Emperor) Temple,** at 70 meters above sea level, with a good view of the city. The temple building is original, the tower built in 1984, and the memorial arch in 1876. A 600-year-old white pomegranate tree here still bears fruit. Nearby is another garden, ''Little Penglai,'' inspired by the real one to the north.

A visit to the **Zhang Yu Wine Company** 张裕葡萄酒厂 and the **Woolen Embroidery Factory** 绒绣厂 are also recommended if you are interested. The wine-making and the embroidery date from imperialist days, the needlepoint probably taught by missionaries. Some of the patterns are European. The woolen embroidery of China's mountains in Chairman Mao's Mausoleum in Beijing was made here.

If you have more time: On **Yantai Hill,** a lighthouse was built on top of a Ming dynasty beacon tower. It has a good view of the harbor.

Yangma Dao (Horse Racing Island) (a.k.a. Elephant Island, because of its shape) is 11 km by ship or 1 hour by road away. Here the first Qin emperor raised horses and visited three times. A 4-km horse-racing track with bleachers opened in 1985, but no gambling at this time. The island is being developed for tourists, with bathing beaches and hotels (including one owned by Xinhua News Agency and People's Daily). It already has farms for raising prawns, harvested in October.

Yantai has two bathing beaches in the city proper: **No. 1 Bathing Beach** 海水浴场 , in central Yantai, and **No. 2 Bathing Beach** farther east (tel. 5440). Both have all facilities. C.I.T.S. here claims that Yantai has no sharks, but rival summer resort Qingdao does! In addition to the beaches on Horse Racing Island, a summer resort is 120 km from the city in Haiyang County, incorporating a 10,000-meter-long beach of golden sand. Currently, there is a small hotel. The swimming season goes from June to early September.

Yantai is a pioneer in **home-stay** programs "for tourists bored by temples." Visitors can pay to live very comfortably in the relatively substantial homes of rich peasants or fishermen, and learn about life in the countryside (usually two days and one night). Visitors can also sail with fishermen. Much of the fishing here is done with fixed nets, which are checked every one or two days.

By Chinese standards, some of the rural villages here are incredibly wealthy, and a visit will explain why. **Xiguan Village** 西关村 , 23 km away, is one of the places where you can spend the night with a family (usually part of a package, and not cheap).

Kongtong Isle 崆峒岛 is 4.5 nautical miles off Yantai, and visitors can see a fishing village here. Lots of wild rabbits. **Kunlun Mountain,** 30 km away, should have 33 square km set aside for hunting wolves, foxes, rabbits, geese, and badgers. Guns and mopeds are available for rent.

C.I.T.S. here seems to try harder because it doesn't have all that many attractions. It says it can organize Wedding Tours complete with a traditional red Chinese gown and the bridal chamber at the Zhifu Hotel. It also has tours for bicycles and motorcycles, fishing (small ones only), picking your own apples, and visits to vineyards.

See also "Weihai," "Qingdao," and "Jinan."

ENTERTAINMENT

Evening dance parties near Yantai Hill Guest House on Chaoyang St. Best arranged through C.I.T.S., but you can find it from the noise. Cheap.

SHOPPING

Riesling wines, vermouth, Gold Medal Brandy, lace, tablecloths, wooden-framed clocks, and partially completed woolen needlepoint pieces (very cheap). Yantai sells gold necklaces and chains. **Yantai Tourist Products Service,** near the museum, has a limited selection of locally made products. The best selection is at the **Exhibition Building.**

FOOD

Seafood, of course! Shandong food is not peppery hot or overly sweet. Lots of garlic, onions, and salt. Yantai people say that Beijing duck originated when two indigent Yantai peasants went to Beijing and found a dead duck on the road. Improvising an earthen oven, they cooked the duck. An official happened by, liked the smell, and asked for a taste. Pleased, he presented the dish to the emperor, who rewarded the official and the poor peasants. See Shandong section under ''Food'' for some dishes.

Huibinlou Restaurant 会宾楼 • *268 Shengli Rd.* • Mainly seafood. Big scallops and prawns.

HOTELS
C.I.T.S. considers the Zhifu Hotel tops, then the Dongshan and #3 the Overseas Chinese and Hongkou.

Dongshan Hotel 车山宾馆 • *Eastern Suburbs. Dist.A.P.17km, Dist.R.W.7km* • 1968. 2 stories. 90 rooms and 13 suites. Quiet hotel in garden setting. Six villas, near beach and pier. Good for joggers. Some rooms upgraded (joint venture) to top quality.

Hongkou Hotel • *111 Dama Rd. Dist.A.P.20 km, Dist.R.W.4 km* • 1985. 138 rooms and 19 suites. Renovated 1987, villa style. Near beach.

Huaqiao (Overseas Chinese) Hotel 华侨宾馆 • *15 Huanshan Rd. Telex 32566 OCGYT CN. Dist.A.P.18km, Dist.R.W.6km, eastern suburbs* • 1983; renovated 1988. 6 stories. 92 rooms and 5 suites.

Yantai Shan Hotel 烟台山宾馆 • *34 Haian Rd. Dist.A.P.20km, Dist.R.W.2km* • 1984. Renovated 1987. 4 stories. 100 rooms and 7 suites. Best location in old city for people-watching and evening walks by the seashore and up into Yantai Hill. Hong Kong J.V. restaurant overlooking the sea.

Zhifu Guesthouse • *Kangfu Rd. Dist.A.P.20km, Dist.R.W.8km. eastern suburbs. Telex 32561 ZFHYT CN* • 1981, ren. 1987, extension 1988. 6 stories, over 116 rooms. Near beach # 2, C.I.T.S. on premises. IDD, no C.C.

OTHER IMPORTANT ADDRESSES
Bank of China: Currency exchange offices in the main hotels, the Department Store, and embroidery factory.
C.I.T.S. 国际旅行社 : 17 Yuhuang Ding Xi Rd., tel. 225626.
C.T.S. 中国民航 : 15 Huanshan Rd.; tel. 224431. Cable 0294.
CAAC 中旅社 : Airport. Southern suburbs; tel. 226605. Ticket office: 6 Dahaiyang Rd.; tel. 225908.

YINCHUAN 银川

Northwest China. Capital of the Ningxia (Ningsia) Hui Autonomous Region, which lies between Inner Mongolia and Gansu on the north central border of China. It is linked by air with Beijing (4 hours) and Xi'an (2 hours). It is also linked by train with Beijing and is on the Lanzhou-Baotou line. Yinchuan is in the northern part of the province, a few km west of the Huanghe (Yellow) River. It is in the middle of a mesh of irrigation canals in the plains, but close to mountains and classic sand deserts. Weather: In the province the coldest temperature ranges from $^-13°C$ to $^-7°C$ in January; the hottest is 17°C to 26°C in July. Very little rain. Sandstorms, which blow hard in spring and autumn, mean having to take some cloth to cover your nose and eyes. At times, everything appears covered with sand.

Yinchuan has only recently been opened to tourists, and whoever goes there has to be adventurous. It is not as far from Beijing as the Silk Road, but the weather is severe, and it is still in the early stages of being developed for tourists.

Ningxia was inhabited 30,000 years ago, and 8000-year-old neolithic relics have also been found here. It was home to the Yong and Di tribes in the Western Zhou. The first Qin emperor conquered the tribes and connected parts of the Great Wall here. He sent thousands of men to settle and defend this area.

Ningxia was close enough to the trade routes for Persian coins to be found in its Northern Wei tombs. It exists because parts have been irrigated by the Yellow River for the last 2000 years. Its fight against the relentless sands is admirable, and visitors from areas like California should be especially interested in how the Chinese here manage. A great deal of the region is covered by the Liupan Mountains, through which the Long March passed in 1935.

Ningxia Hui Autonomous Region was founded in 1958, and many people were moved here from other parts of China in the '60s during the Cultural Revolution. Today, it has many national minorities, including the Huis (31.7%), Mongolians, Manchus, Turfans, and others. The provincial population is 3.89 million.

Ningxia now produces rice, wheat, melons, fruit, and the black hairlike moss called *facai*. The region exports coal and also produces petroleum, mica, asbestos, and lime.

Yinchuan (formerly Xingqing) was founded in the Tang and had a variety of other names until 1947. It was the capital of the Western Xia during the early part of the Song (1038) when it was known as Xingqing. The Xia kings reigned for about 190 years, but the dynasty was destroyed by Genghis Khan. Very little is known about the Western Xia, as there are no records.

Today, 370,000 people live in the urban part of Yinchuan, about 20% Huis, Moslem descendants of those who came 700 years ago to develop this region.

Of importance to visitors is the **Chengtian Monastery Pagoda** 承天寺宝塔 , built in A.D. 1050 (Western Xia) and renovated in the Qing. Like many of the area's pagodas, it is unusually plain. The old **Tanglai Canal** (Tang) and **Hanyan Canal** 汉延古渠 (Han) should be seen as examples of ancient irrigation efforts. Note the old waterwheels. The **South Gate Mosque** 南关清真寺 is recent, with an onion dome. The **Zhongda Mosque** 中大寺 is more in the Chinese style.

The **Tongxin Mosque** 同心清真寺 is from the early Ming and was repaired in the Qing. It is one of the largest mosques in the region. The imposing **Jade Emperor Pavilion** 玉皇阁 (Ming) is good for photographs, with its delicate towers, as is the unusual **Drum and Bell Tower** 钟鼓楼 . The ∗**Haibao (Sea Treasure) Pagoda (a.k.a. North Pagoda)** 海宝塔 is also unusual, a naked structure without fancy eaves, and appearing more like a strange sort of Masonic temple. Dating from the early 5th century, it was destroyed by an earthquake but rebuilt in the 18th century in its original style. It is 1 km north of the city.

The **Twin Pagodas at Baizi Pass on Mt. Holan** 拜寺口双塔 and the **Western Xia Mausoleum** 西夏王陵 are at the base of Mt. Holan, just west of Yinchuan. The mausoleum is rather crude and of interest primarily to people keen on history. In treeless surroundings, it has a stark kind of primitive beauty. The founder of the Western Xia kingdom built over 70 tombs, most as decoys.

Nine imperial tombs can be visited. For atmosphere, tourists can visit at night when the tombs are illuminated and accompanied by ancient music. The tomb of Li Yuanhao the dynasty's founder can be entered.

Adventurers can also take rides on the river on rafts buoyed by inflated pig skins. How many of your friends at home have ever, ever done that! Normal watercraft are also available. At **Qingtongxia** 青铜峡 south of the city, is a gorge and an impressive dam. Nearby on a barren hill, the mysterious 108 white dagobas are arranged in the shape of a triangle in 12 rows from one to 19 in odd numbers. The smallest one is about six feet and three arm-spans around. No one seems to know the significance of the site and the layout. They do look magnificent from a distance.

The city also has a **museum** 博物馆 and a Russian Orthodox Church. The Guyuan grottoes, the mosque in Tongxin county, the Kangji Buddhist Pagoda in Tongxin County, and the Wanshou Pagoda (the latter two both dating from A.D. 1038 to 1227) are among the attractions renovated for Ningxia's 30th anniversary in 1988.

Also in the region: **ancient rock paintings on Holan Mountain** 贺兰山古石画 ; the ruins of the **Great Wall** 长城 (Warring States: 475–221 B.C.) are mainly earthen mounds, no stone. Especially important are the *****Buddhist grottoes on Mt. Xumi** (a.k.a. Sumeru) 须弥山 in Guyuan County. They are Northern Wei to the Tang (A.D. 618–907) and have a 19-meter-tall bust of Buddha rising from the floor of a cave. In the south of the province, these caves are impressive, although many of their 300 statues are damaged. Unless they have been recently built, few, if any, sidewalks and stairs connect the 132 caves. This cave temple covers an area 1 by 2 km and the trip is rugged.

The **Gao Temple,** in Zhongwei County in the western part of the province, is striking because of its sandy monotone. A temple for Confucianism, Buddhism, and Taoism, it also has statues of the Jade Emperor, the Holy Mother, and Guan Yu, the god of War. These point to the eclecticism of Chinese religion. Multipurpose temples of this broad range, however, are rare.

C.I.T.S. can make arrangements for tourists to visit Moslem homes.

SHOPPING

The region produces sheepskin garments, licorice root, Holan inkstone carvings, rugs, and blankets.

Food is mainly Moslem (mutton, no pork). Corn on the cob and oil sticks (like long donuts) are delicious.

RESTAURANTS

Yinbinlou Restaurant • *Jiefang Xi St.* • Moslem food.

Wu Yi Restaurant • *204 Jiafangdong St.* • Han food.

HOTELS

Ningxia Hotel • *3 Gongyuan St., Yinchuan.*

Ningxia Tourism Hotel • *Wen Hua St.* • 1988.

Yinchuan Hotel • *25, Jiefang Xi St.*

Zhongwei Hotel • *Zhongwei County.*

CAAC: 14 Minzu Bei St.; tel. 2143.
C.I.T.S.: 150, Jiefang Xi St.; tel. 22466, 24720; telex 70191 TBNXY
CN.

YIXING 宜兴

(Yihsing, Ihsing, Yising) East China. Due west of Shanghai and
Suzhou, on the west side of Lake Tai (Taihu) in SE Jiangsu province, Yixing is best known for its purple stoneware pottery and
limestone caves. Population: one million.

If you like caves and pottery, this can be a two-day trip. **Shanjuan
Cave**   , 25 km SW of the city, is named after a poet who lived
here 4000 years ago after refusing to accept political responsibilities.
Historical records mentioned the cave 2000 years ago (Spring and Autumn Period). It totals 5000 square meters and is divided into three
layers with four caves all joined together: a foggy (23°C) upper cave,
and a spacious middle cavern with a 50-by-20-meter chamber and a
"lion" and "elephant." In the lower, narrow cavern, one can hire a
rowboat on a 120-meter-long underground river. At the entrance to the
middle cave is a stalagmite seven meters high, probably 35,000 years
old. The rocks are shaped like dragons, horses, sheep, cats, and fruit,
and are bathed in colored lights. Tourists walk less than 700 meters and
a visit takes about an hour.

Near the entrance is a hotel, a stone monument telling about the
"Bixian Nunnery," and the tombstone of Zhu Yingtai's musical instrument and sword. The nunnery existed in A.D. 345. It was once rented
by Zhu Yingtai, an early feminist, as her study room in the Jin (A.D.
265–420). One old legend says that Liang Shanbo and Zhu were star-
crossed lovers. Liang died and Zhu was allowed to visit his tomb before
her forced marriage to another man. Amid thunder and lightning, the
tomb opened and she jumped in. The two became butterflies!

The **Zhonggong Cave**   in Yufeng Hill, 22 km SW of Yixing, goes back over 2000 years in mythology, the home of an old
hermit, Gengsang Chu. Zhang Daoling, one of the founders of Taoism,
lived here in the Han, as did Zhang Guolao in the Tang. Zhang Guolao

was one of the Eight Taoists Immortals. Zhanggong consists of 72 small, interconnected caves, of varying sizes and temperatures, totaling 3000 square meters. Tourists can walk 1 km, and up and down 1500 stone steps, but most do not. Look for the Dragon King Hall and ''Carps Frolicking in the Water.''

All the **pottery factories** are in **Dingsu** 鼎蜀镇 , the most famous being the Purple Sand 紫砂陶工厂 . Made here also are celadon, and Jun-glazed 均陶厂 . Dingsu claims to be the pottery capital of China, but some people might argue in favor of Jingdezhen. Arrangements to visit must be made through C.I.T.S. The huge **Pottery Exhibition Hall** 陶瓷陈列馆 (tel. 411) shows 10,000 pieces.

Other places of interest include the **Yiangxian Tea Plantation** 阳羡茶园 , 4 km from Zhonggong Cave, where visitors can see tea being grown and processed. Takes about an hour. The **Bamboo Ocean** 竹海, near the tea plantation, is a garden of various kinds of bamboo, with toilets and rest houses.

The **Linggu Cave** 灵谷洞 , 30 km SW of Yixing, is in a tea plantation, 8800 square meters. Walk of 1200 meters. Some of the graffiti dates from the Tang.

Muli Cave is 35 km. from Yixing. It covers 8000 sq. meters with a 150-meter-long stream and boats. The cave is hidden in a sea of bamboo and chestnut trees.

The **Free Market** here is different from that of other cities. C.I.T.S. can also arrange for you to see fish hawks catching fish.

The **Friendship Store** is in the Yixing Guest House (tel. 2880).

Local specialties include spiced wild duck 香酥野鸭 , diced chicken with ginkgo nuts 白果鸡丁 , lily-bulb soup with sweet osmanthus flower 桂花百合羹 , and Xushe sweet pastry 徐舍酥糖 (sent as tribute to the Qing emperors).

HOTELS
Shanghai Hotel ● *Park Rd., Dingshan.*

Yixing Guest House 宜兴宾馆 ● *1 Renmin Nan Rd. Telex 34077 YXJSC CN* ● 1980. An extension was completed in 1987. 200 beds. This is the best hotel.

C.I.T.S. 中国国际旅行社 : South Renmin Rd. Telex 34077 YXJSC CN. Tel. 2559, 2493.
Taxis: Yixing Guest House; tel. 2560.

YUEYANG 岳阳

(Yoyang, Yochow) South China. On the north shore of Lake Dongting   in northern Hunan, just south of the Yangtze, 2000 year old Yueyang is sometimes a side trip from Changsha, 140 km south. It can be a pleasant, relaxing day's visit.

Yueyang Tower 岳阳楼 was first built in A.D. 716 in the Tang as a place for officers to train the navy. The site was a Warring States military burial ground. The tower was destroyed and rebuilt many times, the latest time in 1867 in the original Tang style. At that time it became the west gate of the city. It is made of wood, is 19 meters high, and covers 240 square meters. One of the eight Taoist genii—Lu Tung-pin, with the supernatural sword—was a Tang scholar who became a priest after failing the imperial examinations. He is said to have magically saved the original tower from collapsing. He is also said to be responsible for the creation of the long, silver-white fish in Lake Dongting. On the right of the tower is the Drunk Three Times Pavilion, named after the occasions Lu became drunk here; on the left is the Fairy Plum Pavilion, named because a stone slab with imprints was found under the foundation during renovations in the Ming. The main tower is now a museum.

In 1962 a pavilion was built nearby to commemorate the 1250th birthday of famous Tang poet Tu Fu.

Junshan Island 军山岛 , 15 km west across the lake, has 72 hills on 247 acres of land. The highest hill has a celebrated view of the 740,000-acre lake, which is one of the settings of the novel and movie *The Sand Pebbles*. The island grows the famous Junshan Silver Needles Tea, many species of bamboo, and a tree with red leaves on one side and green on the other. It is a bird-watcher's paradise. The island also abounds in myths, so expect your guide to tell you many of the stories as you sip tea made from Liu Yi well water. Try to imagine the time during the Song when 10,000 troops were stationed here.

HOTELS

Yueyang Hotel • 26 Dong Ting North Rd., 414000; Cable 3453. Telex 994008 YHLTD CN. Dist.A.P.130 km. Dist.R.W.3 km • C.C. 1988. 10 stories, 265 rooms. Business center, IDD. H.K.J.V.

Yunmeng Hotel • *25 Chengtong Rd., 13 km from harbor on Yangtze. Dist.R.W.1km* • Ren. 1986. 3 stories. 44 rooms and 2 suites.

C.T.S. • tel. 22482. Cable 0948.

ZHANGZHOU (CHENGCHOW) 漳州

South China. In southern Fujian reached by road west from Xiamen, Zhangzhou is in the best rice-growing area in the province. It is famous for its narcissus flowers, streets lined with magnolia trees, and its many plants for industrial and medicinal use. Zhangzhou also grows a lot of fruit and makes fruit wines. The Zhangzhou Arts and Crafts Factory produces the famous Longxi puppets. Zhangzhou was first recorded over 1200 years ago. Its hottest temperature has been 37°C in July or August, its coldest 3°C in February or March. The annual precipitation is 1500 mm, mainly from February to April. It is off-the-beaten-track and for this reason may appeal to people looking for something unusual.

Most important are Nanshan Temple, the Zhangzhou Arts and Crafts Factory, and Baihua Hamlet.

The **Nanshan Temple** 南山寺 , 2 km from the O.C. Hotel in the southern suburbs, has a large Tang Buddha, a copper bell from the Yuan, and a white jade Buddha. Flower lovers should be interested in **Baihua (Hundred Flower) Village** 百花村 and the **Home of Narcissus** 南山寺 , which specializes in growing these spring flowers. The **Zhangzhou Arts and Crafts Factory** is half a kilometer and the **Mu Mian pavilion** 14 km from the O.C. Hotel.

In the northern suburbs, **Mysterious Pond** 仙字潭 has some writing on a cliff no one has been able to decipher completely. **Yundong Rock** 云洞岩 is in the eastern suburbs.

Zhangzhou with five recent world women's volleyball championships offers volleyball coaching at its Sports Training Base. Contact C.I.T.S. in Xiamen.

Local specialties include Jiangdong perch, fried oysters, rice noodles, and noodles with fried bean curd.

SHOPPING

Narcissus bulbs, Pian Zai Huang tablets, cotton patchwork, and fruit. **Friendship Store** (tel. 23976); **Department Store** (tel. 3320); **Arts and Crafts Service Department** (tel. 3657); **North Yan'an Drug Store** (tel. 4970).

HOTELS

Fujian Zhangzhou Overseas Chinese Hotel ● *38 North Yan'an Rd., 69 km from Xiamen Airport, 1.5 km from railway station, and within view of central bus station* ● 1951; renovated 1984. Central location close to shops, post office, and theaters.

A second **Zhangzhou Overseas Chinese Hotel** ● *North Xinhua Rd. next to the Zhangzhou Gym, near railway station and bus stop.* ● 1988, 12 stories.

Zhangzhou Guest House 漳州宾馆 ● *4 Shengli (Victory) Rd.* ● 1956; renovated 1983.

Zhangzhou New Times Hotel 漳州新时饭店 ● *4 Victory Rd.* ● 1988.

CAAC: 38 North Yan'an Rd.; tel. 26443, 23882.
C.I.T.S. 国际旅行社 and **C.T.S.** 中旅社 : 38 North Yan'an Rd.; tel. 26614. Cable 4357.
Taxi: Overseas Chinese Hotel; tel. 26443.
Bus Station: 汽车站

ZHANJIANG 湛江

(Chanchiang) a.k.a. Ft. Bayard, Kwangchow-wan. South China. This deepwater port is in a bay on the little hook-shaped peninsula on the SE Guangdong coast just north of Hainan Island. Reached by plane from Guangzhou in about an hour and from Hong Kong in less than an hour, Wednesdays and Saturdays. It is also a direct 486-km air-conditioned bus ride from Guangzhou, the terminal beside C.I.T.S. and the train station there. It is a 22-hour train trip from Guangzhou via Guilin and Luizhou in Guangxi province, and also an 8-hour sea voyage from Haikou. On the same latitude as Florida, it is subtropical too. The population of Zhanjiang is 880,000. It is one of the 14 Open Coastal Cities, one of the centers of oil exploration, and a naval base.

Zhanjiang was leased to the French in 1898, at which time it was a coaling station.

If you only have one day in the city, C.I.T.S. recommends: **Huguanyuan Garden** 湖光岩公园 , **Friendship Store, Haibin Garden** 海滨公园 , the **tropical plant experimentation station** 热带植物园 , , a demonstration of **acupuncture** and **moxibustion,** and a **kindergarten.**

If you have more time, there's the **Hedi Reservoir Resort of Lianjiang** 廉江鹤地水库 , 75 km away in Haikang, with a hotel and swimming. At the **Leizhou Ancient Town** 雷州古镇 , 80 km away, is the old **San Yuan Pagoda** 三元塔 , **Pavilion of Su Dong-po** 苏公亭 , Sihu Garden 西湖公园 , Yuansi Academy 阳生师院 , and **Siyi Temple** 十览寺 . The rocky **Fangji Islet** 放鸡岛 (120 km away) is for scuba diving, with parrot fish, pomfret, and lobsters. Also of interest are the **Yangchun resort area** 阳春风景区 (245 km) and **Xie Lu Villa** of Luchuan 陆川榭鲁山庄 .

The **Tachun Island** scenic spot 特星岛风景区 (1½ nautical miles away from Zhanjiang) has a bathing beach, diving service company (rentals), pine tree forest, holiday village, amusement park, and rifle range. The **Huguang Village Club** 湖光乡村俱乐部 (20 km away) has a hotel, holiday village, golf course (being built), shooting and hunting ranges, and archery field.

Haikou, on Hainan Island, is 185 km away, and a half-hour's plane ride. See separate listing.

FOOD

Seafood, of course! These taste better than they sound.

Crab meat roasted with fish maw; steamed crab roe; braised northern mushroom with duck feet; steamed fish with only delicious vegetables; savory and crisp duck; fragile skin deep-fried chicken 脆皮炸子鸡; deep-fried chicken with four nice colors 四彩大拼盆; fried shrimps with chicken and vegetables 碧绿麒麟鸡; fried rice Yangzhou style 杨州炒饭; steamed lobster 清蒸龙虾; sea warfare with cold vegetables

HOTELS

C.T.S. says the top hotel is the Canton Bay, then the Haibin. C.I.T.S. says the top hotel is the Haibin, then the Universal.

Canton Bay Hotel • *22 Renmin Rd., Xiashan. Cable 9918. Dist.A.P.7 km. Dist.R.W. 3 km* • 1960, ren. 1987. Four stories, 300 rooms. C.C. (no Diner's). IDD expected in 1989. Business center, bicycles.

Haibin Hotel 海滨宾馆 • *Haibin Rd., Xiashan, 9 km from airport* • This is the top hotel.

Overseas Chinese Hotel 中国华侨旅社 • *22 Renmin Ave.*

Universal Hotel • *Xia Chi Rd., Chichang. Dist.A.P.8 km* • This is No. 2.

Youyi (Friendship) Hotel 友谊宾馆 • *Renmin Ave., Xiashan, 6 km from airport.*

Nanhai Hotel • *at the Potou oil base* • Houses foreign technicians.

OTHER IMPORTANT ADDRESSES

Bank of China 中国银行 : Honwa Rd., Xiashan.
CAAC 中旅社 : tel. 224415.
C.I.T.S. 国际旅行社 : 33 Renmin Ave., Xiashan; tel. 222559. Telex 45232 CYHZJ CN.
C.T.S.: tel. 224966. Telex 35029. Cable 9918.

ZHAOQING 肇庆

(Chaoching) East China. About 110 km west of Guangzhou on the west bank of the Xijiang River, Zhaoqing is famous for its scenery and Duan inkstones. It can be reached by ship or bus from Hong Kong or Guangzhou or by a railway from Guangzhou and soon direct trains from Shenzhen. The population is about 200,000. The weather is subtropical, with an annual precipitation of 1599 mm, mainly from April to August.

Seven Star Crags, so named because they appear placed like the seven stars of the Big Dipper, has been described by one tourist as "prettier than Hangzhou." The mountains are very much like those of Guilin, including caves with grotesque limestone formations and an underground stream for boat riding. Seven Star Crags (or Cliffs) is like a potted miniature garden.

Known since ancient times, Zhaoqing was the home for six years of the Italian Jesuit missionary Matteo Ricci, his first in China. He lived in "Shuihing" in the 1580s. While no one knows exactly where Ricci's house was, an educated guess places it between the boat landing and the Ming pagoda in the old city by the river. The district here has a Song dynasty gate with houses that look like they haven't changed since Ricci's time. The earthen wall circles the old city and can be walked or cycled for an interesting experience. Zhaoqing was also one of the starting points of the Northern Expedition in 1926, and was not really developed as a resort until 1955. Then, 460-hectare Star Lake was created for irrigation, fish breeding, and scenery. Walkways, bridges, and lights were set up in the caves.

The seven crags are named Langfeng (Lofty Wind), Yuping (Jade Screen), Shishi (Stone Chamber), Tianzhu (Pillar of Heaven), Chanchu (Toad), Shinzhang (Stone Palm), and Apo (Hill Slope). The biggest cave is at the foot of Apo Crag and can be entered by boat. If you hit the rocks at Music Instrument Rock, you get different musical notes.

Zhaoqing also boasts the **Baiyun (White Cloud) Temple,** built in the Tang (618–907) and the **Chongxi, Wenming, and Xufeng pagodas. Qingyun Temple** is at the middle of 1000-meter-high Dinghu (Tripod) mountain, 18 km NE of Zhaoqing. You could also look for the **Yue-jiang Tower,** and the **Water and Moon Palace,** from the Ming. These were damaged during the Cultural Revolution but are now renovated.

The mountain, which is a nature preserve, has a 30-meter-high waterfall on its NW side.

The **Xinghu Amusement Park** is near Xinghu Lake and the Memorial Arch in town. The city also has restaurants, swimming pools, and an art gallery. Golf is planned.

Shopping

In addition to the famous inkstones, locally made are ivory and bone carvings, sandalwood fans, paintings, straw products, umbrellas, and jewelry. Ginseng Beer is made here. **Guangdong Zhaoqing Duanxi Factory of Famous Ink Stones** (Gongnong Rd.; tel. 23975. Cable 4551). A good-sized shopping center juts out into the lake near the Overseas Chinese Hotel.

HOTELS

The best hotel by the lake is the Songtao. In town, it's the Overseas Chinese Hotel. 100 km. from closest airport in Foshan; 130 km. from the airport in Guangzhou.

Pines Villa • *on lake next to Songtao Hotel.* • 1985. Ren. 1987. 13 rooms.

Songtao Hotel • *Seven Star Crags. Cable 9038. Telex 44386 MIMET CN. Dist. bus station 4 km. by road, 2 km. by boat across the lake. Dist. river port 6 km. Hotel is across lake from city in park.* • Renovated 1985. Attractive but not luxury class garden-style hotel between two of the crags (one 90 meters high). Major credit cards. Will telex answer for reservation. 3 and 4 stories. 211 rooms. Good stores. Should have pool in 1988. IDD to Hong Kong only.

Overseas Chinese Hotel. • *Cable 5838. Near bus station, stores, night market, and lake.* • 1987–88 complete renovations.

C.I.T.S.: tel. 22758.
C.T.S. 2–3 Arch St. East, tel. 25351, 25813.
Guangdong Zhaoqing Tourist Trade Development General Corporation: 53 Qixingyanpaifang Dongjie; tel. 23952, 24627; cable: 8888.

Recommended reading: *The Wise Man from the West—Matteo Ricci and His Mission to China* by Vincent Cronin.

ZHENGZHOU 郑州

(Chengchow) Northwest China. On both the Beijing-Guangzhou and the Shanghai-Xi'an railway lines, this capital of Henan province is also a 2-hour flight south of Beijing. It can also be reached by air from several other Chinese cities including Hong Kong. It is about 20 km south of the Yellow River on the main railway line between Luoyang and Kaifeng. In the province, the coldest average temperature is ⁻17°C in January; the hottest is 29°C in July. Annual rainfall is 500–900 mm, especially July through September. Population: urban 1 million.

Zhengzhou is historically important as one of the first cities to be built in China. This was during the Shang dynasty 3500 years ago. It is also important because of its proximity to Shaolin Monastery, known to every *kung fu* fan.

For historians, Zhengzhou has one of the best museums because Henan was a big part of the cradle of Chinese civilization. It was in Anyang that the oracle bones with one of the first Chinese writings were found. The capitals of the Eastern Zhou, Han, Wei, Jin, Northern Song, Tang, and Liang were in this province. At least one of the capitals and possibly four of the five other capitals of the Xia dynasty were also in this province. The Xia was China's first dynasty, and until recently was clouded in legend, traditionally dating from the 16th century B.C. China's first Buddhist temple, the Luoyang Grottoes, and the earliest astronomical observatory are also located here.

Zhengzhou was the site of the February 7th Beijing-Hankou Railway Workers' General Strike of 1923, part of a larger workers' movement for better wages and conditions. Over 100 railroad workers were killed. The strike is commemorated with a modern 14-story double pagodalike clock tower in February 7th Square, built in 1971.

If you only have one day in Zhengzhou, you have a hard choice to make. One day is only time for sightseeing along the Yellow River, hopefully from the top of **Mangshan Mountain** 邙山 (28 km from the International Hotel). There is time also for the Provincial Museum and nearby Shang palace ruins and old city walls.

Near the Provincial Museum is also the **Yellow River Museum,** which gives detailed geological data on that monstrous yet beloved river, recordings of floods, construction work, etc. It will help you understand the regard the Chinese people have for it.

Dahecun Village 大河村 , a 5000-year-old site for Yangshao and Longshan neolithic cultures and Shang ruins, is NE about 12 km and can also be included.

Songshan Mountain takes at least one day, and if you have a third day, then there are Mixian and Gongxian counties.

Songshan Mountain 嵩山 is about 75 km SW of Zhengzhou in **Dengfeng County** 登封层 . It stretches more than 60 km east to west. The highest peak is 1512 meters above sea level. It is one of China's Five Sacred Mountains, and emperors came here to worship. During the Southern and Northern Dynasties (A.D. 420–589), 72 temples and monasteries flourished here.

Songshan is the home of **Shaolin Monastery** 少林寺 , world famous because of the popularity of China's martial arts. Here is where one of the better kung-fu movies was filmed in the early 1980s. If you have a chance, see *Shaolin Monastery*. This Hong Kong-China production should make ancient China seem more vivid to you.

Shaolin was first built in A.D. 495–496 and became famous because 13 fighting monks from here supported the first Tang emperor. (There is a famous story about a group of monks from Shaolin involved in a conspiracy against the Manchus, but they were from a lesser-known Shaolin Monastery in Fujian.)

At this Shaolin temple 13 km NW of Dengfeng County town, you can see the depressions in the floor worn by generations of monks practicing martial arts. (The Shaolin Martial Arts Training Center is close to the temple.) Among the murals and frescoes are some of 500 arhats (Ming), but also some depicting fighting monks. At one time, 2000–3000 monks lived here. The **Ta Lin (Forest of Pagodas)** 塔林 is the largest group of memorial pagodas in China. A cemetery for abbots, it has over 230 miniature pagodas grouped here, dating from the Northern Wei.

Northwest of the temple is a cave where the sixth century Indian missionary Bodhidharma, was reputed to have spent nine years in meditation before achieving Nirvana. He was the founder of Chan Buddhism, more popularly known as Zen, and is frequently depicted in art in his robes, crossing the Yangtze River standing on a reed. The cave is marked with a memorial arch.

The 40-meter-high ***Songyue Pagoda** 嵩岳寺塔 at **Fawang Temple** 法王寺 is the oldest proven extant pagoda in China. Built of brick in about A.D. 520 (Northern Wei), it is also unusual because it has 12 sides and is curved like an Indian *sikhara* tower. It is of extreme importance to those studying pagoda architecture. The **Songyang Shuyuan (Songyang Academy of Classical Learning)** 嵩阳书院 at the foot of the mountain has two cypress trees said to be over 2000 years old, each measuring 12 meters in circumference. The school was one of the four imperial academies preparing students for the imperial examinations.

Zhongyue Miao (Central Mountain Temple) 中岳庙 , at the base of Taishi Peak and 4 km east of Dengfeng County, was founded in the Qin and moved here in the Tang. It has four feisty 3½-meter-high iron figures (Northern Song) guarding it. One of the earliest Taoist temples, it is huge, the largest extant monastery in the province. It was enlarged during the Qing, along the lines of the Forbidden City in Beijing. The *Taishi Tower 太室阙 is from the Eastern Han. One can climb to the top of Huanggai Peak for an overall view of the 400 or so buildings and the 300 Han cypresses.

The *Shaoshi Tower 少室阙 and the *Qimu Tower 启母阙 , also on the mountain, are from the Eastern Han too. The *Astronomical Observatory 观星台 was built early in the Yuan and is the oldest in China. Located in Dengfeng, it was able to prove that the earth revolved around the sun once every 365.2425 days, 300 years before the Gregorian calendar.

A search for the first Xia capital, China's oldest dynasty, has been centered in Dengfeng County, ½ km west of the town of **Gaocheng** 告城 at **Wangcheng Gang (Royal City Mound)** 皇城岗 . This site is not usually included in a tour, but people interested in archaeology might ask about it. Uncovered have been city walls, skeletons (probably of slaves, buried alive in a foundation pit), wine vessels, bronze fragments, and ceramic pots. However, Wangcheng Gang was found to be of a later date (5th century B.C.).

Across the river and ½ km NW of Gaocheng is another site where the earliest bronze vessels in the province were found and carbon-dated to 2000 B.C. This is now thought to be the earliest Xia capital. These sites are about 40 km SW of Zhengzhou.

Also SW of Zhengzhou, but closer to the city, are the **Han Tombs at Dahuting (Tiger-hunting) Pavilion** 打虎亭村汉墓 in **Mixian County** 密县 . They are worth a short stop for their paintings and stone carvings. A few km north of Mixian is the *Gongxian County Cave Temple, dating from A.D. 517 (Northern Wei) to Song, some of its 7743 Buddhist sculptures in an excellent state of preservation. They are not as big or as impressive, though, as Luoyang's, but they are certainly worth a look.

The *Song Tombs, 75 km west of Zhengzhou and also in Gongxian, are from the Northern Song, when that illustrious dynasty had its capital in Kaifeng. They are impressive for their huge stone guardians, among them foreign envoys wearing turbans. The tombs themselves have so far proved less spectacular than those of the later Ming and Qing emperors and are spread over an area 15 km long. They were built in a much shorter time than those of their successors, and without the personal supervision of the emperor who was going to reside there. One of the imperial tombs is expected to be opened in the near future.

Gongxian was also the home county of Tang poet Du Fu (Tu Fu). **Du Fu's Native Place,** the cave where he was born, has been embellished with brick walls and can be visited. The famous three-color Tang porcelain (horses, camels) of which you see reproductions in every Friendship Store in the area, were first made in a kiln at **Xiaohuangye.** One can also visit the 300-year-old **Manor of Landlord Kang Baiwan** for a good insight into how the aristocracy lived then. Just imagine yourself living here as a servant! In what did you cook? Where did the sewage go? How could you deliver clandestine notes to the young mistress from her secret lover?

In Yanshi county are the ruins of a capital of the early Shang dynasty, at least 3000 years old, one of the earliest, largest, and best-preserved ancient cities.

If you have more time, there's a lovely stone dragon at **Huishan Temple** and one of the oldest extant octagonal brick pagodas in the country built in A.D. 746 (Tang). The **Fengxue Temple** 9 km NE of Linru county, is from the Wei. It has a 22-meter-high pagoda. Can you tell just by looking how old it is?

In the province, there's also Kaifeng (70 km away), Luoyang, and Anyang. For destinations close by in Shanxi province, across the Yellow River, see "Taiyuan." For Hebei province, see "Shijiazhuang."

SHOPPING

Made here are reproductions of three-color Tang porcelain figures, jade and lacquerware, calligraphy and paintings. It's a good place to buy Chinese writing brushes, paper, inkstones, and inkbars. Made in the province are also Jun porcelain and embroidery from Kaifeng.

RESTAURANTS

A suggested specialty is mentioned. The following have other dishes too.

Restaurant on the Water • *tel. 23317* • for live Yellow River carp (cooked, of course).

Zhengzhou Roast Duck Restaurant 郑州烤鸭店 • *tel. 24582* • for Zhengzhou's version of this favorite dish.

Shaolin Restaurant 少林餐厅 • *tel. 22441* • for fried monkey head-shaped fungus.

HOTELS

International Hotel 国际饭店 • *East Section, 114 Jinshui Rd.* • 1982, ren. 1989. 8 km from airport. 250 rooms. This is the main tourist hotel.

Regent Plaza (Lijing Mansion) • *113 Jinshui Rd. Cable 2166* • Next door to International Hotel. Close second best. Suites.

Songling Guest House • *Gongxian County.*

Songshan Guest House • *Dengfeng County.*

Zhengzhou Guest House • *115 Jinshui Rd.*

C.I.T.S. 国际旅行社 : 16 Jinshui Rd.; tel. 32070, 25396; telex 46041 CITSZZ CN.
CAAC 中国民航 : tel. 24517.

ZHENJIANG 镇江

(Chinkiang, Chenchiang, Chenkiang: to pacify the river) East China, in central Jiangsu province, where the Grand Canal meets the south bank of the Yangtze. About 1 hour by train (63 km) east of Nanjing, and about 4 hours (220 km) NW of Shanghai. The closest airport is at Nanjing. It is a historic old city, its streets lined with plane trees, some of its houses small and whitewashed like Suzhou's, others black brick with courtyards. It is bound on three sides by hills and on the north by the Yangtze River. Weather: Coldest—⁻8°C from the mid to the end of January; hottest—38°C, July and August, with breezes from the Yangtze. Annual precipitation 1000 mm, mainly in July. Population: 390,000.

Zhenjiang was founded in the Zhou, when it was called Guyang, and then Dantu. It boasts 2500 years of history, including seven as capital of the Eastern Wu (third century), when it was called Jingko (entrance to Nanjing). Many battles were fought in the area and the city is mentioned in *The Romance of the Three Kingdoms.*

During the Yuan, Zhenjiang was visited by Marco Polo. The first British missionaries arrived in the 17th century. Toward the end of the First Opium War, it was the only city that strongly resisted the imperialists. After that failed, however, about 1000 foreigners, mainly merchants and missionaries from Britain, Germany, and the United States lived here. The foreigners left their mark on some of the architecture.

In 1938, Marshall Chen Yi's New Fourth Army was stationed about 50 km away, and some skirmishes with the Japanese took place in the area. In April 1949, the British warship H.M.S. *Amethyst,* while rescuing British citizens upriver, was caught in the crossing of the Yangtze by the People's Liberation Army and held for over three months here. The captain refused to cooperate or admit his ship fired first. Under cover of a passing passenger boat, the *Amethyst* finally escaped.

The American Nobel Prize-winning author Peal Buck (1892–1973) grew up here, studied in what is now the Zhenjiang Second Middle School, and taught here. Her home can be visited; it is part of the Zhenjiang Semiconductor Factory.

Today, Zhenjiang has 500 factories and mines, and makes industrial chemicals, textiles, silk, and paper (from rice stocks) for export.

If you only have one day, C.I.T.S. suggests Jinshan Hill, Jiaoshan Island, the museum, and the Thousand-Year-Old Street. This street, which is 4 km from the Jinshan Hotel, has an unusual stupa built above the sidewalk.

Jiao Hill 焦山 (150 meters high) on Jiao Shan Island, less than ½ km from the city (13 km from the Jinshan Hotel), is named after an Eastern Han scholar, Jiao Guan. A slightly larger than life-size white statue of the hermit meditating in the dim light of his actual cave is at the base. Up 250 steps later is a magnificent view of the Yangtze—all three of Zhenjiang's hills have magnificent views of the Yangtze—and one can see the place where the *Amethyst* was held. What would you have done if you were captain?

Back at the base of Jiao Hill, you can look at the **Battery,** which was used against the British in 1842. It was originally on the river. Also below is a garden with steles of many calligraphers, including that of the father of modern calligraphy, Wang Hsi-chih of 1500 years ago. The original tablet was broken, but it was retrieved from the river in 1713. At the loquat orchard and the **Din Hui Buddhist Temple** most of the Ming statues were destroyed by the Red Guards. The existing statues were made in 1979.

Jinshan (Golden Hill) 金山 , 1 km from the Jinshan Hotel, looks better from afar than close up. The temple here was first built 1500 years ago (Jin) and rebuilt several times since, a victim of lightning, fire, and weather. The current pagoda was finished in 1900 with animal carvings, in time for the Empress Dowager Cixi's birthday. It reflects her crude tastes. Seven stories tall, 30 meters high, it is easier climbing up the 119 steps than down because of the shallow steps.

But there are some fun **caves,** all the more interesting because of the presence in one of the white, ghastly-looking, life-size figure of the monk Fa Hai, and in another the two beautiful women said to be the White Snake and the Blue (sometimes Green) Snake, both fairies. The cave is said to reach Hangzhou!

Guides avoided telling such traditional stories in the 1960s, and it has only been since the late 1970s that one has heard them again. The White Snake's is also the plot of a famous Beijing opera. Briefly, the several-thousand-year-old White Snake from Mount Emei (the Blue Snake is the maid) becomes a beautiful woman and goes to Hangzhou. There at the Tuanqiao (the Bridge of Breaking Up), she falls in love with a scholar, and eventually the two marry. The White Snake, using her magic powers, takes money from a government official to build a house, but because the official's seal is still on the money, the young man is arrested and ordered beaten for theft. The White Snake again uses her magic so that whenever her husband is beaten, the official's wife feels the pain. Consequently, the young man is expelled to Zhenjiang. After his arrival, the monk master Fa Hai, jealous of their happiness, tries to separate the couple, but the White Snake floods the area, including Jin Shan temple. They are reunited at the Tuanqiao. The unrelenting monk master retaliates by imprisoning the White Snake under the Leifeng pagoda in Hangzhou. There she is rescued by the Blue Snake. The White Snake, her husband, and her son are reunited and live happily ever after.

This is a popular Chinese tale and a study of the significance of its symbolism and the psychology of its popularity could keep a folklorist busy for years.

Museum: Housed in the former British consulate building next door to the former Southern Baptist Convention buildings, this museum was opened in 1958. It is 4 km from the Jinshan Hotel. Its permanent collection includes an anchor from the British ship *Amethyst* and a land lease dated 1933 referring to the "former British Concession lot." It has the well-preserved 720-year-old corpse of a scholar, buried with his precious Imperial University entrance certificate in hand. A tiny silver coffin found under the nearby Iron Pagoda contains two gold coffins and the ashes of a Buddhist saint. Charming is the Song porcelain pillow in the shape of a sleeping child.

If you have more time, the **Bei Gu (North Consolidated) Hill,** 9 km from the Jinshan Hotel, is the site of the temple where Liu Pei, founder of the Shu Han dynasty and hero of *The Romance of the Three Kingdoms,* was married to the sister of Sun Chuan. After he died, his wife mourned for him at the pavilion on top of the hill now called Mourning over the River Pavilion. On this hill also is an 11th-century Iron Pagoda (Northern Song), originally nine stories high. Struck by lightning several times, it was repaired in 1960 and now has only its first, second, fifth, and sixth stories.

Zhenjiang also offers **boat tours** on the Yangtze and the Grand Canal, a **Children's Palace** (6 km away), and a **Silkworm and Mulberry Research Institute** (6 km away).

Yangzhou, a pleasant, cultured city, is 25 km away by road and ferry across the Yangtze. **Yixing,** 150 km away, has famous caves and ceramics. See separate listings.

SHOPPING

Dashikou 大市口 is Zhenjiang's main shopping area—department store, antique stores, arts and crafts, and Friendship Store. Zhenjiang's factories make elaborate palace lanterns and are famous for their "crystal" meat and vinegar. Also made in the city are silk, jade carvings, paper cuttings, and silk birds. **Friendship Store,** tel. 21478.

RESTAURANTS

A local specialty is crab cream bun, a steamed meat pastry. Make a hole first and slurp out the soup inside. Food here is concerned with fragrance, shape, and color, and is neither too sweet nor too salty. You might find your hors d'oeuvres looking like butterflies, peacocks, or fans. Everything can be dipped in vinegar.

Jingjiang Restaurant 京江饭店 ● *111 Jiefang Rd.; tel. 22842.*

Tongxinglou Restaurant 同兴楼饭店 ● *218 Zhongshan Rd.; tel. 23942.*

HOTELS

Jinshan Hotel 金山饭店 ● *1, Jinshan Rd. West; 5 km from railway station* ● 1979; renovated 1985. Tennis courts, swimming pool, joint-venture coffee shop, theaters, dance halls, Chinese and Western food. This is the best hotel.

No. 1 Spring Hotel 一泉饭店 ● *1 Yiquan Rd.* ● 1981; renovated 1984.

CAAC: 38 Bei Erqi Rd.; tel. 24339.

C.I.T.S. 中国国际旅行社 : 25 Jianking Rd.; tel. 33287. Telex 360025 ZJJSH CN.
Taxis 计程车 : 1 Jinshan Rd. W.; tel. 22142.
Railway Station 火车站

ZHONGSHAN 中山

(Chung Shan) South China in Guangdong province. Close to the Portuguese colony of Macao, across the Pearl River delta south of Hong Kong, this city can be directly reached by 1½-hour Hovercraft from Hong Kong at least 4 times a day, or via Macao. It is 90 km. (2 to 4 hours by road, depending on the traffic) SW of Guangzhou.

A 1-day tour from Hong Kong usually includes a visit to the former residence of Dr. Sun Yixian (Sun Yat-sen) 孙中山故居 in **Cuiheng** village 翠亨村 . The house was designed by the father of the Chinese republic himself and is a blend of Spanish and local style. The Sun Yixian Memorial Middle School is a couple hundred meters away. Tourists have taken lunch in **Shiqi** 石岐 and visited the Long Rui Village before returning to Macao or Hong Kong, or going on to other places in the area.

For more about Dr. Sun Yat-sen see Nanjing.

Shiqi (Shekki, Shekket) is the cultural, economic and political center of Zhongshan City which has 25 urban and rural districts. The urban population of Shiqi is 170,000. It is in water country, full of intriguing waterways begging to be explored. It has a lot of activity, and new buildings. We experienced a traffic jam in downtown Zhongshan! Yet the water, the age-old river boats, reminds one of a much smaller, old Bangkok.

In the center of the city are floating restaurants (one of them a smaller version of Hong Kong's Jumbo), and a night market with fancy awnings.

Visas for the whole of China can be obtained at the port about 10 km. from Shiqi in 15 to 20 minutes. Instant camera available.

The **Zhongshan (Chung Shan) Hot Spring Golf Club**

Is close to the Zhongshan Hot Spring Resort. The 18-hole, par 72 golf course was designed by the Palmer Course Design Company, named after Arnold Palmer. For those coming from abroad, the club can arrange visas. The address is: Sanxiang Commune, Zhongshan City; tel. 24019; cable: 3306; telex: 44828 CSHS CN. In Hong Kong, telephone 5–8335666, 5–8335723. In Macao, tel. 71702. Bookings also from major hotels in Guangzhou.

SHOPPING

Made locally are straw handicrafts, clothing, embroidery, and sequinned articles.

HOTELS

The top hotels in Zhongshan District City: #1 Zhongshan International; #2 Fu Hua; #3 Hot Spring; #4 Chuiheng. Reservations recommended weekends and Hong Kong holidays. The Fu Hua and Zhongshan International are close together at the bridge in the center of Shiqi near the night market and floating restaurants.

Cuiheng Hotel • *Cuiheng Village, about 29 km. southeast of Shiqi; 24 km. from Zhongshan ferry port. Across road from post office and bus station, and a couple hundred meters from the home of Dr. Sun Yat-sen.* • 1988. Very modern looking hotel, with hotel's Rolls Royce parked in front. 3 stories, 242 rooms. Villas. Pool. Health center planned. Wax museum on hill behind hotel. Amusement park.

Fu Hua Hotel • *Overseas Chinese Building, West Suburb, Shiqi. Cable 0294. Telex 44782 CTSZS CN. Fax 28678. 15 km. from Zhongshan port. Opposite bus station.* • Will telex answer to request for reservation. 1986. 19 stories, 242 rooms. Owned by C.T.S. Revolving restaurant on roof. Exterior elevator. Business center. Bowling. Major credit cards. Lounge open to 2 a.m.! Snooker open to midnight. Separate building for sports.

King Hua Hotel • *Ki Guan Dong Rd., Shiqi. Cable 8123. Telex 44415 KHHZS CN. Fax 24688 X 500.* • Small, attractive hotel in residential area with limited services. Inconvenient location. Business center. Owned by C.T.S. 1985. 4 stories. 90 rooms. IDD. (For budget travelers).

Zhongshan (Chungshan) Hot Spring Hotel • *Shanxiang Township. Cable 3306. Telex 44828 CSHS CN. 20 km. NW. of Macao. 37 km. south of Shiqi.* • 1980. 15 villas. Hong Kong j.v. Will telex answer to request for reservation and charge for telex upon guest arrival. Isolated rural setting next to golf course. Attractive garden style. Major credit cards. Ren. 1987. 400 rooms. Shooting gallery. Horses. Children's playground. Two swimming pools. IDD to Hong Kong. Fax and business center expected 1988.

Zhongshan International Hotel • *2 Zhongshan Rd., Shiqi. Cable 6662. Telex 44715 ZSIH CN. Fax 24736.* • 1986, ren. 1988. T.R., C.C. 22 stories. 369 rooms. First-class well maintained modern hotel in the center of the city. Revolving restaurant. Business center. Good quality stores. IDD.
C.I.T.S. 2 Zhongshan Rd., Shiqi. Tel. 22243, or 24788 X 322. Telex 44715, ZSIH CN. Fax 24736. Cable 6662.
C.T.S Fu Hua Hotel, West Suburb, Shiqi. Tel. 22034. Cable 0294. Telex 44782 CTSZS CN. Fax 28678.

ZHUHAI 珠海

South China, Guangdong Province. Adjacent to the Portuguese colony of Macao across the Pearl River delta southwest of Hong Kong, this Special Economic Zone can be directly reached by ferry from Hong Kong or Shekou, and by road via Macao. It is a 2-hour drive from Guangzhou if no traffic jams. Otherwise, 4 to 5 hours. Heliport with service to Taishan. 3-day visa can be acquired upon arrival without photos, and can be extended in Zhuhai (photos needed). An international airport is planned.

Zhuhai says it is one of the five largest tourist destinations in China with visitors mainly from Hong Kong and Macao, but also many from abroad.

In the vicinity are the Lenzan cave and the birthplace of Dr. Sun Yat-sen. Also in the vicinity is the Banyan Cave with a temple, and beaches. The best beach is at Juizhou Islet, an area now being developed with a 2-km-long cable car, an old style fishing village, bird garden and motor boats. It should be ready in 1992 or so. The sea water is generally very murky in this region.

Also an 18-hole golf course and international trade and exhibition center.

See "Zhongshan." The urban population is 160,000.

The architecture of the Jiu Zhou Cheng shopping center (Jing Shan Rd.; tel. 22959, 22958; cable 3188) was inspired by Beijing's Forbidden City.

Zhuhai International Golf Club/Pearl Land Amusement Park are adjacent, over 30 minutes north of the city. The amusement park is huge and has an 1.8 km. roller coaster, and a 36-seat, 4-abreast ferris wheel. The golf club has a restaurant, Japanese-style bath, visa service, and cheap pick-up at Zhuhai port on the border. Bookings can be made at Japan Golf Promotion Co. Ltd., Room 1009, Gloucester Tower, The Landmark, 11 Pedder St., Hong Kong. Tel. 5–262325.

HOTELS AND RESORTS

Zhuhai has at least 83. C.I.T.S. says the best is the Yindu Hotel, number two is the Zhuhai Resort, and third is the Gongbei Palace Hotel. The Zhuhai Resort, Shi Ching Shan and Garden are close together near the large Jiuzhoucheng Shopping Centre, Zhuhai International Trade and Exhibition Centre, and small amusement park, about 2 km. from the Zhuhai dock. They are about 3 km. from the Gong Bei Palace, 5 km. from the Macao ferry pier and a 20 minute drive to Pearl Land and the golf club.

Reservations needed weekends, July–August and Hong Kong holidays.

Gongbei Palace Hotel • *Shuiwan Rd., Gongbei District. Telex 45638 GBPHC CN. 10 min. walk from Customs House at Macao border.* • 1984. Major credit cards. Very attractive garden-style hotel with villas. 1984. 290 rooms. Gym. Pool. Beach. No business center. Hong Kong j.v.

Shi Ching Shan Tourist Centre • *1 Ching Shan Rd. Cable 2828. Telex 45617 SCST CN. Fax 333511.* • 1981, ren. 1988. Will answer telex for reservation only if no room. Garden style. 115 rooms. Shooting gallery, boating, tennis, pool. IDD. No business center, but this hotel has ties with the exhibition center.

Zhuhai Resort • *Zhuhai Shi. Cable 6333. Telex 45618 ZHRT CN. Fax 332339* • 1983. Hong Kong and Macao J.V. C.C. Attractive garden-style hotel with villas. Well maintained. Three stories, 283 rooms. Should have IDD by now. Stop-smoking and male-fertility clinics. Business center. Tennis. Pool.

C.I.T.S. ● *Zhuhai Resort, Jingshan Rd.; tel. 332822. Telex 45637 CITS CN. Cable 1954. Fax 332339. Hong Kong office tel. 3–686181. Macao tel. 566622. Guangzhou tel. 669900 X 1283.*

Zhuhai Travel Service Corporation ● Binhai Rd., Gongbei, Zhuhai. Tel. 85376, 85902.

North China. In Shandong, on the Beijing-Shanghai express-train route, it can also be reached by air via Jinan. Zibo is near **Linzi,** the capital of Qi (859–221 B.C.), where 150 ancient tombs have yielded a large mirror, horse skeletons, bronzes, crossbows, and bronze coins from that era. A new museum in the Qi style has been put at the site of the Qi capital. Zibo itself makes good porcelain, artistic pottery and glassware, and silk. C.I.T.S., 189 Zhongxin Rd.; tel. 225441, 224407; cable 6030. The top hotel is the Zibo Guest House.

(Tsunhua) North China. Hubei province, about 125 km NE of Tianjin and 135 km east of Beijing but most people go there from Beijing. It takes 3 or 4 hours to get there because the road is congested with donkey and horse carts, trucks, and creeping tractors.

Among the imperial Qing tombs at nearby **Dongling** (Eastern Tombs) are those of Qianlong (Chien Lung) at Yuling. Qianlong is the emperor who snubbed Britain's envoy. He is buried with his five wives. A devout Buddhist, his tomb is covered with religious statues and sutras in Indian, Tibetan, Chinese, Manchurian, and Mongolian.

The tombs of Empress Dowager Cixi (Tzu Hsi) and Empress Ci'an are together at **Dingdongling.** The empress dowager was the fascinating, outrageous, scheming, brilliant, scandalous but short-sighted woman who built the Summer Palace in Beijing. Her tomb, covered with phoenixes deliberately and arrogantly placed *above* the dragons (symbolizing the emperor), was completed in 1881 and renovated in 1895, with an additional 4590 taels of gold as decoration. She died in 1908. Both mausoleums can be entered. The carving is more elaborate than that in the Ming tombs, with Buddhist sutras (in Tibetan and Sanskrit) and figures inside. You can see an exhibition of her clothes, utensils, and photos. Her tomb was robbed in 1928 by a Nationalist warlord who used explosives to open it. He stripped over 500 pearls off her clothes.

Like the Ming tombs, there is also an animal-lined Sacred Way, the figures here smaller but more elaborately carved. It seems each dynasty tried to outdo its predecessors, the Ming being more elaborate than the Song (see "Zhengzhou"). The tombs of the emperors and empresses have yellow glazed roofs. Those of persons of lesser importance have green roofs.

The attendants here are dressed in Qing imperial costumes with eye catching Manchu hats, and high heels attached to the center of their shoes. Some heels are in the shape of vases or bells.

Another word of warning: No decent bathrooms nor running water exist except in the guesthouse in the courtyard to the right of Qianlong's Tomb.

The **Xiling (Western Tombs),** 120 km SW of Beijing at **Yixian** are not as illustrious. The 14 mausoleums hold the remains of emperors Yongzheng (Tailing), Jiaqing (Changling), Daoguang (Muling), and Guangxu (Chongling), plus the usual retinue of wives and children. Visitors can enter Chongling, the last royal tomb in China but it has no funeral objects as it was robbed.

SPECIAL FOR OVERSEAS CHINESE

Overseas Chinese who speak no Chinese should take C.I.T.S. or C.T.S. tours if they are interested primarily in getting the best accommodations and facts in English while sightseeing. If you want to be treated more like family, sometimes taking second place to foreign guests, but getting cheaper rates, go C.T.S. or C.Y.T.S. If you want to learn about China, try to find a family, especially yours, to live with.

I have gone to China all three ways. Emotionally it's a strain, because with a C.I.T.S. group, I get annoyed at the higher prices and furious with foreigners joking about *my* people. With one C.T.S. Hong Kong group, our tour director had a lot of *guanxi,* and we were met not just by a guide, but by the manager of C.T.S., and given the same rooms as Foreign Friends for cheaper prices. Our trip down the Yangtze was a riotous floating poker game, interrupted only by glances at the Three Gorges. I missed much of the commentary because it was all in Cantonese and Mandarin, but we had a ball!

With relatives, I learned more about China than any of the group tours, but in a different way. The first time we met, they pointed out a long-forgotten photograph on the wall of my Canadian family taken 20 years before. My aunt knew everyone by name. Until I started planning a trip to China, I didn't know she existed. In her home, I saw how a six-course meal could be cooked in one wok in one hour. I learned how politeness smooths over a multitude of sins, all ignoring my embarrassing encounter with a naked nephew who was bathing behind a screen in the kitchen (there was nowhere else to bathe). On the streets they pointed to the strange-looking foreigners, *my* fellow Westerners, who had then just started to invade Xinhui. I didn't learn much about the history of the city, but I sure learned a lot about Chinese people and myself.

I think people of Chinese ancestry in particular should visit China. If you feel this bicultural conflict as many of us do, it would be good to explore the Chinese part of your roots. If nothing else, it will help you understand your parents, your grandparents, and your great-grandparents. It might even help you understand things about yourself.

In my father's village in Taishan, I was shocked to learn he had been born in a mud house. I found the watch towers where he used to look out for bandits, and imagined him riding the water buffalo. My grandfather's grave was a simple mound. I expected something more elaborate, considering the money my father said he sent back to the village.

I highly recommend a visit to your ancestral village. Even if you have no relatives there, at least you can look around and see how you would have lived if your ancestors had not emigrated. If you find relatives, you might find your name, if you're male, in a family history book. Part of my novel *Beyond the Heights* is about this experience, which can be traumatic.

But you don't have money to take expensive presents? Don't be silly! People outside China send back presents to family partly to show off. They also send because they feel a strong family obligation. People in China ask for expensive luxury presents like Omega watches because they want to keep up with the Wongs. Remittances have supported a few idlers. If you don't want to contribute to idleness and foolish pride, don't give an expensive gift.

So what do you think will happen if you don't take them a video? Do you think your relatives are going to be rude to you? Of course not. If they ask, tell them you couldn't afford it. My relatives were pleased with the U.S.$20 watch I took in once, especially after I showed them the U.S.$16 Timex I wore myself. Making friends and learning about China are much more important.

You should take some presents, of course. You'd take a bottle of wine to a hostess in the United States, wouldn't you? In China, you and your F.E.C.s are in a privileged position. You could accompany aunts, uncles, and cousins to the Overseas Chinese store and buy them what they want, in exchange for R.M.B. Then you could use the R.M.B. to treat them to dinner at a restaurant, a nice gesture, especially if you're staying with them.

You may find you have nothing in common with Chinese people. On the other hand, you may find that you do. You may have no feelings of obligation to help, dismissing their comparative poverty as their, not your, bad luck. So be it. At least you went and had a look.

For those who do feel pangs of conscience, I think you should be sensitive to opportunities to help. They would trust you more than any other foreigner and would be less reticent to ask you for help.

You can teach—simple skills like English. The children, especially, are learning. You can teach swimming! Imagine my surprise at finding that no one in my village knew how to swim! You can inspire them with technical advances in your home country, drawing pictures if you can't speak the language.

Developing industries and markets have high priority, and never before have the opportunities been so ripe. Every rural village in Guangdong and Fujian seems to be building a hotel for visiting relatives. And restaurants! You may be asked your opinion. The handicraft industry, especially tourist souvenirs, is flourishing. They need ideas on cottage industries that would appeal to foreigners.

New enterprises no longer need approval from Beijing, and you could help them with foreign exchange and expediting imports of machinery and materials from abroad. But do read something about appropriate technology, spare parts, and maintenance before you do. Photocopy machines have lain idle for years because no one knew how to fix them. You may want to set up a joint venture as many other Overseas Chinese and compatriots have done.

Paying for education is also important. Government schools have been free, but a very small percentage of students have been able to qualify. Private schools, including universities, have now sprung up, but fees are needed, of course. These are much cheaper than schools in your home country, and may be more relevant to China's needs. You might be interested in setting up a scholarship fund for people from your ancestral village. I discovered that no one from my father's village had ever gone to university in China. You may want to invest in a private school yourself. Or stay and teach. Of course, living in China takes a special kind of person, one with a great deal of patience and, particularly, a good sense of humor. It is not easy for someone used to Western affluence and efficiency to adapt to Chinese standards, but many do.

Sponsoring a Chinese student to study abroad is also helpful, but only if the student returns to apply his knowledge in China. Nothing is really solved if the student sends back only foreign exchange to an increasingly greedy family. China needs scientists and technicians *in China.*

Help to emigrate is of debatable value. China cannot modernize if her best brains leave the country.

SPECIAL FOR BUSINESS PEOPLE

Advice: Trading with China is not like trading with other countries. As one trade official put it, "If you want to play in the Chinese sand pile, you have to play by Chinese rules."

These rules are much too complicated to put into a travel guide. There are lots of books, business guides, and experienced people to give advice. But to get you started: Trading with China is done primarily through foreign trading corporations, a list of which can be obtained from a Chinese mission. Joint ventures are negotiated through the China International Trust and Investment Corporation.

People who know say:

1. It is possible sometimes for a member of a tour group to get a business appointment.

2. Don't come with the attitude, "We're going to liberate the Chinese." These aren't Chinese laundrymen you're talking to. They'll ask you questions like "Why did you reduce the number of your employees from 500 to 200 last year?" Be prepared. The Chinese know b.s. when they hear it.

Do your homework before you go to China. Visit Chinese trade fairs in North America. Talk with trade officials in the Chinese consulates, your state, provincial or national trade offices, and China trade councils. Find out about government feasibility studies, trade missions, and funding programs. Question people who are doing business in China.

You could sound out the trade department of your own consulate in China about your plan, find out about your competition, and ask for some direction on how to proceed.

3. The Chinese want specific proposals. Don't give them general statements. However, whatever proposal you make won't be accepted anyway. Do not quote rock-bottom figures. The Chinese like to negotiate.

4. Be patient. If you lose patience, you've lost the negotiating battle.

5. Keep accurate notes. The Chinese do. But no tape recorders. The Chinese use interpreters even though they can speak good English. There is plenty of time to make notes. Record who is present, dates, and what was said. Later the Chinese may say to you, "On such a date you said . . . Why are you now saying . . . ?"

6. There is no need to take your own interpreter—too expensive. Chinese interpreters are competent.

7. A Memorandum of Understanding means two parties have identified a field where there is reason to believe there are grounds for possible future negotiations, which, if exploited should lead to a possible contract. It is not a contract, even if it mentions prices.

Trade consultant Kees de Zwager of Gates to China puts it this way: "A Letter of Intent confirms that the parties have met and some prospect exists for a continuation of talks. This letter is not to be taken lightly, as the Chinese might refer to it later.

"A contract is a starting point for further negotiations and is the next step on the road. The negotiating process is continuous. This is an ancient Chinese tradition. One negotiates daily even after all is settled."

8. If the Chinese give you a welcoming banquet, you should return a banquet. Get advice from your embassy.

9. Gifts must be modest: an appointment calendar or a small calculator or some useful novelty. Cash is out. In fact, in late 1988, all gifts to government departments were banned. It should be interesting to see how and if this is enforced.

10. The atmosphere in China among foreign traders is very informal and friendly. Fairs are among the best places to get advice from fellow traders unless you happen to meet a competitor. They are also good places to establish contacts with Chinese officials, and working with trusted partners is how the Chinese prefer to do business.

Says Kees de Zwager, "The Canton Trade Fair is good for new traders to China. What they can see and achieve in three days would otherwise take six weeks of travel in China. The fair represents 30 provinces. Other fairs are provincial or regional.

"But the Canton Trade Fair is not a good place to buy because many fair-goers are tourists and the prices are not the best. But one can make contacts and appointments.

"One must be aware in China, business is not done through strangers."

11. Your host unit in China can book you a hotel, arrange for transportation to meet you upon arrival if you wish, and book tickets for your next destination. You must tell your unit what class of hotel you want or you might be booked into something you don't want.

Do not expect decisions to be made as quickly as elsewhere. You may need two or three visits as an introduction to show the sincerity of your interest.

12. Do take a pile of your business cards preferably with a Chinese translation on the flip side. It would also be helpful to take a one-page introduction of your company in Chinese. Exchanging cards with both hands is now part of the ritual when people meet for business.

13. China has been improving its communications and constructing industrial buildings, especially in the Special Economic Zones and 14 Coastal Cities. IDD telephone communications, luxury hotels, international airports, branches of foreign banks, new labor regulations, tax breaks, and decentralized decision making are among China's efforts to encourage foreign investment.

14. Spouses can come along on a business trip but are not usually included in business functions like banquets. Many spouses should be left in big cities where there is more for them to do, rather than going to tiny communities with dumpy hotels and no English. But this depends on the spouse.

15. Remember that the Chinese are primarily interested in technology transfers with minimal amounts of foreign exchange spendings. They are looking for the training of Chinese personnel, and joint-venture investments.

16. It could take up to two years before you have any results, so you must budget enough for product development. If a project is big, it could take three to five years.

17. You might find that hiring a China trade consultant is a more efficient way for you to do business with China.

Best News Sources on Trade with China: *Asian Wall Street Journal* (daily); *South China Morning Post* (Hong Kong daily); *Asian Wall Street Journal Weekly; Far Eastern Economic Review* (weekly).

Very Helpful: "China Trade Report" (monthly), *Far Eastern Economic Review; The China Business Review* (bimonthly), U.S.-China Business Council; *Business China* (bimonthly); *China Trader Weekly Bulletin; China Briefing* (quarterly and free), Hongkong Shanghai Banking Corporation; *Amcham Magazine* (of the American Chamber of Commerce, Hong Kong, a monthly that focuses several times a year on China); *China Trader,* and *China Daily.*

Also Helpful: *Economic Reporter,* English Supplement; *China's Foreign Trade; Ta Kung Pao Weekly; China Phone Book and Address Directory.*

Books: *China,* Business Profile Service. The Hong Kong and Shanghai Banking Corporation, Hong Kong; anything from the U.S.-China Business Council. Arne J. de Keijer's *The China Business Handbook* and *China*, by Robert Delfs and Thomas D. Gorman, published in Hong Kong by the Far Eastern Economic Review. Susan Goldenberg's *Hands Across the Ocean: Managing Joint Ventures with a Spotlight on China and Japan*, Roderick Macleod's *China, Inc.: How to do Business with the Chinese*.

Trade Councils: Established in 1973, the U.S.-China Business Council is a private, not-for-profit membership association of more than 400 American firms engaged in trade and investment with the People's Republic of China. The Council's primary objective is the promotion and facilitation of bilateral economic relations, and its activities include delegations, seminars, and briefings on various topics related to trade with China. Other services provided member firms include practical business assistance, advice on the development and expansion of their trade with China, and up-to-date information through the resources of its library in Washington and offices in Beijing.

The Canadian equivalent is the Canada-China Trade Council, "founded in 1978 as a federally incorporated non-profit organization to serve as the private sector link between Canadian companies doing business in China and counterpart Chinese organizations. . . . Council members represent a broad spectrum of Canadian industry and service, and range from companies first exploring the Asian Pacific markets to those who have their own offices in China. . . . CCTC's Beijing Office is one of the largest Canadian commercial presences in China . . ." and ". . . offers a practical and cost-effective alternative to opening a company office in China, utilizing shared infrastructure and experience."

The British equivalent is the Sino-British Trade Council.

For Australian and other business addresses, see "Important Addresses."

See also *Individually as a Business Person* in "The Basics" and "Introduction."

USEFUL PHRASES

These are designed so you will be able to communicate with people who speak only Chinese. In most cases you need only point to the Chinese and you will get a "yes" (shi de) or "no" (bu shi) answer or a reassuring smile or an attempt to look up an answer from this book.

Read through the phrases at your leisure so you will know what is available. If you think you need other phrases, get a Chinese-writing friend to do them for you.

Pinyin romanization is courtesy of Beijing Tourism Administration.

Numbers refer to tones: 1 for high; 2 for rising; 3 for a low falling and rising tone; 4 for falling. Words without numbers are neutral. The correct tone is essential. To avoid misunderstandings, point out the phrases in this book to the people with whom you want to communciate as you try to say them.

See "Quick Reference" for the pronunciation of this romanization.

TRAVEL

Arrivals

I am looking for the interpreter who is supposed to meet me.

我正在找一位翻译，他是来接我的。
Wo zheng zai zhao yi wei fan yi, ta shi lai jie wo de.

He is from ———. 他是 ——————— 的人。
Ta shi———ren.

C.I.T.S.　　　　　　中国国际旅行社。
Zhong guo guo ji lu xing she

the Foreign Ministry　　外交部
Wai jiao bu

Foreign Trade Corporation　外贸公司
Wai mao gong si

Academy of Sciences

科学院
_{1   2   4}
Ke xue yuan

All-China Sports Federation

中华全国体育总会
_{1   2   2   2   3 4 3   4}
Zhong hua quan guo ti yu zong hui

Committee for Cultural Relations with Foreign Countries

对外文委
_{4   4   2   3}
Dui wai wen wei

Chinese People's Association for Friendship with Foreign Countries

对外友协
_{4   4   3   2}
Dui wai you xie

People's Institute for Foreign Affairs

中国人民外交学会
_{1   2   2   2   4   2   2   4}
Zhong gua ren min wai jiao xue hui

When do I get my passport back?

什么时候能将护照还给我？
_{2   2   4   2   2   1   4   2   3   3}
Shen me shi hou neng jiang hu zhao huan gei wo?

Where do I get my checked luggage?

我托运的行李在那里取？
_{3   1   4   2   4   3 3 3}
Wo tuo yun de xing li zai na li qu?

That bag is mine. Please give it to me.

那个手提包是我的。请递给我。
_{4   3   2   1   4   3   4   3}
He ge shou ti bao shi wo de. Qing di gei wo.

Is there someone here who can carry my bag for me?

有没有人可以帮我拿手提包？
_{3   2   3   2   3 3 1   3   2   3   2 1}
You mei you ren ke yi bang wo na shou ti bao?

Please call a taxi for me.

请代我叫一辆出租汽车。
_{3   4   3   4   2 4   1   1   4   1}
Qing dai wo jiao yi liang chu zu qi che.

How long will it take for the taxi to get here?

出租汽车要多久才能到达这里？
_{1   1   4 1   4   1   3 2   2   4   2   4 3}
Chu zu qi che yao duo jiu cai neng dao da zhe li?

minutes 分钟
_{1   1}
fen zhong

hours 小时
_{3   2}
xiao shi

Is there a bus I can take to the city?

You jin cheng de gong gong qi che ma?

How can I get to the city?

我怎样可以到城里去？

Wo zen yang ke yi dao cheng li qu?

City Travel

Do you have a map of this city in English?

你有一张这个城市的英文地图吗？

Ni you yi zhang zhe ge cheng shi de ying wen di tu ma?

. . . with city bus routes? 有公共汽车路线图的？

You gong gong qi che lu xian tu de?

I want to go to ———.

我要去 ———。

Wo yao qu ———.

China International Travel Service	中国国际旅行社
	Zhong guo guo ji lu xing she
CAAC office	中国航空公司
	Zhong guo hang kong gong si
Bank of China	中国银行
	Zhong guo yin hang
hotel	旅馆
	lu guan
hovercraft terminal	气垫船终点站
	qi dian chuan zhong dian zhan
train station	火车站
	huo che zhan
ferry terminal	渡船码头
	du chuan ma tou
airport	飞机场
	fei ji chang
bus station	公共汽车站
	gong gong qi che zhan

trade center (as planned for Beijing) 商业中心（像为北京设计的）

shang ye zhong xin (xiang wei bei, jing she ji de)

Guangzhou (Canton) Export Commodities Fair 广州出口商品交易会

guang zhou chu kou shang pin jiao yi hui

Where can I get a ———? 我在哪里可以叫／乘 _____?

wo zai na li ke yi jiao/cheng ———?

taxi 一辆出租汽车

yi liang chu zu qi che

motorscooter 摩托车

mo tuo che

bicycle rickshaw 三轮车

san lun che

city bus 市内公共汽车

shi nei gong gong qi che

subway 地下铁道列车

di xia tie dao lie che

About how much would it cost? 大约要多少钱？

Da yue yao duo shao qian?

City Bus

What number city bus do I take to go from here to ———?
我从这里到_____应该乘那一路公共汽车？
Wo cong zhe li dao ——— ying qai cheng na yi lu gong gong qi che?

Please show me where I can get that bus.
请告诉我在那里上车。
Qing gao su wo zai na li shang che.

Across the street?
过街？
Guo jie?

This side?
这一边？
Zhe yi bian?

Please tell me where I get off for ———.
请告诉我到_____去应该在那儿下车。
Qing gao su wo dao ——— qu ying gai zai nar xia che?

Do I need to change to another bus?

我要不要换车？

₃ ₄ ₂ ₄ ₁

Wo yao bu yao huan che?

What number?

几路？

₃ ₄

Ji lu?

Taxi

Please drive more slowly.

请开的慢一些。

₃ ₁ ₄ ₄ ₁

Qing kai de man yi xie.

Please drive faster.

请开的快一些。

₃ ₁ ₄ ₄ ₁

Qing kai de kuai yi xie.

Please wait for me.

请等我一会。

₃ ₃ ₃ ₄ ₄

Qing deng wo yi huir.

I will be about ——— minutes.

我要耽搁＿＿＿分钟。

₃ ₄ ₁ ₁ ₁ ₁

Wo yao dan ge ——— fen zhong.

How much does it cost for you to wait?

等我得付多少钱？

₃ ₃ ₃ ₄ ₁ ₃ ₂

Deng wo dei fu duo shao qian?

An hour?

一小时？

₁ ₃ ₂

Yi xiao shi?

Where will you wait?

你在哪里等我？

₃ ₄ ₃ ₃ ₃ ₃

Ni zai na li deng wo?

I want to be sure there is a taxi for me early tomorrow morning at ——— o'clock.

我要确定能在明天早晨＿＿＿点种叫到一辆出租汽车。

₃ ₄ ₄ ₄ ₂ ₄ ₂ ₁ ₃ ₂ ₃ ₁

Wo yao que ding neng zai ming tian zao chen ——— dian zhong

₄ ₄ ₂ ₄ ₁ ₁ ₁

jiao dao yi liang chu zu che.

Could you order a taxi for me for that time?

你能为我订一辆那个时候要的出租汽车吗？

Ni neng wei wo ding yi liang na ge shi hou yao de chu zu che ma?

Buying a Ticket (see also Permission)

I want to buy a ticket to go to ———.

我要买一张到_____去的车票。

Wo yao mai yi zhang dao ——— qu de che piao.

One-way	单程	Return	来回
	dan cheng		lai hui

Can I make the return reservation now?

现在我能订回来的票吗？

Xian zai wo neng ding hui lai de piao ma?

I want to go ———. 我要在_____走。

Wo yao zai ——— zou.

in the morning	早晨	in the afternoon	下午
	zao chen		xia wu
in the evening	晚上	today	今天
	wan shang		jin tian
tomorrow	明天	the day after tomorrow	后天
	ming tian		hou tian
next week	下星期	earlier	早一些
	xia xing qi		zao yi xie
later	晚一些	as soon as possible	尽早地
	wan yi xie		jin zao de
soft class	软席	hard class	硬席
	ruan xi		ying xi
berth	卧铺	seat	座位
	wo pu		zuo wei

What times does it leave?

什么时候开车？

Shen me shi hou kai che?

What time does it arrive?

什么时候到？

Shen me shi hou dao?

Where does it leave from?

车从哪儿开出？

Che cong nar kai chu?

Please write that address here.

请你把地址写在这里。

Qing ni ba di zhi xie zai zhe li.

What time should I be there?

我应该在什么时候到那里？

Wo ying gai zai shen me shi hou dao na li?

How much is it?

多少钱？

Duo shao qian?

Do you have a schedule in English?

你有一个英语时间表吗？

Ni you yi ge ying yu shi jian biao ma?

Cancellations

Do you think someone might cancel a ticket later?

你想等一等会有人退票吗？

Ni xiang deng yi deng hui you ren tui piao ma?

Could I take his place?

能把他的位子给我吗？

Neng ba ta de wei zi gei wo ma?

When should I try again?

我应该什么时候再来问？

Wo ying gai shen me shi hou zai lai wen?

Can I exchange this reservation for another time?

我能把订的这张票换一个别的时间的吗？

Wo neng ba ding de zhe zhang piao huan yi ge bie de shi jian de ma?

Is there a service charge?

要付服务费吗？

Yao fu fu wu fei ma?

I would like to cancel this ticket and get a refund.

我想把这张票退掉。

Wo xiang ba zhe zhang piao tui diao.

If I wait here, is there a possibility I can get a ticket?

如果我等在这里，有可能买到一张票吗？

Ru guo wo deng zai zhe li, you ke neng mai dao yi zhang piao ma?

Someone may not show up.

可能有人不来。

Ke neng you ren bu lai.

It is an emergency.

这是一个紧急情况。

Zhe shi yi ge jin ji qing kuang.

(For waiting list, see Hotel section of this chapter.)

Private Car

Checkpoint 检查站

Jian cha zhan

Do you have permission to pass here?

你有通行证吗？

Ni you tong xing zheng ma?

I didn't know we needed permission.

我不知道我们需要办通行证。

Wo bu zhi dao wo men xu yao ban tong xing zheng.

I didn't see a sign.

我没有看见牌子。

Wo mei you kan jian pai zi.

We are only sightseeing.

我们只是在观光。

Wo men zhi shi zai guan guang.

We are traveling from ——— to ———.

我们是从_____旅行到_____。

Wo men shi cong ——— lu xing dao ———.

We are lost.

我们迷路了。

Wo men mi lu le.

Could you please tell me how to go from ——— to ———?

请告诉我从_____到_____怎么走。

Qing gao su wo cong ——— dao ——— zen me zou.

How far is it from here?

从这里去有多远？

Cong zhe li qu you duo yuan?

Please mark where we are now on this map.

请在地图上把我们现在所在的地方做个记号。

Qing zai di tu shang ba wo men xian zai suo zai de di fang zuo ge

ji hao.

Please draw a map for us.

请给我们画个地图。

Qing gei wo men hua ge di tu.

here	there
这里	那里
zhe li	na li

Do you have a telephone?

你有电话吗？

Ni you dian hua ma?

We are ———.   我们是。_____。

Wo men shi ———.

diplomats   外交官

wai jiao guan

guests of the China International Travel Service

中国国际旅行社的客人

zhong guo guo ji lu xing she de ke ren

Overseas Chinese   华侨

hua qiao

foreign experts   外国专家

wai guo zhuan jia

Where can we find a(n) ———?   哪里有_____？

Na li you ———?

gas station?   加油站

jia you zhan?

restaurant?   饭馆

fan guan?

lavatory?   厕所

ce suo?

hotel? 旅馆
　　　　²　³
　　　　lu guan?

English-speaking person? 会说英语的人
　　　　　　　　　　　⁴　¹　¹　³　²
　　　　　　　　　　　hui shuo ying yu de ren?

Please circle the location on this map.
请在这个地图把那个位置圈一下。
³　⁴　⁴　⁴　⁴ ² ³　⁴　⁴　⁴　⁴　¹　²　⁴
Qing zai zhe ge di tu ba na ge wei zhi quan yi xia.

Permission

Is permission necessary?
需不需要先申请？
¹　⁴　¹　⁴　¹　¹　³
Xu bu xu yao xian shen qing?

Do I need permission to come back to this city?
再回这个城市我还需要先申请吗？
⁴　²　⁴　⁴　²　⁴　³　²　⁴　¹　¹　¹　³
Zai hui zhe ge cheng shi wo hai xu yao xian shen qing ma?

Where do I get permission to go there?
到哪里办申请？
⁴　³　³　⁴　¹　³
Dao na li ban shen qing?

Please write that address down here.
请把地址写在这里。
³　³　⁴　³　³　⁴　⁴ ³
Qing ba di zhi xie zai zhe li.

Alien Permit

Where is the office of the Security Police? I want to get permission to go to the following cities:
公安局在哪里？我要申请到以下几个城市去：
¹　¹　²　⁴　³ ³　　³　⁴　¹　³　⁴　³　⁴　³　⁴　³　⁴　²　　⁴　⁴
Gong an ju zai na li? Wo yao shen qing dao yi xia ji ge cheng shi qu:

When? 什么时候？
　　　²　　²　⁴
　　　Shen me shi hou?

Passport? 护照？
　　　　⁴　⁴
　　　　Hu zhao?

What hotel are you staying in? 你住在哪一个旅馆？
　　　　　　　　　　　　³　⁴　⁴　³　²　³　³
　　　　　　　　　　　　Ni zhu zai na yi ge lu guan?

Who invited you to China? 谁邀请你来中国的？
　　　　　　　　　　²　¹　³　³　²　¹　²　　²
　　　　　　　　　　Shui yao qing ni lai zhong guo de?

Come back tomorrow.	请明天再来。 　　3　2　1　4　2 Qing ming tian zai lai.
Come back in two days.	两天后再来。 　　3　1　4　4　2 Liang tian hou zai lai.
What time?	什么时间？ 　2　　2　1 Shen me shi jian?
Is there any charge?	要付钱吗？ 　4　4　2 Yao fu qian ma?

Departures (see also City travel)

Is it time to board yet?
还不该上车吗？
　2　4　1　4　　1
Hai bu gai shang che ma?

Which platform?
哪一个站台？
　3　2　4　4　2
Na yi ge zhan tai?

Which coach?
哪一辆车箱？
　3　2　4　　1　1
Na yi liang che xiang?

Where is the ———?
————在哪里？
　　　4　3　3
——— zai na li?

waiting room	侯车室 　4　1　4 hou che shi	
schedule in English	英语时间表 　1　3　2　1　3 ying yu shi jian biao	
restaurant	餐馆 　1　1 can guan	
retail store	商店 　1　　4 shang dian	
ticket	车／船／飞机票 　1　2　1　1　4 che / chuan / fei ji piao	passport 护照 　　　4　4 hu zhao

customs declaration form

海关报税单
3 1 4 4 1
hai guan bao shui dan

foreign exchange receipt

外汇兑换收据
4 4 4 4 1 4
wai hui dui huan shou ju

identification badge

身份证章
1 4 4 1
shen fen zheng zhang

Lost and Found

I have lost my ———,

我的＿＿＿＿丢了。或：我找不到我的＿＿＿＿。
3 1 4 3 2 4 3
Wo de ——— diu le huo : zhao bu dao wo de ———.

spouse	丈夫／妻子 4 1 zhang fu / qi zi	luggage	行李 2 xing li
tour group	旅行团 3 2 2 lu xing tuan	watch	手表 3 3 shou biao
glasses	眼镜 3 4 yan jing	wallet	皮夹子 2 1 pi jia zi
umbrella	伞 3 san	camera	照像机 4 4 1 zhao xiang ji
purse	钱包 2 1 qian bao	tape recorder	录音机 4 1 1 lu yin ji
typewriter	打字机 3 4 1 da zi ji	shoe	鞋 2 xie
luggage wheels	推行李的小车 1 2 tui xing lide xiao che	package	包裹 1 3 bao guo

Have you seen it? 你看见了吗？
3 4 4
Ni kan jian le ma?

Is there a lost-and-found here? 这儿有失物招领柜吗？
4 3 1 1 3 4
Zher you shi wu zhao ling gui ma?

If someone finds it, could you 　如果有人找到了，
2 3 3 1 2 3 4
Ru guo you ren zhao dao le,

please mail it to me at this address? 请寄到这个地址给我。

3 4 4 4 4 4 3 3 3
qing ji dao zhe ge di zhi gei wo.

HOTEL

General Information

Where do I register? 我在哪儿登记？

3 4 3 1 3
Wo zai nar deng ji?

I have a reservation for today. 我已经订了今天的房间。

3 3 1 4 1 1 2 1
Wo yi jing ding le jin tian de fang jian.

single 单人房　　　double 双人房　　　suite 套房

1 2 2　　　　　　1 2 2　　　　　4 2
dan ren fang　　　shuang ren fang　　　tao fang

——— persons 个人

4 2
———ge ren

cheapest 最便宜的　　　whatever is available

4 2 2
zui pian yi de

most expensive 最贵的　　　不管有什么都行

4 4　　　　4 3 3 2 1 2
zui gui de　　　bu guan you shen me dou xing

old wing 老厅　　　in between 中间的

3 1　　　　　　1 1
lao ting　　　　　zhong jian de

private bath or shower 私人浴室或淋浴　　　new wing 新厅

1 2 4 4 4 2 4　　　　　1 1
si ren yu shi huo lin yu　　　　xin ting

air-conditioned 有冷气的　　　not air-conditioned 没有冷气的

3 3 4　　　　　　　　2 3 3
you leng qi de　　　　　　　mei you leng

4
qi de

better view 看出去风景较好的。

4 1 4 1 3 3 3
kan chu qu feng jing jiao hao de

Can I wait in the lobby until a room is available?

我在前门大厅等到有房间空出来行不行？

3 4 2 1 4 1 3 4 2 2 1 1 2 2 2
Wo zai qian men da ting deng dao you fang jian kong chu lai xing

4 2
bu xing?

Please put me on the waiting list.

请把我的名字登记上。

3 3 3 2 3 1 4 4
Qing ba wo ming zi deng ji shang.

I will check with you tomorrow morning.

明天早上我再来问。

Ming tian zao shang wo zai lai wen.

I would like to make a reservation for a future date.

我想订一个房间。

Wo xiang ding yi ge fang jian.

I am looking for a friend.

我在找一个朋友。

Wo zai zhao yi ge peng you.

Please show me the registration forms so I can find his room number.

请将登记本给我查一下他的房间号数。

Qing jiang deng ji ben gei wo cha yi xia ta de fang jian hao shu.

His nationality?

他的国籍？

Ta de guo ji?

Is there someone to carry my bags to my room?

有人帮我把行李拿到房间里去吗？

You ren bang wo ba xing li na dao fang jian li qu ma?

Where is ———?

——— 在哪儿？

——— zai nar?

barber shop	理发店
	li fa dian
hairdresser	理发师
	li fa shi
masseur	按摩师
	an mo shi
bank	银行
	yin hang
post office	邮局
	you ju
cable office	电报局
	dian bao ju

English	Chinese	Pinyin
Telex	用户电报	yong hu dian bao
clinic	诊疗所	zhen liao suo
retail store	零售商店	ling shou shang dian
bar	酒吧间	jiu ba jian
coffee shop	咖啡馆	ka fei guan
When does it open?	什么时候开门？	Shen me shi hou kai men?
When does it close?	什么时候关门？	Shen me shi hou guan men?
Do you have ————?	你有_____吗？	Ni you ———— ma?
Where?	在那里？	Zai na li?
ping-pong	乒乓	ping pang
billiards	台球	tai qiu
badminton	羽毛球	yu mao qiu
racket	拍子	pai zi
bird	羽毛球	yu mao qiu
net	球纲	qiu wang
volleyball	排球	pai qiu
swimming pool	游泳池	you yong chi

hot spring 温泉
wen quan

nearby park for jogging 附近可供步行锻练的公园
fu jin ke gong bu xing duan lian de gong yuan

scales for weighing luggage 秤行李用的磅秤
cheng xing li yong de bang cheng

Chinese newspaper
中国报纸
zhong guo bao zhi

typewriter
打字机
da zi ji

meeting room for ——— people
_____人开会用的会议室
——— ren kai hui yong de hui yi shi

professional photographer
职业摄影师
zhi ye she ying shi

simultaneous translation equipment
同声翻译设备
tong sheng fan yi she bei

interpreter
翻译
fan yi

movie projector 放影机
fang ying ji

35 mm. 35毫米
san shi wu hao mi

8 mm. 8毫米
ba hao mi

super 8 超8
chao ba

slide projector 幻灯机
huan deng ji

tape recorder	录音机	lu yin ji
spool	录音胶带	lu yin jiao dai
cassette	暗盒	an he
8-track	八声道	ba sheng dao
microphone	扩音机	kuo yin ji
megaphone	传声筒	chuan sheng tong
refrigerator	冰箱	bing xiang
freezer	致冷器	zhi leng qi

What is the rental price?

租金多少？

Zu jin duo shao?

Can you organize a cocktail party for ——— people?

你能为_____人安排一个鸡尾酒会吗？

Ni neng wei ——— ren an pai yi ge ji wei jiu hui ma?

Please show me the room.

请你让我看看那个房间。

Qing ni rang wo kan kan na ge fang jian.

How much for hors d'œuvres and canapes?

小吃多少钱？

Xiao chi duo shao qian?

How much for liquor?

酒多少钱？

Jiu duo shao qian?

How much if we supply our own liquor and you supply the ice and glasses, waiters, and bartender?

我们带自己的酒，你供应冰块、玻璃环、服务员和酒
Wo men dai zi ji de jiu, ni gong ying bing kuai, bo li bei, fu wu

吧问招待员，要多少钱？
yuan he jiu ba jian zhao dai yuan, yao duo shao qian?

What is your cable address?

你的电报挂号是什么？
Ni de dian bao gua hao shi shen me?

What is your telephone number?

你的电话号码是什么？
Ni de dian hua hao ma shi (shen me?) duo shao?

Dining Room

Where is the dining room?

餐厅在哪里？
Can ting zai na li?

Chinese food

中餐
Zhong can

Western food

西餐
xi can

upstairs?

楼上
lou shang?

downstairs?

楼下
lou xia?

What time does it open? close?　餐厅什么时候开？关？
Can ting shen me shi hou kai? guan?

Laundry

If I give you my laundry now when will it be done?

如果我现在把要洗的东西给你，什么时候可以洗好？
Ru quo wo xian zai ba yao xi de dong xi ge ni, shen me shi shou
ke yi xi hao?

I must have it by tomorrow morning. I am leaving at ———.
我明天早上一定要。我＿＿＿＿点钟动身。
Wo ming tian zao shang yi ding yao. Wo ——— dian zhong dong
shen.

Where is my laundry? I gave it to the attendant yesterday and he promised to have it done now. 我交去洗的东西在哪里？
Wo jiao qu de dong xi zai na li?
我是昨天交给服务员的，他答应我现在可以洗好。
Wo shi zuo tian jiao gei fu wu yuan de, ta da ying wo xian zai ke
yi xi hao.

man's	男人的 nan ren de
woman's	女人的 nu ren de
child's	小孩的 xiao hai de
shirt	男式衬衫 nan shi chen shan
trousers	长裤 chang ku
blouse	女人衬衫 nu ren chen shan
underpants	内裤 nei ku
undershirt	内衣 nei yi
socks	短袜 duan wa
dress	衣裙 yi qun
pajamas	睡衣 shui yi

tie
领带
ling dai

suit (man's)
西装
xi zhuang

dry cleaning
干洗
gan xi

I am leaving this morning.
我今天早上走。
Wo jin tian zao shang zou.

I don't have anything else to wear.
我没有别的衣服可穿了。
Wo mei you bie de yi fu ke chuan le.

I need it today
我今天要。
Wo jin tian yao.

I need it right now.
我现在就要。
Wo xian zai jiu yao.

Rooms

There are mosquitoes in this room. Can you give me an incense coil to burn?

这个房间里有蚊子。你能给我一盘蚊香吗？
Zhe ge fang jian li you wen zi. ni neng gei wo yi pan wen xiang me?

Do you have a mosquito net?

你有蚊帐吗？
Ni you wen zhang ma?

extra blanket?

你还有毯子吗？
Ni hai you tan zi ma?

Please give me some hot water in a thermos.

请给我一暖瓶热水。
Qing gei wo yi nuan ping re shui.

I need enough hot water for a bath.

我需要足够洗一个澡的热水。
Wo xu yao zu gou xi yi ge zao de re shui.

Please bring me _____ 请给我拿 _____ 来。

Qing gei wo na ——— lai.
                3   3   3 2

ice	冰	beer	啤酒	tea	茶
	bing 1		pi jiu 2 3		cha 2

orange soda 橘子汽水 Coke 可口可乐 glasses 玻璃杯
ju zi qi shui   ke kou ke le   bo li bei
2 3   3   3   3   3 4   1 1 1

cup 杯子   towel 毛巾   soap 肥皂
bei zi   mao jin   fei zao
1   2   1   2 4

clean 干净的 fan 电风扇／扇子
gan jing de   dian feng shan / shan zi
1   4   4

Something is broken in my room. 我房间的_____坏了。

Wo fang jian de ——— huai le.
        3 2 1

toilet	厕所	light	电灯
	ce suo 4		dian deng 4
telephone	电话	chair	椅子
	dian hua 4 4		yi zi 3
bed	床	air conditioner	冷气机
	chuang 2		leng qi ji 3 4 4
fan	电风扇	mosquito net	蚊帐
	dian feng shan 4 1 4		wen zhang 2 4
television	电视机	radiator	暖气
	dian shi ji 4 4 4		nuan qi 3 4

There isn't enough heat. 不够热
Bu gou re.
4 4 4

This is dirty. 这个不干净
Zhe ge bu gan jing.
4 4 4 1 4

Could someone fix it immediately?
能叫人立刻来修吗？
Neng jiao ren li ke lai xiu ma?
2   4   2 4 2 4 1

No. 不能   Yes. 能   I will try. 我试试看
bu neng.   neng.   wo shi shi kan.
4 2   2   3 4 4

I will ask my director.

我问一下主任。
Wo wen yi xia zhu ren.

Can I get a discount on my room if it is not fixed before I leave?

如果在我离开以前没有修好，我是否可以少付房钱？
Ru guo zai wo li kai yi qian mei you xiu hao, wo shi fou ke yi
shao fu fang qian?

Can I have a hot water bottle?

能给我一个热水袋吗？
Neng gei wo yi ge re shui dai ma?

Telephones

How do I get an outside line on the telephone?

我怎样打外线电话？
Wo zen yang da wai xian dian hua?

Please telephone this person and ask him/her to meet me at the hotel at
——— o'clock. My name is ——— and my room number is ———

请你给这个人打一个电话·让他／她在＿＿＿点钟到
旅馆来找我。我叫＿＿＿＿住在＿＿＿＿号房间。
Qing ni gei zhe ge ren da yi ge dian hua, rang ta zai ———
dian zhong dao lu guan lai zhao wo. Wo jiao ——— zhu zai ——
— hao fang jian.

I would like to make an international telephone call.

我想和国外通一个电话。
Wo xiang he quo wai tong yi ge dian hua.

I would like to call long distance in China.

我想打个中国国内的长途电话。
Wo xiang da ge zhong guo guo nei de chang tu dian hua.

Can I take it in my room?

我能在我房间里接吗？
Wo neng zai wo fang jian li jie ma?

Can I pay for it with a credit card?

我能用信用卡付款吗？
Wo neng yong xin yong ka fu kuan ma?

collect call

收话人付款的长途电话。
Shou hua ren fu kuan de chang tu dian hua.

FOOD

Banquets 宴会

(Arrangements can be made at service counter at hotel.)

Can you recommend a good restaurant for me?

你能推荐一家好的餐馆吗？

Ni neng tui jian yi jia hao de can guan ma?
3 2   1   4   1 1 3   1   3

One noted for good food, moderate prices. I don't care what it looks like.

一家菜闻名，而价钱公道的，我不在乎餐馆的样子
如何。

Yi jia cai wen ming er jia qian gong dao de. Wo bu zai hu can
1 1   4   2   2   2   4   2   1   4   3 4   4   1 1
guan de yang zi ru he.
3   4   2   2

One noted for beautiful surroundings and good food.

一家环境优美，菜又好的餐馆。

Yi jia huan jing you mei, cai you hao de can guan.
1 1   4   1   2   4   1   3   4   1   3   1   3

Could you please make a reservation for me for ——— people at ——— each. The chef can decide the menu.

请你代我订_____人一桌的菜。每人_____元的。
菜单由厨师决定。

Qing ni dai wo ding ——— ren yi zhuo de cai. Mei ren ———
3   3   4 3   4   2   1   1   4   3   2
yuan de. Cai dan you chu shi jue ding.
2   4   1   2   2   2   1 2 4

Yes, I understand we have to pay extra for drinks.

对，我知道喝的要另外算。

Dui, Wo zhi dao he de yao ling wai suan.
4   3   1   4   1   4   4   4   4

Can we bring our own bottles of liquor?

我们能自已带酒吗？

Wo men neng zi ji dai ju ma?
3   2   4 3 4 3

Is it possible to include one dish of ——— for that price?

这个价钱能不能有个_____菜？

Zhe ge jia qian neng bu neng you ge ——— cai?
4   4   2   2   2   4   2   3   4   4

Please make the reservation for ——— o'clock.

请代我订在_____点钟。

Qing dai wo ding zai ——— dian zhong.
3   4   3   4   4   3   1

today 今天
jin tian
1 1

tomorrow 明天
ming tian
2 1

the day after tomorrow 后天
hou tian
4 1

Please write down the name and address for the taxi driver.
请将名字和地址写给司机。
Qing jiang ming zi he di zhi xie gei si ji.
3 1 2 2 4 3 3 3 1 1

Small Noodle or Bun Shops (food is usually in sight)

I understand Foreign Friends and Overseas Chinese do not have to give ration coupons.
我听说外国朋友和华侨不需要给粮票。
Wo ting shuo wai guo peng you he hua qiao bu xu yao gei liang piao.
3 1 1 4 2 2 3 2 2 2 4 1 4 3 2 4

Please, I would prefer to stand in line with everyone else.
啊，我愿意和大家排在一起。
A, wo yuan yi he da jia pai zai yi qi.
4 3 4 4 2 4 1 2 4 1 3

Hotel Dining Rooms and Other Restaurants

I am in a hurry. 我有急事，请你快一点
Wo you ji shi, qing ni kuai yi dian.
3 3 2 4 3 3 4 1 3

Please bring me ———. 请给我_____。
Qing gei wo ———.
3 3 3

a bowl of noodle soup 一碗汤面
yi wan tang mian
1 3 1 4

fried noodles 炒面
chao mian
3 4

fried rice 炒饭
chao fan
3 4

an assortment of meat dumplings 肉馅饺子／馄饨
rou xian jiao zi / hun tun
4 4 3 4 2

a dish of meat 一盘肉菜

1 2 4 4

yi pan rou cai

anything that can be
prepared quickly 任何快餐都行

4 2 4 1 1 2

ren he kuai can dou xing

I would like a Chinese breakfast. 我要一份中式早餐

3 4 1 4 1 4 3 1

Wo yao yi fen zhong shi zao can.

rice congee	大米粥 4 3 1 da mi zhou	baked buns	烧饼 1 3 shao bing
pickles	泡菜 4 pao cai	oil sticks	油条 2 2 you tiao
salted eggs	咸蛋 2 4 xian dan	dim sum	点心 3 1 dian xin
peanuts	花生米 1 1 3 hua sheng mi	soy milk	豆浆 4 1 dou jiang
tea	茶 2 cha		

I would like a Western breakfast. 我要一份西式早点

3 4 1 4 1 4 3 3

Wo yao yi fen xi shi zao dian.

fruit or juice 水果或水果汁

3 3 4 3 3 1

shui guo huo shui guo zhi

toast or buns 烤面包或小园面包

3 4 1 4 3 2 4 1

kao mian bao huo xiao yuan mian bao

eggs	鸡蛋 1 4 ji dan	butter	黄油 2 huang you
bacon or ham	咸肉或火腿 2 4 4 3 xian rou huo huo tui	coffee	咖啡 1 1 ka fei
jam	果酱 3 4 guo jiang	milk	牛奶 2 3 niu nai
sugar	糖 2 tang		

If you have a menu in English, please bring it.

如果你有英语菜单，请拿给我看一看。

Ru guo ni you ying yu cai dan, qing na gei wo kan yi kan.

What do you recommend that is good but not expensive?

你可以介绍什么好而又不贵的菜吗？

Ni ke yi jie shao shen me hao er you bu gui de cai ma?

What is the specialty of this restaurant?

这里的特菜是什么？

Zhe li de te cai shi shen me?

Please bring enough food for one person.

请你给够我一个人吃的饭菜。

Qing ni gei gou wo yi ge ren chi de fan cai.

Please bring enough food for all of us. Total cost no more than ———— per person.

请你给够我们大家吃的饭菜，每人不超过_____。

Qing ni gei gou wo men da jia chi de fan cai, mei ren bu chao guo

————.

Please bring me one order of ————.

请你给我一份_____。

Qing ni gei wo yi fen ————.

beef	牛肉 niu rou	vegetables	蔬菜 shu cai
chicken	鸡 ji	celery cabbage	芹菜 qin cai
pigeon	鸽子 ge zi	green beans	青豆 qing dou
goose	鹅 e	green onions	葱 cong
pork	猪肉 zhu rou	bean sprouts	豆芽 dou ya
fish	鱼 yu	bamboo shoots	竹笋 zhu sun
crab	螃蟹 pang xie	water chestnuts	荸荠 bi qi

lobster	龙虾 long xia	watercress	水芹菜 shui qin cai
shrimp	虾 xia	cabbage	白菜 bai cai
sea cucumber (or slug)	海参 hai shen	mushrooms	蘑菇 mo gu
bean curd	豆腐 dou fu	cloud's ears (fungus)	银耳 yin er
Beijing (Peking) duck	北京鸭 beijing ya	pine nuts	松子 song zi
duck	鸭子 ya zi		
monkey	猴子 hou zi	cashews	枥如树果 ru shu guo
snake	蛇 she	peanuts	花生 hua sheng
dog	狗 gou	walnuts	核桃 he tao
frogs' legs	蛙腿 wa tui	eggs	蛋 dan
civet cat	香猫 xiang mao	caviar	鱼子 yu zi
turtle	甲鱼 jia yu	hors d'œuvre	小吃 xiao chi
lotus seed	莲子 lian zi	black or yellow bean	黑或黄豆 hei huo huang dou
heart	心 xin	gizzard	胗 zhen
liver	肝 gan	kidney	腰子 yaozi

brains	脑 nao	spareribs	排骨 pai gu
hocks	蹄膀 ti bang	tongue	舌 she
steak	牛排 niu pai	fillet (boneless)	里脊 liji
slices	肉片 rou pian	balls	丸子 wanzi
soup	汤 tang	stomach	肚子 du zi
minced	剁碎的 duo sui de	shark's fins	鱼翅 yu chi
bird's nest	燕窝 yan wo		

stir-fried	快炒 kuai chao	roasted	烤 kao
deep-fried (in batter)	炸(裹鸡蛋面) zha (guo ji dan mian)	cooked in wine	酒焖的 jiu men de
poached	烫熟的 tan shu de	barbecued	烧烤 shao kao
steamed	蒸的 zheng de	baked	烘烤 hong kao
fried in paper	包纸炸的 bao zhi zha de	baked in mud	泥烤 ni kao
scrambled	炒 chao	baked in salt	盐烤 yang kao
boiled (hard)	煮（老的） zhu (lao de)	boiled (soft)	煮（嫩的） zhu (nen de)

sweet and sour sauce	糖醋汁 tang cu zhi		
hoisin sauce	甜面酱 tian mian jiang	bland	淡的 dan de

oyster sauce	牝蛎酱 3 4 4 mu li jiang	no salt	无盐的 2 2 mi yan de
soy sauce	酱油 4 2 jiang you	sour	酸 1 suan
mustard	芥茉 4 jie me	spicy hot	麻辣 2 4 ma la
hot pepper	辣椒 4 1 la jiao	sweet	甜 2 tian
plum sauce	梅子酱 2 4 mei zi jiang	no sugar	无糖 2 2 wu tang
sesame oil	芝麻油／香油 1 2 1 2 zhi ma you / xiang you	salty	咸 2 xian
peanut oil	花生油 1 1 2 hua sheng you	1000-year-old eggs	皮蛋 2 4 pi dan
coriander	芫荽 2 1 yan sui	white rice	白米饭 2 3 4 bai mi fan
honey	蜂蜜 1 2 feng me	ginger	薑 1 jiang
salt	盐 2 yan	garlic	蒜 4 suan
vinegar	醋 4 cu		
canned	罐头的 4 2 guan tou de	fresh	新鲜的 1 1 xin xian de
sweet cakes	甜饼 2 3 tian bing	apples	苹果 2 3 ping guo
bananas	香蕉 1 1 xiang jiao	oranges	橘子 2 ju zi
apricots	杏子 4 xing zi	plums	李子 3 li zi
olives	橄榄 3 3 gan lan	kumquats	金橘 1 2 jin ju

pomelo	柚子 4 you zi	lichees	荔枝 4 1 li zhi
pineapple	菠萝 1 2 bo luo		

What kind of tea do you have?

你们有什么茶?

 3 3 2

 Ni men you shen me cha?

jasmine	茉莉花茶 4 4 1 2 mo li hua cha	lung ching	龙井茶 2 3 2 long jing cha
woo lung	乌龙茶 1 2 2 wu long cha	bo ni	普洱茶 3 3 2 pu er cha
chrysanthemum	菊花茶 2 1 2 ju hua cha	ginseng	人参茶 2 1 2 ren shen cha
milk (hot)	热牛奶 4 2 3 re niu nai	milk (cold)	冷牛奶 3 2 3 leng niu nai
unsweetened	未加糖的 4 1 2 wei jia tang de	soft drink	饮料 3 4 yin liao
beer	啤酒 2 3 pi jiu	Coca Cola	可口可乐 3 3 3 4 ke kou ke le
red wine	红酒 2 2 3 hong pu tao jiu	fruit juice	果子汁 3 3 1 guo zi zhi
white wine	白酒 2 2 4 bai pu tao jiu	fermented mare's milk	发酵的马奶 1 4 3 3 fa jiao de ma nai
mao tai	茅台酒 2 2 3 mao tai jiu		
mineral water	矿泉水 4 2 3 kuang quan shui	buttered tea	油茶 2 2 you cha
cold drinking water	冷开水 3 1 4 leng kai shui	cocoa	可可 1 1 ke ke

This tastes terrible. Please bring me something else.

这个很难吃／喝。 请给我来点别的。

 4 4 3 1 1 3 3 2 3 2

 Zhe ge hen nan chi / he. Qing gei wo lai dian bie de.

Enough! 够了！
　　　　　　4
　　　Gou le!

We cannot eat any more. Please cancel the other dishes!

我们吃不下了，请把别的菜取消罢！
　　3　1　4　4　4　　　3　4　2　4　2　4
Wo men chi bu xia le. Qing ba bie de cai qu xiao ba!

Western food

西餐
1　1
Xi can

bread	面包	hot dog	热狗
	4　1		4　1
	mian bao		re gou
sandwich	三文治	hamburger	面包夹牛肉饼
	1　2　4		4　1　2　4
	san wen zhi		mian bao jia niu
			4　3
			rou bing
ice cream	冰淇淋	popsicle	冰棍
	1　1　2		1　4
	bing ji ling		bing gun

Please write down the name of this dish so I can order it again.

请将这个菜名写下来，我以后好再要。
　3　　1　　4　4　4　2　　3　4　2　3　4　3　4　4
Qing jiang zhe ge cai ming xie xia lai wo yi hou hao zai yao.

I am a strict vegetarian. I would like to order a dish of only vegetables, cooked in vegetable oil. What do you recommend?

我是一个真正的素食者。我想要一个素
油炒的蔬菜。你能给我介绍几个这样的菜吗？
　3　4　1　4　1　4　2　4　3　　3　4　4　1　4　4
Wo shi yi ge zhen zheng de su shi zhe. Wo xiang yao yi ge su
　1　3　4　　1　3　4　3　4　3　4　4　4
you chao de shu cai. Ni neng gei wo jie shao ji ge zhe yang de
　4
cai ma?

I am a Moslem. I do not eat pork or anything cooked in lard. What do you recommend?

我信伊斯兰教。我不吃猪肉或猪油烧的东西。你有什么我可以吃的呢？
　3　4　1　1　2　4　　3　4　1　1　4　　4　1　2　1
Wo xin yi si lan jiao. Wo bu chi zhu rou huo zhu you shao de
　1　3　3　2　3　3　1
dong zi. Ni you shen me wo ke yi chi de ne?

I am a diabetic. I cannot eat anything with sugar in it.

我有糖尿病，我不能吃任何有糖的东西。
　3　3　2　4　4　　3　4　2　4　2　3　2　1
Wo you tang niao bing. Wo bu neng chi ren he you tang de dong
xi.

TELEPHONE (see also Hotel Telephones)

Finding a Public Telephone

Please show me where I can find a telephone.

请告诉我哪里有电话？

Qing gao su wo na li you dian hua.

How much for using the telephone?

打一次电话多少钱？

Da yi dian hua duo shao qian?

Can you find out the telephone number for ————?

你能帮我找一找＿＿＿＿的电话号码吗？

Ni neng bang wo zhao yi zhao ———— de dian hua hao ma ma?

the China International Travel Service in this city?

这里的中国国际旅行社？

zhe li de zhong guo guo ji lu xing she?

the CAAC office in this city?

这里的中国航空公司？

zhe li de zhang guo hang kong gong si?

someone who speaks English?

会说英语的人。

hui shuo ying yu de ren?

Please telephone this person. I want to talk to him.

请给这个人打一个电话。我要和他说话。

Qing gei zhe ge ren da yi ge dianhua. Wo yao he ta shuo hua.

I want to make ————. 我要一个＿＿＿＿。

Wo yao yi ge ————.

a long-distance call in China 中国境内的长途电话。

zhong guo jing nei de chang tu dian hua.

an international telephone call 国际长途电话。

guo ji chang tu dian hua.

Can I take the call in my room?

我能在我房间里接吗？

Wo neng zai wo fang jian li jie me?

Can I pay for it with a credit card?
我能用信用卡付款吗？

Wo neng yong xin yong ka fu kuan me?

collect call
收话人付款的长途电话。

Shou hua ren fu kuan de chang tu dian hua

How long will it take?
要多久可以接通？

Yao duo jiu ke yi jie tong?

EMERGENCIES

If Lost

Help!　救命！

Jiu ming!

Excuse me.　对不起。

Du bu qi.

I am lost. Which way to this
address?
我迷路了，到这个地址去走那一条路？

Wo mi lu le, dao zhe ge di zhi qu zou na yi tiao lu?

the closest hotel?
最近的旅馆在哪里？

Zui jin de lu guan zai na li?

the nearest English-speaking person?
在哪个最近的地方可以找到会说英语的人？

Zai na ge zui jin de di fang ke yi zhao dao hui shuo ying yu de ren?

Can you ask someone to take me there?
你能叫人带我去吗？

Ni neng jiao ren dai wo qu ma?

I am very tired.
我很累。

Wo hen lei.

Please don't push me.
请不要推我。

Qing bu yao tui wo.

Where can I find a telephone?

哪里有电话？

_{3 3 3   4   4}
Na li you dian hua?

Embassies

Please contact the embassy of ———.

请你和＿＿＿＿大使馆接个电话。

_{3 3}
Qing ni he ——— da shi guan jie ge dian hua.

I will speak to them on the telephone.

我要和他们说话。

_{3 4 2 1   1 4}
Wo yao he ta men shuo hua.

Please tell their representative to come here.

请告诉他们的代表到这儿来。

_{3 4 4 1   3 4 4 2}
Qing gao su ta men de dai biao dao zher lai.

Australia	澳大利亚 _{4 4 4} Ao da li ya
Belgium	比利时 _{3 4 2} Bi li shi
Britain	英国 _{1 2} Ying guo
Canada	加拿大 _{1 2 4} Jia na da
France	法国 _{3 2} Fa guo
India	印度 _{4 4} Yin du
Indonesia	印尼 _{4 2} Yin ni
Italy	意大利 _{4 4 4} Yi da li
Japan	日本 _{4 3} Ri ben
Malaysia	马来西亚 _{3 2 1 4} Ma lai xi ya

Mexico	墨西哥 Mo xi ge
Netherlands	荷兰 He lan
New Zealand	新西兰 Xin xi lan
Pakistan	巴基斯坦 Ba ji si tan
Philippines	菲律宾 Fei lu bin
Portugal	葡萄牙 Pu tao ya
Singapore	新加坡 Xin jia po
Spain	西班牙 Xi ban ya
The Federal Republic of Germany	德意志联邦共和国 De yi zhi lian bang gong he guo
The German Democratic Republic	德意志民主共和国 De yi zhi min zhu gong he guo
Switzerland	瑞士 Rui shi
Thailand	泰国 Tai guo
U.S.A.	美国 Mei guo

Miscellaneous Emergencies

Stop, please.

请停下来。

Qing ting xia lai.

I need a lavatory. Please show me the closest one.

我需要上厕所。请告诉我最近的一个在哪里。

Wo xu yao shang ce suo. Qing gao su wo zui jin de yi ge zai na li.

women's	女人的　（如指厕所则是：女厕男厕） 　　　　3　2　　2　1　4　　3　2　4　　3　4　2　4 nu ren de (ru zhi ce suo ze shi) nu ce nan ce
men's	男人的 　2　2 nan ren de
Stay away!	站开点！ 　4　1　3 zhan kai dian!
Danger!	危险！ 　1　3 wei xian!
Run away!	跑开！ 　3　1 pao kai!
Follow me!	跟着我！ 　1　　3 gen zhe wo!
Please hurry!	快些！ 　4　1 kuai xie!
air attack	空袭 　1　1 kong xi
air-raid shelter	防空洞 　2　1　4 fang kong dong
boat sinking	船在沉 　2　4　2 chuan zai chen
Fire!	失火了！ 　1　3 shi huo le!
Explosion!	爆炸了！ 　4　4 bao zha le!
Earthquake!	地震了！ 　4　4 di zhen le!

Get outside, away from falling debris.

到外面去，躲开掉下来的碎砾。
　4　4　4　4　　3　1　4　4　2　　4　4
Dao wai mian qu, duo kai diao xia lai de sui li.

Riot!	暴动！ 　4　4 bao dong!
accident	意外。 　4　4 yi wai

flood 水灾。
shui zai

Please call someone who speaks English.
请叫一位能说英语的来。
Qing jia yi wei neng shuo ying yu de lai.

Please call the China International Travel Service.
请叫中国国际旅行社的人来。
Qing jiao zhong guo guo ji lu xing she de ren lai.

Medical Emergencies

Is anyone hurt? 有人受伤吗？
You ren shou shang ma?

Is there someone here who can help us?
这里有那一位能帮助我们吗？
Zhe li you na yi wei neng bang zhu wo men ma?

Please ask people to stand back and give us some air.
请你叫人们靠后站，使我们能吸到些空气。
Qing ni jiao ren men kao hou zhan, shi wo men neng xi dao xie
kang qi.

Please call a doctor.
请叫一位医生来。
Qing jiao yi wei yi sheng lai.

Please bring ———. 请你拿＿＿＿＿来。
Qing ni na ——— lai.

blanket 一床毯子
yi chuang tan zi.

stretcher 一个担架
yi fu dan jia

oxygen 氧气
yang qi

ice 冰
bing

splints 夹板
jia ban

bandages	绷带 beng dai
drinking water	喝的水 he de shui
Stop the bleeding.	止血 Zhi xue.
Call an ambulance.	叫救护车来 Jiao jiu hu che lai.
Get him to a hospital.	送他去医院 Song ta qu yi yuan.
Hurry.	快！ Kuai!
Help him breathe.	帮助他呼吸 Bang zhu ta hu xi.
A bone caught in the throat.	喉咙里卡了一根骨头。 Hou long li qia le yi gen gu tou.
Help him lie down.	帮他躺下。 Bang ta tang xia.
Raise his head.	把他的头抬起来。 Ba ta de tou tai qi lai.
Lower his head.	把他的头放下去。 Ba ta de tou fang xia qu.
Raise his feet.	把他的脚抬起来。 Ba ta de jiao tai qi la.
Give heart massage.	给他按摩心脏。 Gei ta an mo xin zang.
Give mouth-to-mouth resuscitation.	做口对口的呼吸急救。 Zuo kou dui kou de hu xi ji jiu.
Get him cool.	让他凉快凉快。 Rang ta liang kuai liang kuai.
Fan him.	给他扇一扇。 Gei ta shan yi shan.

appendicitis	阑尾炎 lan wei yan
bleeding	流血 liu xie
Broken bone. Do not move it.	骨头断了，不要挪动。 Gu tou duan le. Bu yao nuo dong.
burn	烧伤 shao shang
diabetic	糖尿病 tang hiao bing
drowned	淹了 yan le
drunk	喝醉了 he zui le
epileptic fit	癫痫发作 dian xian fa zuo
heart attack	心脏病发作 xin zang bing fa zuo
high fever	高烧 gao shao
insect bite	虫咬了 chong yao le
poisoned	中毒了 zhong du le
snake bite	蛇咬了 she yao le
stroke	中风 zhong fang
vomit	呕吐 ou tu

Medical (see also Medical Emergencies)

Where can I find a doctor to treat this ———?

在哪里能找到一位医生治这_____?

Zai na li neng zhao dao yi wei yi sheng zhi zhe ———?

itch	痒 yang
pain here	这儿痛 zher tong
bleeding here	这儿流血 zher liu xie
common cold	受凉感冒 shou lian gan mao
diarrhea	腹泻 fu xie
cough	咳嗽 ke sou
headache	头痛 tou tong
fever	发烧 fa shao
difficulty in breathing	呼吸困难 hu xi kun nan
hives	荨麻疹 xun ma zhen
sore throat	喉咙痛 hou long tong
acupuncture	针刺治疗 zhen ci zhi liao
compress	纱布垫 sha bu dian
injection	打针 da zhen
soak	浸湿 jin shi

bandage　　　　　　　　用绷带包扎
$\overset{4}{\text{　}}\overset{1}{\text{　}}\overset{4}{\text{　}}\overset{1}{\text{　}}\overset{1}{\text{　}}$
yong beng dai bao zha

Go to the hospital.　　　去医院
$\overset{4}{\text{　}}\overset{1}{\text{　}}$
Qu yi yuan.

How long bed rest?　　　要卧床多久?
$\overset{4}{\text{　}}\overset{4}{\text{　}}\overset{2}{\text{　}}\overset{1}{\text{　}}\overset{3}{\text{　}}$
Yao wo chuang duo jiu?

When can he continue on his
journey?　　　　　　他什么时候可以继续旅行?
$\overset{1}{\text{　}}\overset{2}{\text{　}}\overset{2}{\text{　}}\overset{4}{\text{　}}\overset{3}{\text{　}}\overset{3}{\text{　}}\overset{4}{\text{　}}\overset{4}{\text{　}}\overset{3}{\text{　}}\overset{1}{\text{　}}$
Ta shen me shi hou ke yi ji xu lu xing?

What is his temperature?　　他的体温是多少?
$\overset{1}{\text{　}}\overset{3}{\text{　}}\overset{1}{\text{　}}\overset{4}{\text{　}}\overset{1}{\text{　}}\overset{3}{\text{　}}$
Ta de ti wen shi duo shao?

What is that in Fahrenheit?　华氏多少度?
$\overset{2}{\text{　}}\overset{4}{\text{　}}\overset{3}{\text{　}}\overset{3}{\text{　}}\overset{4}{\text{　}}$
Hua shi duo shao du?

Is it a high fever?　　　体温高吗?
$\overset{3}{\text{　}}\overset{1}{\text{　}}\overset{1}{\text{　}}$
Ti wen gao me?

Is it normal?　　　　　正常不正常?
$\overset{4}{\text{　}}\overset{2}{\text{　}}\overset{4}{\text{　}}\overset{4}{\text{　}}\overset{2}{\text{　}}$
Zheng chang bu zheng chang?

Dental

dental　　　　　　　牙齿的。
$\overset{2}{\text{　}}\overset{3}{\text{　}}$
ya chi de

I have a pain here.　　　我这儿痛。
$\overset{3}{\text{　}}\overset{4}{\text{　}}$
Wo zher tong.

I think I have lost a filling. 我想我有一个牙齿的充填物掉了。
$\overset{3}{\text{　}}\overset{3}{\text{　}}\overset{3}{\text{　}}\overset{3}{\text{　}}\overset{1}{\text{　}}\overset{4}{\text{　}}\overset{2}{\text{　}}\overset{3}{\text{　}}\overset{1}{\text{　}}$
Wo xiang wo you yi ge ya chi de chong
$\overset{2}{\text{　}}\overset{4}{\text{　}}\overset{4}{\text{　}}$
tian wu diao le.

Can you give me a temporary
filling?　　　　　　　能给我临时补一下吗?
$\overset{2}{\text{　}}\overset{3}{\text{　}}\overset{3}{\text{　}}\overset{2}{\text{　}}\overset{2}{\text{　}}\overset{3}{\text{　}}\overset{1}{\text{　}}\overset{4}{\text{　}}$
Neng gei wo lin shi bu yi xia ma?

Please do not pull out the tooth. 请不要把那个牙拔掉。
$\overset{3}{\text{　}}\overset{4}{\text{　}}\overset{4}{\text{　}}\overset{3}{\text{　}}\overset{4}{\text{　}}\overset{4}{\text{　}}\overset{2}{\text{　}}\overset{2}{\text{　}}\overset{4}{\text{　}}$
Qing bu yao ba na ge ya ba diao.

Please pull out this tooth.　　请把这个牙拔掉。
$\overset{3}{\text{　}}\overset{3}{\text{　}}\overset{4}{\text{　}}\overset{4}{\text{　}}\overset{2}{\text{　}}\overset{2}{\text{　}}\overset{4}{\text{　}}$
Qing ba zhe ge ya ba diao.

Can you give me something to ease
the pain?
你能给我什么止痛的药吗？

Ni neng gei wo shen me zhi tong de
yao me?

Pharmacy (see also Medical)

traditional Chinese herbal medicine 中国草药

zhong guo cao yao

Western medicine 西药

xi yao

allergy to antibiotics 对抗生素过敏

dui kang sheng su guo min

aspirin 阿司匹灵

a si pi ling

insulin for diabetic 治疗糖尿病的胰岛素。

zhi liao tang niao bing de yi dao su

How many teaspoons a day? 一天服几匙？

Yi tian fu ji shao?

How many times a day? 一天服几次？

Yi tian fu ji ci?

How many pills? 几丸？

Ji wan?

For how long? 服多久？

Fu duo jiu?

How much water? 多少水？

Duo shao shui?

Boil and drink like tea? 熬后像喝茶一样喝下去吗？

Ao hou xiang he cha yi yang he
xia qu ma?

All of it? 全喝吗？

Quan he ma?

With sugar? 加糖吗？

Jia tang ma?

Is it bitter?	苦不苦？ Ku bu ku?
Any more injections?	还要打针吗？ Hai yao da zhen ma?
aphrodisiac	催欲剂 cui yu ji
ginseng	人参 ren shen
sea horse	海马 hai ma
pearl	珍珠 zhen zhu
sleeping pill	安眠药 an mian yao
snake	蛇 she
insects	昆虫 kun chong
herb	草药 cao yao
mineral	矿石 kuang shi
animal	动物 dong wu
deer horn	鹿角 lu jiao

WEATHER

What is the temperature today?
今天的温度是多少？
Jin tian de wen du shi duo shao?

Is it hot? 今天热吗？
Jin tian re ma?

cold   冷
3
leng

rainy   有雨
3   3
you yu

snowing   下雪
4   3
xia xue

sunny   晴
2
qing

Do I need to take a ———?   我需要带_____。
3 1 4 4
Wo xu yao dai ———?

coat   一件外套
1 4 4 4
yi jian wai tao

sweater   一件毛衣
1 4 2 1
yi jian mao yi

umbrella   一把伞
1 3 3
yi ba san

swimming suit   游泳衣
2 3 1
you yong yi

suntan lotion   一瓶防晒油
1 2 2 4 2
yi ping fang shai you

RENTALS

Where can I rent a ———?   哪里可以租_____?
3 3 3 3 1
Na li ke yi zu ———?

bicycle   一辆自行车
1 4 4 2 1
yi liang zi xing che

rowboat   一条划艇
1 2 2 3
yi tiao hua ting

tennis racket   一个纲球拍
1 4 4 2 1
yi ge wang qiu pai

car (with driver)   一辆有司机开的汽车
1 4 4 1 1 1 4
yi liang you si ji kai de qi che

How much for an hour? 多少钱一小时？

Duo shao qian yi xiao shi?
<small>1 2 4 3 2</small>

a day? 一天？
<small>4 1</small>
yi tian?

deposit? 押金多少？
<small>1 1 1 3</small>
ya jin duo shao?

I will return in about ———
hours. 我大概在＿＿小时后送还。
<small>3 4 4 4   1 2 4 4 2</small>
Wo da gai zai ——— xiao shi hou song huan.

CONVERSATIONS

Courtesies

hello!	你好！	Ni hao!
Good-bye!	再见！	Zai jian!
I'm sorry. (or) Excuse me!	对不起（或）请原谅!	Dui bu qi (or)
Please	请	Qing. Qing yan liang!
Thank you.	谢谢你！	Xie xie ni.
You're welcome.	不客气。	Bu ke qi.
Yes.	是。	Shi de.
No.	不是。	Bu shi.
Maybe.	可能。	Ke neng.
Wait awhile.	等一会。	Deng yi hui.

Please tell me how to say this in Chinese.
请告诉我这个用中国话怎么说。
<small>3 4 4 3 4 4 4 1 2 4 3 1</small>
Qing gao su wo zhe ge yong zhong guo hua zen mo shuo.

Please say it again slowly.
请再慢一些说一遍。
<small>3 4 4 4 1 1 2 4</small>
Qing zai man yi xie shuo yi bian.

Would you feel offended if I gave you a small token of my appreciation?
如果我送你一件小纪念品以表示我的谢意，你会不会不高兴？
<small>2 3 3 4   3 2 4   3 4 4   3 3 3   4 3   4 4</small>
Ru guo wo song ni yi jian xiao ji nian pin yi biao shi wo de xie yi,
<small>3 4 2 4 4 1 4</small>
ni hui bu hui bu gao xing?

It is not necessary.
你不需要这样做。
<small>3 4 1 4   4 4   4</small>
Ni bu xu yao zhe yang zuo.

But you have been so kind and I feel I will be indebted to you for the rest of my life.

但是你对我这样好，使我觉得此生欠了你很大
的情份。

Dan shi ni dui wo zhe yang hao, shi wo jue de ci sheng qian le ni hen da de qing fen.

It is not convenient.

我不便接受。

Wo bu bian jie shou.

In that case, I will not feel offended.

如果是这样的话，我就不会不高兴了。

Ru guo shi zhe yang de hua, wo jiu bu hui bu gao xing le.

Meeting Strangers (Please have someone fill in the blanks beforehand in Chinese.)

Hello.

I am sorry, I do not speak Chinese.

对不起，我不会说中文。

Dui bu qi, wo bu hui shuo zhong wen.

I speak English.

我说英文。

Wo shuo ying wen.

My name is ———.

我的名字是_____。

Wo de ming zi shi ———.

I am from ———.

我是_____人。

Wo shi ——— ren.

I am in China for ——— weeks.

我要在中国_____周。

Wo yao zai zhong guo dei ——— zhou.

——— months.

_____个月。

——— ge yue.

I arrived ———.

我是在_____到的。

Wo shi zai ——— dao de.

I expect to leave ———.

我预定在_____离开。

Wo yu ding zai ——— li kai.

Please write that down and I will have someone translate it later.	请把它写下来，以后我将找人翻译。 Qing ba ta xie xia lai, yi hou wo zai zhao ren fan yi.
I am visiting ———, ———, ———, ———, ———, and ———.	我将到_____ ____ _____ Wo jiang dao ——— ——— _____ _____ _____去观光。 ——— ——— ——— ——— qu quan guang.
Where do you work?	你在哪里工作？ Ni zai na li gong zuo?
factory	工厂 gong chang
commune	公社 gong she
hospital	医院 yi yuan
office	办公室 bang gong shi
restaurant	饭馆 fan guan
transportation	运输部门 yun shu bu men
hotel	旅馆 lu guan
school	学校 xue xiao
cultural organization	文化机构 wen hua ji gou
government organization	政府机构 zheng fu ji gou

I am a ——————.

(profession)

我是一个_____
Wo shi yi ge ——

（职业）
(zhi ye)

Do you work in this city?

你在这个城市工作吗？
Ni zai zhe ge cheng shi gong zuo
ma?

Where were you born?

你出生在哪里？
Ni chu sheng zai na li?

How many children do you have?

你有几个孩子？
Ni you ji ge hai zi?

Are they all in school?

他们都进学校了吗？
Ta men dou jin xue xiao le ma?

How old are they?

他们多大？
Ta men duo da?

How much money do you make a month?

你一个月赚多少钱？
Ni yi ge yue zhuan duo shao
qian?

How much do you pay for rent?

你的房租多少？
Ni de fang zu duo shao?

for food?

你吃饭花多少钱？
Ni chi fan hua duo shao qian?

What hours do you work?

你什么时间上班和下班？
Ni shen me shi jian shang ban he
xia ban?

Do you have any relatives in my country?

你有亲属在我的国家吗？
Ni you qin shu zai wo de guo jia ma?

Do you have any friends in my country?

你有朋友在我的国家吗？
Ni you peng you zai wo de guo jia ma?

How many years of schooling have
you had? 你曾在学校读过多少年书？
Ni ceng zai xue xiao du guo duo shao nian shu?

How much time have you spent doing manual labor in the countryside?
你下乡干体力劳劲的时间有多久？
Ni xia xiang gan ti li lao dang de shi jian you duo chang?

When was the last time, and for how long?
你最后一次是什么时候去的，去了多久？
Ni zui hou yi ci shi shen me shi hou qu de, qu le duo jiu?

Especially for People with Chinese Relatives

I am very happy to meet you.
见到你我很高兴。
Jian dao ni wo hen gao xing.

Could you join me for a meal?
你能和我一起吃饭吗？
Ni neng he wo yi qi chi fan ma?

For tea? 你能和我一起喝茶吗？
Ni neng he wo yi qi he cha ma?

In the hotel? 我们在旅馆里吃好吗？
Wo men zai lu guan li chi hao ma?

Then follow me. 那么，咱们去吧！
Na me, zan men qu ba!

In a nearby restaurant? 到附近的饭馆去吃好吗？
Dao fu jin de fan guan qu chi hao ma?

Do you know of a good place? 你知道有什么好饭馆吗？
Ni zhi dao you shen me hao fan guan

ma?

Please lead the way, but you are my
guest. 请你带我去，不过让我请客。
Qing ni dai wo qu, bu guo rang wo qing ke.

Could you please order? 你点菜好吗？
Ni dian cai hao ma?

Anything you like. 随便什么你喜欢吃的菜都行。
Sui bian shen me ni xi huan chi de cai dou xing.

I don't know how to do it in
Chinese. 我不知道怎样用中国话说。
Wo bu zhi dao zen yang yong zhong guo hua shuo.

Not too much. I don't like to waste
food. 不要点太多菜。我不愿意浪费。
Bu yao dian tai duo cai. Wo bu yuan yi lang fei.

Did you know my father? 你认识我的父亲吗？
Ni ren shi wo de fu qin ma?

Did you know my grandfather? 你认识我的祖父吗？
Ni ren shi wo de zu fu ma?

Have you visited my ancestral
village lately? 你最近去过我的家乡吗？
Ni zui jin qu guo wo de jia xiang ma?

How is it? 那儿怎么样？
Nar zen me yang?

Poor? 挺穷吗？
Ting qiong ma?

Prosperous? 富裕吗？
Fu yu ma?

Far away? 很远吗？
Hen yuan ma?

Just getting along? 还过得去吗？
Hai guo de qu ma?

Can you take me there for a short
visit? 你能带我去看一看吗？
Ni neng dai wo qu kan yi kan ma?

One of your children? 你的孩子？
Ni de hai zi?

Can you help me make
arrangements? 你能帮我安排吗？
Ni neng bang wo an pai ma?

As soon as possible. 愈快愈对。
Yu kuai yu hao.

When I get back from my tour. 我参观回来的时候。
Wo can guan hui lai de shi hou.

Should I make the application now? 我要不要现在就申请？
Wo yao bu yao xian zai jiu shen
qing?

Tomorrow? 明天？
ming tian?

I am sorry I know so little about
you. 我很遗憾对你不够熟悉。
Wo hen yi han dui ni bu gou shu xi.

What do you do for entertainment? 你参加什么娱乐活动？
Ni can jia shen me yu le huo
dong?

sports 运动？ yun dong?		movies? 看电影？ kandian ying?	
parks? 去公园？ qu gong yuan?		visiting friends? 看朋友？ kan peng you?	
no time 没有空？ mei you kong?		television? 看电视？ kan dian shi?	

How many ration coupons do you
get for a month for ———? 你一个月有多少_____？
Ni yi ge yue you duo shao ———?

肉票 meat rou piao		公斤 kg. gong jin	
粮票 grain liang piao		斤 catties jin	
布票 cotton cloth bu piao		米 meters mi	
油票 cooking oil you piao		两 ounces liang	

肥皂 soap 块 bars
fei zao kuai
2 4 4

Is it sufficient for your needs? 它够不够？
Ta gou bu gou?
1 4 4 4

Do you have ———? 你有＿＿＿＿＿吗？
ni you ——— ma?
3 3

a bicycle 一辆自行车
yi liang zi xing che
1 4 4 3

a sewing machine 一架缝纫机
yi jia feng ren ji
1 4 2 4 1

a television set 一个电视机
yi ge dian shi ji
1 4 4 4 1

a fan 一个风扇
yi ge feng shan
1 4 1 4

a radio 一个无线电
yi ge wu xian dian
1 4 2 4 4

your own kitchen 一个自已的厨房
yi ge zi ji de chu fang
1 4 4 3 2 2

a refrigerator 一个冰箱
yi ge bing xiang
1 4 1

a gas stove 一个煤气炉
yi ge mei qi lu
1 4 2 4 2

Where is the closest school to your
house? 离你家最近的学校在哪里？
Li ni jia zui jin de xue xiao zai na li?
2 3 3 4 4 2 4 4 3 3

primary 小学
xiao xue
3 2

middle 中学
zhong xue
1 2

Do your children walk to school?
你的孩子是不是步行去学校？
Ni de hai zi shi bu shi bu xing qu xue xiao?
3 2 4 4 4 2 4 2 4

Do your children take a public bus?

你的孩子是乘公共汽车去吗？

Ni de hai zi shi cheng gong qi che qu ma?

How much does it cost for ———? _____是多少钱？

——— shi duo shao qian?

tuition	学费	xue fei
room and board	膳宿费	shan su fei
university	大学	da xue

How many people are there in your household who make money?

你们家里有几人赚钱？

Ni men jia li you ji ren zhuan qian?

How much money did you all make last year?

去年你们全家的收入是多少？

Qu nian ni men quan jia de shou ru shi duo shao?

Do you have any savings?

你们有储蓄吗？

Ni men you chu xu ma?

How much did you spend for ———?

你（你们）_____化多少钱？

Ni (ni men) ——— hua duo shao qian?

clothing	穿	chuan
food	吃	chi
rent	房租	fang zu
entertainment	娱乐	yu le
transportation	交通	jiao tong

medical expenses 医药
yi yao

per month? 一个月？   per year? 一年？
yi ge yue?   yi nian?

May I see your house?
我能看看你的房子吗？
Wo neng kan kan ni de fang zi ma?

How many people sleep here?
多少人睡在这里？
Duo shao ren shui zai zhe li?

Where do they all sleep?
他们都睡在哪里？
Ta men dou shui zai na li?

Who does the cooking?
哪一位烧饭？
Na yi nei shao fan?

Who takes care of the children while you are working?
你上班的时候，谁照顾孩子？
Ni shang ban de shi hou, shui zhao gu hai zi?

Do you have a clinic with a full-time doctor nearby?
你们附近有没有一个长驻大夫的诊所？
Ni men fu jin you mei you yi ge chang zhu dai fu de zhen suo?

How much does it cost for a visit if you are sick?
每看一次病要付多少钱？
Mei kan yi ci bing yao fu duo shao qian?

Do you get your salary if you are sick and cannot work?
如果你病了不能上班，工资是不是照发？
Ru quo ni bing le bu neng shang ban, gong zi shi bu shi zhao fa?

How much does it cost per day in the hospital?
住院一天要多少钱？
Zhu yuan yi tian yao duo shao qian?

How many days maternity leave does a woman get with pay?
有工资的产假是多少天？
You gong zi de chan jia shi duo shao tian?

If she is nursing her baby, how many hours with pay does she get a
day to feed it?　如果自已照顾婴儿，不扣工资的喂奶时间
一天有几小时？

Ru guo zi ji zhao gu ying er, bu kou gong zi de wei
nai shi jian yi tian you ji xiao shi?

How many years of school have you had?　你上过几年学？

Ni shang guo ji nian xue?

primary	小学	xiao xue
middle	中学	zhong xue
university	大学	da zue
technical school	技术学校	ji shu xue xiao
on-the-job training	在职训练	zai zhi xun lian

Please forgive me if I am asking too personal questions,
如果我的问题人冒昧，希望能得到你的凉解。

Ru guo wo de wen ti tai mao mei, xi wang neng de dao ni de
liang jie,

but I am very curious about the way of life in China.
但是我很想知道中国的生活情况。

Dan shi wo hen xiang zhi dao zhong guo de sheng huo qing kuang.

Are you happy here?
你在这里幸福吗？

Ni zai zhe li xing fu ma?

Do you like the government?
你喜欢这个政府吗？

Ni xi huan zhe ge zheng fu ma?

Do you want your children to study abroad?
你想让你的孩子到国外去读书吗？

Ni xiang rang ni de hai zi dao guo wai qu du shu ma?

I think I can help you.

我想我可以帮你的忙。

Wo xiang wo ke yi bang ni de mang.

I am sorry I cannot help you.

很抱歉，我不能帮你的忙。

Hen bao qian, wo bu neng bang ni de mang.

It is very expensive to travel abroad.

出国路费很贵。

Chu guo lu fei hen gui.

It is very expensive to go to school abroad.

到国外读书要化很多钱。

Dao guo wai du shu yao hua hen duo qian.

I am not wealthy.

我不是一个富裕的人。

Wo bu shi yi ge fu yu de ren.

Especially for Villages

What is the name of this ———? 这个_____叫什么？

zhe ge ——— jiao shen me?

How many people are in this ———? 这个_____有多少人？

zhe ge ——— you duo shao

ren?

commune 公社？

gong she

production brigade 生产大队？

sheng chan da dui

production team 生产队？

sheng chan dui

live here 在这里生活。

zai zhe li sheng huo

work here 在这里工作。

zai zhe li gong zuo

How much money did you make last year?

你去年的收入是多少？

Ni qu nian de shou ru shi duo shao?

Can a woman make the same amount as a man if she does the same job—like drive a truck?

男女是否同工同酬？例如驾驶卡车。

Ran nu shi fou tong gong tong chou? Li ru jia su ka che.

How big is your private vegetable plot?

你的蔬菜自留地有多大？

Ni de shu cai zi liu di you duo da?

(1 hectare = 15 mou; 1 mou = 10 fen)

Do you raise for your own use ———?

你饲养的＿＿是给自已吃的吗？

Ni si yang de ——— shi gei zi ji chi de ma?

     pigs   猪

                 zhu

     poultry   鸡

                 ji

Did you raise enough meat to sell some on the free market?

你饲养的家畜和家禽除自已食用，还有没有多余的
拿到自由市场去卖？

Ni si yang de jia chu he jia qin chu zi ji shi yong, hai you mei you
duo yu de na dao zi you shi chang qu mai?

Did you sell vegetables on the free market?

你在自由市场卖过蔬菜吗？

Ni zai zi you shi chang mai guo shu cai ma?

If so, how much money did you make selling your surplus?

你卖了多少钱？

Ni mai le duo shao qian?

Your household?

这是你的家吗？

Zhe shi ni de jia ma?

How many earners are there in your household?

你家里有几口人？

Ni jia li you ji ge ren zhuan qian?

How many people are there in your household?

你家里有几个人赚钱？

Ni jia li you ji kou ren?

Is there anyone here who speaks English?

这里有人会说英语吗？

Zhe li you ren hui shuo ying yu ma?

Can I meet them?

我能见见他们吗？

Wo neng jian jian ta men ma?

Are your grown-up children living in this village?

你的成年子女住不住在这个村里？

Ni de cheng nian zi nu zhu bu zhu zai zhe ge cun li?

If you are sick and unable to work, does the commune take care of you?

如果你病了不能工作，公社照顾你吗？

Ru guo ni bing le bu neng gong zuo, gong she zhao gu ni ma?

Your family? 你家里的人？

Ni jia li de ren?

What if you have no family? 如果你没有亲属怎么办？

Ru guo ni mei you qin shu zen me ban?

Is there a pension when you get too old to work?

你们有养老金吗？

Ni men you yang lao jin ma?

Do you still have ———? 你们还有_____吗？

Ni men hai you ——— ma?

ancestral tablets 祖宗牌位

zu zong pai wei

ancestral temple 祖庙

zu miao

ancestral family book 家谱

jia pu

Do you decorate the graves during the Qing Ming still?

你们清明还去上掼吗？

Ni men qing ming hai zu shang fen ma?

Is this pond for fish? 这是养鱼池吗？

Zhe shi yang yu chi ma?

ducks? 这是养鸭池吗？

Zhe shi yang ya chi ma?

May I see your ———? 我能看看你们的_____吗？

Wo neng kan kan ni men de ——— ma?

composting techniques 堆肥技术

dui fei ji shi

irrigation system 灌溉系统

guan gai xi tong

old watchtower 老的守望塔

lao de shou Wang ta

retail store 零售店

ling shou dian

tractor 拖拉机

tuo la ji

school 学校

xue xiao

house 房子

fang zi

private plot 自留地

zi liu di

pigs 猪

zhu

source of drinking water 饮水源

yi shui yuan

latrine 厕所

ce suo

clinic—for family planning 诊所——负责节育的

zhen suo—fu ze jie yu de

motorized water pumps 机器水汞

ji qi shui beng

Who takes care of the children while you work?

你工作的时候谁照顾孩子？

Ni gong zuo de shi hou shui zhao gu hai zi?

What is the name of that ———? _____叫什么？

——— jiao shen me?

tree	那棵树
	na ke shu
vegetable	那种菜
	na zhong cai
building	那幢房子
	na zhuang fang zi

Please write down the name here in Chinese so I can have it translated later.

请用中文把名字写在这儿，以后我再让人翻译。

Qing yong zhong wen ba ming zi xie zai zher, xi hou wo zai rang
ren fan yi.

Especially for Factories

How many people work here?

有多少人在这儿工作？

You duo shao ren zai zher gong zuo?

Salary range a month, i.e., lowest-highest?

最高和最低的月工资是多少？

Zui gao he zui di de yue gong zi shi duo shao?

How much do most workers make?

大多数工人的收入是多少？

Da duo shu gong ren de shou ru shi duo shao?

What is the age range?

最年轻和最老的工人的年纪有多大？

Zui nian qing he zui lao de gong ren de nian ji you duo da?

How long does it take to make one
of those?

做一个那样的东西需要多长时间？

Zuo yi ge na yang de dong xi xu yao duo chang shi jian?

days 大
tian

months 月
yue

weeks 星期
xing qi

cooperative? 合作社?
he zuo she?

state-owned? 国有的?
guo you de?

Where do you get your raw materials? 你的原料是从那里来的?
Ni de yuan liao shi cong na li lai de?

Where do you sell most of your products? 你的产品大多在那里出售?
Ni de chan pin da duo zai na li chu shou?

Do you have a store where I could buy something like this?
你们有出售这样产品的商店吗?
Ni men you diu shou zhe yang chan pin de shang dian ma?

How old are you?
你多大岁数啦?
Ni duo da sui shu la?

How many years have you worked here?
你在这里工作几年啦?
Ni zai zhe li gong zuo ji nian la?

How much money do you make a month?
你一个月赚多少钱?
Ni yi ge yue zhuan duo shao qian?

How many hours do you work a week?
你一星期工作多少小时?
Ni yi xing qi gong zuo duo shao xiao shi?

Do you live in factory-provided housing?
你住在厂里给的房子吗?
Ni zhu zai chang li gei de fang zi ma?

How much rent do you pay?

房租多少？

Fang zu duo shao?
2   1   1   3

How many years of training have you had to do this?

你经过多少年的训练才能做这个工作？

Ni jing guo duo shao nian de xun lian cai neng zuo zhe ge gong
3   1   4   4   1   3   2   4   4   2   2   4   4   4   1

zuo?
4

It is interesting.　　很有趣

Hen you qu
3   3   4

        beautiful.　　漂亮

piao liang
4   4

        very difficult.　很难

hen nan
3   2

SHOPPING

For Daily Necessities

What do you recommend for ———?

_____你说吃什么好？

——— ni shuo chi shen me hao?
3   1   1   2   3

motion sickness　晕船（晕车）

yun chuan (yun che)
1   2   1   1

Do you have any ———?　你有_____吗？

ni you ——— ma?
3   3

aspirin　　　　　　　　　阿司匹灵

a si pi ling
1 1 1 2

toothpaste　　　　　　　牙膏

ya gao
2   1

toothbrush　　　　　　　牙刷

ya shua
2   1

razor　　　　　　　　　　剃刀

ti dao
4   1

razor blades　　　　　　剃刀刀片

ti dao dao pian
4   1   1   4

toilet tissue	卫生纸	wei sheng zhi
mild soap	咸性不大的肥皂	xian xing bu da fei zao
hand soap	肥皂	fei zao
laundry detergent	洗衣粉	xi yi fen
shampoo	洗头水	xi tou shui
sanitary napkins	卫生巾	wei sheng jin
sanitary belt	卫生带	wei sheng dai
ball-point pen	圆珠笔	yuan zhu bi
notebook	笔记本	bi ji ben
letter-writing paper	信纸	xin zhi
airmail paper	航空信封	hang kong xin feng
envelopes	信封	xin feng
foreign film	外国胶卷	wai guo jiao juan
something to cover this	可以包扎这个＿＿＿＿的东西。	ke yi bao zha zhe ge ——— dong xi
cut	伤口	shang kou
blister	水疱	shui pao

something to keep my shoe from hurting

有什么东西可以防止我的鞋子把这儿磨疼。

you shen me dong xi ke yi fang zhi wo de xie zi ba zher mo teng

an antiseptic ointment or cream

消炎药膏或软膏

xiao zai yao gao huo ruan gao

menstrual cramps

月经痛

yue jing tong

Mending

Where can I get this mended?	这个在什么地方可以修理？ Zhe ge zai shen me di fang ke yi xiu li?
How soon will it be finished?	多快能修好？ Duo kuai neng xiu hao?
Can it be done faster?	能够快一些吗？ Neng gou kuai yi xie ma?
I will have it done later.	我以后再修。 Wo yi hou zai xiu.
Please do it now.	请你现在就修。 Qing ni xian zai jiu xiu.
How much will it be?	要多少钱？ Yao duo shao qian?

You may not be here when I come to get it. Please write down here
what I should ask for.

我来取的时侯你可能不在。请将我要取的东西写在这儿。

Wo lai qu de shi hou ni ke neng bu zai. Qing jiang wo yao qu de

dong xi xie zai zher.

Shopping in General

Please show me on the map where there is a ———.

请指给我看地图上哪里是＿＿＿＿＿。

Qing zhi gei wo kan di tu shang na li shi ———.

Please take me to a ———.

请带我到一个＿＿＿＿去。

Qing dai wo dao yi ge ——— qu.

Please point the way to a ———.

请指给我看到＿＿＿＿怎么走。

Qing zhi gei wo kan dao ——— zen me zou.

How many blocks is it?

要过几条街？

Yao guo ji tiao jie?

left	左面
	zuo mian
right	右面
	you mian
department store	百货商店
	bai huo shang dian
foreign-language bookstore	外文书店
	wai wen shang dian
cloth store	布店
	bu dian
Arts and Crafts Store	手工艺品商店
	shou gong yi pin shang dian
Friendship Store	友谊商店
	you yi shang dian
Chinese traditional medicine store	中国药店
	zhong guo yao dian
antique store	古董铺
	gu dong pu
more expensive	更贵一些的
	geng gui yi xie de
less expensive	便宜一些的
	pian yi yi xie de
bigger	大一点的
	da yi dian de

smaller

小一点的

xiao yi dian de

Do you have others the same as this?

你还有这样的东西吗？

Ni hai you zhe yang de dong xi ma?

Different color?

不同颜色的？

Bu tong yan se de?

Different design?

不同图案的？

Bu tong tu an de?

How old is this?

这个有多少年了？

Zhe ge you duo shao nian le?

Will I be able to take it out of China?

我能把它带出中国吗？

Wo neng ba ta dai chu zhong guo ma?

What dynasty?

什么朝代的？

Shen me chao dai de?

Can you wrap it so it won't break when I mail it?

能不能把它包好免得会在邮寄时打破。

Neng bu neng ba ta bao hao mian de hui zai you ji shi da po?

Where can I have this wrapped and shipped?

哪里可以包装及运出这个？

Na li ke yi bao zhuang ji yun chu zhe ge?

I'm sorry, I don't have ration coupons.

很抱歉我没有布票。（粮票、工业券）

Hen bao qian wo mei you bu piao. (liang piao, gong ye quan)

I was told I didn't need ration coupons.

人家告诉我我不需要给布票。

Ren jia gao su wo wo bu xu yao gei bu piao.

Will you be getting more within the next three days?

三天之内你们会有更多的来货吗？

San tian zhi nei ni men hui you geng duo de lai huo ma?

Can it be washed in soap and water without damage?

这能用肥皂和水洗吗？

Zhe neng yong fei zao he shui xi ma?
  4   2   2   2   4   2   3 3

Should it be dry-cleaned?

需要不需要干洗？

Xu yao bu xu yao gan xi?
 1   4   1   4   1   3

Arts and crafts—also for Sightseeing

What is it made of?　这是用什么东西做的？

Zhe shi yong shen me dong xi zuo de?
 4   4   4   4

bamboo	竹子 zhu zi 　2	marble	大理石 da li shi 4 3 2
bone	骨头 gu tou 　3	metal alloy	合金 he jin 2 1
brick	砖 zhuan 1	mother-of-pearl	螺母 luo mu 2 3
bronze	铜 tong 2	palm straw	棕榈章 zong lu zhang 1 2 1
carved	雕刻的 diao ke de 1 4	(for baskets and mats) （编篮子和席子用） (bian lan zi he 1 2 xi zi yong) 2 4		
celadon	青瓷 qing ci 1 2		
ceramic	陶瓷 tao ci 2 2	paper	纸 zhi 3
clay	泥 ni 2	pearl	珍珠 zhen zhu 1 1
cloisonné	景泰兰 jing tai lan 3 4 2	plastic	胶料 jiao liao 1 4
coconut	椰子 ye zi 1	rattan	藤 teng 2
coral	珊瑚 shan hu 1 2	rayon	人造纤维 ren zao xian wei 2 4 1 2

cotton	棉花 mian hua	rice husks	谷壳 gu ke
dough (flour mixture)	揉面 rou mian	rice paper	宣纸 xuan zhi
eiderdown	绒毛 rong mao	satin	缎子 duan zi
enamel	搪瓷 tang ci	silk	丝 si
filigree	金丝 jin si	silver	银子 yin zi
glass	玻璃 bo li	soapstone	皂石 zao shi
glaze	釉料 you liao	stone	石头 shi tou
iron	铁 tie	turquoise	松石 song shi
ivory	象牙 xiang ya	wire	铁丝 tie si
gold	金子 jin zi	wood	木头 mu tou
jade	翡翠 fei cui	wool	羊毛 yang mao
lacquer	漆器 qi qi	animal	动物 dong wu
lapis lazuli	青金石 qing jin shi	vegetable	蔬菜 shu cai
leather	皮子 pi zi	mineral	矿石 kuang shi
malachite	孔雀石 kong que shi		

What is it? (Animate objects) 这是什么？
zhe shi shen me?

banyan tree 榕树
rong shu

bird 鸟
niao

bodhisattva (Lohan) 罗汉
luo han

Buddha 佛
fo

camel (two-humped) 骆驼（双峰）
luo tuo (shuang feng)

cypress tree 柏树
bai shu

dragon 龙
long

（five-toed imperial) 五爪金龙
wu zhao jin long

dromedary (one-humped) 单峰骆驼
dan feng luo tuo

emperor 皇帝
huang di

empress 皇后
huang hou

fairy 仙女
xian nu

god 神
shen

goddess 女神
nu shen

goddess of mercy 观音
guan yin

flames
火焰
huo yan

horse
马
ma

imperial family
皇室
huang shi

lion
狮子
shi zı

leaders
领袖
ling xiu

Mao Tse-tung
毛泽东
Mao Ze Dong

Chou En-lai
周恩来
Zhou En Lai

lotus
莲花
lian hua

Lu Hsun (author)
鲁迅（作家）
Lu Xun (zuo jia)

mandarin
橘子
ju zi

monkey
猴子
hou zi

mountains
山
shan

mountains of Kweilin
桂林的山
gui lin de shan

mythical animal
神兽
shen shou

peach
桃子
tao zi

phoenix
凤凰
feng huang

poet	诗人 shi ren		
revolutionary hero	革命英雄 ge ming ying xiong		
Soldier Lei Feng	战士雷锋 Zhan Shi Lei Feng		
Dr. Norman Bethune	白求恩大夫 Bai Qiu En Dai Fu		
revolutionary theme	革命题材 ge ming ti cai		
e.g., episodes on the Long March	如长征组歌 ru chang zheng zu ge		
scales of the dragon	龙鳞 long lin		
scholar	学者 xue zhe		
temple guardian	庙祝 miao zhu		
tiger	老虎 lao hu		
tortoise	龟 gui		
What language?	哪一国文字？ Na yi guo wen zi?		
ancient Chinese	中国古文 zhong guo qu wen	Mongolian	蒙文 meng wen
Arabic	阿拉伯文 a la bo wen	Sanscrit	梵文 fan wen
Chinese	中文 zhong wen	Tibetan	藏文 zang wen
Manchu	满族文 man zu wen		

(Inanimate objects)

What is it?	这是什么？ 4 4 2 Zhe shi shen me?
bell	钟、铃 1 2 zhong, ling
Buddha's footprint	佛的脚印 2 3 4 fo de jiao yin
chariot	战车 4 1 zhan che
cooking utensil	炊具 1 4 chui ju
cosmetic box	化妆品盒 4 1 3 2 hua zhuang pin he
costumes—theatrical	戏装 4 1 xi zhuang
drum	鼓 3 gu
fan	扇子 4 shan zi
food-serving utensils	餐具 1 4 can ju
funeral objects (buried with deceased)	陪葬品 2 4 3 pei zang pin
gong	锣 2 luo
house	房子 2 fang zi
incense burner	香炉 1 2 xiang lu
inkstand	墨水台 4 3 2 mo shui tai
jar	坛子 2 tan zi

jewelry	手饰	shou shi [3] [4]
jug	盂	yu [2]
mask—theatrical	戏台用面具	xi tai yong mian ju [4] [2] [4] [4]
mirror	镜子	jing zi [4]
moon	月亮	yue liang [4] [4]
musical instrument	乐器	yue qi [4] [4]
ornament	装饰品	zhuang shi pin [1] [4] [3]
paperweight	纸镇	zhi zhen [3] [4]
pearl (flaming usually)	夜明珠	ye ming zhu [4] [2] [1]
pillow	枕头	zhen tou [3]
poem	诗	shi [1]
by Chairman Mao	毛主席的诗	mao zhu xi de shi [2] [3] [2] [1]
snuff bottle	鼻烟壶	bi yan hu [2] [1] [2]
spirit screen	招魂幡	zhao hun fan [1] [1]
toilet box	梳妆盒	shu zhuang he [1] [1] [2]
tool	工具	gong ju [1] [4]

toy	玩具 2　4 wan ju
vase	花瓶 1　2 hua ping
water buffalo	水牛 3　2 shui niu
weapon	军器 1　4 jun qi
wheel of the law	法轮 3　2 fa lun
wine goblet	酒杯 3　1 jiu bei
yin-yang symbol	太极图 4　2　2 tai ji tu
calligraphy	书法 1　3 shu fa
carving	雕刻 1　4 diao ke
copy	抄本、摹本、复制品 1　3　2　3　4　4　3 chao bei, mo bei, fu zhi pin
drawing	画 4 hua
embossing	浮雕 2　1 fu diao
embroidery	刺绣 4　4 ci xiou
engraving	雕刻 1　4 diao ke
etching	蚀刻 2　4 shi ke
fresco	壁画 4　4 bi hua

handmade	手工的	shou gong de
ink	墨水	mo shui
machine-made	机制的	ji zhi de
original	原本	yuan ben
print	印刷	yin shua
rubbing	摹拓	mo ta
scroll	卷轴	juan zhou
sculpture	雕塑品	diao su pin
sketch	速写	su xie
watercolor	水彩	shui cai
woodcut	木刻	mu ke
woven photograph	丝织像	si zhi xiang
hand loom	手织机、纺车	shou zhi ji, fang che

Paying

How much does that cost?

那个多少钱？

Na ge duo shao qian?

Please write down that price here.

请你将价钱写在这儿。

Qing ni jiang jia qian xie zai zher.

That's too expensive.

太贵了。

Tai gui le.

How about half the price?

半价怎么样？

Ban jia zen me yang?

How much then?

那样是多少钱？

Na shi duo shao qian?

yuan/kwai/renminbi

元／块／人民币

yuan / kuai / ren min bi

mao (1/10 of a yuan)

毛（1／10元）

mao (1/10 yuan)

fen (coin)

分（硬币）

fen (ying bi)

Do you know how much that is in U.S. money?

你知道合成美金是多少？

Ni zhi dao he cheng mei jin shi duo shao?

Please bring my bill.

请把帐单给我。

Qing ba zhang dan gei wo.

Do I pay you or the cashier?

我把钱付给你还是付给出纳员。

Wo ba qian fu gei ni hai shi fu gei chu na yuan?

I am leaving early tomorrow morning. Can I pay the bill tonight?

我明天一早就走。我可以不可以在今晚付帐？

Wo ming tian yi zao jiu zou. Wo ke yi bu ke yi zai jin wan fu zhang?

May I have a receipt, please?

能给我一个收据吗？

Neng gei wo yi ge shou ju ma?

Can I pay with ———?　我能用＿＿＿＿付款吗？

Wo neng yong ——— fu kuan ma?

a Bank of China traveler's check　中国银行的旅行支票

zhong guo yin hang de lu

xing zhi piao

a foreign traveler's check　外国旅行支票

wai guo lu xing zhi piao

a personal check　私人支票

si ren zhi piao

a company check　公司的支票

gong si de zhi piao

a credit card　信用卡

xin yong ka

BUILDINGS

What is the name of this place?

这个地方叫什么名字？

Zhe ge di fang jiao shen me ming zi?

Please write it in Chinese.

请把它用中文写下来。

Qing ba ta yong zhong wen xie xia lai.

What was it before Liberation?

解放前这个地方是做什么用的？

Jie fan qian zhe ge di fang shi zuo shen me yong de?

What dynasty was it built in?

它是那个朝代建造的？

Ta shi na ge chao dai jian zao de?

What date?

什么年代？

Shen me nian dai?

How high is it?　它有多高？

Ta you duo gao?

stories?　多少层？

duo shao ceng?

meters?	多少公尺？		
	duo shao gong chi?		
Can I get a closer look?	我能走近一些看看吗？		
	Wo neng zou jin yi xie kan kan ma?		
Can I go inside?	我能进去吗？		
	Wo neng jin qu ma?		
What direction is it?	这是什么方向？		
	Zhe shi shen me fang xiang?		
north	北 bei	south	南 nan
east	东 dong	west	西 xi

ancient?	古代的？
	gu dai de?
minorities?	少数民族的？
	shao shu min zu de?
imperial?	宫殿式的？
	gong dian shi de?
modern?	现代的？
	xian dai de?
post-Liberation?	解放后的？
	jie fang hou de?
revolutionary?	革命的？
	ge ming de?
for children?	为孩子的？
	wei hai zi de?
for workers?	为工人的？
	wei gong ren de?
Is it religious?	是不是宗教性的？
	Shi bu shi zong jiao xing de?
ancestral	祖先的
	zu xian de
atheistic	无神论的
	wu shen lun de

Buddhist	佛教的 fo jiao de
Christian	基督教的 ji du jiao de
Confucian	孔教的 kong jiao de
Lamaist/Tibetan	喇嘛的／西藏人的 la ma de / xi zang ren de
Moslem	伊斯兰教的 yi si lan jiao de
Taoist	道教的 dao jiao de
Is it any of these?	它是这其中的一种吗？ Ta shi zhe qi zhong de yi zhong ma?
air-raid shelter	防空洞 fang kong dong
apartment building	公寓 gong yu
aqueduct	沟渠 gou qu
aquarium	水族馆 shui zu guan
archaeological site	考古现场 kao gu xian chang
bridge	桥 qiao
cemetery	公墓 gong mu
church	教堂 jiao tang
cinema	电影院 dian ying yuan

dagoba (Indian stupa)

舍利子塔（印度神龛）
she li zi ta (yin du shen kan)

democracy wall

民主墙
min zhu qiang

drum or bell tower

鼓或钟楼
gu huo zhong lou

exhibition hall

展览馆
zhan lan guan

fort

堡垒
bao lei

factory

工厂
gong chang

garden

花园
hua yuan

gate

大门
da men

hotel

旅馆
lu guan

house

房子
fang zi

kiln

窑
yao

library

图书馆
tu shu guan

military camp

军营
jun ying

moat

护城河
hu cheng he

monastery

寺
si

monument—commemorative

纪念碑
ji nian bei

mosque	清真寺	qing zhen si
museum	博物馆	bo wu guan
observatory	天文台	tian wen tai
office building	办公大楼	ban gong da lou
pagoda	塔	ta
palace	皇宫	huang gong
park	公园	gong yuan
pavilion	馆、楼阁	guan, lou ge
playground	操场	cao chang
restaurant	饭馆	fan guan
resort	胜地	sheng di
school	学校	xue xiao
primary	小学	xiao xue
middle	中学	zhong xue
university	大学	da xue
shipyard	船坞	chuan wu

shrine	神龛	shen kan
sports stadium	运动场	yun dong chang
stele	石碑	shi bei
grave	墓	mu
historical event	历史性的	li shi xing de
poem	诗	shi
subway	地下铁道	di xia tie dao
temple	庙	miao
theater	戏院	xi yuan
tomb	墓	mu
train station	火车站	huo chen zhan
wall	墙	qiang
watchtower	瞭望台	liao wang tai
water tower	水塔	shui ta
zoo	动物园	dong wu yuan

May I take a photo of you?

我能给你拍张照片吗?

Wo neng gei ni pai zhang zhao pian ma?

Please smile.

请微笑。
Qing wei xiao.

Can I have a photo of you and me together?

我能和你合拍一张照片吗？
Wo neng he ni he pai zi zhang zhao pian ma?

I would like to show my friends what nice people there are in China.

我想让我的朋友看看在中国有多么友好的人。
Wo xiang rang wo de peng you kan kan zai zhong guo you duo me
you hao de ren.

I would like to show my friends who cannot visit China what things look like here. 我想让我那些不能来访问中国的朋友看看
中国是什么样子。
Wo xiang rang wo na xie bu neng lai fang wen zhong guo de peng
you kan kan zhong guo shi shen me yang zi.

Could you please take my photo in front of this place with my camera?

请用我的照像机给我在这里拍一张照。
Qing yong wo de zhao xiang ji gei wo zai zhe li pai yi zhang zhao.

It is all set. Just press here. 都对好了，你只要在这里按一下。
Dou dui hao le. Ni zhi yao zai zhe li an
yi xia.

Closer. 靠近一些。
Kao jin yi xie.

Back up. 退后一些。
Tui hou yi xie.

I'm sorry, I don't have any more film.

对不起我没有胶卷了。
Dui bu qi, wo mei you jiao juan le.

I'm sorry, I didn't know I couldn't take photographs here.

对不起，我不知道不许在这儿拍照。
Dui bu qi, wo bu zhi dao bu xu zai zher pai zhao.

May I have my camera back?

能将我的照像机还给我吗？
Neng jiang wo de zhao xiang ji huan gei wo ma?

Where can I get film developed?
哪里可以冲洗胶卷？
Na li ke yi chong xi jiao juan?

Black and white?
黑白的。
Hei bai de?

Color slides?
彩色幻灯片？
Cai se huan deng pian?

Color prints?
彩色照片？
Cai se zhao pian?

Do you cut the film and mount the slides?
你们切装幻灯片吗？
Ni men qie zhuang huan deng pian ma?

How much for each print?
印一张多少钱？
Yinyi zhang duo shao qian?

How long will it take?
要多长时间？
Yao duo chang shi jian?

What size film do you have?
你们有几号胶卷？
Ni men you ji hao jiao juan?

Do you have any foreign film?
你们有外国胶卷吗？
Ni men you wai guo jiao juan ma?

ENTERTAINMENT

Is there a good cultural presentation on now in this city?
现在这里有没有一个好的文艺节目在上演？
Xian zai zhe li you mei you yi ge hao de wen yi jie mu zai shang
yan?

movie　　　　电影　　　　ballet　　　　芭蕾舞
dian ying　　　　　　　　　　　ba lei wu

acrobats	杂技 za ji	traditional opera	京戏 jing xi
play	话剧 hua ju	martial arts	武术 wu shu
puppet	木偶戏 mu ou xi	concert	音乐会 yin yue hui
Chinese	中国的 zhong guo de	foreign	外国的 wai guo de
English subtitles	英文字幕 ying wen zi mu	sports competition	运动比赛 yun dong bi sai

Where can I buy tickets? 在哪里买票？
Zai na li mai piao?

What is the address?
什么地方？
Shen me di fang?

I would like tickets ———. 我要＿＿＿＿票。
Wo yao ——— piao.

 for today. 今天的。
jin tian de.

 for tomorrow. 明天的。
ming tian de.

 for the day after tomorrow. 后天的。
hou tian de.

What are the times? 有那些时间的？
You na xie shi jian de?

How much do the best seats cost? 最好的座位多少钱一张？
Zui hao de zuo wei duo shao qian
yi zhang?

Do you have seats close to the stage so I can take photographs?
有没有靠近舞台可以让我拍照的位子？
You mei you kao jin wu tai ke yi rang wo pai zhao de wei zi?

How about an aisle seat?

侧厢的座位怎么样？

Ce xiang de zuo wei zen me yang?

Is the theater air-conditioned?

戏院有冷气吗？

Xi yuan you leng qi ma?

Is the theater heated?

戏院有暖气吗？

Xi yuan you nuan qi ma?

What time is the performance over?

演出什么时候完？

Yan chu shen me shi hou wan?

Will you be my guest?

我请你看好吗？

Wo qing ni kan hao ma?

Can you buy the tickets for me?

你能代我买票吗？

Ni neng dai wo mai piao ma?

Where will I meet you?

我们在哪里碰头？

Wo men za na li peng tou?

What time?

什么时候？

Shen me shi hou?

I have to cancel my tickets.

我得退票。

Wo dei tui piao.

Can I have my money back?

能把钱退给我吗？

Neng ba qian tui gei wo ma?

Would you like to use my tickets instead?

你愿意要我的票吗？

Ni yuan yi yao wo de piao ma?

Can we go backstage to meet the performers?

我们能去后台看看演员吗？

Wo men neng qu hou tai kan kan yan yuan ma?

I must tell you how very much I enjoyed the performance.

我一定要告诉你我是多么欣赏你的演出。

Wo yi ding yao gao su ni wo shi duo me xin shang ni de yan chu.

I hope someday you can come to perform in my country.

我希望有一天你能来我的国家演出。

Wo xi wang you yi tian ni neng lai wo de guo jia yan chu.

May I touch your costumes?

我能摸摸你的戏装吗？

Wo neng mo mo ni de xi zhuang ma?

May I touch your musical instruments?

我能摸一摸你的乐器吗？

Wo neng mo yi mo ni de yue qi ma?

May I take a photograph with you?

我能和你合拍一张照片吗？

Wo neng he ni he pai yi zhang zhao pian ma?

Can you show me how this works?

你能告诉我这个怎么用？

Ni neng gao su wo zhe ge zen me yong?

How much training have you had?

你受过多久的训练？

Ni shou guo duo jiu de xun lian?

At what age did you start?

几岁开始的？

Ji sui kai shi de?

Will you be giving another performance here?

你在这里还将再演出一次吗？

Ni zai zhe li hai jiang zai yan chu yi ci ma?

When?

什么时候？

Shen me shi hou?

Will it be the same?

还是这个节目吗？

Hai shi zhe ge jie mu ma?

Where is there a dance party in this city?

这个城市里什么地方有午会？

Zhe ge cheng shi li shen me di fang you wu hui?

When? What day and time?

什么时候？那一天？几点钟？

Shen me shi hou? Na yi tian? Ji dian zhong?

How much does it cost?

多少钱？

Duo shao qian?

MISCELLANEOUS

Colors

red	红色	hong se	blue	蓝色	lan se
orange	橙色	cheng se	purple	紫色	zi se
yellow	黄色	huang se	black	黑色	hei se
green	绿色	lu se	brown	褐色	he se

Directions

near	近	jin	far	远	yuan
up	上	shang	down	下	xia
above	上面	shang mian	below	下面	xia mian
inside	里面	li mian	outside	外面	wai mian
right	右	you	left	左	zuo
center	中间	zhong jian			

Months of the Year

January	一月 yi yue	July	七月 qi yue
February	二月 er yue	August	八月 ba yue
March	三月 san yue	September	九月 jiu yue
April	四月 si yue	October	十月 shi yue
May	五月 wu yue	November	十一月 shi yi yue
June	六月 liu yue	December	十二月 shi er yue

Days of the Week

Sunday	星期天 xing qi tian	Thursday	星期四 xing qi si
Monday	星期一 xing qi yi	Friday	星期五 xing qi wu
Tuesday	星期二 xing qi er	Saturday	星期六 xing qi liu
Wednesday	星期三 xing qi san		

Today, Yesterday, and Tomorrow

today 今天 jin tian
yesterday 昨天 zuo tian
tomorrow 明天 ming tian

Seasons

spring	春	chun	summer	夏	xia
autumn	秋	qiu	winter	冬	dong

Terms and Names

attendant (term used for room boy, waitress)
服务员
fu wu yuan
2 4 2

interpreter (term used for guide)
翻译
fan yi
1 4

cadre (also leading member)
干部
gan bu
4

management committee
管理委员会
guan li wei yuan hui
3 3 3   4

party member
党员
dang yuan
3   2

Communist Party of China
中国共产党
zhong guo gong chan dang
1   2   4   3   3

Politburo
政治局
Zheng Zhi Ju
4   4 2

State Council
国务院
Guo Wu Yuan
2   4   4

peasant
农民
nong min
2   2

worker
工人
gong ren
1   2

People's Liberation Army
中国解放军
Zhong Guo Jie Fang Jun
1   2   3   4   1

Four Modernizations
四个现代化
Si Ge Xian Dai Hua
4 4   4   4   4

agriculture
农业
nong ye
2   4

national defense
国防
guo fang
2   2

technology
技术
ji shu
4   4

science	科学	ke xue
Is there a campaign on now?	现在有运动吗？	Xian zai you yun dong ma?
Chairman Mao	毛主席	Mao Zhu Xi
socialism	社会主义	she hui zhu yi
dictatorship of the proletariat	无产阶级专政	wu chan jie ji zhuan zheng
democratic centralism	民主集中制	min zhu ji zhong zhi
Gang of Four	四人帮	Si Ren Bang

Numbers

one	一	yi	eleven	十一	shi yi
two	二	er	twelve	十二	shi er
three	三	san	twenty	二十	er shi
four	四	si	twenty-one	二十一	er shi yi
five	五	wu	thirty	三十	san shi
six	六	liu	forty	四十	si shi
seven	七	qi	fifty	五十	wu shi
eight	八	ba	hundred	百	bai
nine	九	jiu	thousand	千	qian
ten	十	shi	ten thousand	万	wan

MILESTONES IN CHINESE HISTORY

The Chinese interpret history in Marxist terms, pointing out that dynasties fell primarily because of peasant unrest and uprisings. Roughly, this is how they see history (here with place names in the new spelling and historical names in the old). See "Quick Reference" for new spellings of dynasties.

c. 1,000,000–4000 years ago—primitive society.

c. 21st century–476 B.C.—slave society. Slave holders owned all the means of production including slaves captured in wartime. Slaves were killed and buried with their deceased owners supposedly to continue their work of servitude in the afterworld.

475 B.C.–A.D. 1840—feudal society. While slaves were kept after the end of the 5th century, slave holders ceased to own all the means of production. A new class of landowners found that giving slaves some freedom resulted in better production. Land was contracted to them as serfs in return for a large part of the harvest. If the serf did not produce, the fields were contracted to someone else. The transition to feudal society took place in the Warring States period, and after 476 B.C. slaves were no longer sacrificed.

1840–1919—semi-colonial and semi-feudal society. Pure feudalism ended with the Opium Wars and the advent of foreign domination. In 1919 the May 4th Movement marshaled anti-imperialist and nationalistic sentiments.

The Chinese also call *1912–1927* the period of the First Revolutionary War, which failed when Chiang Kai-shek betrayed the revolution and massacred the Communists. They also consider this war a failure because of the divisions within the Communist Party itself.

August 1927–July 1937 was the Second Revolutionary War, a period of armed struggle against the Nationalists and the warlords from the first armed Communist uprising to the beginning of the Japanese war.

In July 1937 the Japanese invaded China and there was some attempt at cooperation between the Communists and Nationalists again. After the Japanese surrender in 1945, the civil war resumed. That war and the semi-colonial and semi-feudal society ended with Liberation in 1949. Now is the socialist society.

With earlier dates approximations, the milestones are:

c. 8,000,000 years ago—Ramapithecus (Lufeng, Yunnan).

c. 1,000,000 years ago—Yuanmou Man.

c. 600,000–700,000 years ago—Lantian Man.

c. 400,000–500,000 years ago—Peking Man. (See Zhoukoudian under "Beijing.")

c. 20,000–30,000 years ago—Liuchiang Man (Guangxi), Hotao Man (Inner Mongolia), and Upper Cave Man (Zhoukoudian).

c. 5,000–7,000 years ago—Lungshan Culture (Shandong) and Yangshao Culture (Henan). (See "Xi'an"—Banpo Museum.)

Dynastic dates overlap because different dynasties controlled different parts of China at the same time. Eastern and Western usually refer to periods of the same dynasty with different capitals, e.g., Changan or Luoyang. Northern and Southern Sung refer to the Kaifeng and Hangzhou capitals.

c. 21st–16th centuries B.C.—HSIA: beginning of the slave system; irrigation and flood control work; rudimentary calendar; the earliest form of writing. (Some scholars now say the first writing dates from 2400 to 2300 B.C.)

c. 16th–11th centuries B.C.—SHANG: earliest glazes, wine, and silk; highly developed bronze casting primarily of ritual vessels; jade handles on swords and spears; ivory cup inlaid with jade; iron; cowry shells used for money; trade outside of China; development of writing; ancestor worship; divination by tortoise shells; beginning of cities (Zhengzhou and Anyang). Celadon.

c. 11th century–771 B.C.—WESTERN CHOU and 770–249 B.C.—EASTERN CHOU: welded bronze; flat building tiles; first lacquer; copper coins; crossbows; walled cities; elaborate rituals and music using jade as well as bronze vessels.

770–476 B.C.—SPRING AND AUTUMN PERIOD: warring states fighting for power; Confucius preached a return to the Chou rituals and tried to stabilize society by insisting on obedience to the emperor, father, husbands, older brothers, etc. Beginnings of feudalism; cylindrical tile sewer pipes; iron implements and oxen for plowing; steel; metal spade-shaped coins; knowledge of multiplication tables, mathematics, astronomy; medicine.

475–221 B.C.—WARRING STATES: transitional period to feudalism; *Master Sun's Art of War* written; Taoism, Mohism, and Mencius; first large scale irrigation and dams including erosion control; iron farm tools widely used; mining; use of arch in tomb and bridge building; discovery of magnets; carpenter's saw, plane, and square; manure for fertilizer; salt production; medical diagnosis through feeling the pulse; the first books on astronomy.

221–206 B.C.—CHIN: unification of China for the first time; building of Great Wall; standardization of weights and measures; strict legal code; unification of currency; standardization of writing; first clay burial figures; the burning of all historical records except those dealing with the Chin, medicine, and agriculture; the execution of some scholars.

206 B.C.–A.D. 220—EASTERN AND WESTERN HAN: water wheel, windmill, the first plant-fiber paper, seismograph, water-powered bellows for smelting;

first important Chinese medical text; the first armillary sphere; the discovery that moonlight comes from the sun; the use of general anaesthesia in surgical operations, and acupuncture and moxibustion; jade burial suits and gold-coated bronze; Szuma Chien, China's first historian.

2nd century B.C.—14th century A.D.—The Silk Road: The Chinese exchanged silk, tea, iron and steel, knowledge of deep-well digging, paper making, peach and pear trees. They received grapes, pomegranate and walnut trees, sesame, coriander, spinach, the Fergana horse, alfalfa, Buddhism, Nestorianism, and Islam. Trade was with India, West Asia, and even Rome, and the main stops in China west from Xi'an were Lanzhou, Wuwei, Dunhuang, north through Turpan or south through Ruoqiang. Arab and Persian traders settled in Xi'an and Yangzhou (Yangchow).

A.D. 68—First Buddhist temple built by Emperor Han Ming-ti in Luoyang.

220–265—THREE KINGDOMS (Wei, Shu, and Wu): development of a water pump, celadon, and ships big enough to carry 3,000 men.

265–420—WESTERN AND EASTERN TSIN and 420–589—SOUTHERN (Sung, Chi, Liang, Chen) and NORTHERN (Wei, Chi, Chou) DYNASTIES: first arched stone bridge, widespread use of celadon, two crops a year. Northern Wei dynasty started Buddhist statues at Luoyang and Datong.

581–618—SUI: built the Grand Canal (2,000 km. long), ships up to 70 meters long, and an arched stone bridge still in use today (Zhaoxian county, Hebei).

618–907—TANG: one of China's most prosperous and culturally developed dynasties; three-color glazes, snow-white fine porcelains, inlaid mother-of-pearl, gold and silver, wood-block printing, fine silks, the weaving of feathers; water wheel and adjustable curved-shaft plow; attempt at land reform; the most prosperous period of the Silk Road and the opening of a special office for foreign trade in Guangzhou, a city where a mosque was built by Arab traders; cultural expansion—Tang princess took Buddhism to Tibet; Chinese monks took Buddhism to Japan and Korea (Kyoto is modeled on Xi'an); Chinese monk Hsuan Tsang went to India 629–645 to obtain Buddhist sutras. Chinese travelers also went to Persia, Arabia, and Byzantium; Tang poets still the most famous. Look for fat faces in paintings and sculptures—they are most likely Tang.

907–960—FIVE DYNASTIES (Liang, Later Tang, Later Tsin, Later Han, Later Chou): a transitional warring period.

916–1125—LIAO: controlled Inner Mongolia and part of southern Manchuria; invaded China and occupied Beijing; built extant 66.6-meter wooden pagoda, Ying Xian, Shaanxi.

960–1279—NORTHERN AND SOUTHERN SUNG: another of the most prosperous and culturally developed dynasties; first paper money, moveable type, compass, gunpowder, rocket-propelled spears; fine porcelains; red lacquer; the development of acupuncture and moxibustion; progress in mining and metallurgy; Hangzhou, then known as Qinsai, was the largest, richest city in the world.

1038–1227—WESTERN HSIA: controlled today's Gansu and western Inner Mongolia.

1245—Franciscan friars arrived at Inner Mongolia.

1115–1234—KIN (a.k.a. CHIN): captured Beijing and controlled Kaifeng, the Wei River valley, Inner Mongolia, and northwestern China.

1271–1368—YUAN (a.k.a. Mongol): water clock; improved cotton spinning and weaving; developed blue-and-white and underglaze red porcelain; cloisonne; controlled all of today's China and areas north and east including Moscow, Kiev, Damascus, Baghdad, and Afghanistan.
1275–92—Marco Polo visited China, serving in court of Kublai Khan.

1368–1644—MING: imported corn, potato, tobacco, peanut, sunflower, tomato (seeds that is) from America; refined blue-and-white porcelain; polychrome porcelain; sea links with Malacca, Java, Ceylon, East Africa; opium first introduced as a narcotic.
1513—First European to south China—Jorge Alvares of Portugal.
1557—Macao "lent" to the Portuguese.
1582—First Christian missionary, Matteo Ricci, S.J., to Macao and then in *1601* to Beijing.
1623—Dutch colony in "Formosa," a.k.a. Taiwan—until 1662.

1644–1911—CHING (a.k.a. Manchu): made some of the best porcelains in early part of dynasty; had to cope most with foreign powers; Cheng Chengkung, a.k.a. Koxinga, drove out Dutch from Taiwan; expanded into Russia, Korea, Vietnam, Burma, Sikkim at first, but later lost a great deal of territory.
1683—Taiwan became part of China.
1757—All foreign trade in south confined to Chinese trading associations (Cohongs) in Guangzhou (Canton). Families of foreign traders live in Macao.
1784—First U.S. trading ship, *Empress of China*—Guangzhou.
1793—First British mission—Lord Macartney.
1807—First Protestant missionary, Robert Morrison of Britain.
1830—First U.S. missionaries.
1839—Chinese attempted to stop opium trade. Burned 20,000 chests near Guangzhou, more than half one year's trade.
1840–42—Opium War, mainly over freedom to trade with China and of course British objection to the government's opium policy. Britain needed to sell China opium to balance trade. British forces with French help seized a few cities along the coast and threatened Nanjing. The Chinese gave in, ceding Hong Kong to Britain and opening to foreign trade Guangzhou (Canton), Xiamen (Amoy), Fuzhou (Foochow), Ningbo (Ningpo), and Shanghai. This was the beginning of the foreign exploitation of a militarily weak, and badly-led China until 1949. Also involved were Germany, Italy, Japan, Belgium, Russia and the U.S.
1841—Uprising of people of Sanyuanli, Guangzhou, against the foreign imperialists.
1844—Treaty of Wang-hsia. First U.S. treaty with China.
1844—Emperor agreed to tolerate Christian churches.
1848–50—Chinese emigration to America and Australia started.
1851–64—Taiping Heavenly Kingdom, a rebellion against the Manchus led by a Christianity-inspired Cantonese who believed himself the younger brother of Jesus Christ. Starting in January 1851 in Jin Ting Village, Guangxi. This was the largest peasant movement in Chinese history. At one time or another it occupied most of China, including Zhejiang (but not Shanghai), Guilin, Suzhou,

and almost Chongqing. It established a capital at Nanjing for eleven years, where there is now a Taiping museum. It was defeated in part by a foreign mercenary army led by a British officer Charles Gordon, known as Chinese Gordon, who was later killed in the Sudan. "Taiping" means "great peace."

1856–60—Second Anglo-Chinese War, a.k.a. Arrow war, and more unequal treaties. British took Kowloon.

1860—British and French sacked Beijing, burned down Summer Palace.

1870—China started to send thirty students a year to U.S. to study. Students also to Britain and France.

1870—Tientsin Massacre of French missionaries (see "Tianjin").

1885—French took Vietnam (then a tributary state of China) and turned over Taiwan and Pescadores to China.

1886—British took Burma.

1895—Sino-Japanese War. Japan took Taiwan, the Pescadores, and the Liaoning peninsula from China.

1898—Britain leased area north of Kowloon and about 235 islands around Hong Kong for 99 years.

1898–1908—The Kuang Hsu Emperor kept under house arrest by Empress Dowager Tzu Hsi for defying her and passing reforms that attempted to modernize China.

1899—"Open Door" notes on China, whereby the U.S. unilaterally declared that foreign powers should not cut up China into colonies, that all nations should be free to trade with China. Only Britain bothered to reply, but because of these notes, China looked for a while to the U.S. as its only foreign friend.

1900—Boxer Rebellion, a.k.a. the Rebellion of the Society of the Righteous and Harmonious Fists, a reaction, at times encouraged by the Manchu Empress Dowager, against the increasing foreign domination of China. Attacks on foreigners and Chinese Christians. (See "Beijing.") Foreign powers, including the Americans, responded by capturing Beijing, sacking it, and forcing another humiliating treaty on China.

1904—Russian-Japanese War fought on Chinese soil. A year later southern Manchuria taken by Japanese.

1908—Death of Empress Dowager. Succeeded by two-year-old Pu-yi.

April 1911—Most important of several small abortive attempts by Dr. Sun Yat-sen against the Qing. Huanghuagang Insurrection, Guangzhou.

October 10, 1911—First victory of Sun Yat-sen's republican revolutionists following an accidental explosion in one of their bomb factories. Hankou.

January 1, 1912—Dr. Sun Yat-sen declared provisional president of the Chinese Republic, with its capital at Nanjing.

1912—Outer Mongolia with Russian help declared independence from China.

1913—Yuan Shih-kai elected president of the new republic.

August 27, 1914—Japan declared war on Germany. Under guise of attacking German concession at Kiaochow Japanese troops gained foothold in China, also taking over naval base at Qingdao (Tsingtao).

1915—Yuan agreed to many of Japan's Twenty-one Demands. Much protest. More protest after Yuan proclaimed himself emperor.

June 11, 1916—Death of Yuan in Beijing of heart attack. Warlords controlled country.

1917—China sent coolies to France to dig trenches along Western Front.

1919—Versailles Treaty concluding World War I. Japanese kept gains in China. Western powers retained their pre-war concessions.

May 4, 1919—Student demonstrations against the Versailles Treaty mark the beginning of the nationalistic and cultural upsurge known as the *May Fourth Movement*, the training ground for many Communist revolutionaries.

July 1, 1921—Founding of the Chinese Communist Party in Shanghai with Russian Communist help, although the Soviets, for tactical reasons, preferred to support Sun Yat-sen.

1923—Sun Yat-sen agreed to cooperate with Russian and Chinese Communists. Chiang Kai-shek sent to Moscow for military training. Mikhail Borodin and General Vassily Blucher arrived as advisers. Communists were allowed to join the Nationalist Party as individuals. Sun Yat-sen could not be sure of help from Britain and America.

1924—Chiang Kai-shek established Whampoa Military Academy, Guangzhou, with Chou En-lai in charge of political indoctrination. The Soviet Union voluntarily gave up privileges and concessions in China and recognized Outer Mongolia as part of China.

March 12, 1925—Dr. Sun died of cancer in Beijing.

May 30, 1925—Demonstrations in the International Settlement in Shanghai.

1926—Northern Expedition started out led by Generalissimo Chiang Kai-shek and Whampoa-trained officers with Communist cooperation and Soviet supplies. It attempted to unify China, wrest control from the warlords, and fight the unequal treaties. The Nationalists aimed for support from merchants, landlords, and warlords; the Communists concentrated on the peasants and urban proletariat.

March 1927—The Northern Expedition took Nanjing.

April 12, 1927—Chiang purged Communists in Shanghai. Chou En-lai escaped. Chiang later killed Communists in other cities.

August 1, 1927—Nanchang Uprising. Founding date of the Chinese Red Army. (See ''Nanchang.'')

April 18, 1927—Chiang declared Nanjing his capital.

September 8, 1927—Autumn Harvest Uprising led by Mao. Miners from Anyuan, some students, peasant cadres, and a peasant militia set out to take Changsha. Ill-prepared, they withdrew to Jinggang Shan (Chingkang Mountains), Jiangxi (Kiangsi), where they met up with the army from the Nanchang Uprising and established the first Chinese soviet, distributing land to the peasants in the area.

June 4, 1928—Nationalists took Beijing, renaming it Peiping (Northern Peace).

1930—Communists unsuccessfully attacked Nanchang and Changsha. Chiang retaliated with three ''extermination'' campaigns which almost succeeded against Jinggang Shan.

September 18, 1931—Japanese invaded Manchuria and set up puppet government under Pu-yi. Chiang returned to Nanjing to head the defense. With no international help available, Chiang accepted a humiliating truce in 1933.

1933—Chiang renewed attack on Communists on Jinggang Shan with a ''scorched earth'' policy.

October 16, 1934—The Communists, aware they could no longer hold their base on Jinggang Shan, started out with 80,000 troops on what is now known as the *Long March*. It was not until they arrived three months later in Xunyi (Tsunyi), Guizhou (Kweichow), that they decided on northern Shaanxi as their goal, since that was the only Communist base big enough. In addition, there was the added incentive of being able to fight the Japanese invaders in that area. At that meeting also, Mao Tse-tung took over as leader of the March.

From Xunyi, the march continued in spite of Nationalist bombs and persistent Nationalist pursuers. The major battles were fought at Loushan Pass (February 1935) and Luting suspension bridge over the Tatu River, which forward units had to cross on its three chains under fire, the enemy having ripped up most of the wooden floor boards. There were uninhabited grasslands, snow-capped 16,000-foot mountains, and hostile tribesmen. Edgar Snow gives a good account of the march in *Red Star Over China*. Some of the important battles have been immortalized in ivory or porcelain.

During the Long March, the original Central Army was joined by other Communist armies. It officially ended in Wuqi in northern Shaanxi on October 20, 1935. For the original marchers now reduced to 8,000, including thirty women, it had been a journey of 12,500 kilometers.

From Wuqi, the Communists eventually moved to Bao An where Edgar Snow visited them and researched his classic book. The move to Yan'an was made in January, 1937 (see "Yan'an").

1934—Chinese Communists declared war on Japan but Chiang concentrated on eliminating the Communists.

1936—Xi'an Incident. Chiang kidnapped by one of his own officers at Huaqing Hot Spring and forced into a wartime coalition with the Communists against the Japanese.

July 7, 1937—Marco Polo Bridge Incident. Killing of Japanese soldiers near Beijing set off *1937–45* war between Japan and China. Japan occupied most urban areas. Chiang moved capital to Hankou and finally to Chongqing (Chungking). Western powers remained neutral. Many warlords with their private armies rallied in fight against Japanese. Badly armed, the warlords were destroyed.

Although Nationalists blocked supply routes, Communist Eighth Route Army and New Fourth Army waged guerrilla warfare against Japanese, engaged in political and economic work among peasants, and developed strategy, discipline, and plans for takeover of rest of China. (See "Yan'an.")

1938—Canadian surgeon Dr. Norman Bethune joined Eighth Route Army and died the following year of blood poisoning while operating without antiseptics. Because of his skills at improvisation and selfless devotion to duty, Bethune later became a Chinese national hero. (See "Shijiazhuang.")

December 7, 1941—The U.S. declared war after Japan's attack on Pearl Harbor. It increased aid to Chiang via the Burma Road until 1942, and then via transport planes over the Himalayan "hump" to Chongqing and Kunming. U.S. tried to reconcile Mao and Chiang against the Japanese.

1943—Treaties with U.S. and Britain abolishing concessions and extraterritorial rights. At the Cairo Conference, Chiang promised to make more effort to fight Japan; Roosevelt and Churchill promised more military aid and China's repossession of Manchuria, Taiwan and the Pescadores after Japan's defeat.

February 1945—Yalta Conference declared Outer Mongolia to be independent, Manchuria to be under Russian sphere of influence.

August 6 & 9, 1945—U.S. dropped atomic bombs on Hiroshima and Nagasaki, Japan. Russia invaded Manchuria.

August 14, 1945—Japanese surrender. Lin Piao, leading Communist Army, advanced into Manchuria to receive Japanese surrender. Chou En-lai and Mao Tse-tung met with Chiang in Chongqing.

October 1945—Nationalists and Communists clashed in Manchuria.

November 1945—Chongqing talks broke off. U.S. President Truman ordered end of all aid to Nationalists, because the U.S. would otherwise be involved in a civil war. Civil war continued. Communists advanced because of severe inflation, Nationalist government corruption, breakdown of law and order, mass Nationalist troops defections, and the Communists' exemplary work in winning the hearts and minds of the peasants.

October 1, 1949—Known as *Liberation*. Chairman Mao proclaimed the birth of the People's Republic of China from the Gate of Heavenly Peace in Beijing. Later Chiang and troops and officials loyal to him fled to Taiwan. Refugees flooded Hong Kong. Communists tried but failed to take offshore islands of Matsu and Quemoy across from Taiwan.

December 1949—Mao visited Moscow.

February 1950—Sino-Soviet Treaty of Friendship and Alliance.

1950—Trials started against landlords. Two million people believed executed. Social reforms instigated. Remolding of intellectuals.

January 5, 1950—Britain resumed diplomatic relations.

1950–1953—Land reform. .15–.45 acres per peasant.

1950–51—Campaign to assert control over Tibet opposed by Khamba tribesmen. People's Liberation Army (PLA) took Tibet, September 1951.

1950—North Korea invaded south. In October, Chinese forces joined North Koreans after United Nations and South Koreans counterattacked north of 38th parallel border and threatened China.

In China, many foreign missionaries, teachers, and scholars jailed and then expelled as imperialist spies. China accused U.S. of poison gas and germ warfare and circulated maps showing American bases surrounding China. U.S. and Canada decided against resuming diplomatic relations.

1951—Americans began an embargo which wasn't lifted until the 1970s.

1953—China started to use Hong Kong and Macao as trading centers and sources of foreign exchange.

1954—Chiang signed mutual defense treaty with U.S.; French defeat and beginning of U.S. involvement in Indochina.

1954–55—Countryside reorganized into cooperatives with pooling of labor and land.

1955—Bandung Conference of nonaligned nations of Asia and Africa to continue "struggle against imperialism and colonialism" and to assert idea of peaceful coexistence. Attended by Chou En-lai.

1955—Khamba rebellion in Tibet.

1956–57—*Hundred Flowers Movement*. Free expression of opinion temporarily encouraged.

1957—*Anti-Rightist Campaign*. Public criticism and jailing of "Rightists," many of whom were not released until 1978.

1958–60—Great Leap Forward. Mobilization of masses to increase production; communes established; backyard furnaces smelted scrap metals. Mao resigned presidency to concentrate on this campaign, which apologists claim succeeded because it mobilized the masses. In 1979 the Chinese leadership admitted it was an economic disaster.

August 1958—Chinese attempted to capture Quemoy. Russia refused to give help, except to threaten retaliation if the Americans intervened. Nationalist air force outfought the Communists.

1959—Mao accused Russians of being revisionists, or giving in to capitalism and to nuclear blackmail. Chinese rejected Russia's offer of nuclear weapons in exchange for bases in China. Dalai Lama fled to India.

June 1960—Bucharest Conference. Rift between Russia and China became extremely bitter.

1959–62—Period of extreme economic difficulties due to "natural calamities." Some scholars also blame bad planning. Government insisted on repaying Russians for military aid immediately.

August 1960—Khrushchev ordered end of all Soviet aid to China. Advisers left many unfinished projects and took the plans back to Russia.

1962—Liu Shao-chi became president. Mao chairman of the Communist Party.

October 1962—India asserted control of disputed border territory. China sent punitive invasion force into India. It defeated the Indians and then unilaterally announced ceasefire in November and withdrew.

1963—China started to supply Hong Kong with fresh water.

October 1964—First atomic bomb exploded at Lop Nor testing grounds in Xinjiang (Sinkiang).

1964—Chiang Ching, wife of Mao Tse-tung, started campaign to make culture serve the revolution. Traditional Peking opera abolished. From this time until her downfall, only eight revolutionary operas allowed, all written by committees.

1965—PLA under Lin Piao abolished all outward display of rank.

November 1965—Publication of article instigated by Mao in a Shanghai daily *Wen Hui Pao* brought the Cultural Revolution into the public eye for the first time.

May 25, 1966—First important "Big Character Poster" put up at Beijing University.

July 29, 1966—Chairman Mao swam the Yangtze River at Wuhan (9 miles) to show he was still powerful.

August 18, 1966—First of many Red Guard rallies in Tian Anmen Square, Beijing, in support of Chairman Mao with PLA Commander Lin Piao at his side. Schools closed so that students could travel and learn how to make revolution. From this time until the end of the Cultural Revolution, much violence took place; the British embassy was sacked (August 22, 1967) by a group of extremists called the May 16th Detachment, which also took over the Foreign Ministry and the media at the same time.

The *Great Proletarian Cultural Revolution* was started by Chairman Mao to regain lost power, an attempt to return to his ideals of the Chinese Communist revolution. Supporters of "revisionism" as propagated by President Liu Shao-chi had been promoting, among other things, an intellectual elite and an urban base. One big quarrel was over which incentives to use to increase production: bonuses versus pure political idealism. Liu wanted bonuses. (He was to succeed in 1978.)

Chairman Mao had always taught that the workers and the peasants, not the intellectuals, are the basis of the Chinese revolution. So as Mao regained his power with Red Guard and army help, many party cadres were sent to May Seventh Cadre Schools to be reeducated in the "correct" political thinking by learning to respect and love physical labor. Police chiefs pounded beats; doctors swept floors to help them identify with the masses and understand their problems. Officials who took privileges like personal use of office cars and the acceptance of "gifts" were violently attacked.

Red Guards, riding free on the trains and sleeping in school dormitories while fed by the municipalities, traveled around the country taking part in revolutionary movements such as the "Four Olds." In this, they physically destroyed many religious statues, buildings, ancestral tablets, and opposed many of the old virtues like long life, happiness, and personal wealth. They changed the names of streets and parks from old dynastic names to "The East Is Red" and "Liberation," stripped some women of their tight trousers (it was the style then), and cut off long "bourgeois" hair. They sought to eliminate "old ideas, old culture, old customs, and old habits." They also attacked elements of foreign influence. They believed all these were obstacles to completing the course of the revolution. Teng Hsiao-ping was denounced. Liu was deposed in 1968 and has since died. He was officially rehabilitated in 1979.

1967—Communist-inspired riots in Macao and Hong Kong.

1969—Border clashes with Soviet Union. Schools reopened with emphasis on "more red than expert." Students were chosen for university, after they completed at least two years of manual labor, by fellow peasants and workers according to level of political consciousness—how well they knew Maoist theory and how enthusiastic and selfless they were in serving the people.

1970—First Chinese satellite launched.

1971—U.S. Secretary of State Dr. Henry Kissinger and U.S. table tennis team visited China. Lin Piao accused of plotting to overthrow Mao, killed in plane crash while fleeing to Soviet Union. Death announced in 1973. China took United Nations seat from Taiwan. Canada resumed diplomatic relations.

1972—President Richard Nixon's historic visit.

1973—Campaign criticizing Lin Piao and Confucius. Teng Hsiao-ping rehabilitated and became Vice-Premier in charge of planning.

1974—Chinese aided Frelimo guerrillas in Mozambique and Angolan guerrillas against Portuguese. Asserted control in Paracel Islands. Seized stray Russian helicopter. One million Soviet troops along border. Russian tanks within 600 miles of Beijing. Teng Hsiao-ping announced Three Worlds policy in speech of United Nations.

1975—Death of Chiang Kai-shek in Taiwan.

January 1976—Death of Premier Chou En-lai. Succeeded by Teng Hsiao-ping (Deng Xiao-Ping) as acting premier.

April 1976—Tian Anmen incident (see "Beijing"). Supporters of Chou put wreaths on monument honoring former premier. Chiang Ching, Mao's wife, ordered removal. Clash ensued. Teng blamed.

July 1976—Tangshan earthquake. China refused all outside help.

September 9, 1976—Death of Mao Tse-tung. Hua Kuo-feng succeeded.

October 6, 1976—Gang of Four arrested. *The Gang of Four,* along with Lin Piao, are blamed for many of the country's ills. They are Chiang Ching, widow of Chairman Mao, and three leaders from Shanghai who rose to prominence during the cultural revolution.

1977—Split with Albania, for many years China's only ideological friend.

August 1977—Teng completely rehabilitated. Resumed previous posts.

1978—Democracy walls flourished for four months.

1979—The U.S. and China resumed full diplomatic relations. Because of continued Vietnamese "armed incursions" Chinese forces invaded Vietnam. Border clashes since then. Government bans posters critical of Communists. See "Local Customs."

January 1, 1980—First of series of new laws on crime and judicial procedures officially came into effect.

1980–81—Multicandidate county-level elections.

1980—Zhao Ziyang succeeded Hua Guo-feng as premier. Leaders tried to improve living standards and eliminate "left deviation, i.e. over-rigid and excess control of economic system, the rejection of commodity production, and the mistaken attempt to transfer prematurely the ownership of all enterprises to the state." Admitted financial deficit. Began economic reassessment and retrenchment. Banned all Democracy Walls. Wei Jingsheng, one of the leaders, sentenced to 15 years' imprisonment.

December 1980—Pan-Am flew first direct U.S.-China flight in 30 years. China protested Netherland's plan to sell two submarines to Taiwan.

1981—Chinese officials stated that Mao Tse-tung's contribution to China outweighed his mistakes. China modified the commune system, making the family the basic economic unit, and diminished the role of the Communist Party in just about every aspect of life. Chiang Ching (Jiang Qing) and one other member of the Gang of Four were given suspended death sentences following trials the previous November. Hua Guo-feng, Mao's chosen successor, was replaced by Hu Yaobang as Chairman of the Communist Party.

1982—The United States agreed not to increase arms sales to Taiwan; China reiterated that she would use force to regain Taiwan only if all else failed. British Prime Minister Margaret Thatcher visited Beijing to discuss Hong Kong's future.

Relations with the Soviet Union started to improve again but China restated objections to Soviet intervention in Afghanistan and Indochina, and to the large numbers of Soviet troops near Chinese borders. Relations with the Netherlands deteriorated even more with a Dutch airline flying to Taipei.

China announced centralized economic controls only for some essential commodities, and gradual changes in prices based on market forces. The Chinese fiancee of a French diplomat was arrested (and later released).

1983—Beijing ordered the round-up of 50,000 criminals and executions of 10%, in its campaign against the increase in crime. Public sentencing rallies, marches of condemned criminals through the streets, and posting of photos of executed prisoners continued the following year.

U.S. Defense Secretary Caspar Weinberger visited, and permitted the sale of some U.S. military technology to China. The United States grant of political asylum to a visiting Chinese tennis player disrupted cultural and sports exchanges between the two countries. Hijackers forced a CAAC plane to fly to Seoul. Marriages between most Chinese and foreigners were now permitted with one month's notice. The campaign against "spiritual pollution" (immoral foreign influences) was vigorously pursued and gradually slowed down.

Record harvests took place in spite of a decrease in agricultural lands. These, along with a sharp increase in cash crops, encouraged the continuation of the new economic policies. All state-owned companies were ordered to make a profit and pay taxes. Foreign oil companies under joint ventures started drilling in Guangdong province and the Yellow Sea area.

1984—another abundant harvest, the fourth in a row. Foreign exchange reserves hit a record high, and China went on an importing spree. The Cultural Revolution was denounced completely. The Communist Party booted out thousands of leftists. Intellectuals started being sought out and encouraged to contribute to modernization. The Italian correspondent for *Der Spiegel* was expelled.

Factories became independent, making their own production and marketing decisions. An American demographer reported 250,000 female infanticides in China since 1979. U.S. President Ronald Reagan visited. China protested the release to Taiwan of Chinese hijackers imprisoned in Seoul. Clashes continued with Vietnam.

Britain and China agreed on Hong Kong's future: It will all revert back to China in 1997. Deng proclaimed a one-country, two-systems policy in dealing with Taiwan and Hong Kong. Premier Zhao Ziyang toured the United States, Canada, France, and Belgium. The rift with the Netherlands was patched up. Foreign Minister Wu Xueqian met with Soviet Foreign Minister Andrei Gromyko at the United Nations.

The Communist Party spelled out its plan for the next three to five years and explained "socialism with Chinese characteristics." China started drafting up bankruptcy laws. The chronic shortage of electricity continued.

1985—The riot following China's loss to Hong Kong in a soccer match in Beijing left 30 policemen hurt, 25 vehicles damaged, and 127 arrested. An end-of-1985 deadline was set for firing incompetent managers of state enterprises. Two-hour lunch breaks were reduced to one hour for factory workers.

A Chinese demographer pointed out that sex ratios in demographic figures do not necessarily mean infanticide, and admitted to a few isolated cases.

Nine aging members of the Politburo resigned to make way for younger leaders, whose average ages are 50–59. Over one million elderly party members also resigned. President Li Xiannian visited the United States and Canada. Unauthorized resale of imported motor vehicles in Hainan Island created a big corruption scandal. Such shopping sprees helped to deplete foreign exchange reserves, and restrictions again were imposed for a few months.

1986—Taiwan negotiated release of its cargo plane hijacked to Canton. Sweden became the first customer for China's satellite launching service. China joined the Asian Development Bank. Some government-owned factories allowed to issue stock.

A Shenyang factory declared the first case of bankruptcy since Liberation. Queen Elizabeth II visited. First stock market since Liberation opened in Shanghai. The government announced that all new factory workers would be under limited contracts instead of lifetime assignments. In addition, the government also started a federal unemployment insurance and pension scheme.

1987—Student demonstrations for more freedom led to the resignation of leaders advocating "bourgeois liberalization." This included the Communist Party general secretary. University students were given improved teaching of Marxist-Leninist theories, trips to the countryside and factories, and military training. Two foreign heroin smugglers were executed in Kunming.

Chinese student Yang Wei, who studied in the U.S., was sentenced to two years imprisonment for conducting "demagogical propaganda for counter-revolutionary ends." He was reported as being involved with the demonstrations, the Chinese Alliance of Democracy, and the journal *China Spring*.

Demonstrations by Tibetans in Lhasa for the separation of Tibet from China resulted in the closing of Tibet to all foreign tourists except those in prepaid tours. Some foreigners expelled from Tibet.

Taiwan permitted its citizens to visit the mainland. Many tearful, dramatic reunions took place between family members who had not seen each other since Liberation. Mail, telegram, and telephone service also resumed.

China Travel Service official sentenced to death for "illegal sales of foreign exchange and motor vehicles." Shortages of pork, beer, and grain.

Three AIDS deaths so far in China; one a foreigner, one an Overseas Chinese; and one a child who had been given a transfusion of imported blood.

1988—China opened the rostrum on the Gate of Heavenly Peace to tourists. Hainan became 31st province. First visit of Chinese foreign minister to Moscow since 1957. Sino-Soviet summit planned. A few relatives from China visited Taiwan. US$35 billion foreign debt. Cut-back on non-capital enterprises to control inflation. More demonstrations for independence in Tibet. Ugly demonstrations against African students, especially in Nanjing.

1989—40th anniversary of the founding of the People's Republic of China. Big celebrations planned. Death of Panchen Lama. About late Sept. *1990*—China host to Asian Games in Beijing.

1990s—Shanghai subway and Euro-Asia Bridge railway line from Rotterdam to Lianyungang should be completed.

See also "Introduction."

IMPORTANT ADDRESSES AND INFORMATION

SOME CHINESE MISSIONS ABROAD

	Telephone
Australia	
Embassy of the People's Republic of China	412447
247 Federal Highway	412446
Watson, Canberra, A.C.T. 2602	
Canada	
Embassy of the People's Republic of China	(613) 234–2706
415 St. Patrick St.	234–2682
Ottawa, Ont., K1N 5H3	234–2718
Consulate General of the People's Republic of China	
240 St. George St.	
Toronto, Ont., M5R 2P4	(416) 964–7260
Consulate General of the People's Republic of China	(604) 736–3910
3380 Granville St.	
Vancouver, B.C. V6H 3K3	
England	
Embassy of the People's Republic of China	(01) 636–5726
31 Portland Pl.	
London, W1N 3AG.	
France	
Embassy of the People's Republic of China	361005
11, Ave. Georges V	361096
75008, Paris	361097
Japan	
Embassy of the People's Republic of China	
4-33, Moto-Azabu 3-chome	
Minato-ku, Tokyo	(03) 403–3389

Malaysia
Representative of the People's Republic of China
229, Jalan Ampang
Kuala Lumpur   428495

New Zealand
Embassy of the People's Republic of China   721382
2–6/6 Glenmore St.   721383
Wellington

Philippines
Embassy of the People's Republic of China
2038 Roxas Blvd. (Visa Office), Metro Manila   57.25.85
or 4896 Pasay Rd., Dasmarinas, Metro Manila   86.77.15

Singapore
Office of the Commercial Representative of the People's Republic of China
70–76 Dalvey Rd.
Singapore 1025   7343360

Thailand
Embassy of the People's Republic of China
57 Rachadapisake Rd.   Telex 82014 HSHUABK TH.
Bangkok   2457044

U.S.A.
Embassy of the People's Republic of China
2300 Connecticut Ave., N.W.   (202) 328–2517 (visa)
Washington, DC 20008   (202) 328–2500 (chancery)

Consulate General of the People's Republic of China
104 S. Michigan Ave., Suite 1200
Chicago, IL 60603   (312) 346–0288

Consulate General of the People's Republic of China
3417 Montrose Blvd.   (713) 524–4311
Houston, TX 77066   (713) 524–0778

Consulate General of the People's Republic of China
502 Shatto Place
Suite 300   (213) 380–2507
Los Angeles, CA 90020   (213) 380–2506

Permanent Mission to the People's Republic of China to the United Nations
520 12th Ave.
New York, NY 10036

Consulate General of the People's Republic of China
520 12th Ave.   (212) 330–7409
New York, NY 10036   (212) 868–7409

Consulate General of the People's Republic of China
1450 Laguna St.   (415) 563–4857
San Francisco, CA 94115   (415) 563–4885

China Tourist Offices

China Tourist Office, 55 Clarence St., 11 fl., Sydney NSW 2000, Australia
China Tourist Office, 4 Glentworth St., London NW1, England
Office Du Tourisme de Chine, 51 Rue Sainte-anne 75002, France
China Tourist Office, Eschenheimer Anlage 28, D-6000 Frankfurt am Main-1, Federal Republic of Germany
China Tourist Office, Lincoln Building, 60 E. 42nd St., Suite 3126, New York, N.Y. 10165, U.S.A.
China Tourist Office, 333 West Broadway, Suite 201, Glendale, CA 91204

TOUR ORGANIZERS AND TRAVEL AGENTS
Australia

Cathay Pacific Airways, 28 O'Connell St., Sydney 2000.
Hertz Asia Pacific Ltd., 6th floor, 10 Dorcas St., South Melbourne, Vic. 3205

Canada

Bestway Tours & Safaris, 202–2676 W. Broadway, Vancouver, B.C. V6K 2G3 (For Karakoram Hwy. From Pakistan to China.)
Blyth & Co., 68 Scollard St., Toronto, Ont. M5R 1G2.
Canadian Travel Abroad Ltd., 80 Richmond St. W., Suite 2007, Toronto, Ont., M5H 2C6. Tel. 1–800–387–1876. Fax (416) 364–6951.
China Travel Service (Canada) Inc., P.O. Box 17, Main Floor, 999 West Hastings St., Vaciuverm, B.C. V6C 2W2. Tel. (604) 684–8787. Telex: 04–54219. Fax: (604) 684 3321.
Conference Travel of Canada, 102 Bloor St. W., Suite 620, Toronto, Ont., M5S 1M8. (416) 922–8161, 1–800–387–1277 (Ont.-Que.), 1–800–387–1488 (rest of Canada).
Cultural Tours, 360–2600 Granville St., Vancouver, B.C. V6H 3V3. 1–800–663–1751, 1–800–282–8898 (US). Offices also in Toronto, Los Angeles, Honolulu, and Hong Kong.
Fujian Tourism Bureau, North American Office, Suite 603, 1112 West Pender St., Vancouver, B.C. V6E 2S1. Tel. (604) 687–7435. Fax: (604) 687–2639.
Tour East Holidays, 1030 Bay St., Suite 317, Toronto, Ont. M5S 3A5. Tel. 1–800–263–2808. Fax: (416) 972–1734.

China (See also Beijing)

China International Travel Service, Head Office, 6, East Chang'an Ave., Beijing. Telex: 22350 CITSH CN. Cable: LUXINGSHE BEIJING. Addresses of domestic branches in "Destinations."
China International Travel Service, FIT Division, Room No. 1302, Chongwenmen Hotel, Beijing. Telex: 22004 CIFIT CN. Cable: LUXINGSHE BEIJING.
China Travel Service and Overseas Chinese Travel Service, 8 Dong Jiao Min Xiang, Beijing. Tel. 550031–271. Telex: 22487 CTSHO CN. Cable: 2464. Try also China Travel Service in Hong Kong.

China Sports Service, 9 Tiyuguan Rd., Beijing. Tel. 5112859. Telex: 222283 CIST. Cable: SPORTSCHINE BEIJING.
CCPIT, Telex: 218214 CEX CN
CICCST (China International Conference Center for Science and Technology), Friendship Hotel, Beijing 100086. Tel. 8313172. Telex: 222337 ICCST CN. Fax: 898116.

In addition to the provincial travel departments of C.T.S., C.I.T.S., and China Youth Travel Service, travel agents authorized to deal with foreign travelers include: China Swan International, China Civil International Tourists Co., China International Sports Co., China Women's Travel Service, China Workers' Travel Service, China Everbright Travel Inc., China Golden Bridge Travel Service, China Peace International Tourism Corp., China Merchants International Travel Co., China Kanghui Travel (for handicapped travelers), and CITIC Travel Inc.

Hong Kong

China International Travel Service (H.K.), 6th Fl., Tower II, South Seas Centre, 75 Mody Rd., Tsimshatsui, Kowloon. Tel. 3–7215317. Telex: 38449 CITC HX. Cable: 2320 Hong Kong; 618 Swire House, 11 Chater Rd. C. Tel. 5–8104282.
China Merchants International Travel Service (For Yangtze River Cruises), Rm. 301, China Merchant Bldg., 15–16 Connaught Rd. W., Hong Kong. Tel. 5–419914.
China Travel Service (H.K.), Head Office; 4/F, C.T.S. House, 78–83 Connaught Rd. C., Hong Kong. Tel. 5–8533533. Telex 85222 HCTSF HX. Fax: 5–419777 Branches: 77, Queen's Rd. C., Hong Kong. Tel. 5–252284, 5–236222. Cable: TRAVELBANK. *Branches:* 27–33, Nathan Rd., 1/F (entrance on Peking Rd.), Kowloon, tel. 3–7211311, 3–7214481. 24–34 Hennessy Rd., Wan Chai, Hong Kong, tel. 5–280102; Hung Hom Railway Station, Kowloon, tel. 3–330660; Tai Kok Tsui HK/Guangzhou Pier, tel. 3–929403. Has Independent Travelers Branch.
China Youth Travel, Rm. 606, Wing On House, 71, Des Voeux Road, C., Hong Kong. Tel. 5–410975, 5–259075. Telex: 61679 YOUTH HX. Cable: HONSHANC. Fax 5–8106063.
Club Med, 3/F, BCC House, 10 Queens Rd. Central, Hong Kong.
Hong Kong Student Travel Ltd., Room 833–835 Star House, Tsimshatsui, Kowloon, Hong Kong. Tel. 3–696323. Fax: 3–7219407. Telex: 52988 ACSTB.
Jin Jiang Travel (HK) Ltd., 9–11 fl., Chiao Chi Bldg., 877 Lai Chi Kok Rd., Kowloon. Tel.3–7446110. Fax 3–7452881.
Rosalind Henwood, G.P.O. Box 6768, Hong Kong. Tel. 5–232237 or 5–260623. Telex 61309 STL HX.
Time Travel Services, Block A, 16/fl., Chung King Mansion. Tel. 3–7239993, 3–666222. Telex 37670 TRVEL HX. Fax 3–7395413.
The Travel Advisers Ltd., Room 1006, 10/F, Silvercord, Tower One, 30 Canton Rd., Tsimshatsui, Kowloon. Tel. 3–698321. Telex: 44430 ADVSR HX. (Across from Marco Polo Hotel.) Branch in Swire House.
Zhuhai Tours (HK) Ltd., Room 3207 New World Tower, 16–18 Queen's Rd., C., Hong Kong. Tel. 5–232136, Telex: 74493 HMHCO HX.

Macao

C.I.T.S. Zuhai Branch, 6A–4C, R/C Rua de Sacadura Cabral. Tel. 566622.
China Travel Service, 33 rua Vis. Paco de Arcos. Tel. 88922.

New Zealand

Globetrotter Tours (NZ), P.O. Box 6145, 47 Lorne St., Auckland.

Pakistan

Pakistan Tourism Development Corporation Ltd., House No. 2, Street 61,
F-7/4, Islamabad. For information on Karakoram Hwy. (See also Canada for
Bestway Tours.)

U.S.A.

AFS International/Intercultural Programs, 313 E. 43rd St., New York, N.Y.
10017
Arunas Travel Co., 630 Third Ave., 4th floor, New York, NY 10017. 1–
800–842–1989.
Avia Travel, 441 California Ave., Palo Alto, CA 94306. (415) 321–3824. Fax
(415) 321–7518. Telex 3716433 VOLASIA. (Cheapest airfare.)
CET, 1110 Washington St., Lower Mills, Boston, Ma., 02124. Tel. 1–800–
225–4262.
China International Travel Service (GD), 138B, World Trade Center, San
Francisco, CA 94111. (415) 362–7477. Fax (415) 989–3838.
Chinasmith, Inc., 324 W. 42nd St., New York, NY 10036. 1–800–US–CHINA.
Euro-Asia Express, 475 El Camino Real, Penthouse Suite, Millbrae, CA 94030.
1–800–782–9624, 1–800–782–9625. For cheaper air fares.
Hemphill Harris Travel Corp., 16000 Ventura Blvd., Suite 200, Encino, CA
91436. 1–800–421–0454; 1–800–252–2103. Canada 1–800–367–8075.
Indoculture Tours, 5601 W. Slauson Ave., Suite 272, Culver City, CA 90230.
1–800–234–4085. Telex 4933128 CULTURE.
Kuo Feng Corporation, 15 Mercer St., New York, N.Y. 10013. Tel. 1–800–
233–8687, 1–800–821–8177; 644 Broadway, Suite 401, San Francisco, CA
94133.
Lindblad Travel, Inc., 1 Sylvan Rd. N., P.O. Box 912, Westport, CT 06881.
Tel. 1–800–243–5657.
Mountain Travel, 6420 Fairmont Ave., El Cerrito, CA 94530. Tel. 1–800–
227–2384.
Pacific Delight Tours, Inc., 132 Madison Ave., New York, NY 10016. Tel.
1–800–221–7179. (Offices also in Los Angeles, San Francisco, Minneapolis,
and Seattle.)
Sino-American Tours, 221 Canal St., Suite 501, New York, NY 10013. Tel.
1–800–221–7982.
U.S. China Travel Service, Main Office, 500 Sutter St., Suite 621, San Francisco, CA 94102. Tel. (415) 398–6627, 1–800–332–2831, 1–800–553–8764.
Also 223E, Garvey Avenue, Suite 138, Monterey Park, CA 91754. Tel. (818)
288–8222.

CHINA FRIENDSHIP ASSOCIATIONS

Australia-China Society, c/o Mrs. Kathleen Godfrey, National Tour Organizer, 20 Barkly St., Brighton, 3186, Victoria. (03) 5925653.
Federation of Canada-China Friendship Associations, Suite 204, 2420 Douglas St., Victoria, B.C. V8T 4L7.
Society for Anglo-Chinese Understanding, 152 Camden High St., London, NW1, England.
New Zealand-China Friendship Society, 52 Customs St. East, P.O. Box 3460, Auckland, New Zealand.
U.S.-China Peoples Friendship Association, National Office, 2025 Eye St. N.W., Washington, DC 20006, U.S.A. 1–800–368–5883.

FOR SCHOLARS, STUDENTS, AND FOREIGN EXPERTS
Australia

Australia-China Council, c/o Department of Foreign Affairs, Canberra, ACT 2600, Australia.
Department of Employment, Education and Training, GPO Box 9880, MLC Tower, Woden, Canberra ACT 2606.

Canada

Association of Universities and Colleges of Canada, 151 Slater St., Ottawa, Ont. K1P 5N1.
China Desk, Canadian Council of Churches, 40 St. Clair East, Toronto, Ont., M4T 1M9.
Canadian Executive Service Organization, Operations Centre, Suite 2000, 415 Yonge St., Toronto, Ont. M5B 2E7.
Canadian International Development Agency, 200 Promenade du Portage, Hull, Quebec K1A 0G3.
Chinese Education Association for International Exchanges, c/o P.O. Box 80383, Burnaby, B.C. V5H 3X6. (604) 266–3300.

China

Foreign Experts Bureau, Friendship Hotel or Ministry of Education, 37 Da Mu Cang Hu Tong, Beijing. Tel. 66–1758. **Foreign Experts' Bureau of the State Council,** P.O. Box 300, Beijing. It is quicker to write directly to the Office of the President or the Foreign Affairs Office of the school where you wish to teach, as the Foreign Experts Bureau is primarily a central clearing house. Foreign Affairs Division, **Arts Education Bureau,** Ministry of Culture, Beijing. Tel. 44–6571X515 (for teachers in the performing arts).
Foreign Student Affairs Division, Foreign Affairs Dept., Ministry of Education, Beijing. Tel. 66–1917.
International Liaison Dept., **State Science and Technology Association,** Beijing. Tel. 86–8361X714 (for teachers of science and technology.)

England

Education Office of the **British Council,** Clarendon House, Spring Gardens, London SW1.
Great Britain-China Centre, 15 Belgrave Square, London SE1X 8PG.

Hong Kong

University Service Center, China newspaper collection, USC Unit, Basement, General Library, Chinese University of Hong Kong, Shatin, N.T.

U.S.A.

China Affairs Division, United States Information Agency, Washington, DC 20547.
Committee on Scholarly Communication with the People's Republic of China, National Academy of Sciences, 2101 Constitution Ave., NW, Washington, DC 20418.
Council for International Exchange of Scholars (CIES), 11 Dupont Circle, Suite 300, Washington, DC 20036-1257. (Fulbright).
International Education Programs, U.S. Department of Education, 400 Maryland Ave., S.E., ROB 3, Room 3082, Washington, DC 20202.
National Association for Foreign Student Affairs, 1860 19th St. NW, Washington, DC 20009.
National Committee on U.S./China Relations, 777 United Nations Plaza, New York, NY 10164.
Peace Corps, 806 Connecticut Ave., NW, Washington, D.C. 20526. 1–800–424–8580 X243.

OTHER IMPORTANT ADDRESSES

Australia

Air/China, 104 The Waldorf, 57–67 Liverpool St., Sydney, 2000, Suite 11, 6th fl., 422 Collins St., Melbourne 3000.
Australia-China Business Co-operation Committee, P.O. Box 14, Canberra, ACT 2600. Independent body for the promotion of trade between Australia and China and to provide a forum for the exchange of up-to-date material on China.
Australia-China Chamber of Commerce and Industry, c/o Melbourne Chamber of Commerce, 60 Market St., 21st Floor, Melbourne, Victoria 3000. A nonprofit organization to promote trade; to serve as liaison between governments on trade matters; to assist counterpart organizations in China; to promote social and cultural contacts between the two countries, etc.
Bank of China, 65 York St., Sydney, N.S.W. 2000.
Department of Trade, Edmund Barton Building, Kings Ave., Barton, ACT 2600. Ask for booklet.
NSW-ACT Chamber for China Trade and Commerce, Suite 69, 6/F, 104 Bathurst St., Sydney, NSW 2000.

Canada

Air China, Unit 15, 131 Bloor St. W., Toronto, Ont., M5S 1R1; 1040 West Georgia St., Vancouver, B.C. V6B 4H1.
Amnesty International, 130 Slater St., Ste. 900, Ottawa, Ont., K1P 6E2.
Bank of China, Ste. 1116, National Bank Building, 181 University Ave., Toronto, Ont., M5H 3M7.
Canada-China Programme, Canadian Council of Churches, 40 St. Clair Ave. East, Toronto, Ont. M4T 1M9.
Canada-China Trade Council, Suite 310, 133 Richmond St. W., Toronto, Ont. M5H 2L3.
Convention Administrator, Canadian Wildlife Service, Environment Canada, Ottawa, Ont. K1A OE7.
Customs Office, 360 Coventry Rd., Ottawa, Ont. K1K 2C6.
Export Development Corporation, Box 655, Ottawa, Ont., K1P 5T9.
IAMAT International Association for Medical Assistance to Travellers, 1287 St. Clair Ave. W., Toronto, Ont., M6E 1B8.

China

Air China, Capital Airport, Beijing 100621. Tel. 5138833. Telex 210322 RAPEK CN.
China Eastern Airlines, Hongqiao International Airport, Shanghai. Tel. 518550.
Amity Foundation, 13 Da Jian Yin Xiang, Nanjing.
CAAC, 155 Dongsi St. West, Beijing. Tel. 558861.
China Daily, 2, Jintai Xi Rd., Beijing. Tel. 596231.
China Tourism News, English Edition, Room 1408, Chongwenmen Hotel, Beijing 100062. 5122211 X254, 253.
China Travel and Tourism Press, Room 304, Chongwenmen Hotel, Beijing. Tel. 5122211 X 302.
   For other addresses in China, see each city under "Destinations," especially "Beijing," "Guangzhou," "Shanghai," and "Shenyang."
China Welfare Institute, Mme. Du Shu Zhen, Dep. Secy.-Gen., 157 Changzhu Rd., Shanghai.
Soong Ching-ling Foundation. For donations, Bank Account 71402496, General Office of the Bank of China, Beijing.

England

Air China, 41 Grosvenor Garden, London SW1W OBP.
China Travel Service (UK) Ltd., 24 Cambridge Circus, London WC2H 8HD. Tel. (01) 836–9911. Fax (01) 836–3121.
Sino-British Trade Council, 5/F, Abford House, 15 Wilton Rd., London SW1V 1LT.
Sitara Travel Consultants (PVT) Ltd., 4, Christ Church Ave., Turnbridge Wells, Kent TNI UW.

Hong Kong

American Chamber of Commerce, 1030 Swire House, Hong Kong.

Asian Wall St. Journal, G.P.O. Box 9825, Hong Kong.

Australian Commission, Hong Kong Harbour Centre, 25 Harbour Rd., Wan Chai, (G.P.O. Box 820), Hong Kong.

Bank of China, 2A Des Voeux Rd. Central, Hong Kong.

CAAC, G/F Gloucester Tower, Pedder St., Hong Kong; 34/F United Center, 95 Queensway. 5–8610288.

Canadian Chamber of Commerce, 11/F, One Exchange Square, 8 Connaught Pl., G.P.O. Box 1587, 5–251143.

Canadian Commission, Box 11142, GPO, 11/14 F, Tower I, Exchange Square, 8 Connaught Rd., Hong Kong.

Cathay Pacific, Swire House, 9 Connaught Rd., Central, Hong Kong.

China Phone Book Co. Ltd., GPO Box 11581, Hong Kong.

China Resources Co., Causeway Center, Gloucester Rd., Hong Kong.

Chinese Arts and Crafts (H.K.) Ltd. *Branches:* Star House (at Star Ferry Terminal), Kowloon: 233 Nathan Rd., Kowloon; Shell House, Queen's Rd., Central, Hong Kong.

Dragonair, 12/F, Tower 6, China Hong Kong City, 33 Canton Rd., Tsimshatsui, Kowloon. Tel. 3–7383388. Telex 45936 DRAGH HX. Fax 3–7360833.

Far Eastern Economic Review, G.P.O. Box 160, Hong Kong.

Hertz Asia Pacific, 2/F Pacific Star Bldg., 2 Canton Rd., Tsimshatsui, Kowloon. Tel. 3–671021.

Hong Kong Bank China Services, Level 13, 1 Queen's Rd. C. Hong Kong.

Hongkong China Liaison Office, World Division, Board of Global Ministries, The United Methodist Church, 2 Man Wan Rd., C–17, Kowloon.

Hong Kong Tourist Association, Connaught Centre, 35/F, Hong Kong. (Represented abroad by offices in San Francisco, New York City, Chicago, Los Angeles, Wellington, Sydney, London, Rome, Paris, Frankfurt, Singapore, Tokyo, and Osaka, and by Cathay Pacific Airways.)

Peace Book Co., Rm. 1502, Wing On House, 71 Des Voeux Rd., C.

Shanghai Airlines, c/o Wen Wei Newspaper, 197 Wanchai Rd., Hong Kong. Tel. 5–722211.

South China Morning Post, G.P.O. Box 47, Hong Kong.

Ta Kung Pao—Weekly supplement, 342 Hennessy Rd., 7/F, Hong Kong.

Tao Fong Shan Ecumenical Center, P.O. Box 33, Shatin, N.T.

United States Consulate, 26 Garden Rd., Hong Kong.

Visa Office, Ministry of Foreign Affairs of the People's Republic of China in Hong Kong. 5/F, Lower Block, 26 Harbour Rd., Wanchai. Tel. 5–744163. 9 a.m.–noon and 2–5 p.m. daily. Saturdays 9 a.m.–noon.

Yue Hwa—Chinese Products Emporium Ltd., 301–309 Nathan Rd., Kowloon; 54–64 Nathan Rd., Tsimshatsui.

U.S.A.

Air Ambulance International Medical Service Inc, P.O. Box 9091, Incline Village, NE 89450. Tel. (702) 832–7961.

Amnesty International, 322 Eighth Ave., New York, NY 10001.

Asian Wall St. Journal Weekly, 200 Liberty St., New York, NY 10281.
Bank of China, 410 Madison Ave., New York, NY 10017; 444 S. Flower St. Suite 3900, Los Angeles, CA 90071.
CAAC, 45 E. 49th St., New York, NY 10017; 51 Grant Ave., San Francisco, CA 94108; 2500 Wilshire Blvd., Los Angeles, CA 90057.
China Books and Periodicals, 2929 24th St., San Francisco, CA 94110 (retail and mail orders); 126 W. 18th St., New York, NY 10011, 55 E. Washington, Suite 1003, Chicago, IL 60602. (hours are irregular—call first, (312) 782–6004).
China Daily Distribution Corp., 15 Mercer St., Suite 401, New York, NY 10013.
Federal Wildlife Permit Office, United States Department of the Interior, 1000 North Glebe Rd., Room 611, Arlington, VA 22201.
IAMAT (International Association for Medical Assistance to Travelers), 417 Center St., Lewiston, NY 14092.
International SOS, Tel. (215) 244–1500, 1–800–523–8930 (U.S.A.), 1–800–441–4767 (Canada). Fax (215) 244–9617. Telex 831598 ISOS PHA.
National Council of Churches, China Program Administrative Committee, 374 Riverside Dr., 6/F, New York, NY 10115.
United States Customs Service, Public Information Division, Washington, DC 20229.
U.S.-China Business Council, 1818 N St. NW, Suite 500, Washington, D.C. 20036.
Asia Travel Trade, 190 Middle Rd. #14, 10 Fortune Center, Singapore 0718.

CHINA IDD DOMESTIC TELEPHONE CODES

Only a few hotels have a list of domestic long-distance codes. The China Hotel (Guangzhou), with the longest one found so far, has given us permission to reprint theirs. We have added some codes from Teleglobe Canada.

Anyang 372; Anshan 412; Baoding 312; Beijing 1; Changchun 431; Changsha 731, Chengde 314; Chengdu 28; Chongqing 811; Chaozhou 7681, Chunzhou 735.

Dalian 411; Dandong 415; Foshan 757; Fuzhou 591; Guangzhou 20; Guiyang 851; Haikou 750; Harbin 451; Hefei 551; Hangzhou 571; Huaxian 2091; Huizhou 752; Jinan 531; Jilin 432; Jinzhou 416; Jiangmen 7682.

Kaifeng 378, Kaiping 7658; Kunming 871; Lanzhou 931; Liaoyang 419; Maanshan 555; Maoming 7683; Meixian 7631; Nanchang 791; Nanjing 25; Nanning 771; Ningbo 574.

Qingdao 532; Qinhuangdao 335; Quanzhou 595; Shantou 754; Shanghai 21; Shaoguan 751; Shenyang 24; Shenzhen 755; Sijiazhuang 311; Siping 434; Shaoxing 575; Shunde 7653; Suzhou 512; Taishan 7657; Taiyuan 351; Tianjin 22.

Weifang 536; Wuhan 27; Wuzhou 772; Xiamen 592; Xian 29; Xinhui 7656; Xining 971; Xuzhou 516; Yanan 911; Yantai 535; Yinchuan

951; Yueyang 730; Zhanjiang 759; Zhaoqing 758; Zhengzhou 371; Zhenjiang 571; Zhongshan 7654; Zhuhai 756; Zhangzhou 596.

CHINESE CUSTOMS REGULATIONS

Upon entrance every tourist is requested to fill in a Baggage Declaration in duplicate to be handed in to Customs.

Articles for personal use carried by a tourist including foodstuffs to be consumed during the trip, 2 bottles of wine (not exceeding 750 grams each) and 400 cigarettes may be imported duty free. Wristwatches, recorders (including multi-purpose combination sets), cameras and cinecameras for personal use may be imported but may not be transferred or sold privately and are to be taken out of the country at the time of exit. Gifts for friends and relatives or articles carried on behalf of others are to be declared to the Customs.

Tourists should retain the duplicate copy of the baggage declaration issued by the customs at the entry port. Upon exit tourists should fill in the blanks for exit declaration which is to be submitted to the customs for inspection.

Invoices for purchases made in China in reasonable quantities for personal use should be produced to the customs upon exit. Shipped goods are exportable with the export permit which is obtained upon application.

Import of the following articles is prohibited:

(1) Arms, ammunition and explosives of all kinds;

(2) Radio transmitter receivers and principal parts;

(3) Renminbi;

(4) Manuscripts, printed matter, films, photographs, gramophone records, cinematographic films, loaded recording tapes, video-tapes, etc. which are detrimental to China's politics, economy, culture and ethics;

(5) Poisonous drugs, narcotics and opium, morphia, heroin, etc;

(6) Animals, plants and products thereof infected with or carrying disease germs and insects pests;

(7) Insanitary foodstuffs and germ-carrying foodstuffs from infected areas; and

(8) Other articles the import of which is prohibited by state regulations.

Export of the following articles is prohibited:

(1) Arms, ammunition and explosives of all kinds:

(2) Radio transmitter-receivers and principal parts;

(3) Renminbi and securities, etc. in RMB;

(4) Foreign currencies, bills and securities in foreign currencies (with the exception of those allowed to be taken out);

(5) Manuscripts, printed matter, films, photographs, gramophone records, cinematographic films, loaded recording tapes, video-tapes, etc. which contain state secrets or which are otherwise prohibited export;

(6) Valuable cultural relics and rare books relating to Chinese revolution, history, culture or art;

(7) Rare animals and rare plants and their seeds;

(8) Precious metals and articles made thereof, jewelry, diamonds and ornaments made thereof (with the exception of those which have been brought in and declared to the Customs); and

(9) Other articles the export of which is prohibited by state regulations.

Overseas Chinese with foreign passports can import, duty-free, to be left in China on one's first visit each year, one of an item worth ¥200 to ¥1000 RMB such as a TV, washing machine, refrigerator, or motorcycle, or any five of the following worth ¥50 to ¥200: bicycle, sewing machine, fan, radio, typewriter, electronic organ, electric kettle. Also a "reasonable amount of clothing." A Chinatown or Hong Kong travel agent specializing in Overseas Chinese tours can give you more details.

Duty if levied, is high. You might pay ¥600 on a Rolex watch; ¥275 on a Chinese-made 12–15-inch color television, ¥350 on a similar foreign-made one. If you don't want to pay the duty, leave the item with Customs and pick it up on the way out.

BIBLIOGRAPHY

Ahrens, Joan Reid and Malloy, Ruth Lor. *Hong Kong Gems and Jewelry*. Hong Kong: Delta Dragon, 1986.

Austin, Alvyn J. *Saving China—Canadian Missionaries in the Middle Kingdom, 1888–1959*. Toronto: University of Toronto Press, 1986.

Barber, Noel. *The Fall of Shanghai*. New York: Coward-McCann and Geoghegan, Inc., 1979.

Barr, Pat. *To China with Love—the Lives and Times of Protestant Missionaries in China, 1860–1900*. New York: Doubleday & Co., Inc., 1973.

Bauer, E. E. *China Takes Off—Technology Transfer and Modernization*. Seattle: University of Washington Press, 1986.

Behr, Edward. *The Last Emperor*. Toronto: General Paperbacks, 1987.

Booz, Elizabeth, B. *Tibet*. Hong Kong: Shangri-la Press, 1986. Lincolnwood, IL: Passport Books.

Bredon, Juliet. *Peking*. Shanghai: Kelly and Walsh, Ltd., 1931; Hong Kong: Oxford University Press. 1982.

Buck, Pearl S. *The Good Earth*. New York: J. Day, 1977.

Buckley, Michael, and Samagalski, Alan. *China—A Travel Survival Kit*. Victoria and Berkeley: Lonely Planet.

Catchpool, Brian. *A Map History of Modern China*. London: Heinemann Educational Books Ltd., 1977.

Chen, Jack. *A Year in Upper Felicity*. New York: Macmillan, 1973.

Chen, Jerome. *Mao and the Chinese Revolution*. Oxford, 1976.

Chen Yuan-Tsung. *The Dragon's Village*. New York: Pantheon, 1980.

Ching, Frank. *Ancestors*. New York: William Morrow, 1988.

Coye, Molly Joel, etc., editor. *China, Yesterday and Today*. New York: Bantam Books, 1984.

Cronin, Vincent. *The Wise Man from the West, Matteo Ricci and His Mission to China*. London: Collin, Fount Paperbacks, 1984.

Daubier, Jean. *A History of the Chinese Cultural Revolution*. New York, Toronto: Vintage Books, 1974.

Dawson, Raymond. *Imperial China*. New York: Pelican Books, 1976.

De Keijzer, Arne J. *The China Business Handbook*. San Francisco: China Books & Periodicals, Inc., 1986.

Er Si, etc. *Inside Stories of the Forbidden City*. Beijing: New World Press, 1986.

Fairbank, John K. *The United States and China*. Cambridge: Harvard University Press, 1983.

Fitzgerald, C. P. *The Tower of Five Glories—A Study of the Min Chia of Ta Li, Yunnan*. West Point, CT: Hyperion Press, 1973.

Fleming, Peter. *Bayonets to Lhasa*. New York: Oxford University Press, 1985.

Gernet, Jacques. *Daily Life in China on the Eve of the Mongol Invasion. 1250–1276*. Stanford, Ca.: Stanford University Press, 1973.

Goede, William. *Love in Beijing and Other Stories*. Dunvegan, Ont: Cormorant Books, 1988.

Goldenberg, Susan. *Managing Joint Ventures With a Spotlight on China and Japan*. Harvard Business School Press, 1988.

Gu Hua. *A Small Town Called Hibiscus*. Beijing: Panda Books, 1983.

Haldane, Charlotte. *The Last Great Empress of China*. New York: Bobbs-Merrill, 1965.

Han Suyin. *The Crippled Tree*. New York: Bantam, 1972.

———. *A Mortal Flower*. London: J. Cape, 1966.

———. *Birdless Summer*. New York: Putnam, 1968.

Harrer, Heinrich. *Return to Tibet*. London: George Weidenfeld & Nicolson Ltd., 1984.

———. *Seven Years in Tibet*, London: The Adventure Library, Rupert Hart-Davis, 1957; London: Granada, 1984.

Hersey, John A. *A Single Pebble*. Chicago and Montreal: Bantam Books, 1961.

Hollingworth, Clare. *Mao and the Men Against Him*. London: Jonathan Cape, 1985.

Lampton, David M., etc. *A Relationship Restored—Trends in U.S.–China Educational Exchanges, 1978–1984*. Washington, D.C., National Academy Press, 1986.

Latsch, Marie-Luise. *Peking Opera as a European Sees It*. Beijing: New World Press, 1980.

Li Nianpei, *Old Tales of China—a tourist guidebook to better understanding of China's stage, cinema, arts and crafts*. Beijing: China Travel and Tourism Press, 1981.

Li Xueqin, *The Wonder of Chinese Bronzes*. Beijing: Foreign Languages Press, 1980.

Liang Heng and Shapiro, Judith. *Son of the Revolution*. New York: Vintage Books, 1984.

Lin Yutang. *Moment in Peking*. New York: John Day, 1939.

Ling, Ken. *The Revenge of Heaven*. New York: G.P. Putnam's Sons, 1972.

Lo Kuan-chung. *Three Kingdoms*. Robert Moss, trans. & ed. New York: Pantheon, 1976.

Macleod, Roderick. *China, Inc. How to do Business With the Chinese*. New York: Bantam Books, 1988.

Malloy, Ruth Lor. *Beyond the Heights*. Hong Kong: Heinemann Educational Books Ltd. (Asia), 1980.

McCawley, James D. *The Eater's Guide to Chinese Characters*. Chicago and London: The University of Chicago Press, 1984.

McKenna, Richard. *The Sand Pebbles*. Greenwich, Conn.: Fawcett, 1962.

Medley, Margaret. *A Handbook of Chinese Art*. New York: Icon Ed., 1974.

Richardson, Hugh E. *Tibet and Its History*. Boston and London: Shambala, 1984. Random House distributor.

Schram, Stuart. *Mao Tse-tung*. New York: Penguin, 1967.

Seagrave, Sterling. *The Soong Dynasty.* New York and Sydney: Harper & Row.

Sharman, Lyon. *Sun Yat-sen, His Life and Its Meaning.* Stanford: Stanford University Press, 1978.

Snow, Edgar. *Red Star Over China.* New York: Penguin, 1977.

Spence, Jonathan. *To Change China: Western Advisers in China. 1620–1960.* Boston, Toronto: Little, Brown, 1969.

Stalberg, Roberta Helmer. *Shopping in China, Arts, Crafts and the Unusual.* San Francisco: China Books & Periodicals, Inc., 1988.

Sullivan, Michael. *The Arts of China.* Los Angeles, Berkeley, London: University of California Press, 1977.

Tolley, Kemp. *Yangtze Patrol: The U.S. Navy in China.* Annapolis, Md.: Naval Institute Press, 1971.

Tsao Hsueh-Chin. *The Dream of the Red Chamber* (Hung Lou Meng). New York: The Universal Library, Grosset & Dunlop, 1973.

Turner-Gottschang, Karen, etc. *China Bound—A Guide to Academic Life and Work in the PRC.* Washington, DC: National Academy Press, 1987.

UNESCO. *Tibet and the Chinese People's Republic: A Report to the International Commission of Jurists by its Legal Inquiry Committee on Tibet.* Geneva: International Commission of Jurists.

U.S. Government. *Post Report on China.* Government Printing Office, Washington, DC.

Warner, Marina. *The Dragon Empress: The Life and Times of Tz'u-Hsi, Empress Dowager of China, 1835–1908.* New York: Macmillan, 1972.

White, Theodore. *In Search of History.* New York: Warner, 1978.

Williams, C.A.S. *Outlines of Chinese Symbolism and Art Motives.* New York: Dover Publications, 1976.

Witke, Roxanne. *Comrade Chiang-Ching.* Waltham, MA: Little, Brown, 1977.

Woodcock, George. *The British in the Far East.* New York: Atheneum, 1969.

Wu Zuguang. *Peking Opera and Mei Lanfang.* Beijing: New World Press, 1981.

———. *Doing Business in Today's China.* The American Chamber of Commerce in Hong Kong.

———. *Zhonghua Renmin Gongheguo Fen Sheng Dituji.* (Atlas of China). Beijing: Xinhua Shudian, 1971.

———. China City Guide Series. Beijing: Travel and Tourism Press. 1983. Guides of Beijing, Guangzhou, Guilin, Hangzhou, Kunming, Nanjing, Shanghai, Taiyuan, Tianjin, Xiamen, etc.

QUICK REFERENCE

Official Chinese Holidays

January or February	Spring Festival/New Year, the date depending on lunar calendar (3 days).
May 1	Labor Day
October 1 and 2	National Day, celebrating the founding of the People's Republic of China in 1949.

In addition, the following are celebrated with special programs, but offices and schools are open.

March 8	International Working Women's Day
March 12	Tree-planting day, south China
April	Tree-planting day, north China (first Sunday)
May 4	Youth Day (May 4th Movement)
June 1	Children's Day
July 1	Founding Day of the Communist Party of China
August 1	Founding Day of the People's Liberation Army
Sept. 10	Teacher's Day
Sept. 27	World Tourism Day. Celebrated by different cities in turn. Special events, gifts for tourists.

The Chinese also celebrate several other traditional holidays. The Lantern Festival is the last day of the old lunar new year celebrations. The Dragon Boat races commemorate the untimely death of an upright official. Originally, the boats raced to feed the fish so they wouldn't eat him! (But no one thinks of that now.) The Mid-Autumn Festival celebrates the most beautiful full moon of the year.

Check with C.I.T.S. about special events related to the festivals (not necessarily on the specified day). Daylight-savings time about the second Sunday in April until 2nd Sunday in September.

Some major festivals are listed here. For regional festivals, please look up individual destinations like Weifang (for the kite festival), Kunming (for the Water-splashing Festival and Third Moon Market), and Guiyang for festivals of the nationalities.

Since the dates for the traditional festivals fluctuate (like Easter) according to the lunar calendar, the Western equivalents are:

	1990	1991	1992
Lunar New Year	Jan. 27	Feb. 15	Feb. 4
Lantern Festival (15th day, 1st month)	Feb. 10	Mar. 1	Feb. 18
Dragon Boat Festival (5th day, 5th month)	May 28	June 16	
Mid-Autumn Festival (15th day, 8th month)	Oct. 3	Sept. 22	Sept. 11
Confucius's Birthday (27th day, 8th month)	Oct. 15	Oct. 4	
Buddha's Birthday	May 2	May 21	
Qingming	Apr. 5	Apr. 5	Apr. 5

	Old Spelling	*Pinyin*	*Province in Pinyin*
厦门	AMOY	Xiamen	Fujian
鞍山	ANSHAN	Anshan	Liaoning
安阳	ANYANG	Anyang	Henan
常州	CHANGCHOW	Changzhou	Jiangsu
长春	CHANGCHUN	Changchun	Jilin
长沙	CHANGSHA	Changsha	Hunan
肇庆	CHAOCHING	Zhaoqing	Guangdong
樟州	CHENGCHOW	Zhangzhou	Fujian
郑州	CHENGCHOW	Zhengzhou	Henan
承德	CHENGTEH	Chengde	Hebei
成都	CHENGTU	Chengdu	Sichuan
嘉峪关	CHIAYUKUAN	Jiayuguan	Gansu
景洪 (西双版纳)	CHINGHUNG, HSISHUANG PANNA	Jinghong, Xishuangbanna	Yunnan
井冈山	CHINGKANG MOUNTAINS	Jinggang Shan	Jianxi
景德镇	CHINGTECHEN	Jingdezhen	Jianxi
镇江	CHINGKIANG (also Chenkiang)	Zhenjiang	Jiangsu
秦皇岛	CHINWANGTAO	Qinhuangdao	Hebei
酒泉	CHIUCHUAN	Jiuquan	Gansu
九华山	CHIUHUA MOUNTAINS	Jiuhua Shan	Anhui
曲阜	CHUFU	Qufu	Shandong
重庆	CHUNGKING	Chongqing	Sichuan
福州	FOOCHOW	Fuzhou	Fujian
佛山	FASHAN (also Fatshan)	Foshan	Guangdong
抚顺	FUSHUN	Fushun	Liaoning

海口	HAIKOW	Haikou	Guangdong
杭州	HANGCHOW	Hangzhou	Zhejiang
邯郸	HANTAN	Handan	Hebei
哈尔滨	HARBIN	Harbin	Heilongjiang
衡阳	HENGYANG	Hengyang	Hunan
合肥	HOFEI	Hefei	Anhui
襄樊	HSIANGFAN	Xiangfan	Hubei
湘潭	HSIANGTAN	Xiangtan	Henan
新会	HSINHUI (also Sunwai)	Xinhui	Guangdong
咸宁	HSIENNING	Xianning	Hubei
锡林浩特	HSILINHOT	Xilinhot	Nei Monggol
新乡	HSINHSIANG	Xinxiang	Henan
西柏坡	HSIPAIPO	Xibaipo	Hebei
徐州	HSUCHOW	Xuzhou	Jiangsu
黄山	HUANG MOUNTAINS	Huang Shan	Anhui
呼和浩特	HUHEHOT	Hohhot	Nei Monggol
辉县	HUIHSIEN	Hui Xian	Henan
宜兴	IHSING (also Yising)	Yixing	Jiangsu
开封	KAIFENG	Kaifeng	Henan
江门	KIANGMEN (also Kongmoon)	Jiangmen	Guangdong
吉林	KIRIN	Jilin	Jilin
九江	KIUKIANG	Jiujiang	Jiangxi
巩县	KUNGHSIEN	Gongxian	Henan
昆明	KUNMING	Kunming	Yunnan
广州	KWANGCHOW (also Canton)	Guangzhou	Guangdong
桂林	KWEILIN	Guilin	Guangxi
桂平	KWEIPING	Guiping	Guangxi
拉萨	LHASA	Lhasa	Xizang (Tibet)
兰州	LANCHOW	Lanzhou	Gansu
连云港	LIENYUNKANG	Lianyungang	Jiangsu
林县	LINHSIEN	Linxian	Henan
柳州	LIUCHOW	Liuzhou	Guangxi
乐山	LOSHAN	Leshan	Sichuan
洛阳	LOYANG	Luoyang	Henan
路南—石林	LUNAN—STONE FOREST	Lunan—Stone Forest	Yunnan
马鞍山	MAANSHAN	Ma'anshan	Anhui
莫干山	MOKAN MOUNTAINS	Mogan Shan	Zhejiang

紫金山	MT. CHIKING	Zijin Shan	Jiangsu
庐山	MT. LUSHAN	Lushan	Jiangxi
峨嵋山	MT. OMEI	Emei Shan	Sichuan
南昌	NANCHANG	Nanchang	Jiangxi
南京	NANKING	Nanjing	Jiangsu
南宁	NANNING	Nanning	Guangxi
宁波	NINGPO	Ningbo	Zhejiang
北雁荡山	NORTH YENTANG MOUNTAINS	Bei Yandang Shan	Zhejiang
包头	PAOTOW	Baotou	Nei Monggo
北戴河	PEHTAIHO (also Peitaihe)	Beidaihe	Hebei
北京	PEKING	Beijing	
宾阳	PINYANG	Binyang	Guangxi
三门峡	SANMEN GORGE	Sanmenxia	Henan
上海	SHANGHAI	Shanghai	
绍兴	SHAOHSING	Shaoxing	Zhejiang
韶山	SHAOSHAN	Shaoshan	Hunan
沙市	SHASHIH	Shashi	Hebei
沙石峪	SHASHIHYU	Shashiyu	Hebei
胜利油田	SHENGLI OIL FIELD	Shengli Oil Field	Shandong
沈阳	SHENYANG	Shenyang	Liaoning
石家庄	SHIHCHIACHUANG (also Shihkiachwang)	Shijiazhuang	Hebei
石河子	SHIHHOTZU	Shihezi	Xinjiang
西安	SIAN	Xi'an	Shaanxi
苏州	SOOCHOW	Suzhou	Jiangsu
汕头	SWATOW	Shantou	Guangdong
大寨	TACHAI	Dazhai	Shanxi
大庆油田	TACHING OIL FIELD	Daqing Oil Field	Heilongjian
泰安(泰山)	TAIAN (Mt. Tai)	Tai'an (Mt. Tai)	Shandong
太原	TAIYUAN	Taiyuan	Shanxi
大港油田	TAKANG OIL FIELD	Dagang Oil Field	Tianjin
大连	TALIEN	Dalian (also Luda)	Liaoning
唐山	TANGSHAN	Tangshan	Hebei
丹江	TANKIANG	Danjiang	Hubei
大同	TATUNG	Datong	Shanxi
天津	TIENTSIN	Tianjin	
济南	TSINAN	Jinan	Shandong
青岛	TSINGTAO	Qingdao	Shandong
从化	TSUNGHUA	Conghua	Guangdong

Chinese	Wade-Giles	Pinyin	Province
遵化	TSUNHUA	Zunhua	Hebei
敦煌	TUNHUANG	Dunhuang	Gansu
吐鲁番	TURFAN	Turpan	Xinjiang
淄博	TZUPO	Zibo	Shandong
乌鲁木齐	URUMCHI	Urumqi	Xinjiang
万县	WANHSIEN	Wan Xian	Sichuan
潍坊	WEIFANG	Weifang	Shandong
温州	WENCHOW	Wenzhou	Zhejiang
武汉	WUHAN	Wuhan	Hubei
芜湖	WUHU	Wuhu	Anhui
武鸣	WUMING	Wuming	Guangxi
无锡	WUSIH	Wuxi	Jiangsu
扬州	YANGCHOW	Yangzhou	Jiangsu
阳泉	YANGCHUAN	Yangquan	Shanxi
阳朔	YANGSHUO	Yangshuo	Guangxi
延安	YENAN	Yan'an	Shanxi
烟台	YENTAI	Yantai	Shandong
岳阳	YOYANG	Yueyang	Hunan
禹县	YUHSIEN	Yuxian	Henan

DYNASTIES-pinyin (old spelling)

Chinese	Dynasty	Period
夏	Xia (Hsia)	c. 21st–16th century B.C.
商	Shang (Shang)	c. 16th–11th century B.C.
西周	Western Zhou (Chou)	c. 11th century–771 B.C.
春秋	Spring and Autumn Period	770–476 B.C.
战国	Warring States Period	475–221 B.C.
秦	Qin (Chin)	221–206 B.C.
西汉	Western Han (Han)	206 B.C.–A.D. 24
东汉	Eastern Han (Han)	25–220
三国	The Three Kingdoms	220–265
魏	Wei (Wei)	220–265
蜀	Shu (Shu)	221–263
吴	Wu (Wu)	222–280
西晋	Western Jin (Tsin)	265–316
东晋	Eastern Jin (Tsin)	317–420
南北朝	Southern and Northern Dynasties	420–589
南朝	Southern Dynasties	420–589
宋	Song (Sung)	420–479
齐	Qi (Chi)	479–502

梁	Liang (Liang)	502–557
陈	Chen (Chen)	557–589
北朝	Northern Dynasties	386–581
北魏	Northern Wei (Wei)	386–534
东魏	Eastern Wei	534–550
西魏	Western Wei	535–556
北齐	Northern Qi (Chi)	550–577
北周	Northern Zhou (Chou)	557–581
隋	Sui (Sui)	581–618
唐	Tang (Tang)	618–907
五代	Five Dynasties	907–960
辽	Liao (Liao)	916–1125
宋	Song (Sung)	960–1279
北宋	Northern Song (Sung)	960–1127
南宋	Southern Song (Sung)	1127–1279
西夏	Western Xia (Hsia)	1038–1227
金	Jin (Kin)	1115–1234
元	Yuan (Yuan)	1271–1368
明	Ming (Ming)	1368–1644
	Hongwu (Hung Wu)	1368–1399
	Jianwen (Chien Wen)	1399–1403
	Yongle (Yung Lo)	1403–1425
	Hongxi (Hung Hsi)	1425–1426
	Xuande (Hsuan Teh)	1426–1436
	Zhengtong (Cheng Tung)	1436–1450
	Jingtai (Ching Tai)	1450–1457
	Tianshun (Tien Shun)	1457–1465
	Cheng Hua (Cheng Hua)	1465–1488
	Hongzhi (Hung Chih)	1488–1506
	Zhengde (Cheng Teh)	1506–1522
	Jiajing (Chia Ching)	1522–1567
	Longqing (Lung Ching)	1567–1573
	Wanli (Wan Li)	1573–1620
	Taichang (Tai Chang)	1620–1621
	Tianqi (Tien Chi)	1621–1628
	Chongzhen (Chung Cheng)	1628–1644
清	Qing (Ching)	1644–1911
	Shunzhi (Shun Chih)	1644–1662
	Kangxi (Kang Hsi)	1662–1723
	Yongzheng (Yung Cheng)	1723–1736

Qianlong (Chien Lung)	1736–1796
Jiaqing (Chia Ching)	1796–1821
Daoguang (Tao Kuang)	1821–1851
Xianfeng (Hsien Feng)	1851–1862
Tongzhi (Tung Chih)	1862–1875
Guangxu (Kuang Hsu)	1875–1908
Xuantong (Hsuan Tung)	1908–1911

HOW TO PRONOUNCE CHINESE LETTERS

Following is a table of the Chinese phonetic alphabet showing pronunciation with approximate English equivalents. Letters in the Wade-Giles system are in parentheses.

"**a**" (a), a vowel, as in far;

"**b**" (p), a consonant, as in be;

"**c**" (ts), a consonant, as in "ts" in its; and

"**ch**" (ch), a consonant, as in "ch" in church, strongly aspirated;

"**d**" (t), a consonant, as in do;

"**e**" (e), a vowel, as "er" in her, the "r" being silent; but "**ie**," a diphthong, as in yes and "**ei**," a diphthong, as in way;

"**f**" (f), a consonant, as in foot;

"**g**" (k), a consonant, as in go;

"**h**" (h), a consonant, as in her, strongly aspirated;

"**i**" (i), a vowel, two pronunciations:
1) as in eat
2) as in sir in syllables with the consonants c, ch, r, s, sh, z and zh;

"**j**" (ch), a consonant, as in jeep;

"**k**" (k), a consonant, as in kind, strongly aspirated;

"**l**" (l), a consonant, as in land;

"**m**" (m), a consonant, as in me;

"**n**" (n), a consonant, as in no;

"**o**"(o), a vowel, as in "aw" in law;

"**p**" (p), a consonant, as in par, strongly aspirated;

"**q**" (ch), a consonant, as "ch" in cheek;

"**r**" (j), a consonant pronounced as "r" but not rolled, or like "z" in azure;

"**s**" (s, ss, sz), a consonant, as in sister; and "**sh**" (sh), a consonant, as "sh" in shore;

"**t**" (t), a consonant, as in top, strongly aspirated;

"**u**" (u), a vowel, as in too, also as in the French "u" in "tu" or the German umlauted "u" in "Muenchen";

"**v**" (v), is used only to produce foreign and national minority words, and local dialects;

"**w**" (w), used as a semi-vowel in syllables beginning with "u" when not preceded by consonants, pronounced as in want;

"**x**" (hs), a consonant, as "sh" in she;

"**y**" used as a semi-vowel in syllables beginning with "i" or "u" when not preceded by consonants, pronounced as in yet;
"**z**" (ts, tz), a consonant, as in zero; and "**zh**" (ch), a consonant, as "j" in jump."

—from *China Reconstructs,* March 1979

CELSIUS-FAHRENHEIT CONVERSION TABLE

Centigrade (Celsius)		Fahrenheit
−40°		−40°
−20°		− 4°
0°	Freezing Point	32°
10°		50°
20°		68°
30°		86°
40°		104°
50°		122°
60°		140°
70°		158°
80°		176°
90°		194°
100°	Boiling Point	212°

To convert Fahrenheit to Celsius subtract 32, multiply by 5, and divide by 9. To convert Celsius to Fahrenheit multiply by 9, divide by 5, and add 32.

MILE-KILOMETER CONVERSION TABLES

Miles	Kilometers	Kilometers	Miles
1	1.6093	1	.621
2	3.2186	2	1.242
3	4.8279	3	1.863
4	6.4372	4	2.484
5	8.0465	5	3.105
6	9.6558	6	3.726
7	11.2651	7	4.347
8	12.8744	8	4.968
9	14.4837	9	5.589
10	16.093	10	6.21
20	32.186	20	12.42
30	48.279	30	18.63
40	64.372	40	24.84
50	80.465	50	31.05
60	96.558	60	37.26
70	112.651	70	43.47
80	128.744	80	49.68
90	144.837	90	55.89

Distances Between Main Tourist Cities

(Shortest distance between cities by rail in kilometres)

	Beijing	Shanghai	Tianjin	Guangzhou	Nanning	Changsha	Shaoshan	Wuchang	Nanjing	Wuxi	Suzhou	Hangzhou	Jinan	Qingdao	Xi'an	Kunming	Chengdu	Chongqing	Zhengzhou	Shijiazhuang	Dalian	Shenyang	Changchun
Shanghai	1462																						
Tianjin	137	1325																					
Guangzhou	2313	1811	2450																				
Nanning	2565	2063	2702	1334																			
Changsha	1587	1187	1724	726	978																		
Shaoshan	1718	1216	1855	755	1007	131																	
Wuchang	1229	1534	1366	1084	1336	358	489																
Nanjing	1157	305	1020	2116	2368	1492	1521	1229															
Wuxi	1334	128	1197	1939	2191	1315	1344	1406	177														
Suzhou	1376	86	1239	1897	2149	1273	1302	1448	219	42													
Hangzhou	1651	189	1514	1622	1874	998	1027	1356	494	317	275												
Jinan	494	968	357	2284	2536	1689	1820	1200	663	840	882	1157											
Qingdao	887	1361	750	2677	2929	2082	2213	1593	1056	1233	1275	882	393										
Xi'an	1165	1511	1302	2129	2381	1534	1665	1045	1206	1383	1425	1700	1177	1570									
Kunming	3179	2677	3316	2216	1501	1503	1532	1950	2982	2805	2763	2488	3119	3512	1942								
Chengdu	2048	2353	2185	2544	1829	1831	1860	1887	2048	2225	2267	2542	2019	2412	842	1100							
Chongqing	2552	2501	2689	2040	1325	1327	1356	1774	2552	2729	2771	2312	2523	2916	1346	1102	504						
Zhengzhou	695	1000	832	1618	1870	892	1023	534	695	872	914	1189	666	1059	511	2453	1353	1857					
Shijiazhuang	283	1266	420	2030	2282	1304	1435	946	961	1138	1180	1455	298	691	923	2865	1765	2269	412				
Dalian	1238	2426	1101	3551	3803	2825	2956	2467	2121	2298	2340	2615	1458	1851	2403	4417	3286	3790	1933	1521			
Shenyang	841	2029	704	3154	3406	2428	2559	2070	1724	1901	1943	2218	1061	1454	2006	4020	2889	3393	1536	1124	397		
Changchun	1146	2334	1009	3459	3711	2733	2864	2375	2029	2206	2248	2523	1366	1759	2311	4325	3194	3698	1841	1429	702	305	
Harbin	1388	2576	1251	3701	3953	2975	3106	2617	2271	2448	2490	2763	1608	2001	2553	4567	3436	3940	2083	1671	944	547	242

MILE-KILOMETER CONVERSION TABLES

Miles	Kilometers	Kilometers	Miles
100	160.93	100	62.1
200	321.86	200	124.2
300	482.79	300	186.3
400	643.72	400	248.4
500	804.65	500	310.5
600	965.58	600	372.6
700	1126.51	700	434.7
800	1287.44	800	496.8
900	1448.37	900	558.9
1000	1609.3	1000	621.

(Prepared by Linda Malloy)

WEIGHTS AND MEASURES

China uses both the metric system and the Chinese system

1 gong-jin (kilogram)	= 2.2 pounds
1 jin or gun (catty)	= 1.33 pounds = .604 kg.
1 dan (picul) = 100 catties	= 133 pounds or 60.47 kg.
1 mi (meter)	= 39.37 inches
1 gong li (kilometer)	= .6 mile = 1 km.
1 li (Chinese mile)	= .3106 mile = ½ km.
1 mu	= .1647 acres
1 hectare	= 2.471 acres = 10,000 sq. meters
100 hectares	= 247.1 acre = 1 sq. km.
259 hectares	= 1 sq. mile

LEADERS

In early 1989, Li Peng was premier, Deng Xiaoping was usually described as "leader" or "elder statesman," and Zhao Ziyang was general secretary of the Communist Party. Yang Shangkun was president.

GLOSSARY

arhats—Buddhists who have attained Nirvana.

bodhisattvas—Buddhist saints who have attained Nirvana but have returned to help others. See "What Is There to See and Do?"

CAAC—formerly China's only airline. See "Getting Around."

cadre—in Chinese *kanpu,* meaning "core element." Any person who plays a leadership role.

QUICK REFERENCE TO WORLD TIME ZONES

All of China is in one time zone. At 8 a.m. in China the time is 1 a.m. in West Germany or 7 a.m. in Singapore. The time in China is 13 hours later than in the eastern United States. For example, 8 a.m. in China is 7 p.m. Eastern Standard Time, or 6 p.m. Daylight Savings Time, the *previous* day in New York City.

C.I.T.S.—China International Travel Service.

C.T.S.—China Travel Service (the travel agency for Overseas Chinese and Compatriots).

dagoba—similar to an Indian stupa, a bell-shaped tower under which is buried a Buddhist relic or the ashes of a monk.

Dist. A.P.—distance airport.

Dist. R.W.—distance railway station.

F.E.C.s—Foreign Exchange Certificates.

F.F.—Foreign Friend

feng-shui—literally, wind and water. Geomancy. The belief that the placement of buildings in relation to water, and the contours of the land, affects the fortunes of the people who live in or near them; in the case of tombs, the placement affects the fortunes of the descendants.

guanxi—connections. See ''Local Customs.''

H.K.—Hong Kong

J.V.—joint venture; a business arrangement involving several parties. China has entered into many joint ventures with foreign businessmen.

lohan—the Chinese word for *arhat*.

Luxingshe—the Chinese name for C.I.T.S.

Manchu—the group from northeast China who ruled China under the dynasty name *Qing*.

Mongol—the group of people from north China who ruled China under the dynasty name *Yuan*.

neolithic—pertaining to the Stone-Age period in which man developed pottery, weaving, and agriculture, and worked with polished stone and metal tools.

penjing—the art of growing miniature trees and plants. Similar to Japanese *bonsai*.

P.L.A.—People's Liberation Army (currently being reorganized).

pinyin—the new system of romanizing the Chinese language now adopted as official.

pusa—the Chinese word for bodhisattva.

qigong—Chinese yoga. Health and healing through breathing exercises and magnetism.

ren.—renovated.

res.—reservation.

R.M.B.—*ren min bi*—people's money, one of the terms used to refer to Chinese currency. R.M.B. is not the same as F.E.C., above.

stele—a large stone tablet used to commemorate an event, a life, or an important piece of writing.

Wade-Giles—the most commonly used of the old systems of romanizing the Chinese language.

W.C.—water closet. Toilet.

wok—a large, round pan fitted into a stove for cooking.

work unit—every salaried worker belongs to one of these.

X—telephone extension

¥—yuan, similar to a dollar. See ''Budget.''

Names of People in *pinyin* and Wade-Giles

Pinyin	*Wade-Giles*
Bainqen Lama	Panchen Lama
Cixi	Tzu Hsi, (Tsu-hsi, Qing Empress Dowager)
Deng Xiaoping	Teng Hsiao-ping
Feng Yuxiang	Feng Yu-hsiang (general)
Guan Yu	Kuan Yu (Three Kingdoms)
Guo Moruo	Kuo Mo Ruo
Hua Kuofeng	Hua Guo-feng (former Party chairman)
Jiang Jieshi	Chiang Kai-shek
Jiang Qing	Chiang Ching (widow of Mao Tse-tung)
Lin Biao	Lin Piao
Liu Shaoqi	Liu Shao-chi (former president)
Mao Zedong	Mao Tse-tung
Sun Yixian	Sun Yat-sen (father of republican China)
Xuan Zang	Hsuan-tsang (Tang dynasty monk)
Yuan Shikai	Yuan Shih-kai (2nd president of China)
Zhong Shan	Chung Shan (the honorific name of Dr. Sun Yat-sen)
Zhou Enlai	Chou En-lai (former premier of China)
Zhu Yanzhang	Chu Yuan-chuan (first Ming Emperor)

BUDGET AND HOTEL QUICK REFERENCE

HOW MUCH MONEY SHOULD YOU TAKE TO CHINA?

Be aware that (a) only a few credit cards are accepted only by the larger and more expensive hotels and some restaurants, and stores for foreign visitors. Cash advances cost 4%. See "Important Addresses and Information." Find out before you go the latest regulations regarding credit card usage in China from your credit card company; (b) personal checks are not generally accepted, but some can be cashed at the Bank of China with some credit cards; (c) companies and embassies established in China can pay by check if known to the person cashing the check; (d) it takes five banking days to cable money to you in China, assuming everyone knows his job and has your passport number; (e) you might ask your embassy to cash a personal check, but I wouldn't count on it.

These all mean, of course, that you should take enough **cash or traveler's checks.** Cash brings a slightly lower foreign exchange rate than traveler's checks, leaving you with less money. Acceptable traveler's checks are listed below.

For current foreign exchange rates, check business newspapers, your local bank, or *China Daily*. For rates at press time, see below.

Prepaid travelers booking through a travel agent usually have to pay the full price of the tour prior to their arrival in China. You may have to pay extra at the end of your trip. A final accounting is tallied toward the end of the tour. If there are to be additional expenses, you are usually consulted during the trip. For example, flights delayed by weather might mean an option of paying for an additional day or cutting out another part of the tour.

Many travel agencies cover any small additional costs themselves rather than antagonize their clients. On the other hand, you might get some money back.

So how much money should you take to China?

Read ahead and then budget in addition to the price of your China tour:

¥ _____ (a) at least ¥300 per week for "unforeseen circumstances" that one hopes won't happen. How much would it cost if you lost your passport and had to spend a couple of extra nights in a hotel in Shanghai?

¥ _____ (b) for "optional tours" that might mean you would otherwise be wandering around the city alone.

¥ _____ (c) for whatever you want for shopping. It's painful to resist buying things you've watched being made, especially if you know they are more expensive at home; don't forget film and film processing (if you can't wait to do it before you get home).

¥ _____ (d) if you socialize a lot and enjoy buying a round of drinks in the evening.

¥ _____ (e) if you take people out to dinner.

¥ _____ (f) for laundry, cheap at modest hotels; more at international standard hotels.

¥ _____ (g) for a massage at a modest hotel barber shop, or for about ¼ of that at a public bath house.

¥ _____ (h) for a barber or hairdresser.

¥ _____ (i) for miscellaneous extras—overweight luggage, telephone calls, medical expenses, postage, photography, etc.

After you total this up, add about 20%, and you should have sufficient.

¥ _____ Total.

Pay-as-you-go travelers should budget in addition to the above:

¥ _____ (j) for a hotel room (one or two people). The highest prices are for luxury, international standard hotels. The lowest prices listed are for adequate but crude accommodations, almost always with private bath in the smaller cities. In the larger cities you may have to book an expensive hotel room.

¥ _____ (k) for food and drinks.

¥ _____ (l) for transportation (between and inside cities), permits, etc. Count on airport tax each time you leave China. Less energetic people tend to use taxis more, and could spend a maximum of ¥190 a day on taxis.

¥ _____ (m) for entrance fees to most tourist attractions.

¥ _____ (n) bus or boat tours

¥ _____ (o) C.I.T.S. charges.

¥ _____ (p) entertainment

¥ _____ (q) unforeseen circumstances like currency fluctuations, medical treatment, and price changes. Give yourself ample. Be sure you are covered by medical insurance.

¥ _____ **Grand Total.** Now figure out what that comes to in your own currency.

Overseas Chinese and backpackers should calculate 10% to 40% less on hotels and transportation if they're good at arguing.

Those who want to save money have to take much more time, and not care about the highest available standards of cleanliness and comfort.

If you go on your own, save first **before** going to China. Look for bargain airfares. Haggle with managers in travel agencies and airline offices (especially Air China, CAIL, KAL, PAL, SIA, and CAL). You have nothing to lose but your pride. Read the youth travel columns in newspapers. Talk to backpackers about cutting costs. Find out about flying as a courier. Check out travel agents in local Chinatowns. What about the train from London to Beijing via Moscow? Tickets on the Trans-Siberian railway are said to be much cheaper if bought in an East European country.

Or how about the special air rates between London and Hong Kong for British citizens? Or excursion fares? Across the Pacific, check out Euro Asia Express or Avia Travel. Look into tour prices from Canada. How about via Manila? C.I.T.S. and CAAC discount from December 1 to March 31 on some routes and tours. Hotels too.

Let the Chinese pay your way, or at least part of it. Go as **a teacher or foreign expert,** or while you are in China offer to teach at a school for a few months. The Chinese will hire qualified teachers more readily if you pay your own airfare to get there, and will give you a modest bit of pocket money besides, and possibly travel discounts. You'll get a much less superficial experience than as a tourist, and teaching can be very satisfying.

Organize your own tour group. In a group of 15 persons (sometimes 10), inclusive service in China is free for one to two travelers, and airlines might give one free seat.

In China

At each **hotel,** do not be afraid to *ask* if there are cheaper rooms. If the clerk says no, keep trying every day, or try other hotels. The Chinese might offer you the most expensive for your own comfort as well as for the higher revenue. Rooms on the uppermost floors are usually more expensive. *Argue* pleasantly. Tell the clerk you're a student (if you have your card), or a foreign expert (even if you've just given *one* lecture). One Overseas Chinese argued successfully for 50% hotel discounts, and he didn't look Chinese! Many hotels have dorms with up to 30 or 40 beds in a room for about ¥10 and up. Try hostels. Share rooms with friends, as most rooms cost the same for one guest as for two. As hotels in big cities are more expensive, stay away from the center of the city. Or take anything you can get for the first night, and then look around.

Ask a **local Chinese** friend to buy you a train ticket (at local prices). You can always pay the difference on the train if the conductor objects—and few conductors so far have objected.

Book **hard-class train.** You might like it. If not, you can frequently upgrade your accommodations, if space is available, by paying more.

Travel with an Overseas Chinese friend and book through **C.T.S.**

Avoid travel agents if you can.

Do not assume that the Chinese are giving you anything free. Always ask, "What is the charge?"

Go by **public bus or boat.** Some of these aren't bad. Some are filthy and noisy. See "Jiangmen" for one kind of boat. Some buses are air-conditioned and reasonable. The price difference between the regular ferry and the luxury tour boats on the Yangtze River is considerable. So are the standards of comfort and privacy. See "Yangtze Gorges."

Eat in bun or noodle shops or at market stalls. These cost considerably less than hotel restaurants and some of them are clean. One backpacker spent 2½ months in China eating cheaply at market stalls and never got sick. But others aren't so lucky.

Avoid tourist restaurants. Invite one of the young people trying to practice English on you to take you to a restaurant where ordinary people eat.

If you're traveling only a few kilometers by **taxi,** it may be cheaper to have your taxi wait than to hire a car by the day or the half-day. Ask about waiting time and maximum distances for the day rate.

Ask your hotel service desk or C.I.T.S. if a **tour bus** you can join goes to the tourist attractions. For one or two people, this may be cheaper than taking taxis. You might try to hitch free rides with tour groups. Or try to interest other individual travelers in sharing taxis or minibuses. How about renting a bicycle?

Stay with friends or relatives. Courtesy demands you take them presents, but this could be anything from a bag of fruit, candy, or cookies, to a video or refrigerator. See *Gifts* in "What to Take" and "Special for Overseas Chinese."

Foreign hitchhikers have traveled around China successfully, sleeping in hostels for local Chinese (after much persistent pleading), sometimes for less than ¥1 a night. (Take your own bedding and don't be surprised at bedbugs.)

Travel during low tourist season. The south is pleasant in the wintertime.

Search out backpackers, who are usually happy to exchange travel tips. Look for them in dormitories at hotels like the Chongwenmen in Beijing, and the Chungking Mansions in Hong Kong.

RECENT PRICES

These are listed primarily to help you plan. Since the mid-1980s, China has been allowing market forces to set prices, and many of the following will go up or down. Yes, some prices might go *down* 10 to 50% in winter. Prices depend on supply and demand. Budget travelers should shop around for everything.

These prices will also help you avoid being ripped off by China's new class of private enterprisers, with whom you are expected to haggle over prices. Do start at one-quarter of the asking price and see what happens when you feign lack of interest, and don't pay more than you would in a government fixed-price store.

Most quotes here are FEC unless otherwise specified. Most hotels mentioned are top hotels.

Note that tourist facilities like Friendship Stores and hotels are usually paid in F.E.C.s.

10% service and 3 or 5% sales tax are added to bills in some joint venture retaurants and hotels.

Some establishments have two sets of prices—the higher for R.M.B.; the lower for F.E.C.

Your highest prices are usually in the big cities, especially Beijing. Guangzhou is cheaper. The more expensive the hotel, the higher the cost of other services like laundry, food and hair cuts. US$1 = HK$7.8.

Businesses are named here to give you some options. Mention does not necessarily mean endorsement.

Collected in late 1988 and early 1989, prices listed here are subject to inflation, but they should give you an idea of what to expect.

The black market rate is roughly ¥1 FEC to ¥2 RMB, but unless you are staying a long time we urge you to avoid it.

Air fares

Cheapest air fares from North America found so far: One Canadian dollar is roughly US$.78. Add US$13 tax for flights from the U.S., Can.$19 to each Canadian flight. Be sure to ask about special conditions, like advance payment, open return, restricted departure days. Maybe your own travel agent can match these prices.

Atlanta or New York to Hong Kong: US$885 (Avia Travel)

New York to Beijing: US$1259 (Avia Travel)

New York to Beijing: US$1123. New York to Hong Kong US$799 (Kuo Feng)

S.F. or L.A. to Hong Kong: US$606; to Beijing: US$780 (Avia Travel)

West Coast to Shanghai: US$710 to $850; to Beijing: $740 to $899 (Euro Asia Express)

Toronto to Shanghai: Can.$1040 to $1190 Toronto to Shanghai to Hong Kong: Can.$1265. (Air China). Westbound, overnight in Shanghai, hotel paid by Air China. Returning Sundays with one-hour layover in Shanghai: (Tour East Holidays).

Toronto to Seoul to Hong Kong: Can.$990. Two-hour layover in Seoul going; overnight hotel in Seoul or New York returning, included in price. (Tour East Holidays)

Sample return airfares from Hong Kong by scheduled charters in US dollars (courtesy of U.S. China Travel Service): Chengdu ($344–$349), Dalian ($464), Fuzhou ($264), Guilin ($226), Haikou ($194), Nanjing ($336), Shenyang ($476), Xi'an ($368).

Sample China domestic one-way airfares: Beijing to Changsha (¥304), Beijing to Guangzhou (¥553) Beijing to Guilin (¥425), Beijing to Urumqi (¥735), Beijing to Xi'an (¥242).

Prices for domestic flights in China can be obtained from many travel agents in North America.

Airport tax:
For international flights (including Hong Kong)——¥20.

Barber Shops, Hairdressers, Massages:
Whole body massage——¥16 to ¥80.
Man's haircut——¥12 to ¥16.
Fingerwave——¥10 to ¥20.

Business Centers:
Garden Hotel and China Hotel (Guangzhou); Nikko (Shanghai).

English typing ¥12–¥24 per page. *Chinese typing* ¥20–¥28 per page. *Shorthand typing* ¥20 –¥25 per page. *Photocopying* 60 fen–90 fen per copy. *Secretarial service* ¥150–¥280 per (7- or 8-hour) day or ¥28–¥50.

Interpreter: English-Chinese ¥95–¥130 per (8-hour) day. More for technical and negotiations.

Rentals 6 to 8 pax conference room ¥40 an hour or ¥240 to ¥20. VCR and TV screen——¥20 an hour or ¥120 per 7-hour day. Electric typewriter——¥20–¥30 an hour or ¥120 per 7-hour day. Manual typewriter——¥10 per hour or ¥60–¥80 per day. Word processor——¥50–¥80 (with operator), ¥25 per page.

Printing name cards——¥80–¥100 for one side, ¥120 for two sides. 100 pieces.

Cigarettes:
American——about ¥5 to ¥5.50 a pack.

Clinic:

(From cost of medicines only to ¥40 for a consultation plus medicines.) At the Jianguo Hotel (Beijing): Acupuncture therapy ¥30, acupuncture to stop smoking ¥35, acupuncture and herbal medicines to lose weight ¥35. Hospitals could cost ¥300 a day.

Communications:

Three-minute *telex* ¥11.60 to ¥15 for China, ¥24 to ¥34 for Hong Kong, ¥48.30 to ¥60 for North America.

Fax service charge ¥15 for first page, then ¥5 and up each page. To China ¥10 to ¥20; to Hong Kong ¥26; to North America ¥50 to ¥72.

International Direct Dial telephone call ¥14.60 per minute to U.S. ¥18 per minute to Canada. *Person-to-person* ¥14.60 plus ¥14.60 per minute to the U.S.

Postage:

Airmail to North America 10 gms ¥1.60; 20 gms ¥2.

Airmail postcard ¥1.30.

Letters inside China about 20 fen for 20 gms.

Food and Beverages:

Western Breakfast Buffet: ¥10 to ¥26.

Chinese Breakfast: ¥8 to ¥18.50.

Continental Breakfast: ¥5 to ¥20.

Chinese banquets: 10 people per table is ideal, although four people can also have a good banquet. The following prices are per person for 10 people.

Beijing: Movenpick US$18 or $25 plus beverages. Comes with live entertainment such as Chinese opera or traditional Chinese dances. Sichuan food.

Guangzhou: Kwangchow Restaurant, Guangzhou. ¥40 to ¥50 gives you a simple banquet. ¥80 to ¥100 is more elaborate. Big portions. China Hotel says ¥80 to ¥100 for a good banquet. Garden Hotel says ¥60 for a simple banquet, ¥70 up to ¥660 for more elaborate.

Shanghai: Hua Ting Sheraton says ¥30 for a simple banquet, ¥60 to ¥80 for more elaborate. Xiqiao Guest House says ¥40 for simple banquet, ¥100 for more elaborate.

Western Food:

Movenpick, Coffee Shop: appetizers ¥16 to ¥22; soups ¥8 to ¥9; fish and seafood ¥24 to ¥46; children's entrees ¥12 to ¥16; sandwiches ¥12 to ¥24; salad bar ¥9 to ¥14; steaks ¥30 to ¥58; hamburgers ¥18; other entrees ¥20 to ¥48.

Kentucky Fried Chicken: ¥10 for chicken, salad, and potatoes.

Rainbow Hotel (Shanghai): sandwiches ¥9 to ¥11; hot dogs ¥7; eggs ¥4; omelets ¥3 to ¥5.50; noodles and rice ¥5 to ¥12; hamburgers

¥10 to ¥15; entrees ¥6 to ¥24; salads and soups ¥4.50 to ¥10; juices ¥5.50; coffee ¥2.50; fresh milk ¥4; beer or Coca-Cola ¥4; mineral water ¥2.

Budgeting: at medium-priced hotels or the cheaper restaurants of some of the top hotels (Guangzhou especially), you can do well with ¥60 a day. You can eat even cheaper in less expensive hotels, local restaurants, and street stalls, or if you take your own granola bars.

Bar: By the bottle: French white wine ¥75 to ¥150, French red wine ¥90 to ¥125; Portuguese wine ¥80; Italian wine ¥75 to ¥85; champagne ¥95 to ¥250. By the glass: Chinese ¥60 to ¥6.50; imported ¥9.50. (Movenpick)

Minibars (in guest bedrooms)

Beijing International: ¥11 to ¥17 for small one-shot bottles of Campari, martinis, Four Roses, Canadian V.O., cognac, and vodka; ¥20 for J.W. and Old Pall, and ¥25 for Chivas Regal. Coca-Cola and local beer ¥7.50. Heineken and juices ¥9. Munchies ¥8 to ¥13.

Novotel Guangzhou Jiang Nan: beer ¥6 to ¥8. Mineral water ¥5. Orange juice ¥7. Coca-Cola ¥6. Peanuts ¥8.

Garden Hotel: one-shot bottles of Scotch, Cognac VSOP, vodka, gin, and rum ¥15 to ¥18; beer ¥10 and ¥12; sodas ¥8; water ¥6 to ¥12; juice ¥6; instant coffee ¥3.

Tea (Coffee Shop of White Swan Hotel, Guangzhou) ¥8 and worth it for the view.

Laundry:

As a general rule, the cheapter the hotel the cheaper the laundry. Cheap does not necessarily mean bad, but your chances of a good job improve with higher prices.

Wet wash: man's shirt ¥2.50 to ¥6; trousers ¥3 to ¥6; underpants ¥1.50 to ¥2; blouse ¥1.50 to ¥6; woman's sweater ¥3.50 to ¥9.

Dry cleaning: two-piece suits ¥11 to ¥18; tie ¥2 to ¥5; trousers ¥4.50 to ¥8; blouse ¥3.50 to ¥7.

Photography:

Beijing Friendship Store: developing film ¥2FEC or ¥3 RMB. Prints 50 fen FEC or 70 fen RMB. Takes two days.

Most tourist stores have low-speed 35 mm color-print film at varying prices. It is difficult to find other varieties and sizes, especially Polaroid. Cheapest film found: Guangzhou Friendship Store 36-exposure 35 mm Kodacolor ASA 100 ¥9.20 (other stores about ¥11); ASA 200 ¥11.60. Fujicolor 100 ¥9. Fujichrome 100 ¥19.

Porters:

In hotels, ¥3 to ¥5 per load. Generally, ¥1 to ¥1.50 each bag. At railway stations, they might ask for ¥20 but don't give it to them.

Recreation:

Movenpick: Aerobics class ¥15; live concerts (symphonies, etc.) US$5; tennis ¥18; free movies and swim for guests.

Jin Sha: Disco ¥15.

Nikko: Disco ¥35 (free to guests); free in-house movies two times a week; free use of pool and gym for guests; Karaoke bar ¥10.

Dong Fang: Karaoke bar ¥40.

Shopping:

Shanghai Art and Curio Store (Shanghai). Cloisonne: package of 7 bangles ¥18; bracelet ¥9.80; 5 panda pins ¥4.90; 2″ picture frames ¥7. Silk ties from ¥6.80. Brocade clutch bag ¥7.60.

Free Market (between Jianguo Hotel and Friendship Store, Beijing). First asking price (you can probably bargain for at least 50% of this if you pay F.E.C. "wai hui"): Mongolian boots ¥130; down coats ¥140; beautiful silk camisole and panty sets ¥40; silk panties ¥10. Much more. Good buys if you check goods carefully.

Beijing Friendship Store: Bicycles Chinese ¥254 to ¥301; 4-speed Bugatti ¥570; fur hats ¥76 to ¥585; cashmere sweaters for women (plain) ¥180 to ¥840; 7″ miniature violin with own bow and case ¥58.50.

Guangzhou Friendship Store: Embroidered placemats ¥2 and up (if you're lucky; usually cheapest ¥12). Beaded purses ¥4.50 to ¥51. Silk blouses ¥59 to ¥90. Embroidered coats ¥121 to ¥328. Men's cashmere sweaters ¥121 to ¥315. Table cloths cheaper here than Beijing and Shanghai.

Shanghai Airport Transit Lounge: Beautiful white-on-white silk happy coats ¥52.50. Most other items more expensive than Friendship Store.

Shanghai Friendship Store: Men's cotton-polyester dress shirts ¥14. Women's cashmere sweaters ¥172 and up; men's ¥195 and up. Fur caps ¥25 to ¥420. Black leather jackets and coats ¥265 to ¥477. Women's skirts ¥290; women's trousers ¥452. Silk: beautiful white-on-white dressing gowns ¥120; jackets ¥130; women's pajamas ¥145; camisoles ¥14; panties ¥6; men's briefs ¥9; men's dress shirts ¥46.50; textiles ¥19.80 and up per meter. Kites ¥23 to ¥86. Brass hot pots ¥112 to ¥143.

Sightseeing:

Transportation in land cruisers with four passengers: *Holiday Inn Lhasa Hotel, Tibet:* Day trip to Yamdrok Lake ¥500; Three-day Xigatse trip about ¥1600. *Beijing:* C.I.T.S. day tour ¥65; half-day tour ¥30. Great Wall and Ming Tombs ¥90. Summer Palace and Lama Temple ¥65. Pick up at Lido, Grat Wall, Jinglun, Kunlun, or Jianguo. Not all daily. These tours are the cheapest with English-speaking guides.

Bus tour to Great Wall and Ming Tombs with Chinese-speaking

guide ¥12. City Bus Tour ¥20. Stops at some tourist attractions. Guide on bus only.

The price for one or two people sightseeing alone can be very high, about ¥112 to ¥300 for one person per day.

Entrance to most tourist attractions ¥1.50 to ¥4.50. Cable cars can be much more expensive.

Luggage Storage: 50 fen to ¥1.50 per bag per day. Some hotels free. Airports about ¥1.50 a day.

Tours: Cheap does not necessarily mean bad. Some tours are the least expensive because of volume, good relations between tour operator and organizer, and winter discounts. Businesspeople might want to take advantage of these packages too. Ask about conditions, quality of hotels, and additional expenses like tips and taxes.

Hong Kong: Seven days US$959 and up, five nights' hotel accommodation, half-day sightseeing in Hong Kong, transfers, and service of a local English-speaking guide. From New York. (Sino-American Tours Inc.)

Beijing-Nanjing-Wuxi-Hangzhou-Suzhnou-Shanghai: Two weeks from Vancouver, Can.$2099; from Toronto, Can.$2279 plus $20 visa. All-inclusive winter price. (Tour East Holidays)

Beijing-Jinan-Taishan-Qufu-Suzhou-Shanghai: Two weeks from Toronto, Can.$1995 plus $20 visa. All-inclusive winter price. (Conference Travel of Canada)

Out of Hong Kong:

Mini-package (no food). Guangzhou (1N), Shanghai (2N), Xi'an (2N), Beijing (3N): double hotel occupancy, air or train tickets, transfers, visa handling. US$765. (China Youth Travel)

Soft sleeper to Guangzhou (2N), to Beijing (5N), and hard sleeper train to Moscow: double ocupany US$858. (China Youth Travel)

Transfers   from airport: Garden Hotel ¥18. Hua Ting Sheraton ¥18. Some hotels free.

Transportation:

Bicycles: ¥1 an hour, ¥5 to ¥40 a day.

Taxis: Generally ¥1.20 per km all over China. Some smaller communities might have ¥1 per km.

Flagfall Beijing ¥6.80 per 4 km. Full day ¥187.20 (8 hours and maximum of 120 km, though we bargained one driver down to about ¥150. Flagfall Guangzhou ¥3.60 first 3 km, then ¥1.20 per km. ¥30 an hour if inside the city. Sometimes a small surcharge is added. Flagfall Shanghai ¥10.50 per 5 km for taxis that charge ¥1.20 per km. Waiting time: ¥ 1.20 for five minutes. ¥156 per 8-hour day. Fiat taxis are ¥3 per 5 km and 50 fen per km, but are uncomfortable. Mini-buses are ¥2.40 per km.

Train: Shanghai to Urumqi ¥402; to Guangzhou or Beijing ¥105 for hard berth; ¥200 for soft berth. Includes service charge. (C.I.T.S. Shanghai)

Ship: from Shanghai to Hong Kong ¥246 to ¥1036, including bed and food. (Jin Jiang Shipping Co.)

Ferry: Second class through Yangtze Gorges, Chongqing to Yichang, ¥200 not including meals which are about ¥30 to ¥50 a day.

Standard luxury cruise ship: ¥800 plus ¥30 to ¥50 a day for food. ¥100 each excursion.

Travel agents: High prices in big tourist cities. Service charges for booking train tickets range from ¥2 to ¥30 (mostly for big cities). A guide for one person costs ¥50 to ¥100 per day. Service charges for booking air tickets ¥4 (Beijing Hotel) to ¥20.

Visa service: China visas for individual travelers during high season (when you normally need a letter from a host in China) US$30. (Avia Travel) You can probably get a visa with just a confirmed hotel reservation. Try that first. Visas at a consulate US$7, Can.$8, H.K.$50.

HOTELS

Like everything else, these prices are subject to change, and in some cases, negotiation (depending on supply and demand). They are for a double room with bath which frequently costs the same for one or two people (except in top hotels). Prices are listed to help you budget and should not be considered absolute. Updated quotes from hotels will be published whenever possible by *Travel China Newsletter*.

Prices are quoted in F.E.C.'s, H.K., or U.S. dollars depending upon the information received from hotels. F.E.C. prices are lower than R.M.B. prices. Surcharges of 10 to 15% could be added in some hotels. (Some of these hotels include these taxes in the quoted price.) Payment however is usually made in F.E.C.'s.

The agency from whom you book your hotel should be able to tell you the latest price, but don't count on it unless the hotel is top international standard. Agents have trouble getting information too.

Please note that the telephone numbers are the latest we could possibly obtain. In the late 1980s, China has been in the process of upgrading its telephone service, and therefore changing many of its telephone numbers.

Reservations have been necessary April through October in major tourist areas such as Shanghai, Beijing, Wuhan, Chengdu, Xi'an, and Guilin.

$ means US$ unless otherwise specified. Most beds in a dorm for backpackers range from ¥10 to ¥20. *One US$ = Hong Kong $7.8.*

	telephone	rate in F.E.C.s.	page
Anshan:			
Anshan	27931	¥100	185
Shengli	25958, 27911	¥68–¥120	186
Anyang:			
Anyang	2012, 2157, 2244		187
Baotau:			
Baotou	26612		189
Qingshan (Blue Mountain)	24615	¥110	189
Beidaihe: (Low tourist season: Oct. 2–April 30)			
Beidaihe Hotel for Diplomatic Personnel	41807		191
Jinshan	41678		191
Xishan (West Hill)	2338 X364, 2678		191
Beijing:			
Beijing	5137766	$100–120	216
Beijing International	5126688	$105–125	217
Beijing-Toronto	5002266	$110	217
Chang Fu Gong	5125711	$120–140	217
China World	5005258	$180	217
Club Med	281931 X426		217
Diaoyutai	866250, 868831	US$140	217
Exhibition Center	8316633	¥242	218
Fragrant Hills	285491	$60	218
Grand Hotel			218
Great Wall	5005566	$130	218
Guang Hua	592931	¥130	218
Holiday Inn Lido	5006688	$110	219
Hilton International			219
Huadu	5001166	¥150–160	219
Huaqiao Hotel (O.C.)	4016688	¥165	219
Huiqiao	4214061	¥86	219
Jianguo	5002233	$115–275	220
Kunlun	5003388	$110–120	220
Lu Song Yuan	440436		220
Ming Yuan	654931–2870		220
Movenpick Dragon Spring	3014366, 8773366	$70–85	220
Palace	5128899	$120–160	221
Peace	5128833	$55–98	221
Qianmen	3016688	¥172	221
Shangri-La	8312211	US$110	221
Summer Palace G. H.	285198–462	¥150	221

Xiyuan	8313388	$64–106	221
Yanxiang	5006666	$55	222
Youyi (Friendship)	890621, 8901961	¥117–160	222
Zhaolong	5002299	$86	222
Changchun:			
Changbaishan	883551	¥70–120	228
Nanhu	883571	¥120	229
Provincial Changyi	38495	¥90 a suite	229
Changsha:			
Xiangjiang (Xiang River)	26261	$35	233
Changzhou:			
Changzhou	26971		234
Jiangnanchun		$35	234
Chengde:			
Qiwanglou			239
The 33 Yurt Hotel			239
Chengdu:			
Chengdu	444112, 443312	$40	245
Jinjiang (Brocade River)	24481	$30	245
Minshan International	27101/52611		245
Sichuan College of Education	53981 X19		245
Chongqing:			
Chongqing (Bingguan)	52611		249
Chongqing Fan Dian	49301	¥125–160	249
Holiday Inn City Center	766999	$75–150	250
Shaping Grand	663293, 663257	¥120	249
Renmin (People's)	53421		250
Yuzhou	23829, 23610		250
Dalian:			
Bangchuidao (Ginseng Islet)	235131	¥150	253
Furama	230888	$70	254
Holiday Inn	807467	$65–75	254
International	238238	$55–75	253
Regent	282811	¥150–170	254
Nanshan	238751	¥76–160	254
Datong:			
Datong G.H.	32467, 32333		258
Datong Mining Co.	32431		258
Yungang Hotel	24274, 24284		258
Dazu:			
Dazu	100		260
Dunhuang:			
Dunhuang	74, 2325, 2492		

Foshan:

Foshan	85775, 23338		265
Huaqiao (O.C.)	86511		
Rotating Palace	85622		266

Fushun:

Friendship		¥70	268
Fushan	24481	¥50	268
Oriental Cherry	29004, 29049	¥80	268

Fuzhou:

Foreign Trade Centre Hotel	550154	$30–35	270
Hot Spring Hotel	551818	$40	270
Huaqiao (O.C.)	557603	¥95–135	271
Lakeside	539888	¥183	271

Guangzhou: Reservations absolutely necessary then and also during the Spring Festival. (H) High seasons are during the Trade Fairs; (L) Low seasons at other times.

Baitian E (White Swan)	886968	(H) $140–160; (L) $80–90	287
Baiyun	333998	(H) ¥207; (L)¥138	285
Central	678331	(H) ¥415; (L) ¥170	285
China	666888	(H) $190; (L) $75–90	285
Dong Fang	669900	(H) $100; (L) ¥230–260	285
Garden	338989	(H) $145; (L) $75	285
Guangdong	332950	(H) ¥222; (L) ¥138	286
Guangzhou	338168	(H) ¥143; (L) ¥128	286
Holiday Inn City Center	766999	(H) $150; (L) $75–90	286
Huaqiao (O.C.) Mansion	336888	(H) ¥160–¥180; (L) ¥150–¥160	287
Huaqiao (O.C.) (at Railway Station)	663488	(H) ¥130–¥160; (L) ¥105	287
International	758888	¥130–220	286
Liuhua	668800	(H) ¥160; (L) ¥130	286
Nanhu (South Lake)	706706	(H) ¥90–¥260; (L) ¥90–150	287

New Mainland	673638, 678638	(L) ¥120;	286
		(H) $61	
Novotel	418888	$60–66	287
Ocean	765988	(H) $120;	287
		(L) ¥196	
Shamian	888124	(H) ¥120;	287
		(L) ¥99	

Guilin:

Dangui (Osmanthus)	334300, 332261	$33–52	295
Garden	442411, 443611	$80–160	295
Guilin Jiashan	2240, 2986, 4712		295
Guilin Riverside Resort	222294, 222291	$65–70	295
Gui Shan	443388	$90	294
Holiday Inn Guilin	223950	$75–80	294
Hong Kong	333889	$55–65	295
Li Jiang (Li River)	2881		296
Pine Garden Holiday Resorts	442311		296
Ronghu (Banyan)	223811		295
Sheraton Guilin	225588	$75–90	296
Yangshuo	2260		296

Guiyang:

Huaxi	25973		299

Haikou:

Haikou Hotel	22634, 23234		301
Haikou International Financial	22988		301
Center			
Haikou Tower	23990		301

Handan:

Handan	3168	¥80–¥130	302

Hangzhou:

Dragon	554488	$75–85	309
Friendship	22951		309
Huagang	71324, 72481		309
Huaqiao (O.C.)	23401	¥100–¥170	310
Linping	27415, 53559		310
Shangri-La	22921	$50–100	310
Wanghu	71024		310
Xihu (West Lake)	27196		310
Xiling	28301, 22921		
Xin Qiao	26911, 24991		310
Zhejiang	25601		311

Harbin:

Guoji (International)	31441, 33001	¥58–98	314
Heping Cun (Peace Village)	220101	¥110	314
Swan	22020	¥76–98	305

Hefei:

Daoxinglou	52548		316
Jianghuai	52221		316
Luyang	61814, 60851		316

Hohhot:

Inner Mongolia	41183		322
Xincheng (New City)	23107		322

Huangshan:

Beihai (North Sea)	241		324
Taoyuan (Peach Spring)	295, 381		324
Yupinglou (Jade Screen)	303		324

Jiangmen:

Capital	32524, 35516		326
Donghu (East Lake)	33611		326

Jilin:

Dongguan Hotel	54272	¥70–¥80	328
Milky Way	43717		328
Xi Guan	43141	¥60–¥150	328

Jinan:

Jinan	35351, 3695119	80	332
Nan Jiao	613931		332
Qilu Hotel	47961	¥140–¥160	332
Shadong Teachers University	43711		332
Shungeng Mountain Villa	615901		332

Jingdezhen:

Jingdezhen	4927		334

Jiujiang:

Nanhu	2140		335

Jiuquan:

Jiuquan	2943		337

Kaifeng:

Kaifeng Hotel	22669, 23901		339

Kunming:

Golden Dragon	33104, 33015	¥130–150	345
Green Lake	22192, 23514	¥84	345
Kunming	22063, 23918	¥110–¥130	345

Lanzhou:

Lanzhou	22987, 22985		348
Jincheng	27931		348

Leshan:

Hongzhushan	2528		350
Jia Zhou	22301, 22419	¥84	350

Jiu Ri Feng	2850		350
Lan Lou	2811, 2827		350
Lhasa:			
Banak Shol	23829		360
Holiday Inn Lhasa	22221	$76	360
Kirey	23462		359
No. 1 Hotel	22500		
Snowland	23687		359
Tibet Guest House	24966		360
Lianyungang:			
Shen Zhou	23080, 23088		
Liuzhou:			
Liujiang	25021		361
Liuzhou	24921		361
Luoyang:			
Youyi (Friendship)	22991, 22689		366
Lushan:			
Lulin	282100, 282120	¥90	370
Lushan Hotel	282932, 282060		370
Lushan Mansion	282860, 282160		370
Yunzhong (Amidst the Clouds)	282547		370
Ma'anshan:			
Ma'anshan Guest House	2970		
Ma'anshan Steel Co. Hostel	3098		
Ma'anshan	2970		
Yushanhu	3270, 3251	¥160–200	
Nanchang:			
Jiangxi	64124, 64861		371
Qingshanhu (Green Mountain Lake)	65615, 63473		371
Nanjing:			
Dingshan	685931		381
Jinling	742888, 741999		382
Nanjing	639831, 634121		382
Shengli (Victory)	643035, 643880		
Shuangmenlou	685961, 685535		382
Nanning:			
Ming Yuan	28923		386
Xi Yuan	29923		385
Yongjiang (Yong River)	28123		385
Nantong:			
Tian Nan Hotel	518151	¥120–220	
Ningbo:			
Asia Garden			389

Huaqiao (O.C.)	63175		389
Ningbo	66334		389
Qingdao:			
Badaguan	26800		394
The Guesthouse	26120		394
Huanghai	84215, 85965		394
Huaqiao (O.C.)	86738–9, 85738		394
Huiquan	85215–6, 84220		394
Qiqihar:			
Hubin	23566, 23574, 27991		
Quanzhou:			
Golden Fountain	25078		399
Huaqiao (O.C.)	2366, 2310	¥80–90	399
Qufu:			
Queli	300, 303		403
Kong Family Mansion Hotel			403
Shanghai:			
Cherry Holiday Village	328350		418
City	551133	$75–95	420
Cypress	329388	$55	418
Heping (Peace)	211244, 218050	North Bldg. $50–63	420
Hongqiao (Rainbow)	593388	$60	420
Huaqiao (O.C.)	276226	¥150	420
Hua Ting Guest House	386800	¥180	418
Hua Ting Sheraton	386000	$79–99	418
Jing An	551888	¥157	419
Jin Jiang	534242, 582582	¥136–195	419
Jin Jiang Tower	534242, 582582	$110–130	419
Jinsha	546000	¥$169	419
Mandarin		$135–185	418
Nikko Longbai	593636, 59888	$105	419
Park (Guoji)	275225	$53	420
Seagull	251500	¥132	420
Shanghai	312312	¥144–192	420
Shanghai Hilton International	550000	$135–185	421
Shanghai International Airport	518888		421
Shanghai Mansions	246260	¥150–180	421
Tian Ma	328100	$46	421
Xijiao	328800	$70	421
Westin Pacific	329126		421
Yangtze	595157, 595380		422
YMCA	261040		422
Shantou:			
International	51212	$47–52	426
Longhu	60706	¥85–128	426

Shaoguan:

Green Lake Villa	75109, 74928	$25	428
Jin Yuan Villa	668800	¥70	428
Shaoguan	81870, 81871	¥70	428

Shaoshan:

Shanshan	2127		429

Shaoxing:

Shaoxing	2156, 2142, 3483		432

Shekou:

Nanhai	692888	HK$480–650	433

Shenyang:

Huaqiao (O.C.)	734214		
Liaoning Hotel	734582	¥95–¥120	436
Liaoning Mansions	62546		436
Phoenix	66501, 66507	¥160	436
Youyi (Friendship)	66581	¥100	436

Shenzhen:

Bamboo Garden	222934, 221848	HK$260	438
Century Plaza	220888	HK$450–700	438
Dong Hu (East Lake)	22727, 22728		438
Huaqiao (O.C.)	22811		436
Shenzhen International	259369	$50	436
Shenzhen Overseas Forum	236333		438
Silver Lake Resort Hotel	222827, 222834	HK$385	436

Shihezi:

Shihezi	2587, 2588		440

Shijiazhuang:

Hebei Guest House	48961		441
Shijiazhuang	45866		441

Suzhou:

Bamboo Grove	25407	$65	450
Gusu (Ancient Suzhou)	24689		450
Nanlin	27651, 24641	¥166	450
New World Aster	731888	$50	450
Suzhou	24646, 22298	¥165	450

Tai'an:

Taishan	7211		452

Taishan, Guangdong:

Garden	25890, 25668		455
Huaqiao (O.C.)	24768	¥60	455
Mei Lei Hua	22933, 22934		454
Stone Flower Mountain	25834	$5	455

Taiyuan:

Bingzhou	25924		458

Jinci	29441, 29941		458
San Jin Mansions	23489		458
Yingze	23211		459
Tianjin:			
Astor	32112		465
Crystal Palace	310567	$70	465
Hyatt Tianjin	318888	$80–100	465
Tianjin No. 1	310707		
InterTech	319281, 319115		465
Sheraton Tianjin	333388		466
Victory	985833	$55	466
Youyi (Friendship)	310372-3		465
Turpan:			
Turpan	2847		
Turpan Tourist Hotel			469
Urumqi:			
Friendship	23991, 23951		472
Kunlun	23360, 42411	¥80	472
Xinjiang	22233, 23222		472
Weifang:			
Weifang	2981		474
Weihai:			
Weihai	2426, 2172		
Wuhan:			
Jianghan	21253, 23998		479
Qingchuan	441141		479
Yangtze	562828	¥150–200	479
Wuxi:			
Hubin	668812	US$45	482
Milido	665665		482
Shuixiu	669712		482
Taihu	667901		482
Wuxi Grand	669138, 668163	$60	483
Xiamen:			
Huaqiao (O.C.)	25602, 25701	¥120	489
Jinbao	46888, 26888	HK$320	490
Lujiang	22922, 22203	¥145	489
Seaview Garden Tourist Village	26959, 26958		490
Xiamen Hotel	22265, 24941	¥170	490
Xiamen Mandarin	43333	$40–50	490
Park (Xindeco)	41186	¥128	490
Xi'an:			
Bell Tower	718767, 29203	$100	503
Concord	44460, 44824		503
Dynasty	28870, 713433	$100–120	504

Golden Flower	32981		504
Holiday Inn Xi'an	721882	¥100–110	504
Jianguo	621957	$60–70	504
Jiaolong University	31361		504
Northwest University	715036		504
Renmin (People's)	315111		504
Scarlet Bird	53311	¥160	504
Shaanxi Sports	71344	¥75	504
Tang Cheng	54171, 55921		505
Xi'an	711351	$65	505
Xian Garden	711111		505
Xinhui:			
Kui Yuan	44806		507
Xinhui	62800		507
Xining:			
Qinghai	44365	¥120	509
Xiqiao:			
Baiyun Lou	611		510
Sanhu	342		510
Xiqiao Grand			510
Xuzhou:			
Nanjiao (South Suburban)	23611, 28980	¥140–500	511
Yan'an:			
Yan'an Guest House	2767, 2252		514
Yangzhou:			
Xiyuan	42611	¥65	521
Yangzhou	42611	$40	521
Yantai:			
Dongshan	224501		526
Huaqiao (O.C.)	224431		526
Yantai Hotel	226556		526
Yantai Shan	224491, 224493		526
Zhifu	248421, 248289	$43	526
Yichang:			
Yiling	22110		
Yinchuan:			
Ningxia	2131		529
Yinchuan	3053, 2615		529
Yixing:			
Yixing	2559, 2493, 2179		531
Yueyang:			
Yunmeng Hotel	23011	¥120	533

Zhangzhou:

Huaqiao (O.C.)	3614		534
Zhangzhou	3429, 4714		534
Zhangzhou New Times	4687		534

Zhanjiang:

Canton Bay	224966	¥18	536
Haibin	23555		536
Yuoyi (Friendship)	23555, 24808		536
Zhanjiang	23888, 23788		536

Zhaoqing:

Huaqiao	22952		538
Pines	27521		538
Songtao	24412		538

Zhengzhou:

International Hotel	23413, 26531		543
Regent Plaza	28046		543
Yellow River Hotel	48958		543
Zhengzhou	24255, 29941, 24937	¥60–¥110	543

Zhenjiang:

Jinshan	32971, 32975		546

Zhenning:

Huangguoshu	376		

Zhongshan:

Cuiheng	24091, 24077		548
Fuhua	22034		548
Kinghua	24688	HK$250	548
Zhongshan Hot Spring Resort	22811		548
Zhongshan International	24788	$46	548

Zhuhai:

Garden (Yuanlin)	332568		550
Gongbei Palace	886833, 23831		550
Shi Ching Shan	333518		550
Zhuhai Resort	333718, 332973	¥161	550

Zibo:

Zibo	22138		551

Zunhua:

Beiguan	2651, 2619		

HOTEL CHAINS AND SOME NORTH AMERICAN TOLL-FREE NUMBERS

Hilton International: 1–800–268–9275
Holiday Inn: 1–800–HOLIDAY

Hyatt International Corp.: 1–800–228–9000
Jianguo: 1–800–553–3638
Leading Hotels of the World: 1–800–223–6800
New World Hotels International: 1–800–227–5663 (U.S.),
1–800–387–1456 (Can.)
Movenpick-Radisson Hotels: 1–800–228–9822
Nikko: 1–800–645–5687
Novotel: 1–800–221–4542
Okura: (NY) (212) 755–0733, (LA) (213) 388–1151
Peninsula Group: SABRE SR13132
Ramada Worldwide Reservations: In the U.S., 1–800–2RAMADA; Ont. and Que., 1–800–268–8930; elsewhere in Canada, 1–800–268–8998.
SARA: UTELL International offices worldwide. SAS-THAI offices worldwide.
Shangri-La International: 1–800–457–5050
Sheraton International: 1–800–325–3535
Swiss-Belhotel: 1–800–553–3638 (U.S. only)
Swissair Nestle Swissotel: 1–800–223–0888
Westin: 1–800–228–3000

HOTEL RESERVATION AGENCIES IN NORTH AMERICA

Orient Hotel Reservations: Sino-American Tours, 221 Canal St., Suite 501, New York, NY 10013. 1–800–221–7982. New York state 212–925–3388. SABRE direct access Y/TUR/QSA.

UTELL: 1–800–44UTELL, 1–800–387–1338.

FINANCES

Not all foreign banks and financial institutions have relations with the Bank of China. To avoid inconvenience, always ask if their services can be used in China.

Only some **foreign currencies** are accepted for exchange in China. These are: Australian dollar (A$), Austrian schilling (Sch), Belgian franc (BF), Canadian dollar (Can$), Danish krone (DKr), West German mark (DM), French franc (FF), Japanese yen (¥), Malaysian dollar (M$), Dutch guilder (fl.), Norwegian krone (NKr), Singapore dollar (S$) Swedish krona (SKr), Swiss franc (SF), pound sterling (£), US dollar (US$) and Hongkong dollar (HK$).

Not all **credit cards** are acceptable in China. Some can be used to pay for a limited number of hotels, obtain cash, and pay for purchases in a few designated stores, with a 4% surcharge. Currently accepted are

Federal Card, Visa/MasterCard, American Express, Diner's Club, Million Card, Great Wall, and JCB Card. Payment can also be made with Renminbi Travelers Letter of Credit bought with foreign currencies, drafts and other payment instruments in convertible currencies issued by the Bank of China branches in London, New York, Los Angeles, Toronto, Singapore, Luxembourg and Hongkong and the banks maintaining accounts in convertible Renminbi with the Banking Department, Bank of China, Head Office.

Some travelers, however, have found Letters of Credit difficult to convert into F.E.C.s.

The only **traveler's checks and money orders** accepted are issued by foreign banks that have concluded payment arrangements with the Bank of China. These are:

Rafidain Bank, Baghdad, Iraq. T/C	US.$, £
Arab Bank Ltd., Amman, Jordan. T/C	US.$ £
The National Bank of Australasia Ltd., Melbourne, Australia. T/C	Australian Dollar
Bank of New South Wales, Sydney, Australia. T/C	Australian Dollar
Australia & New Zealand Banking Group Ltd., T/C	$, $A
Commonwealth Trading Bank of Australia, Sydney, Australia. T/C	$, $A
MITSUI-THOMAS COOK T/C	Japanese Yen
Hankyu Express International Co. Ltd., "VISA" T/C	Japanese Yen
Yamaguchi Bank Ltd., "VISA" T/C	Japanese Yen
The Bank of Tokyo, Ltd., Tokyo. T/C	US.$, Yen
The Sumitomo Bank Ltd., "VISA" T/C, Tokyo	Yen
The Fuji Bank, Ltd., Tokyo. T/C	Yen
Barclays Bank International Ltd., "VISA" T/C and International Money Order, London	£, US.$
Lloyds Bank Ltd., London. T/C	£
Standard Chartered Bank Ltd., London. T/C	£, US.$
The Royal Bank of Scotland Group T/C, London	£
Grindlays "VISA" T/C, London	£
National Westminster Bank Ltd., London. T/C	£
Thomas Cook & Sons Ltd., London. T/C	£, US.$, Can.$, A$
The Hongkong & Shanghai-THOMAS COOK T/C	Hongkong Dollar
Standard DM. T/C Issued by 30 German Banks	Deutsche Mark
Societe Francaise Du Cheque De Voyage S.A. T/C	French Frs.
Societe Generale THOMAS COOK T/C	French Frs.
Swiss Bankers T/C, Berne, Switzerland.	Swiss Frs.
Banque Bruxelles Lambert, Brussels T/C	Belgian Frs.
Societe Generale De Banque, Brussels T/C	Belgian Frs.
Algemene Bank Nederland N.V., Amsterdam T/C	Florin
Amsterdam-Rotterdam Bank N.V., Amsterdam T/C	Florin
Nederlandsche Middenstandsbank N.V., Amsterdam. T/C	Florin
Norwegian T/C	Norwegian Krone

The Royal Bank of Canada, Montreal. World Money Order	Can.$, US.$
Bank of America, San Francisco, T/C	US.$
Citicorp, New York, T/C	US.$
Manufacturers Hanover Trust Co., New York, International Money Order	US.$
American Express Co., New York. T/C	US.$, £, F.frs., Can.$, Yen, DM, S.frs.
First National Bank of Chicago "VISA" T/C, Chicago	US.$
Republic National Bank of Dallas, Texas. T/C	US.$

SALARIES

As for monthly salaries in China, an average worker makes ¥111. An attendent in a tourist hotel makes ¥100–350 a month including bonus. A taxi driver ¥200–400. A Guangzhou doctor with over 20 years' experience ¥125; a newly graduated doctor ¥75. Rent for an apartment is about ¥15 per month. Profits from each stall in the alley between the Jianguo Hotel and Friendship Store range from ¥20,000 to ¥100,000 a year.

CURRENCY

Chinese money is called Renminbi (RMB)—people's money. The Chinese dollar, known as the *yuan* (or *kuai*) equals 10 *jiao* or 100 *fen*. Yuan notes are in denominations of 10, 5, 2, and 1. The smaller jiao notes are 5, 2, and 1. The coins are 5, 2, and 1 fen.

F.E.C.s are Foreign Exchange Certificates with which you must pay for tourist hotels, tourist restaurants, and some shops.

Foreign exchange rates fluctuate. There is also a slight variation for cash or traveler's checks. Please consult your bank, Bank of China, or the *China Daily*.

The following chart will give you a rough idea of Chinese equivalents. If you cannot find the exchange rate in effect when you go, draw up your own table so that you can convert easily.

IF YOU END UP WITH A LOT OF UNWANTED RMB

The black market in the form of swarthy men whispering "Change money?" loudly outside many tourist hotels can sell you RMB (renminbi, people's money, at about 2 to 1 FEC), but it is almost worthless to tour group members and any traveler on a tight schedule. It is also illegal to change money this way and impossible to change back when you leave.

Most places frequented by tourists take only FEC. One diplomat said Chinese authorities even refused to cremate a dead foreigner unless paid in FEC. And even some post offices are asking for FEC.

Try to avoid collecting a lot of RMB in change, especially if you're on a quick trip or a group tour where you won't have a chance to spend it. Keep a lot of small change in FEC handy.

If you want to use up RMB (as opposed to FEC), use it in taxis, free markets, non-tourist approved stores, and offer it to pay for food in restaurants, even hotel restaurants. The China Hotel in Guangzhou took my RMB in one of its restaurants at the price quoted in the menu.

It is not illegal for foreigners to possess RMB, although some places might charge you extra for paying in RMB. Discuss this (cheerfully, please!) with the clerk, as in "But I don't see a sign that says I have to pay in FEC" or "That's all I have." You may or may not get away with it, depending on your timing. Sometimes the government has a campaign insisting that foreigners pay in FEC; sometimes clerks forget about it.

Some stores with prices quoted in RMB give discounts for FEC.

If you still have RMB left over when you leave China, you could leave it with friends or relatives, or as a charitable donation (at a temple), or to the Amity Foundation (13 Da Jian Yin Xiang, Nanjing). Amity is a Christian social welfare group serving all Chinese, not just Christians.

Another possibility is the Soong Ching-Ling Foundation (see Important Addresses for bank account number). This foundation helps children in China. Also, some airports have a box for the Chinese Red Cross.

DOLLAR TO YUAN CONVERSION TABLE

If you want a handy chart to show you Chinese currency equivalents with your money, enter the current exchange rate into column **C** by multiplying the rate with the number in column **A.** Column **B** contains the Jan. 1989 U.S. dollar rate as an example.

BUYING YUAN

A *Your Currency*	B *Yuan (Jan.)*	C *Current Rate*
1	3.71	
2	7.42	
3	11.13	
4	14.84	
5	18.55	
6	22.26	
7	25.97	
8	29.68	
9	33.39	

BUYING YUAN *(Continued)*

A *Your Currency*	B *Yuan (Jan.)*	C *Current Rate*
10	37.10	
20	74.20	
30	111.30	
40	148.40	
50	185.50	
60	222.60	
70	259.70	
80	296.80	
90	333.90	
100	371.00	
200	742.00	
300	1113.00	
400	1484.00	
500	1855.00	
600	2226.00	
700	2597.00	
800	2968.00	
900	3339.00	
1000	3710.00	

In Jan. 1989, the exchange rates in RMB yuan as printed in *China Daily* were:

Currency		*Per*	*Buying*	*Selling*
Australia	$	100	319.20	320.80
Austria	Sch	100	28.64	28.79
Belgium	Fr	10000	954.56	959.35
			951.62	956.35
Canada	$	100	311.01	312.56
Denmark	Kr	100	51.79	52.04
F.R.G.	Dm	100	201.28	202.29
France	Fr	100	58.73	59.02
Italy	Lira	10000	27.45	27.58
Japan	Yen	100000	2698.35	2912.88
Holland	G	100	178.45	179.34
Norway	Kr	100	55.80	56.07
Singapore	$	100	190.10	191.05
Sweden	Kr	100	59.27	59.56
Swiss	Fr	100	234.31	235.48
U.K.	pound	100	658.63	661.94
USA	$	100	371.27	373.14
Hongkong	$	100	47.49	47.72
ECU		100	459.96	462.27

MAPS

The People's Republic of China
(old spelling)

CHINA'S ADMINISTRATIVE DIVISIONS

XINJIANG

Urumqi

TIBET

Lhasa

QINGHAI

GANSU

INNER MONGOLIA

NINGXIA

Yinchuan

Lanzhou

Xining

SICHUAN

Chengdu

YUNNAN

Kunming

GUIZHOU

Guiyang

GUANGXI

Nanning

SHAANXI

Xi'an

SHANXI

Taiyuan

Hohhot

HEBEI

BEIJING

Shijiazhuang

Tianjin

HENAN

Zhengzhou

HUBEI

Wuhan

HUNAN

Changsha

JIANGXI

Nanchang

GUANGDONG

Guangzhou

Hongkong

Macao

FUJIAN

Fuzhou

ZHEJIANG

Hangzhou

ANHUI

Hefei

JIANGSU

Nanjing

Shanghai

SHANDONG

Jinan

BOHAI SEA

HUANGHAI SEA

EAST CHINA SEA

SHENYANG

LIAONING

JILIN

Changchun

HEILONGJIANG

Harbin

TAIWAN

SOUTH CHINA SEA

Guang

CHINA'S RAILWAYS

Xuzhou

JIANGSU

ANHUI

Yangzhou

Nanjing Zhenjiang

Hefei Wuxi

Changzhou Suzhou

Yangtze River Yixing **Shanghai**

Hangzhou SHANGHAI

Huangshan

Shaoxing Ningbo

ZHEJIANG

Fuzhou

FUJIAN

Quanzhou

Zhangzhou

Xiamen

Z.M. Li

**EAST CHINA
TOURIST REGION**

NORTH CHINA
TOURIST REGION

Shanhaiguan
Qinhuangdao
Beidaihe
Tangshan

Zunhua

Tianjin

Chengde

Beijing

HEBEI

Shizizhuang

Handan

Yantai
Weihai

Qingdao

SHANDONG

Zibo
Weifang

Jinan
Tai'an

Qufu

Yellow River

INNER
MONGOLIA

Datong
Hengshan

Taiyuan
Dazhai

SHANXI

Hohhot

Baotou

Yellow River

Yinchuan

NINGXIA

Z.M. Li

NORTHEAST CHINA
TOURIST REGION

HEILONGJIANG

● Daqing

Harbin
●

JILIN

Changchun   **Jilin**
●   ●

Shenyang
●
LIAONING   Fushun
           ●
       ● Anshan

● Dalian

Z.M. Li

NORTHWEST CHINA, TIBET, AND QINGHAI TOURIST REGION

Z.M. Li

SOUTH CHINA TOURIST REGION

Z.M. Li

Jiujiang

Lushan

Jingdezhen

Yueyang

HUNAN **Changsha**

Nanchang

JIANGXI

Shaoshan

Hengshan

Jinggang
Mountains

Guilin

Shaoguan

Liuzhou

GUANGDONG

GUANGXI

Wuzhou

Shantou

Foshan

Conghua

Zhaoqing

Guangzhou

Guiping

Xiqiao

Shekou

Nanning

Jiangmen

Shenzhen

Taishan

Hong Kong

Xinhui

Zhuhai

Zhongshan

Zhanjiang

Haikou

HAINAN

Sanya

HUBEI

Gezhouba
Shashi
Wuhan

Yangtze River

SICHUAN

Chengdu

Emei
Mountain
Leshan
Dazu
Chongqing
Zigong

GUIZHOU

Guiyang

Kunming
Lunan

Dali
Xiaguan

YUNNAN

Jinghong

**SOUTHWEST CHINA
TOURIST REGION**

Z.M. Li

THE SILK ROAD

Antioch
Palmyra
Tyre
Baghdad
Hamadan
Damghan
Merv
Samarkand
Balkh
Kashi
Hotan
Minfeng
Kuloulan
Kuchar
Turpan
Dunhuang
Wuwei
Lanzhou
...an

Z.M. Li

THE YANGTZE GORGES

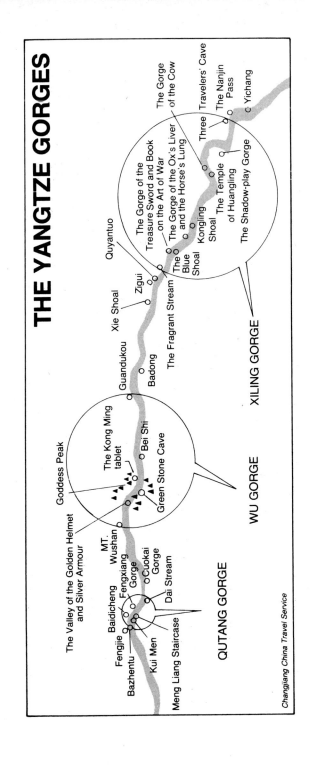

Changjiang China Travel Service

QUTANG GORGE

The Valley of the Golden Helmet
and Silver Armour

Fengjie
Baidicheng
Bazhentu
Kui Men
Meng Liang Staircase
Fengxiang Gorge
Cuokai Gorge
Dai Stream

MT.
Wushan
Goddess Peak
The Kong Ming tablet
Bei Shi
Green Stone Cave

WU GORGE

Guandukou
Badong
Xie Shoal
Zigui
Quyantuo
The Fragrant Stream

XILING GORGE

The Gorge of the
Treasure Sword and Book
on the Art of War
The Gorge of the Ox's Liver
and the Horse's Lung
The Blue Shoal
Kongling Shoal
The Temple of Huangling
The Shadow-play Gorge

The Gorge
of the Cow
Three Travelers' Cave
The Nanjin Pass
Yichang

BEIJING

Z.M.

Tourist Hotels

A. Beijing (Peking)
B. Xin Qiao (Hsin Chiao)
C. Qianmen (Chien Men)
D. Minzu (Min Tzu, Min Dzu) [Nationalities]
E. Youyi [Friendship]
F. Heping [Peace]
G. Huaqiao (Huachiao) [Overseas Chinese]
H. Jianguo Hotel
 I. Yanjing Hotel
J. Great Wall Sheraton
K. Jinglun (Toronto-Beijing) Hotel
L. Chongwenmen Hotel
M. Yanxiang Hotel
N. Holiday Inn Lido
O. Xiyuan Hotel
P. Huadu Hotel and Kunlun

Of Interest to Visitors

1. Tian Anmen [Gate of Heavenly Peace] Square
2. Tian Anmen Gate
3. Forbidden City and Palace Museum
4. Coal Hill Park
5. Great Hall of the People
6. Museums of the Chinese Revolution and Chinese History
7. Temple of Heaven
8. Summer Palace
9. Beihai Park
10. Zhongnanhai (Chung Nan Hai)
11. International Club
12. Friendship Store
13. Lama Temple
14. Temple of Confucius
15. Drum Tower
16. CAAC
17. Beijing Zoo
18. Beijing Library
19. Niujie Mosque

CHANGSHA

Z.M. Li

1. Hunan Provincial Museum
2. Martyrs' Park
3. Hunan Guest House
4. Hunan Exhibition Hall
5. Xiangjiang Guesthouse
6. Friendship Store
7. Rongyuan Hotel
8. Changdao Hotel
9. Railway Station
10. Hunan No. 1 Normal School
11. Tianxin Park
12. Huangxing Rd.
13. Jiefang Rd.
14. Zhongshan Rd.
15. Hunan Embroidery Building
16. Lushan Hotel
17. Fenglin Hotel
18. Aiwan Pavilion

CHENGDU

Tu Fu's Cottage

Temple of Marquis Wu

Wangjianglou
(River Viewing Tower)

Z.M. Li

1. **To Zoo and Divine Light Monastery**
2. **Wenshui Monastery**
3. **Jinjiang and Minshan hotels**
4. **To Leshan and Emel Shan**
5. **Tomb of Wang Jian**
6. **Chengdu Hotel**

CHONGQING

1. Jiatse Cave
2. Bai Gong Guan
3. North Hot Spring Park
4. Chingyun Park
5. Airport
6. South Hot Spring Park
7. South Mountain Park
8. Yuzhou Guest House
9. Railway Station

10. People's Guest House
11. Chongqing (Bingguan) Guest House
12. Chaotianmen Wharf
13. Hongyancun (Red Crag Village)
14. Eling (Goose Neck Park)
15. Loquat Hill
16. Cableway
17. Chongqing (Fan Dian) Hotel
18. Holiday Inn

DATONG

Z.M. Li

1. Railway Station
2. Municipal Carpet Factory
3. Nine Dragon Screen
4. Drum Tower
5. Yungang Guest House
6. Airport
7. Datong Guest House
8. Shanhua Monastery
9. Brassware Factory
10. Huayan Monastery
11. Red Flag Bazaar
12. To Wooden Pagoda, Yingxian County
13. Yungang Caves
14. Guanyin Hall
15. To Temple in Mid-air

GUANGZHOU

1. National Peasant Movement Institute
2. Memorial Gardens to the Martyrs of the 1927 Guangzhou Uprising
3. Mausoleum of the Seventy-two Martyrs at Huanghuagang
4. Guangzhou Zoo
5. Zhenhai Tower
6. Dr. Sun Yat-sen Memorial Hall
7. Temple of the Six Banyan Trees
8. Guangzhou Cultural Park
9. Guangzhou Trade Center
10. C.I.T.S.
11. CAAC
12. Friendship Store
13. Huai Sheng Mosque a.k.a. Guang Ta Monastery
14. Nanfang Department Store
15. Zhoutouzui (Ship Quay)
16. Qingping Free Market
17. Guangxiao Temple
18. Cathedral of the Sacred Heart
19. Folk Arts and Crafts Hall (Zhen Family Temple)

Hotels

A. Dongang (Tung-fang) and China Guangzhou
B. Guangzhou
C. Liu Hua
D. Huaqiao (Overseas Chinese) Mansion
E. Novotel
F. Holiday Inn City Centre
G. White Swan
H. Baiyun and Garden (opposite)

Z.M. Li

GUILIN

1. Li Jiang (Li River) Hotel
2. Ronghu Hotel
3. Jiashan Hotel
4. Osmanthus Hotel
5. Holiday Inn
6. Riverside Resort
7. Sheraton
8. Guishan
9. to Pine Garden
10. to Ming Tomb

ROMY PARIÑA

HANGZHOU

Z.M. Li

1. Lingyin Temple
2. Hangzhou Hotel
3. Baochu Pagoda
4. West Lake
5. Three Pools Mirroring the Moon
6. Six Harmonies Pagoda
7. Children's Palace
8. Baidi Causeway
9. Autumn Moon on Calm Lake
10. Temple of Yue Fei
11. Jade Spring
12. Sudi Causeway
13. Nanshan Rd.
14. Hubin Rd.
15. Liulangwenying Park
16. Huagang Park
17. Nine Creeks and Eighteen Gullies
18. Dragon Well
19. Yan'an Rd.
20. Jiefang Rd.
21. Overseas Chinese Hotel
22. Huajiashan
23. Huagang Hotel
24. Xihu Hotel
25. Zhejiang Hotel
26. Dragon Hotel
27. Qiantang River
28. Friendship Hotel
29. Wanghu Hotel

KAIFENG

1. Iron Pagoda
2. Kaifeng Embroidery Factory
3. Painter's Studio
4. Caomen Gate
5. Songmen Gate
6. King Yu's Terrace
7. Pota Pagoda
8. Railway Station
9. South Gate
10. Guest House
11. Yanqing Taoist Temple
12. Baofu Pit
13. West Gate
14. Dragon Pavilion
15. Yangjia Lake
16. Panjia Lake
17. North Gate
18. Xiangguo Monastery

KUNMING

1. Yuantongshan Mountain
2. Zhui Hu (Green Lake) Park
3. Green Lake Hotel
4. Daguan Lou (Grand View Pavilion)
5. Kunming Hotel and C.I.T.S.
6. Railway Station
7. To Airport
8. Dianchi Lake
9. To Western Hills

NANJING

Z.M. Li

1. Nanjing Hotel
2. Drum Tower
3. Jinling Hotel
4. Stone Citadel
5. Mochou Park
6. Chaotian Palace
7. Wuchao Gate and
   Ming Palace ruins
8. Nanjing Provincial
   Museum
9. Ming Tomb
10. Sun Yat-sen Mausoleum
11. Linggu Pagoda
12. Yuhuatai Mausoleum
13. To Airport
14. Taiping Museum and
    Confucian Temple
    Market
15. Observatory
16. Xuanwu Lake
17. Friendship Store
18. Shuangmenlou Hotel
19. Dingshan Hotel

QINGDAO

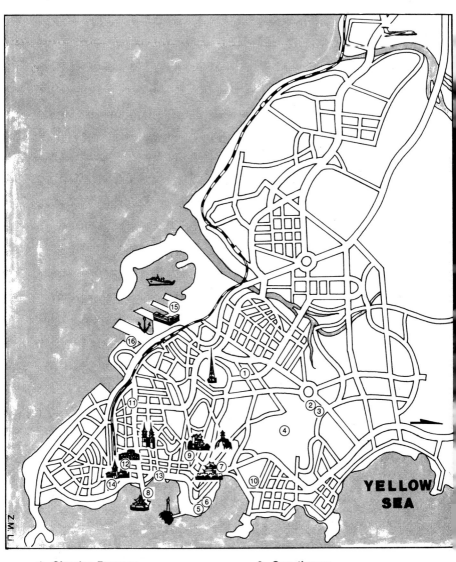

1. Qingdao Brewery
2. Embroidery Factory
3. Jade Carving Factory
4. Zhongshan Park
5. Luxun Park
6. Qingdao Museum of Marine Products
7. Qingdao Museum
8. Pier
9. Guesthouse
10. Huiquan Guesthouse
11. Zhongshan Rd.
12. Huaqiao (Overseas Chinese) Hotel
13. Zhanqiao (Pier) Guesthouse
14. Railway Station
15. Youyi (Friendship) Hotel
16. Passenger Quay

YELLOW
SEA

Z.M. Li

URBAN SHANGHAI

1. **Site of the First National Congress of the Communist Party of China**
2. **Museum and Tomb of Lu Xun (Lu Hsun), Hung Kou Park**
3. **Lu Hsun's Former Residence**
4. **Shanghai Municipal Museum**
5. **Former Residence of Dr. Sun Yat-sen**
6. **Shanghai Industrial Exhibition Hall**
7. **Jade Buddha Temple**
8. **Shanghai Art and Handicraft Research Studio**
9. **Yu Yuan Garden**
10. **People's Square**
11. **Lung Hua Pagoda**
12. **Friendship Store**
13. **Main Shopping area**

SUZHOU

1. Shizilin (Lion Forest) Garden
2. Chang Lang [Gentle Wave Pavilion]
3. Yi [Joyous] Garden
4. Liu [Lingering] Garden
5. Wangshih [Garden of the Master of Nets]
6. Zhuozheng [Humble Administrator's] Garden
7. Hu Qiu [Tiger Hill]
8. North Temple Pagoda
9. Han Shan Temple
10. Xiyuan [West Garden] Temple
11. Purple Gold Nunnery

12. Twin Pagodas
13. Xuan Miao Guan [Taoist Temple]
14. Sky High Hill
15. Divine Cliff Hill
16. Friendship Store
17. Precious Belt Bridge
18. C.I.T.S.
19. Suzhou Hotel and Gusu [Ancient Suzhou] Hotel
20. Nanlin Hotel
21. Nanyuan Hotel
22. Grand Canal
23. Panmen Gate

14. Shanghai Railway Station
15. International Club
16. Foreign Passenger Quay
17. U.S., Japanese, and French consulates
18. New Shanghai Railway Station
A. Jin Jiang and Garden Hotels
B. Huaqiao [Overseas Chinese]
C. He Ping [Peace]
D. Shanghai Da Sha [Shanghai Mansions]
E. Heng Shan
F. Guo Ji [Park]
G. Da Hua Guest House
H. Shanghai
J. Cypress Hotel

K. Western Suburb Guest House a.k.a. Xijiao
L. Chengqiao Hotel
M. Xinyuan (New Garden) Hotel
N. Cherry Tourist Village

P. Hongqiao Hotel
Q. Hua Ting Hotel
R. Jing'an Guest House (New Building)
S. Jing'an Hilton
T. Yan'an Hotel
U. Donghu (East Lake) Guest House
V. Jinjiang New Tower Hotel
W. Ruijin Guest House

TAIYUAN

Z.M. Li

1. Yingze Guest House
2. Chongshan Monastery
3. Provincial Museum No. 1
4. Bingzhou Hotel
5. Shuangta Monastery
6. Railway Station
7. To airport
8. To Long Shan (Dragon Mountain) Taoist caves and Tian Long Shan Caves
9. To Jinci Temple
10. To Jinci Hotel (near the Temple)
11. Yunshan Hotel
12. San Jin Mansions
13. Tang Ming Hotel
14. Shanxi Hotel
15. San Qiao Mansions
16. Provincial Museum No. 2
17. Fen River

WUHAN

1. Xuangong Hotel
2. Wuhan Customhouse
3. Changtian Lou (Long Heaven Tower)
4. Xinyin Ge (Pavilion for Reading Poems)
5. Huguang Ge (Lake Scenery Pavilion)
6. Hubei Provincial Museum
7. Yellow Crane Tower on Snake Hill
8. Qiyi (Uprising Gate)
9. Hongshan Hill

10. Wuchang Railway Station
11. Hanyang Railway Station
12. Guiyang Temple
13. Platform of the Ancient Lute
14. Hankou Railway Station
15. Passenger Quay
16. Airport
17. Shengli Hotel
18. Jianghan Hotel

ANCIENT XI'AN

Locations in different historical periods

1. W. Han—Fengjing
2. W. Han—Haojing
3. Qin—Xianyang
4. Han—Changan
5. Ming and Qing—Xi'an
6. Sui—Daxing
7. Tang—Changan
8. Xi'an today

XI'AN

1. Shaanxi Provincial Museum
2. Big Wild Goose Pagoda
3. Little Wild Goose Pagoda
4. Bell Tower
5. Drum Tower
6. West City Gate
7. Great Mosque
8. Holiday Inn Shenzhou
9. Museum of the Eighth Route Army
10. Renmin, Novotel, and Sofitel
11. Friendship Store
12. Zhonglou (Bell Tower) Hotel
13. Garden Hotel
14. Efang Palace Hotel
15. Golden Flower Hotel (Jinhua)
16. Jianguo
17. Sports Hotel
18. Tangcheng Hotel
19. XI'an (Xiaoyanta Hotel)
20. Scarlet Bird Hotel

INDEX

Accidents, bicycle and car, 124
Acrobats, 157, 211, 252, 281, 322, 338, 380, 407, 414, 434, 461, 478
Air sports, Anyang, 187
Air travel. *See also* Helicopter service and Tours
   within China, 10–12, 105–09
   to China, 34–35
   from Hong Kong, 65
   reconfirming reservations, 73, 105
   regulations, 108
Alien travel permit, 99, 113, 184
Amusement and theme parks, 13, 209, 265, 280–81, 538
Ancestral temples, 176
   Foshan, 265
Ancestral villages, 554
   Guangzhou, 275–76
Ancient towns and capitals. *See also* Ghost city
   Datong, 255–57
   Foshan, 264–66
   ghost city, 468
   Hefei, 315–16
   Jingdezhen, 333–34
   Jiujiang, 335
   Kaifeng, 337–39
   Kashi, 339–40
   Luoyang, 362–66
   Nanjing, 375–82
   Ningbo, 386–89
   Qufu, 399–403
   Shaoxing, 430–32
   Shasi, 432
   Shenyang, 434–36
   Suzhou, 444–50
   Taiyuan, 456–59
   Turpan, 467–469
   Wuhan, 475–80
   Wuxi, 480–83
   Xi'an, 491–505
   Yangtze Gorges, 515–518
   Zhanjiang, 535–37
   Zhengzhou, 539–43
   Zhenjiang, 543–47
   Zibo, 551
Animals. *See also* Birds; Endangered species; Monkeys; Wildlife and nature parks; Zoos

   buying, 146–47
Antiques, 145
   Beijing, 212
   Guangzhou, 282, 283
   where to buy, 145
Archaeological sites. *See also* Bronzes; Terracotta army
   Anyang, 186–87
   Baotou, 188–89
   Dunhuang, 261
   Lanzhou, 347
   Ningbo, 387–88
   Taiyuan, 456–58
   Wuhan, 475–78
   Xi'an, 492–501
   Yinchuan, 528–29
   Zhengzhou, 539–42
   Zibo, 551
Art. *See also* Art museums and galleries; Arts and crafts; Bronzes; Buddhist sites and temples; Painting and calligraphy; Porcelain; Pottery and ceramics; Statuary and carvings
   contemporary, 208
   Revolutionary, 144–45
Art museums and galleries
   Beijing, 208
   Chongqing, 248
   Nanchang, 371
   peasant, 499
   Shanghai, 407–08
   Tianjin, 461
Arts and crafts. *See also specific arts and crafts*
   Beijing, 212–213
   Changsha, 231
   Chongqing, 249
   favorite subjects of, 144
   Foshan, 265, 280
   Guangzhou, 282–83
   Guilin, 294
   Jinan, 332
   Hangzhou, 308
   minority, 472
   Nanjing, 380
   Shanghai, 406, 408, 415
   Shantou, 425, 426
   shopping for, 139–45
   Suzhou, 445

Tianjin, 464
Urumqi, 472
Wuhan, 478
Xiamen, 488
Xi'an, 502
Zhangzhou, 533
Astronomical observatories, 209–210, 375, 541
Automobile travel, 112. *See also* Taxis
Aviation museum, Shanghai, 412

Backpacking, 26, 64, 114, 483. *See also* Hiking and climbing
Bamboo, where to buy, 142
Banks, 233, 245, 296, 386, 394, 422, 466, 505, 526
Beaches. *See also* Water sports
Beidaihe, 190–91
Dalian, 252
Qingdao, 391
Qinhuangdao, 395
Shantou, 426
Taishan, 454
Yantai, 524–25
Beer, 88, 331, 391
Beggars, 122
Beverages, 88
Bicycling, 64, 113–14, 210, 232, 281, 304
Birds, 146, 291, 344, 508
Boat trips, 36–37, 41, 66–67, 115–16, 272, 280, 292, 299, 308, 317, 343, 411, 413, 447, 481, 484, 515–18, 546
Border formalities, 71. *See also* Customs regulations; Passports; Visas
Botanical gardens, 280, 307, 319, 342, 369, 375, 383, 411–12, 486
Bridges, 211, 291, 305, 365, 378, 398, 426, 477
Bronzes, 154–56, 408, 412, 492, 494, 496
Buddhism, 98, 168, 170–72, 352–54
Buddhist sites and temples, 170–72, 205, 237, 242, 261–62, 269, 302, 315, 321, 329–31, 335, 338, 340, 342, 349, 357, 364–65, 374–75, 388, 408–09, 426, 428, 441, 448, 457, 462, 468–69, 477–78, 484–85, 466, 500, 513–14, 524, 529. *See also* Caves and cave temples; Lamaism and Lama temples; Zen Buddhism
Buddhist statuary and carvings, 170–72, 259–60, 261–62, 264, 265, 269, 273, 292, 302, 329–31, 338, 347, 363–65, 374–375, 379, 408–09, 412, 441, 457, 463, 468–69, 473, 484–85, 513–14, 520, 529, 533

Business travelers, tips for, 27, 30, 31, 32, 556–59
Bus travel
to China, 41, 67, 68, 112
within China, 115, 194, 265, 443
Silk Road, 443

CAAC (Civil Aviation Administration of China), 11–12, 41, 69, 106–07, 108–09. *See also* Travel agents and arrangements
Calligraphy. *See* Painting and calligraphy
Camels, riding, Hohot, 320
Canals and irrigation systems, 187, 242, 271, 272, 293, 325–26, 338, 424, 430, 468, 527, 530. *See also* Grand Canal; Reservoirs
Carpets, 462
where to buy, 142
Cathedrals. *See* Churches and cathedrals
Caves and cave temples, 18, 176–77, 256, 261–62, 269, 291–92, 298, 302, 308, 334, 340, 347, 361, 364–65, 383, 428, 469, 471–72, 513–14, 530–31, 541, 545, 549
photography in, 262
Ceramic army. *See* Terracotta army
Ceramics. *See* Pottery and ceramics
Checks, personal, 55
Chiang Kai–shek, sites associated with, 48, 247, 248, 276, 392, 411
Children
books for, 145
traveling with, 33
Children, activities for. *See also* Festivals; Acrobats
amusement and theme parks, 13, 20, 227, 265, 280–81, 538
Chengdu, 241–42
Chongqing, 248
circus, 338
Guangzhou, 277
Harbin, 312–13
Hohhot, 322
Jilin, 327
puppet show troupe, 232
Qingdao, 391
Shanghai, 411, 414
Shenyang, 435
Wuhan, 478
Xiamen, 488
zoos, 177, 241–42, 248, 252, 280, 313, 411
China, learning about, 47–51

China Friendship Associations, 37–38, 50, 669

China International Travel Service (CITS), 10, 26, 31, 35, 69, 101–02, 104, 150. *See also* Travel agents and arrangements
foreign offices, 666, 667, 668

China Sports Service Company, 103

China Travel Service (CTS), 26, 32, 55, 69, 101, 102–03. *See also* Travel agents and arrangements

China Travel & Tourism Press, 100, 671

China Youth Travel Service, 69, 101, 103

Chinese citizens, 126, 150
looking up specific, 44, 127, 128

Chinese language. *See also* Pinyin spellings
characters, 47
learning, 47, 153
useful words and phrases, 119–20, 183, 560–650

Chopsticks, how to use, 87

Chou En-lai. *See* Zhou Enlai

Christianity, 130–32, 460–61, 496

Churches and cathedrals, 132, 177, 280, 414
services, 132, 280

Circus, Kaifeng, 338

City walls
Nanjing, 373–380
Xi'an, 492–501

Cixi, Express Dowager, and sites associated with, 49, 202, 203, 204, 225, 235–36, 462, 463–64, 474, 481

Clay figures
where to buy, 142

Climbing. *See* Hiking

Cloisonne, where to buy, 142, 212, 464

Club, international, 210

Committee on Scholarly Communication with the People's Republic of China (CSCPRC), 28

Communes, 153, 258, 280

Communist revolution, sites associated with, 131, 187, 197–98, 201, 247, 276, 278, 334, 371, 405, 410–11, 440, 476, 492–93, 512–14

Confucian temples, 170, 208, 377, 398, 401, 413, 448–49, 496

Confucius and Confucianism, 18, 170, 331, 399–402, 451

Consulates, 100, 246, 289, 422, 436, 664–65, 672

Conventions, tours for, 32

Cosmetics and toiletries, 58, 59

Courtesy and manners, 57, 89–91, 121, 132–33. *See also* Local customs

Credit cards, 12–13, 54–55

Cross-country skiing, 63

Cruises, 25. *See also* Boat trips

Cultural events, 157–60. *See also* Entertainment and nightlife

Cultural Revolution, 49, 128, 131, 196–97, 405

Customs. *See* Local customs

Customs regulations, 42–44, 51–52, 71, 74, 674–75

Dalai Lama, 48, 61, 83, 238, 353, 354, 355, 356

Dance parties and discos, 160, 209, 211, 270, 305, 525

Dance school, Lanzhou, 347–48

Daylight Savings Time, 15, 73, 679

Deer farm, Jilin, 327

Democracy walls, 134–35

Demonstrations, 124

Department stores, 139

Design motives, traditional, 160–69, 178–81

Diplomatic missions, 100

Dough sculptures, where to buy, 142, 293

Dog corporation, 257

Dream of the Red Chamber, 13, 158, 180, 406, 414, 521
theme park, 209

Drinking water, 77, 81, 325

Driving, 112

Drum towers, 237, 336, 373, 376, 378, 497, 528

Du Fu, sites associated with, 241, 500, 542

Dumpling and noodle shops, 91

Earthquakes, 123, 459

Embassies, 223–24

Embroidery, 232, 233, 281, 331, 338, 449

Emergencies, 45–46, 123, 125–27

Employment for foreigners, 30, 31, 32

Endangered species, 86, 136–37, 146, 228

English corners, 224, 252–53, 281, 378, 406

Entertainment and nightlife, 157–61, 211, 232, 252–53, 265, 270, 305, 313, 322, 380, 414, 478, 525

Exchange students, 27–28

Experts, foreign, 29

Factories, 139, 150
arts and crafts, 139, 195, 281–82, 387–88, 425, 461, 488, 502

Baotou (carpet), 188
Beijing (various), 195
buying of, 140
Changchun (automobile), 227
(fur), 228
Changsha (embroidery), 232
Chengdu (various), 241
Dalian (glass), 252
Foshan (silk), 265
Fuzhou (art), 270
(lacquerware), 270
Guangzhou (various), 277, 281–82
Jinan (embroidery), 331
(fine arts), 331
Jinquan (jade cup), 336
Ningbo (arts and crafts), 387–88
Shantou (arts and crafts), 425
(embroidery), 425
Suzhou (various), 444–45
Tianjin (carpet), 462
(metalcraft), 463
visiting, 139, 182–83, 387–88
Wehai (various), 474
Wuxi, (clay figures), 481
(silk), 481
Xiamen (arts and crafts), 502
Xiaguan (tea brick), 484
Xinhui (fan palm), 506
Yantai (embroidery), 524
Yixing (pottery), 531
Zhangzhou (arts and crafts), 533
Zhenjiang (various), 544
Families, living with, Weifang, 473
Ferries, 93, 115–16, 272, 459, 478, 515–16, 517. See also Boat trips
from Hong Kong, 67–68
Festivals, 180–81
Beijing, 212
Changchun, 227–28
Dalian, 252
Fuzhou, 270
Guangzhou, 281
Harbin, 312, 313
Hohhot, 332
Kunming, 341, 344
Lhasa, 359
Nanning, 384–85
Qingdao, 391
Suzhou, 452
Taichen, 454
Weifang, 473
Wuxi, 481
Yangzhou, 521
Film studio, Changchun, 227
Firecrackers, 135–36

Fishing. See Hunting and fishing
Flirting, 122
Flowers. See also Botanical gardens; Gardens, 279–80, 533
Food and restaurants, 9–10
Anshan, 185
Anyang, 187
background, 84
banquets, 86, 90–91, 93, 557
Beidaihe, 191
Beijing, 195, 200, 202, 204–05, 206, 210, 213–15
beverages, 62–65, 88
to bring with you, 62–63
breakfasts, 88–89
Buddhism and, 98
buffets, 85
Changchun, 228
changes in, 84–85
Changsha, 233
Chengde, 239
Chengdu, 244
for children, 33
Chongqing, 249
chopsticks, using, 87
courtesies, 89–90
Dalian, 253
Datong, 258
desserts, 87–88
endangered species, 86, 313
fast food stalls, 92
Fushun, 267
garden restaurants, 277, 283
for gourmets, 84, 85
Great Wall, 272
Guangzhou, 277, 283–84
Guilin, 294
Guiyang, 299
Hainan, 301
Hangzhou, 309
Harbin, 313–14
health restaurants, 93
Hefei, 316
Hohhot, 322
illness and, 92–93
inviting Chinese to, 89–94
Jilin, 327
Jinan, 322
Jinggang Shan, 335
Kaifeng, 339
Kunming, 345
Lanzhou, 348
Lhasa, 359
Luoyang, 366
Lushan, 369

meat, 83, 93
monosodium glutamate, 93
Nanjing, 381
Nanning, 385
Ningbo, 389
ordering, 85–86
private dining rooms, 85
Qingdao, 393
Qinhuangdao, 396
Russian food, 313
regional dishes, 85, 94–97
Shanghai, 406, 413, 416–17, 422
Shanhaiguan, 425
Shantou, 426–27
Shekou, 433
Shenyang, 435–36
Silk Road, 443
special diets, 86–87
specialities, 85, 94–97, 299, 301, 327,
   345, 348, 369, 472, 482, 525–26, 531,
   534, 536, 546
Suzhou, 449
Taishan, 454
Taiyuan, 458
Tianjin, 464
tipping, 121
Urumqi, 472
vegetarian, 98, 306
Western food, 89, 210, 314
Wuhan, 479
Wuxi, 482
Xiamen, 489
Xi'an, 502
Xining, 509
Yangzhou, 521
Yantai, 525–26
Yinchuan, 529
Yixing, 531
Zhangzhou, 534
Zhanjiang, 536
Zhengzhou, 542–43
Zhenjiang, 546
Foreign affairs offices, 224, 234, 246, 288,
   333, 386, 490
Foreign Exchange Certificates (FEC's), 72,
   85, 94
Foreign experts, 29, 669–70
Foreign Ministry, 224
Forests. See Wildlife and nature parks
Free market, 139–40, 153, 213, 282, 411,
   531
Frescoes, Dunhuang, 261
Friendship stores, 139
Furs, 142, 146, 212, 228, 313, 327

Gang of Four, 197. See also Cultural Rev-
   olution
Gardens. See also Botanical gardens
   Beijing, 200, 204, 209
   Chengde, 237
   Chengdu, 242
   Chongqing, 247
   Guangzhou, 277, 280, 283
   Hangzhou, 304, 307
   Hengshan, 319
   how to visit, 177
   Jiujiang, 335
   Nanjing, 375, 377
   Nanning, 383
   orchid, 280
   restaurants, 277, 283
   Shanghai, 406, 407, 411–12, 413
   Suzhou, 445, 446–47
   tea, 307
   Tianjin, 462
   Weifang, 473
   Wuxi, 480–81
   Xiamen, 486, 488
   Yangzhou, 520
   Zhanjiang, 535
Gates, 196, 376, 451, 475–76
Gems and jewelry
   Beijing, 212
   Guangzhou, 280
Genghis Khan, sites associated with, 189,
   320
Ghost city, Turpan, 468
Gifts, 8, 59–62, 104, 129–30, 458, 557
Glaciers, Urumqi, 470
Glass, artistic
   Chongqing, 249
   Dalian, 252, 253
   where to buy, 142
Gliding, Anyang, 187
Golf courses, 224, 547–48
Government. See Politics
Grand Canal, 267
   Hangzhou, 303
   Nanjing, 373
   Suzhou, 445, 447
   Tianjin, 461
   Wuxi, 481
   Yangzhou, 520
Great Wall, 272–274
   Beijing, 195, 196, 206, 207
   Datong, 257
   Jiuquan, 336
   Shanhaiguan, 424
   Silk Road, 442–43

Tianjin, 463
Yinchuan, 527, 529
Group tours, 24–26
Guanxi, 68, 134
Guidebooks, 100

Health insurance, 46
Helicopter service, 108–09, 195, 273, 425
Herb market, Guangzhou, 282
Hiking and climbing. *See also* Backpacking
    Changsha, 232
    Hangchow, 264
    Hangzhou, 308
    Huangshan, 323
    Lushan, 368
    Tai'an, 351
    Xiamen, 487
    Xi'an, 500
    Xiqiao Mountain, 509
History, 651–63
    books about, 48–50, 676–78
    museums, 201, 231, 247, 331, 363–64, 496–97
Hitchhiking, 113
Home–stay programs, Yantai, 525
Hong Kong, traveling via, 65–70, 109
Horse racing, 322, 525
Horse trading, 344, 484
Hospitality, 129
Hot-air ballooning, Anyang, 187
Hotels, 75–83, 184. *See also* Apartments; Home-stay programs; Kong Family Mansion; Temples, to stay in; Villages, to stay in; Yurts
    Anshan, 185–86
    Anyang, 187–88
    Baotou, 189
    Beidaihe, 191
    Beijing, 215–22
    Changchun, 228–29
    Changsha, 233
    Changzhou, 234
    Chengde, 239
    Chengdu, 244–45
    Chongqing, 249–50
    Dalian, 253–54
    Datong, 258
    Dazu, 260
    deluxe international, 80–82
    Dunhuang, 263
    Emei Shan, 264
    Foshan, 265–66
    Fushun, 268

Fuzhou, 270–71
Guangzhou, 284–88
Guilin, 294–96
Guiyang, 298, 299
Hainan Island, 301, 302
Handan, 302
Hangzhou, 309–11
Harbin, 314
Hefei, 316, 317–18
Hengshan, 319
Hohhot, 322
Huangshan Mountain, 324
Jiangmen, 326
Jilin, 328
Jinan, 332
Jingdezhen, 334
Jinggang Shan, 335
Jiujiang, 335
Kaifeng, 339
Kashi, 340
Kunming, 345
Lanzhou, 348
Leshan, 350
Lhasa, 355, 359–60
Liuzhou, 361
Luoyang, 366
Lushan, 369–370
Nanchang, 371
Nanjing, 380, 381–82
Nanning, 385–86
Ningbo, 389
overbooking by, 13
Overseas Chinese and, 26–27, 553–55
Qingdao, 393–94
Qinhuangdao, 396
quality of, 184
Quanzhou, 398–99
Qufu, 402–03
reservations, 44
Shanghai, 417–22
Shanhaiguan, 425
Shantou, 426–27
Shaoguan, 428
Shaoshan, 429
Shaoxing, 432
Shashi, 432
Shekou, 433
Shenyang, 436
Shenzhen, 438–39
Shihezi, 440
Shijiazhuang, 441
standard foreign tourist, 77–80
Suzhou, 449–50
Tai'an, 452–53

Taishan, 454–55
Taiyuan, 450–59
Tianjin, 464–66
Turpan, 469
Urumqi, 472
Weifang, 474
Weihai, 474
Wuhan, 479
Wuxi, 482–483
Xiaguan, 484
Xiamen, 489–90
Xi'an, 504–507
Xinhui, 507
Xining, 509
Xiqiao Mountain, 510
Xuzhou, 511
Yan'an, 514–15
Yangzhou, 521
Yantai, 526
Yinchuan, 529
Yixing, 531
Yueyang, 533
Zhangzhou, 534
Zhanjiang, 536
Zhaoqing, 538
Zhengzhou, 543
Zhenjiang, 546
Zhongshan, 548–49
Zhuhai, 550
Zibo, 551
Hot springs and pools
Anshan, 185
Chongqing, 248
Conghua, 251
Dazu, 260
Fuzhou, 269
Guilin, 292
Hainan Island, 301
Huangshan Mountain, 323
Jinan, 329, 331
Kunming, 342, 343
Qingdao, 393
Tianjin, 462
Weifang, 473
Weihai, 474
Xiaguan, 484
Xi'an, 493, 495
Zhongshan, 547–48
Hovercrafts, 66
Hunting and fishing, 292, 525

Ice sculpture festival, Harbin, 312
Ice skating, 202
Illness, 92–93, 125–27
Immigration, 71

Immunizations, 43
Industrial Exhibition Hall, Shanghai, 411
Intestinal parasites, 92–93
Islam, 175–76. See also Mosques and minarets
Ivory
  factory, 277, 282
  where to buy, 142, 415

Jade
  factory, 282
  where to buy, 212, 415
Jewish community (Kaifeng), 338
Journalists, tours for, 32
Jungle, Kunming, 341

Ke Lan, 402
Kite festival, Weifang, 473
Kong Demao, 402
Koxinga (Cheng Cheng-Kung), 397, 398, 486, 487, 488
Kublai Khan, 203, 211, 303, 353

Lacquer, where to buy, 142
Lakes, 191, 304, 313, 327, 335, 342, 343, 369, 375–76, 413, 424, 426, 430, 484–85, 508, 532, 537
Lamaism and Lama temples, 172–73, 188–89, 208, 237, 238, 320, 321, 343, 344, 354–57, 508
Land routes, to China, 41, 68, 70–71
Lao Tzu, sites associated with, 248. See also Taoism (Daoism) and sites associated with
Laundry, 57
Law
  breaking the, 125
  court, 440
Leather-silhouette show, Harbin, 313
Liang Heng, 231
Libraries, 304–05, 387, 435
Limestone formations, 343, 539
Lin Zexu, sites associated with, 269
Literary history, sites associated with, 230–31, 236–37, 241, 278–80, 317–18, 341–42, 361, 367, 377, 393, 411, 430, 477, 500, 542
Local customs, 119–37
Local time, 15, 73
Locomotives museum, Shenyang, 435
Lu Xun (Lu Hsun), sites associated with, 278, 410, 430

Maba Man, 427
Macao, traveling via, 70

Magic troupe, Shanghai, 414
Mail service and post offices, 46, 224, 505
Manor, Zhengzhou, 542
Mansions
    Beijing, 210
    Kong Family, Qufu, 401–02
    Nanjing, 377
    to stay in, 403
Mao tai, 88
Mao Zedong (Mao Tse-tung), 49, 130–31, 197–98, 230, 232, 247, 276, 279, 334, 371, 429, 440, 476, 512–14
Marble, Xiaguan, 484
Maritime history, 269, 378, 398
Markets, 282, 407. *See also* Free markets
Martial arts, 18, 157
Medicine and medical treatment, 31, 59, 125–27
Metalcrafts, where to buy, 143
Mines and mining, 255, 267, 427, 476
Mirages, Yantai, 523
Monasteries. *See* Buddhist sites and temples
Money, 12–13, 52–53, 54–55, 72, 121
Monkeys, 232, 248, 264, 301, 338
Mosques and minarets, 175–76, 209, 279, 322, 339, 397, 462, 469, 497, 508, 520, 528
Mosquitoes, 63, 125
Mountain scenery, 20, 185, 211, 243, 257, 263–64, 267, 269, 281, 291, 307, 308, 317, 319, 323–24, 327, 329–30, 334–35, 336, 340, 344, 358, 367, 388, 392, 395, 428, 441, 451, 454, 462, 469, 470, 473, 478, 484–85, 487, 500–01, 509–10, 525, 528, 537, 540
Mummies, 19–20, 231, 317, 468, 477–48
Murals, 242, 262, 347, 357, 442, 463
Museums. *See also* Art museums and galleries; History museums; Natural history museums
    anthropology, 427, 487
    aviation, Shanghai, 412
    Beijing, 201
    Changchun, 226
    Changsha, 231
    Chengdu, 242
    Chongqing, 248
    communications, Quanzhou, 397
    Dalian, 252
    Datong, 256–57
    Foshan, 265
    Guangzhou, 277–78
    Guilin, 292
    Hangzhou, 307
    Harbin, 313
    Hefei, 316
    Hohhot, 322
    Jinan, 331
    Jiuquan, 336
    locomotive, Shenyang, 435
    Luoyang, 363–64
    Lushan, 371
    LuXun, Shanghai, 410
    Mao Zedong, Shaoshan, 429
    military history, Xi'an, 493
    minorities, 471, 487
    Nanchang, 371
    Nanjing, 376, 377, 378
    Nanning, 383
    natural history, 248, 252, 461
    Overseas Chinese, Xiamen, 487
    Qingdao, 392, 393
    revolutionary, 201, 371
    Shanghai, 407–08, 410, 412
    Shijiazhuang, 441
    Taiping, Nanjing, 377
    Shaoguan, 427
    Taiyuan, 457
    Tianjin, 461, 462
    Urumqi, 471
    Weifang, 473
    visting, 153–56
    Weihai, 474
    Wuhan, 476, 478
    Xiaguan, 484
    Xi'an, 493, 494, 496, 497–98, 498
    Yangzhou, 520
    Yantai, 524
    Yellow River, Zhengzhou, 540
    Yinchuan, 529
    Zhenjiang, 545
    Zhou Enlai, Tianjin, 462
    Zibo, 551
Music, 147, 160, 313. *See also* Bells; Opera; Song and dance troupes; Song festivals
Mythology, 179–180

National minorities, 180–81, 209, 298, 300, 320, 341, 344, 362, 383–84, 444, 468, 471, 484, 487, 508, 527–28
Nepal, traveling via, 70
Neolithic sites, 187, 256, 361, 457, 497–98, 540
Newspapers and periodicals, 50, 58, 558
Nunneries, 210, 530

Opera, 157–60, 232, 281, 317, 365, 407, 478

Oracle bones, 186, 539
Overseas Chinese, 26–27
  ancestral villages of, 278–79, 326, 553–55
  Chinese names of, 45
  Chinese relatives and, 44–45, 51
  hotels
    Foshan, 265–66
    Fuzhou, 271
    Guangzhou, 287
    Hainan Island, 301
    Hangzhou, 310
    Shanghai, 420
    Shantou, 426
    Shijiazhuang, 441
    Taishan, 455
    Xiamen, 489
  medical treatment and, 125
  museum, 487
  schools for, 488, 555
  stores for, 140
  tips for, 553–55
  visas for, 26, 42–43, 44

Pagodas, 178–79
  ancient woodframe, 257
  Anyang, 187
  Beijing, 205
  Chengde, 239
  Chengdu, 242
  Datong, 257
  Dunhuang, 262
  Fuzhou, 269
  Guangzhou, 279
  Hangzhou, 305, 306
  Hohhot, 321
  Huangshan, 324
  Jinan, 330
  Jiujiang, 335
  Kaifeng, 338
  Lanzhou, 346–47
  Lhasa, 359
  Luoyang, 363
  Nanjing, 376–77
  Ningbo, 387
  Quanzhou, 397
  Shanghai, 412
  Shashi, 432
  Suzhou, 447, 448, 449
  Taiyuan, 457
  Urumqi, 471
  Wuhan, 477
  Wuxi, 481
  Xiaguan, 485
  Xi'an, 495–96, 500

Xinhui, 506
Yan'an, 513
Yangzhou, 520
Yinchuan, 528
Zhanjiang, 535
Zhengzhou, 540, 540–41
Zhenjiang, 545
Painting and calligraphy, 179. *See also*
  Frescoes; Murals; Rock paintings
  Dunhuang, 261
  Nanchang, 371
  Shanghai, 415
  Tai'an, 452
  where to buy, 143
  Yantai, 524
  Zhengzhou, 540
  Zhenjiang, 544
Pakistan, traveling via, 70–71
Palaces, 203, 344, 355, 377, 378, 398, 434, 457, 471, 500, 538
Paper crafts, where to buy, 143
Parks, 189, 191, 205, 232, 242, 248, 252, 260, 280–81, 291, 293, 305, 315, 326, 327, 329, 336, 346–47, 357, 368, 379, 383, 384, 391, 407, 411, 425, 426, 435, 462, 481, 500
Passports, 42, 46, 123
Peking Man, 211
Penglai Pavillion, Yantai, 523
Photography, 58–59, 122–23, 149, 494
Pilgrims, Ningbo, 388
Pinyin spellings, 14–16, 560–650
Plants, buying, 146–47
Police stations, 152, 225, 234
Politics, 133–34
  asking questions about, 156–57
  joking about, 121–22
Polo, Marco, sites associated with, 211, 303–04, 329, 431, 442, 445, 544
Porcelain, 143, 265, 334, 369, 408
Pottery and ceramics, 231, 265, 302, 334, 531
Prepaid tours, 24–26, 35–36
Prices, 138–40
Prints, woodblock, 143, 473
Pu Songling, 393

Radios, 58
Rafting, 227, 269, 528–29
Rainy season, 23, 26, 63
Religion, 130–32. *See also specific religions and topics*
Renminbi (RMB), 72
Reservoir, 227, 267, 440

Resorts, 235–36, 367, 437, 474, 524, 537, 550
  ancient, 304, 495
Restaurants. *See* Food and restaurants
Restricted areas, 99
Revolutionary art, 141, 144–45
Rickshaws, 114
Rock paintings, 384
Rubbings, stone, buying, 141

Sail-sledding, Harbin, 313
Sandlewood fans, 144, 449
Scholarly visits, 27–29, 669–670
Schools
  Anyang, 187
  Changsha, 232
  Chongqing, 248
  Lanzhou, 347–48
  Luoyang, 365
  Overseas Chinese and, 412, 488
  Shanghai, 408
  Suzhou, 449
  visiting, 23, 151–52
  Xiamen, 488
  Yantai, 524
  Zhengzhou, 541
Scuba diving, 67, 536
Seal engraving, Hangzhou, 305
Shell art, where to buy, 143
Shopping, 52–53, 72, 138–47. *See also* Arts and crafts; *and specific items*
  Beijing, 212–213
  Changchun, 228
  Changsha, 233
  Chengde, 239
  Chengdu, 244
  Chongqing, 249
  comparison, 52–53
  Dalian, 252
  Datong, 258
  Foshan, 265
  Fushun, 267
  Fuzhou, 270
  Guangzhou, 281–83
  Guilin, 293–94
  Guiyang, 299
  Hainan Island, 301
  Hangzhou, 308
  Harbin, 313
  Hefei, 316
  Hohhot, 322
  Hong Kong, 65–66
  Huangshan Mountain, 324
  investment, 141
  Jinan, 331–32
  Kunming, 344
  Lanzhou, 348
  Lhasa, 359
  Luoyang, 365–66
  Lushan, 369
  Luoyang, 365–66
  Nanjing, 380
  Nanning, 385
  Ningbo, 389
  Qingdao, 393
  Qinhuangdao, 395–96
  Quanzhou, 398
  Qufu, 402
  Shanghai, 415–16
  Shantou, 426
  Shaoxing, 432
  Shenyang, 435
  Shijiazhuang, 441
  Suzhou, 449
  Tai'an, 452
  Taiyuan, 458
  Tianjin, 463–64
  tips for, 138–39
  types of stores, 139–40
  Urumqi, 472
  what to buy, 140–47
  Weifang, 473
  Wuhan, 478
  Wuxi, 481
  Xiamen, 488
  Xi'an, 501–02
  Xining, 509
  Yantai, 525
  Yinchuan, 529
  Yixing, 531
  Zhangzhou, 534
  Zhaoqing, 538
  Zhengzhou, 542
  Zhenjiang, 546
  Zhongshan, 548
Silk and silk industry, 143, 306, 481, 546
Silk Road, 442–43
  Dunhuang, 262
  Jiuquan, 336
  Kashi, 339
  Lanzhou, 346
  Luoyang, 362
  Turpan, 468
Skiing, 63, 313, 327
Sky-diving, Anyang, 187
Snake sanctuary, Dalian, 252
Song and dance troupes, 157, 252, 322, 343, 478
Song festivals, 384, 485
Soong Ching-ling, 48, 409, 410

Special Economic Zones, 276, 437, 486
Special tours, 32, 194–95, 281, 292, 316, 344, 373, 448, 481, 526, 546
Specialty stores, 140
Sports. *See also specific sports*
  Anyang, 187
  China Sports Service Company, 103
  competitions, 157
  tours for, 32
  Xiqiao Mountain, 510
  Zhanjiang, 536
Springs. *See also* Hot springs and pools
  Hangzhou, 307
  Jinan, 329
  Jiuquan, 336
Statuary and carvings. *See also* Clay figures; Dough sculptures
  Beijing, 200
  butter, 508
  Chengde, 237, 238
  Chengdu, 242
  Confucian, 260
  Datong, 256
  Dazu, 260
  Fushun, 267
  Great Wall, 273
  Harbin, 312
  ice, 312
  Jinan, 330
  military, 260
  sandstone, 256
  Silk Road, 442
  Suzhou, 445–46, 448
  Tai'an, 452
  where to buy, 143–44
  Xi'an, 496, 498
  Xining, 508
  Zhengzhou, 541–42
  Zhenjiang, 545
Straw crafts, where to buy, 144
Students, 27–29, 31, 669–70
Subways, 115–94
Sun Yixian (Sun Yat-sen), 48, 130, 276, 279, 373–74, 409, 410, 454, 547, 549
Surveillance of foreigners, 122
Swimming, 232, 299, 506. *See also* Beaches
Symbols
  Buddhist, 168, 172, 173
  Taoistic, 174–75
  traditional, 160–69

Tailors, 146, 415
Taiping Revolution, 276, 297, 315, 377, 383–84, 392–93, 449

Tan Kah Kee, 486–88
Taoism (Daoism), sites associated with, 173–75
  Chengdu, 243
  Chongqing, 248
  Kaifeng, 338
  Lushan, 368
  Nanchang, 371
  Qingdao, 392–93
  Quanzhou, 397
  Shantou, 426
  Suzhou, 448
  Wuhan, 476
  Xi'an, 500
  Yantai, 523
  Yixing, 530–31
  Yueyang, 532
  Zhengzhou, 541
Taxis, 12, 72–73, 114–15
Tea and tea production, 88, 307
Telecommunications, 116–17, 333
Telephoning, 116–17, 184
  Beijing, 225
  in hotels, 77
  Suzhou, 450
Television, 58, 157
Temples. *See also* Ancestral temples; Buddhist sites and temples; Confucian temples; Lamaism and Lama temples; Taoism (Daoism) and sites associated with
  ancient woodframe, 257, 387
  Anyang, 187
  Baotou, 188–89
  Beidaihe, 190, 91
  Beijing, 201–02, 204, 205, 206, 208–09, 210
  Changsha, 232
  Chengde, 237–38
  Dhengdu, 241, 242–43
  Datong, 257
  Emei Shan, 264
  Foshan, 265
  Fuzhou, 269
  Guangzhou, 278, 279, 280
  Guilin, 293
  Hainan Island, 300–01
  Hangzhou, 306–07
  Heifei, 316
  Hengshan, 319
  Hohhot, 321
  Jiangmen, 326
  Jinan, 329, 330
  Kaifeng, 338
  Kunming, 342, 343, 344

Leshan, 349
Lhasa, 356
Liuzhua, 361
Luoyang, 363, 365
Lushan, 369
multipurpose, 529
Nanjing, 374–75, 377, 379
Ningbo, 387
Quanzhou, 397, 398
Qufu, 401
Shanghai, 408–09, 412, 413
Shanhaiguan, 424
Shantou, 425, 426
Shaoguan, 428
Shaoxing, 431–32
Shashi, 432
Shihezi, 440
Shijiazhuang, 441
Suzhou, 447–48
Tai'an, 451, 452
Taiyuan, 446, 457
Tianjin, 461
Wuhan, 477, 478
Xiamen, 487
Xi'an, 499–500, 501
Xinhui, 506
Xining, 508
Yangzhou, 520
Yantai, 524
Yinehuan, 529
Zhangzhou, 533
Zhengzhou, 540–41, 542
Zhenjiang, 544
Zhuhai, 549
Terracotta army, 12, 433, 494, 498
Tibet. *See also* Lamaism and Lama temples
  what to bring, 61, 352
Tibetan Buddhism. *See* Lamaism and Lama temples
Tidal bores, Hangzhou, 308
Tile faces, 179
Toiletries, 58
Tombs
  Baotou, 189
  Beijing, 207
  Changsha, 232
  Chengdu, 241, 242
  Fushun, 267
  Great Wall, 273
  Guangzhou, 277, 278–79
  Guilin, 293
  Hainan Island, 301
  Hangzhou, 306–07
  Hefei, 315

Hohhot, 321–22
  Islamic, 397–98
  Jiuquan, 336
  Kashi, 329
  Lhasa, 356, 357
  Liuzhou, 361
  Luoyang, 365
  Nanjing, 374, 375, 379
  Quanzhou, 397–98
  Qufu, 402
  Shanghai, 410, 411
  Shekou, 433
  Shenyang, 435
  Suzhou, 447
  Tai'an, 452
  Taiyuan, 457
  Turpan, 468
  Wuhan, 476
  Xiamen, 488
  Xi'an, 494–95, 498, 499
  Yan'an, 514
  Yangtze Gorges, 518
  Zangzhou, 520
  Yinchuan, 527
  Zhengzhou, 541–42
  Zibo, 551
  Zunhua, 552
Tour guides, 13, 103–05
  gifts for, 61, 104
  on-site, 100
Tours, 24–26, 32, 35–36. *See also* Special tours; Travel agents and arrangements
Towers, 497. *See also* Drum towers
Trade center and fair, Guangzhou, 283, 288
Train travel, 41, 67, 109–12, 437, 443, 507
Travel agents and arrangements, 10, 34–38, 68–70, 101–03, 666–668. *See also* Alien travel permit; Border formalities; Customs regulations; Immunizations; Passports; Tours; Visas; *and specific modes of travel*
Tribal weaving, where to buy, 144
Tropical plants, Zhanjiang, 535
Typhoons, 123

Villages. *See also* Ancestral villages; Communes
  Beidaihe, 190–91
  Guangzhou, 281
  Guilin, 293
  Hangzhou, 307
  Huangsha Mountain, 324
  Jilin, 327
  Nanning, 384
  neolithic, 498–99

Villages (*continued*)
  period restoration, 307, 324
  to stay in, 281, 525
  Suzhou, 445
  Wuxi, 481
  Xi'an, 498–99
  Yan'an, 514
  Yantai, 525
  Yangtze Gorges, 517
  Zhangzhou, 533
  Zhengzhou, 540
Visas, 26, 42–43, 73, 99–100. *See also*
    Alien travel permit; Passports
Voltage, 64

Walking, 116, 149–50, 210–11. *See also*
    Backpacking; Hiking and climbing
War Criminal Prison, 267
Water, 77, 88, 93
Waterfalls, 263, 299, 540
Water-Splashing Festival, 341
Water sports. *See* Beaches; Rafting; Scuba
    diving; Swimming
White Snake, 545
Wildlife and nature parks. *See also* Birds;
    Butterflies; Monkeys; Endangered
    species
  Changchun, 227
  Changsha, 232
  Chengdu, 243–44
  Dalian, 252

  Emei Shan, 263–64
  Hainan Island, 301
  Harbin, 313
  monkey reserve, 301
  Shihezi, 440
  snake sanctuary, 252
  Taishan, 454
  Xining, 508
  Zhaoqing, 537
Wine, 88, 228, 336, 432, 502, 524
Wushu, 157

Yang Guifei (Kuei-fei), 495, 498
Yuan Shikai, 187
Yuan-tsung Chen, 346
Yue Fei, 306–07
Yurts, 239, 321, 470

Zen Buddhism, 387, 540
Zhou Enlai, sites associated with, 247, 276,
    371, 378, 380, 405, 411, 430
Zoos, 177
  Chengdu, 241–42
  Chongqing, 248
  Dalian, 252
  Guangzhou, 280
  Harbin, 313
  Heifei, 315
  Shanghai, 411
  Tianjin, 462

ABOUT THE AUTHOR

Ruth Lor Malloy is a Canadian of Chinese ancestry. She was trained as a social worker, and has been a conference organizer, freelance writer and photographer, travel columnist, and wife and mother. She has lived and traveled sporadically in Asia for over two decades. She now travels there three times a year.

In addition to writing guidebooks on China since 1973, she has written the *Post Guide to Hong Kong, Hong Kong Gems and Jewelry* (with Joan Reid Ahrens, G.G.), and published a novel. She also edits the *Travel China Newsletter* and *China Hotel Guide.* She currently lives in Toronto.

PLEASE HELP US HELP OTHER CHINA TRAVELERS

Please complete this form and mail to *Fielding's People's Republic of China,* c/o William Morrow and Co., 105 Madison Ave., New York, NY 10016. Use more paper if necessary.

I have found the following hotels to be of acceptable international standards.

I have found the following airlines to be unacceptable, due to . . .

I would highly recommend the following guides:

I have found the following different from your book.

Other comments about my China visit:

Dates of visit:
   Name:

   Address (optional—but we might want to contact you for clarification):

   Telephone number (optional):